MASTER THE ART OF Speed Painting

:DIGITAL PAINTING TECHNIQUES

MASTER THE ART OF Speed Painting

:DIGITAL PAINTING TECHNIQUES

3DTOTALPUBLISHING

3DTOTAL PUBLISHING
Correspondence: publishing@3dtotal.com
Website: www.3dtotal.com

Every effort has been made to ensure the credits and contact information listed are present and correct. In the case of any errors that have occurred, the publisher respectfully directs readers to the **www.3dtotalpublishing.com** website for any updated information and/or corrections.

First published in the United Kingdom,
2016, by 3dtotal Publishing.
3dtotal.com Ltd, 29 Foregate Street, Worcester,
WR1 1DS, United Kingdom.

Soft cover ISBN: 978-1-909414-34-1
Printing and binding: Everbest Printing (China)
www.everbest.com

Reprinted in 2016 by 3dtotal Publishing.

Visit **www.3dtotalpublishing.com** for a complete list of available book titles.

Junior editor: Debbie Cording
Proofreader: Melanie Smith
Lead designer: Imogen Williams
Designers: Aryan Pishneshin, Joe Cartwright
Cover designer: Matthew Lewis
Managing editor: Simon Morse

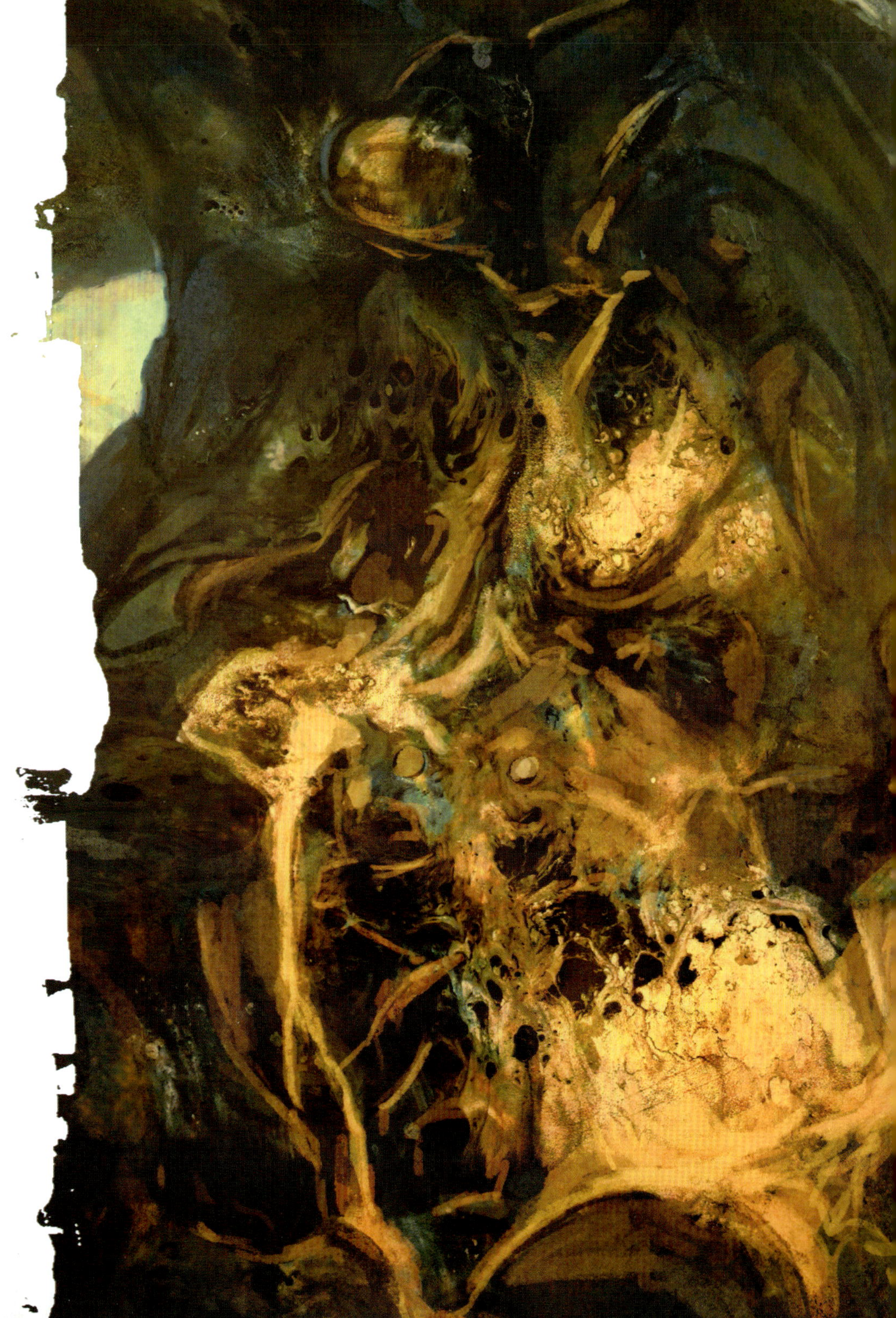

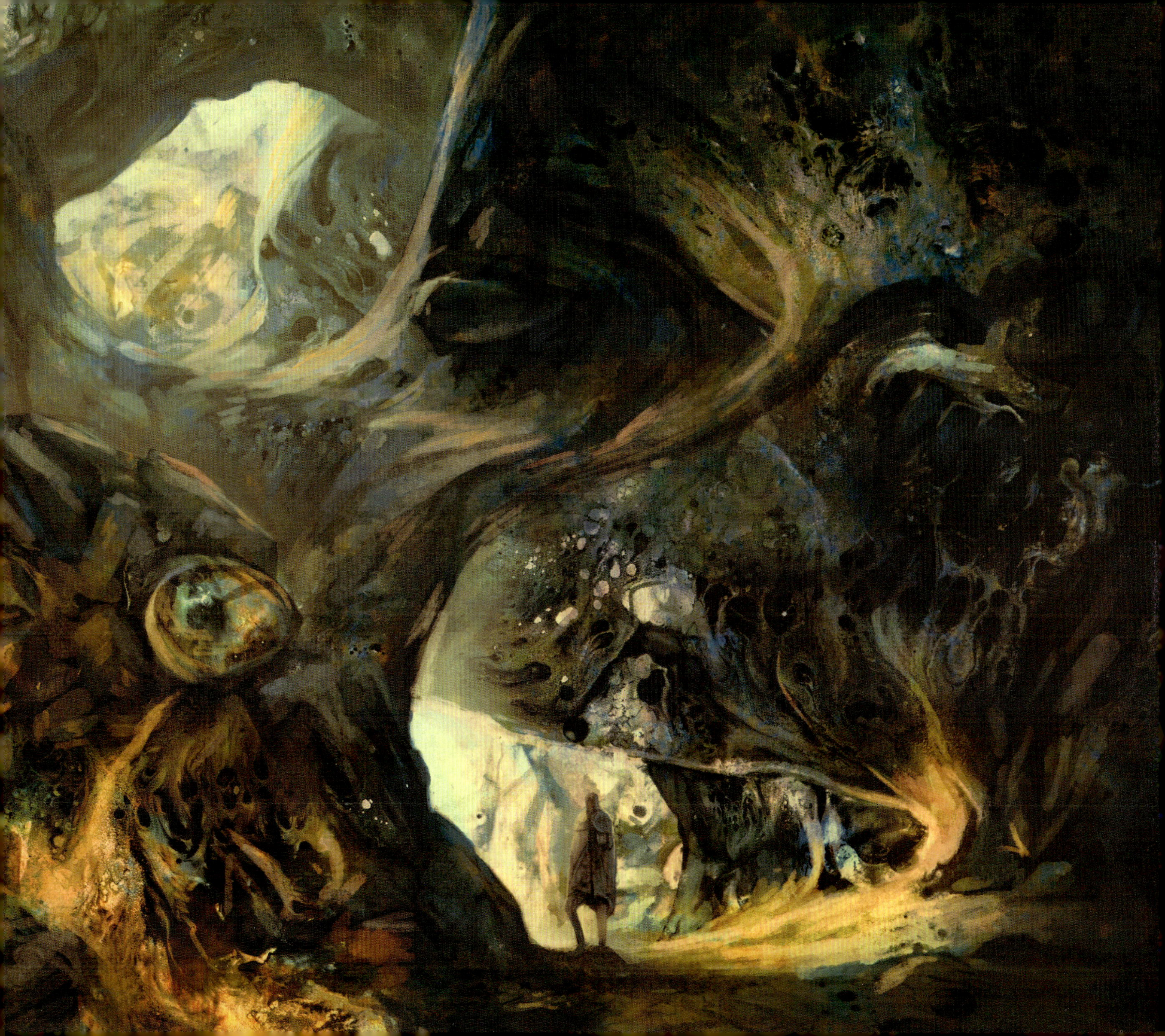

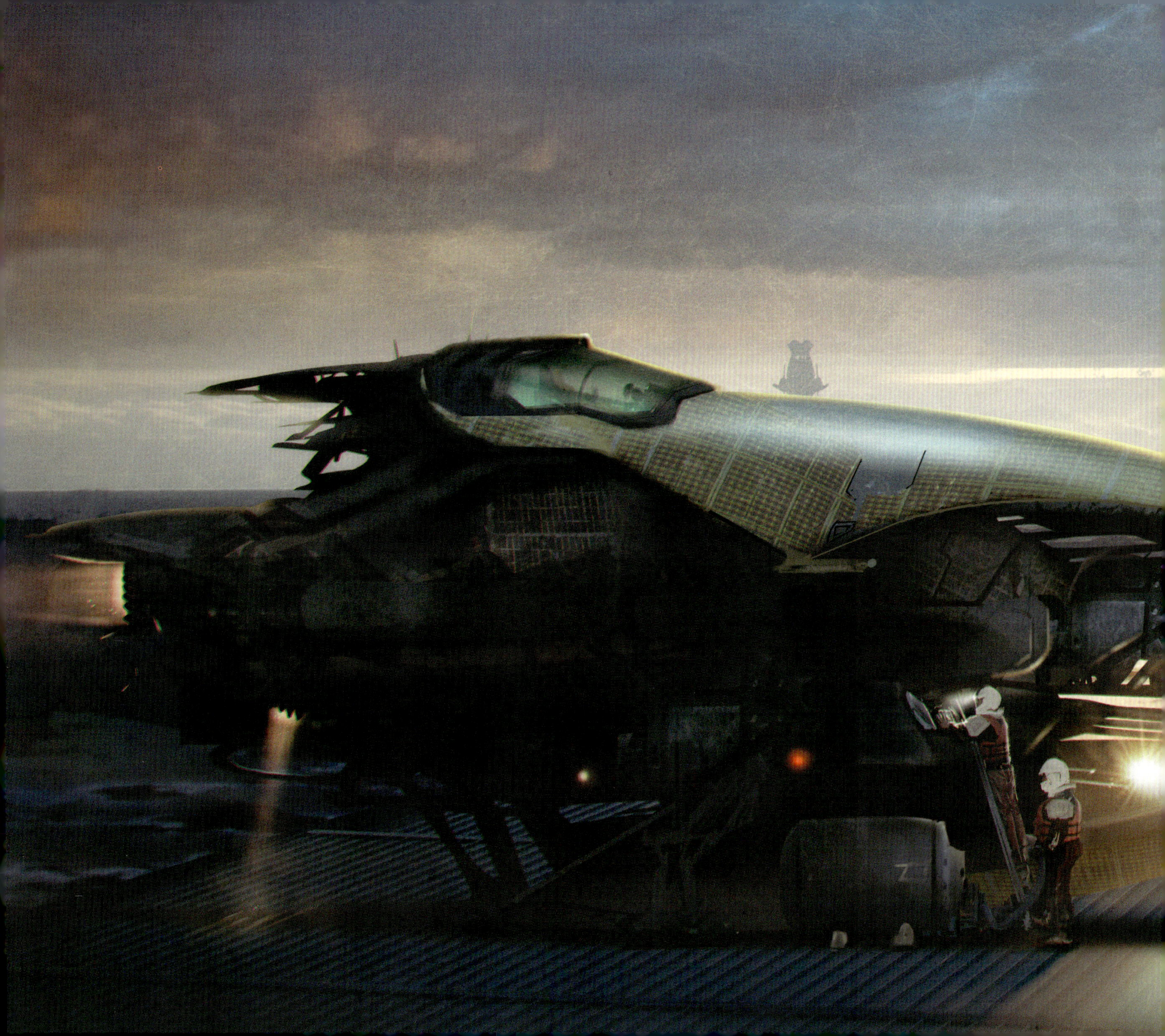

Contents

Foreword

BY NOAH BRADLEY

SPEED PAINTING IS ABOUT ACCEPTING RESTRICTIONS SO WE CAN ENJOY FREEDOM.

Whether those restrictions are time limits, the subject matter, tools, or techniques, the limiting of our options lets us focus more easily on actually creating.

Faced with a blank canvas and infinite possibility, we freeze. But faced with thirty minutes to paint a "futuristic wizard on Mars" with nothing but the Brush tool, our mind immediately starts racing with ideas; thirty minutes later we're looking at a finished piece.

I consider speed painting one of the fundamental exercises for aspiring professional artists. Not because every painting needs to be done quickly, that's not what speed painting is about. Speed painting is about learning efficiency, clear thinking, and decisiveness. When you only have thirty minutes to complete something (or even an hour or two), you don't have the time to try a dozen ideas first; you can't Ctrl+Z that first stroke again and again. You have to put your marks down and make them clear; you have to make your time count. Your original idea has to be perfectly concise, as you won't have hours and hours to refine it. It's that thinking, that ability to make clear, decisive choices in your painting, that is the skill you develop. It's a skill that carries through from the first stroke in any piece to the last one twenty hours later.

Speed painting sometimes gets a bad rap for supposedly encouraging beginners to rush their pieces. But rushing has no place in speed painting because it encourages sloppiness, and if you want to create a good speed painting you can't be sloppy. Speed painting isn't necessarily about doing things quickly, it's often more about doing things well. Beginners have a tendency to see the timer ticking down and to try to put marks down faster, but that just creates mistakes they then have to fix. They keep making sloppy marks to fix their other sloppy marks and at the end they just have a mess in their hands. Eventually they learn that it's better to put something down that's correct. Get it right the first time so you don't have to do it a second time!

You have to make things happen and you have to do so efficiently. This is why I consider speed painting such good practice. While there is certainly time to explore subtlety or try and scrap a bunch of ideas, the ability to take any idea from conception to realization in a short time is crucial. Whether you're showing that piece to a client or just yourself, you need to be able to take the ideas in your head and put them down in the real world.

When I was in art school I did lots of speed paintings and most of them were awful, but it taught me how important it is to get ideas down, to show sketches to clients without wasting hours with unnecessary rendering; it taught me how to start a painting and, in a way, it taught me a lot about how to finish a painting.

It also taught me a lot of different techniques over the years. While some artists do most of their work with just a brush, others incorporate photos, use a quick-shapes tool, or any number of aids they can find to make the process better.

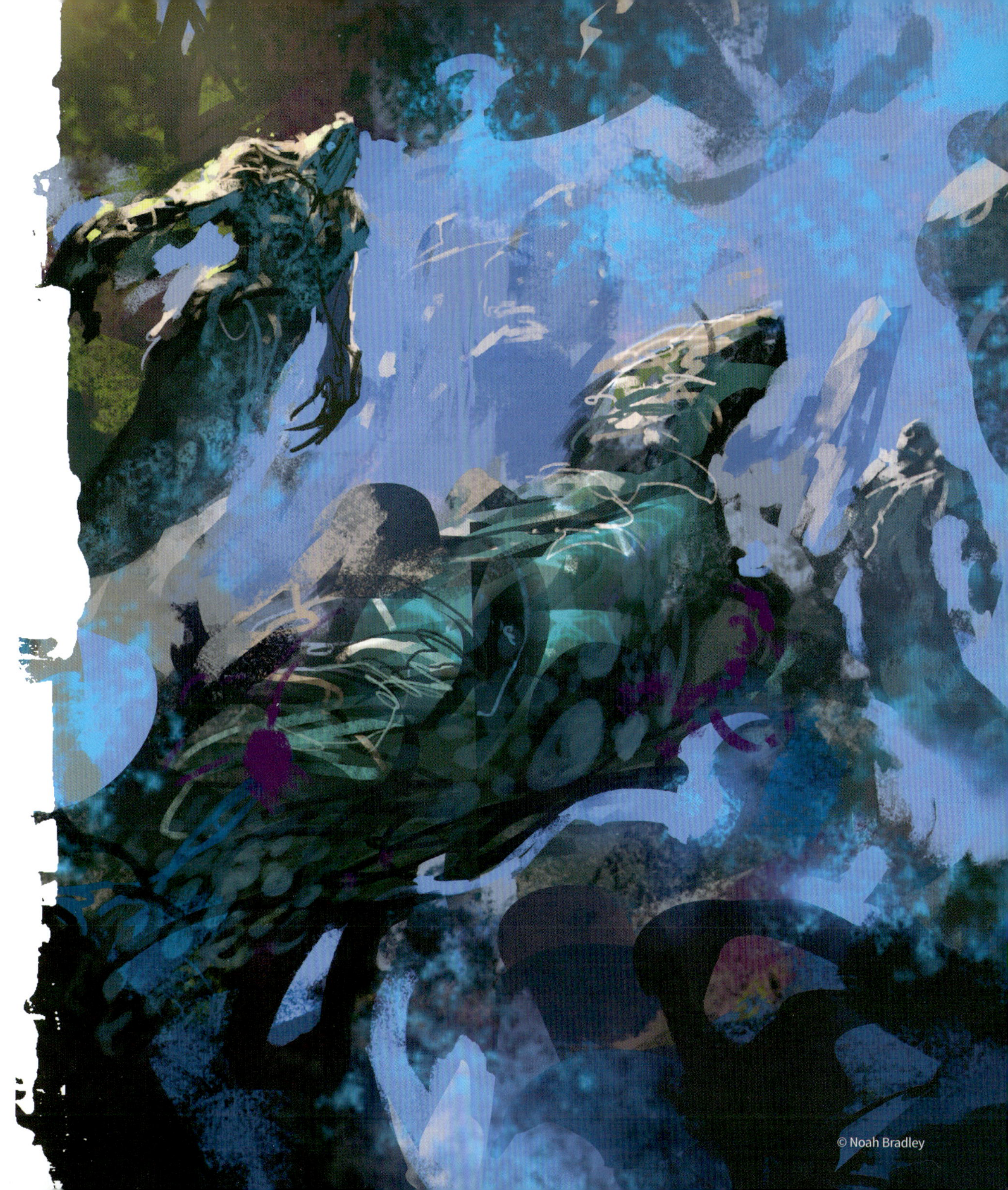
© Noah Bradley

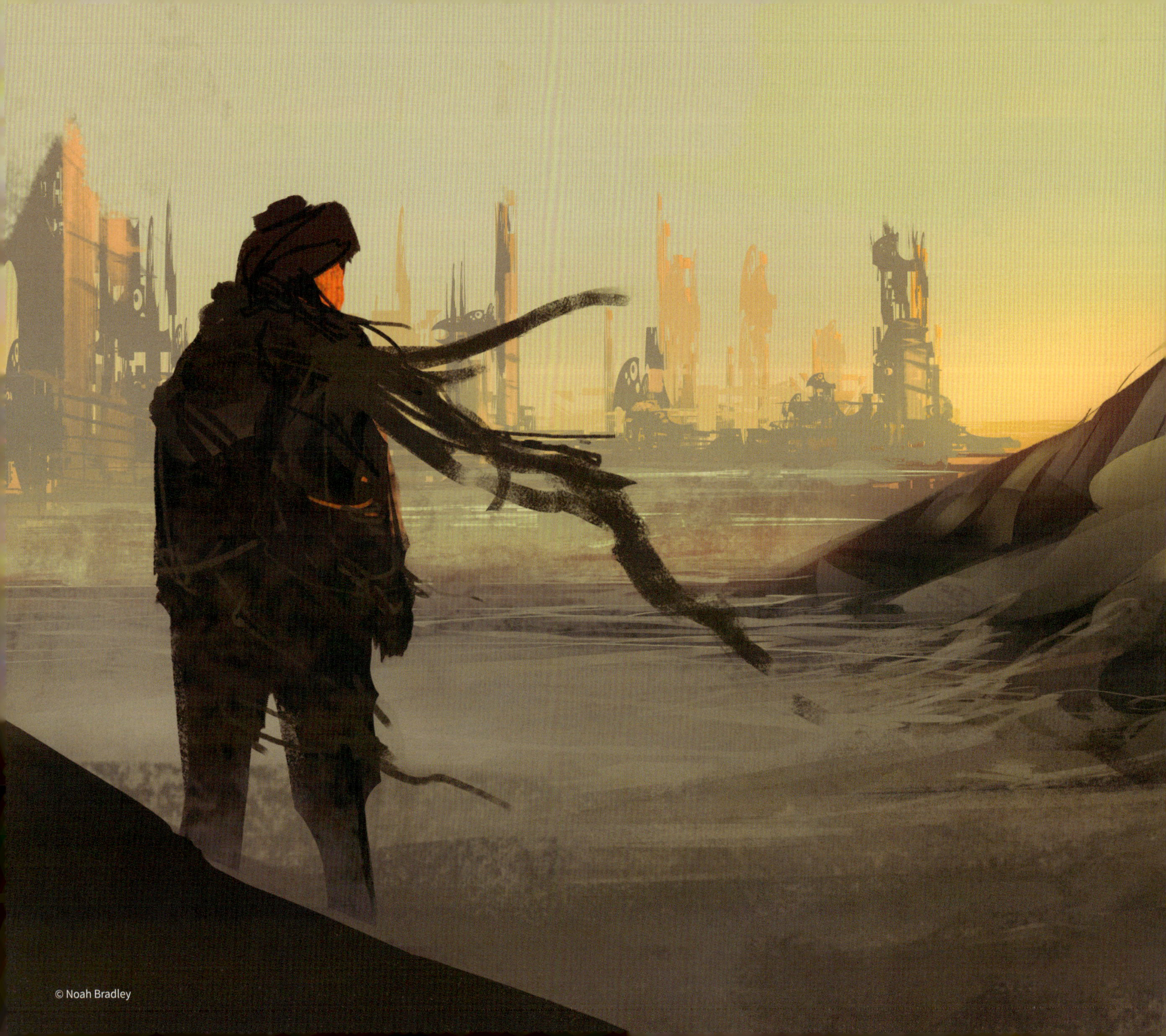

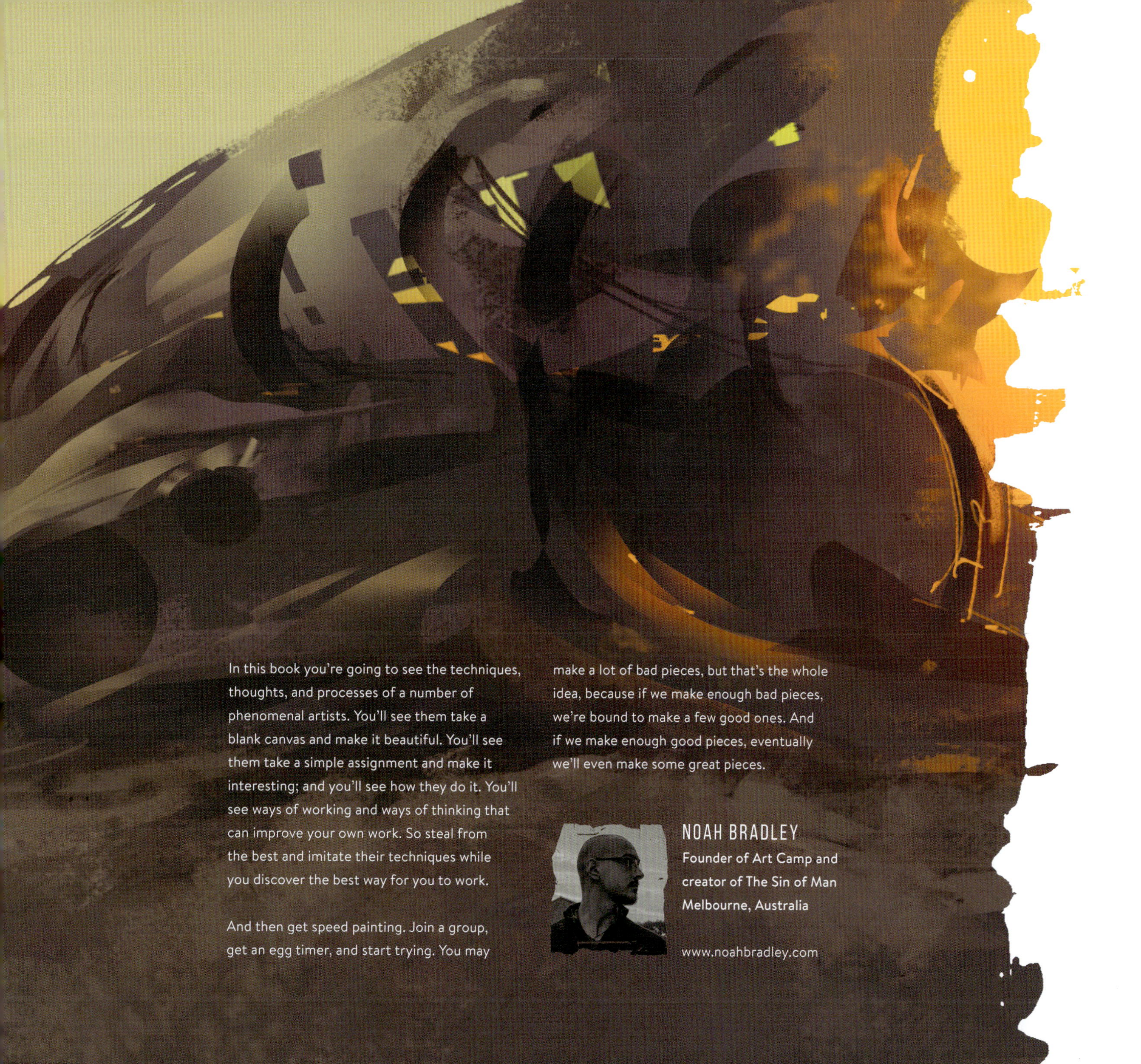

In this book you're going to see the techniques, thoughts, and processes of a number of phenomenal artists. You'll see them take a blank canvas and make it beautiful. You'll see them take a simple assignment and make it interesting; and you'll see how they do it. You'll see ways of working and ways of thinking that can improve your own work. So steal from the best and imitate their techniques while you discover the best way for you to work.

And then get speed painting. Join a group, get an egg timer, and start trying. You may make a lot of bad pieces, but that's the whole idea, because if we make enough bad pieces, we're bound to make a few good ones. And if we make enough good pieces, eventually we'll even make some great pieces.

NOAH BRADLEY
Founder of Art Camp and creator of The Sin of Man
Melbourne, Australia

www.noahbradley.com

Introduction

What is speed painting and how does one master it? To the casual outsider or uninitiated artist speed painting might appear to be a means to an end – a way to quickly work out an idea for a longer, more finished piece or as a concept for a client – rather than an art form in its own right.

Speed painting is the perfect vessel for artists of all abilities to develop and perfect their workflow and process. Even though they are called "speed paintings," speed isn't everything; maybe they should be called "timed" paintings instead. It isn't about racing to the finish line or beating the clock, but about using your time wisely and efficiently. There is a huge difference between randomly slapping down brushstrokes or textures and coming up with a well-considered and methodical composition.

At the same time, remember that you are not producing a finished masterpiece; speed painting is about the journey and what you want to achieve on that journey. Learn to use your time effectively and think about what it is that you want to get done in the time available.

In this book a spectacular selection of professional artists demonstrate their speed-painting workflows, covering commonly used industry approaches and techniques such as photobashing to create compositions and add texture, using custom brushes, and some good old-fashioned "painting." The result is an inspiring compilation of eclectic and useful methods that any artist can use quickly and efficiently to get down their ideas and concepts.

Never be afraid of getting it wrong or making a "mess" as there isn't really a right or wrong way of speed painting; you just need to find what works for you and your workflow. So dive in, but most of all have fun!

Debbie Cording
Junior editor
3dtotal Publishing

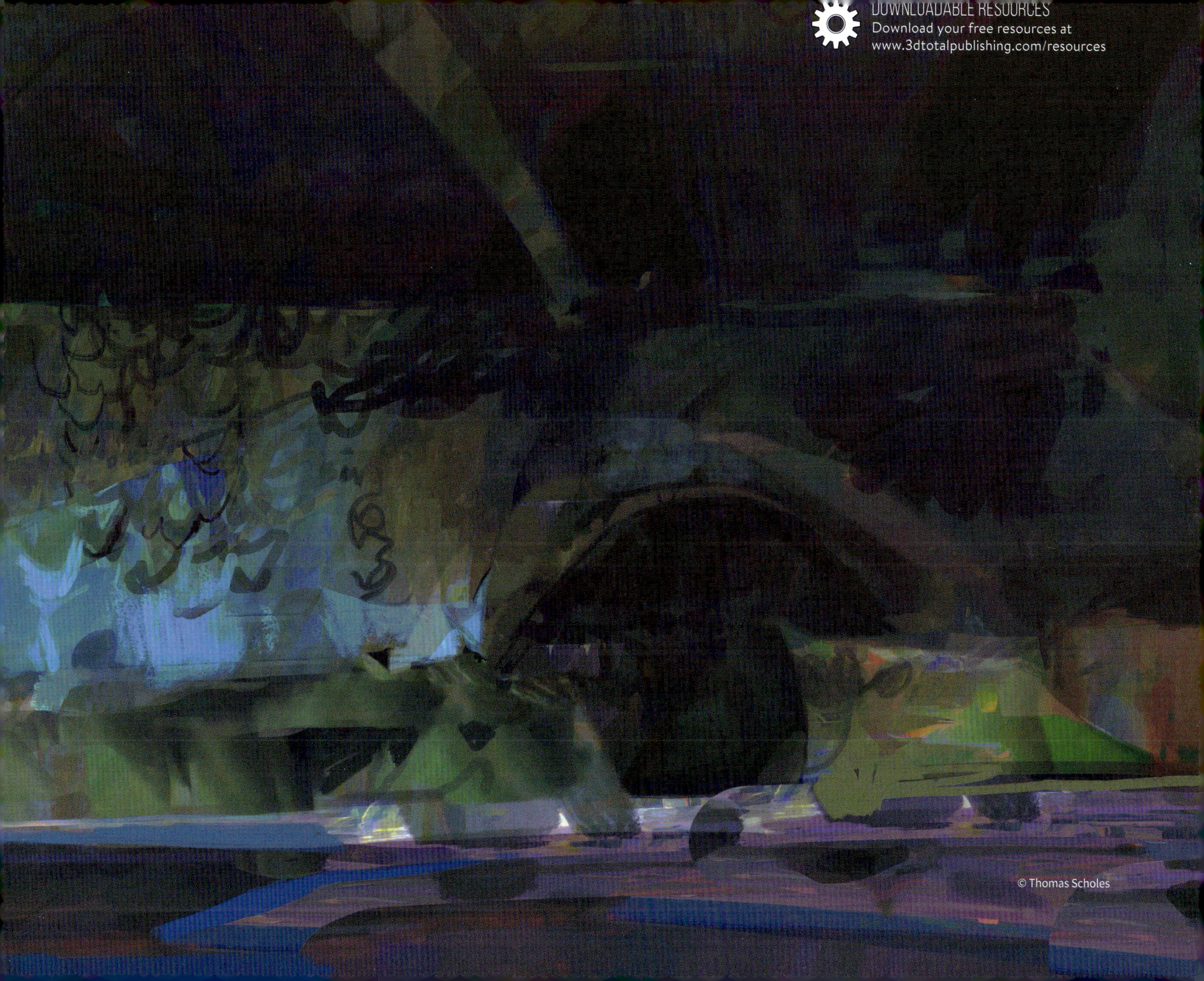
DOWNLOADABLE RESOURCES
Download your free resources at
www.3dtotalpublishing.com/resources
© Thomas Scholes

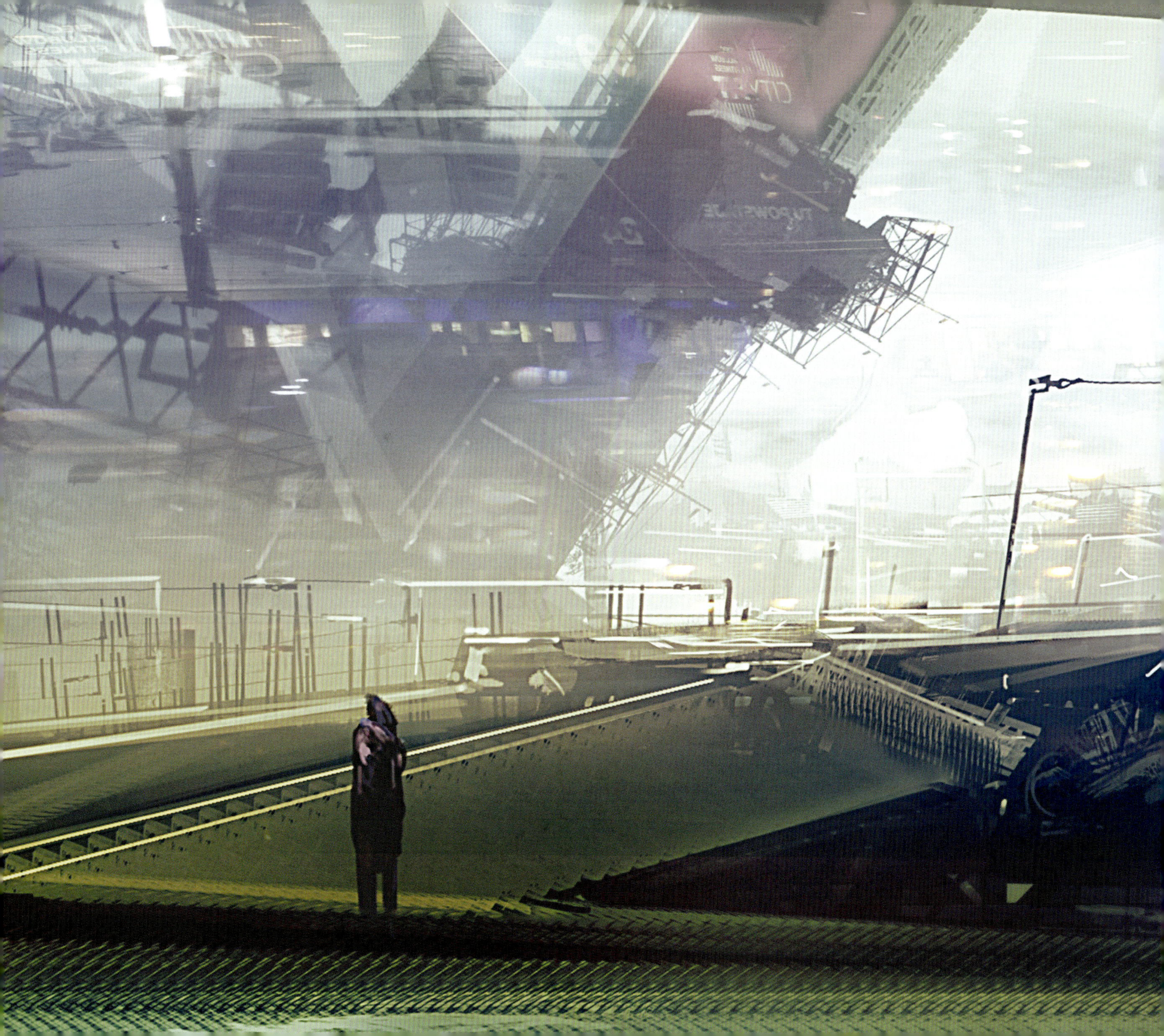

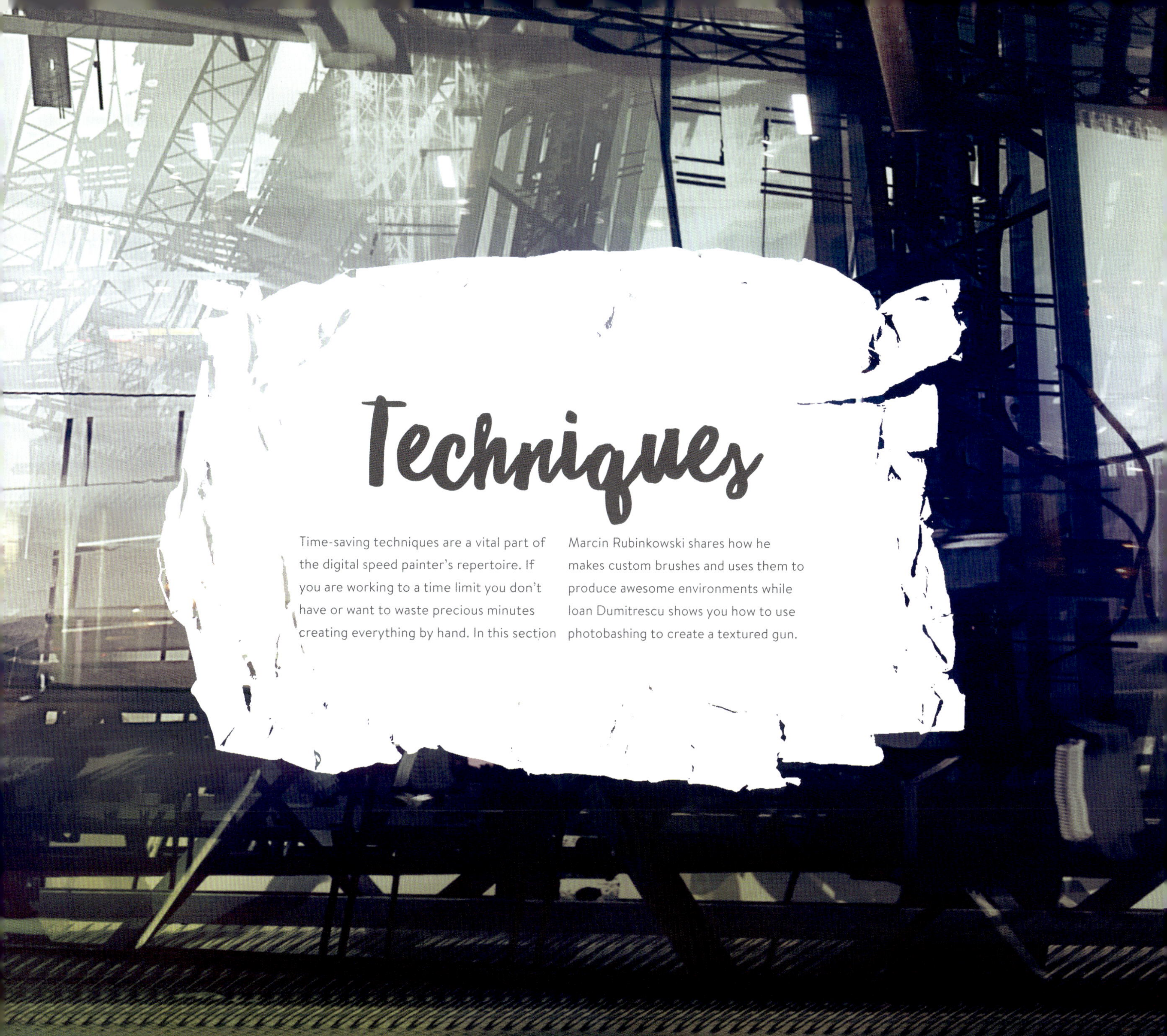

Techniques

Time-saving techniques are a vital part of the digital speed painter's repertoire. If you are working to a time limit you don't have or want to waste precious minutes creating everything by hand. In this section Marcin Rubinkowski shares how he makes custom brushes and uses them to produce awesome environments while Ioan Dumitrescu shows you how to use photobashing to create a textured gun.

CUSTOM BRUSHES
by Marcin Rubinkowski

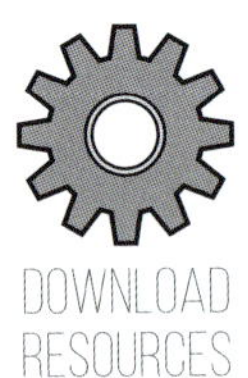

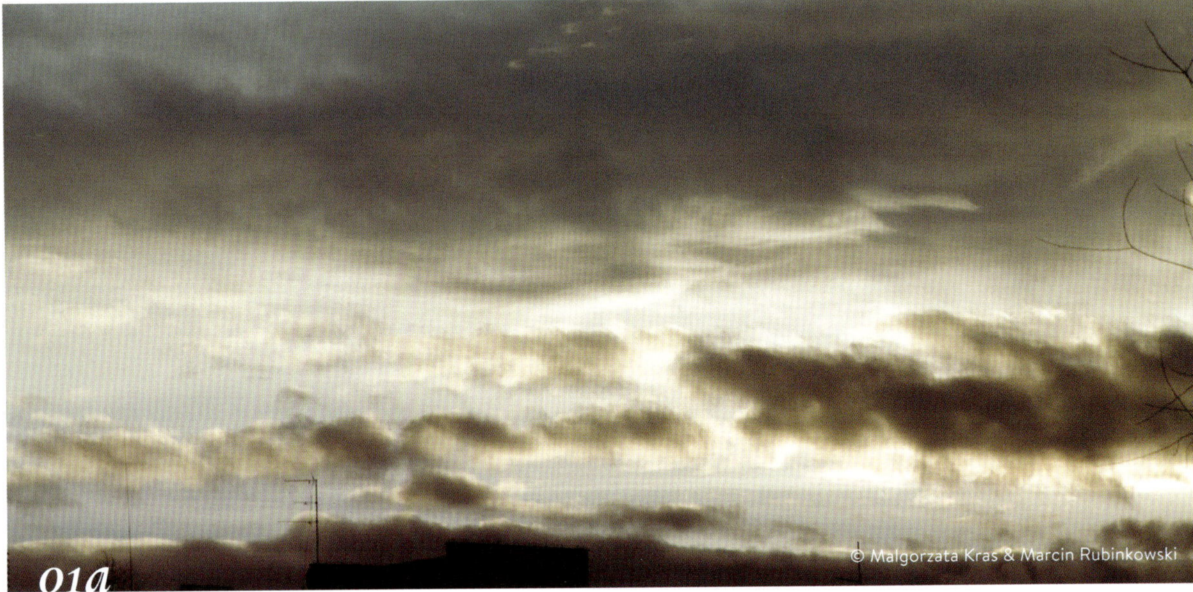

▲ A photo taken by my wife and me for reference purposes

In this chapter we will look at making custom brushes and using them to create environmental concept art. Digital brushes are nothing more than a tool; totally cooler than real-world brushes but still only a tool.

Many artists have a favorite set of brushes, but in my opinion it is not always a good idea to download "new" brushes from the web. The wiser method is to have your own favorite set but upgrade it for each assignment with custom brushes that fit the world you are creating. Why can't we make brushes from a Chinese roof, city lights, or stone pillars? We can – and we can do more than that, as you will come to see later in the chapter.

I will show you that when you are making concepts and collecting references for this task you can go a step further and make brushes from your own references that fit your project as well as basic materials. This will give you an advantage and also more time and opportunity to add a personal twist to the project because you'll already be playing with the subject as a brush. Nobody is forcing you to use a pillar brush as a pillar. The only limit when it comes to using this tool is your creativity, not the tool itself.

Once it comes to using the brushes we will work on two pieces at the same time. Working this way saves time and prevents your brain from getting tired because you can always switch to the other piece when you get stuck. We must keep our mind happy, fed with enjoyment, and avoid artistic block or any other frustrations.

Overall pipeline for the chapter

We will start with photos. Then we will choose and make our custom brushes from them. This part will be in black and white. After we make our brushes with my instructions and categories we will start to paint. I will show you where you should use them, how to manage the mess, and after this we will add quick color to the painting and a couple of finishing touches with a Screen layer. If you follow the instructions, everything should be fine! For all exercises you should make three PSD documents: one for brushes, one for testing, and one for the actual image you will be creating. Use them wisely all the time.

01: Select the right photo material

The first step is to select reference photos. It's important to choose appropriate photos to allow us to get what we need from them. For example from messy weird images we can get brushes with intriguing shapes and textures at the same time; if we are focused on making atmospheric brushes we should use photos of sunsets to get really visible shapes for the clouds.

We can use messy brushes as simple, small, hard brushes for details and finishes and use a soft airbrush or something similar to help us to clean up and create distance in our piece. Don't forget to turn a vector image into pixel format if needed using Layer > Rasterize in Photoshop.

02: Rules for making brushes

The next three steps will lay down some general guidelines for making custom brushes. In the beginning make sure you have another document open to check how your brushes look. When making brushes we will only work in black and white.

Make yourself a new document set to 2000 × 1000 pixels; paste the photos you gathered previously into the document and use the Lasso or Quick Selection tool to cut your shapes. Try to make wide brushes. Note that when it comes to edges, only atmospheric brushes should be blurred at the corners.

The photo material must be modified in Levels to get rid of most of the shade. White will be transparent overall. You can paint or copy everything on it when you are creating messy brushes. It is good to have really weird shapes and content inside the brush. I suggest you use your creativity with brushes from all the categories. Use your imagination but keep in mind what it is they will be used for. Overall, material for brushes should be over-contrasted and sharp on the edges with readable content inside.

Rules for your brushes:

- They should be black and white
- Over-contrast them
- Use sharp edges
- White is transparent

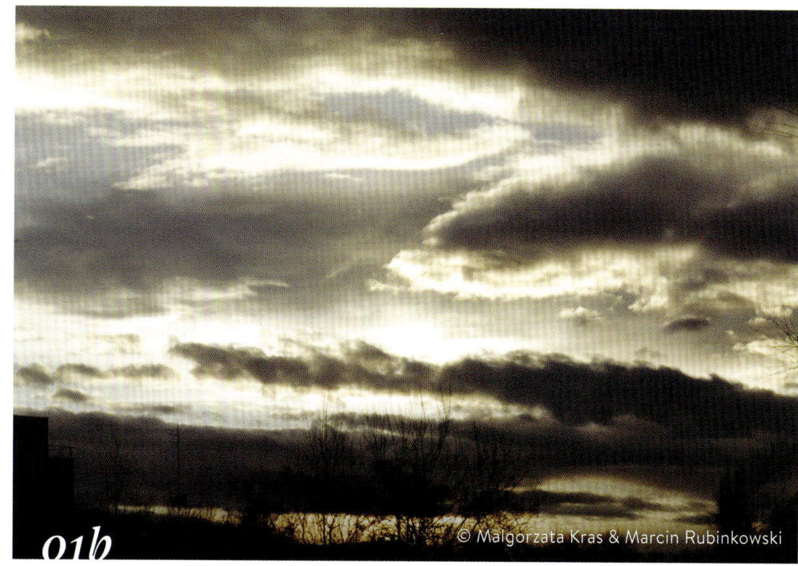

▲ Another photo taken by my wife and me for reference purposes

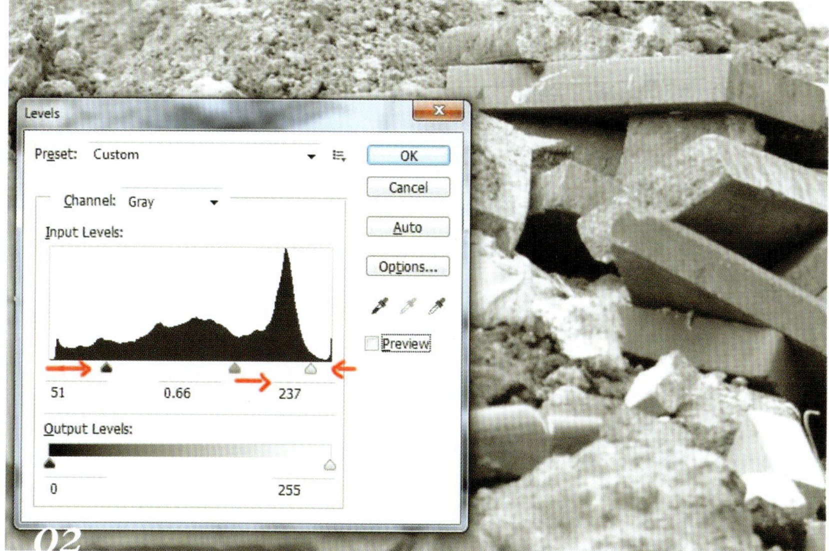

▲ Modify the references to remove all color

Pro tip:

Make use of all tools

Be free with your selection; do not be afraid to use all the Marquee tools such as Lasso and Quick Selection, and mix them with the Alt and Shift keys for a suitable effect. Do not worry, Ctrl+Z will also work on selection tools.

03: Brush categories

I like to categorize brushes as: atmospheric brushes, background ("bg") brushes, and messy brushes. I usually like mixing messy brushes with the Dual Brush option on (see step 09) to gain creative shapes and textures. This saves time and can produce something that is totally out of your comfort zone.

If you have selected your photo material you can start making brushes with the categories mentioned above. We are trying to make a maximum of three brushes for each category.

04: Atmospheric brushes

We will start by making atmospheric brushes with readable content and few or no hard edges. Cut big plates with only cloud-like textures. Avoid boring horizontal lines and focus on catching interesting cloudy spirals and tribal-like shapes (**image 04a**).

When your cloud is ready, go to Adjustments > Exposure or Levels... and increase the gamma and contrast. Then invert the colors (also in Adjustments; **image 04b**). Now you can save the brush preset. At least one brush should have an ellipse or circle shape in this smaller size. All of them should have smoothly erased outer edges.

Turning your black and white image into a custom brush couldn't be easier. With your newly created image open click on Edit > Define Brush Preset... (**image 04c**). Once you have done this a window will appear giving you the opportunity to name your new brush (**image 04d**). Once you have done this your new brush has been created and is ready to use. If

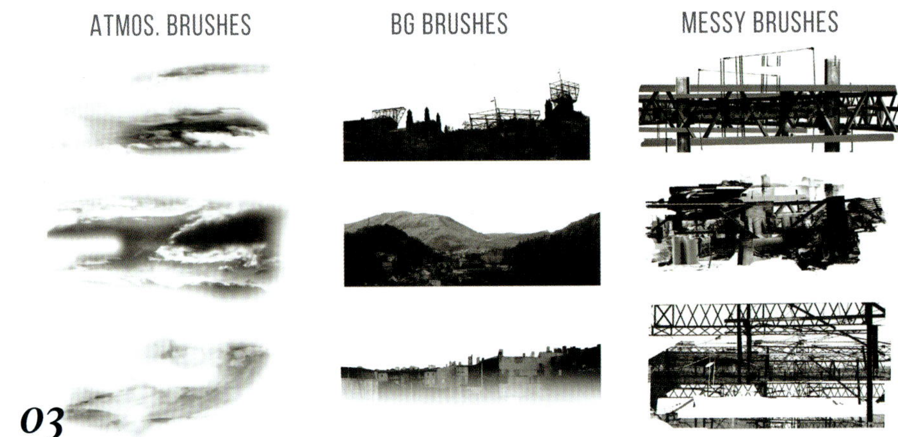

▲ I like to categorize my brushes to save time and for ease of use

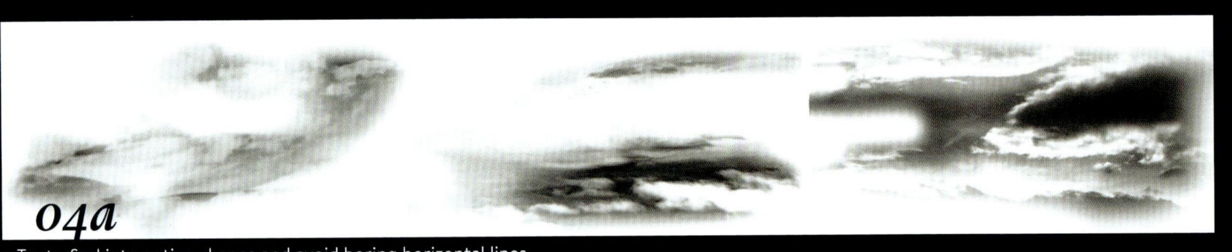

▲ Try to find interesting shapes and avoid boring horizontal lines

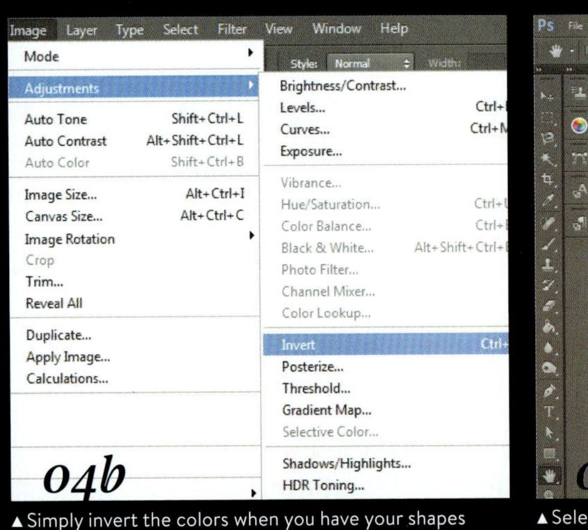

▲ Simply invert the colors when you have your shapes

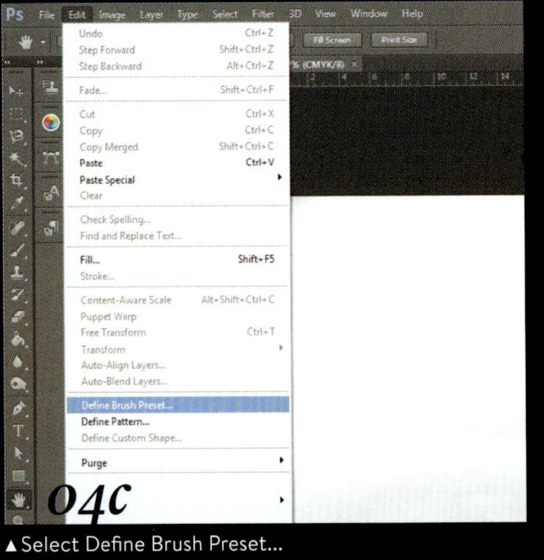

▲ Select Define Brush Preset...

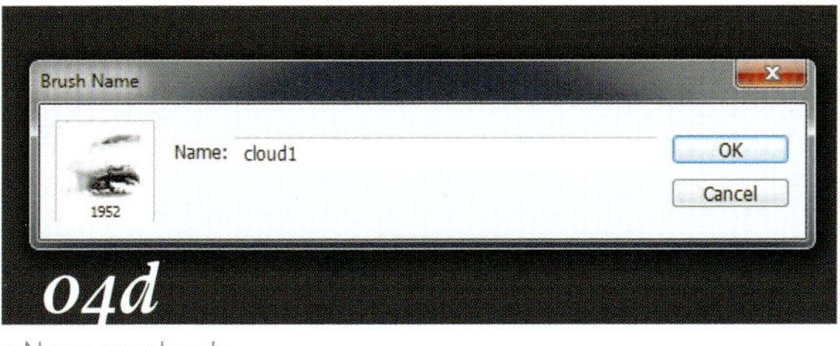

▲ Name your brush

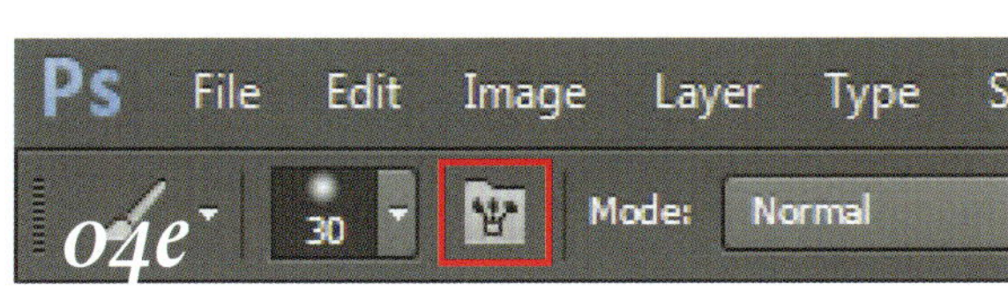

▲ Select the Brushes palette option

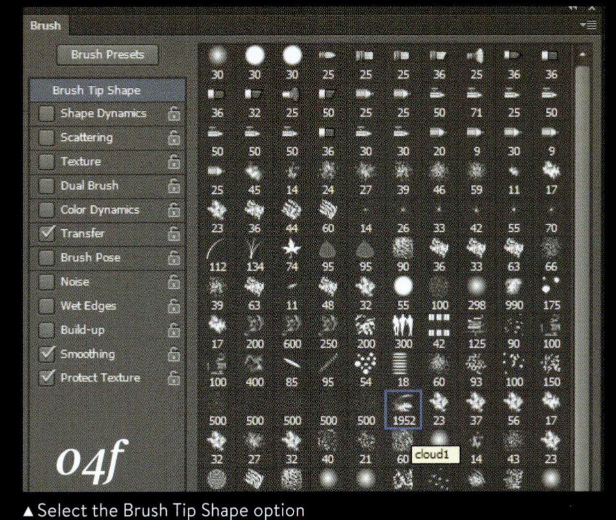

▲ Select the Brush Tip Shape option

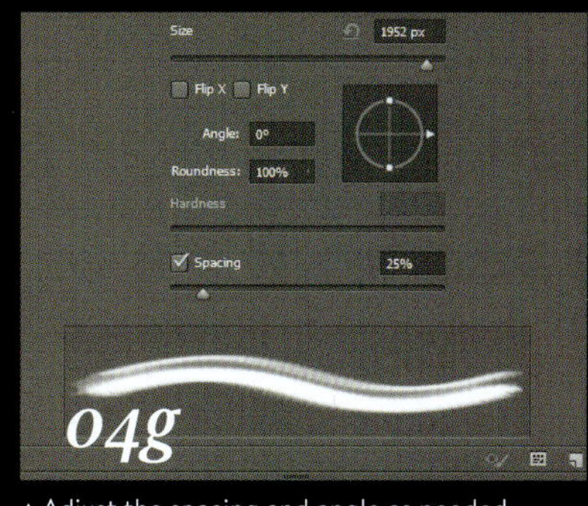

▲ Adjust the spacing and angle as needed

▲ Take the time to test your brushes before

you look at your brushes you will most likely find it at the bottom of your list.

This brush would be fine to use as stamp, but it isn't very versatile as a brush yet. The next step is to click on the Brush tool and then select the Brushes palette option you can see highlighted in **image 04e**. This will open a pop-up window like the one you see in **image 04f**. Scroll down the list and find your new brush and click on it. Select the Brush Tip Shape option and you can very easily change the spacing and angle to make the brush easier to use **image 04g**.

By choosing the other options in this list you can continue to customize your brush and make it ready for use.

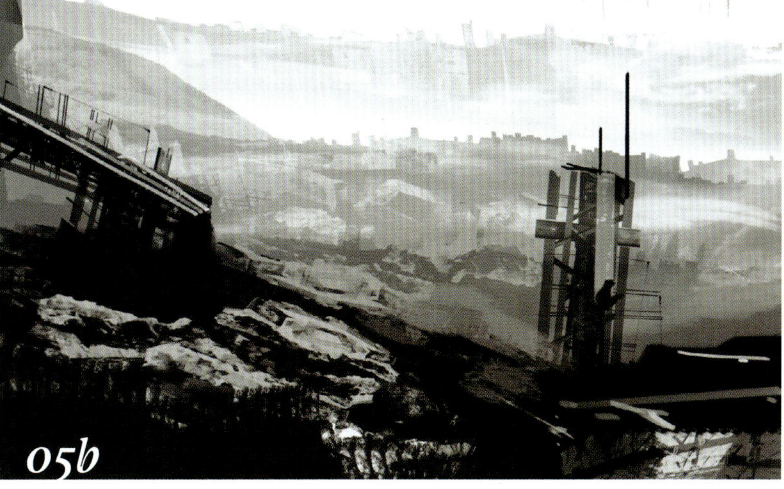

▲ You don't need to be consistent when testing the brushes, it is solely for reference

05: Test your brushes

It's important to test your brushes out to see what they look like. Do this in a separate document so you can refer back to it if needed (**image 05a**). Try not to paint anything consistent on this document; it should only be for review purposes and to help your mind get into the right place to play with your brushes (**image 05b**).

You don't have to stop making brushes when you start painting; it can be good to make brushes in the middle of the pipeline.

Pro tip: More brushes

You can also make new brushes from material you've already used by selecting what you want and pressing [Ctrl+Shift+C] to Copy Merge and paste it into a new document.

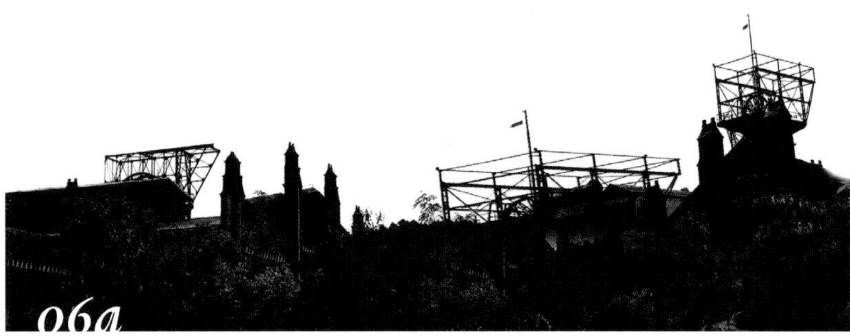

▲ A larger range of reference images means a bigger brush library!

06: Background brushes

Now we will follow a similar process for the background brushes. For this category we will be searching for images such as cityscape silhouettes or other interesting background landscapes such as mountains and fields (**image 06a**). For these, try to have a flat horizontal rectangle shape for your brushes at the end.

All the content should have strongly visible silhouettes without the sky (**image 06b**). Here you shouldn't have any bigger shapes on the left and right sides, also upper corners should be free. Cityscapes or all horizontal objects far away will work well. Try to not have too much information inside the silhouettes as we will be adding more in there in later stages.

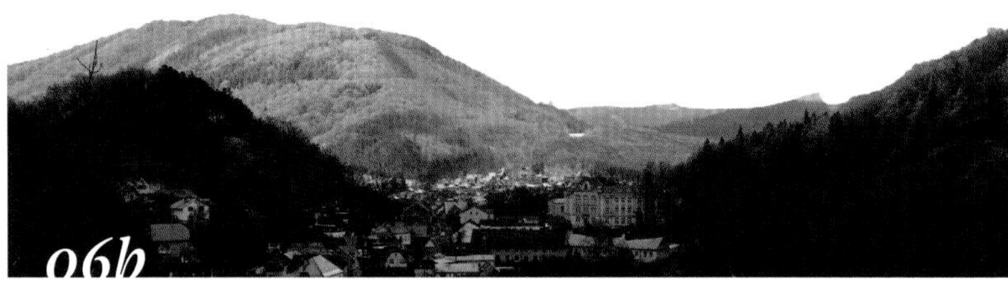

▲ Make sure you have strong silhouettes without a sky

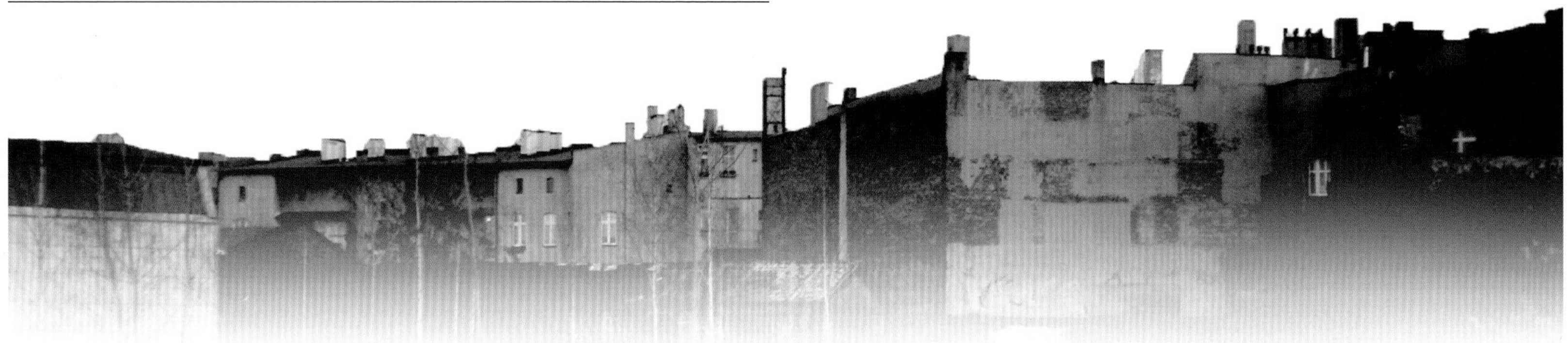

06c

▲ Cityscapes make great background brushes as they save so much time when making a skyline!

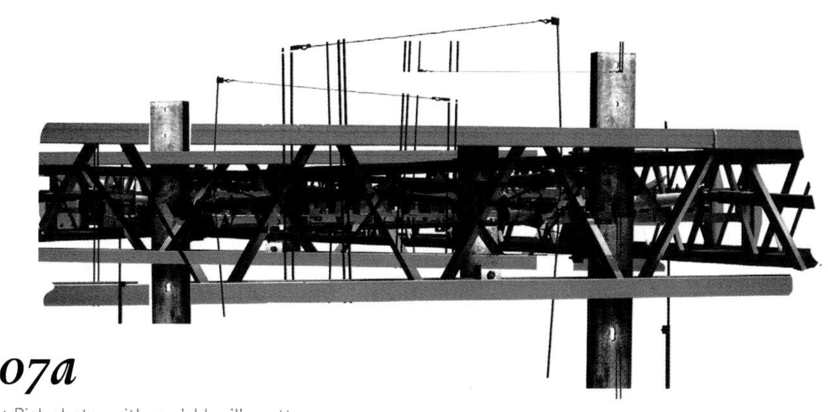
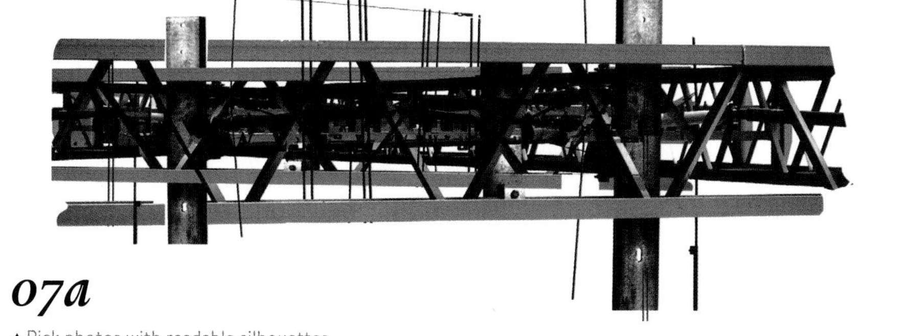

07a

▲ Pick photos with readable silhouettes

You also may consider using a soft airbrush to erase the bottom of the cityscape so that it will blend more easily with the landscape (**image 06c**). Follow the actions in step 04 to create your brushes, then test them.

07: Messy brushes

Use photos with readable silhouettes, without deep shadows or over-contrasting (**image 07a**). We will choose some shapes from this mess. Try to have at least have one brush in a geometric shape such as a rectangle or square; the rest can be your own invention. Choose large source images, with as large a subject matter as you can – you will be using them in a huge form with some kind of texture so you need them to be good quality and have clean edges (**image 07b**).

Make your own set but don't double up the subject of the brush. For messy brushes especially, we should try to have almost black-and-white readable silhouettes, so I suggest using some correction with Levels or Curves to get the correct effect (**image 07c**). Once again, create your brushes as in step 04 and test them.

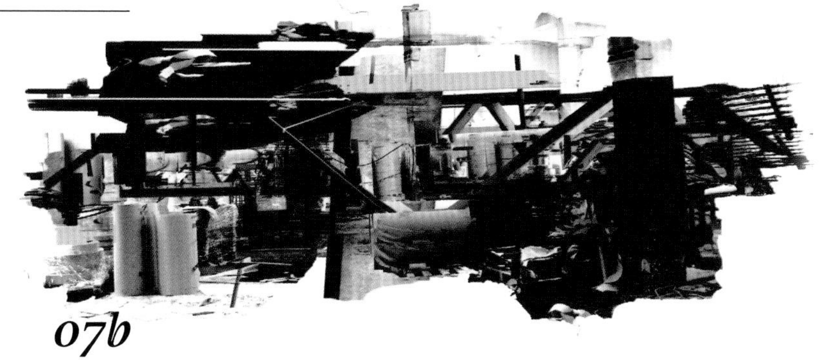

07b

▲ Select big plates with as large a subject matter as possible

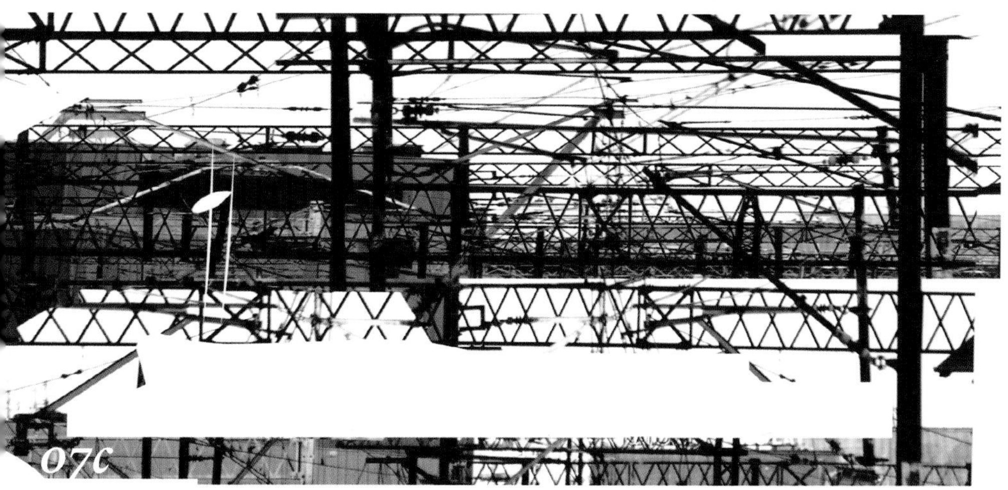

07c

▲ Don't be afraid to mix and match to make interesting shapes

08: Advanced brush configuration

In the end it's up to you and how you will use your tablet or program, but for this exercise set your options to Brush Projection. Set Pen Pressure to Transfer. You can use the [and] keys to change the brush size, or your tablet wheel if you have one. The button on the stylus should be set to the Alt key. If you have another button I suggest you set the right-click mouse button there as it will allow you to quickly access your brushes. I usually set Spacing to 10% but sometimes I change this when painting, as I do with almost all settings in the Brush settings menu. I think it is important to have fun when exploring brush settings, in particular with the Spacing option. Each option can also be used in particular situations to save time and give us what we need (**images 08a** and **08b**). I set my eraser to a soft airbrush.

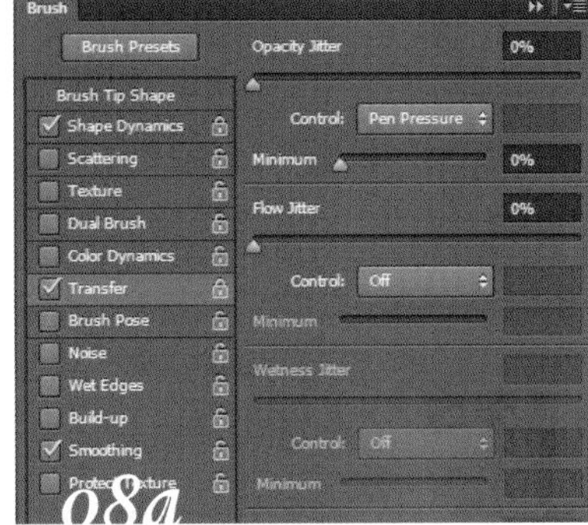

▲ Don't be daunted by all the options

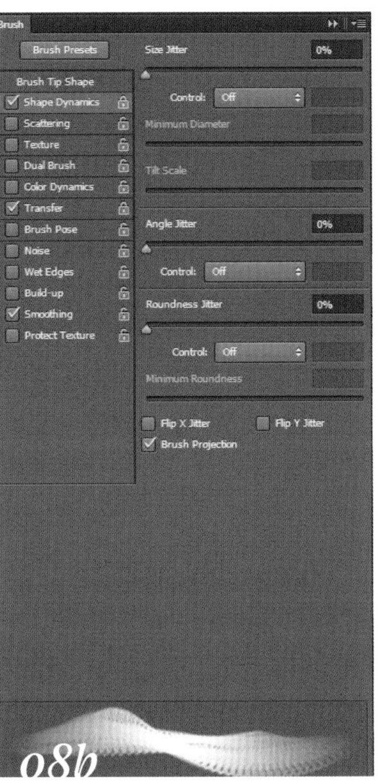

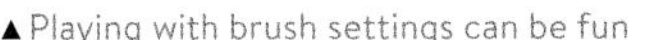

▲ Playing with brush settings can be fun

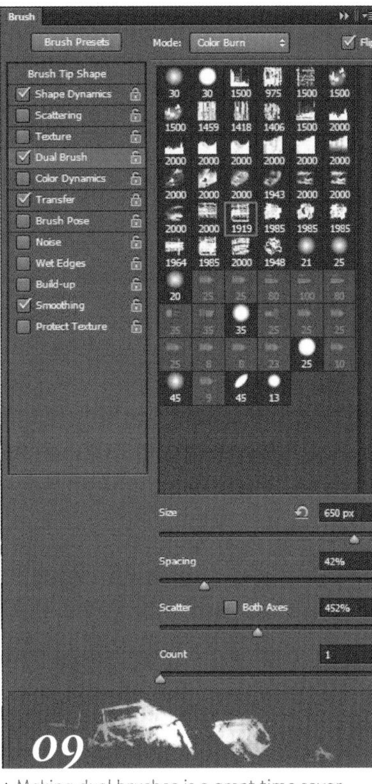

▲ Making dual brushes is a great time saver

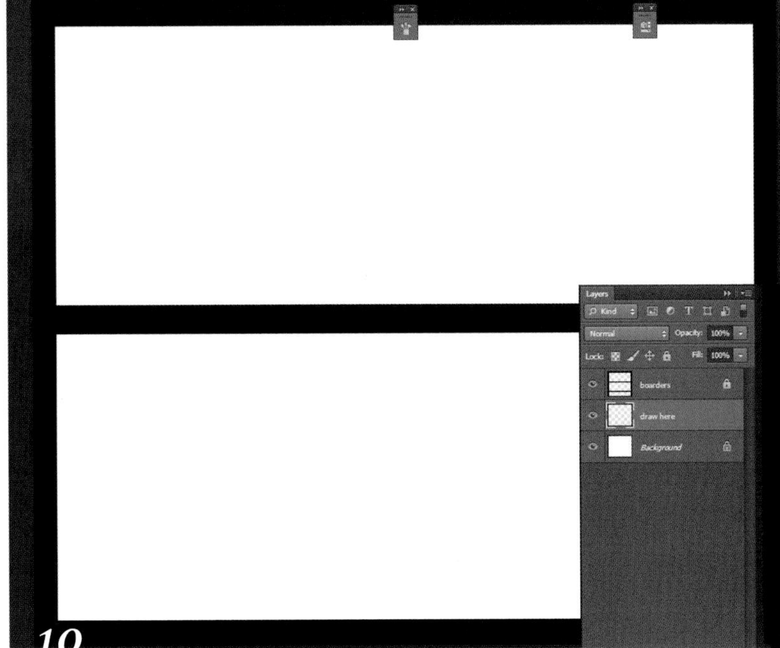

▲ Set up your canvas and keep layers organized

09: Creative Dual Brush

Here we will play with all the creative and time-saving content. Try to mix messy brushes with the background family of brushes using a rather large size for the secondary brush. Mix them with courage and remember to save them as new brushes. Artists should sometimes allow tools to make decisions for them and the Dual Brush is suitable for this. Use of large-sized brushes for both of them will slow down weaker workstations but with other options you can, and should, have lots of fun without a heavily equipped PC.

10: Painting assignment rules

We will now start to create a painting with the custom brushes so open a new document. Keep the resolution evolving in accordance with the progress of the assignment. You should build black border frames to start. For this occasion two wide shots will do. Lock this layer on top of the other layers and paint on the layers below this frame layer. You can organize your layers in order for each painting or not, it's your choice. At this stage it doesn't matter, though later it will. It is important to have a good painting routine but anything that restricts you is not needed. Painting should be fun, or at least have some fun stages, and we should know where we can use our skill and intuition.

11: Start in black and white

We will start with black-and-white compositions in order to use our brushes, at least at the beginning. Take one of the background brushes and make a cool-looking background in light gray tones. Don't mess things up too much, but you can rotate everything, stretch, and have fun with it. Set your horizon line; try to think like a builder, not a painter. You can set something to look far from something else by using the airbrush with a lighter value on the bottom. Make sure you pay attention though to avoid brightening everything too much. Choose tones that dominate in this area of your background. Don't get too far into details. This part should take you about twenty minutes to do.

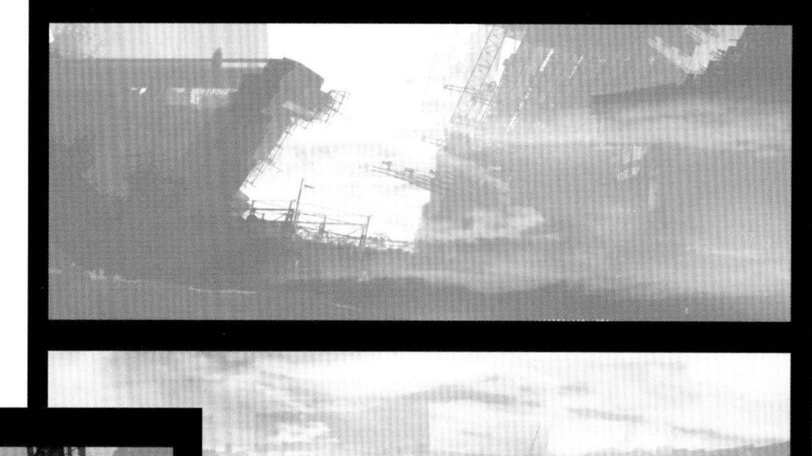

▲ Stick to black and white to begin with – the color will come later

12: Unleash brush creativity

Open a new layer. Here the fun begins. At this stage it is good to zoom out and block in the composition. Use bigger shapes at the beginning and use messy brushes – rotate them and use with a variety of Spacing settings. The goal is to set up the relationship between the two most important parts of environmental concepts: middle ground and background; foreground comes later.

12

▲ Just go for it!

13: Stop that mess! Use an atmospheric brush

Now it is time to relax and use the airbrush or atmospheric brushes to add depth to the composition. Find places in your art where the viewer's eye can slow down and add some clouds or fog to those places.

It is also good to clean up your values at this stage. Open a new layer, use the Quick Selection tool or the Lasso, and mark bigger sections from your middle ground. Also add some brighter tones at the bottom to add depth (not too many though). Depth is the key word for this stage.

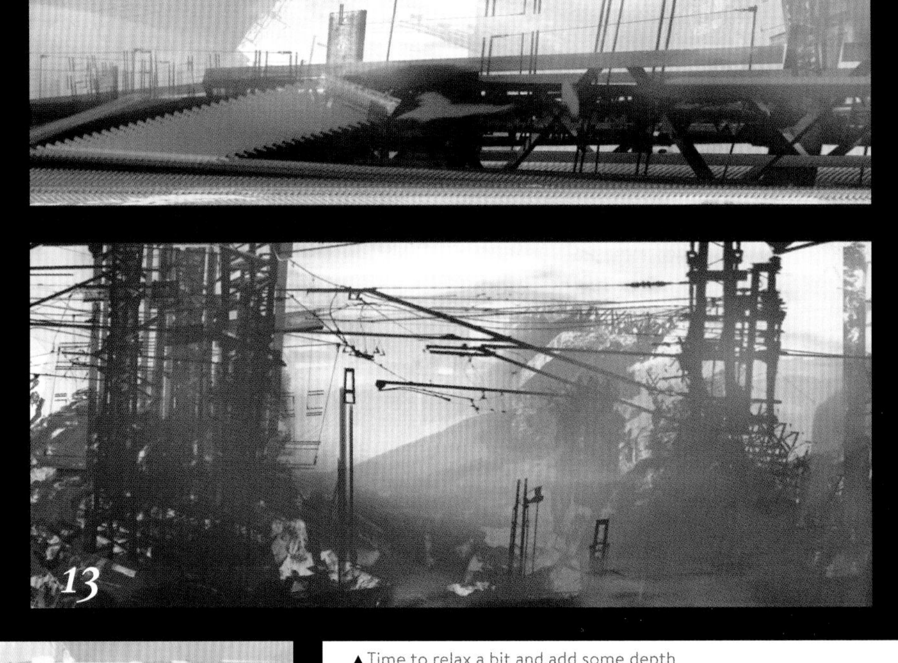

▲ Time to relax a bit and add some depth

14: Again and again

Now we should check our composition and the content we've made up to now. To see if our composition is working we can flip the canvas horizontally. Strong compositions should work both ways. Our mind will get used to seeing what we've created so it's good to check it from a new perspective (**images 14a–14c**). Don't worry, you will not lose anything; you can (and should) flip your work often. You will quickly see how your mind is cheating you sometimes. After doing this, you will see your art differently.

When flipping again, start trying to look at and develop focal points more closely. Here you can start getting into details and textures with dual brushes. You can also start to think about exactly what it is that you are painting. We must make some decisions here. Repeat this process of flipping and using messy and atmospheric brushes a few times at least before you move on to the color phase.

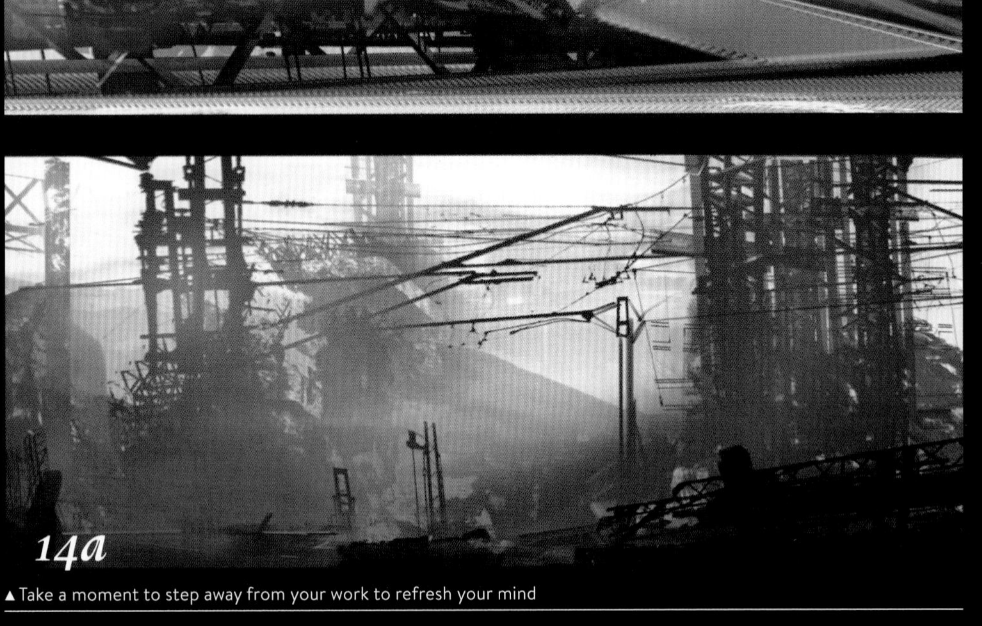

▲ Take a moment to step away from your work to refresh your mind

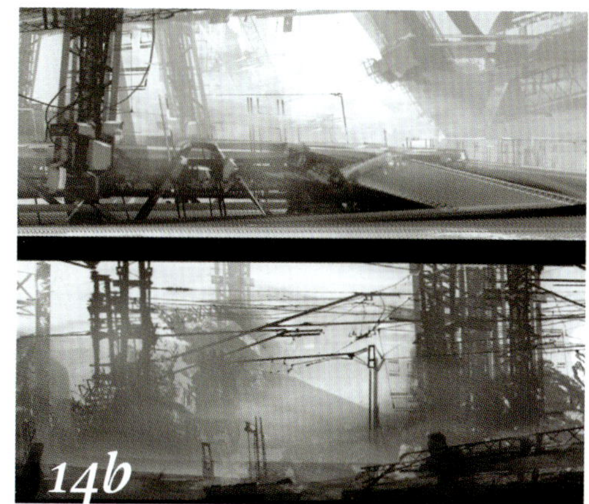

▲ Flipping your canvas allows you to check composition

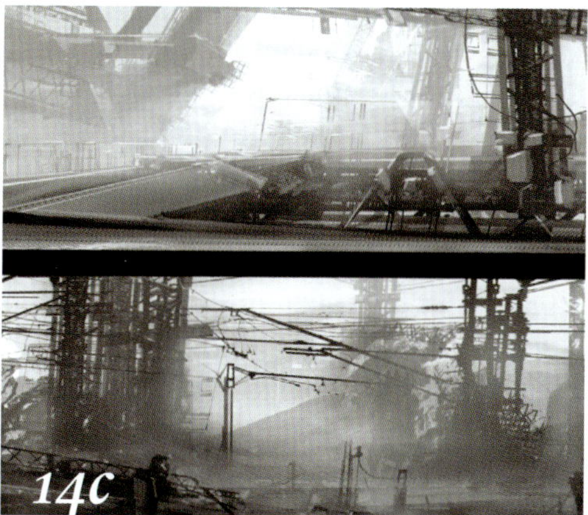

▲ Repeat this stage at least three times

15: Color

Now we must add some color to our piece. You can colorize it using Color, Overlay, and other layer modes according to your preference (**image 15a**). You can also toss a coin a little bit and merge all the content and add color to the image as a gradient effect in the Layers manager with an interesting blend mode. You can then manage the gradient effect with Overlay or correct how much it appears with Curves. I think sometimes when you are feeling tired with your routine you can find new inspiration by setting tasks for your gray cells. You can for example change the way you work (such as by changing the method you add colors to the image). Ultimately, try to make wise color choices (**image 15b**).

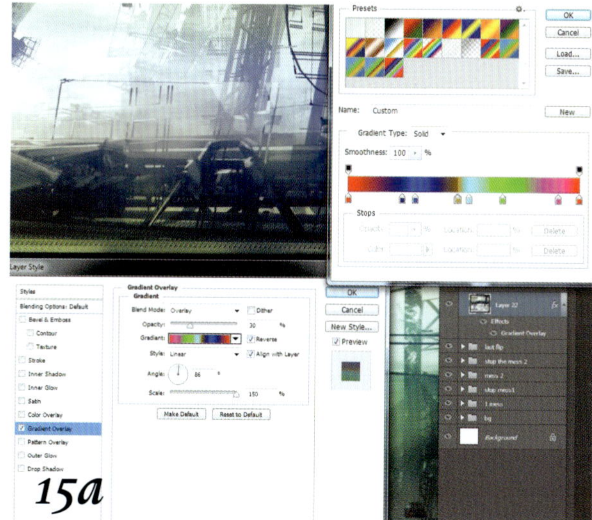

▲ Time for a splash of color

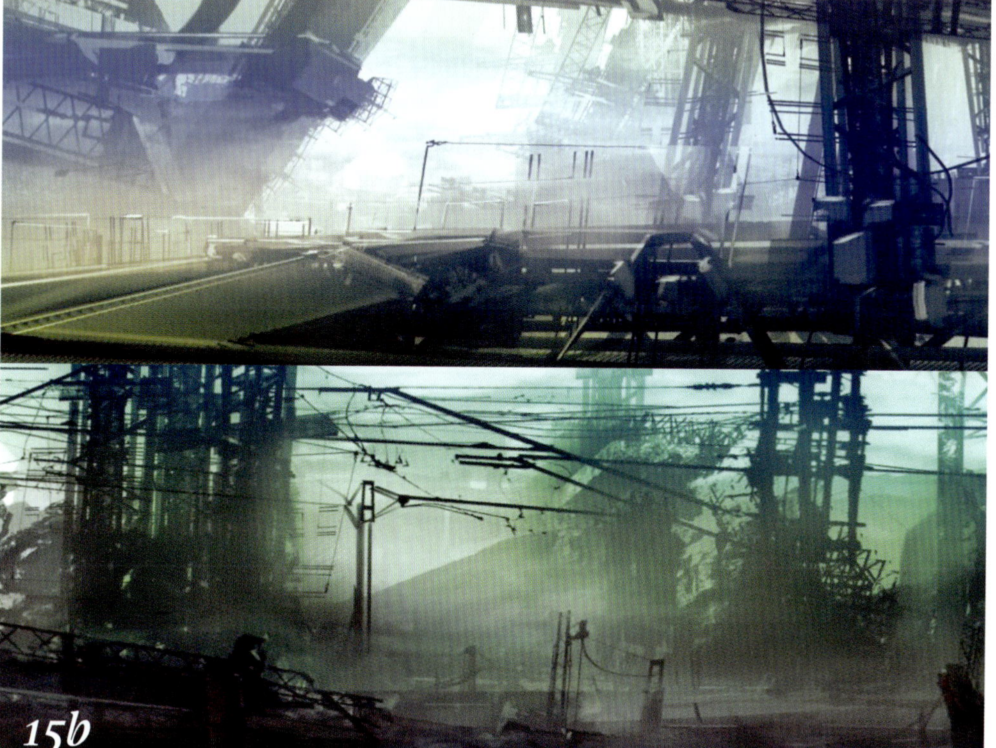

▲ Make wise color choices when colorizing your work

16: Foreground

We now need to check all focal points and consider them in relation to the foreground. Are they leading to what we want? How is the viewer being led around in this environment? It is time to use foreground as a tool to expose composition and tell more story.

I suggest you use messy brushes at almost 100% black for foregrounds. Try not to let the foreground dominate your piece. Sometimes foregrounds should be blurred according to your focal point, and this trick increases the immersion effect of your story.

17: Light fun

We can also use city lights to add emphasis to our focal points. To do this, copy city lights from a photo onto the top of your layer stack. Set the lights layer to Screen or Lighten mode. Go to Levels (Ctrl+L) and increase the contrast with the slider so you have only the city lights. Copy this layer, shrink it, and put it near the focal points. Use it wisely to give your scene more life.

18: Final touches

After all these pipeline stages, and when the entire piece is flattened, I usually play around with colors and Curves to gain an effect that suits me. It is good to use the Smart Sharpen filter on particular elements to enrich the focal points.

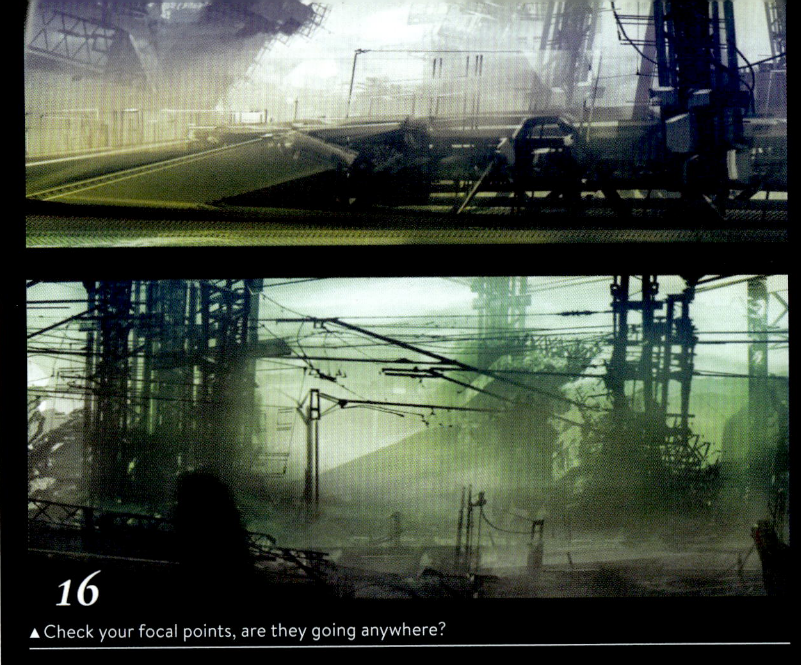

▲ Check your focal points, are they going anywhere?

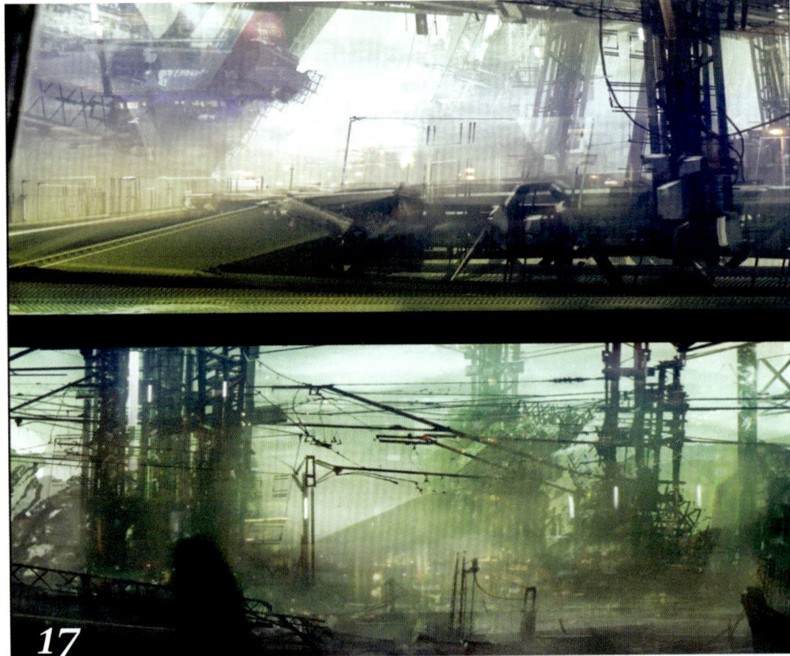

▲ Find some reference images of lights to add focus and life to your work

Sometimes we can add a little character silhouette. While this can look funny, it is also done with the purpose of giving the viewer a sense of the scale and size of elements in the scene, and to make it easier to read and set the viewer's perspective. This stage is for all those lovely little details and last corrections.

This chapter is meant to open you up to free explorations of creating custom and dual brushes and offer you a readable process that leads from beginning to end. Remember that this is only one exercise and you should make hundreds of them – find tasks for yourself and try to explore areas where you lack artistic knowledge. Tackle them with inspiration and with the workflow I have shown you here when necessary.

While following these rules, remember that this is only an exercise and you shouldn't worry about making mistakes or doing something wrong.

If we want to be successful artists we must do thousands of these kinds of exercises and find our own ways to deal with particular assignments. An artist's brain likes to be kept in a well-exercised and excited state, so we must try to have fun all the time. We must spend our time searching out new ways, trying new techniques, and mixing them with our artistic pipeline.

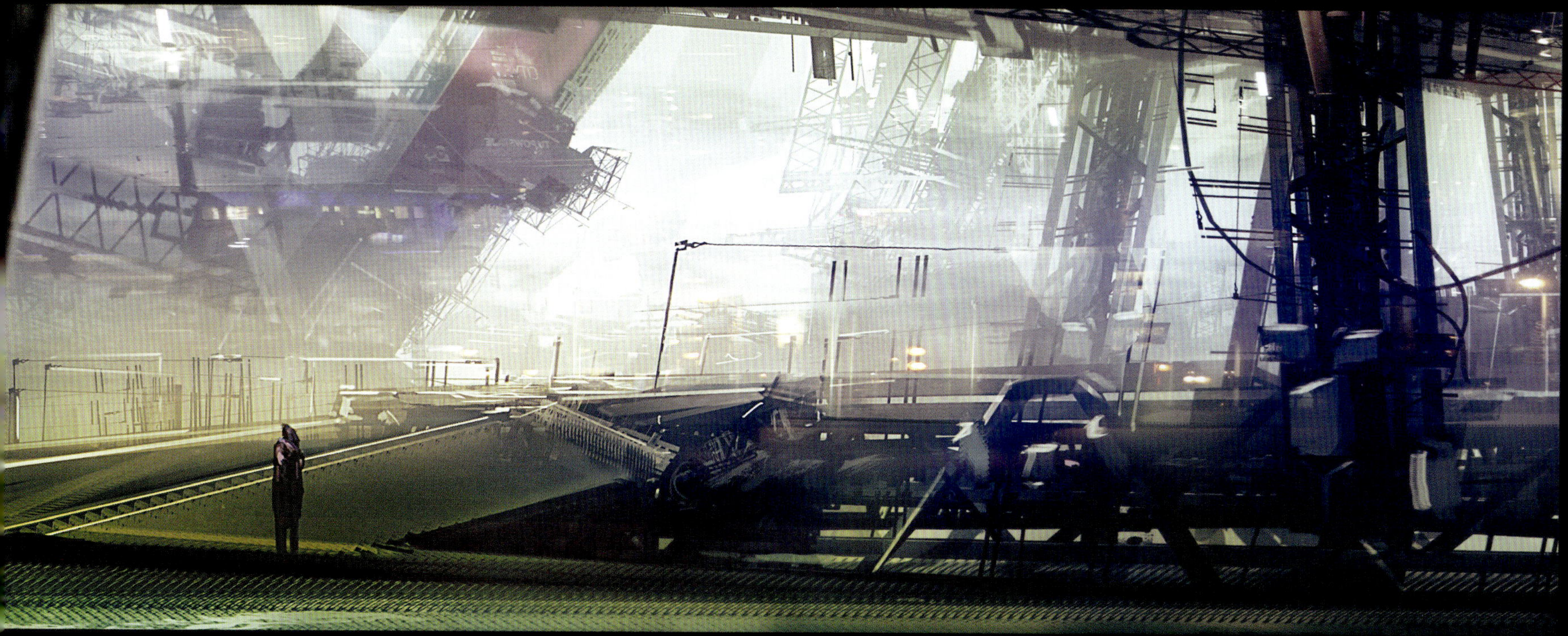

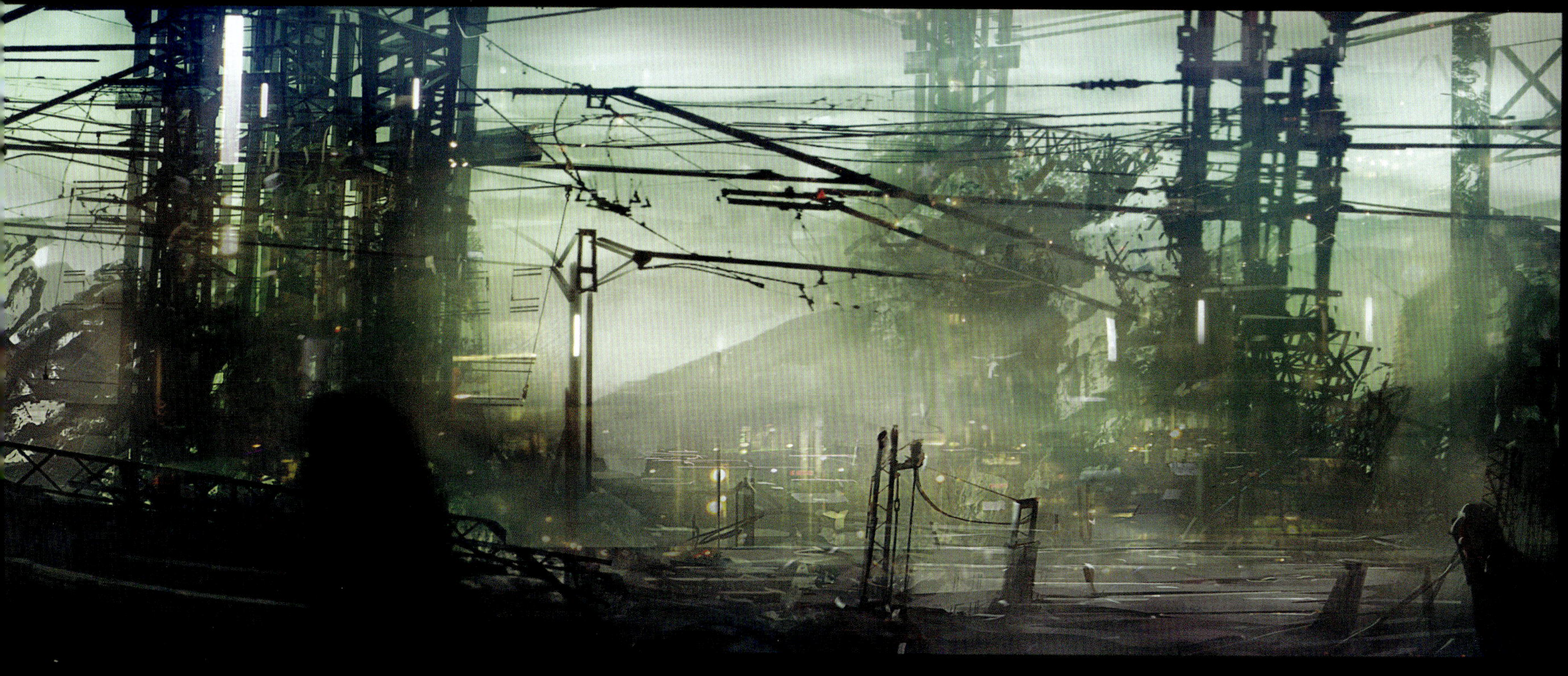

PHOTOBASHING
Ioan Dumitrescu

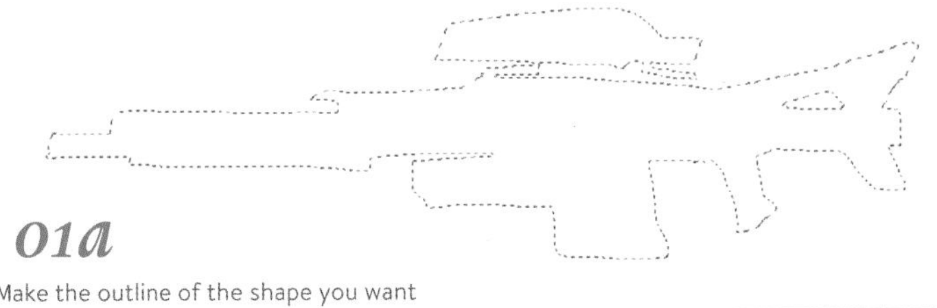

01a

▲ Make the outline of the shape you want

Photobashing is a technique that uses photographic material to quickly obtain textures and effects in an image. Here we will cover some of the basic tools that make up the day-to-day process of Photoshop image making, especially when it comes to developing concepts quickly. To put some of these techniques in context, I'll talk about them while developing a design for a weapon, which will be quite imaginary as far as the idea goes and how reality based it is.

I use a standard Photoshop interface; I don't feel I need to make any adjustments to it. I use keyboard shortcuts for the tools I use, assigned from the Edit menu. When designing a weapon it's usually best to start from a side view. That way you can see the whole silhouette and watch proportions and function. To start we need a basic shape, so what I like to do to block out quick clean shapes with the Lasso tool. Either freeform Lasso or Polygonal Lasso will do! Let's begin.

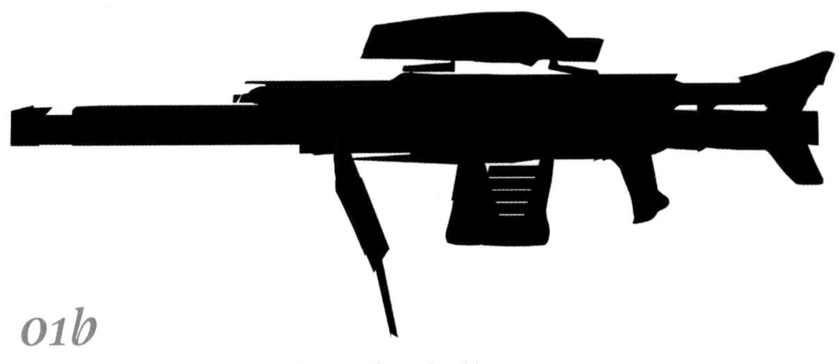

01b

▲ It helps to view the weapon as a silhouette from the side

01: Make shapes

Make a shape and use the Fill tool to fill it in. Make any adjustments to the shape using the Rectangular Marquee tool (**images 01a and 01b**). I like to work by adding and deleting because I find it gives a nice graphic look and feel.

02: References

Now you can fill the shape with the necessary information to give the gun a believable feel. This is where reference libraries come in handy. You can take your own photos or find what you need on the internet (although take care with copyright here).

I don't want to add parts to my design that are already from guns because it would defeat the purpose. We are trying to get something new flowing, explore opportunities, and have fun!

I use an image of a remote micro surveillance camera (**image 02**) – the hard plastic material is good and it has

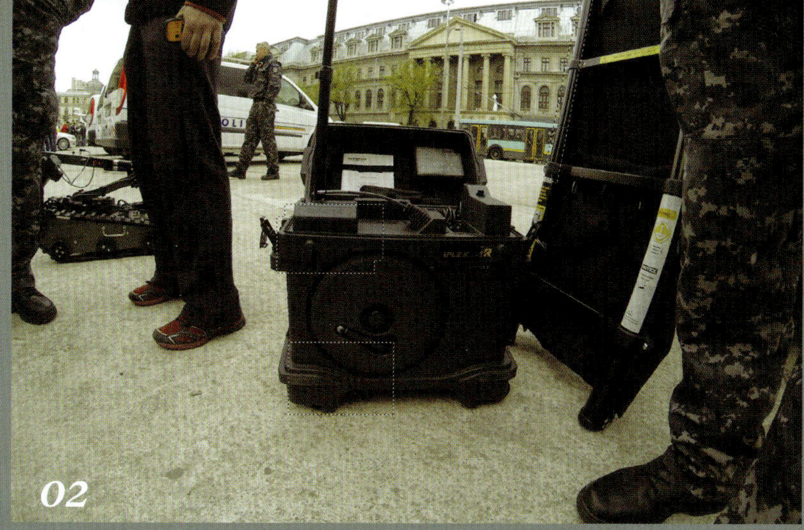

▲ My reference image

some interesting shapes that might help develop a realistic and pleasing look for the gun. I like using a GoPro to shoot references because its high angle distortion can spark a lot of ideas!

03: Select and transform

Start to use parts of the photo on your weapon design to add to the concept. Use the Marquee selection tool; to add another selection press the Shift key. You can do as many selections as you want! I'm going to try to use only photos till the very end, just so that we can go through as many technical aspects as possible.

To allow yourself to focus more on the design, desaturate everything using Hue/Saturation, setting Saturation to 0. This makes all colors turn gray, leaving just tones. Select some shapes you like and create a new separate layer with just these. Now you can select each one and transform them into position (**image 03a**).

I use a lot of Skew, Free Transform, and Warp to help me to place the selections from photos into the shape previously created. I'm not trying to be totally specific at this point; to be more precise, press Ctrl and touch the control points – they will be active and movable. You can also rotate the shape around, and flip it vertically or horizontally (**image 03b**)!

04: Fix the distortion

As mentioned, angle distortion in images is sometimes fun and can trigger new ideas, however in some cases it is unwanted and will need to be fixed as we require some elements to remain straight. Use the Warp tool after Free Transform, using the control points to balance the curves and make them straight.

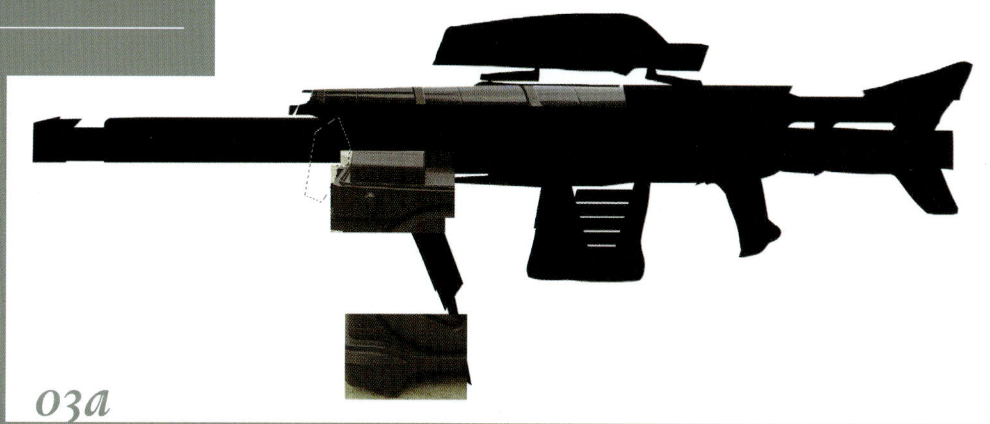

▲ Add selections from your reference photos

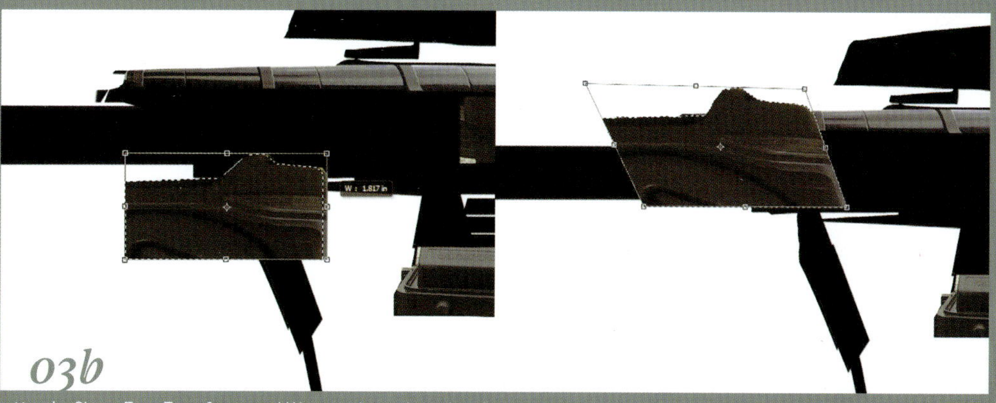

▲ Use the Skew, Free Transform, and Warp tools to place the photo selections

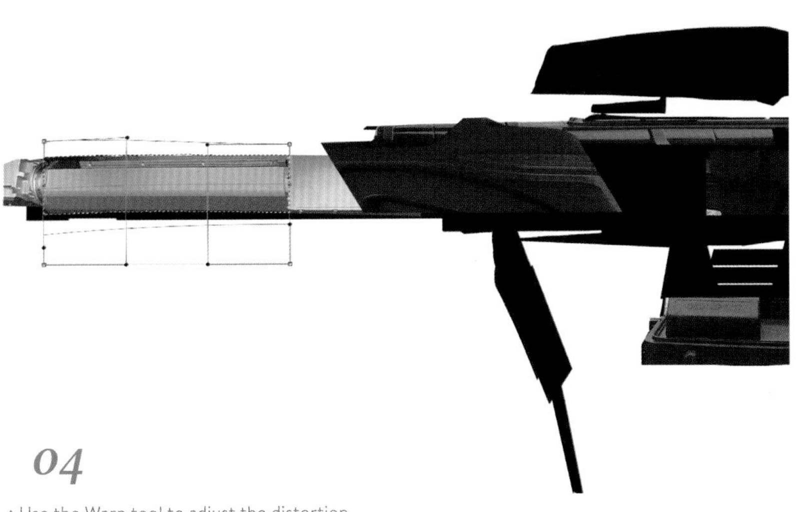

04

▲ Use the Warp tool to adjust the distortion

05

▲ Add the barrel as a simple shape

05: The barrel

Add the barrel as a simple shape as we can detail it later. The start of it has a more rectangular boxy shape. I want to replace it so it becomes a continuous octagon-like profile. I select a portion of it and use Free Transform to stretch it across.

06: Lighting and Curves

I keep bringing photo elements in and feel the need to fill in the black space with more gray. I therefore make a selection with a brush and sweep across to fill the space (**image 06a**).

To give shape to the gun we need lighting. I go for a more studio-lighting effect, with a top light and fill light. You need to see this in your grays, so start using Curves in order to adjust the grays and make shapes pop out (**image 06b**)!

Put simply, the Curves tool controls highlights and darkest darks. In the Curves window, the upper-right control point manages values starting from white, and the lower-left control point manages black. By moving these up and down or left and right, you can get them into the middle, which is a pure 50% gray.

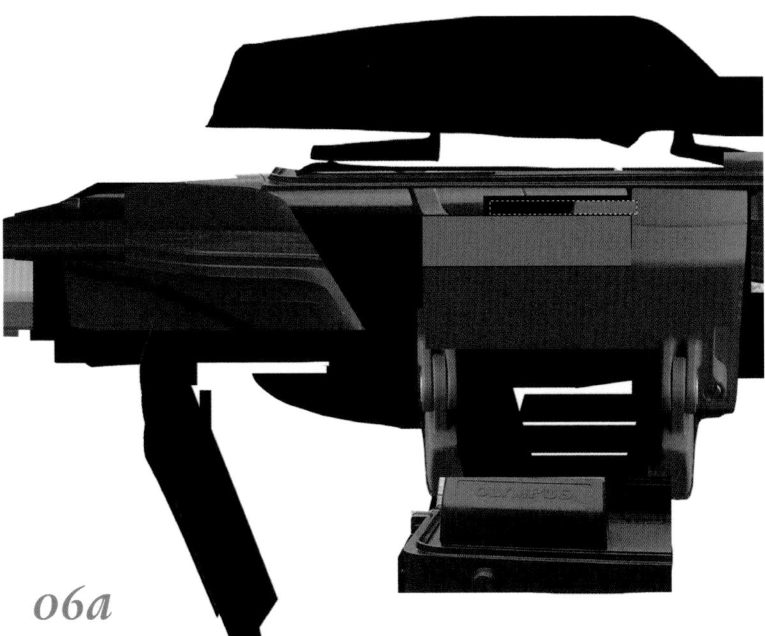

06a

▲ Add more gray to the gun

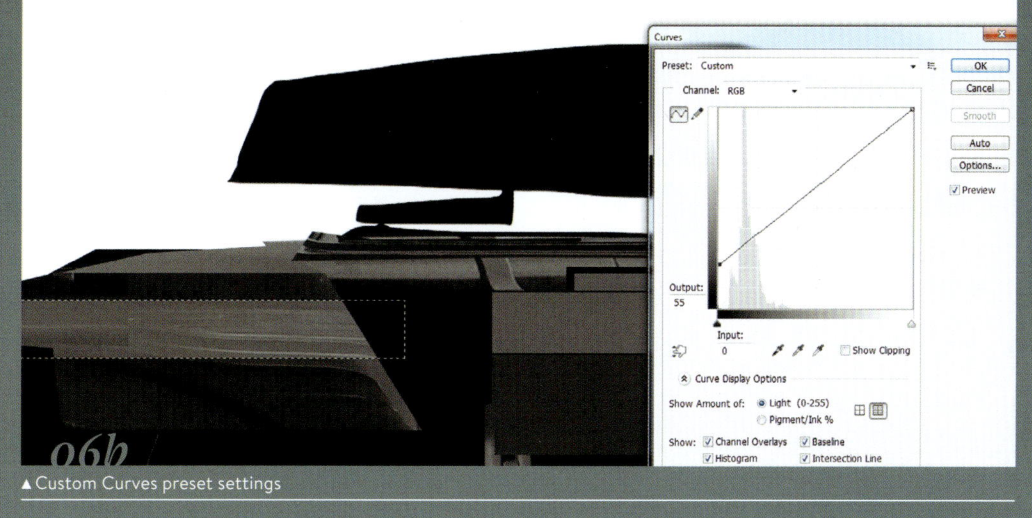

▲ Custom Curves preset settings

"Gradients are useful for giving the appearance of depth"

The best way to look at it is to ask yourself questions: what do I want to do? Do I want to brighten this image? For the gun we need to keep the darks in the creases. Move the white control point to the left towards the dark to increase brightness, and leave the darkest darks where they are (**image 06c**). Once you start playing around with it you'll get the hang of it quickly!

You can also select Curves to change colors; instead of RGB select the channel you want to play with.

07: Gradients

I push photos all over the place to fill my initial black shape and soon I have a base on which to select and define the shapes I feel better about. I also want to fill the background with something more gray because the white is jumping too much and works against me, darkening the whole gun due to contrast. Gradients are useful for giving the appearance of depth. Go to the Gradient Editor, select one of the presets, and start fooling around with the controls. Add as many control points as you want by clicking underneath the gradient line. You can change the type of color/value you want them to have. At the end Photoshop will form a gradient just like that shown in the preview box. Now you can just click and drag in the direction you want the gradient to have, in this case vertical.

08: Edit shapes

A selection technique I use all the time is a very quick and easy way to obtain more complex shapes out of your simple selections. Using the Lasso tool I select the support strut I have added to the gun, knowing that I want to fill it and suggest another part with gray. I also want to leave a few areas untouched for some simple bolts. While holding the selection, press Alt and use the Elliptical Marquee tool to get a circle. Once you release, the circle

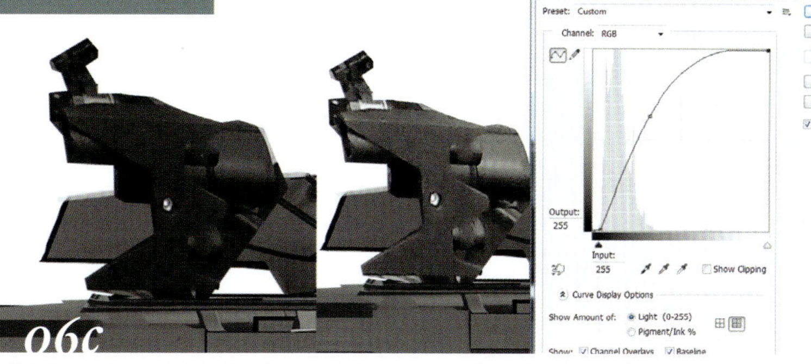

▲ Pull the control points in the Curves window to adjust the values in your image

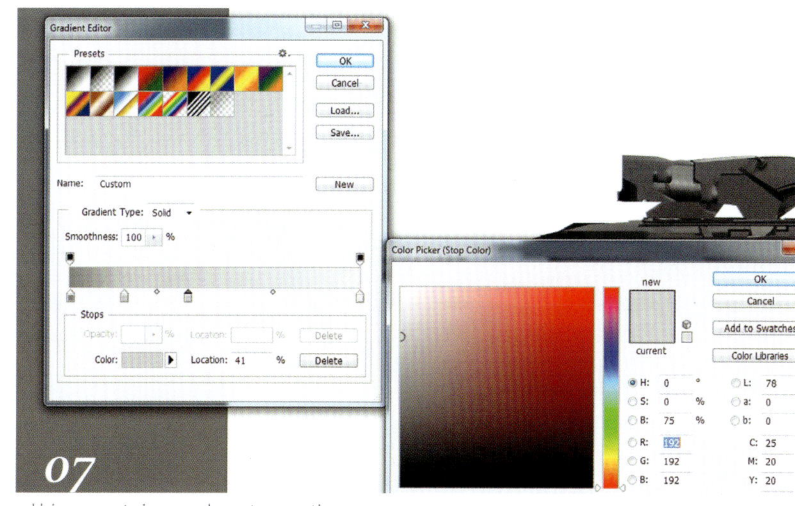

▲ Using presets is a good way to save time

is cut from the selection. Turn to Gradient and choose one of the presets with transparency that doesn't fill everything. This way you can get your values softer inside the shape. Reducing the opacity down to 10–20% also helps (**image 08a**).

The tripod strut has a rubber handle that value-wise is not working for me. How can we fix it using Curves? Go into mask mode by pressing Q. There you can see our area selected, but we need the selection to be more graded so we only affect what we need on this circular part. I select a soft standard brush and use it on the mask. White enlarges the selection and black will reduce it. Of course you can use intermediates, or just rely on pen pressure.

Now press Q again to leave mask mode and you will be left with your selection to modify. Drop down the highlights controller and it will be there (**image 08b**).

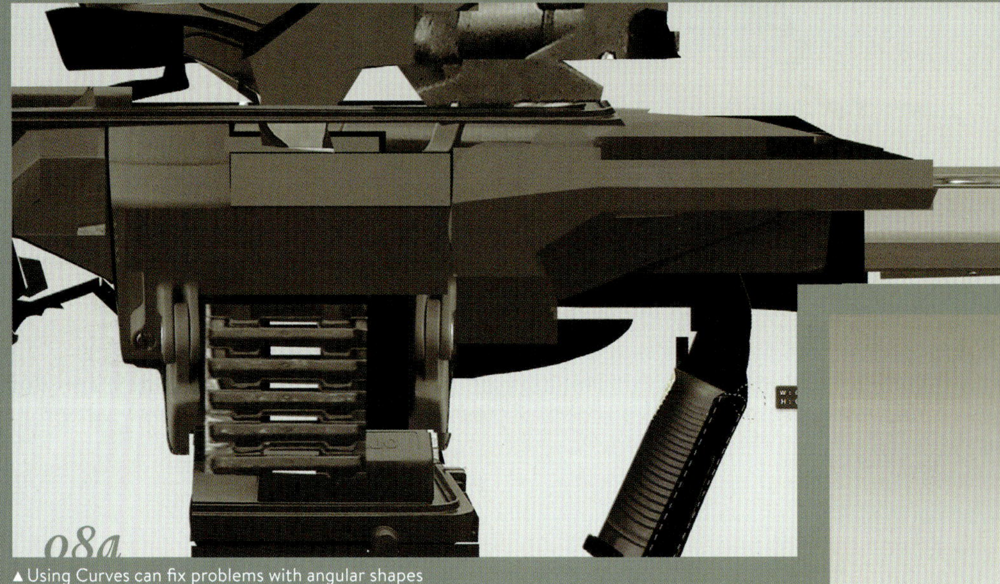

▲ Using Curves can fix problems with angular shapes

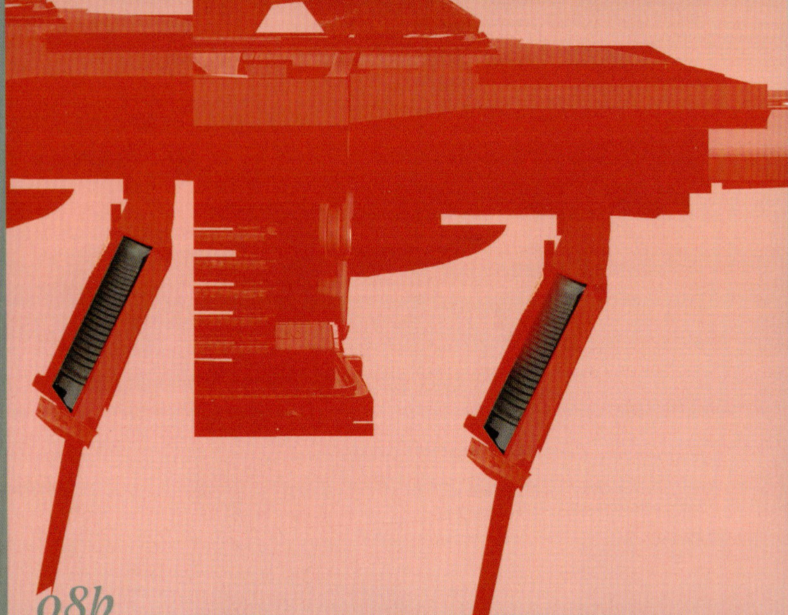

▲ Use a mask when fixing the values of the rubber handles

09: Detailing

I use these various techniques all around to integrate the photos with each other and create the light I want to suggest. To unite them better I use selections that I fill with local value.

Another way to unify your image is to use some layer modes. I usually use Lighten, which lightens everything underneath to the color you use, or Darken, which does the opposite. Whichever is whiter or respectively darker is not affected by these layers. I use a Darken layer to give shadow and occlusion to creases. This will make things believable and sit better together. I find that using the Soft brush or a gradient helps to put the occlusion feeling across.

Now it's time to add more details through photos. I want to add a grill texture to the gun and start going through layer modes. I end up choosing Overlay as the best choice. Use Curves to increase contrast so the darks and whites pop out more. Use Free Transform with Warp to put it into place and the

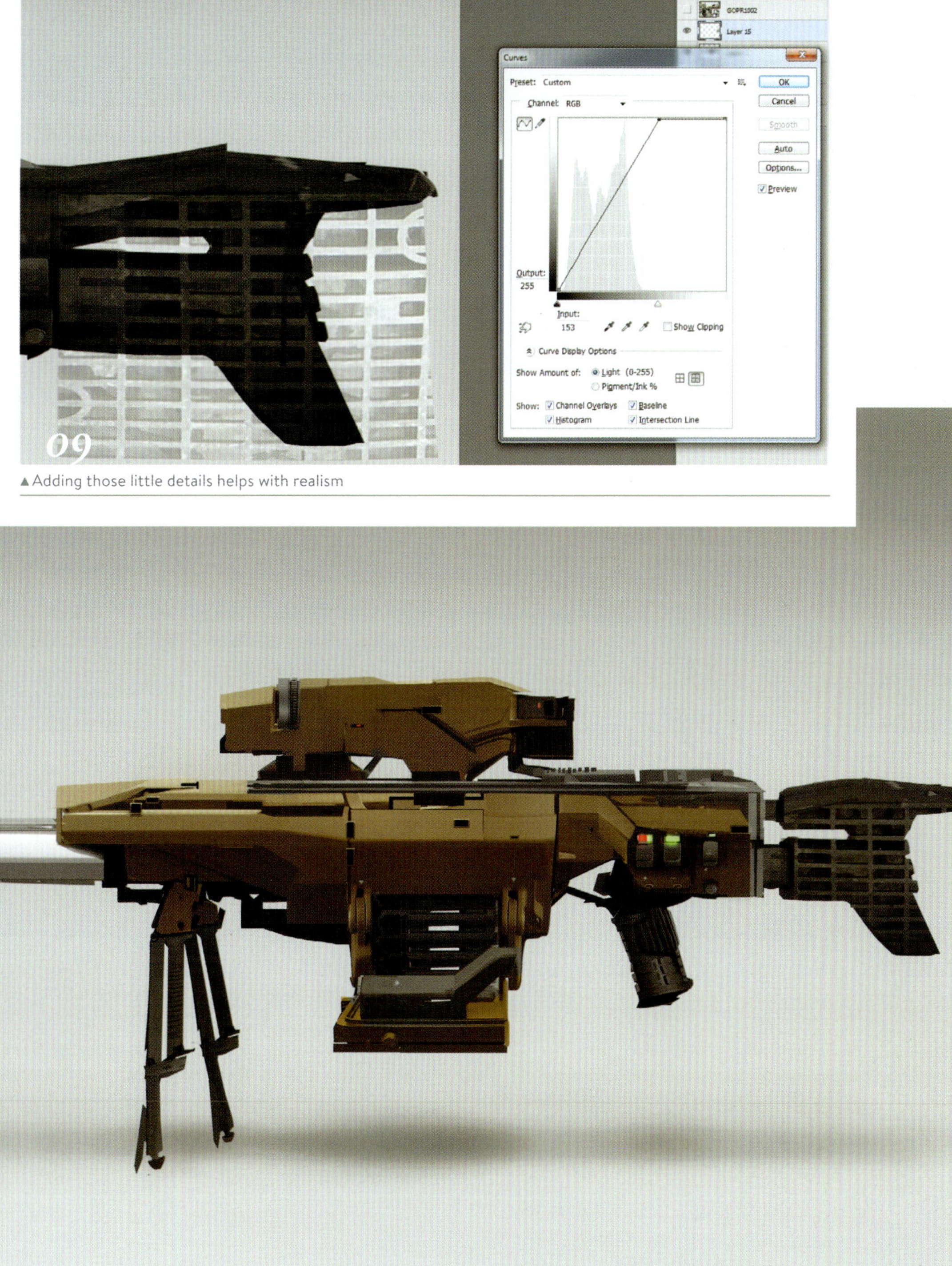

▲Adding those little details helps with realism

correct perspective. Now I just need the texture to be on the gun and not on the background. For this I clip it to the gun layer by clicking in between the layer in the Layers panel. While holding Alt you will see a broken arrow just before you click. This will act as a mask, which will keep everything inside the shape of the gun.

10: Finishing touches

A quick way to detail products is to make little geometric shapes that look like bolts or nuts. For this I usually use the Elliptical or Rectangular Marquee tool. Once I've made all the selections around the gun I use Edit > Stroke... and choose the color and thickness. This will give micro detail that helps the believability and realism of the gun.

Now we should bring in some colors. We can do this through some electronic lights for the optics or gun safety mechanism. Fill in selections with their respective colors and then add a Color Dodge layer to pop it. I'm thinking of making this gun a bit more of a prototype with some production colors on it, something along the lines of orange or yellow. For this make a new layer and turn it to Color Mode. Choose a middle range orangey-brown and bucket it over the whole canvas. Now use the selection of the gun and add a mask to it. From this mask you can erase out the areas you don't want to have this color. Finish your final details and tighten up some shapes with a bit more integration.

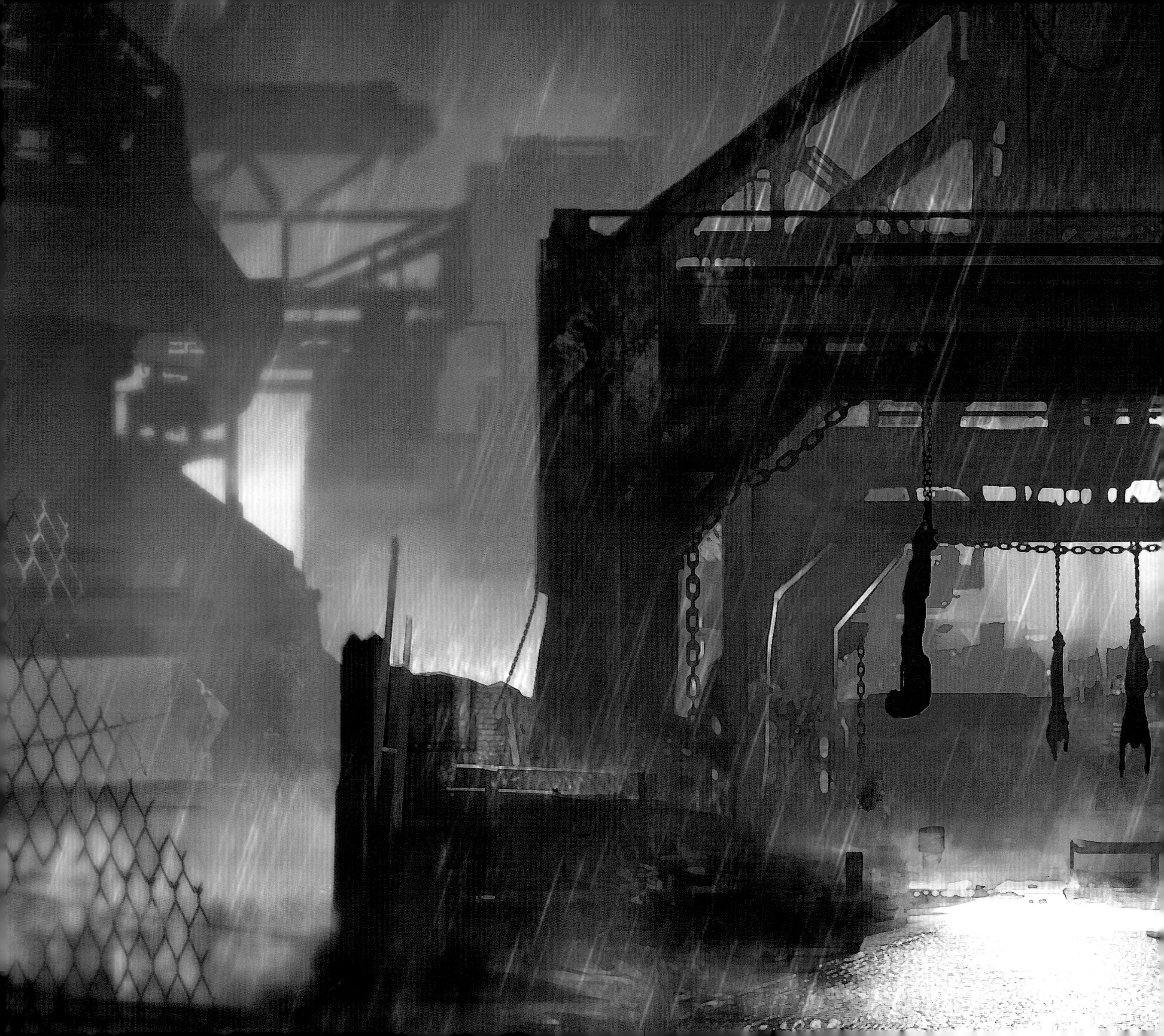

Gallery

Here we have gathered together some fantastic speed paintings from artists around the globe. There are a variety of genres, themes, and styles, including futuristic city concepts, fantasy landscapes, and everything in between. We hope that you find them as beautiful and inspiring as we do.

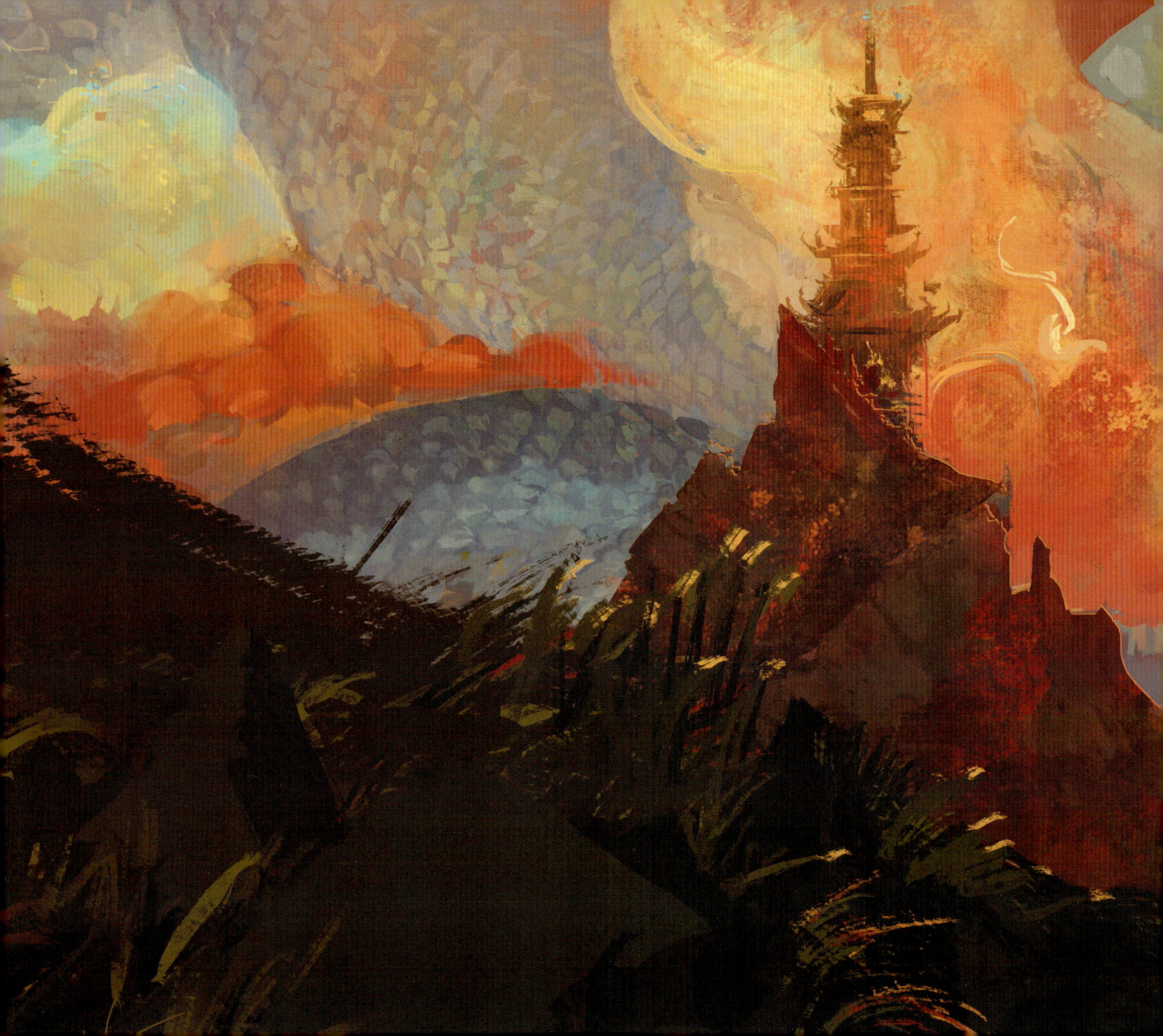

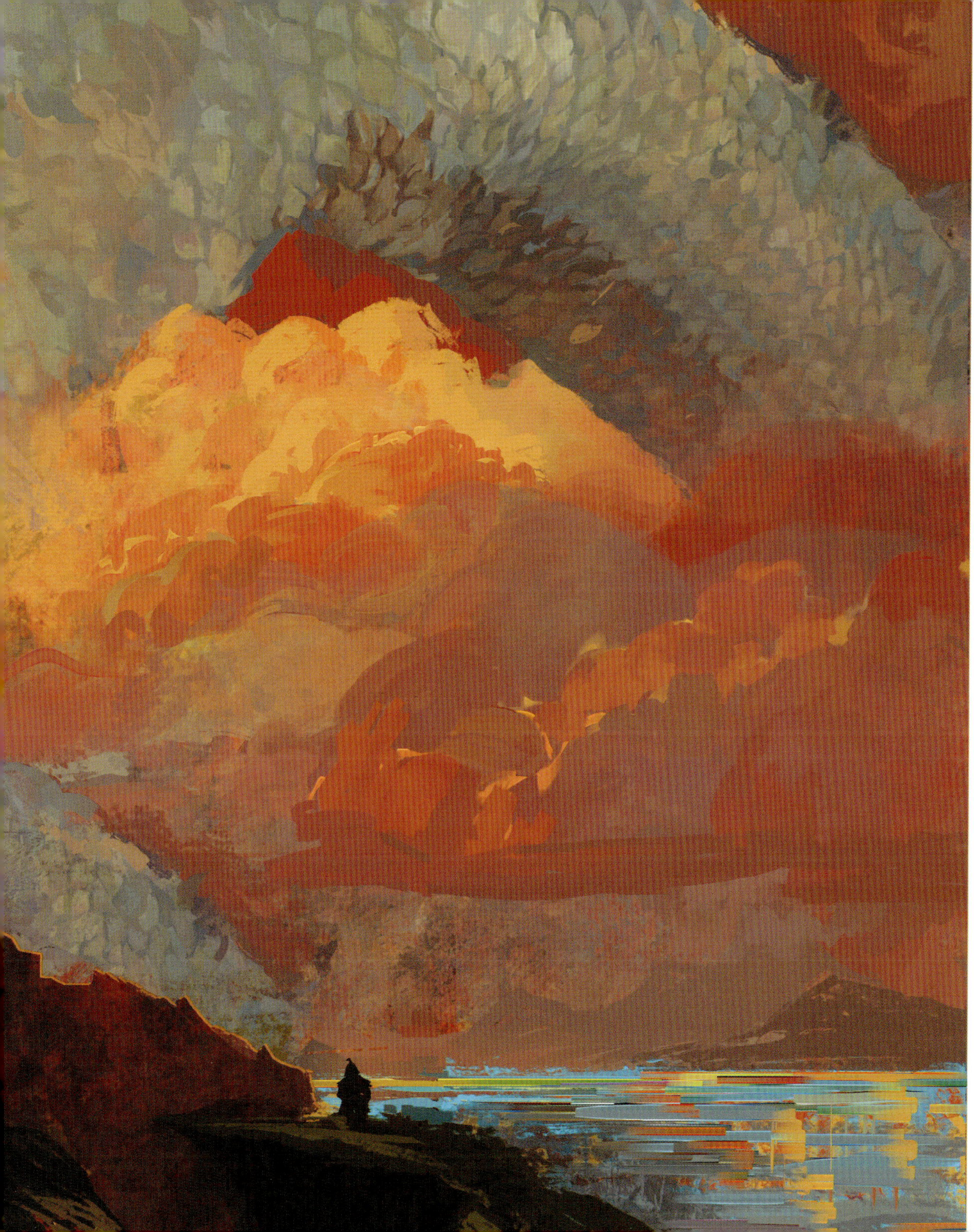

Dragon Temple
Stephanie Cost

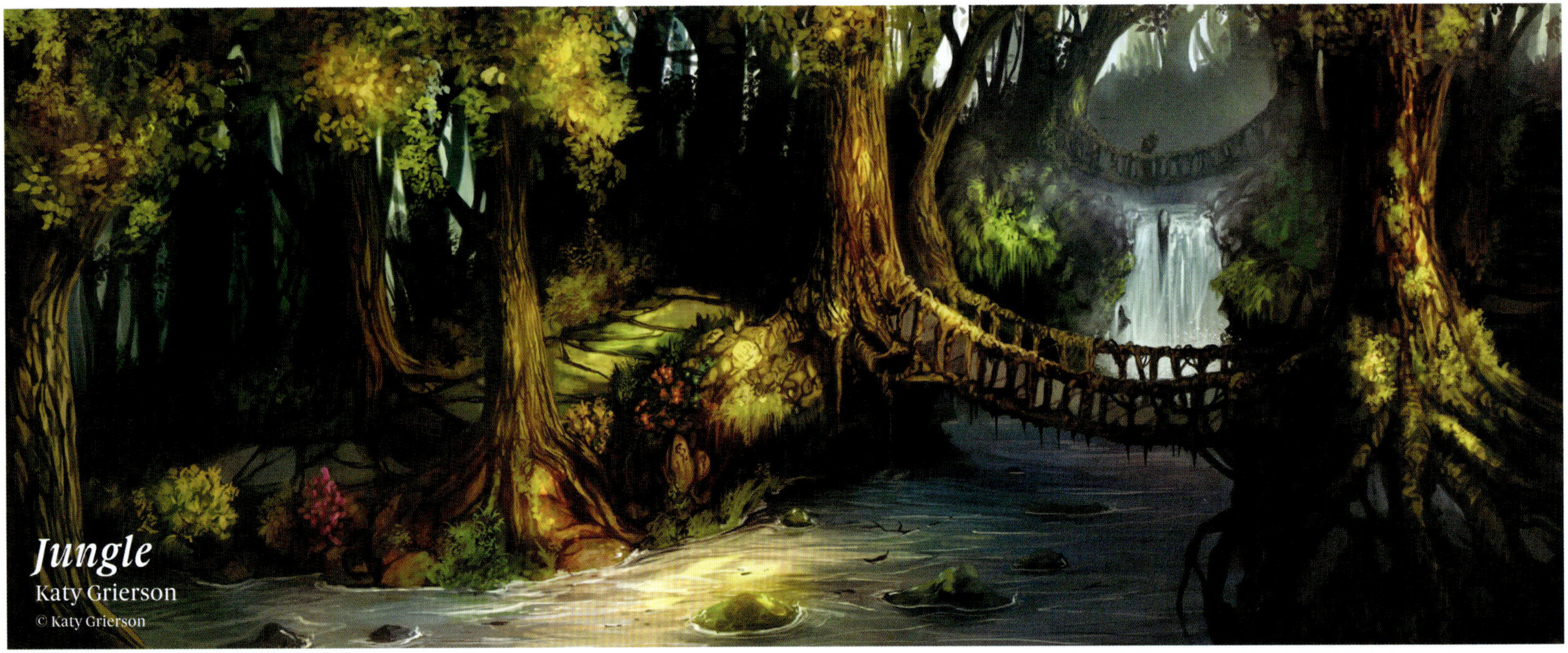

Jungle

Katy Grierson

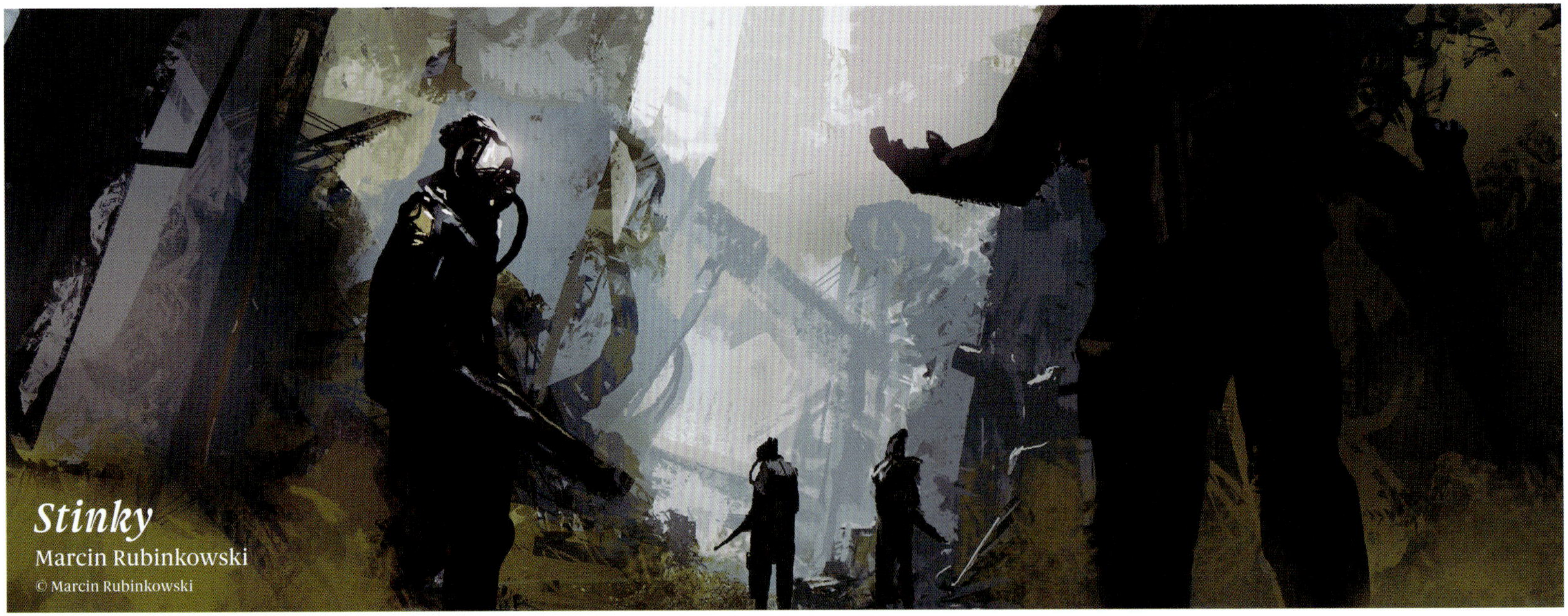

Stinky

Marcin Rubinkowski

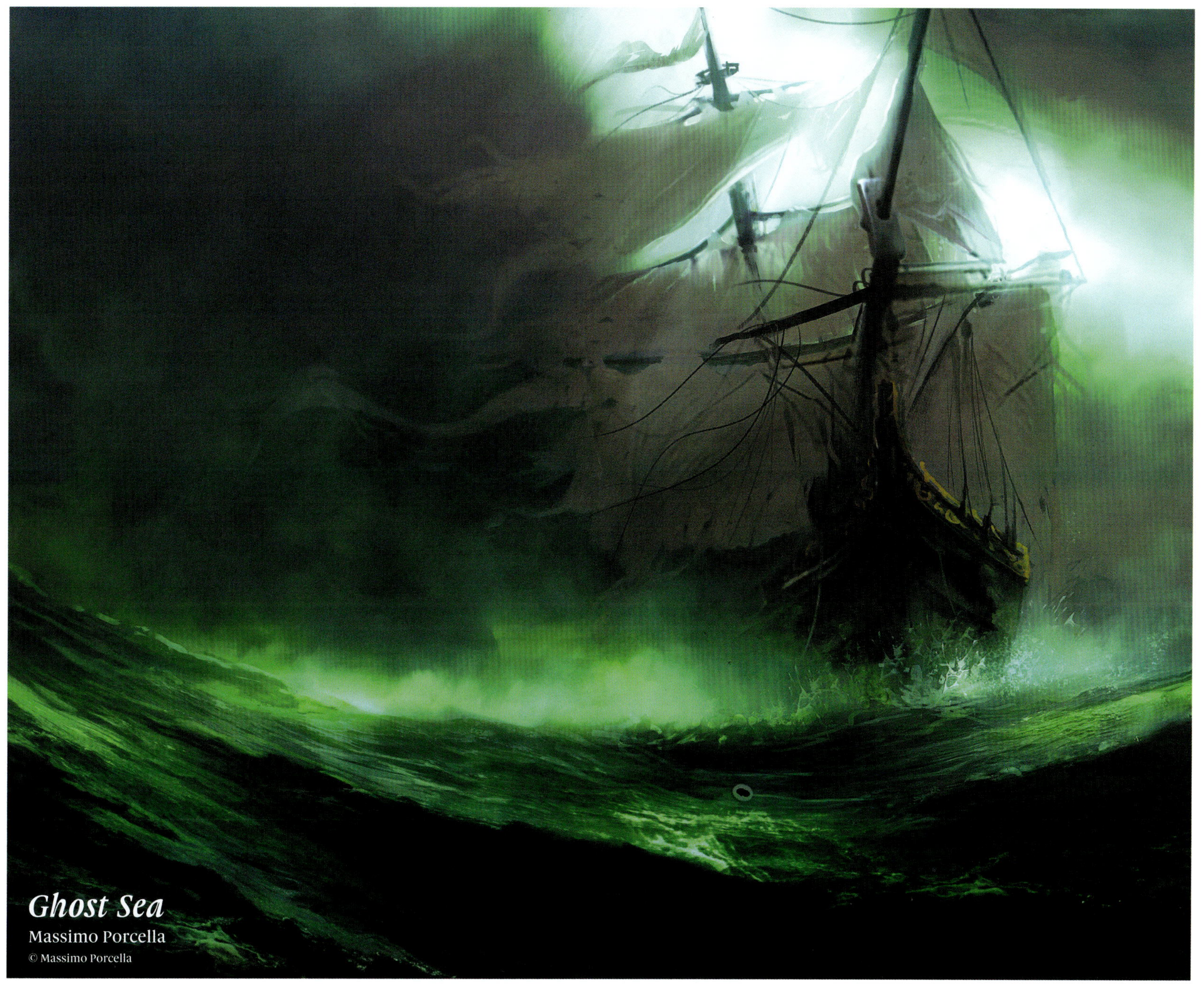

Ghost Sea

Massimo Porcella

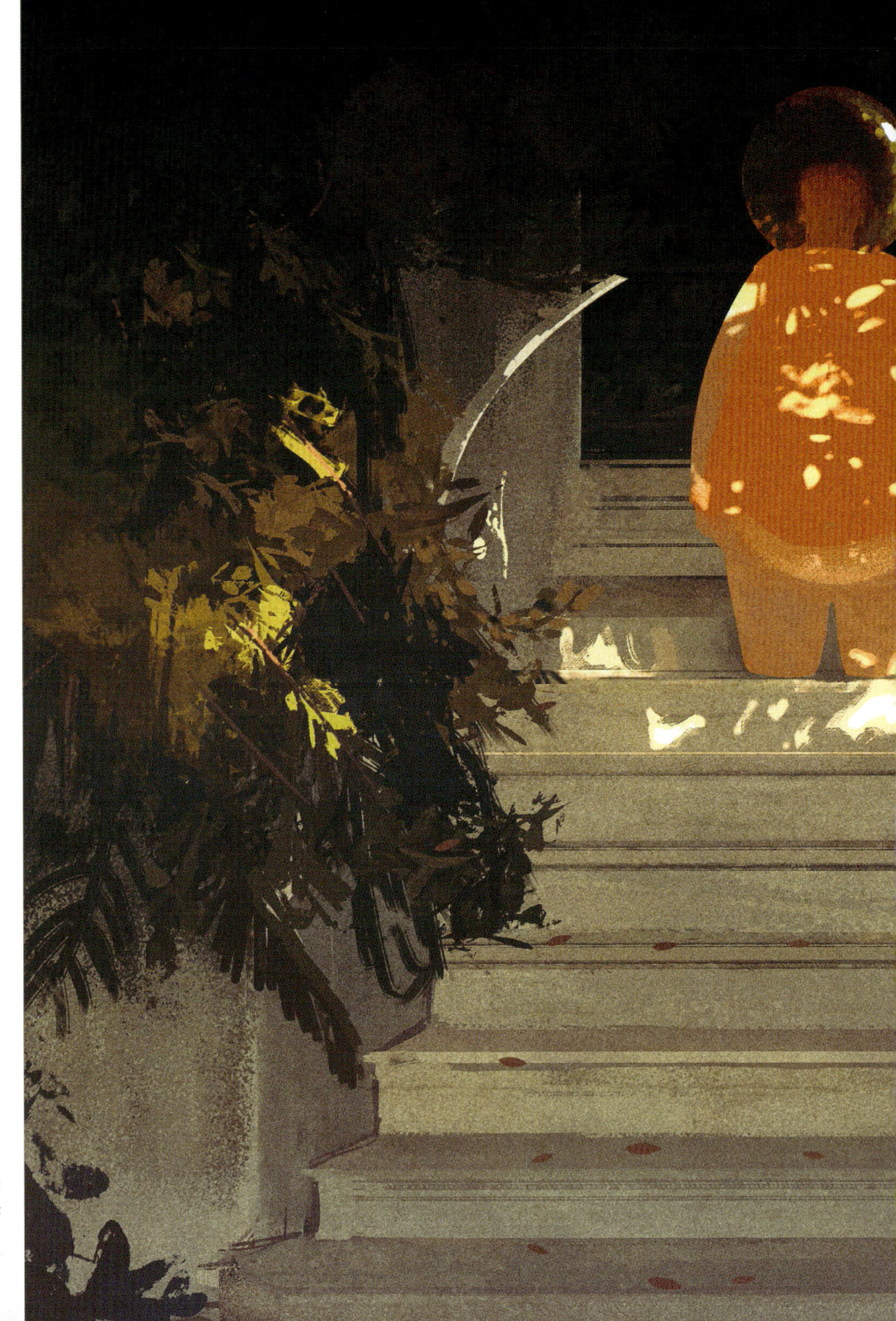

Le Réviel

Florian Aupetit

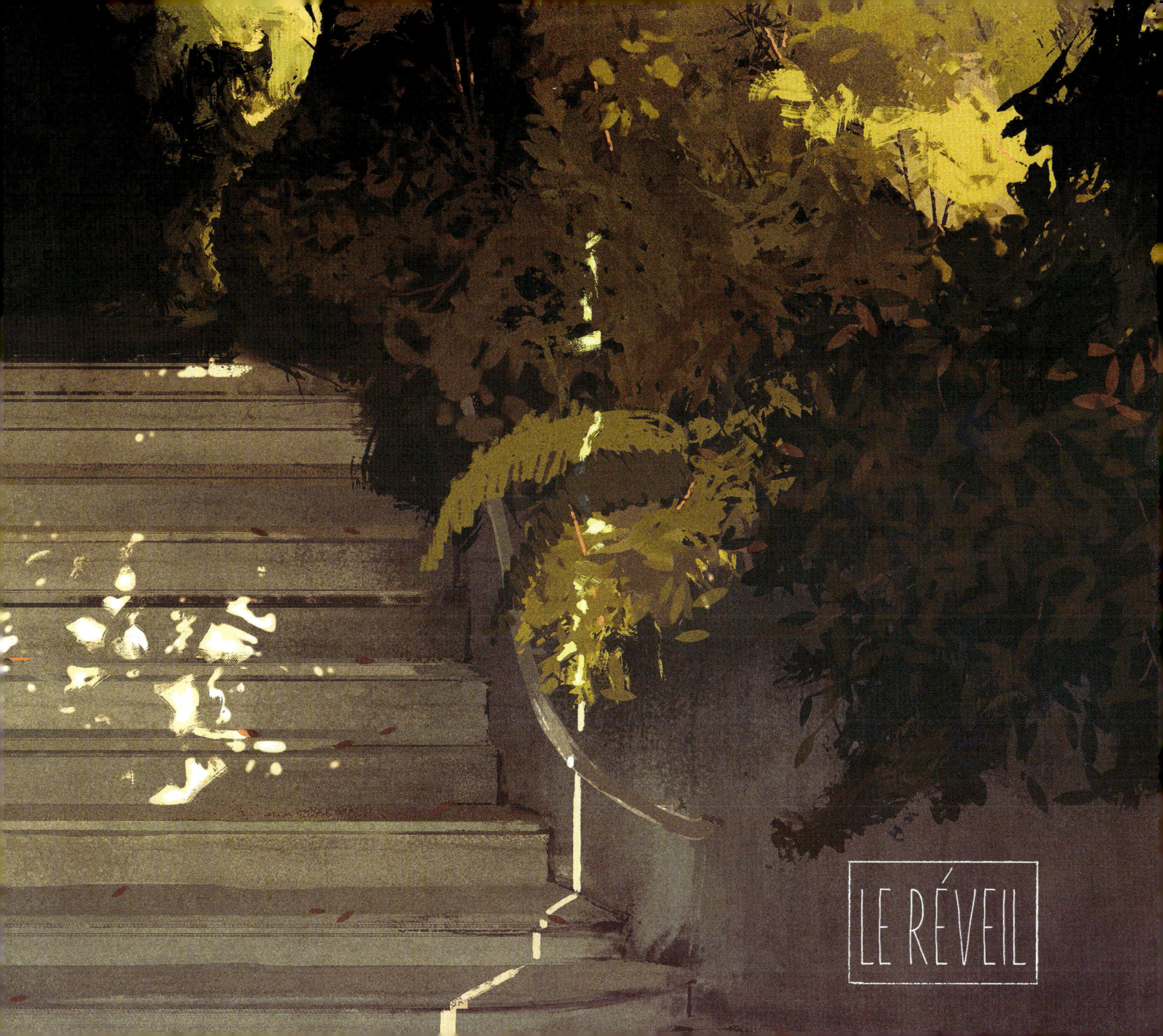
LE RÉVEIL

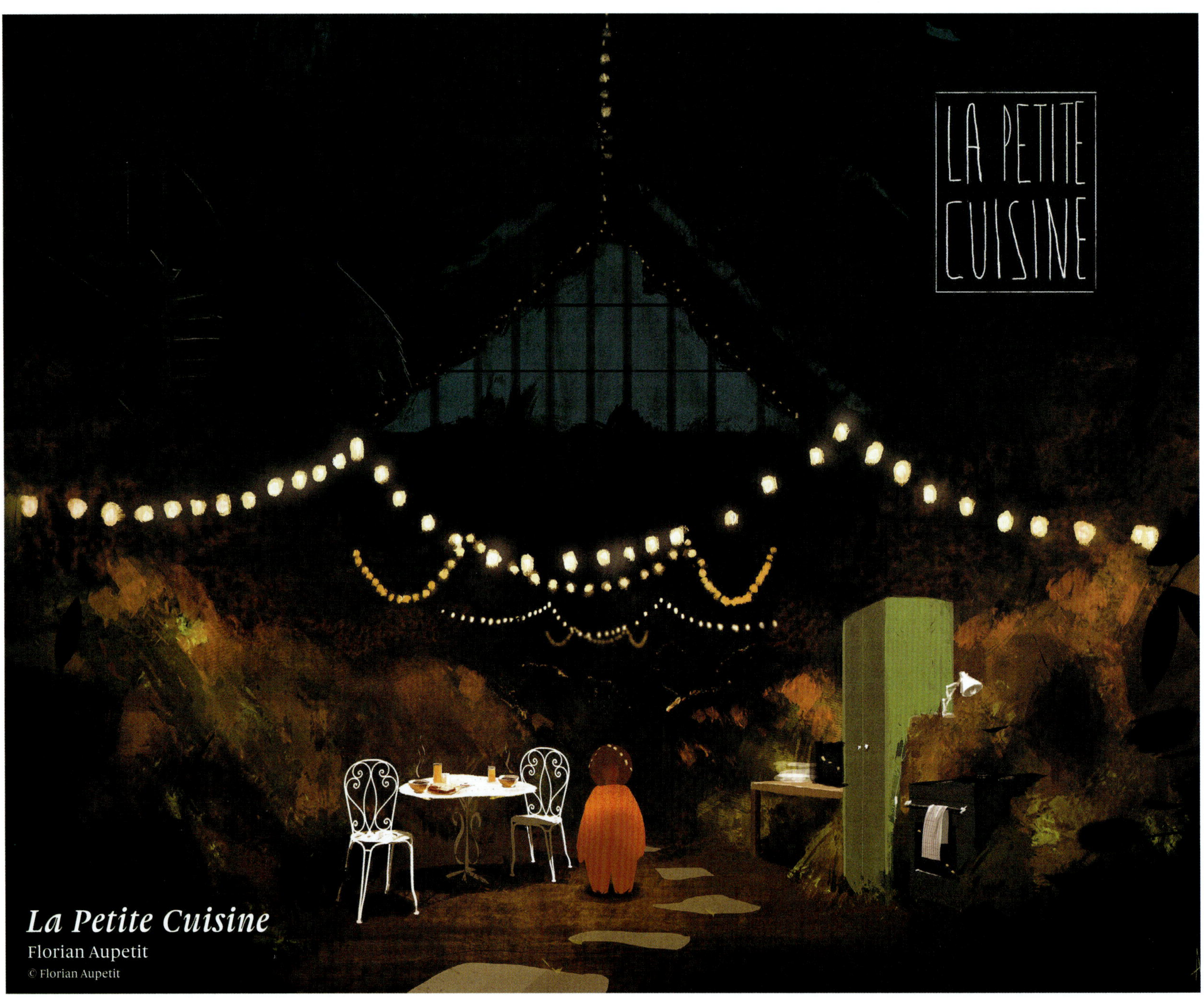

La Petite Cuisine

Florian Aupetit

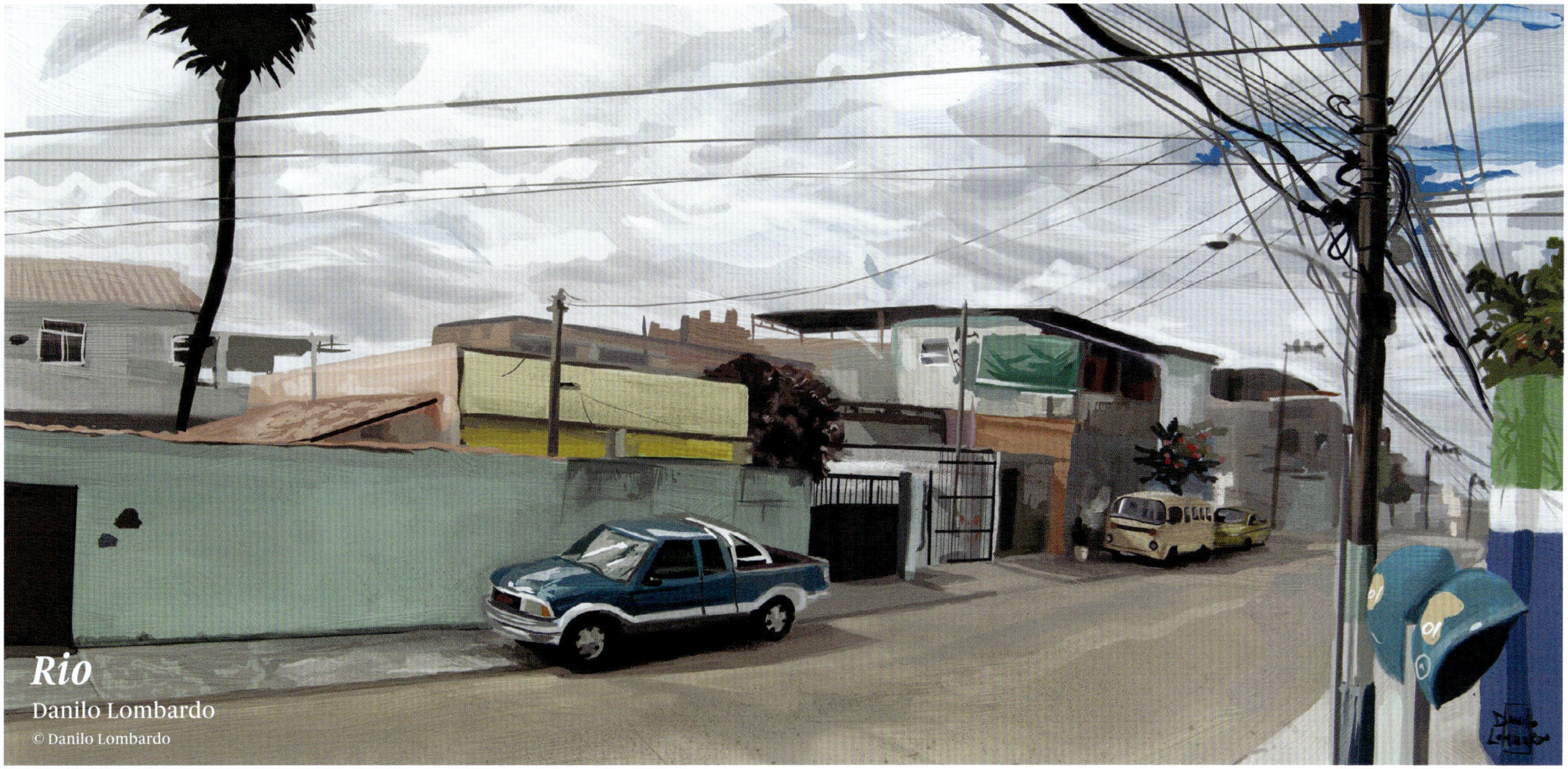

Rio

Danilo Lombardo

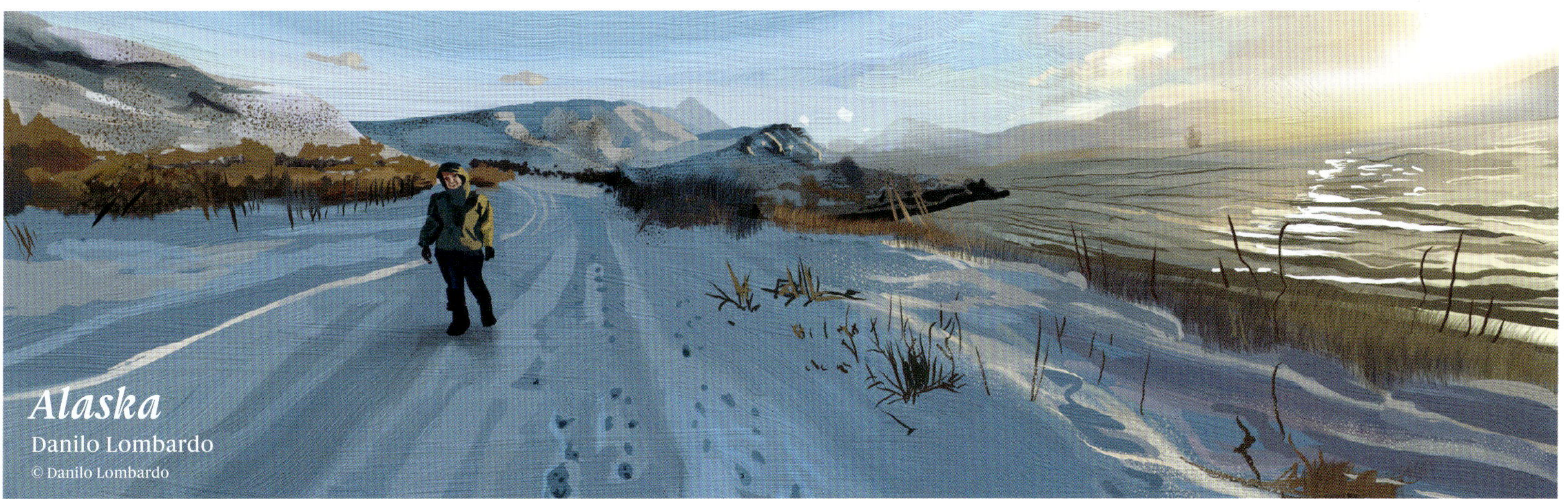

Alaska

Danilo Lombardo

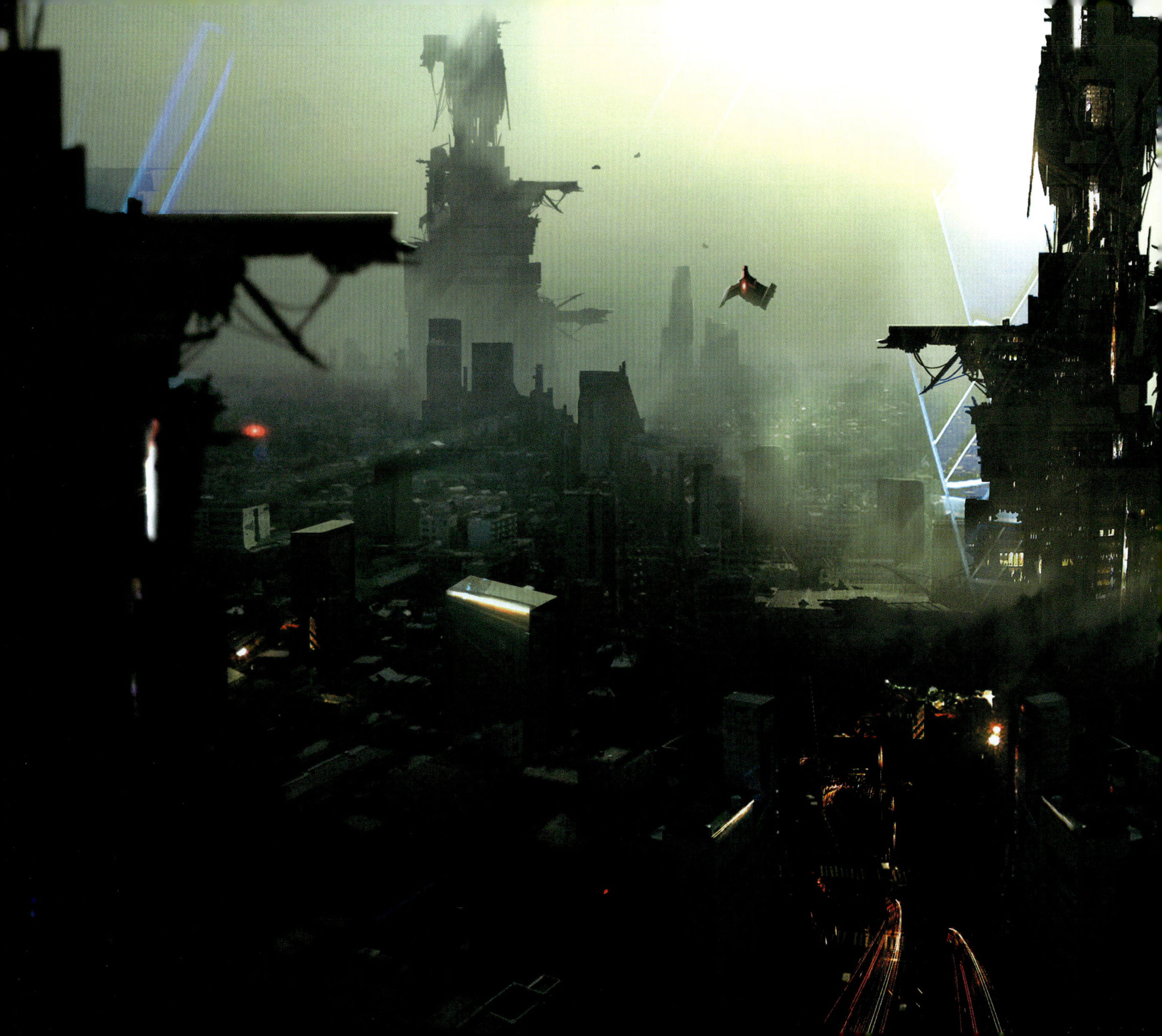

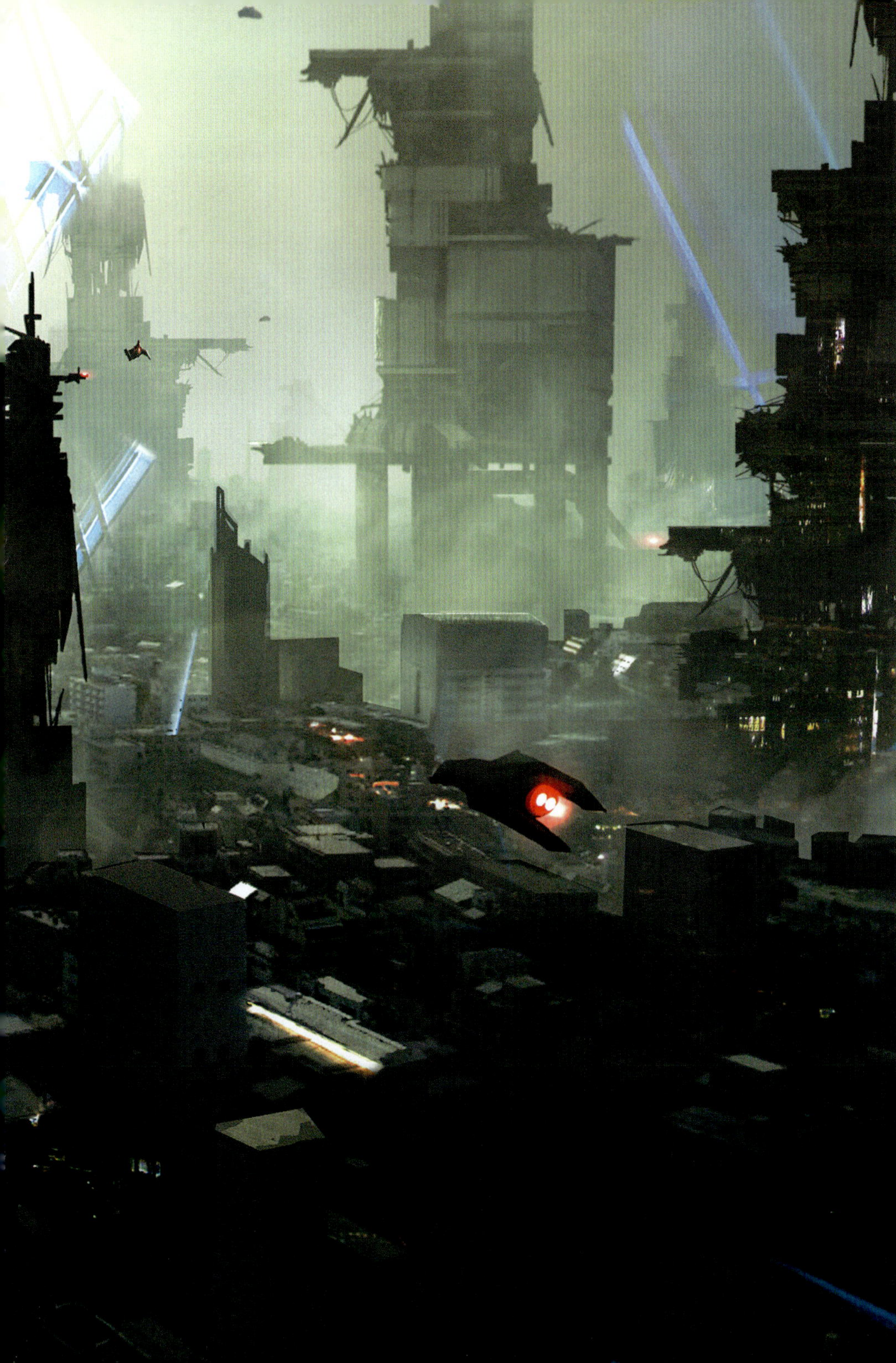

Cyber City
Massimo Porcella

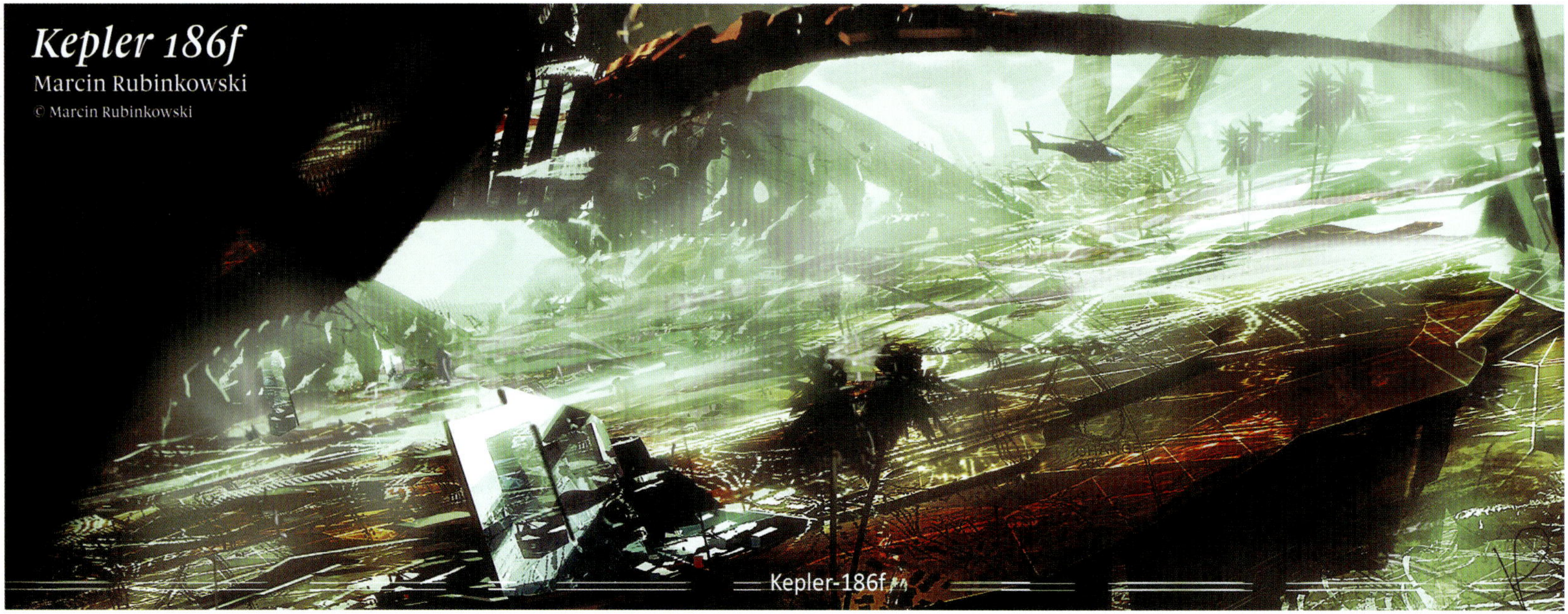

Kepler 186f

Marcin Rubinkowski

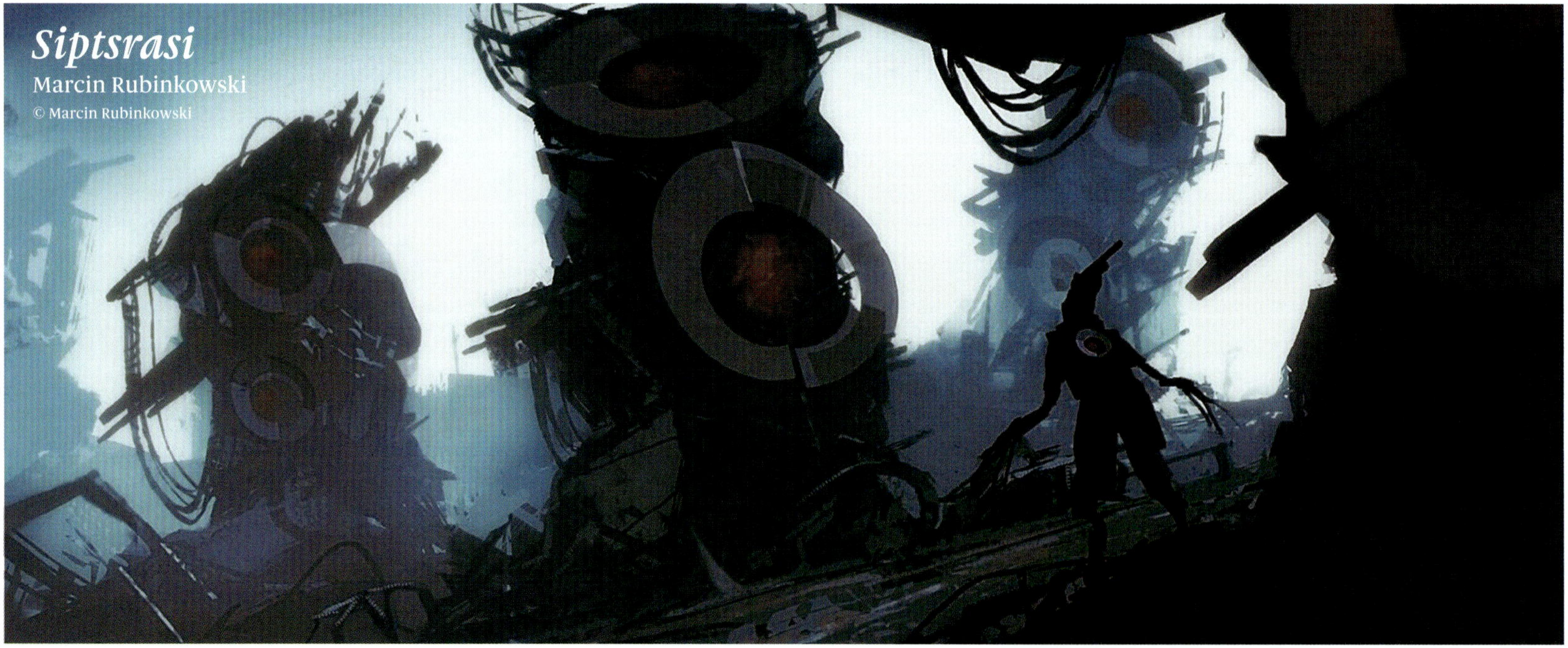

Siptsrasi

Marcin Rubinkowski

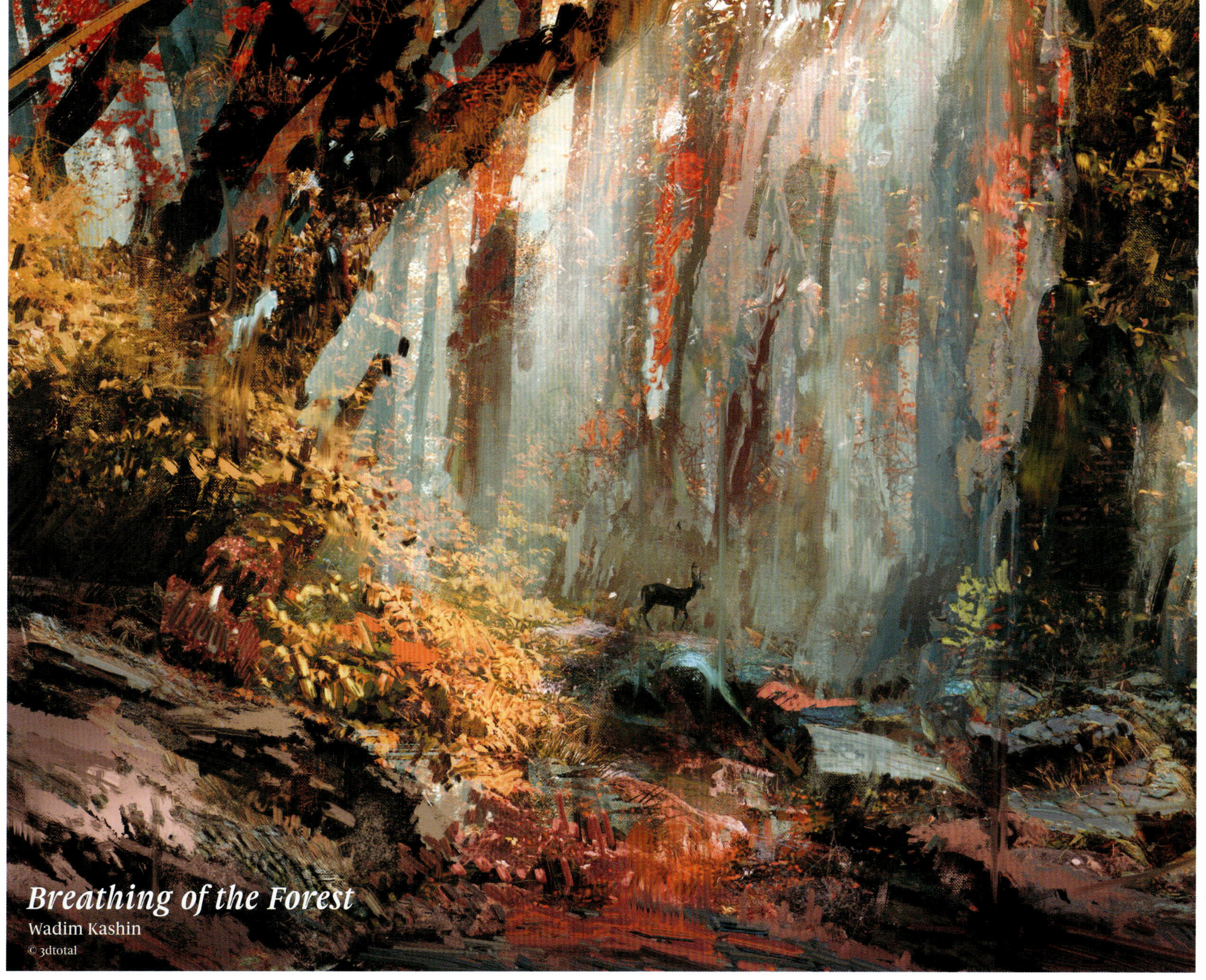

Breathing of the Forest
Wadim Kashin

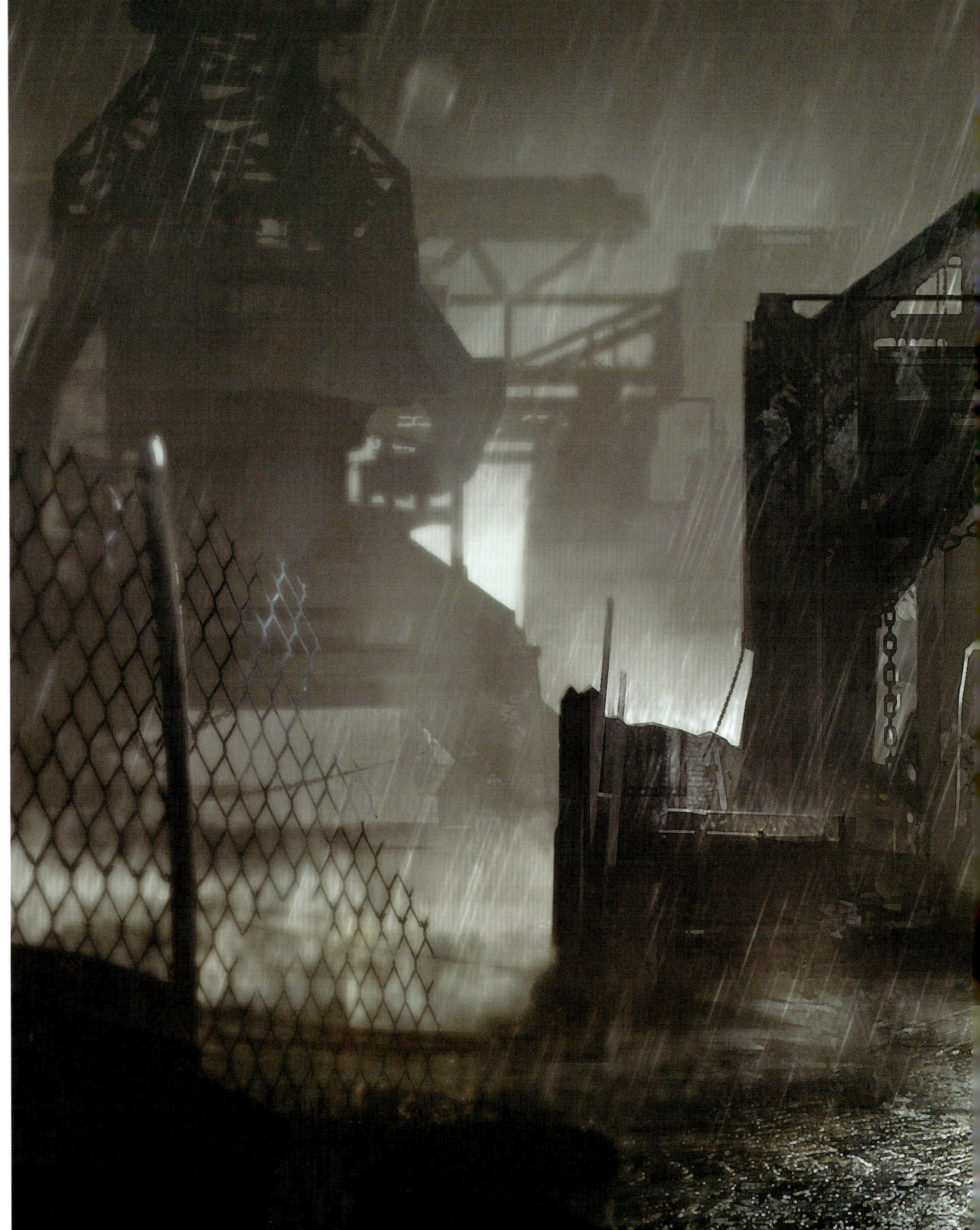

Docks
Massimo Porcella

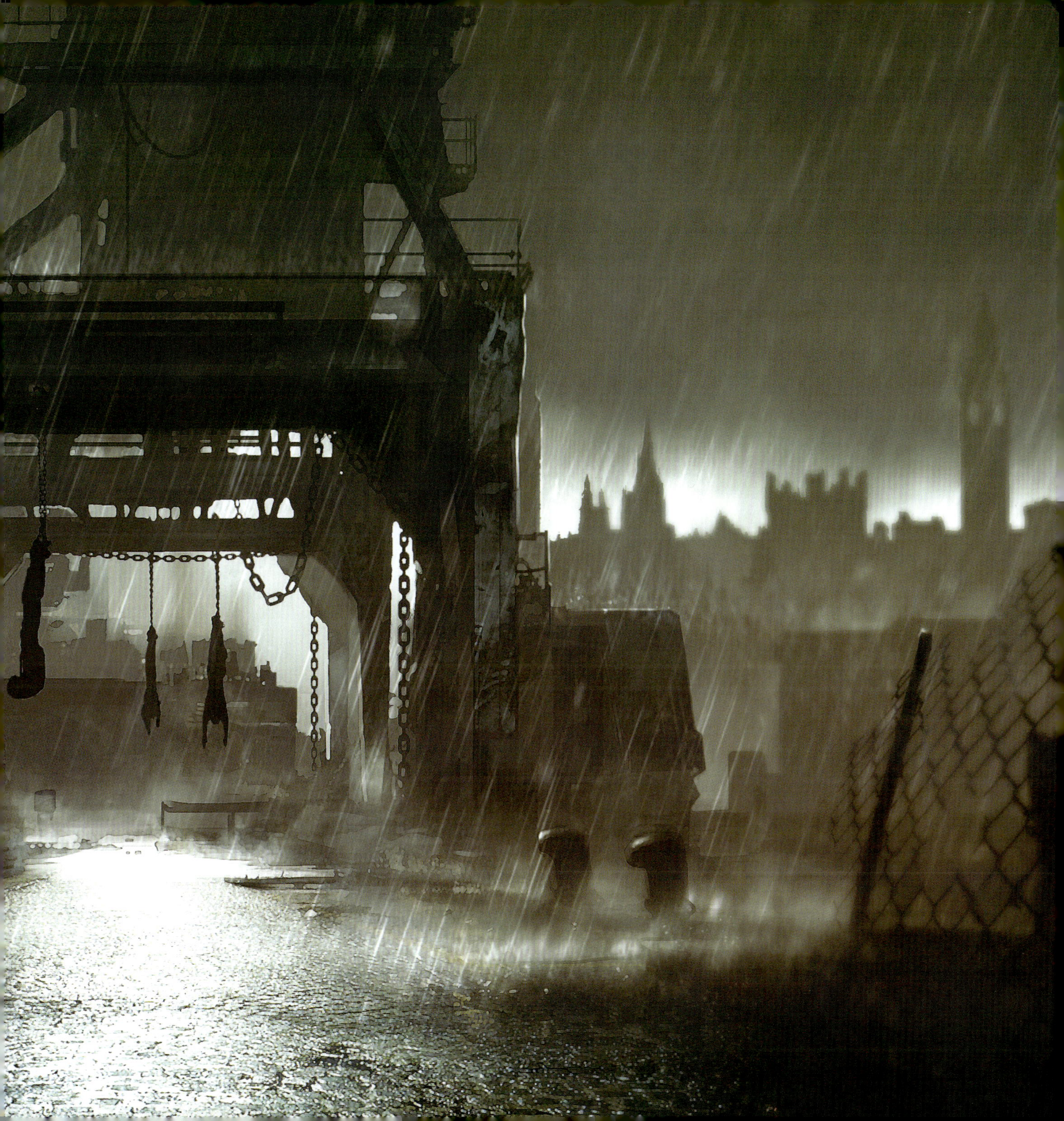

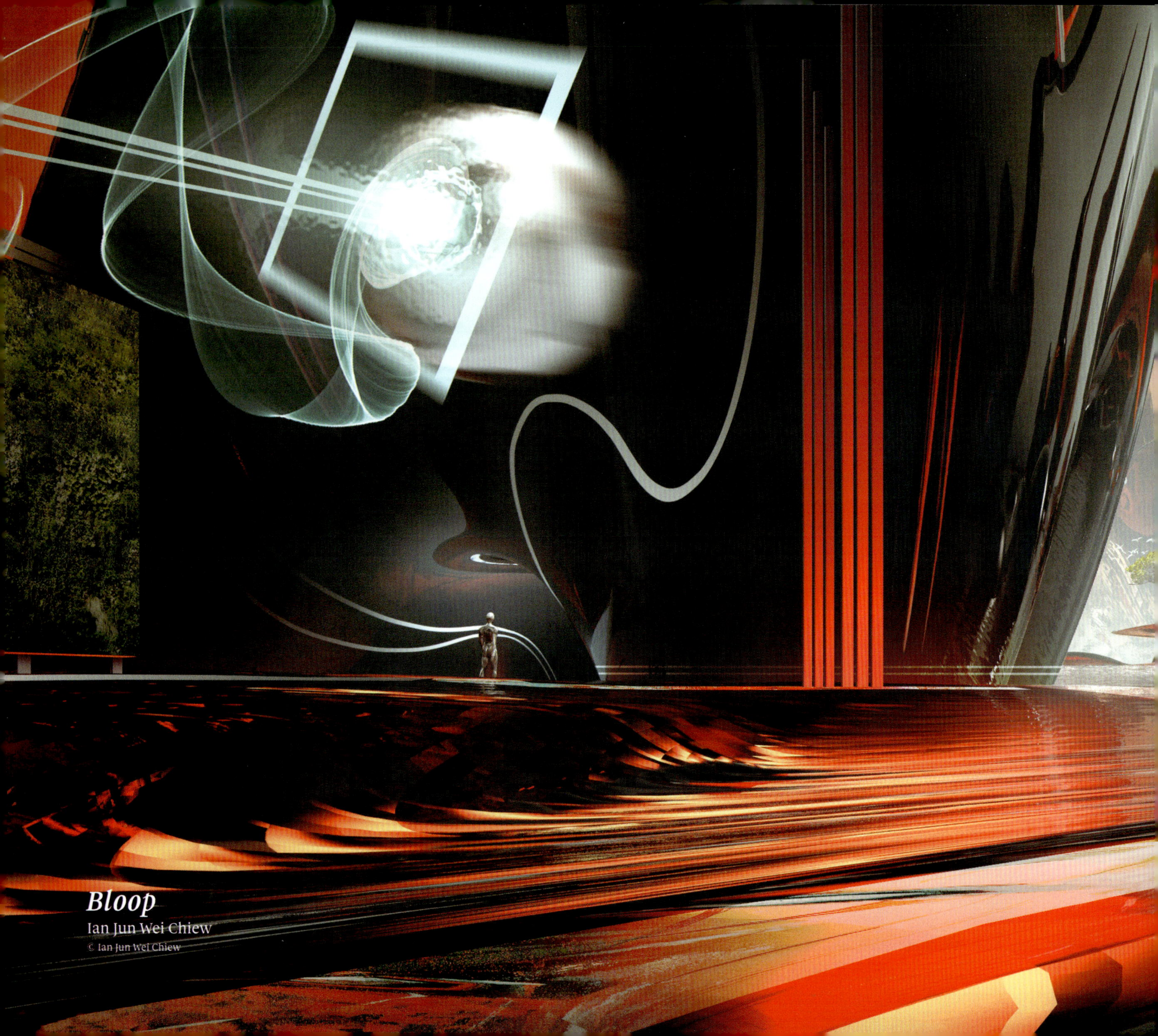

Bloop
Ian Jun Wei Chiew

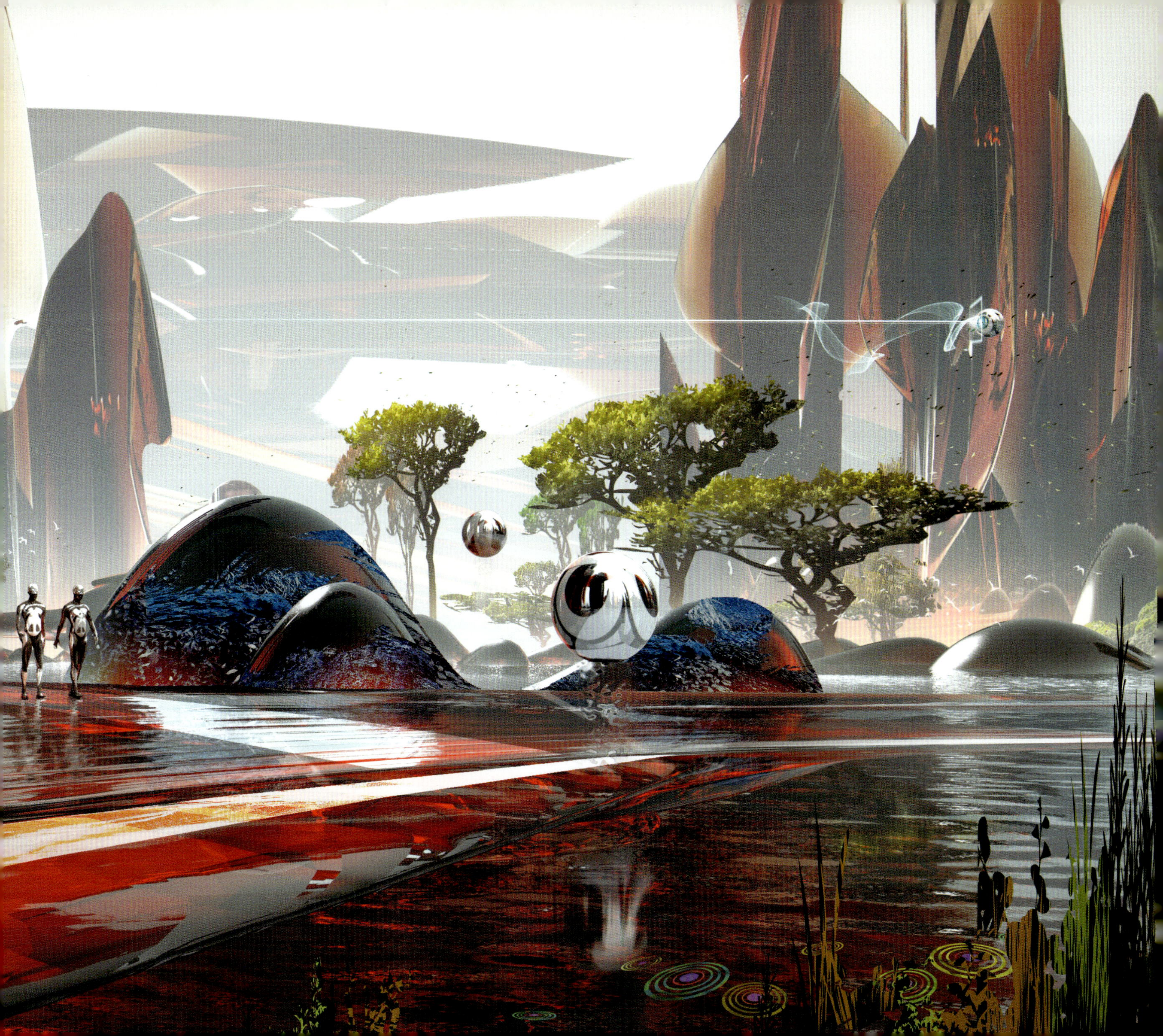

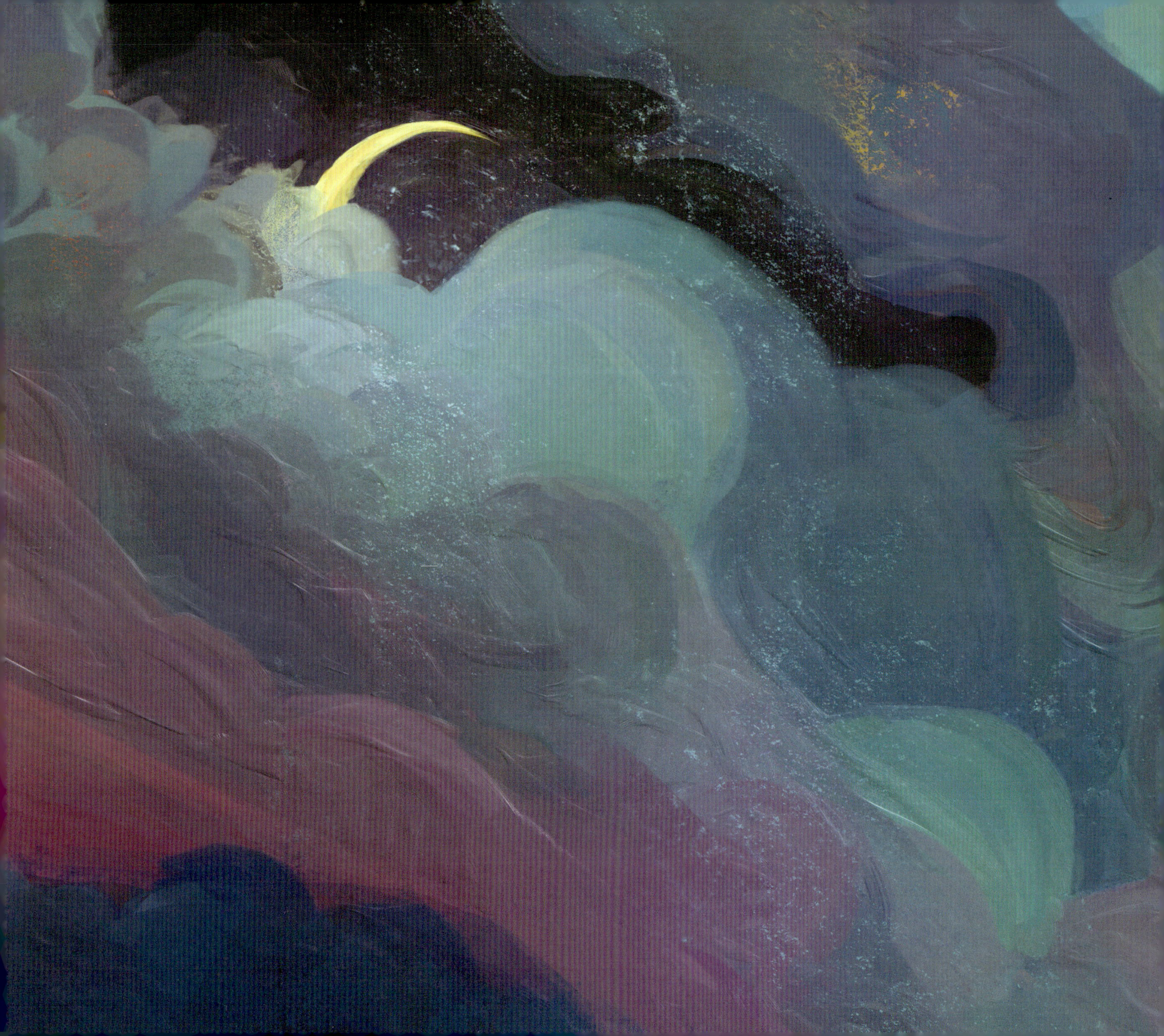

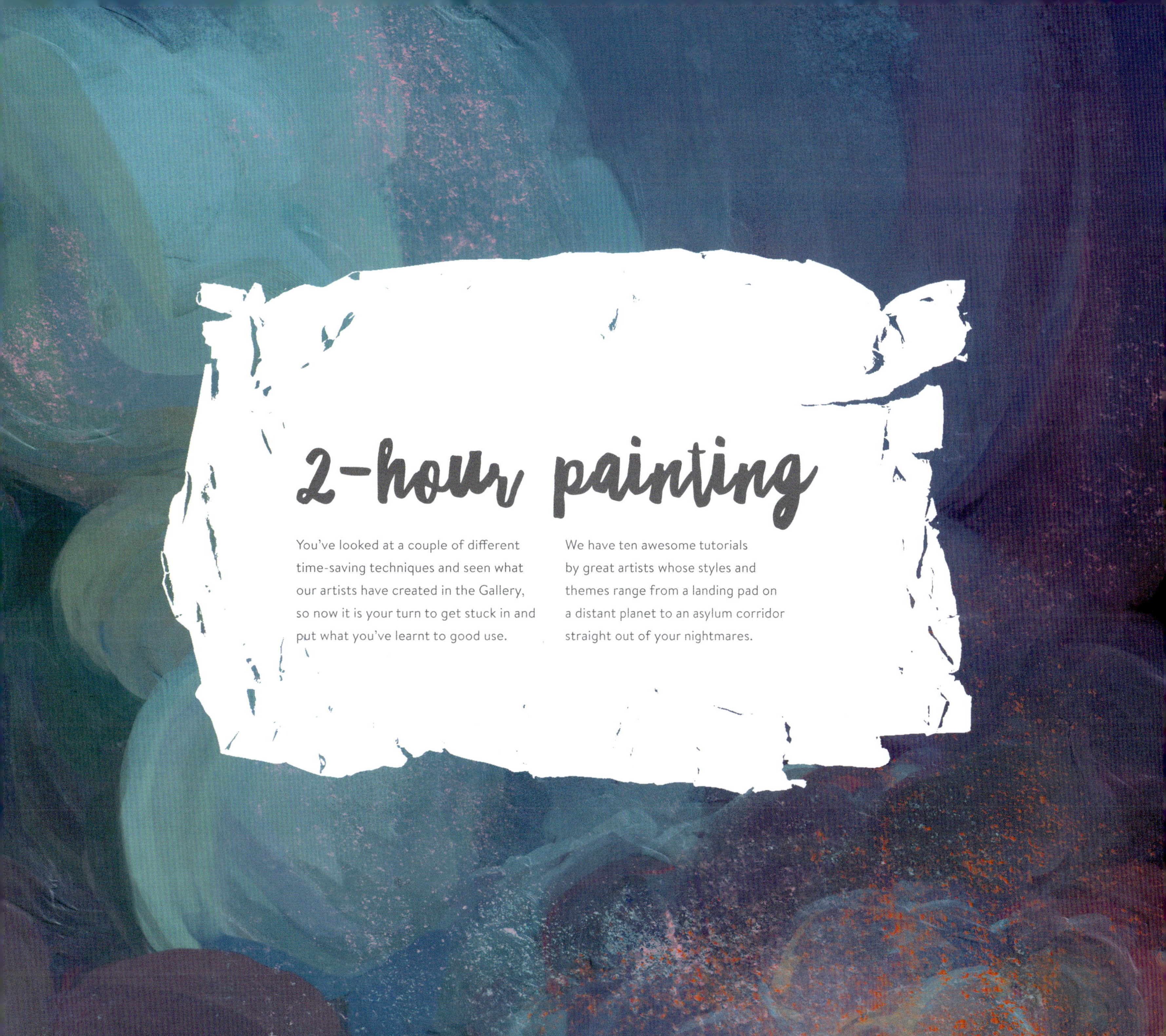

2-hour painting

You've looked at a couple of different time-saving techniques and seen what our artists have created in the Gallery, so now it is your turn to get stuck in and put what you've learnt to good use.

We have ten awesome tutorials by great artists whose styles and themes range from a landing pad on a distant planet to an asylum corridor straight out of your nightmares.

SCI-FI: LATE EXPEDITION

by Alex Olmedo

2 HOURS

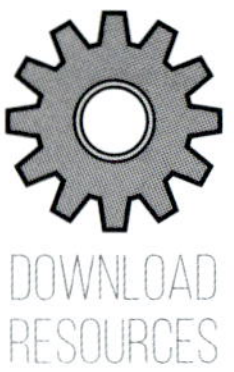

DOWNLOAD RESOURCES

For this image I have a very specific idea of the scene that I want to create: peaceful with a beautifully lit sunset and seaside view where you can see small mountains crowned with futuristic-looking buildings entering the sea and going away from the horizon. The remaining elements of the image, such as ships or characters, will emerge during the creative process, providing a certain narrative to the scene.

As this is a speed painting we can't devote too much time to tweaking individual photos by changing colors or lighting, so it's important to select good reference materials before you start. Looking for scenes that are taken at the same time of day or with the same weather conditions can help save you time.

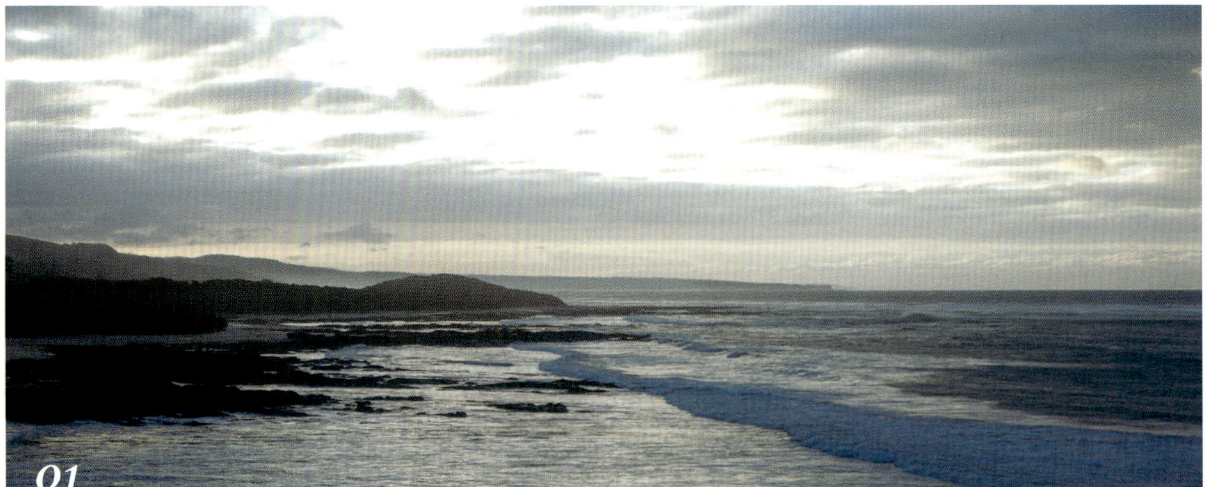

▲ Original photo from the Australian coast, done in the same hour of the day I wanted for this painting. Image supplied courtesy of Noah Bradley (https://gumroad.com/noahbradley)

01: Start from a base

There are lots of images and photos to be found on the internet and many are copyright free. Noah Bradley (**https://gumroad.com/noahbradley**) has a massive collection of photos from all over the world. I select some from his Australia folder for this tutorial. There are also thousands of free photos of space stations, rockets, and space that are perfect reference images for any sci-fi artwork.

I select this photo for its composition, perspective, and mood, all of which are ideal for this tutorial. The silhouettes of small mountains and cliffs, with their different values, help to establish perspective and atmosphere. On the other side of the scene there is a big empty and clear space to place the main focus, which is the perfect base from which to start.

02: Change the sky

If the sky of your original image is too clear and bright you can easily introduce a new one – simply find a reference that you like. I want a richer sky with more color and room to add extra light sources to make it more attractive.

Simply put the photo in a Lighten layer mode and create a mask to erase the parts that don't fit, such as the horizon line. You can place a couple of bluish gradient layers under it to improve the merging with the base image.

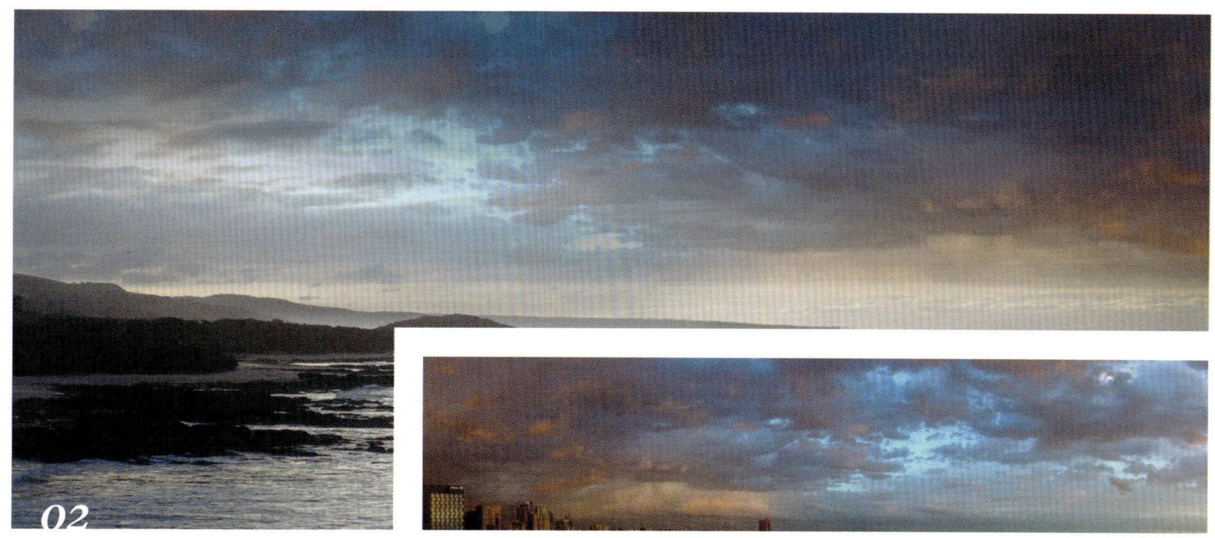

▲ With this sky the painting begins to look more attractive. Image supplied courtesy of Noah Bradley (**https://gumroad.com/noahbradley**)

▲ Image supplied courtesy of Efflam Mercier (**https://gumroad.com/efflam**)

03: Sunset lighting

With the new sky in place you may want to add more intensity and contrast to the evening light. You don't need to put in much effort, just use a Standard brush to paint a yellowish-orange light near the horizon and below the clouds.

Another great place to get royalty-free photos is from Efflam Mercier's gumroad page (**https://gumroad.com/efflam**). I use an image of a rill to change the tidal area of the original beach, which enhances the composition, with only minor transforming.

04: Custom shapes

For this next step I like to use custom shapes. They are super useful tools for artists and are often forgotten by a large majority. They are simple, fast, and fun to make, and are great time savers when designing and speed painting. On those days when you feel uninspired to make art you can make these instead. Simply scribble abstract shapes using a hard brush, then play with them; try copying, repeating, overlapping, and transforming the shapes and using them in your art.

05: Architectural elements

This is a crucial step for defining the overall style and shape language of your painting. Add a few stylized building silhouettes using the custom shapes and color pick from the base photo. Think carefully about the shapes' positions – you want them to emphasize the sunset as well as being part of the composition. This is also a good time to add some reflections to the water. I do this by using a Color Dodge layer on top of the foreground water according to the sky color.

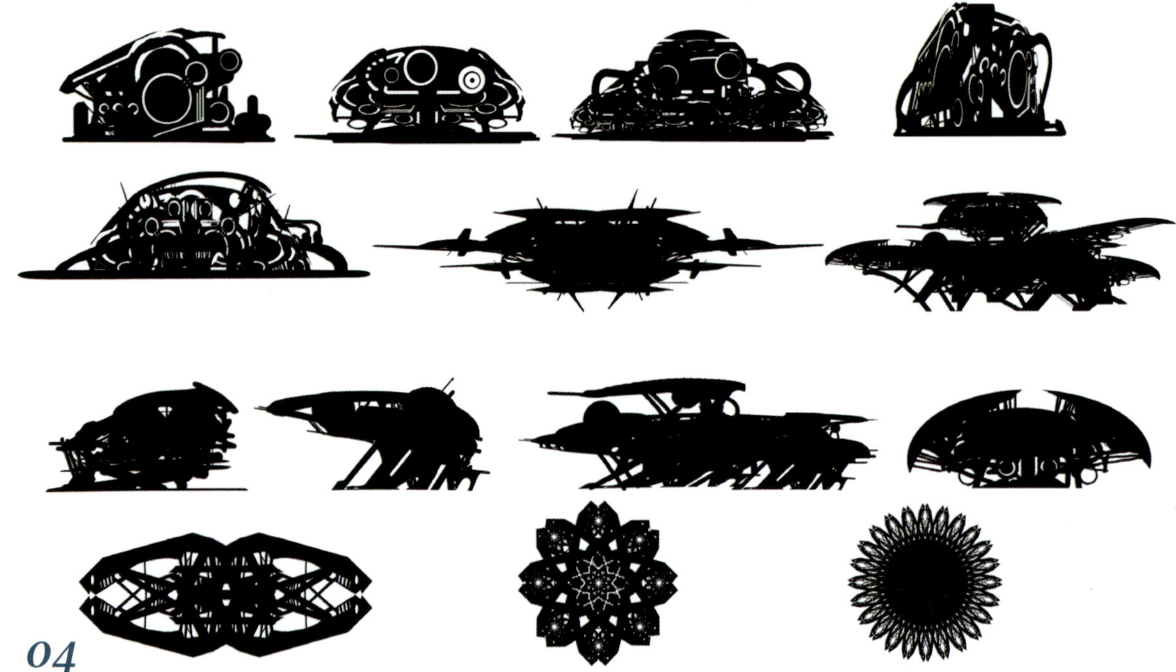

▲ Some examples of my custom shapes which you can download from **www.3dtotalpublishing.com/resources.html** and have a play with

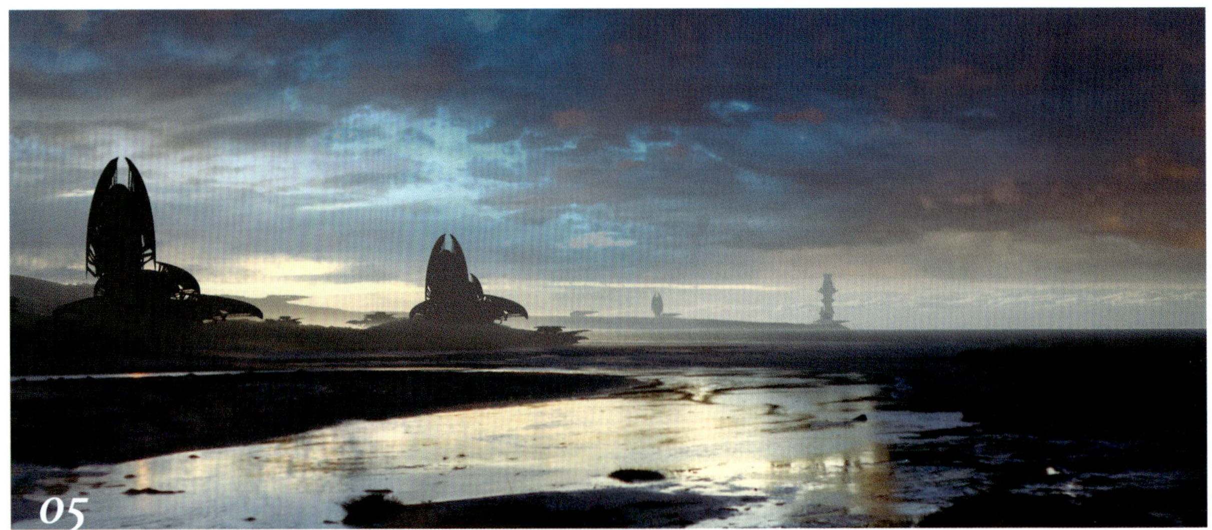

▲ The silhouette of the buildings helps to give the essential sci-fi look to the painting

"The texture's industrial design really helps to break up the natural aspects of the image"

06: Foreground structure

Using another of Noah Bradley's Australian pictures, I find a striped tin-roof texture which helps to strengthen the perspective (**image 06a**). After it has been scaled and moved about I realize it makes the perfect basis for a future object. The texture's industrial design really helps to break up the natural aspects of the image so far (**image 06b**). If you pick the right image you won't need to play around with the values too much!

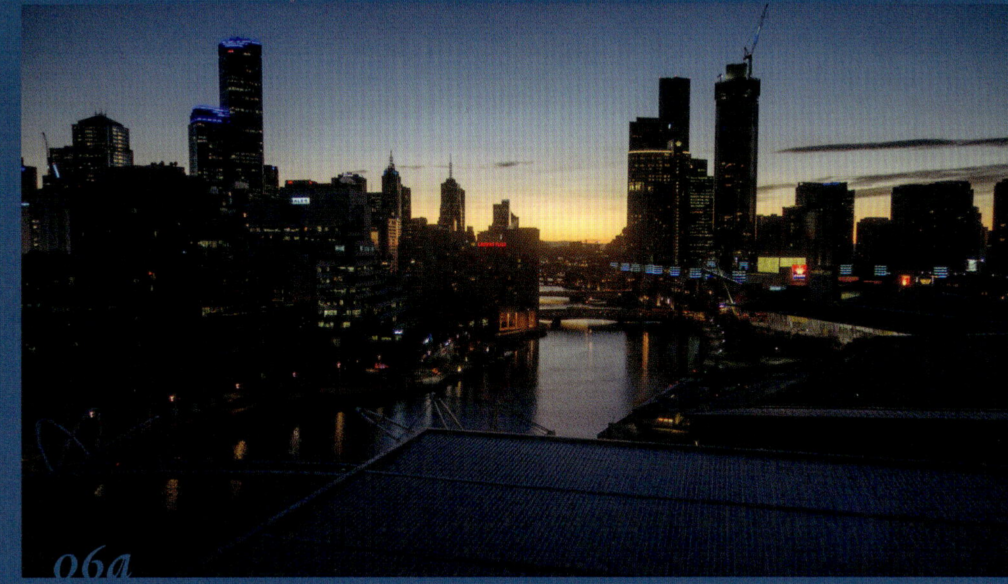

▲ Image supplied courtesy of Noah Bradley (**https://gumroad.com/noahbradley**)

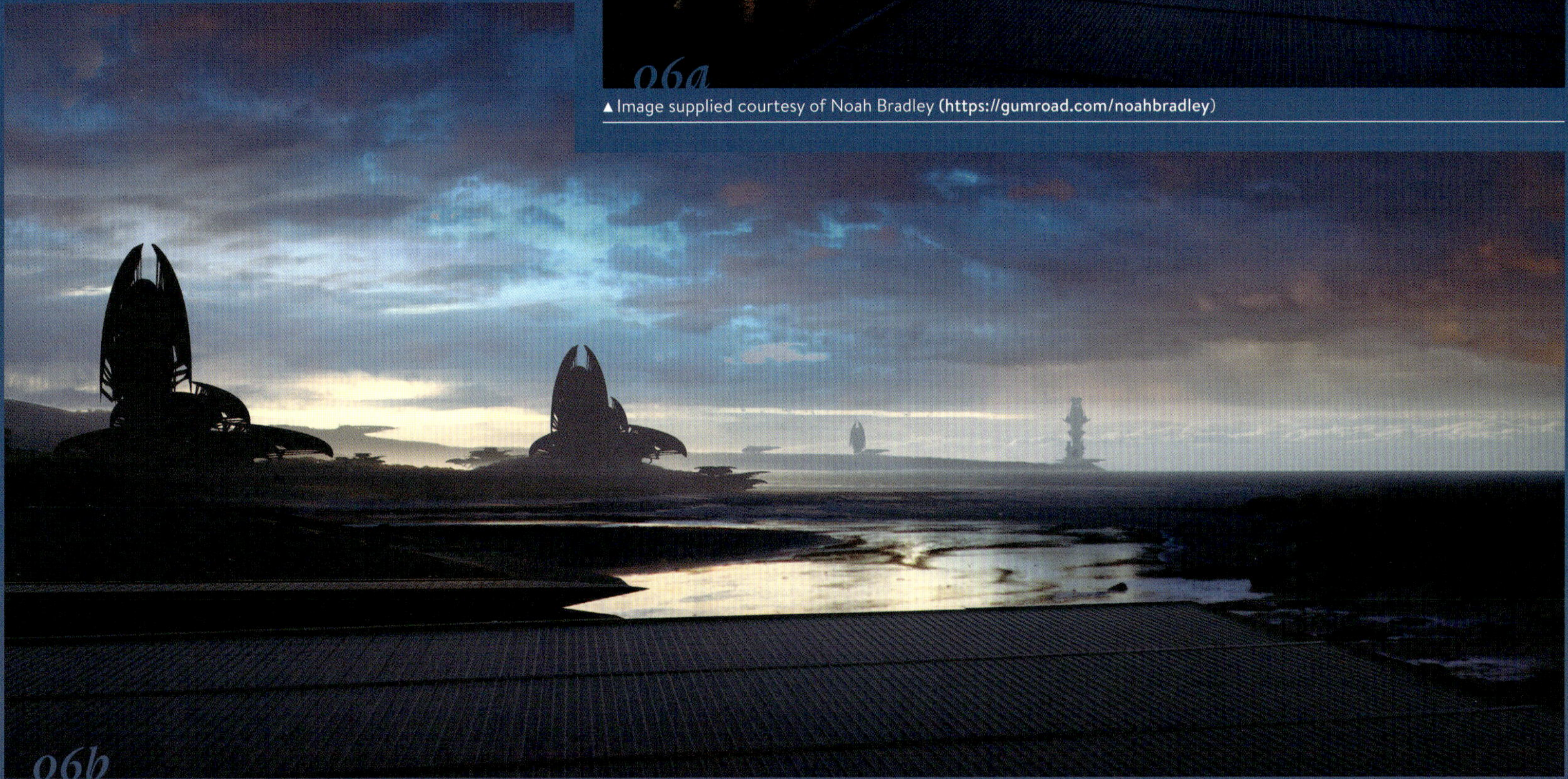

06b

▲ More industrial elements were added to provide a sense of a human-made world

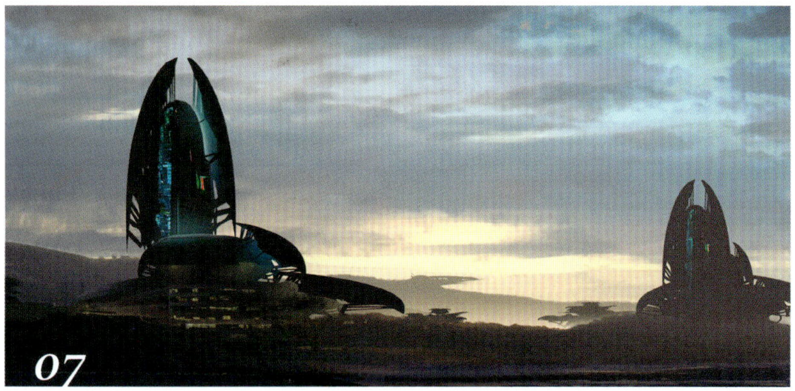

▲ Photos allow you to quickly add artificial lights and textures

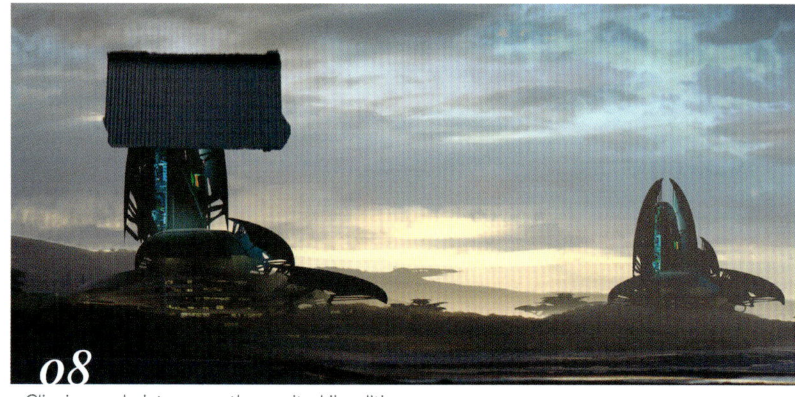

▲ Clipping masks let you see the result while editing

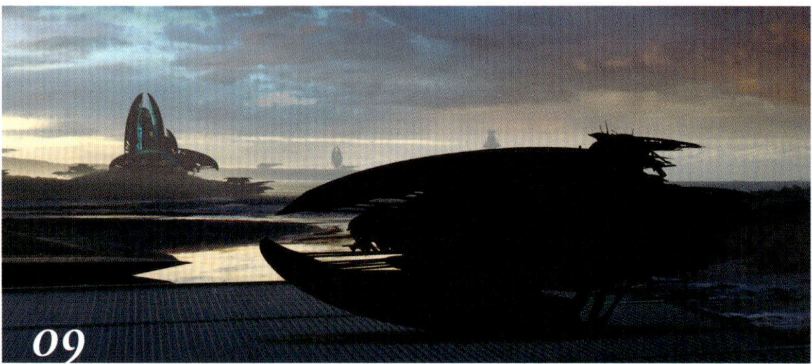

▲ With the same custom shapes but rotated 90 degrees, the silhouette of a spaceship appears

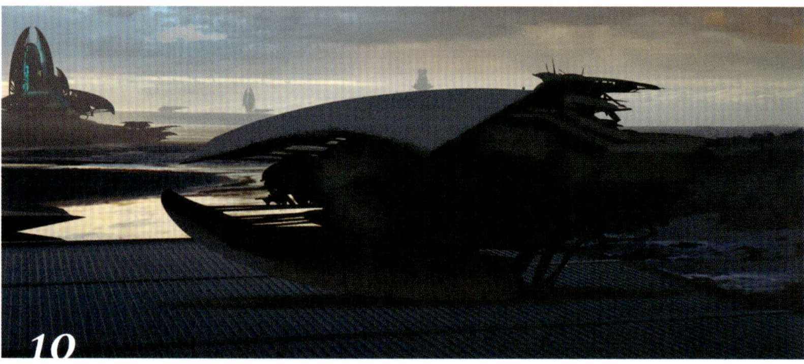

▲ With just a few plane strokes the initial look of the ship starts to become clearer

07: Give life to the buildings

Bringing the building to life is one of the best parts of the whole process. Use a night-time cityscape and select different parts of the image with the Quick Selection tool (which makes for interesting forms because it may choose bits that you wouldn't). Place the selections above the building layer using different layer modes, such as Lighten, Color Dodge, or Screen, to make different lights appear and enliven the empty building silhouettes. Use the Lasso tool and soft brushes to define the shapes further. You can also clone the lights for similar use, adding and removing bits to add realism.

08: Add more texture

With the basic design of the building done it is time to add some texture to the structures. Remember that this is a speed painting so you don't need to worry about the level of detail. Use the same tin-roof texture from step 06 to add texture to the buildings in the middle ground. This repetition of textures helps to keep the overall style of the image consistent.

Once you've extracted, scaled, and transformed the texture, place it and create a clipping mask on the buildings layer; use the Lighten layer mode.

09: Add a ship

Use the custom shapes to come up with a striking and attractive silhouette of a ship. To begin with you should only concentrate on matching the perspective – use the grated roof as a guide. By using the same custom shapes as the buildings to make the ship you are continuing with the same visual language, which helps to promote continuity.

10: Give sense to the silhouette

Spend some time adding brushstrokes to the ship to give it a sense of volume. Paint on some of the defining parts of the fuselage. For me, the silhouette suggests a rounded aerodynamic style. Add more strokes to suggest the machinery, tubes, and wires leading to the rear of the ship where the engine is located, and round out the prow.

11: First detailing pass

Add details using clipping masks of photos; moving and scaling the textures creates abstract and subtle details in the areas you want the eye to linger. As there is no direct light on the ship, try to use Lighten layers when adding the photos and only highlight those areas lit by ambient lighting.

In the design, the contrast is very important, not in terms of colors and lights, but also in the size of the shapes. Balancing large, medium, and small shapes will make your paintings more attractive.

12: Second detailing pass

Using the same methods of adding texture as in previous steps you can add more photo textures – simply scale and rotate them to give uniformity. Pay close attention to where you place them. All this work has to be slowly blended with the image, so paint over the textures with different brushes depending of the material.

13: Add extra details

All spaceships must have a cockpit for the pilot so you need to spend a little time getting this bit right. In a separate layer create the shape you want and add textures and colors using clipping

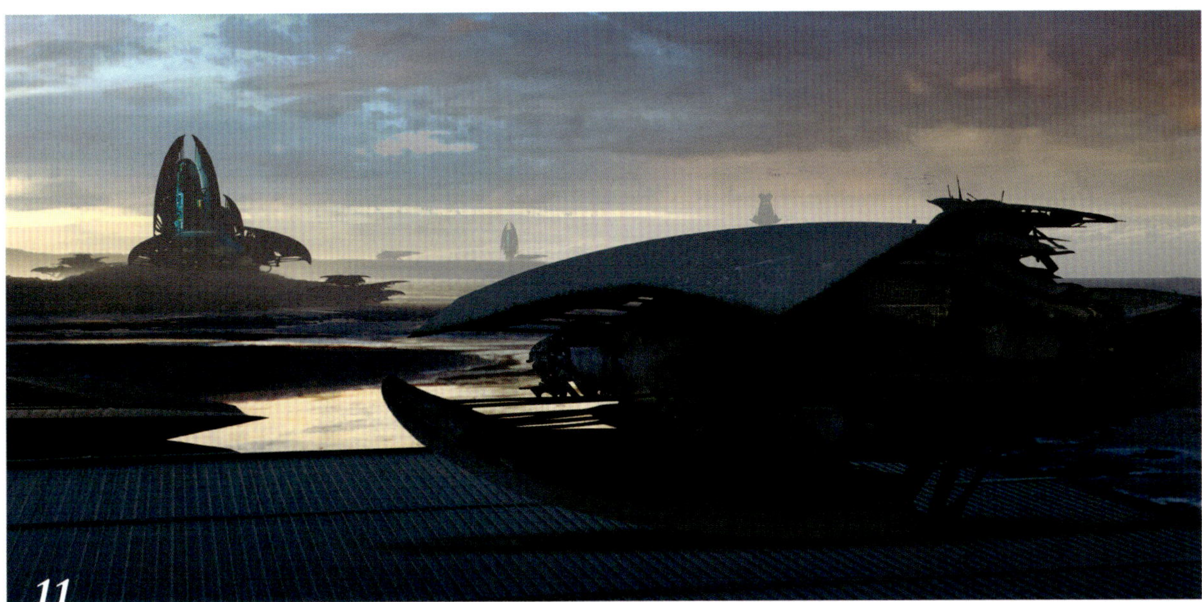

▲ The first few photos I use offer lots of useful details such as gratings, pipes, and screws

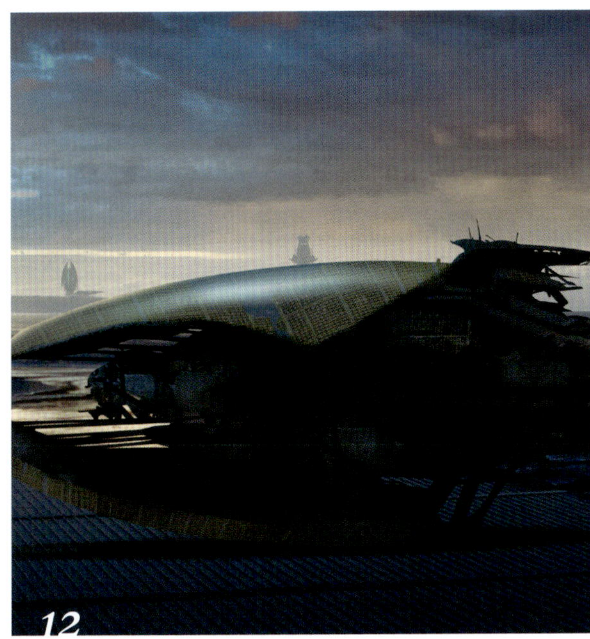

▲ Use repeated textures for the design of the fuselage

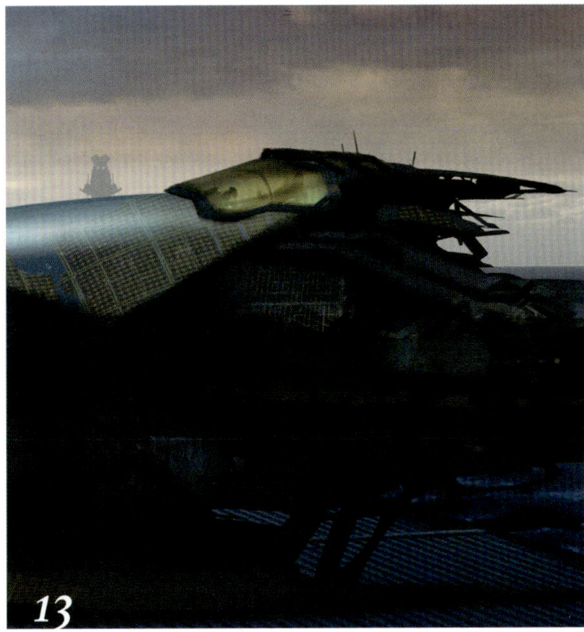

▲ Change the transparency when painting glass

masks. To achieve the appearance of glass, I create a layer on top of everything and lower the transparency, revealing what is painted underneath.

14: Human interaction

For this piece the human element isn't for storytelling but to give a sense of scale, making it easier for the viewer to judge the size of the ship. We are programmed to recognize the human form and people are usually one of the first things we see. Find photos of people working on machinery and add them to the image. To better integrate them you can paint on extras such as armor or tools.

15: Strengthen the focal point

To give more detail and prominence to the ship, plus more realism, paint a few lights here and there using a soft brush in Color Dodge mode. Place a warm and strong light near the prow, making an eye-catcher for the two characters. This needs to be integrated into the picture considering the reflections and lights.

Also add a halo of light coming from the sunset around the ship. Paint the cockpit a bright green, breaking up the blues and oranges of the rest of the image a little.

16: Duplicated ships

An easy way to offer more dynamism to this kind of painting is to add flying objects. In this case simply duplicate the main ship and repeat it a couple of times, then resize and place them further away

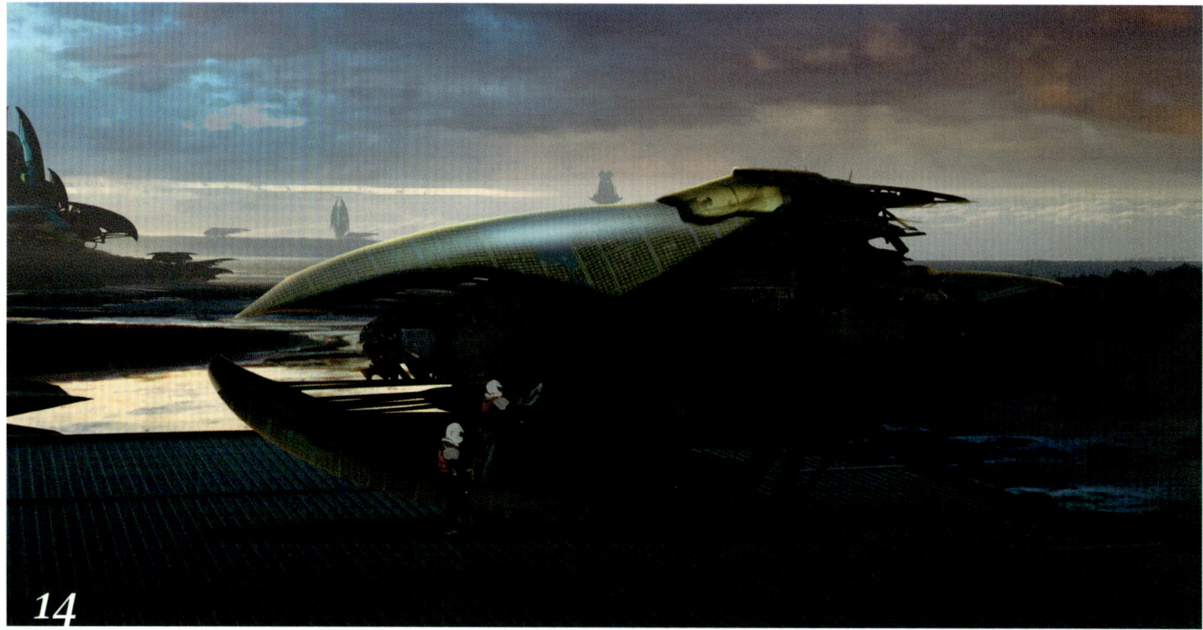

▲ Adding human shapes to your paintings will help to define the scale

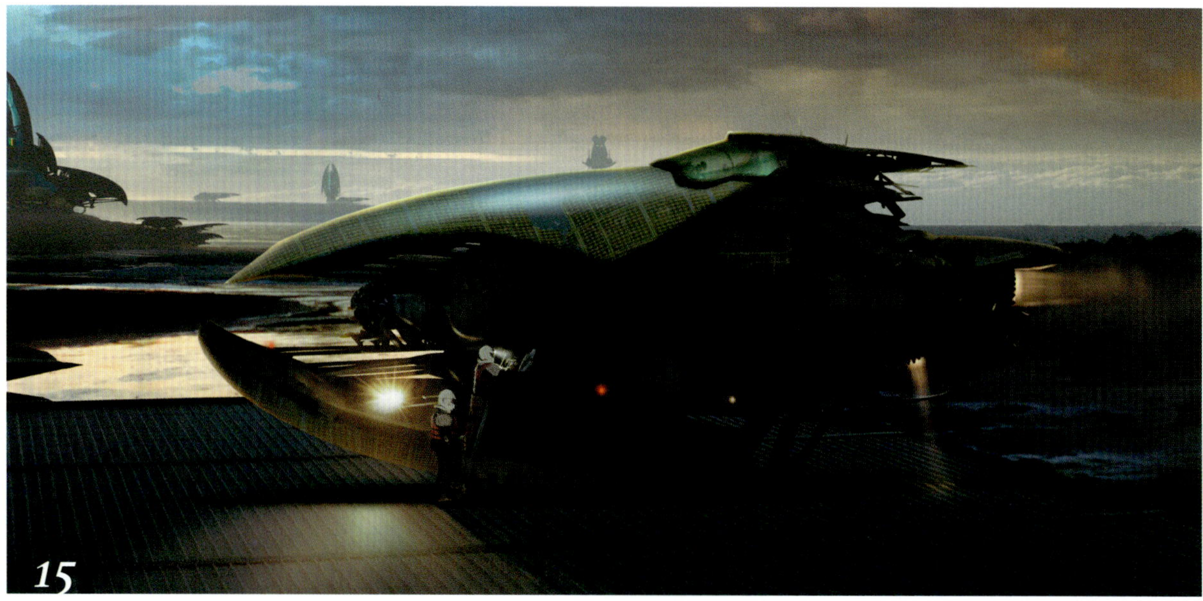

▲ Details such as strong lights are a good way to emphasize the focal points, providing them with more realism

to help with perspective. Remember to adjust the values of each one: the furthest away will be less contrasted and saturated. Add some highlights to show the light hitting the fuselage from the sunset. Placing them near the sun helps the composition, avoiding distracting the viewer from the areas of interest.

17: Light adjustments

Don't add too many details to areas that may distract from the focal points, focus on the overall settings. Adjust the sunlight to give the image more depth and unify the colors. This also helps to make the image look more realistic and convincing. I add a Color Dodge airbrush layer on top of the sun and a splattered texture layer on top of everything to recreate particles in the air (also in Color Dodge mode).

18: Final VFX

To give the image a more photorealistic look you can make some adjustments with Photoshop filters, such as different blurs or lens corrections. First you need to merge everything in a new

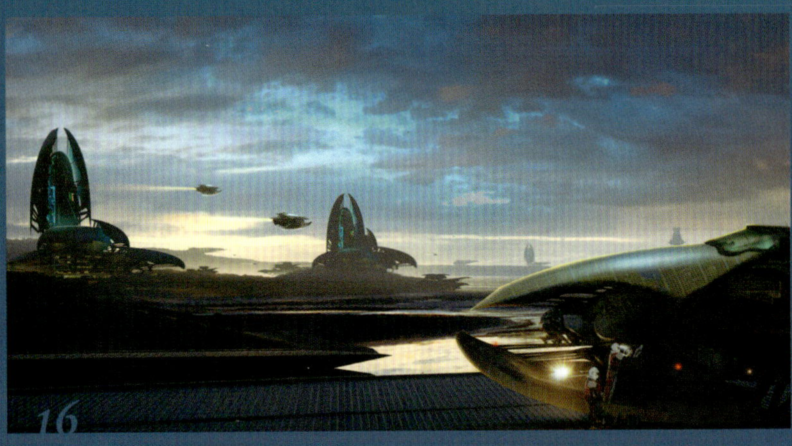

▲ By duplicating the main ship we can add more flying vehicles to the painting, creating more dynamism

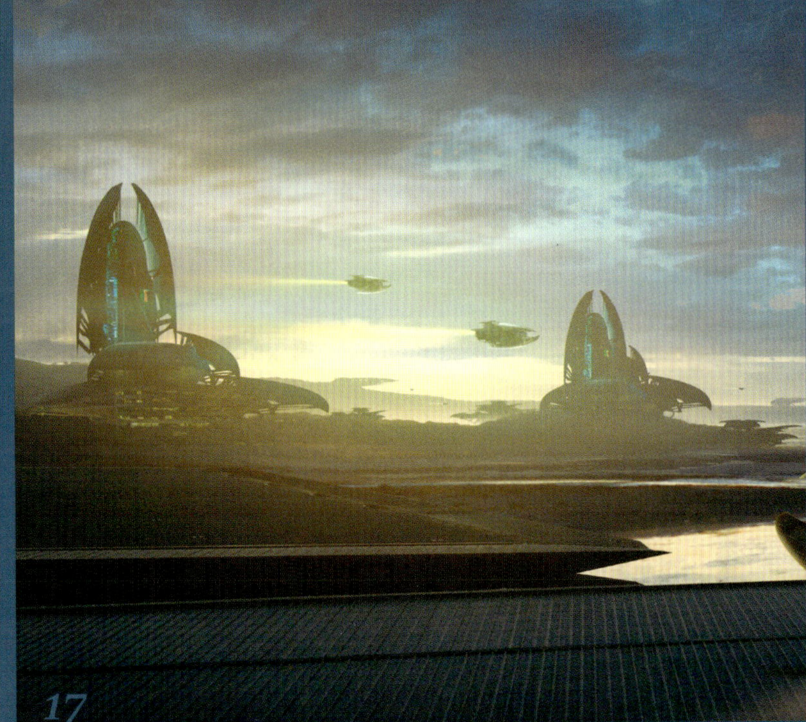

▲ Once almost everything is done I add some layers of soft lights on top of everything to unify the whole painting

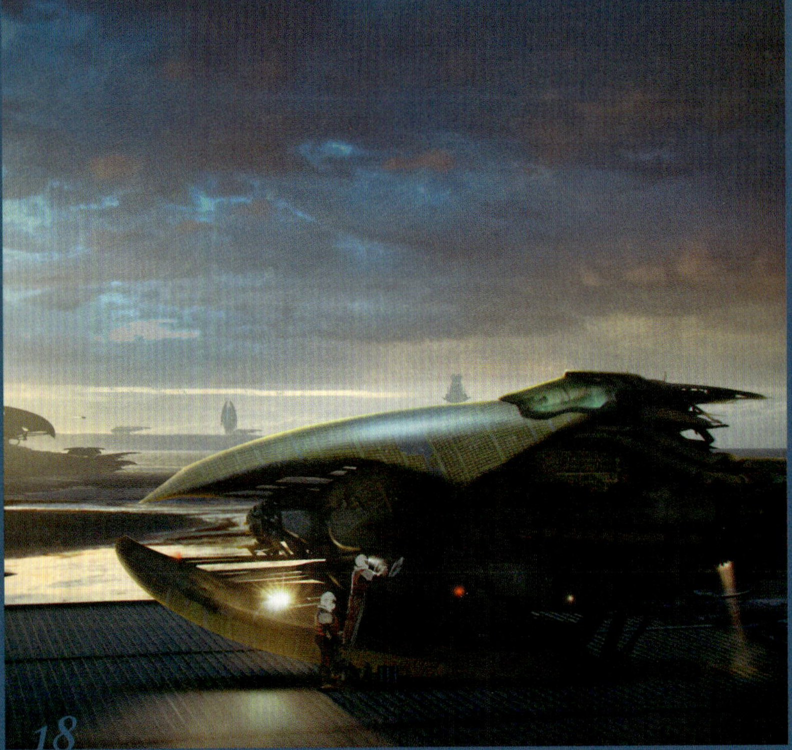

▲ Playing with Photoshop filters and blurs can give your painting a more cinematic look

layer (Shift+Ctrl+E) and on top apply a grainy overlay layer, further unifying the colors and edges. Then make some slight lens corrections, darkening the outline of the image and playing with the Chromatic Aberration sliders. Finally add an Iris blur to remove some of the details around the corners.

19: Last-minute tweaks

If you have a few minutes to spare at the end you can add some more details. For example I notice that some parts of the main ship are a bit undefined so I add a few subtle lines, dots, and shapes, suggesting more different structures. With those tweaks we are done!

Pro tip: Selecting photos

When making photobashing images it is very important to choose the right photos. Often if you try to include a photo with a totally different lighting source compared to others involved in the image you'll end up spending too much time trying to fix the problem and even dismissing the photo.

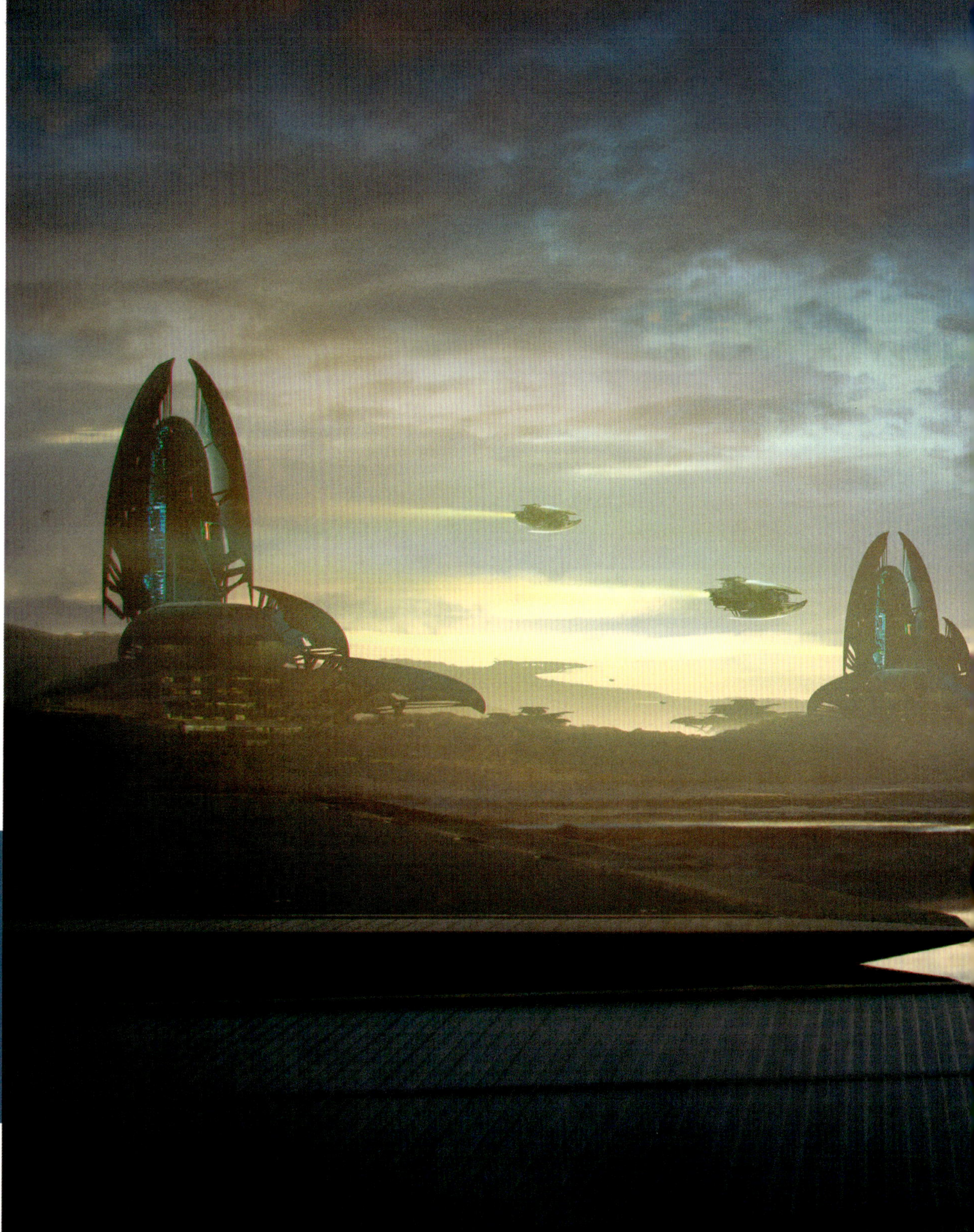

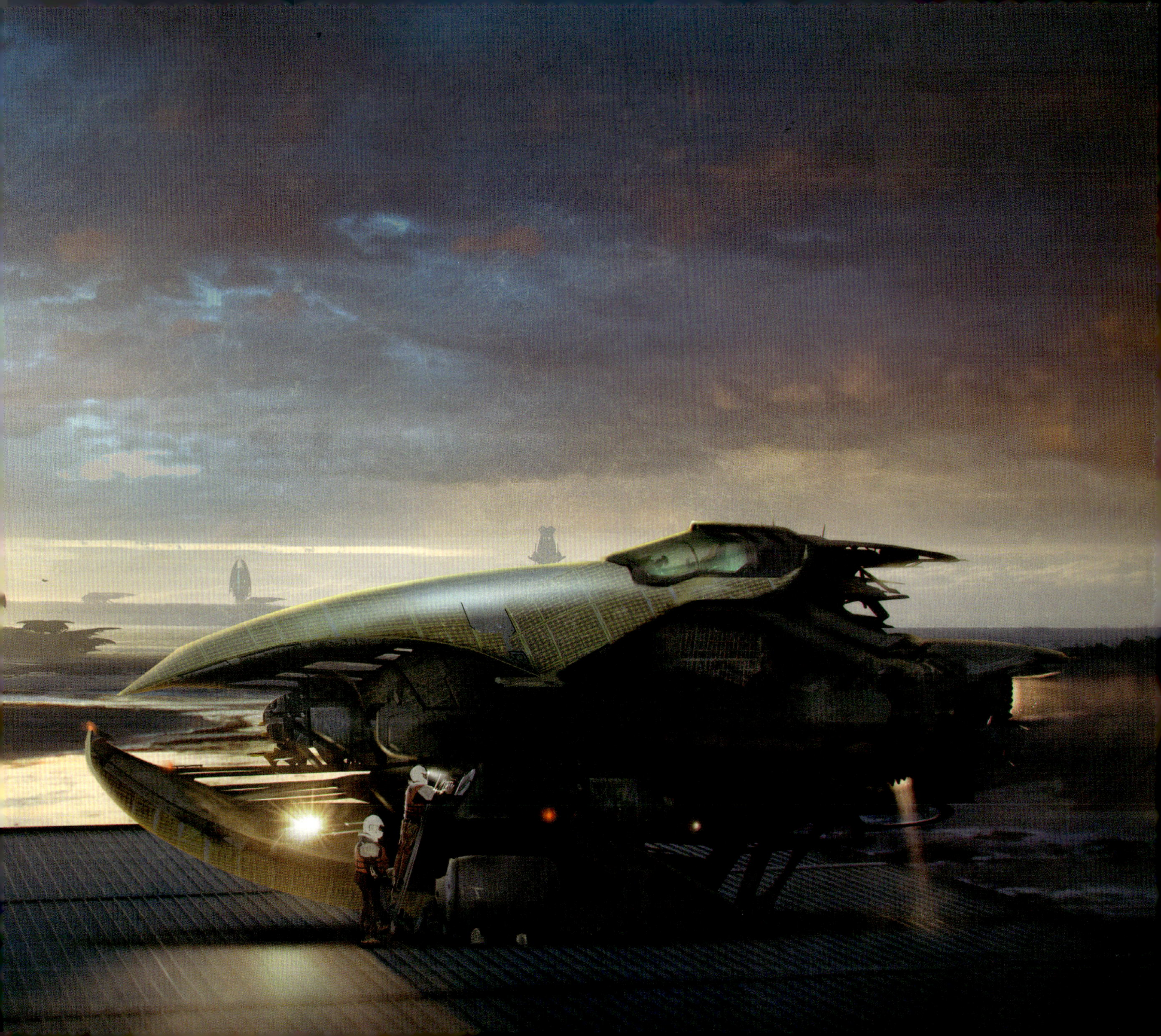

FANTASY: AN UNEXPECTED PLACE
by Jesper Friis

2 HOURS

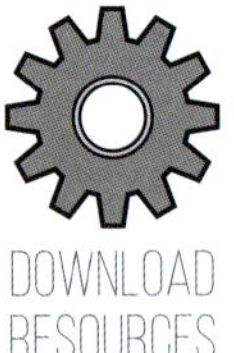

DOWNLOAD RESOURCES

Speed painting is a great way to explore the unexpected and unplanned, the "happy accident," if you will. It is a good way to break from your usual workflow, let loose, and find something new that you would not normally paint.

In this tutorial I hope to show you a different and inventive way to create interesting and fun textures. You will then discover how you can use them to create paintings by establishing an attention-grabbing starting point and allowing an element of randomness into the process and going with the flow.

It's a process that I find quite enjoyable, but how do you set yourself up for a successful "accident"?

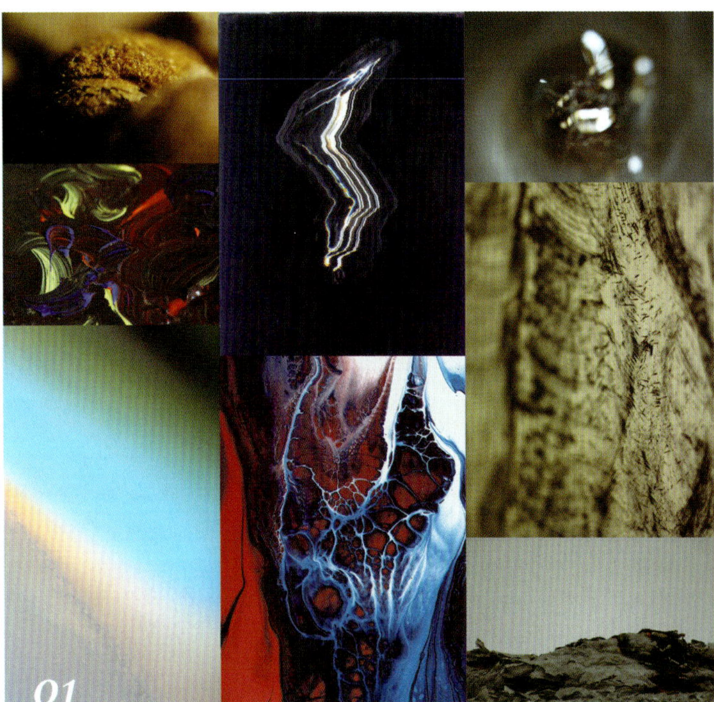

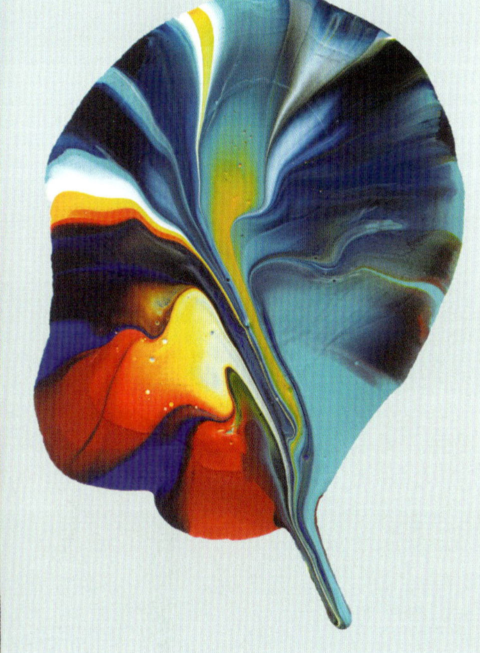

▲ A selection of the different textures I have created

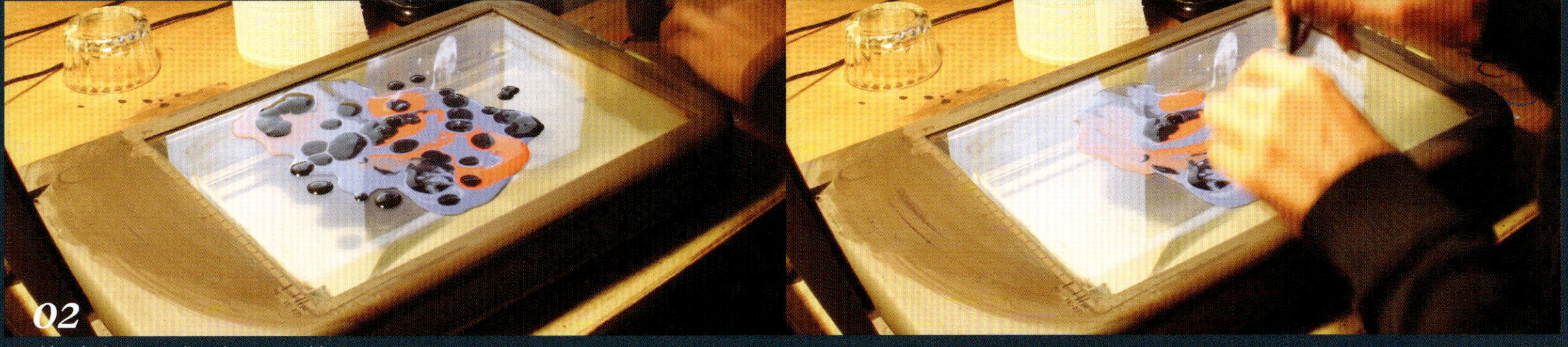

▲ I add and mix the acrylic paint on my old scanner

01: Boredom sparks creativity

In a fit of boredom one day I decided I would drag out my old scanner I had sitting around and started painting on the glass with some watercolor. I closed the lid to see what would come out.

That was really the start for me in terms of using images in my digital paintings. Since then I have been making weird textures this way from time to time. It might seem a little silly at first, but even a day spent experimenting with some of these methods for making textures can give you something in your library that you will keep coming back to, something that's uniquely yours and really can't be recreated. They can serve as a great base for painting, as an effect in another, maybe a new brush, or even in 3D art as a displacement map.

02: Making textures

I make the textures using my trusty old scanner and watered-down acrylic paint (to achieve better mixing when closing the lid). I use some plastic shot glasses to hold the paint and drinking straws to deposit it onto the glass (**image 02**). The results vary quite a bit depending on how thick the paint is; there is a lot of trial and error involved but that is all part of the fun! You do have some control over the results by stacking the paint, using the thicker paints to guide the thinner. Start slowly, see how it looks, and add more to your liking; when it becomes too muddy just wipe it off and start over.

"There is a lot of trial and error involved but that is all part of the fun!"

Keep in mind that it can get very messy so you may want to put down some plastic or old newspaper to protect your work surface – keep plenty of paper towels to hand. Don't use a scanner that you plan to use for anything else, especially important documents. An alternative is to use two pieces of glass and take high-resolution photos.

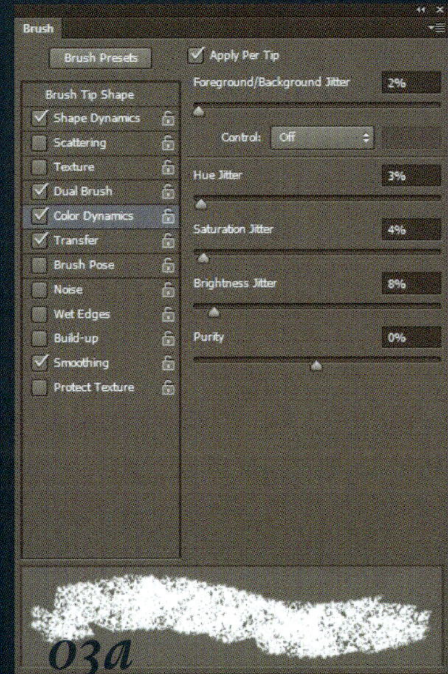

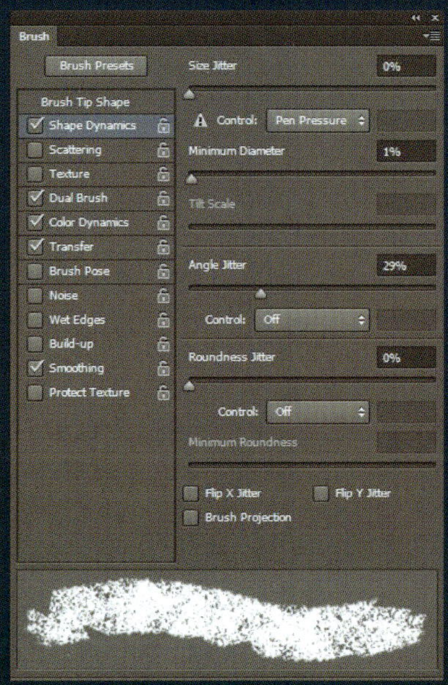

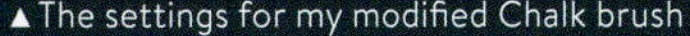

▲ The settings for my modified Chalk brush

You can download some of my textures from **http://friis.deviantart.com** if you don't want to make your own.

03: Brushes and UI

Previously I have experienced some trouble with my brushstrokes when painting over images – the strokes were noticeable and didn't blend very well. I therefore modified one of the default Chalk brushes in Photoshop to get the feel I was looking for; I added more noise, color, and angle jitter (see the settings in **image 03a** above). Along with

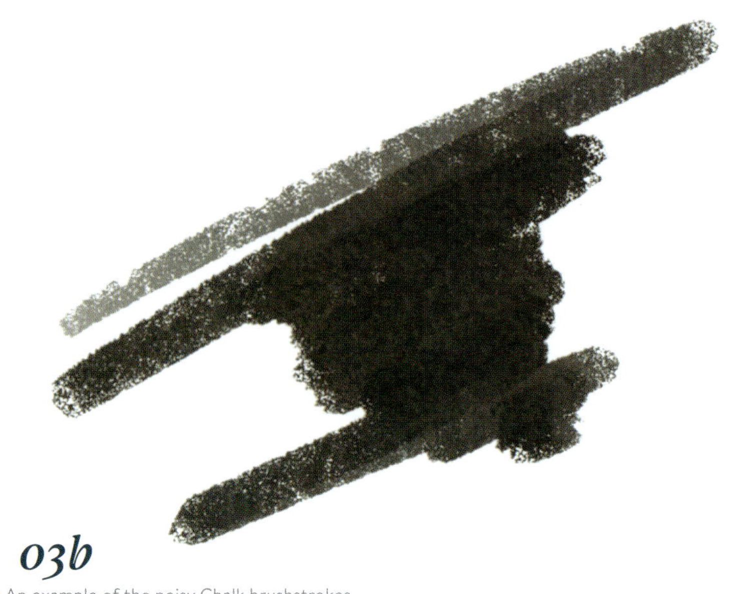

▲ An example of the noisy Chalk brushstrokes

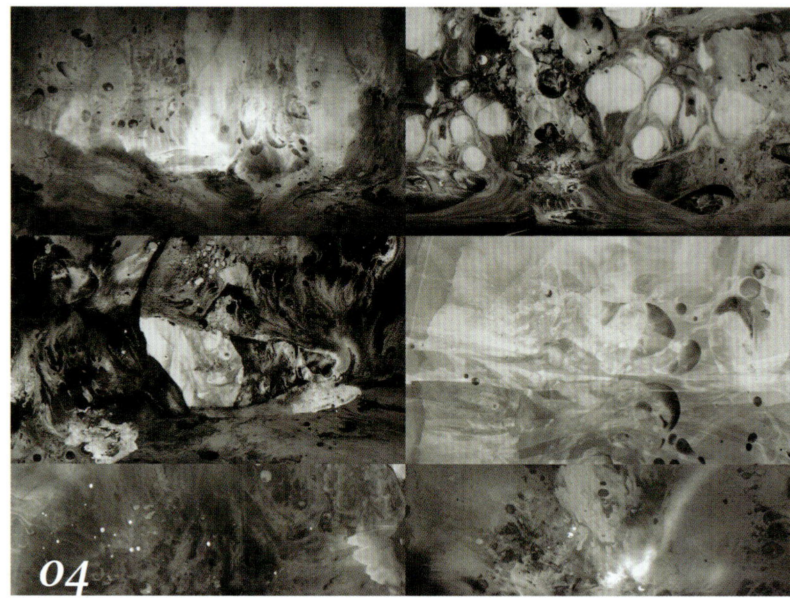

▲ A quick thumbnail is a great way to get ideas down

the Airbrush (soft round), these are the only brushes I use here (**image 03b**).

04: Thumbnails

Starting off with some quick thumbnails is always a good idea. I either use a pre-made grid that I can work under or I make a new file for each thumbnail. The danger here is getting bogged down on one image. Spend a few minutes on each just trying out some blend modes and moving things around to see if anything catches your eye; if not, simply delete and move on.

Simplify things by making it grayscale. I find this gives more flexibility when moving elements around because I don't have to worry about colors and layers

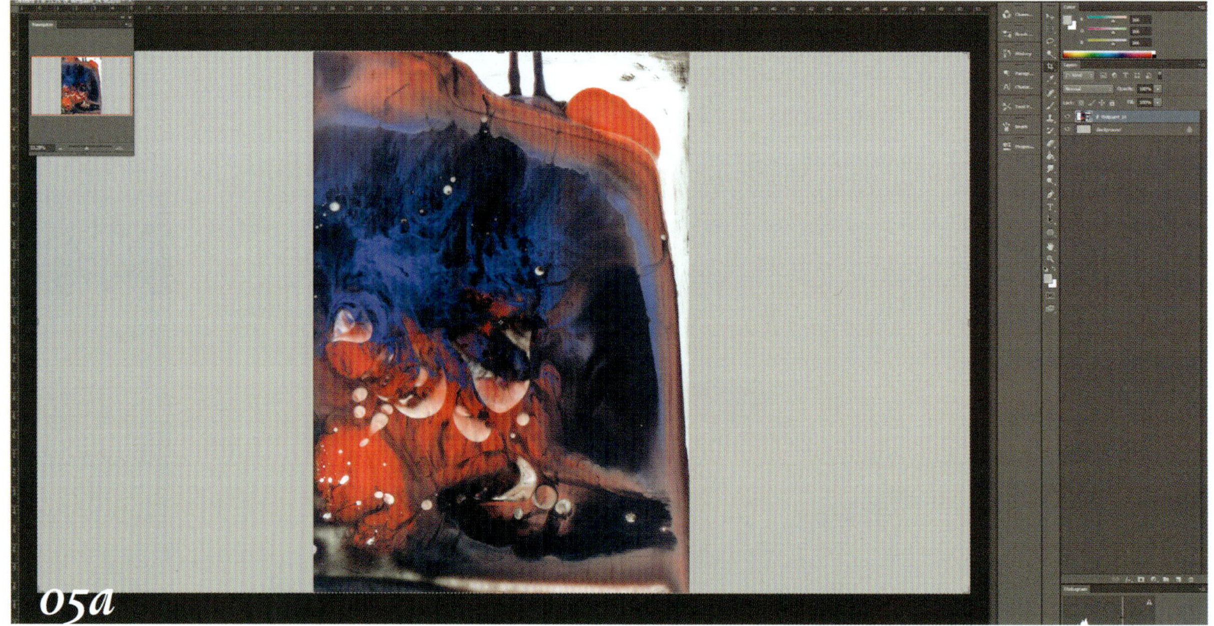

▲ Drag one of your scanned textures into Photoshop

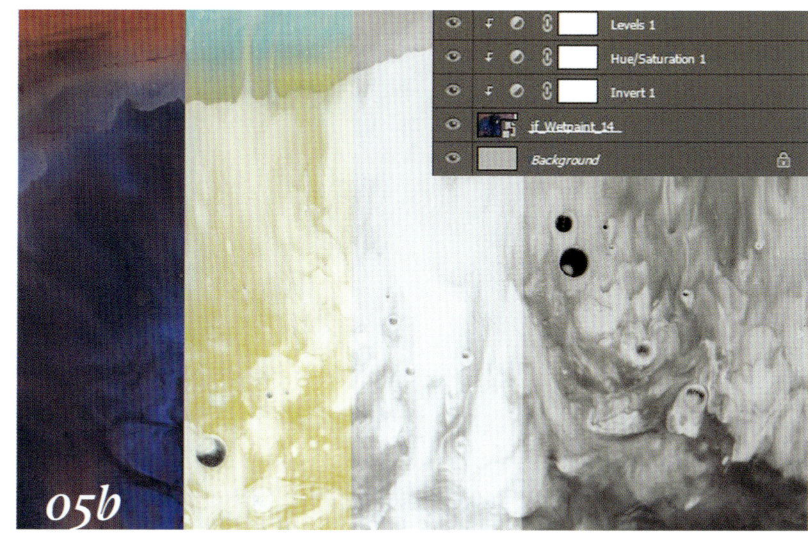

▲Adjustment layers can be applied to all images

overlapping – but fun things can happen when you keep the color! You need to try and find what works for you. You could start with a basic line drawing or blocking in some values and use Overlay or Multiply blend mode to lay down the textures; in this case I want to let the texture form the image naturally.

05: How to make thumbnails

Pick one of the textures you created as a starting point and drag it into Photoshop (**image 05a**): look for one that speaks to you or has interesting landmarks and shapes. Something with lots of details will give more opportunities for "accidents" to happen.

To make your texture grayscale you can use adjustment layers with a clipping mask – use Invert, desaturate (Hue/Saturation), and play with Levels (for contrast). Levels gives you a lot of control over how much and which parts of your image show up when using blend modes. I recommend that you copy the adjustment layers to all the upcoming layers. This will save you a lot of time (**image 05b**).

Drag in a new image and apply the same adjustment layers you made to the first layer (Alt+drag). With a clipping mask (hold Alt and click between the layers), play with different blend modes (I use Hard Light). Flick through the drop-down menu to see how each mode changes the images, combine the images, and move it around using a layer mask to erase what you don't want (**image 05c**).

Like with building blocks you can quickly block out your scene very fast and

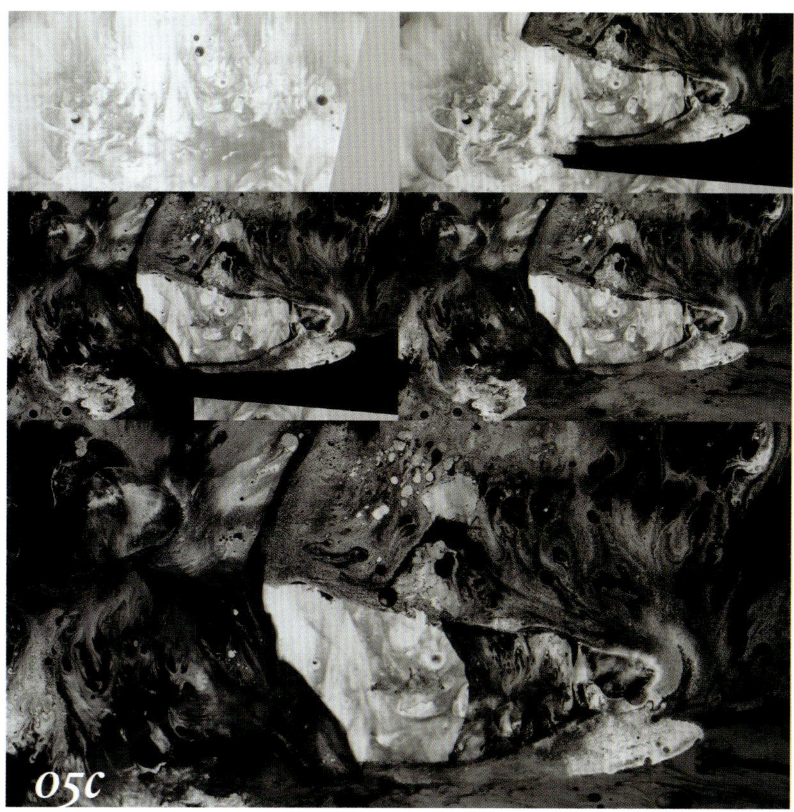

▲Build the thumbnail with different textures

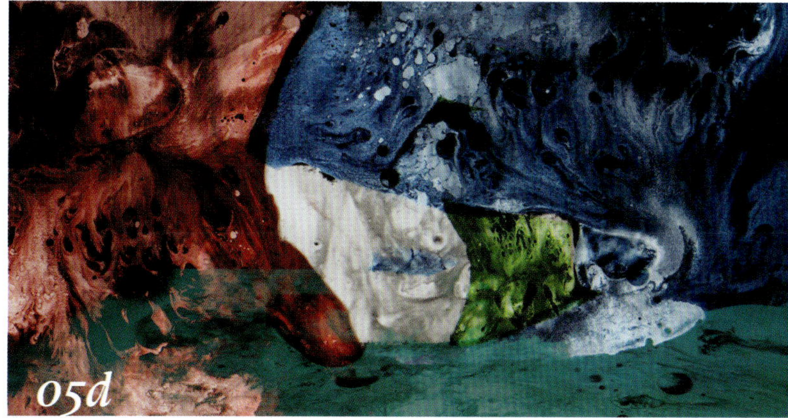

▲Each color shows a different texture

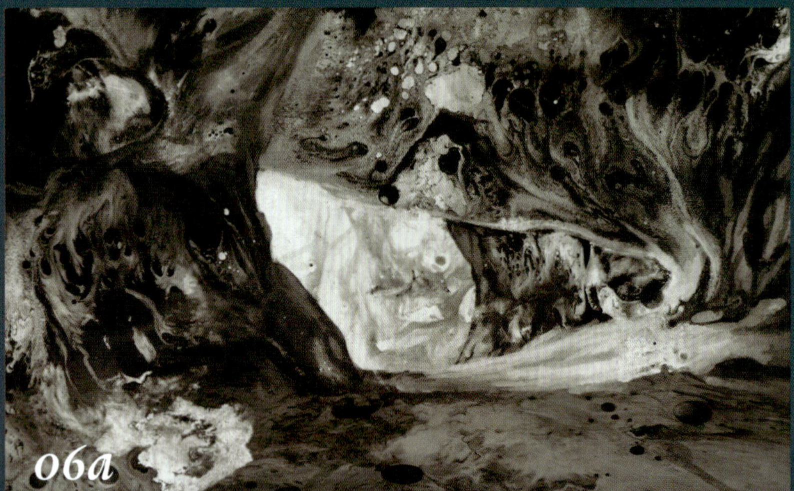

▲ Use the noisy Chalk brush to blend the images

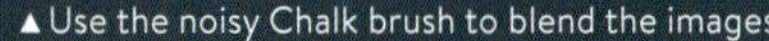

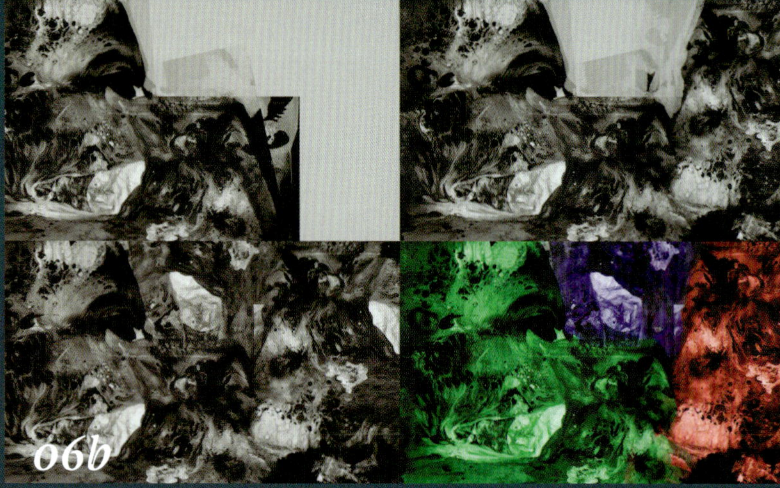

▲ The development of the composition

organically by moving things around and adjusting them as you go; working non-destructively at this stage (using layer masks and adjustment layers) keeps the process fluid and allows for quick changes. However, keep an eye on the file size because it will climb quickly; collapse (Ctrl+E) your layers once you are happy with your work (**image 05d**).

"Using the building-block idea from the previous step you can grow and develop your final composition to make the space a little bigger"

06: Start the painting!

With the thumbnail done you can start painting with the noisy Chalk brush from step 03. Just blend the images together and begin defining the areas you want

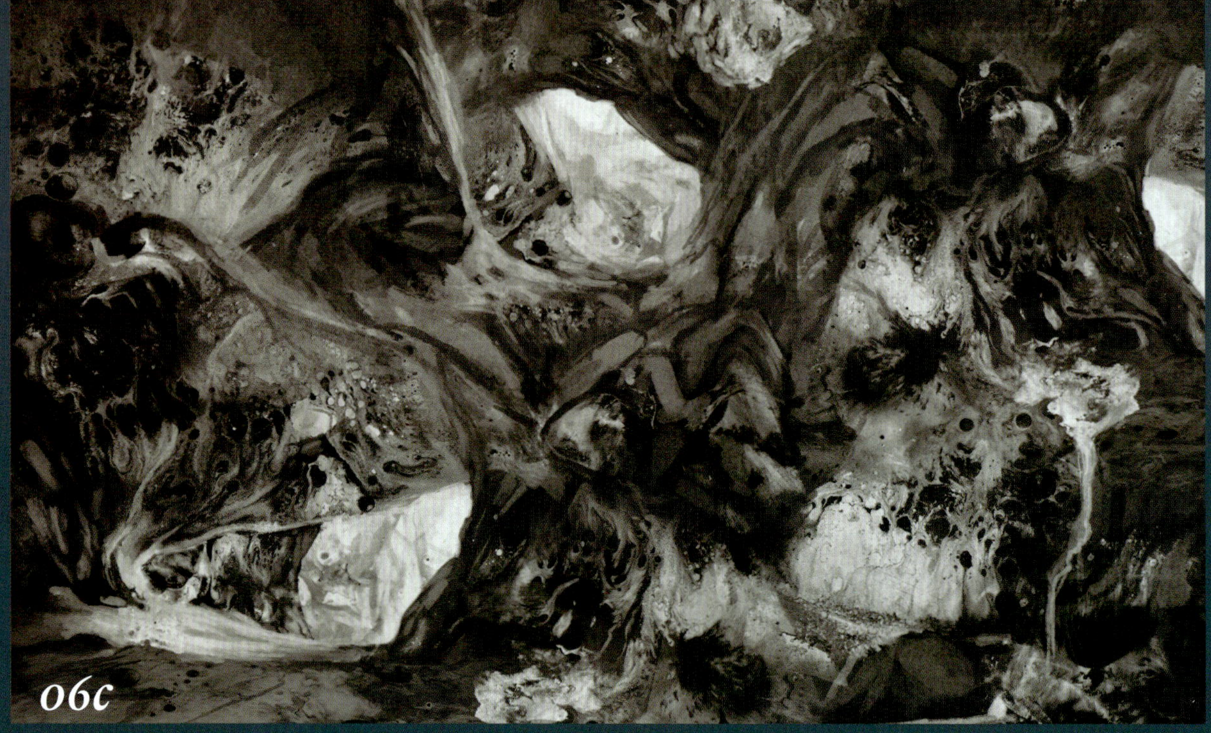

▲ Blend and define the shapes

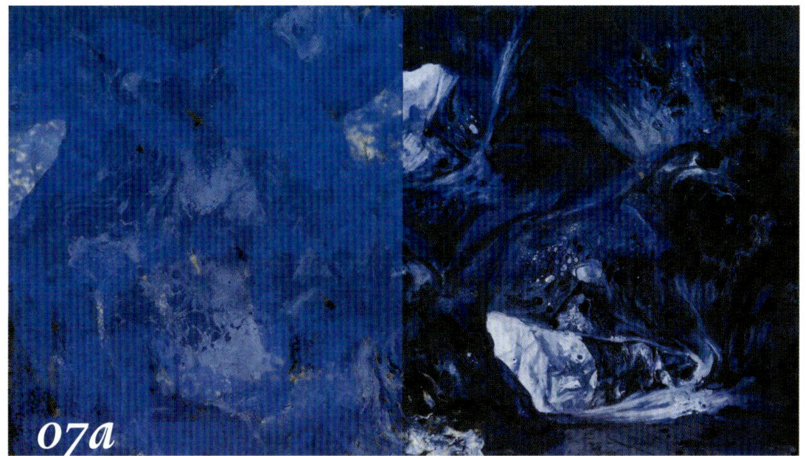

▲ Add a cold blue color

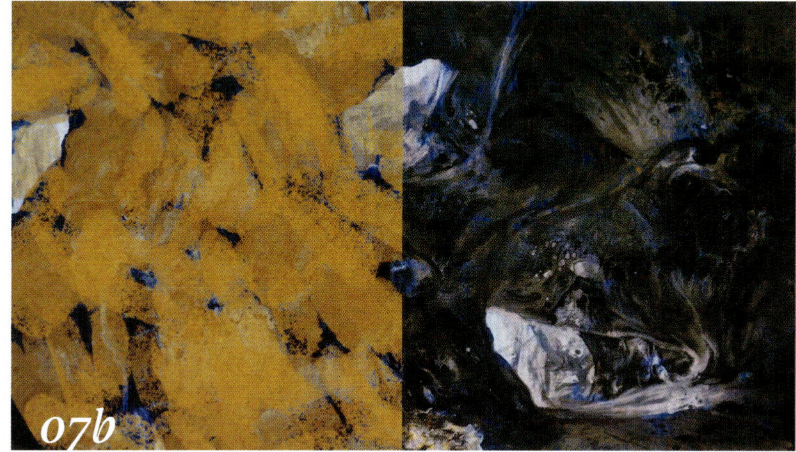

▲ Add a warm brown color

to focus on (**image 06a**). At this stage I feel my image is too small and needs to be bigger before I can continue. Using the building-block idea from the previous step you can grow and develop your final composition to make the space a little bigger.

To make your image bigger start by scaling it down using the Transform tool to make more room for other elements. You can use leftover elements from the thumbnail stage by copying and pasting the layer a few times to build up the rest of the scene (**image 06b**).

Again, there are ugly edges where the images join together so you need to blend and paint over them with the noisy Chalk brush, just the same as before. Using the existing shapes from the textures you can start to define the edges and fill out the blank spots (**image 06c**).

07: Time for some color

Once again using the noisy Chalk brush, fill in a new layer (set to Overlay) with a cold blue (**image 07a** above) and a warm brown (**image 07b**) on top. The Color Jitter on the brush will give brilliant color variety and will help to make the image feel more alive.

I need to separate the shapes and pull back the top part a bit, so with the Lasso tool I select the area that I need to deal with and then use a large soft round brush to paint with color picking from the lightest part of the image. I also use some minor color contrast and color adjustments.

If the image is too dark and you want to lighten it, you can play with Curves and add highlights to make it feel more connected with the background; for example give the image a nice blue tint with the Color Balance tool (**image 07c**).

Go over the lighter areas with a warm color (layer set to Overlay) to add some punch. You can add highlights by color picking from the lights nearby. This will help to give some separation between the foreground and the entrance (**image 07d**).

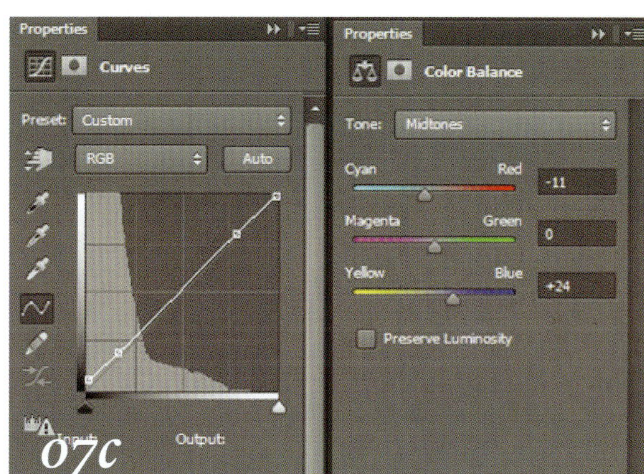

▲ The Curves and Color Balance settings

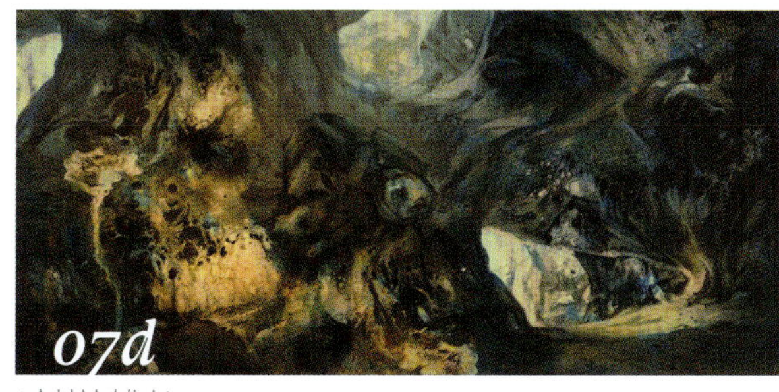

▲ Add highlights

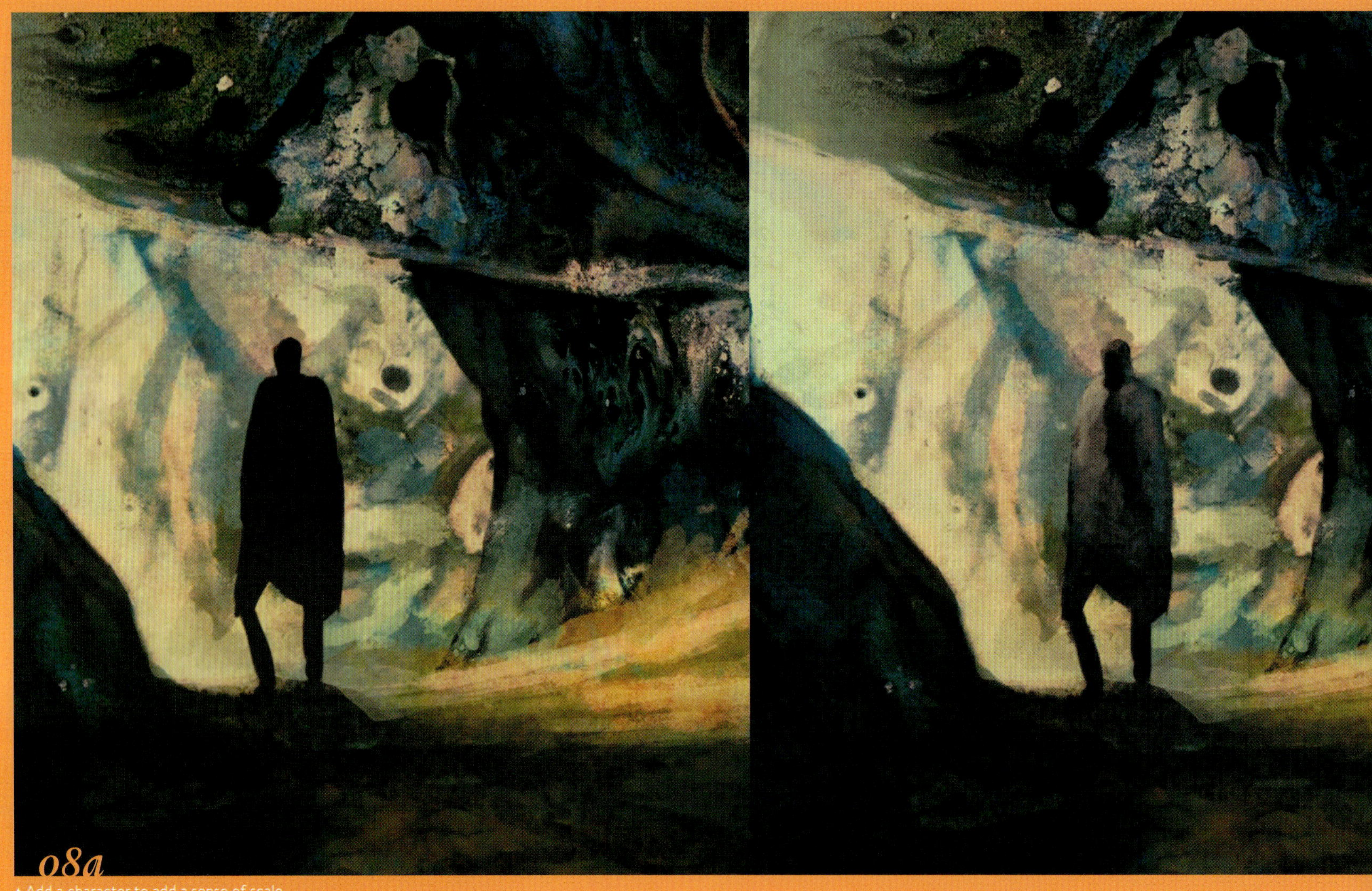

▲ Add a character to add a sense of scale

"I usually spend a long time cleaning up my work and adding details – it is actually kind of refreshing having a time limit and being able to just move on!"

08: Details

This stage is just about fixing up the minor things to tie everything together. If you think (like I do) that the scene is lacking something you can always add someone to explore your world; this will also greatly add to the sense of scale in the environment. To make your explorer, start with a simple silhouette and gradually add detail and highlights to bring them to life (**image 08a**). This is where I usually spend a long time cleaning up my work and adding details – it is actually kind of refreshing having a time limit and being able to just move on! You may want to make the glowing part a little stronger (use the same process as in step 07; **image 08b**).

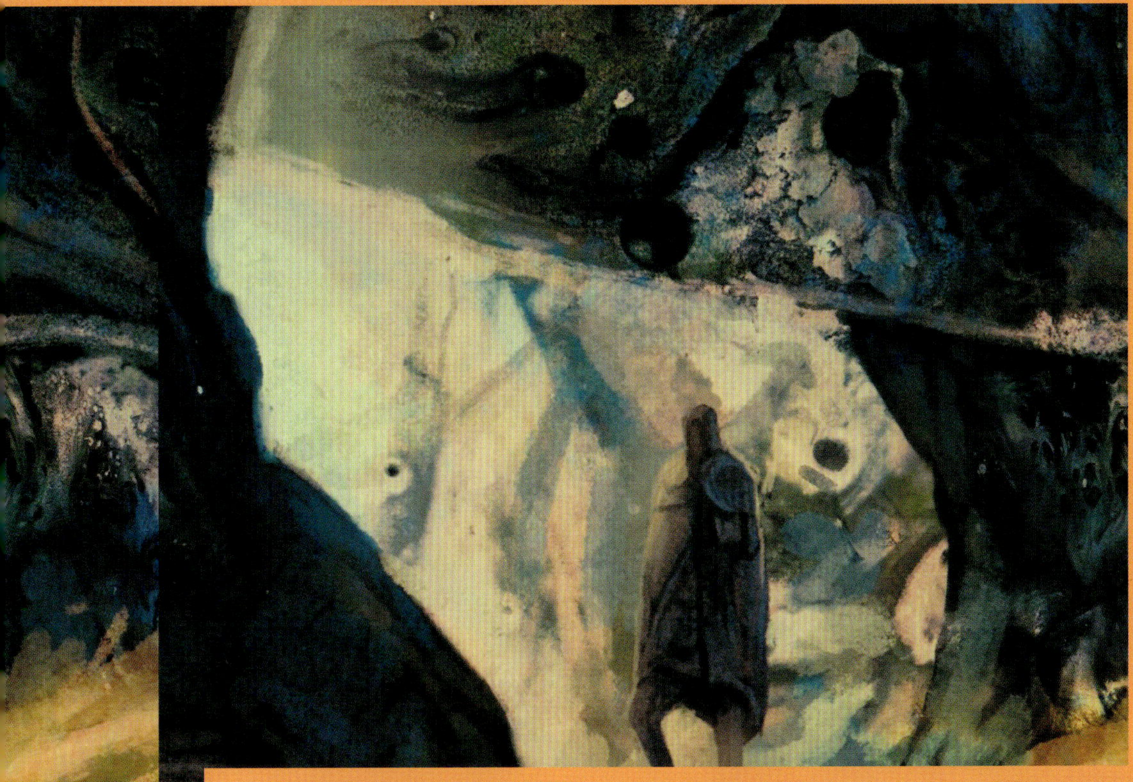

"This is just one way to go about speed painting with textures. The possibilities are endless and you will always see something new – a bit like watching clouds"

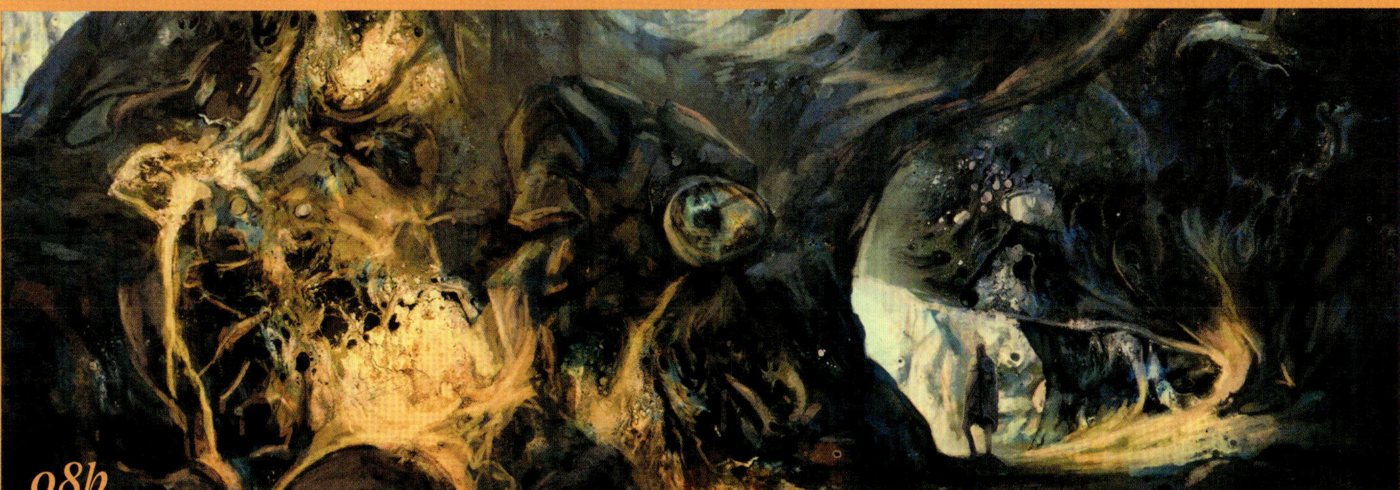

08b

▲ The character brings the image to life

09: Final thoughts

The painting is finished and ready to go, although you may want to make a few final adjustments. For example I adjust the color slightly to make it more yellow/brown because it was a little too blue.

This is just one way to go about speed painting with textures. The possibilities are endless and you will always see something new – a bit like watching clouds. You may find this to be a fun and relaxing way to get some ideas and have a break from your usual work process. I hope you give it a go and see that creating your own library of unique textures will give you something new and exciting to work with!

Pro Tip: Use photography

For some other interesting results, find every-day items and document them in different ways, for example with macro-photography (reverse the kit lens on your DSLR and you have a macro lens) of some seeds, leaves, or scratched-up metal. Drag a glass candle holder across a scanner for some neat lighting effects, and of course play around with paint and strokes on paper, letting wet paint mix and dry on its own, or squishing it between paper or in a scanner.

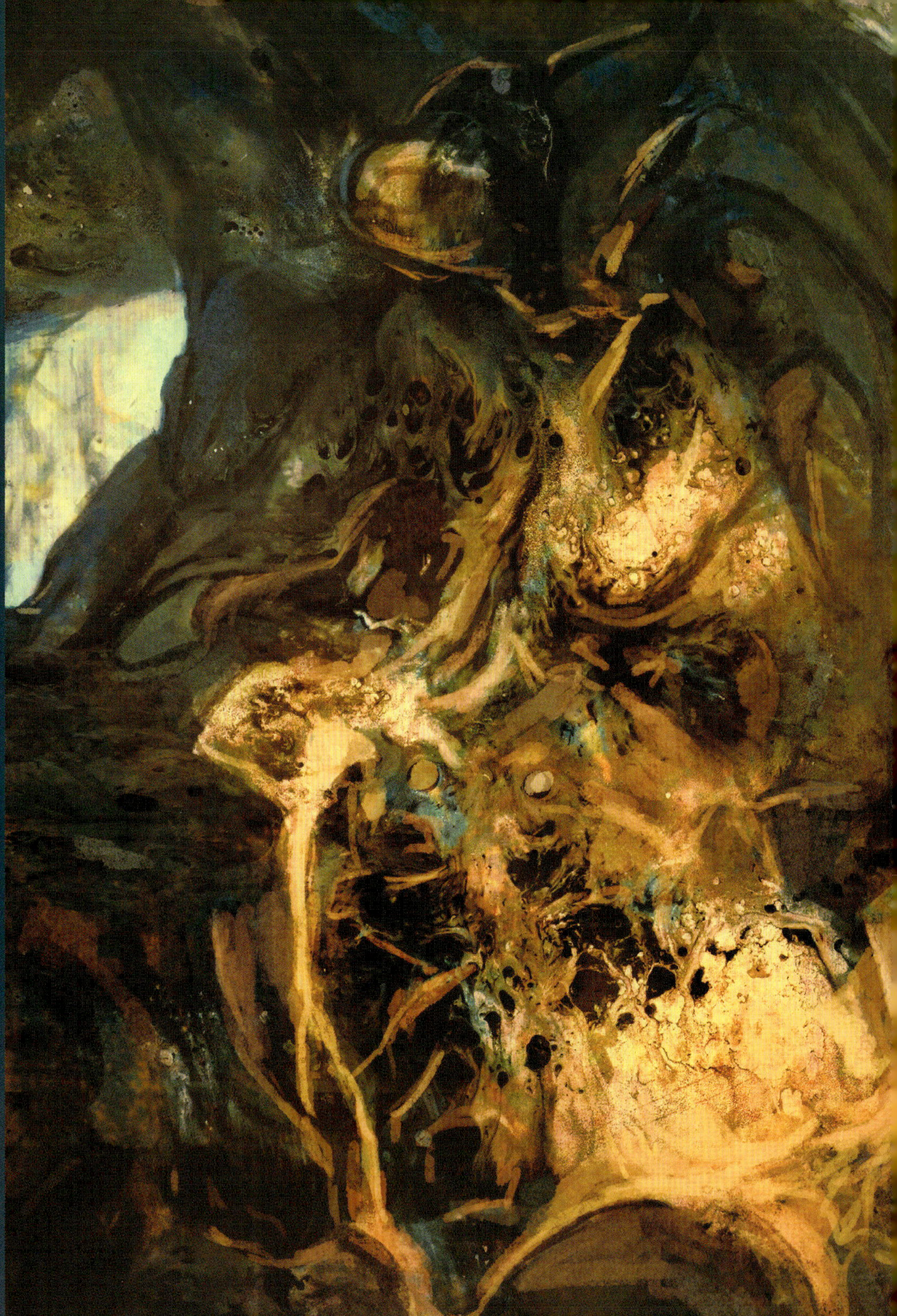

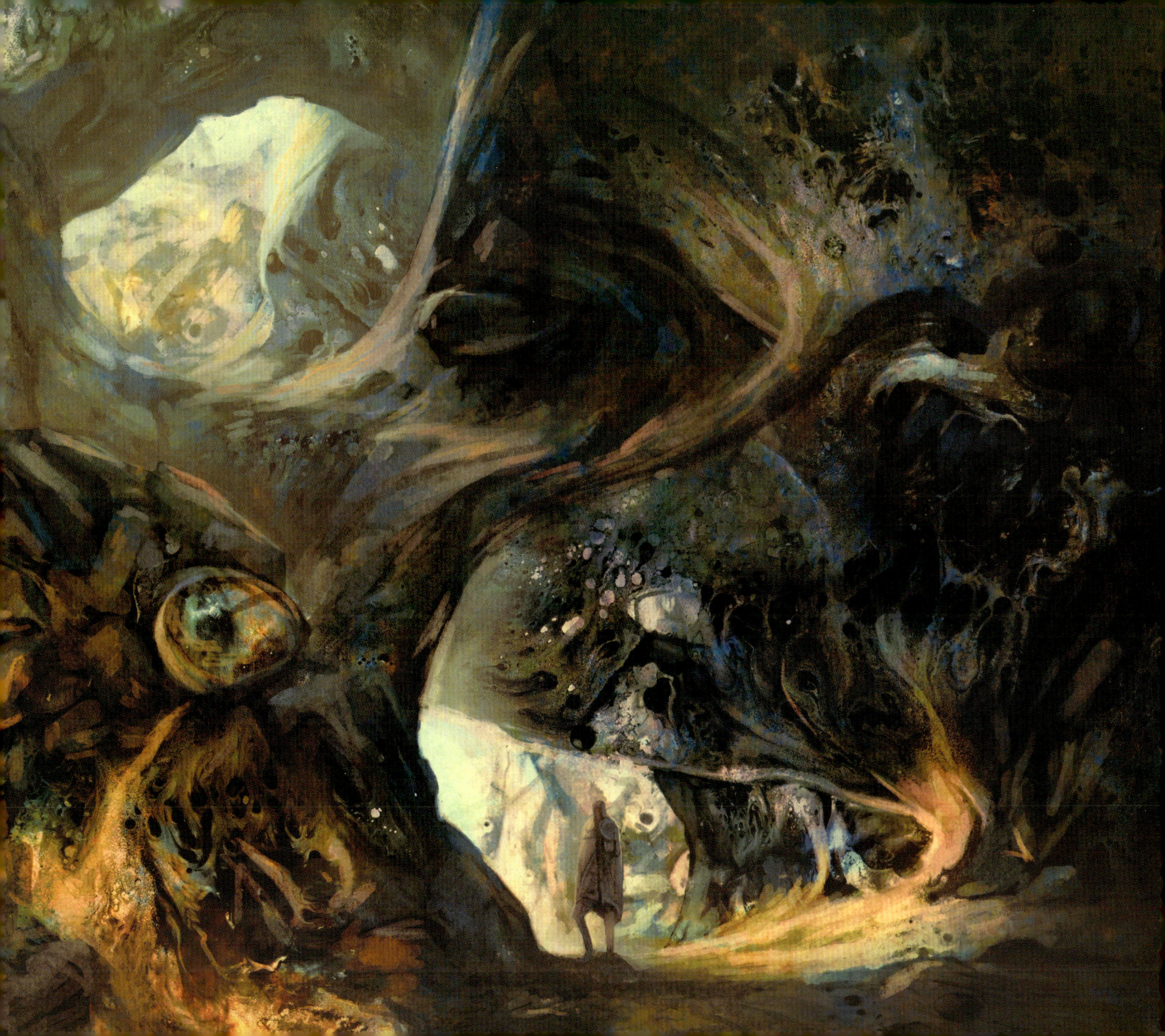

HORROR: WARD AWAY

by Noely Ryan

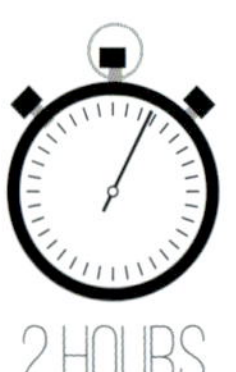

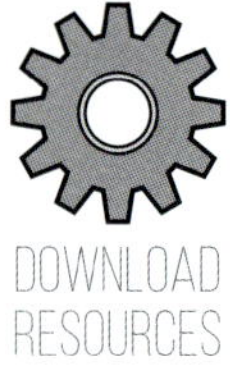

In my experience as a concept artist, speed is a very important factor when it comes to getting ideas and concepts ready for a director, producer, client, or your colleagues to see. It can help immensely when a project demands multiple renditions of the same subject for the sole purpose of exploration.

The task can be finding the right atmospheric mood in a scene or where an establishing shot might begin or end, or even the position of a character in a certain shot. No matter how big or small the demand, speed is the key when there is a budget on the line.

01: Choose a setting

The theme for this tutorial is horror, as here in Ireland, where I am based, we are fortunate to have a number of eerie buildings and ruins. Some may have a grim history but they make the perfect settings for horror! Research is a very important part of any new project; find as many reference images as you can that relate to your theme. These should include mood and atmospheric images as well. Most of the images I looked at were of Hideo Kojima's brilliant *P.T.*,

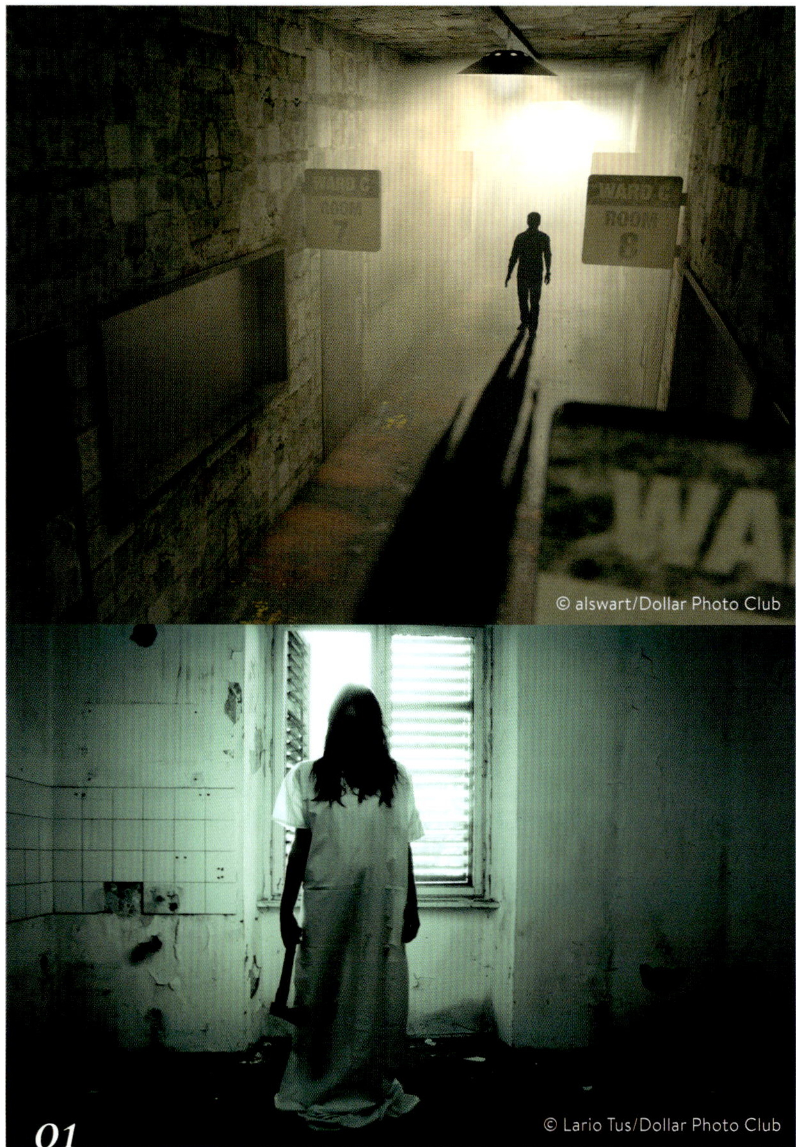

▲ Find some really creepy and atmospheric reference images to get the creative juices flowing

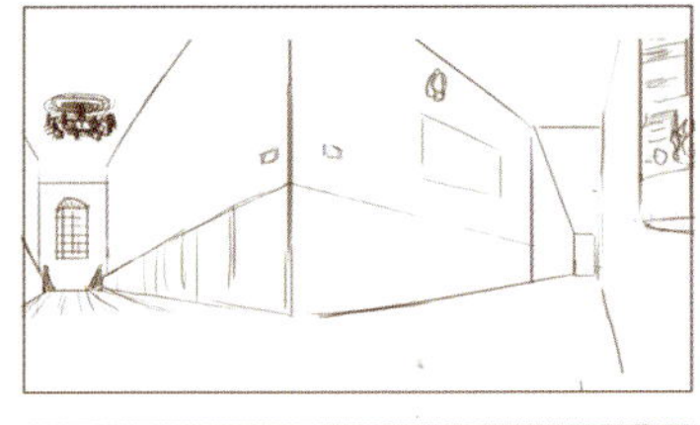
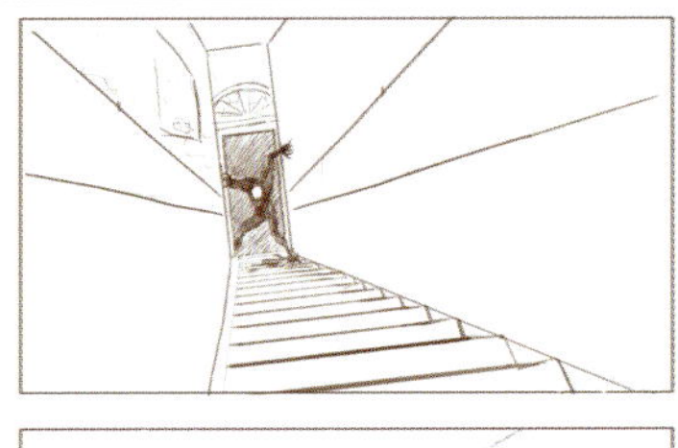
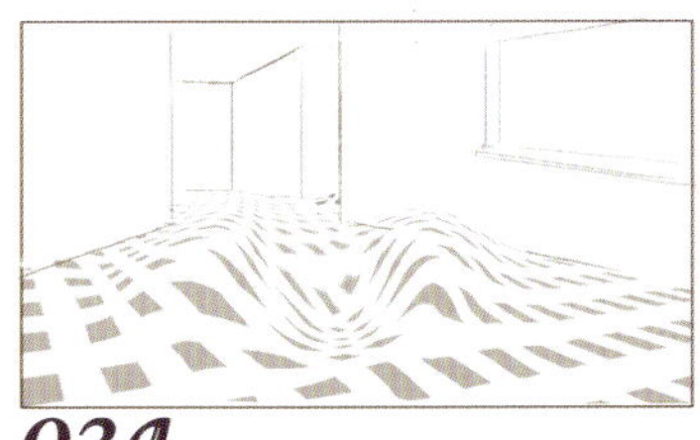
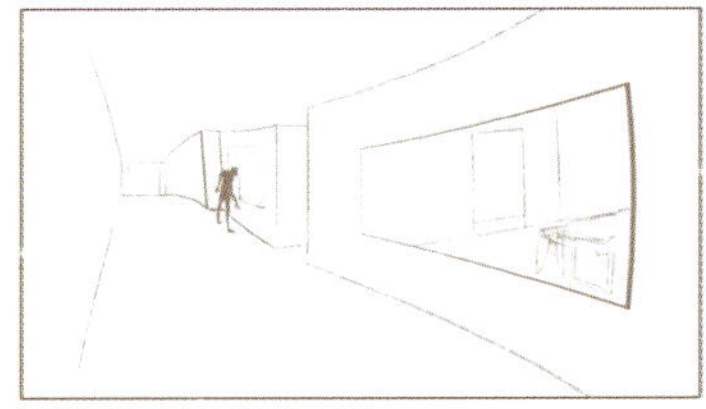

02a

▲ Quick thumbnail sketches can help you to choose the best composition

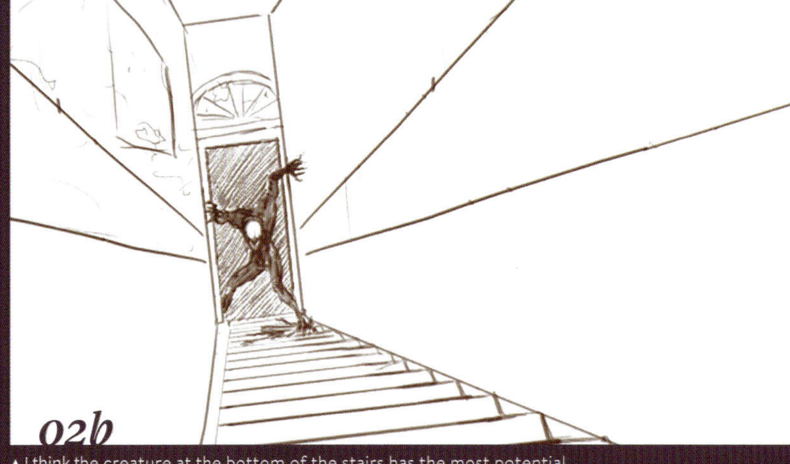

02b

▲ I think the creature at the bottom of the stairs has the most potential

so it's fair to say I was nicely spooked before beginning. You can use any scary film or story as a basis for your art. I decide to go with an asylum location.

02: Thumbnails

Spend a few minutes sketching out some thumbnails of typical asylum settings, such as dark hallways and stairs (**image 02a**). You should go for a scene which portrays a sense of mystery and apprehension, similar to horror movies and games. Just picture a place like this at night with the lights off!

I feel that the thumbnail with the creature at the bottom of the stairs is the strongest composition (**image 02b**). I am going for a scene where the viewer has turned a corner and shines a flashlight down the stairs at a doorway and suddenly a monster crashes through to give chase.

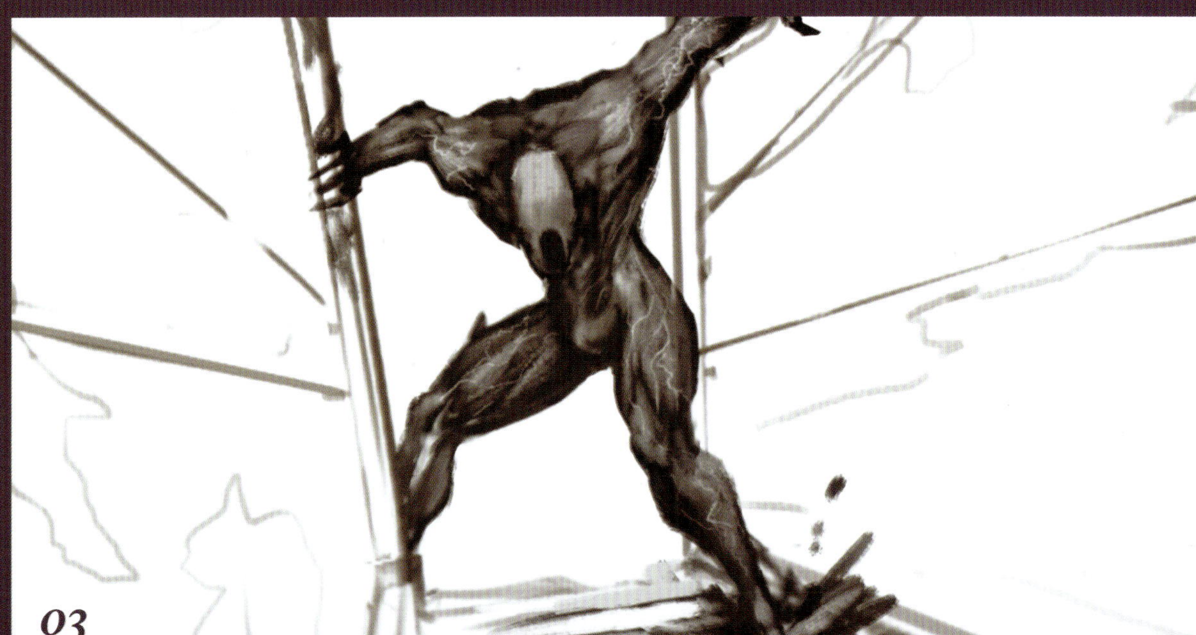

03

▲ As this is the first thing the viewer will look at it is worth spending a little more time here

03: Develop the sketch

If you are happy enough with the lines for the walls and stairs in the sketch, put some time into developing the creature and posing it to enhance the dynamic nature of the scene. Try to make it look like it has sprinted to the doorway and has to grab the wall for balance before it chases up the stairs. The creature is the main focal point of the image so some extra time given to it at this stage will help later on when finishing the image.

04: Refine the sketch and perspective

Perspective is an important part of any image; it needs to draw in the viewer's eye. You can distort the perspective by using the Polygonal Lasso tool (Shift+L). Select the lines of the doorway and the wall above it and free transform the shape (Ctrl+T). To evenly manipulate the angle of the selection, stretch it and hold down Alt+Ctrl to drag the corner of the box.

05: Block in colors

To stay with the run-down and dilapidated state of the building you should try to go with a muted color palette. Some important things to consider when choosing your colors are faded and peeling paint, mold and mildew which might form on long forgotten walls, and maybe even some dated retro wallpaper as well!

You don't need to spend ages agonizing over the colors as they can always be tweaked later if you change your mind.

06: Texture the walls

You will need to find some textures if you don't already have some. All of the textures I use for this image come from free sources such as the texture library at **www.3dtotal.com** or

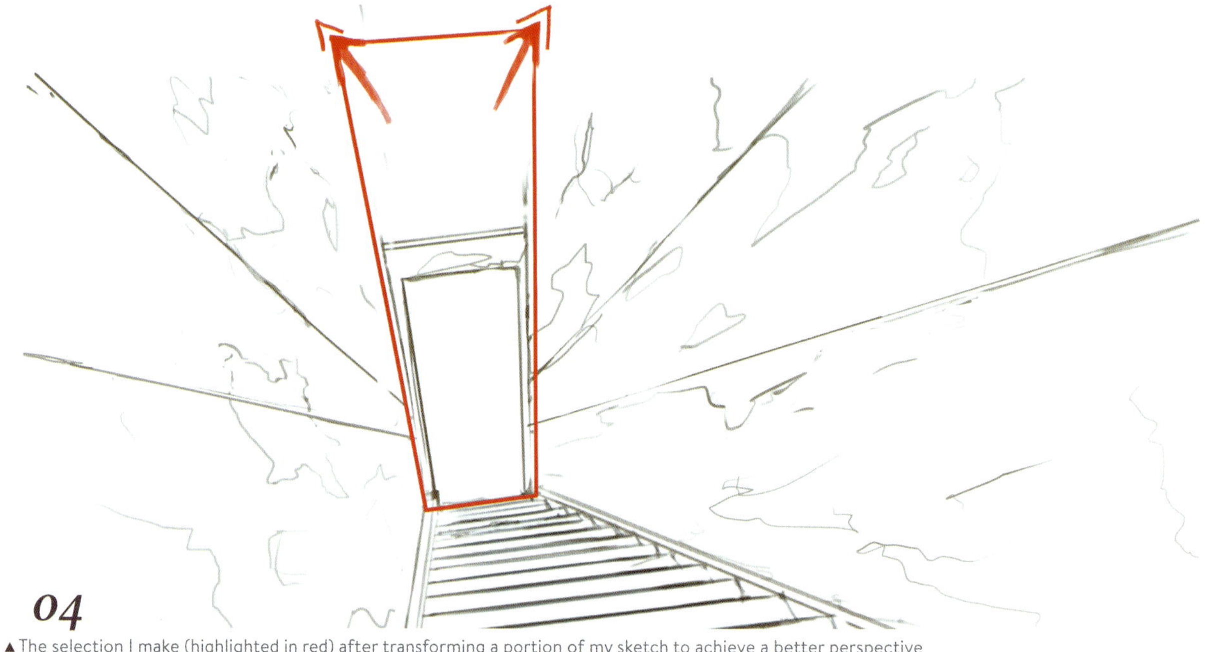

▲ The selection I make (highlighted in red) after transforming a portion of my sketch to achieve a better perspective

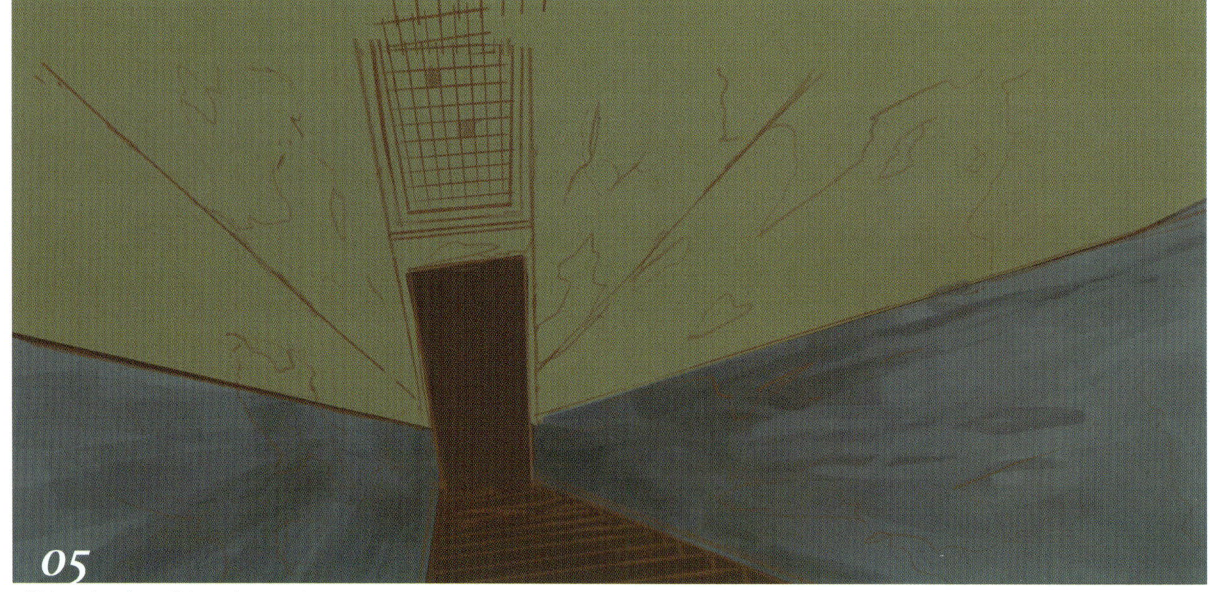

▲ Dirty colors for a dirty environment

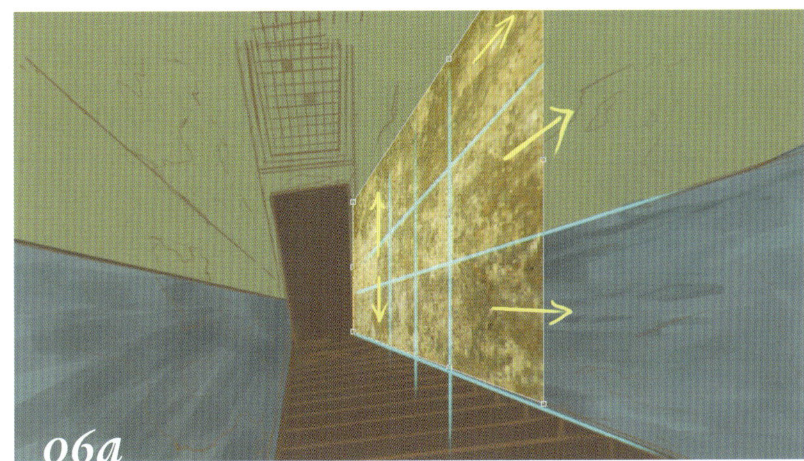

▲ Make your textures follow the contour lines of whatever you are texturing

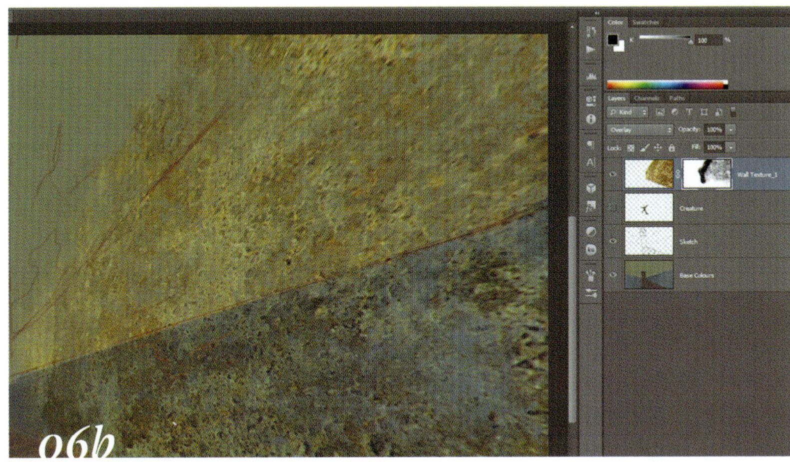

▲ Textures add to the believability of your work

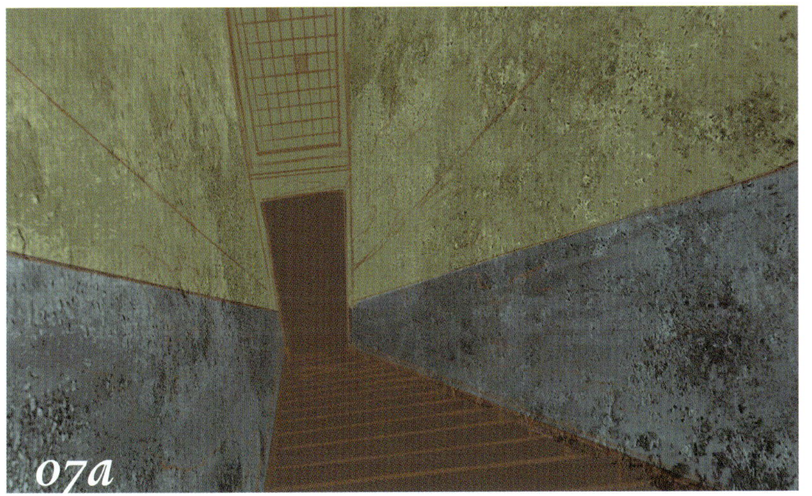

▲ Simply duplicate and flip the texture onto the other wall

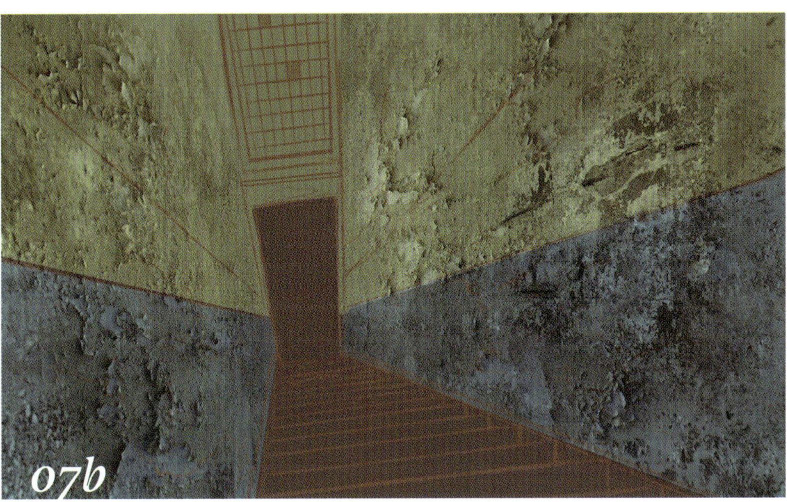

▲ This is a very quick and non-destructive method for texturing the walls

www.textures.com. You will want to search for aged and grungy ones to give your painting a good horror feel.

The first texture I apply is an old pebble-dashed look for the base of the walls. Apply your texture with its blend mode set to Overlay and free transform it so the hard edges roughly follow the perspective lines of your sketch (**image 06a**).

To get rid of the hard edges use a mask and paint them out with a soft round brush. You may want to mask out a few other areas to allow other textures to show through later (**image 06b**).

07: More damage

With the first texture applied you can now add more damage to the scene by using textures such as peeling paint or grungy-looking plaster (**images 07a** and **07b**). Simply drag into Photoshop, rasterize, and free transform them into place. Then set them to Overlay and mask each one. Instead of erasing or deleting areas of something you might reuse later, use masks as they can save you a headache when something is changed later in a project.

Reveal some areas of the texture until you are happy, duplicate the layer, and flip it onto the other wall. This is where masks can come in handy again; use them to reveal new areas to avoid repetition and symmetry.

08: Glass block window

Glass block windows over doors are commonly used in hospital design; they will also add a touch of color to your dark and dreary scene. I choose a glass block window reference with some light reflection on it, which with careful manipulation I could turn into a flashlight reflection.

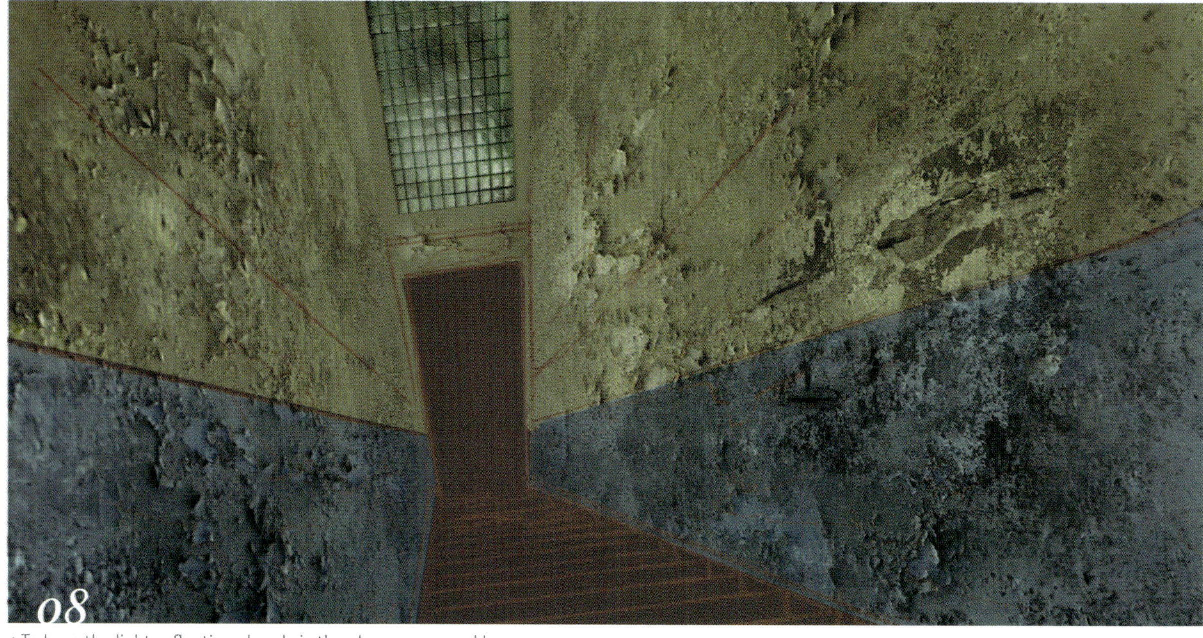

▲To have the light reflection already in the glass was a good bonus

Paint a greenish-blue on a layer underneath the glass; this will push color into the glass texture when it is laid on top. Repeat the texture process from steps 06 and 07 to adjust the texture. I want the window to extend up and off the canvas as if it went up to the ceiling so I select a portion of the dark area at the top of the texture and duplicate it to extend it upwards.

09: Tiling the floor

On a new layer fill the doorway with solid black and use a checkered tile texture for the floor at the bottom of the stairs. If it isn't big enough you can repeat this type of pattern relatively seamlessly; the edges may not match up perfectly but this can easily be fixed by duplicating the layer (Ctrl+J), erasing one edge, and placing it over the layer

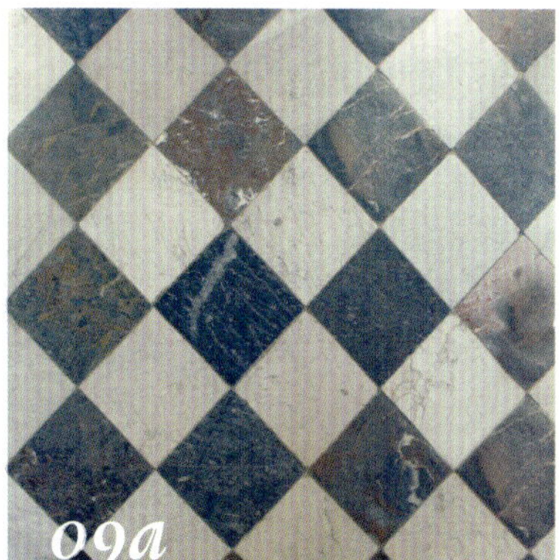

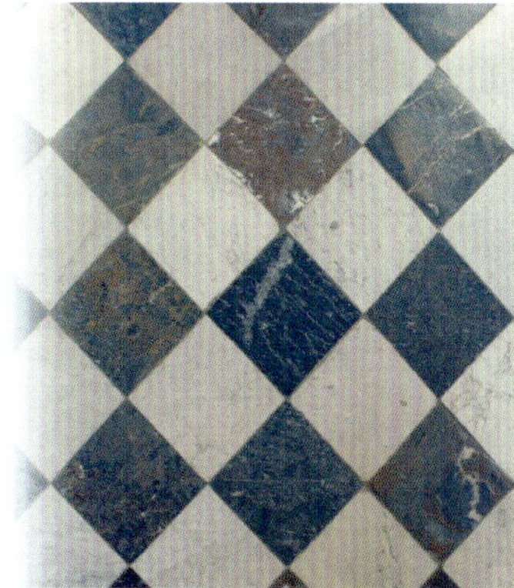

▲The tiles help to tie the image and the perspective together nicely at this stage

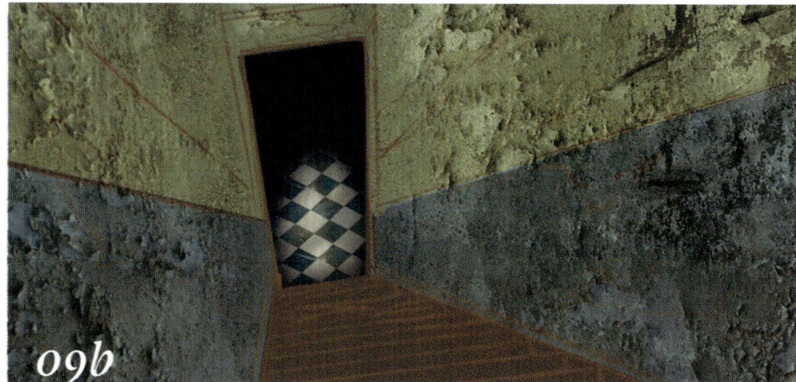

▲Fading the tiles into shadow adds to the eerie vibe of the image

underneath until the tiles match up (**image 09a**). Repeat until you have a big enough image to work with.

Apply a mask to it using a content selection of the black doorway layer: Ctrl+click on the layer's thumbnail, then press the Mask icon on the layer you want to mask. Paint out the area that disappears into the shadows, leaving only the area that would be lit up by the flashlight (**image 09b**).

10: Blood and graffiti

I apply blood textures to the walls using a Multiply blend mode. Having a blood texture on a white background enables the Multiply mode to get rid of the white, leaving only the color information on the canvas.

Use this technique for the graffiti, although my graffiti textures are on grayish concrete walls which show through, darkening the area it covers. You can use a Levels adjustment (Ctrl+L) to brighten the grays to whites until they disappear, leaving only the graffiti artwork.

11: Rotten wood

To add texture to the stairs and door you will need a wood texture, preferably with peeling paint.

Use an Overlay blend mode and play around with Hue/Saturation (Ctrl+U) to change the color. Duplicate the

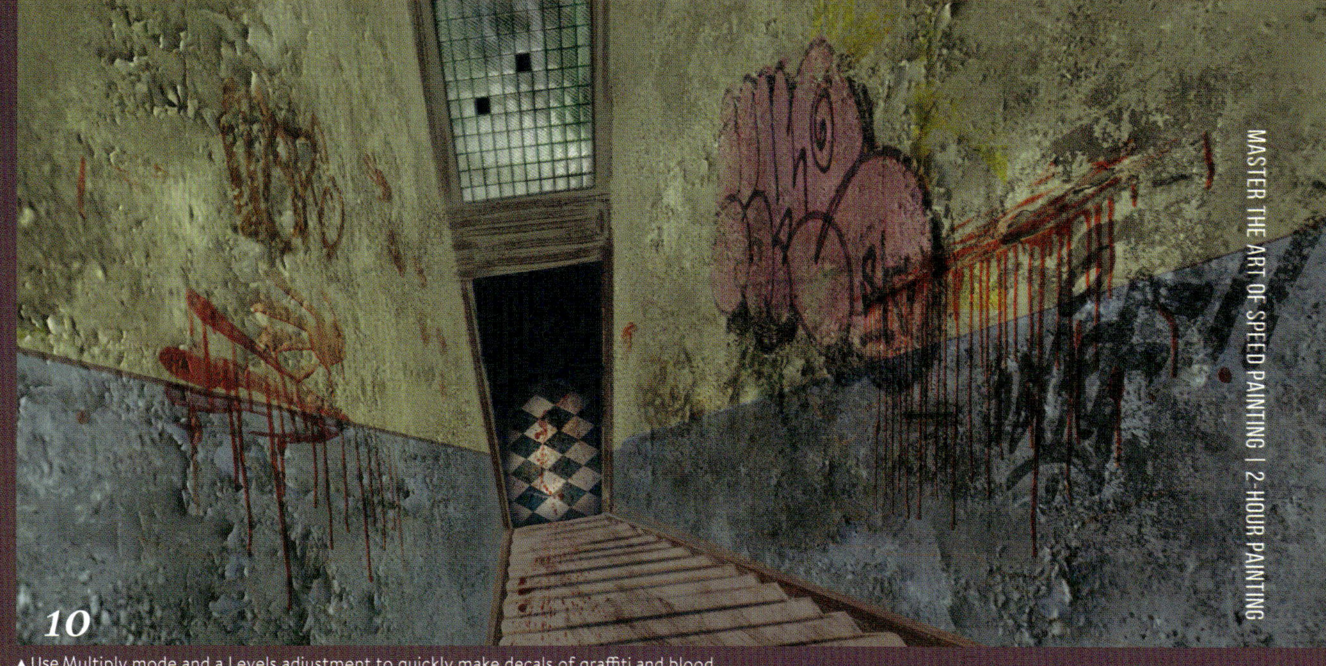

▲ Use Multiply mode and a Levels adjustment to quickly make decals of graffiti and blood

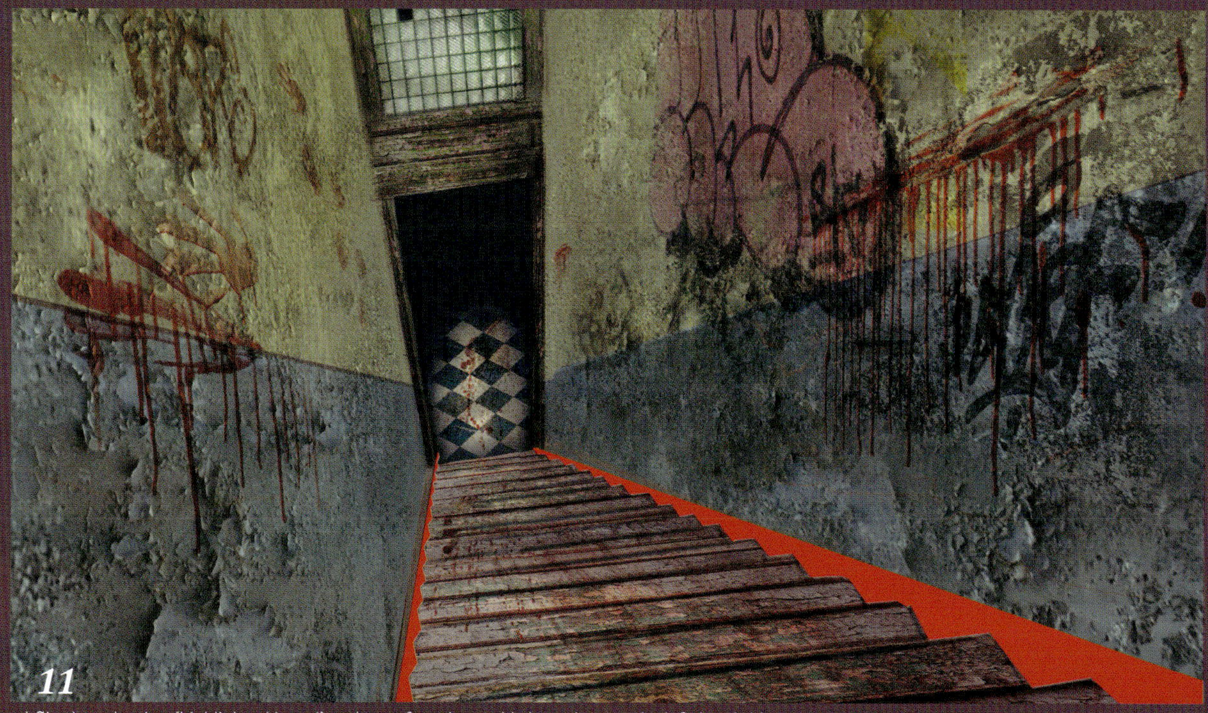

▲ I flip the selection (highlighted in red) and transform it roughly into place on the left-hand side

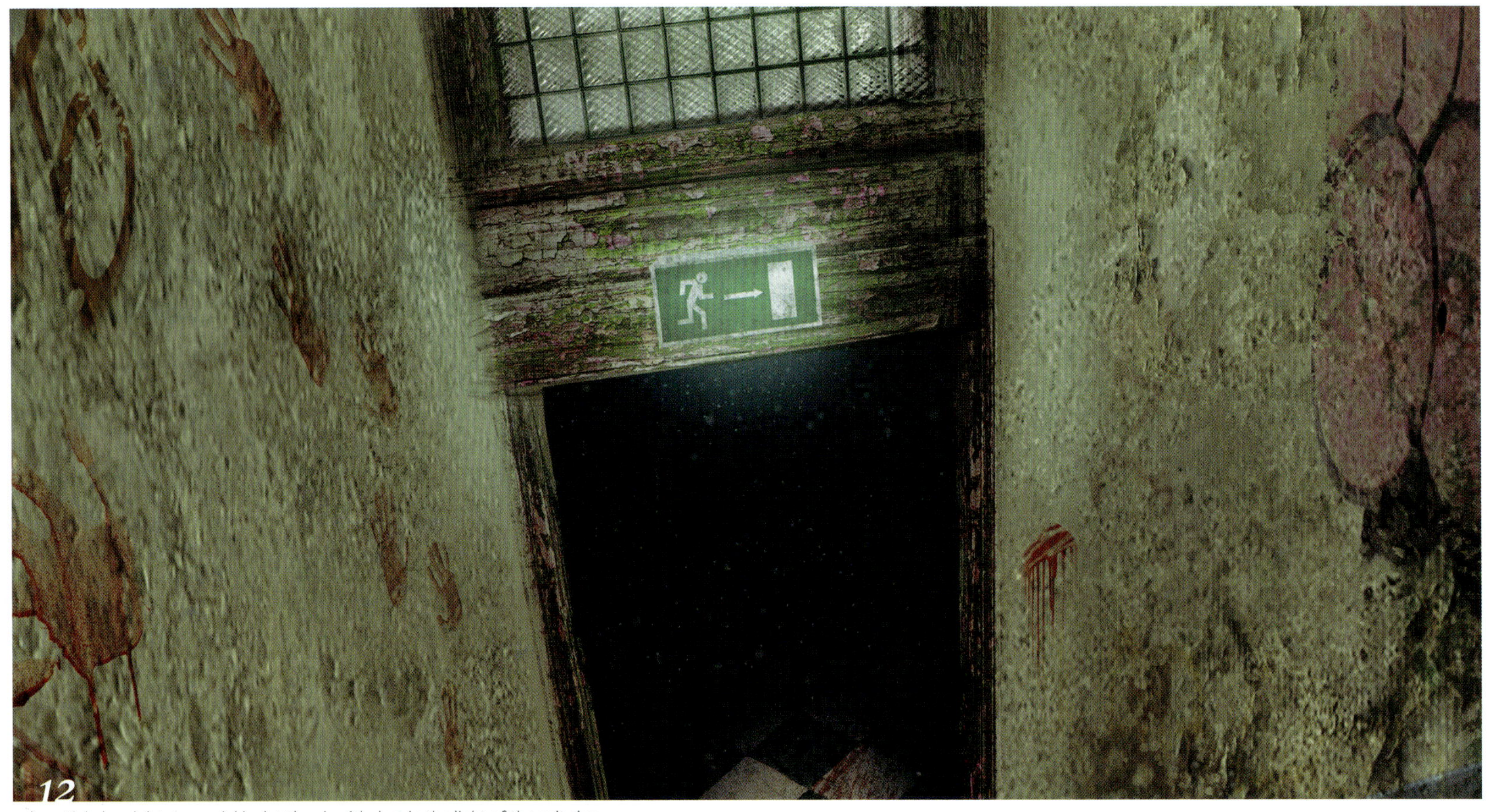
12

▲ A particle brush lets me quickly dot the air with dust in the light of the exit sign

image and make it longer for the stairs, then transform it to follow the downward angle of the stairs. You don't need to worry about precision when applying textures in this image because you are going for a damaged, old look. Use the Polygonal Lasso tool to make a rough selection of the shape of the steps and delete it. To make a door frame, cut strips of the texture and place around the door.

Pro tip: Keyboard shortcuts

I have keyboard shortcuts for flipping a layer horizontally by pressing Ctrl+Shift+-, and vertically by pressing Ctrl+Shift+=. Edit your own shortcuts by going to Edit > Keyboard Shortcuts. I chose these keys because they weren't already used by any other action.

12: Exit sign

Transform an exit sign reference image and place it over the door. Remember to paint the surrounding box. On a new layer, paint a light green glow set to Linear Dodge. I like to think it adds to the story of the image as signaling the only available way out of the asylum.

13: Finish the creature

Spending the time in step 03 working on the creature's forms will save you time here. Duplicate the creature a couple of times; set one copy to Overlay and on another copy colorize it red using the Hue/Saturation tool. I also add color and texture passes on different layers set with clipping masks on the base sketch. Have a play around with the different Overlay layers to paint in highlights and shadows until the creature is to your liking.

For the shadow behind, use a base sketch copy and set the Lightness to complete black using Hue/Saturation. Add a little blur using Gaussian Blur and place it below the creature, off slightly to one side.

14: Flashlight

When you are happy with the final look, create a composite layer (Ctrl+Shift+Alt+E). This allows you to make adjustments and transformations without messing with the original layers, which you will want to do to add a flashlight beam to heighten the creepiness (**image 14a**).

To make the flashlight (**image 14b**), fill a new layer with black and mask out the beam area with a hard brush. Blur the mask using Gaussian Blur to soften the glow, duplicate this layer, and have a

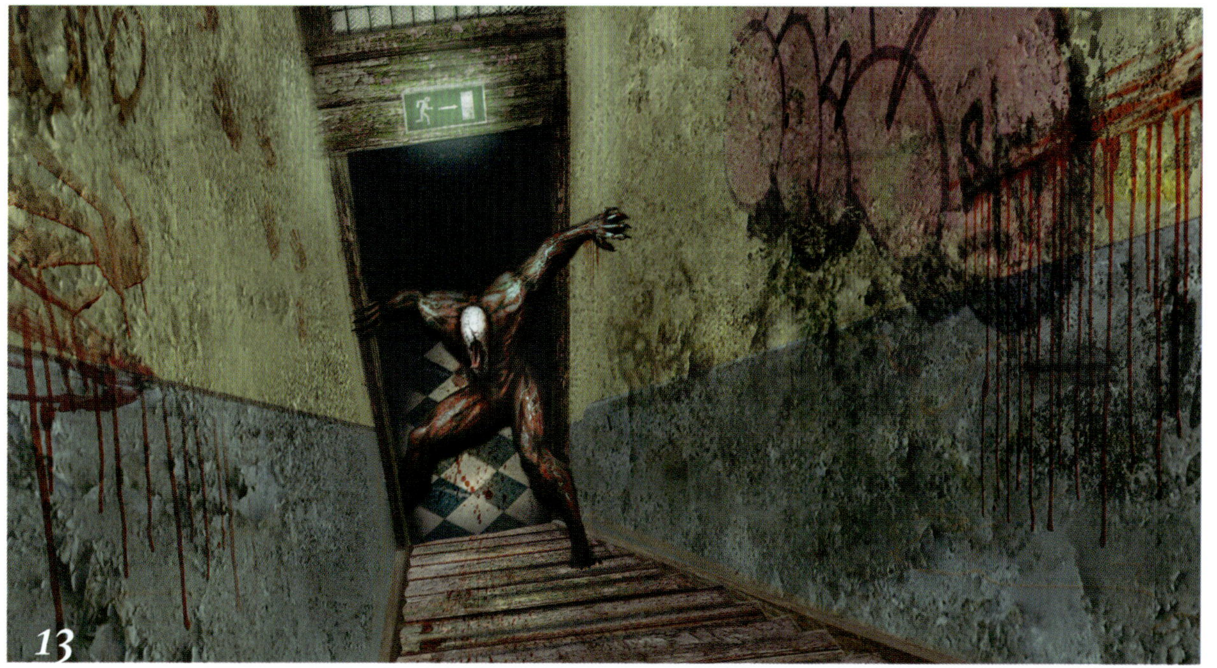

▲ Early preparation allows for a quick finish to the creature by reusing layers

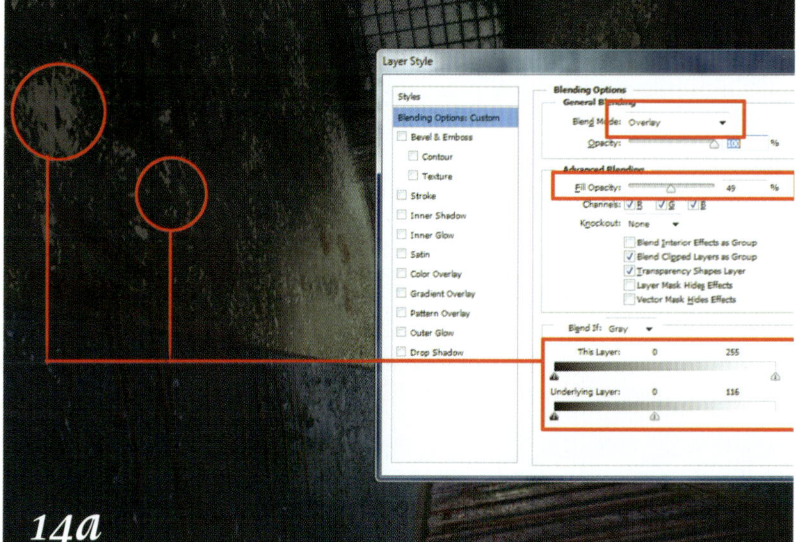

▲ Exploring the blending properties of layers can yield some nice results

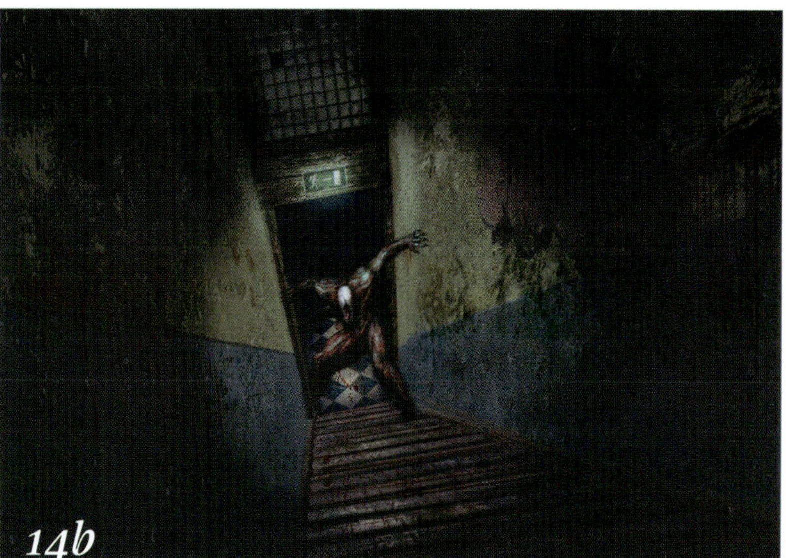

▲ The beam from the flashlight is a creepy touch that adds to the atmosphere

play around with the Layer Style menu to reveal lighter areas underneath the composite layer – the highlights nicely break up the darkness here and there.

15: Finishing touches

On a new layer add some dust using a particle brush; you can also add a Vivid Light layer to bring up the brightness of the flashlight. With these new layers create a new composite layer, add chromatics, make some color corrections, and duplicate it – this can really add to the final look and mood of an image: I also apply a slight Radial Blur to the duplicate and mask away some areas to add some more movement and depth. Finally I add some noise to bring the image together (Ctrl+B).

Pro Tip: Composite layering

The non-destructive method of merging composite layers and playing with the different filters, effects, and masks applied to them allows you to change the final look of the image at any time.

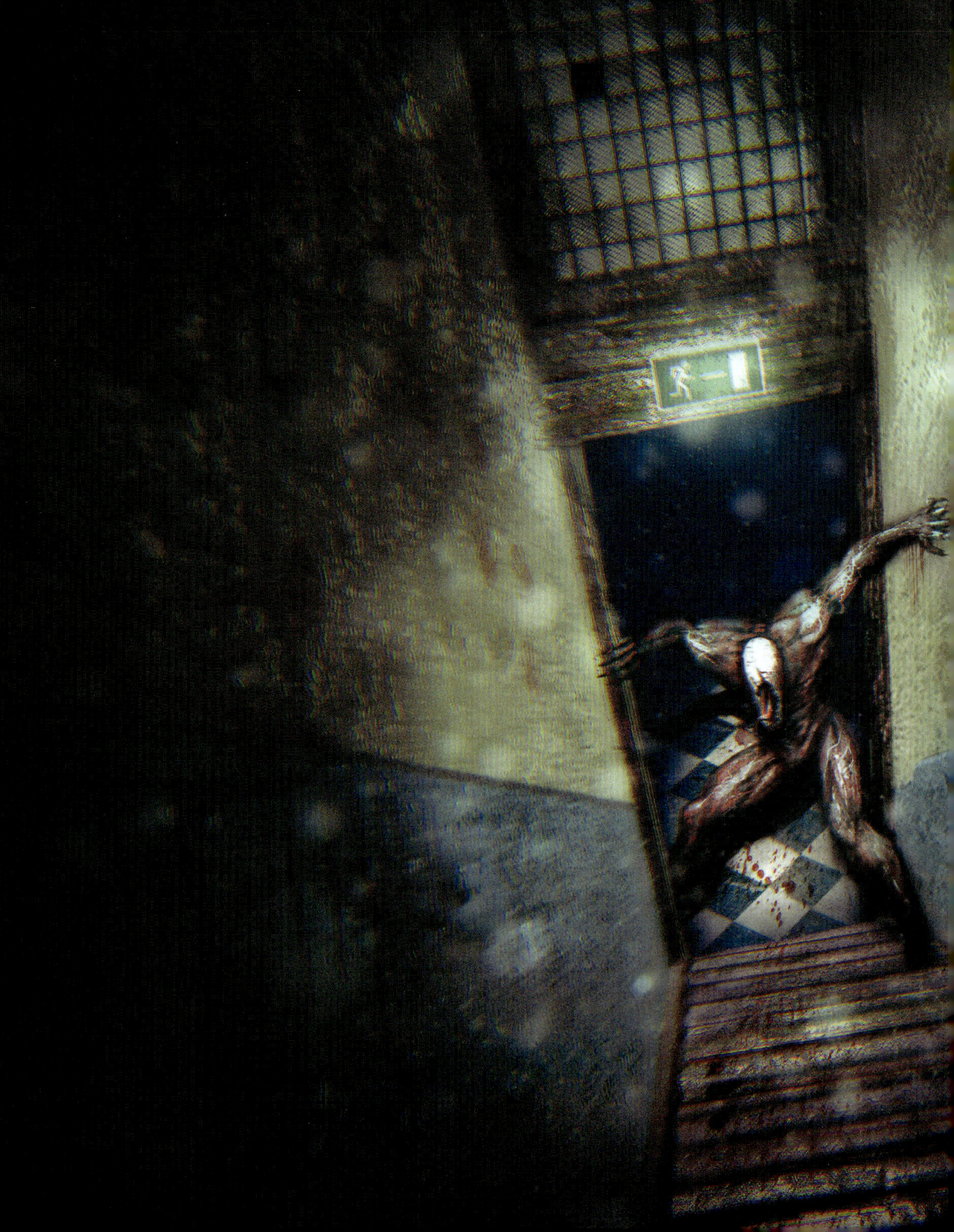

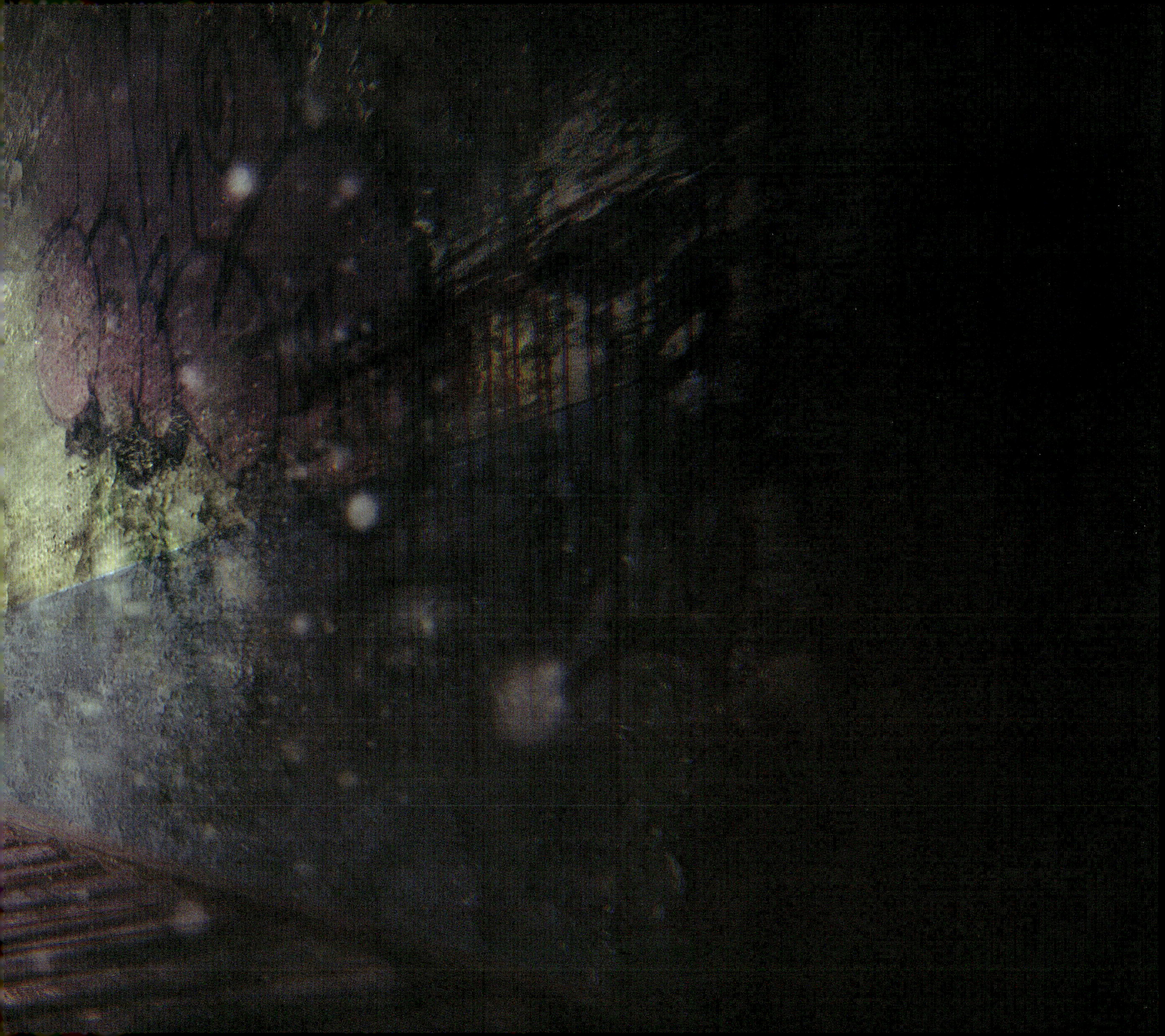

2 HOURS

REAL WORLD: HISTORICAL LANDSCAPE

by Donglu Yu

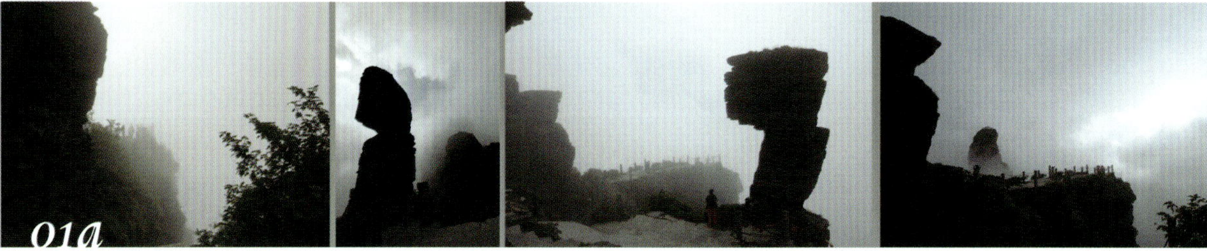

▲ Reference gathering is crucial for you to gain familiarity with specific themes

In this tutorial I will guide you through my approach to creating a historical landscape. The key to a successful speed painting is to capture the essence of your theme within a very limited time constraint, in this case two hours. This requires you to be very familiar with your chosen subject and use common shapes to portray the theme. Such familiarity can be obtained by two methods: years of experience of observation and careful studies of any available image references.

Once you are ready, you can then switch to the technical aspects of speed painting. I will take this opportunity to share a few tricks for coming up with composition variations quickly and efficiently by using custom brushes and shapes. The importance of value relationship and ambience will be elaborated upon as well. We will also discuss lighting and the use of color temperature in order to portray depth.

The tutorial will finish with a few tricks for tightening up whole images, including edge treatment and camera effects.

Throughout, I will do my best to explain not only how to apply certain techniques, but also the reason behind the practice of those techniques. I firmly believe that once you have a logical understanding of your painting approaches, the technical side will become natural to you, therefore you will be able spend

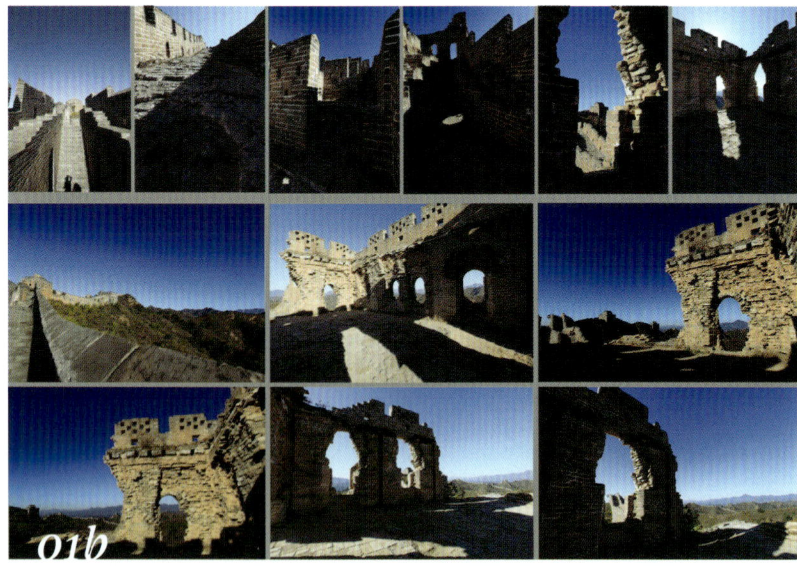

▲ Make a large visual bank from the many resources available to you

your time and energy more effectively on the creative aspects of your artwork.

"Try to limit your selection of brushes for the speed-painting process"

01: Reference gathering

Reference gathering is a key part of any project because it helps you to become familiar with your chosen topic. I personally like to take my own pictures – it can take a lot of time to build up a decent library but it is well worth the effort. You can do this with high-end shots using a professional camera or simply your smartphone or tablet on your way to work.

Alternatively you can do a quick image search on the internet or use image-based websites such as Flickr to build a reference bank. You need to be careful when using images that are not your own however because they may have copyright restrictions and this could lead to trouble if you ever want to publish your work. Fortunately there are solutions: you can use websites such as **www.textures.com** to get access to copyright-free images, although there is sometimes a small membership fee (**images 01a** and **01b**).

02: Warm up with brushes

Before I start working on a speed-painting session I like to warm up with some custom brushes (**image 02a**).

Depending on the theme, try to limit your selection of brushes for the speed-painting process. Working with a limited range of brushes can force you to work more efficiently by thinking about shapes and design rather than brushstrokes. This may take a while to get used to but it will speed up your whole process (**image 02b**).

Another time-saving step you can take is to map the brush set to keyboard hot keys, such as F1, F2, and F3.

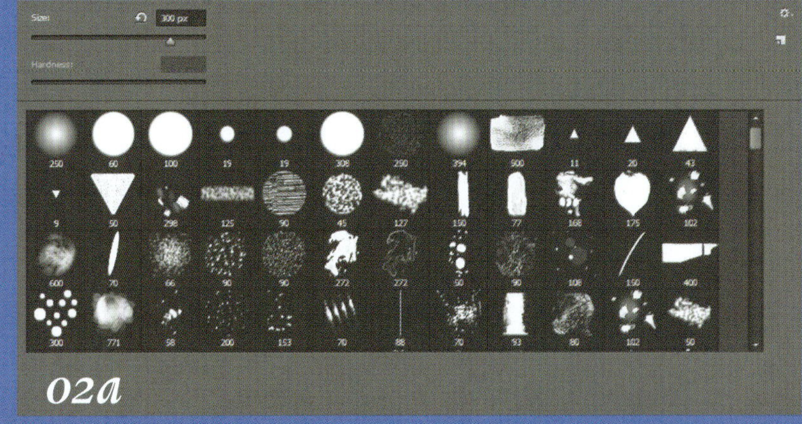

▲A selection of my custom brushes

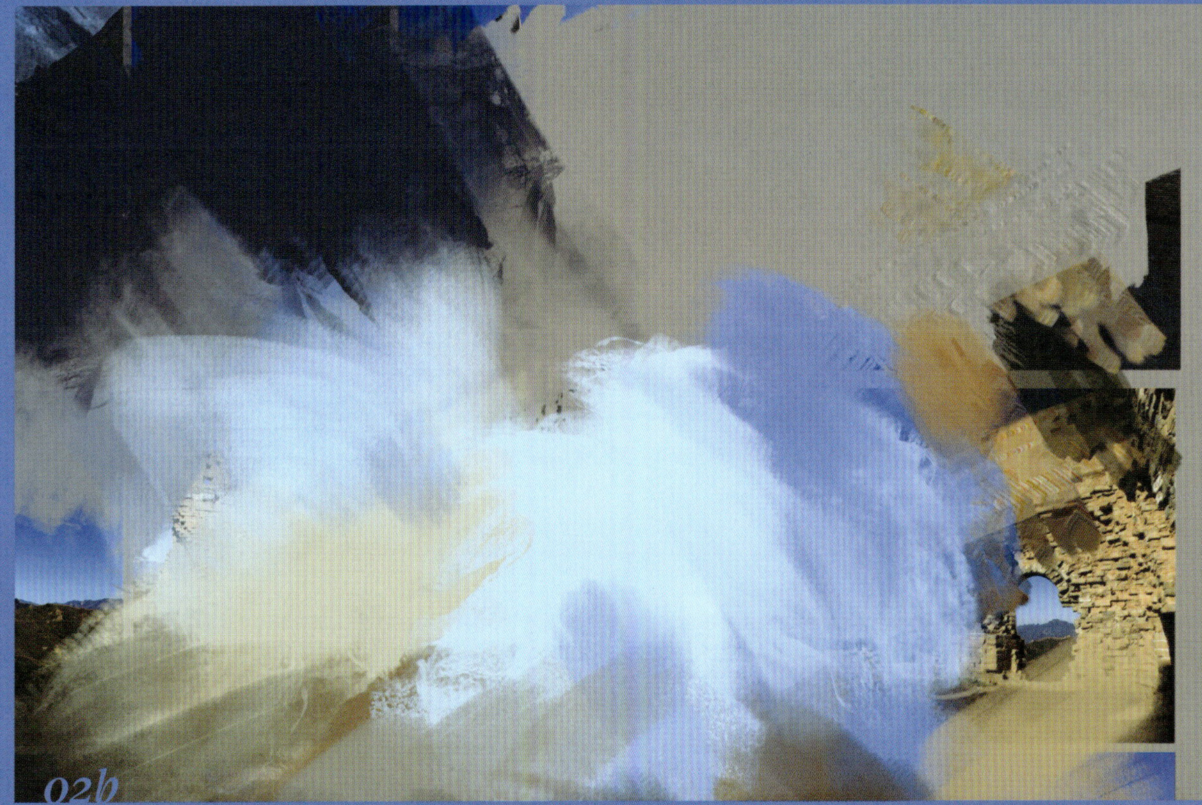

▲Try working with only a limited number of brushes to help you save time and not become distracted by different brush types

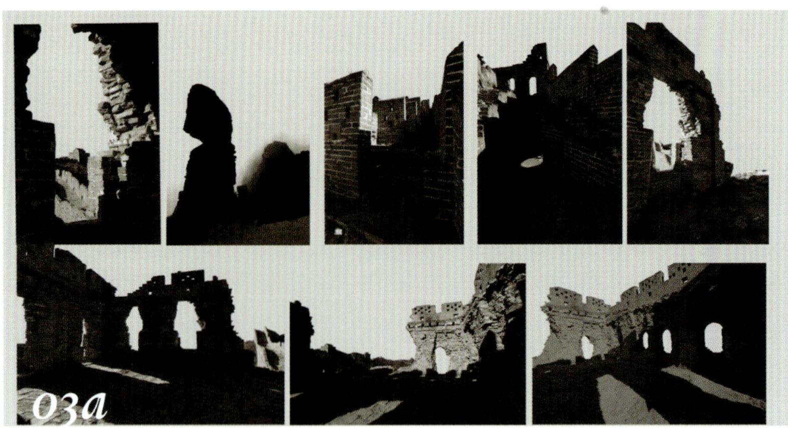

▲Shapes are the most effective visual language to help the viewer understand the image

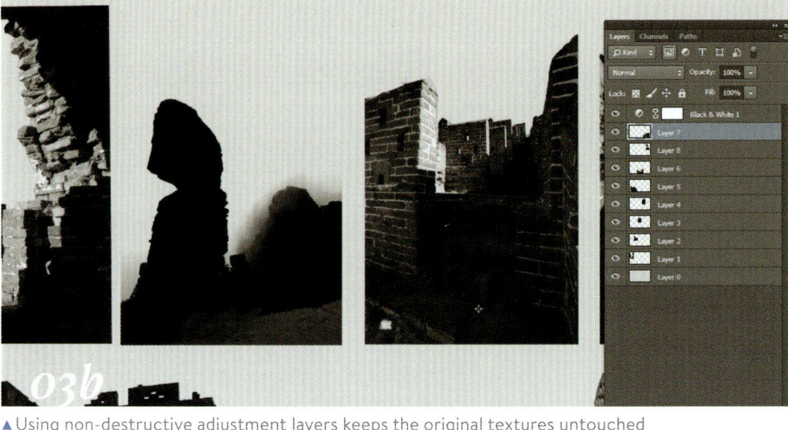

▲Using non-destructive adjustment layers keeps the original textures untouched

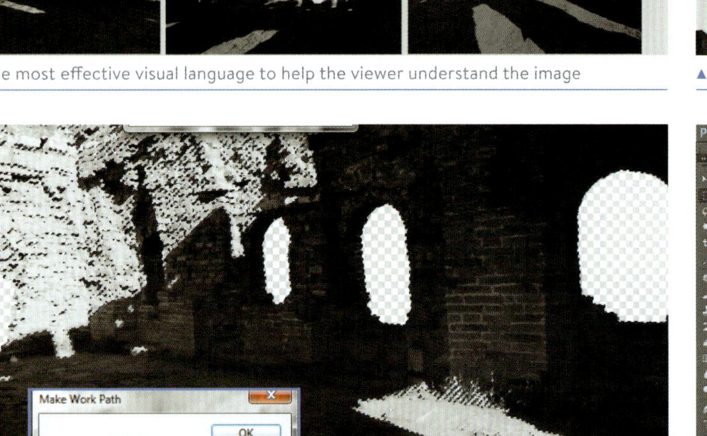

▲To make a custom shape, select Make Work Path... and set the tolerance to 0.5 pixels

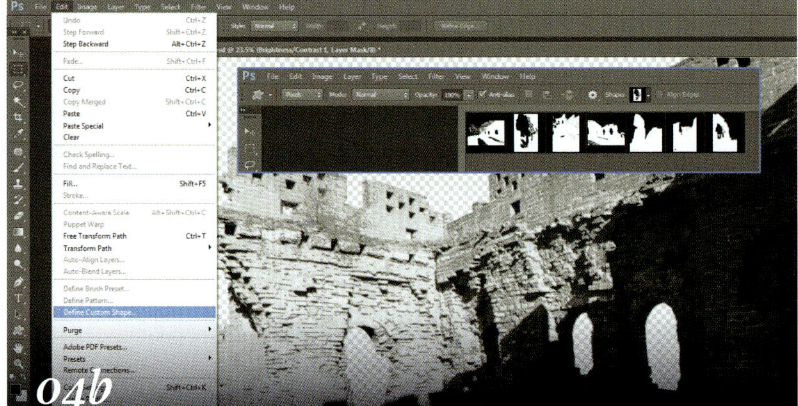

▲Select Edit > Define Custom Shape... and the shape will appear on the Custom Shape toolbar

03: Selection of iconic shapes

Taking the time to collect good reference images bears fruit now because they can be collated together. Shapes are key design elements in making relevant and interesting compositions. In Photoshop open a large blank canvas and copy and paste all the interesting shapes for your theme on it (**image 03a**). I like to visualize my shapes as grayscale graphic elements against a light gray background, so I can better judge their readability and relevance. It is important to understand that shape is also silhouette, so we are taking this opportunity to set up a solid foundation for future composition possibilities.

I prefer to use a non-destructive adjustment layer for the desaturation, so I can still keep all the original textures for later use (**image 03b**).

04: Creation of custom shapes

The use of custom shapes is my favorite alternative to custom brushes. They can be applied much faster on the canvas to generate nearly endless possibilities for the composition. To make a custom shape based on your previous shape selection, go to the Channels tab and select any color channel that will give you the best contrast. Press M on the keyboard, right-click, then select Make Work Path... with a tolerance of 0.5 (**image 04a**). Go to Edit and click on Define Custom Shape.... Now the shape is ready for use when you click on the Custom Shape tool on your toolbar (**image 04b**). Press and drag the shape to have fun with it.

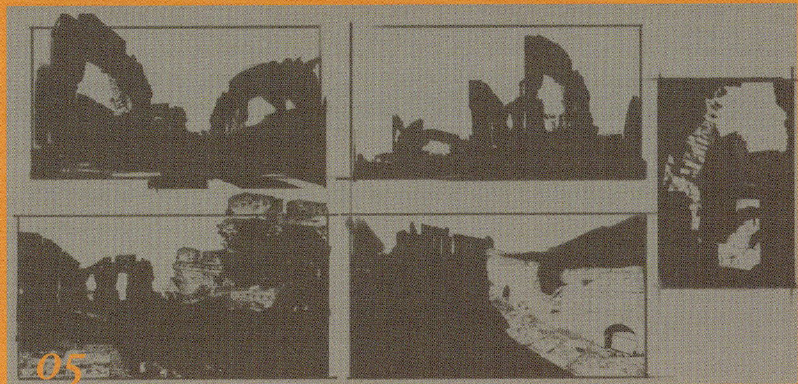

▲ Drag and drop your custom shapes to come up with interesting compositions

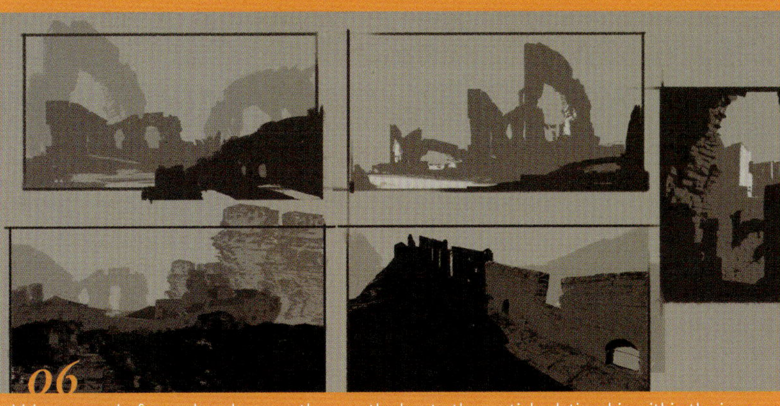

▲ Values come before colors, because they are the key to the spatial relationship within the image

The flexibility and usefulness of custom shapes keeps this approach in my top list of favorite painting techniques.

05: Composition studies

Now we have a small collection of the custom shapes that we have created with our initial shape selections.

Drag them freely on the canvas to see what interesting compositions you can come up with. Since the dragging can create a new aspect ratio of the original shape, you can think outside the box while using the shapes. For example a stone wall can be stretched horizontally and be used as a textured ground texture. A tall tree can be dragged with much smaller proportions and be used as bushes.

You don't need to flip your shapes and create new custom shapes out of them; instead, simply flip your canvas and drag them as you are used to.

06: Value studies

After playing around with shapes and flat black, continue to bring more value nuances to the chosen composition studies.

Depth and ambience are worked out by using controlled values. Atmospheric depth is a key player in this step. When objects are closer to us, they have a high level of contrast compared to the objects that are far away from us. I paint fog or humidity between the shape layers in my Photoshop layers to tweak the spatial relationship within the image. Place your horizon line in a strategic way so the depth is not blocked at the foreground or at the middle ground.

07: Lighting reference gathering

If the first pass of reference gathering is about the shapes, then this pass of reference studying is all about the lighting. Bear in mind the different lighting situations that you encounter in the studies: direct sunlight, overcast, sunset, night time, artificial light, and back light.

The back-lighting scenario is my favorite and this is also the one which can best show off the shapes and structures in your work by casting interesting shadows. I like to categorize all my lighting references on a big blank canvas and use it as my lighting board. This specific step forces you to study the lighting independently, separated from shapes, designs, and colors.

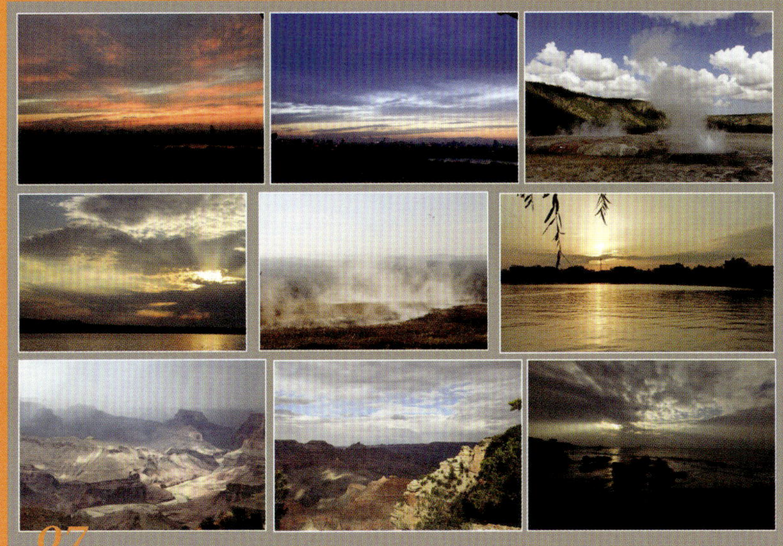

▲ Reference studying is essential, but this time it is more about lighting and colors than shapes

Pro tip: Don't over-tell

My students often like to tell a very complex story with one image. My feedback is always pick the top two or three things that you want to tell through the image, and tell them really well. When a story is too complex, you need to divide your canvas space into smaller portions to distribute it all to the different storytelling elements, making it difficult to come up with an iconic composition.

08: Put down the colors

Once the lighting is set, we can talk about color palette. Even though a lot of speed paintings use a monochromatic approach, I still like to have some subtle contrast in my color temperature. I like to use a warm color temperature for the areas which receive light, and a cold color temperature in the shadow areas. An advantage of using a nice color range in your painting is that it allows you to have the visual impression of a higher contrast level without going into extreme dark and light grays.

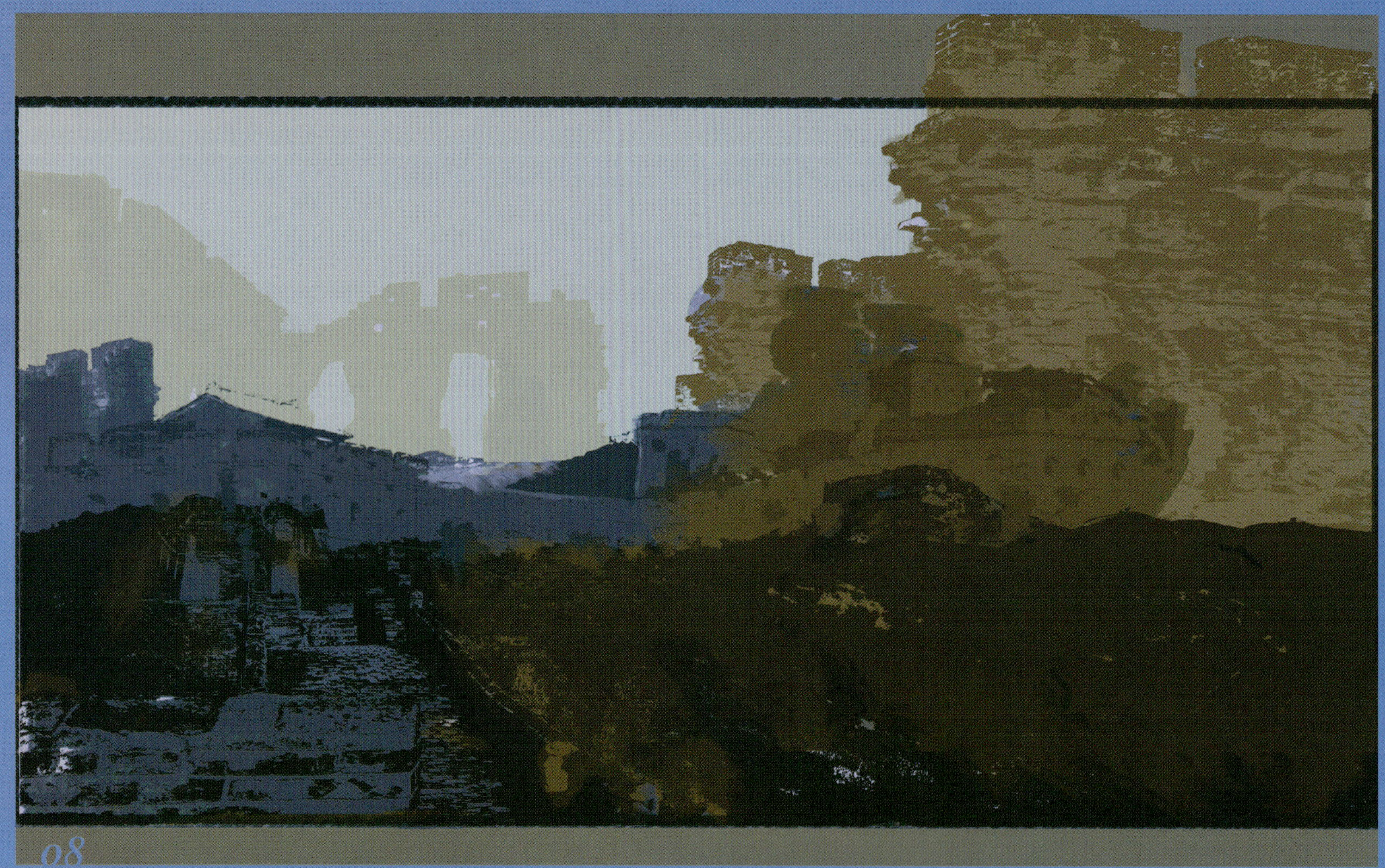

▲ Try to have a nice range of cold and warm colors so you can give more visual vibrancy to your painting

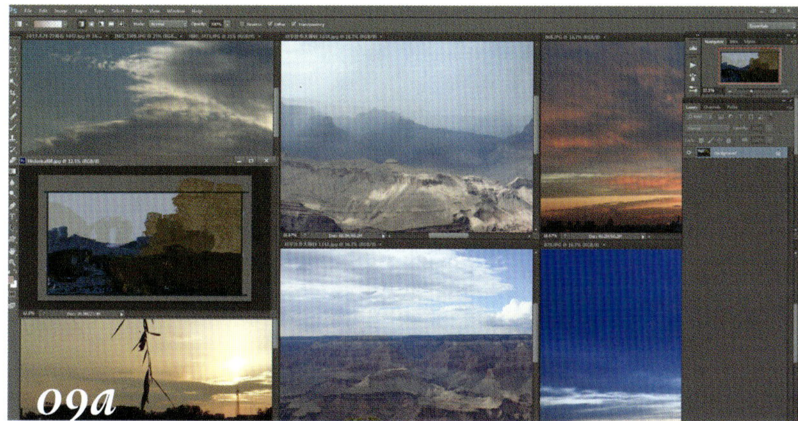

▲ Find lots of reference images and drag them into Photoshop

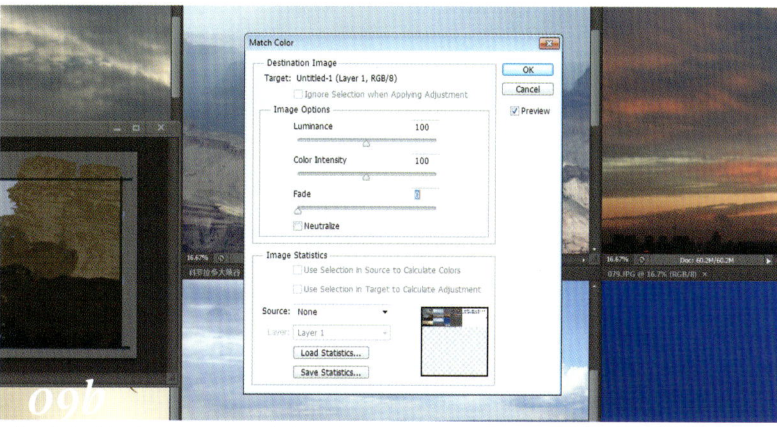

▲ Use Color Match options to tweak the colors

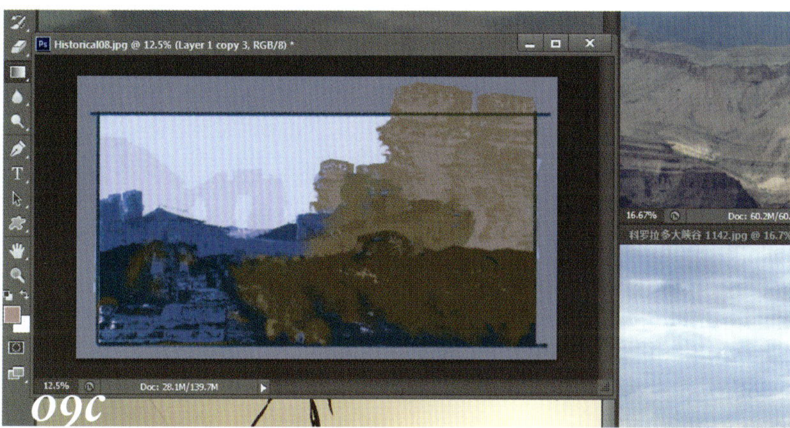

▲ Sometimes "happy accidents" can make for great colors

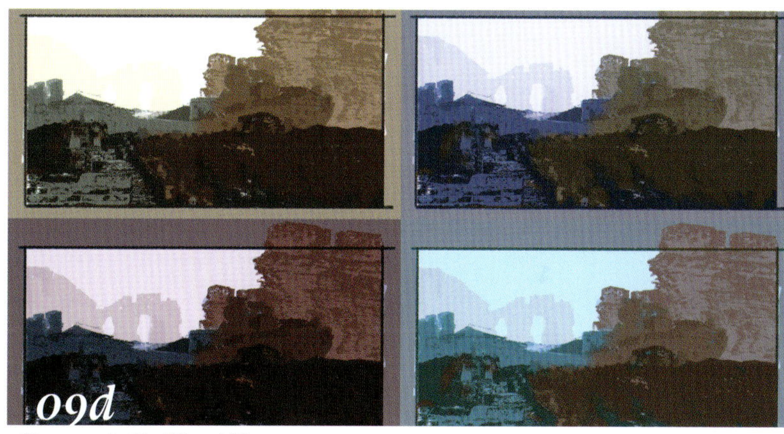

▲ Play around with different filters

09: How to tweak colors

I have two frequently used ways to tweak my color palette. The first one is very straightforward: I simply try out different adjustment layers, such as Color Balance, Hue/Saturation, and Photo Filter.

The second method is more based around discovering "happy accidents." I find all of the photo references that I like and drag them into Photoshop (**image 09a**). Then I select my painting and go to Image > Adjustment > Match Color (**image 09b**). Once I am in the Match Color pop-up window, I go to the Source drop-down menu and go through all the photo references to see which ones would have a better color match with my original painting (**image 09c**). You can use the sliders to get better control of the luminance, color intensity, and fading level (**image 09d**).

10: Double check the values

At this point, I suggest using the Black & White adjustment layer to desaturate the whole painting again in order to see if the values have been messed up at all. This can happen a lot after playing with coloring and photo texture integration as the original value relationship could be disturbed by the additional pixel information.

The reason you should pay so much attention to the values is that the brain reads grayscale values before color information. If the grayscale is wrong, the colors won't help you solve depth inaccuracy.

11: Add details

I use this step to add all the extra details: birds, tree branches, foreground vines, grass, cloud textures, and so on. I usually have a collection of custom brushes for adding those final details – they can save you a significant amount of time.

During this process, constantly check your navigator window so you will always be aware of whether the overall thumbnail still holds up tightly while adding the details.

I also use some photo texture to boost up the color nuance on a large surface. Use the photo textures with subtlety though so they don't damage the value relationship that you have tried so hard to maintain until now.

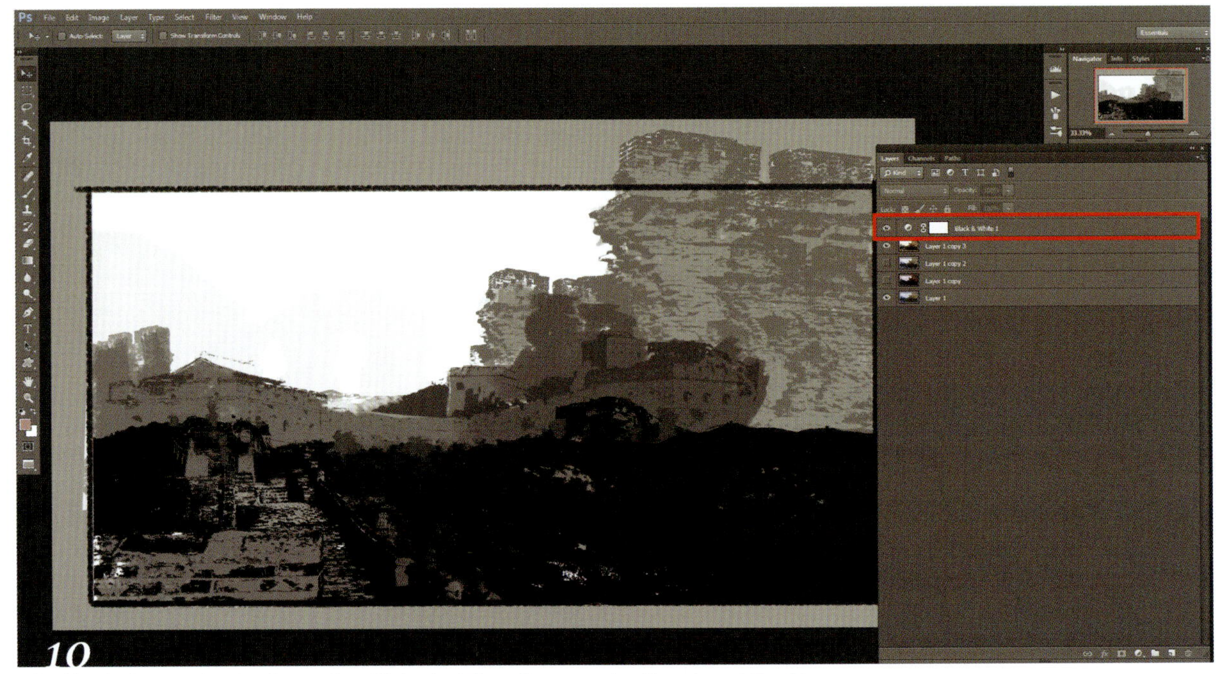

▲Double check your values just in case the added color information messed up the value relationship

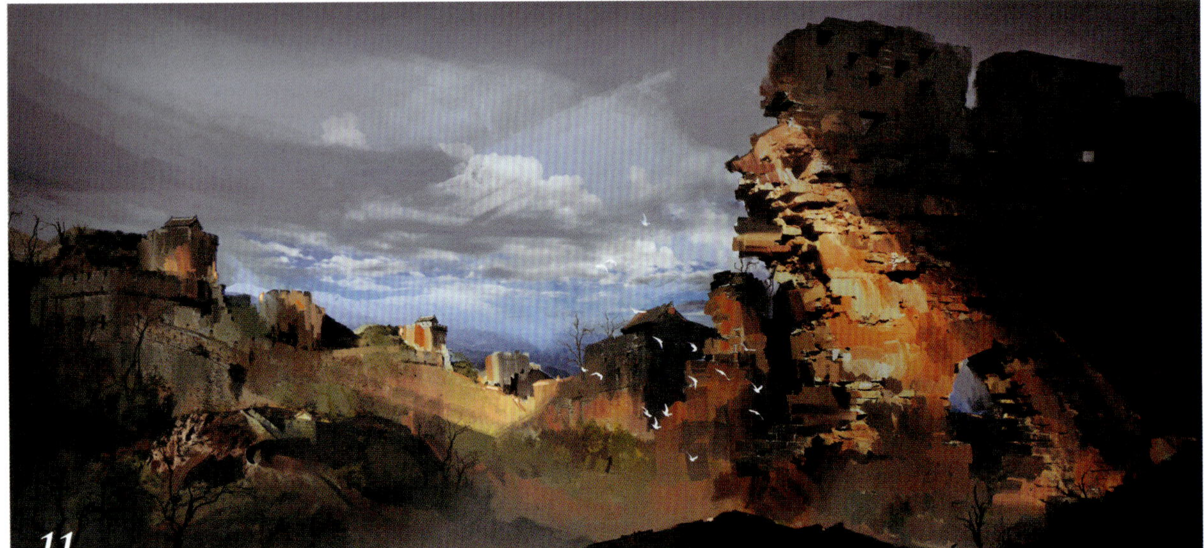

▲Making a small collection of specific brushes can speed up the process of adding details

12: Flip your canvas

Flip your canvas to double check your composition. This should be done throughout the painting process. Before Photoshop existed, traditional painters would check their paintings in the mirror to have their images flipped. You may ask, why go to so much bother?

It is because after all the time you have spent looking at the painting, your brain becomes used to that particular visual representation and always tries make sense out of it. By flipping the canvas, your brain gets a fresh perspective of the painting so it can analyze the image from a more objective point of view.

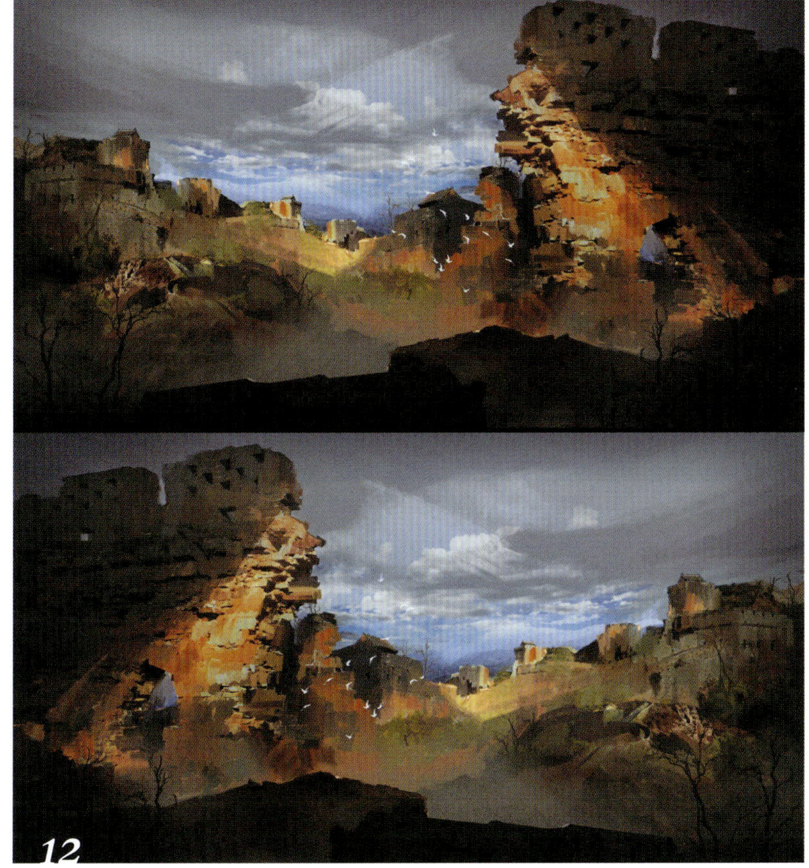

▲ Flip the canvas frequently to give your brain a fresh take on the image

13: Effect: zoom blur

I also like to use a subtle motion blur at the bottom of the image. It fakes a camera effect and adds more movement to the still image. To achieve this effect, go to the Filter tab, select Blur > Radial Blur (**image 13a**), set Amount to 10, and set Blur Method to Zoom (**image 13b**). It will make all your image edges blur into the center of the image. In order to make this effect subtle, create a mask on the layer, erase the areas that you don't need, and reduce the opacity to around 30% (**image 13c**).

14: Effect: chromatic aberration

I would also like to talk about chromatic aberration, even though I prefer to use it for sci-fi scenes rather than a historical image, since such an effect mimics the effect of a modern camera. Chromatic aberration is an effect which appears in

▲ To add subtle motion to your image you can add a Blur filter

▲ You can choose the size and center of the Blur

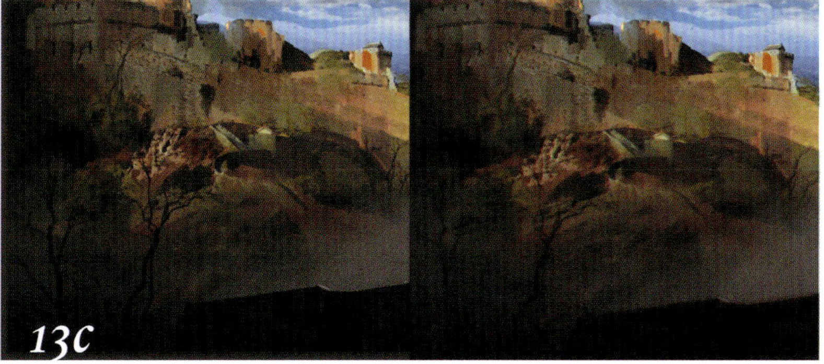

▲ The final effect of adding a Blur filter to your image

photography, where there is some slight blurring of the image caused by the camera lens not focussing on the different colors in light correctly. Although it is considered an error in photography, digital artists mimic the effect to give their images a more cinematic feel.

To apply chromatic aberration, go to Filter > Lens Correction, then go under the custom tab and play with the three sliders in the Chromatic Aberration section. This allows you to offset the RGB channels to mimic a lens effect. Avoid moving the three channel sliders all at the same time, since they may cancel out each other's effect, thus making the effect less apparent.

15: Conclusion

Now we are done with the painting. I would probably walk away from the image for a few hours and come back to check if the whole image is still working well to suit my artistic tastes.

For extra individual training, I recommend that you create a series of other speed paintings based on the references studies and the custom shapes created for this specific theme. Practice makes perfection. I always tell my students not to have too much emotional attachment to their images. I would rather have them spend ten hours on ten different color sketches instead of spending ten hours on one single image.

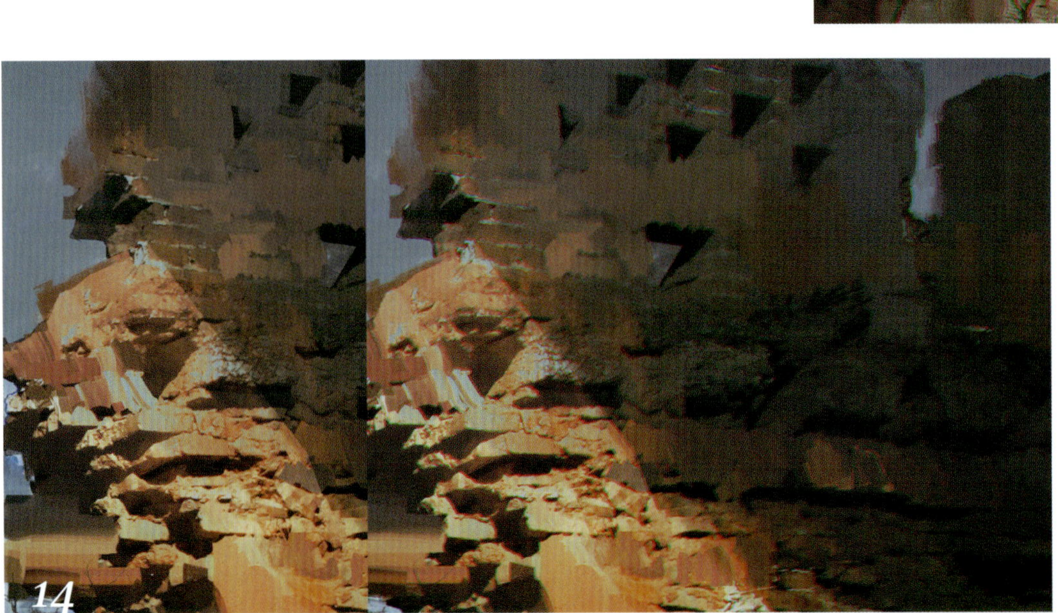

▲ Chromatic aberration mimics the modern camera effect by offsetting the color channels, making the images more cinematic

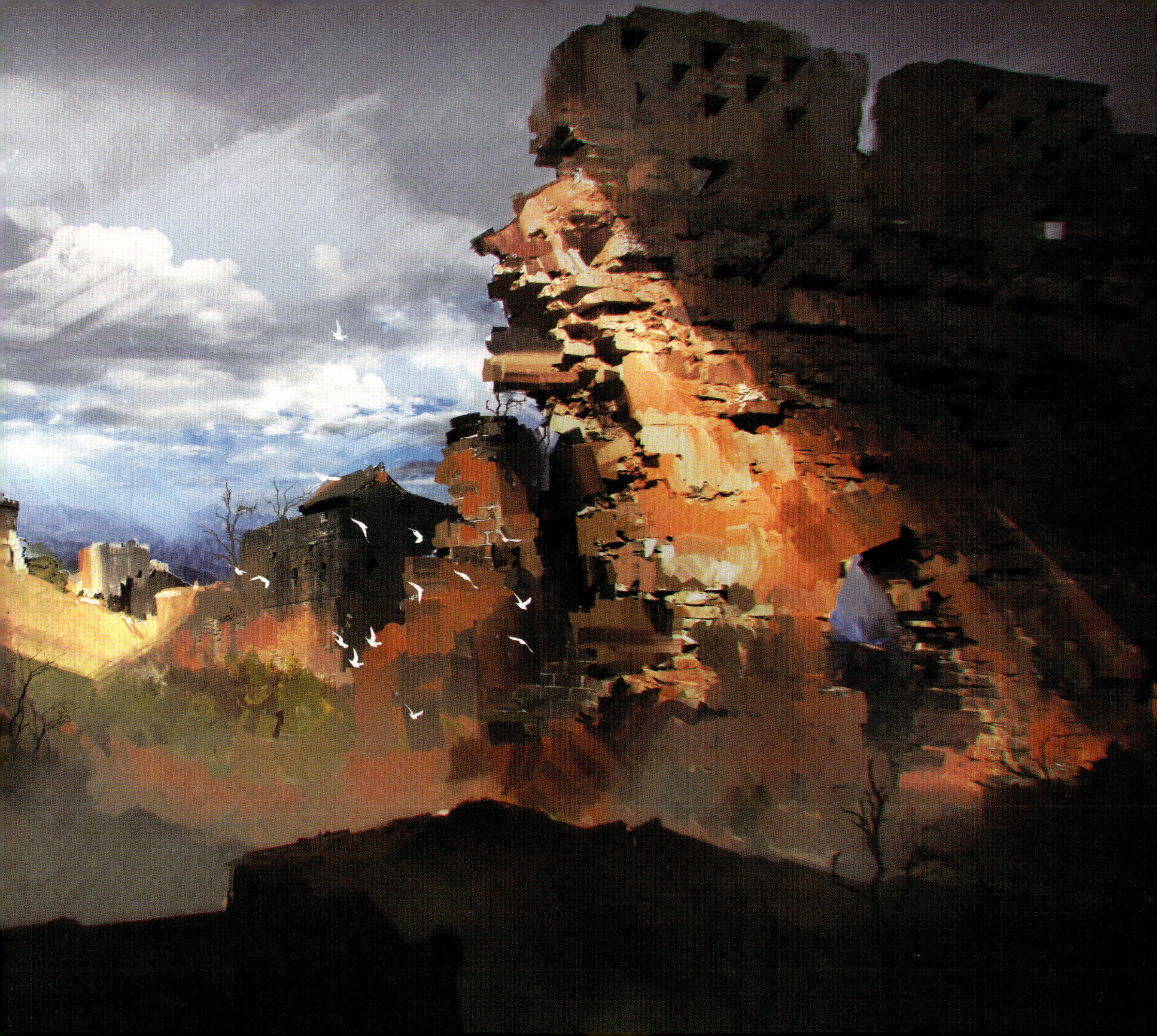

HORROR: DOOM HEAD

by Noely Ryan

In this tutorial I will go through my process of creating a monster concept that could work as an enemy character in a first-person shooter game. It is largely influenced by the monsters and demons that populate the *Doom* and *Quake* game franchises: big, bad, and hell-bent on turning your character into a dead, bloody mess.

Anatomical knowledge is usually essential for most character art, however making monsters allows for more freedom in putting them together – especially when their arms are replaced with a large plasma-spitting gun!

01: Monster shapes

The first step I take with most, if not all, of my character work is to sketch a few thumbnail silhouettes. The silhouette or

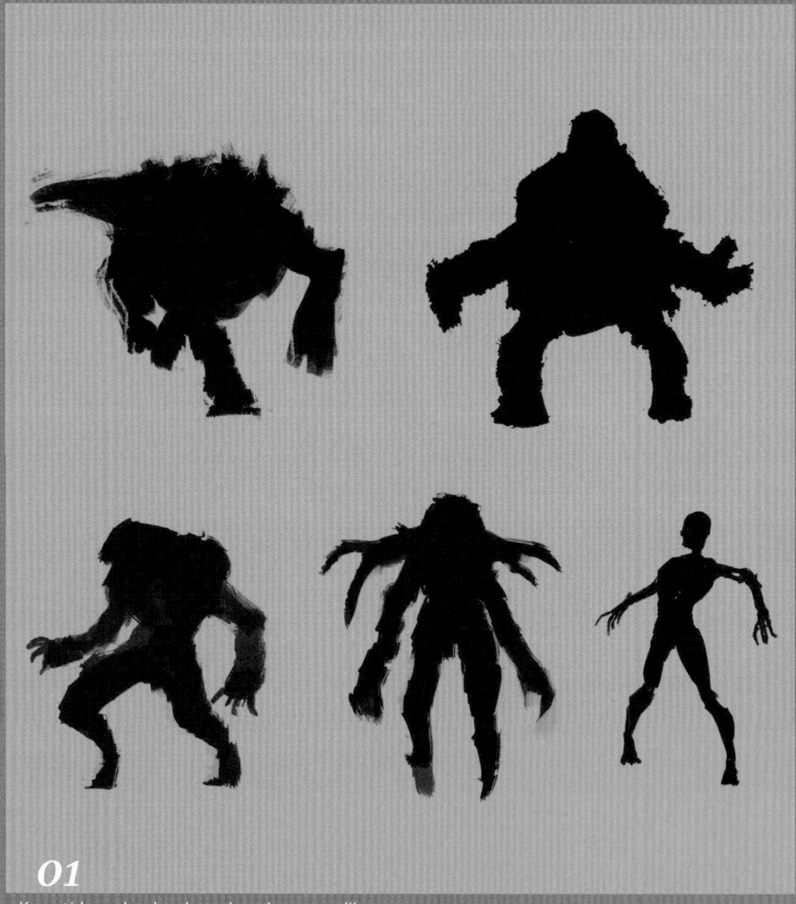

▲ Keep things simple when choosing your silhouette

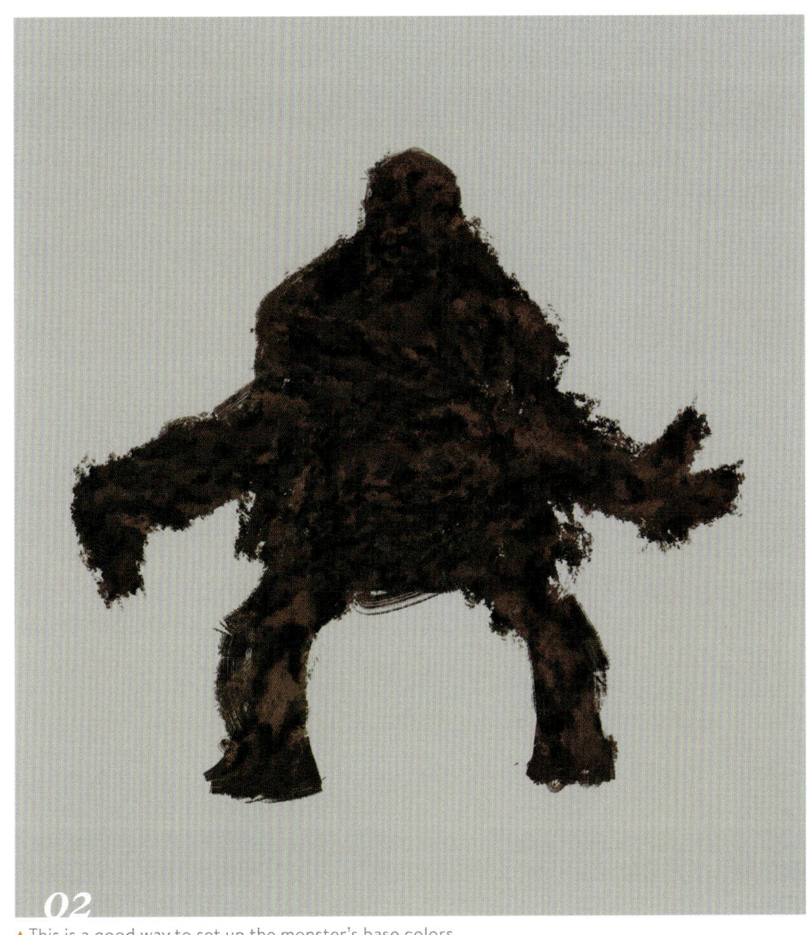
▲ This is a good way to set up the monster's base colors

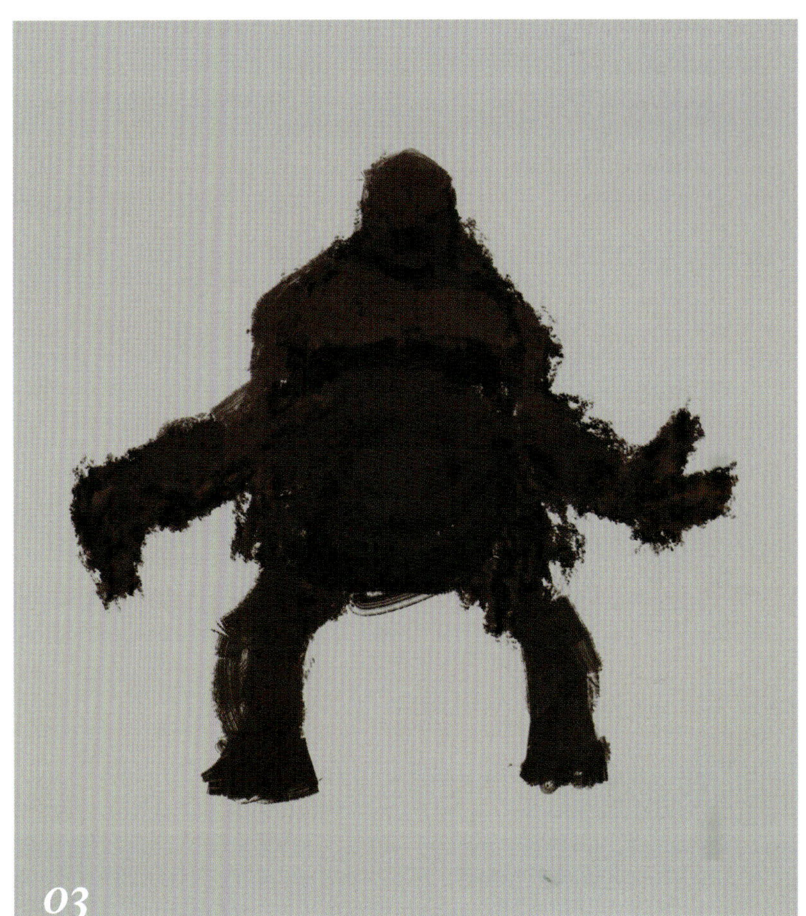
▲ A simple face can add a bit of life

outline shape of an object is usually the first thing the eye picks up on, even if it is not immediately apparent to the viewer. It is a very good sign of how noticeable or recognizable your character is.

Sketching these in a small thumbnail size will allow you to get a few of them done quickly and helps you to visualize the shape of your character.

02: Block in color

Place your chosen silhouette on a new layer and enlarge it to fill the page. Put a new layer above it and create a clipping mask by clicking on the line between the layers while holding down Alt. This mask will hide everything you paint except the shape that is under it. Use downloadable textured brushes or any of your own (with Color Dynamics and Scatter turned on) to randomly add texture to the black shape which should show through later. Don't worry too much if it doesn't, the main purpose is to get rid of the flat black color and give you base colors to work with.

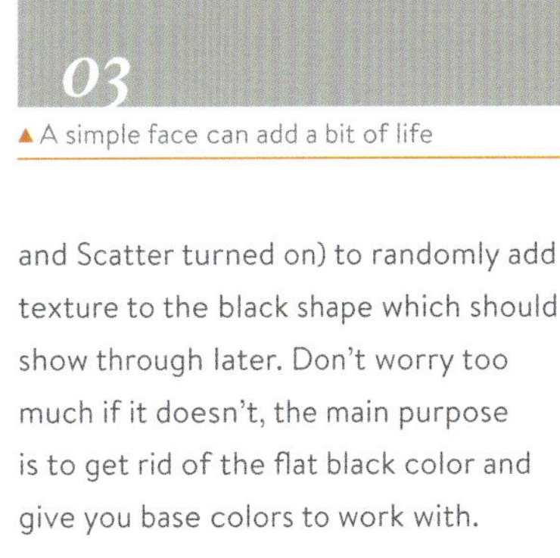

03: Basic forms

Choose whatever colors you want for the monster's skin. I've gone with a brown/ red color. Merge the two layers and use the Eyedropper tool to select colors and paint in the forms of the monster's body. Use the colors to give him a big stomach and paint in the shadows under his chest.

Sketch in a quick face now because even a simple face added early on gives the character a little spark of life and will help you to imagine his attitude.

04: Alternate colors for quick painting

When you are happy with the large forms it is time to add some muscular details. Set the foreground color as a lighter value of the base color and the background as a darker value. By using X to alternate between them, work the muscles of the stomach and arms with large basic strokes.

Then set the opacity of your brush to 50–60%, decrease the size, and alternate the colors again, going in between the large strokes to blend the shadows and lights together. Leave the feet dark and keep the strongest light hitting the top of the head.

05: Further details

Continue this alternating color process (from step 04) to define all the muscular details. As you will be working quickly you may find a few of the forms end up in the wrong place (for me this was the stomach area). Use the Liquify tool to straighten them up. Adding extra detail to the arms and hands is useful here because the hands are one of the places the human eye is drawn to – even if it is subconsciously.

When painting the gun, you will need to keep it simple because of the time constraints – although for me this sometimes takes the longest time to paint and settle on a design. Up to now your time has

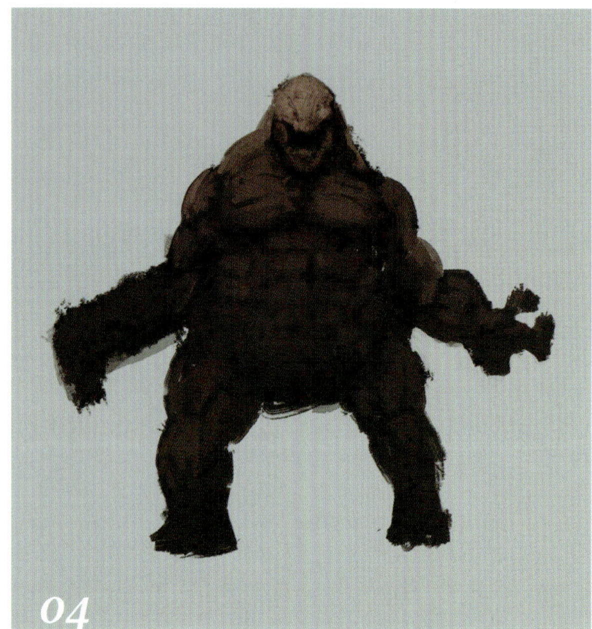

▲ As well as adding muscular detail, define the outline of the monster

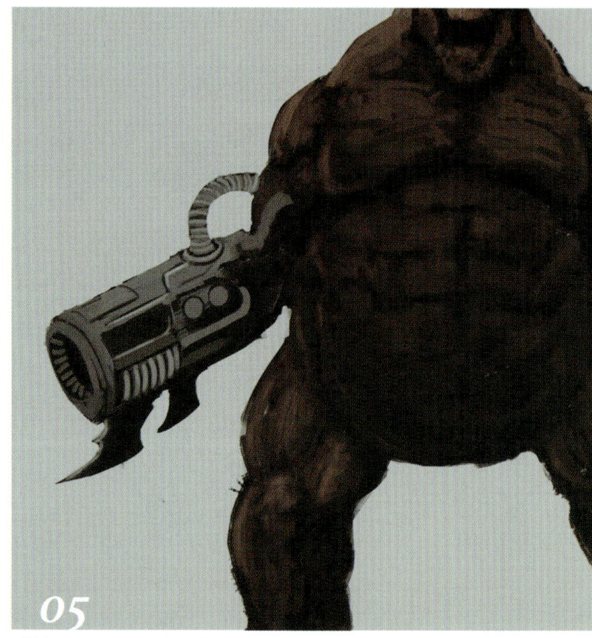

▲ Take the time to slow down when doing the gun

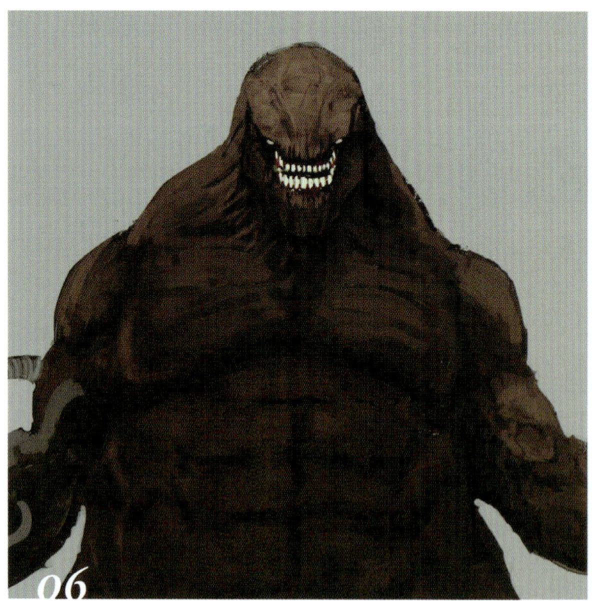

▲ Piercing eyes and a grin of pure evil – welcome to hell!

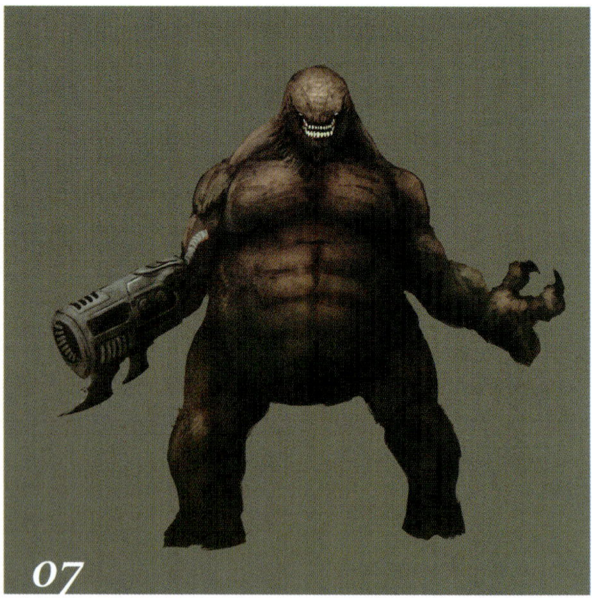

▲ Use custom texture brushes to overlay layer highlights and shadows

consisted of frantic painting but you should take a more controlled approach for the gun. To add interest you can also put in a few extra details such as blades and tubing.

06: Killer grin

At this final stage of the painting process, I want to make sure the grin is the stand-out feature of the monster. I decide to give it teeth that are more human-like than fangs. You can use the Lasso tool to reposition any parts or make adjustments to the size or weight.

This is a good time to refine the outline and add straining neck ligaments to show the beast's fury and bad temper. If you are happy with the forms you can move on to the finishing touches.

07: Dirty color and texture

Add extra colors by creating two or three clipping masks above the monster layer and with a large soft brush (with low opacity) paint various greens and browns over the shadowed areas. Place another clipping mask, set to Overlay, and build up the highlights on the torso and head with a 20% white soft brush. Use a textured brush for this layer to mix up the highlights and textures. Follow the same steps used for the gun to bring out its forms and add vents where the gun's energy will shine out.

08: Blood spatter and droplets

Using the same clipping mask technique as in step 07, add blood spatter with a custom spatter brush on a new layer set to Overlay. To add some raised blood droplets on the skin use the spatter brush to paint red blobs; then duplicate this layer and use Hue/Saturation (Ctrl+U) to drag the Lightness slider all the way up to white. Place the white spatter layer underneath the red layer and, using the Move tool (V) and arrow keys, move the white layer a few pixels up – this will give the appearance of light hitting the top of the drops.

This technique may not give perfectly rendered drops but it is quick and good enough for a speedy concept piece.

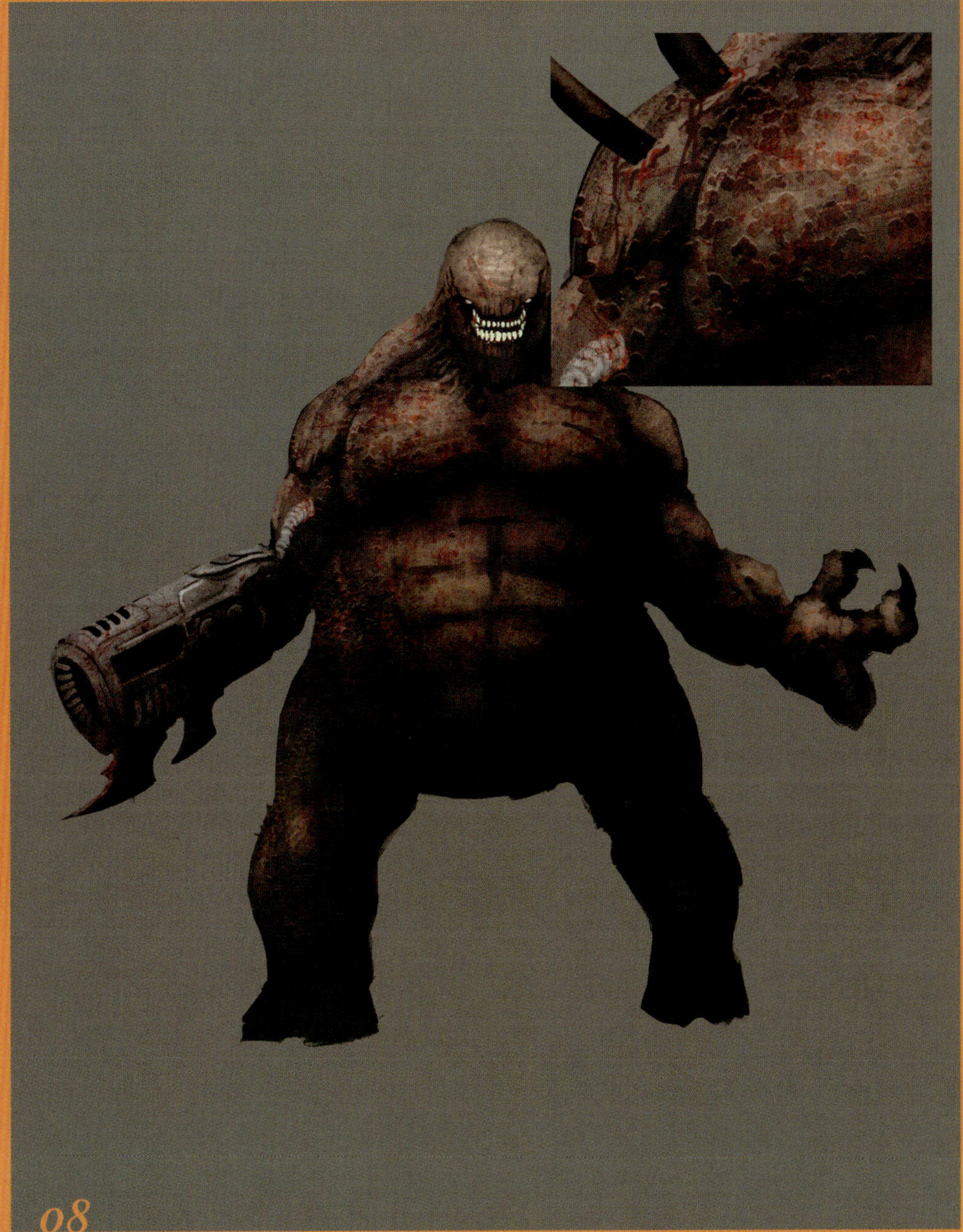

08

▲ Use a custom spatter brush to add gore to the beast

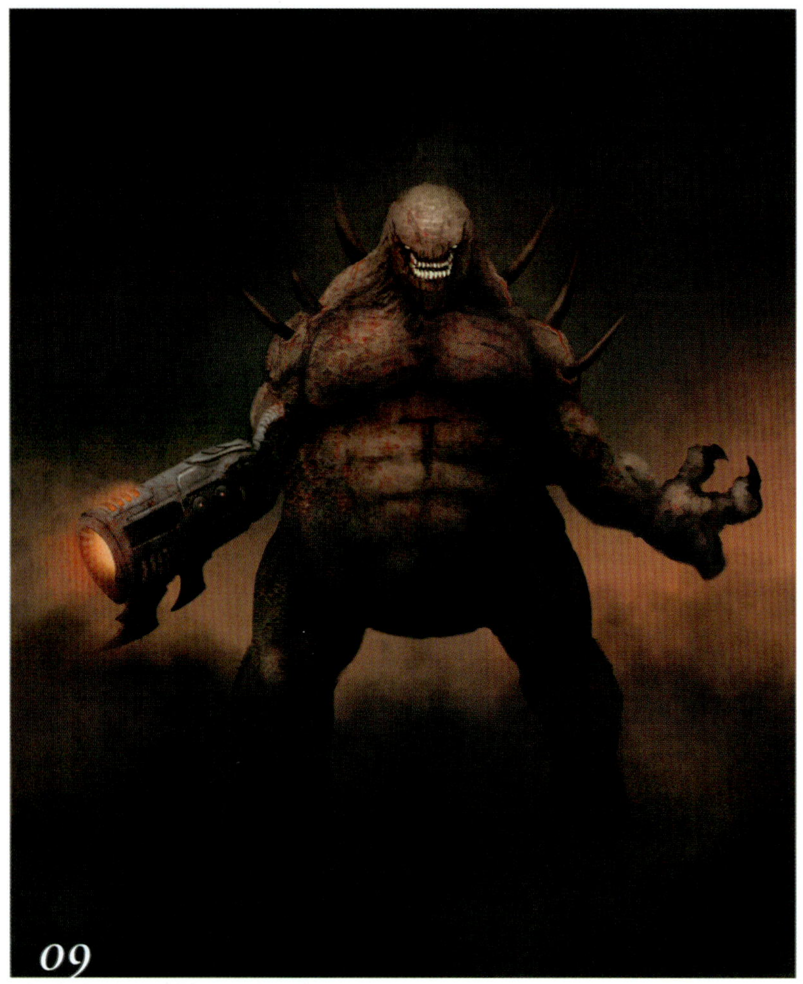

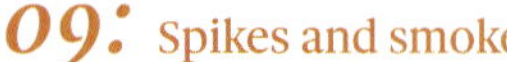

▲Smoke brushes are lifesavers for effects in your images

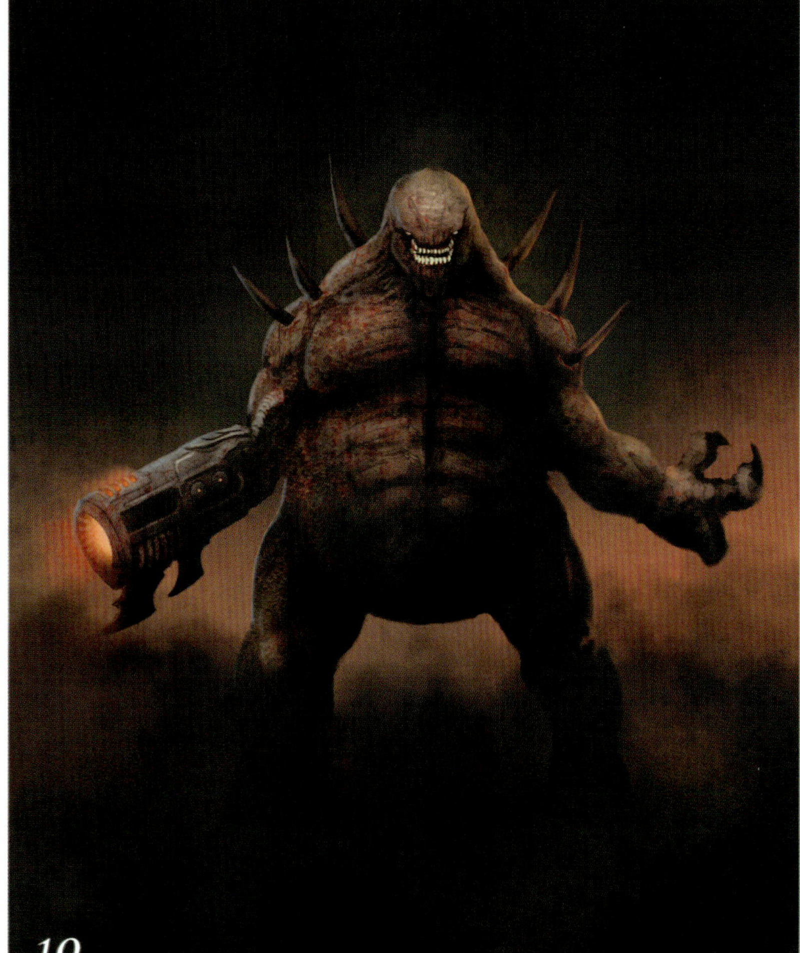

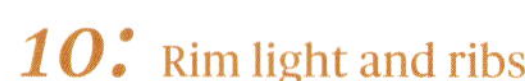

▲Rim lighting can be very effective for adding depth to your characters

09: Spikes and smoke

The shoulders look a bit bare and naked; use the Lasso tool to add some spikes and a soft brush for shading. To give the gun firepower use the custom Smoke brush to paint in a Lasso selection of the gun barrel. I use the same brush to add orange smoke in the background on a layer underneath. On the background layer use the Linear Gradient tool to make a simple lighting gradient. Paint a shadow under the monster with the soft brush. On a new layer use the Smoke brush to add steam coming off the shoulders; you can also add some darker smoke surrounding and in front of the monster.

10: Rim light and ribs

With a suitably creepy and smoky environment and background lighting added, it is time to add some highlights. Add another clipping mask above the shape of the monster and paint some rim lights around the edges with a small soft brush. Pick a complementary blue to do the rim lights on the opposite side. This adds depth to the character and helps to place him in the scene.

For fun and to add more interest to the stomach area I use an anatomy brush (you can find these free on the internet) and stamp a rib cage onto it, warping it into shape and erasing what I don't want with a soft-edged eraser.

11: Final grading and post

Make a composite layer (Ctrl+Alt+Shift+E) of all of the layers and flip it horizontally to check the proportions of the monster. Mine leans a little to one side so I use the Liquify tool to balance it out. With your monster balanced bring up the Curves editor (Ctrl+M) and play with each of the RGB channels to enhance the colors.

To add chromatic aberration use the Lens Correction tool under Filter (Shift+Ctrl+R). Its sliders are in the Custom tab. Play around with them to give your image a filmic edge; then add some noise to take away the clean "digital look." To finalize the environment and give it a bit more believability paint some sparks and cinders using a scatter brush. Do this in two separate layers, one for the background and one for the blurred sparks closer to the viewer. You can see the final image on the right here.

Pro tip: Speeding up the process

For a concept or speedy piece you don't have the luxury of spending hours fine-tuning the shape and details. However, if you can get the character to a stage where the shapes and forms are rough but readable, Photoshop's tools can greatly speed up the process and workflow, which is great if you are working to a deadline.

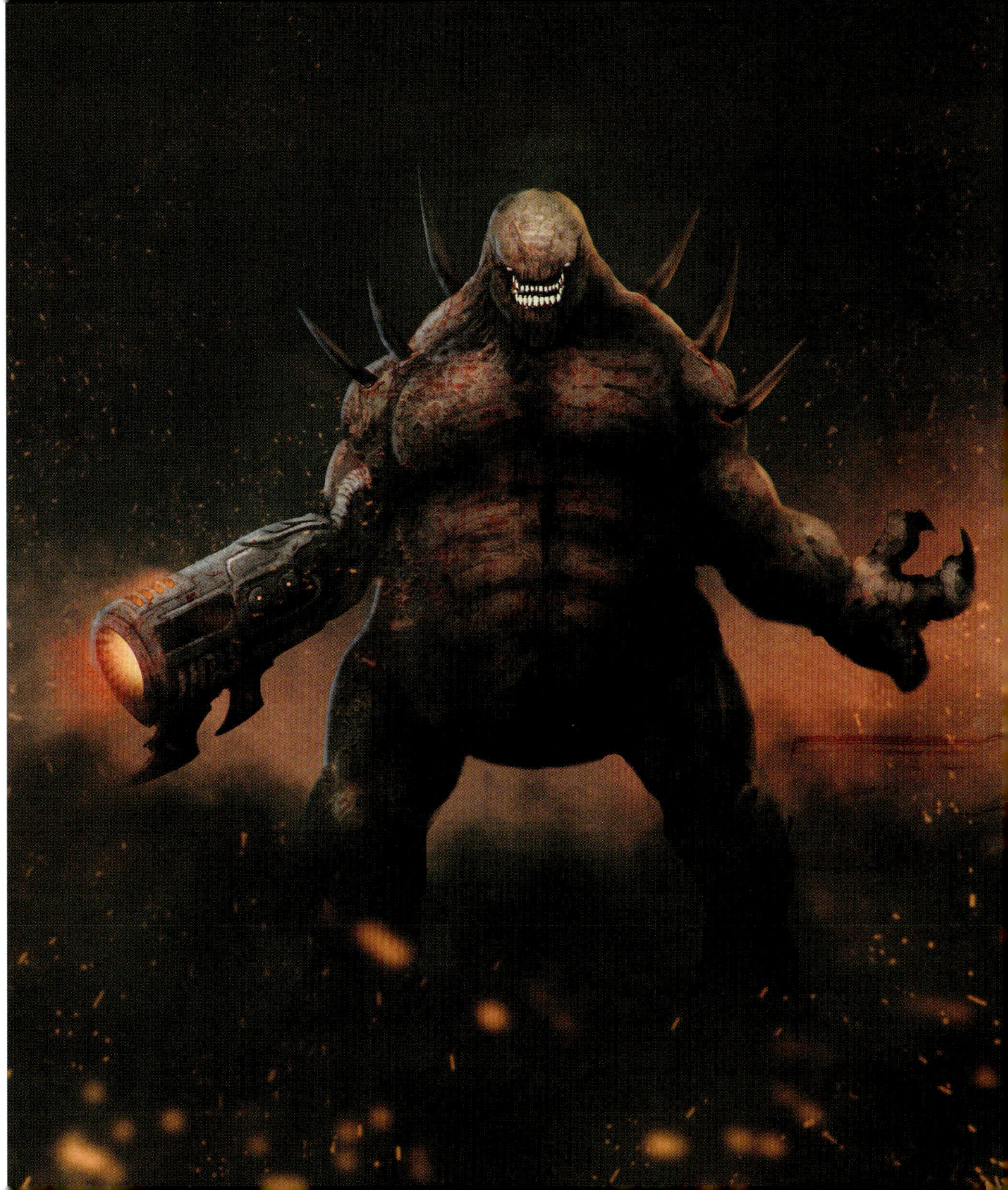

SCI-FI: OLD SHORE
by Wadim Kashin

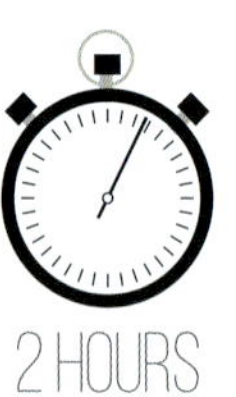

The phrase "speed painting" is often used to describe the process in which artists create quick sketches to generate ideas or to just get a job done quickly in a small amount of time. It is important to point out here, however, that while it can be difficult to maintain quality at fast speeds, all paintings require quality, and this is therefore something that should not be lost during the speed-painting process.

I spend about two hours creating the illustration for this tutorial, during which I manage to think of the composition, create a scene with characters, work on small details, and create an atmosphere. When creating this work I will depart from some of the standard digital painting methods and techniques in order to meet the deadline. While I will be using textures, I will use these alongside brushes in my image.

01: Primary palette

This painting will portray a coastline, surrounded by porous rocks and stones, and will convey an atmosphere of old and wild places. There will also be something futuristic about it; the main focus will be a mech fighting some local people.

For the initial stage of work you need to research images for the color and mood; images of trees and porous rocks

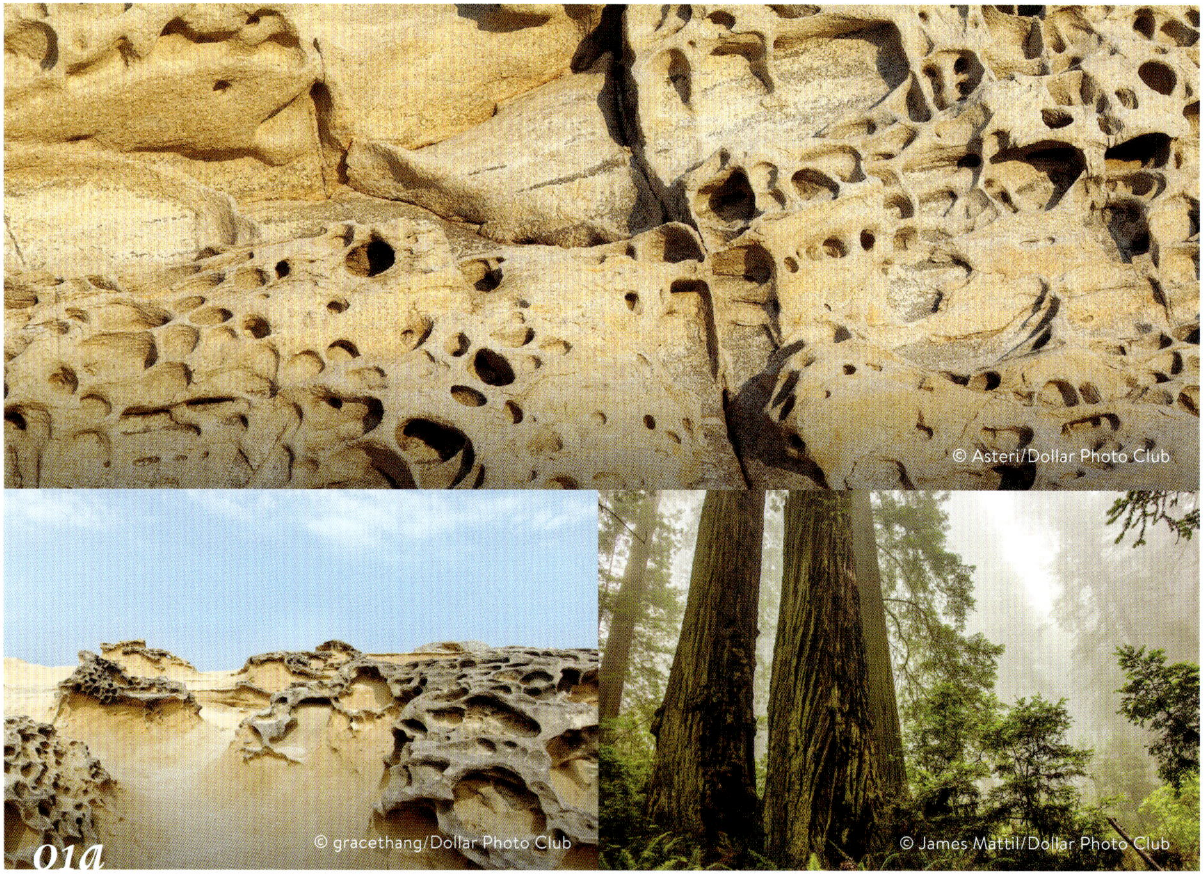

© Asteri/Dollar Photo Club

© gracethang/Dollar Photo Club

© James Mattil/Dollar Photo Club

01a

▲ Find a good range of reference photos

are a good start! I search for a big, looming redwood trees and honeycomb weathered rocks – they have a wonderful holey texture (**image 01a**). With images in hand simply place them on your canvas and apply Motion Blur. This will give you a great base to start from (**image 01b**).

02: Start with your brushes

Sometimes when applying Motion Blur to the image, blurry edges can show up. You can quickly rework these contours using brushes to bring them together. Using a variety of brushes adds chaotic strokes to your work and can help you make a start. In the lower corners of the canvas apply the reference photo of the porous rocks

▲ Using Motion Blur is a great way to start your work

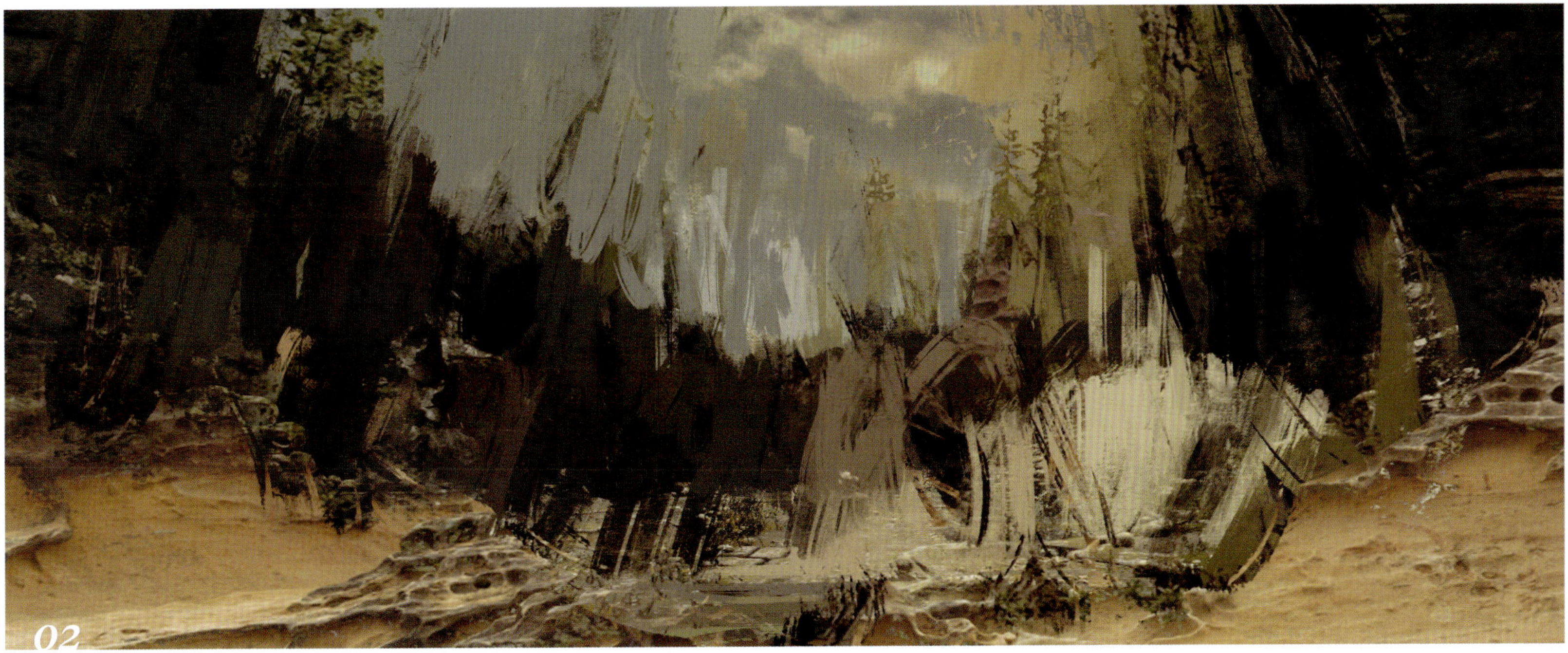

02

▲ Use brushstrokes and reference photos to make a start on your canvas

in Lighten blend mode; for the top use a photo of the sky in Darken blend mode.

03: Quick details

I know artists who spend too much time on this initial stage of creating their work and then the same amount on the rest of the piece. Using photobashing in the following way can be useful for trying to speed up this initial process. I take two pictures, making them one color, then apply either a Lighten or Darken blend mode to each of them, and finally place one under the other. This is a great way to find new and interesting shapes and objects, drawing and editing shapes with brushes in order to get the result you want.

Using a different photo of porous rock, in the same blend modes, fill in random parts of the image that you want to be rocky. To add variety use the Transform and Refine tools to edit the size and shape of the textures. This quickly and efficiently gets details done at an early stage.

04: Correct textures

Here you can use brushes to add strokes to update the areas where you apply your textures. Painting the new parts gives the work more depth. For example the areas close to the ground feel flat so I add a dark green color to give volume to the earth. Remember to think about highlighting some of the areas – the settings can be edited in

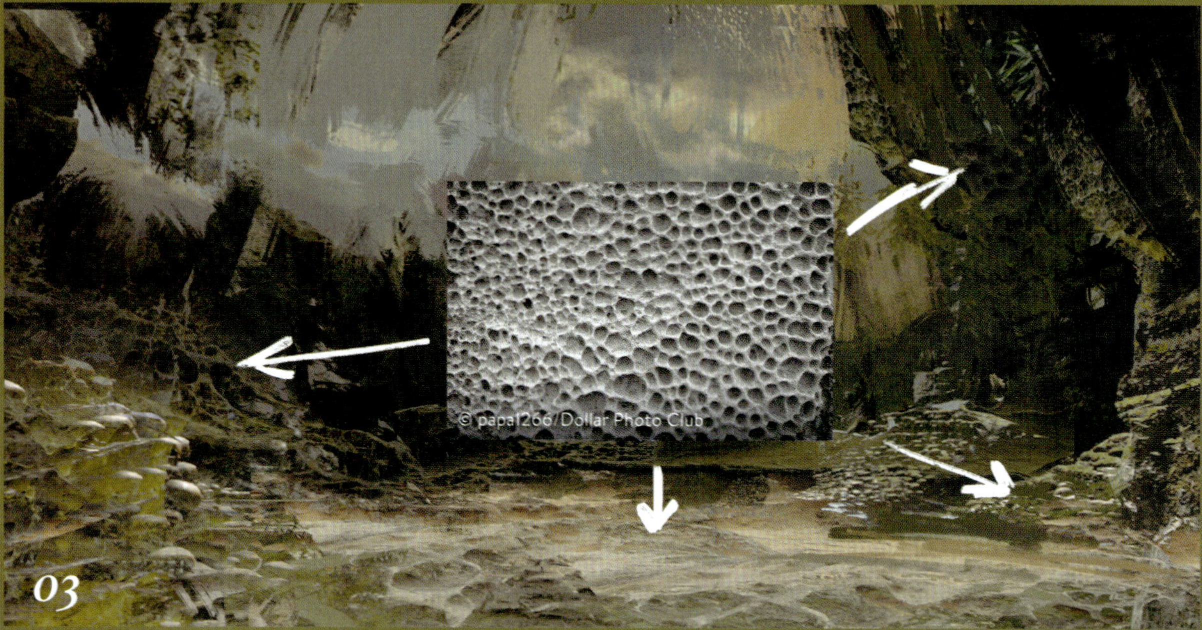

▲ Transform textures to add variety

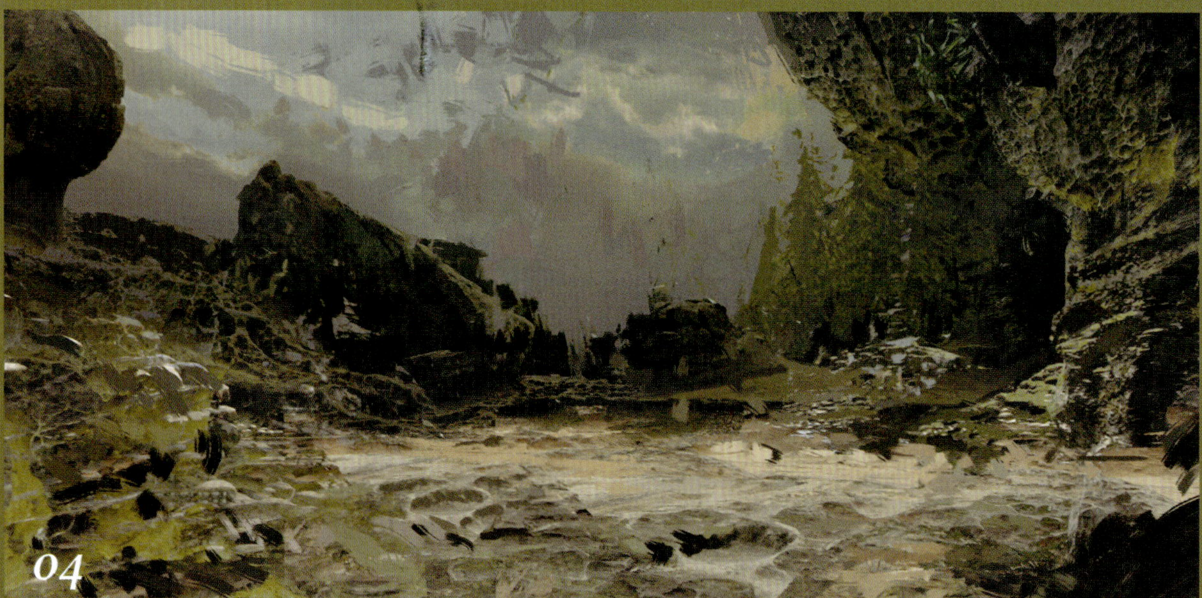

▲ Keep an eye on the perspective and depth; you don't want a flat painting

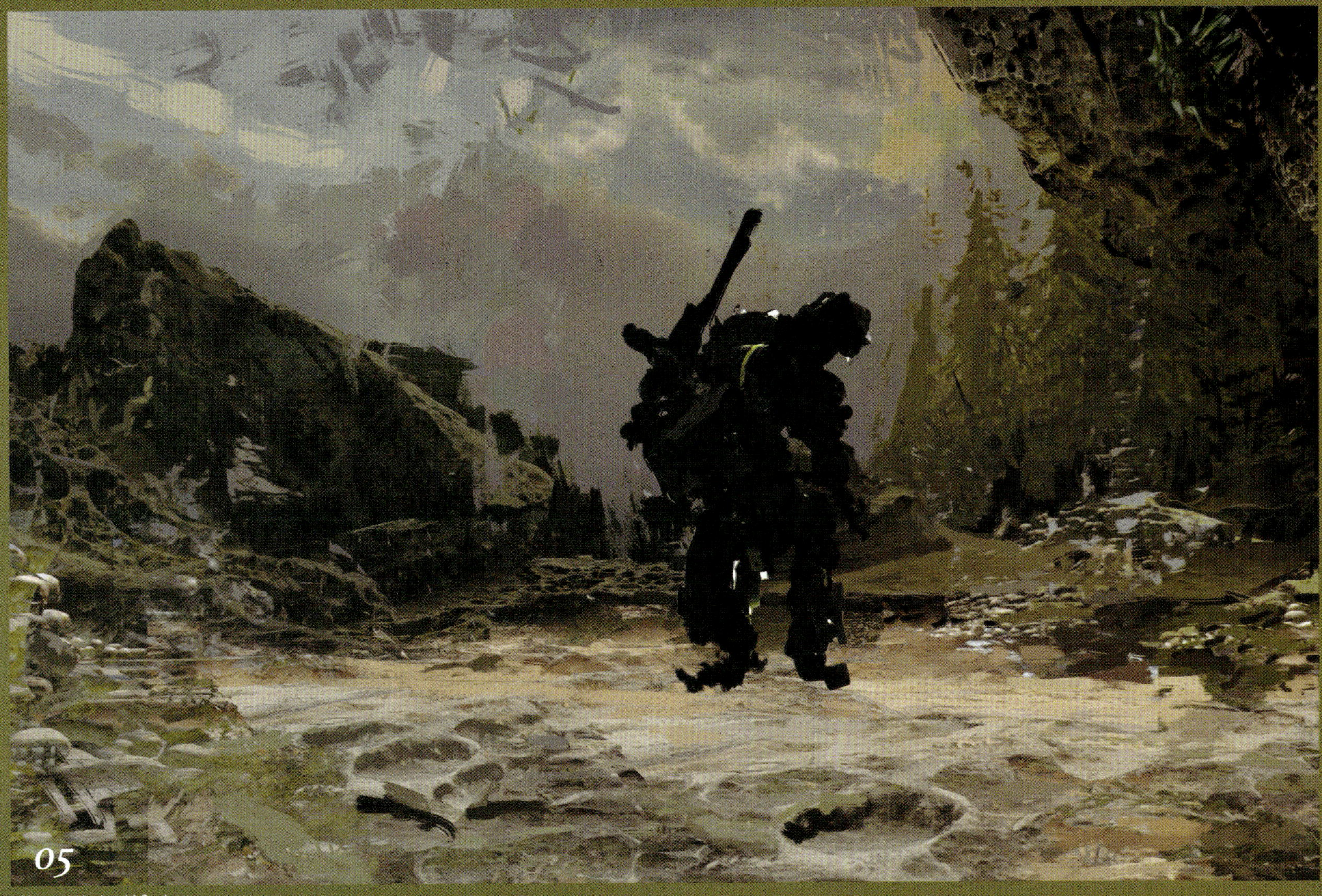

▲ Your mech should fit the scene

the Levels tab. You may find it useful to correct the perspective if the piece seems off in some way; do this by connecting all the layers and applying the Transform tool to make adjustments.

05: The mech

I love mechs and have always been attracted to their maneuverability in difficult terrain. They do not always have to signify the distant future – they show us what we could create if we wanted. Design your mech to show its application and functionality in a variable environment. Start with a silhouette on a separate layer. This makes adding textures much easier later on. You might find it useful to make several different designs (all on separate layers) and overlay them to get new forms and shapes. Remember to think about scale and adjust your mech as needed.

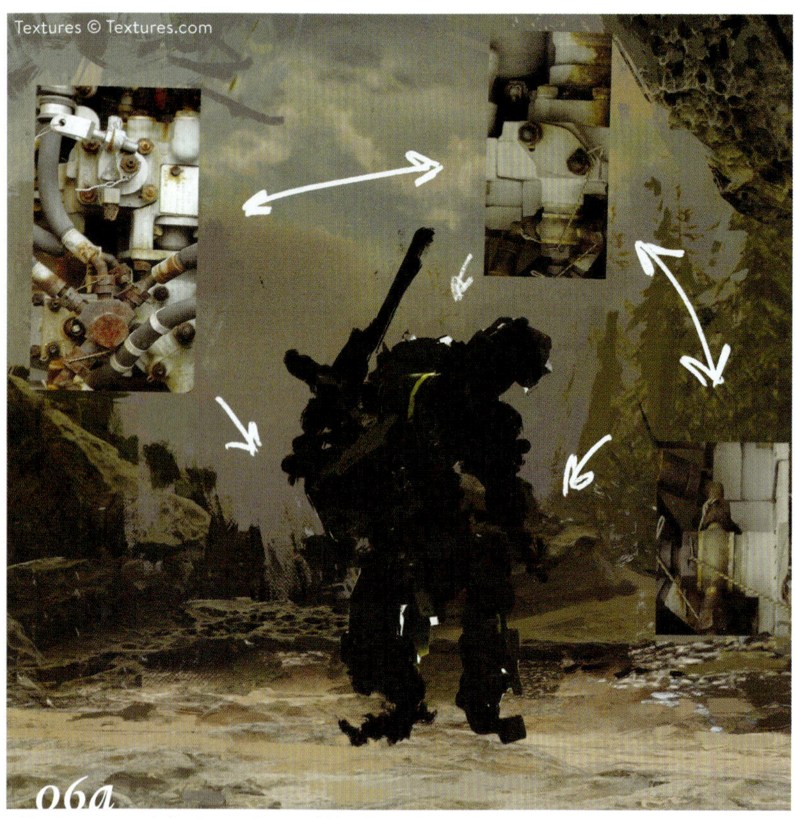

▲ Use textures and clipping masks to add details to the mech

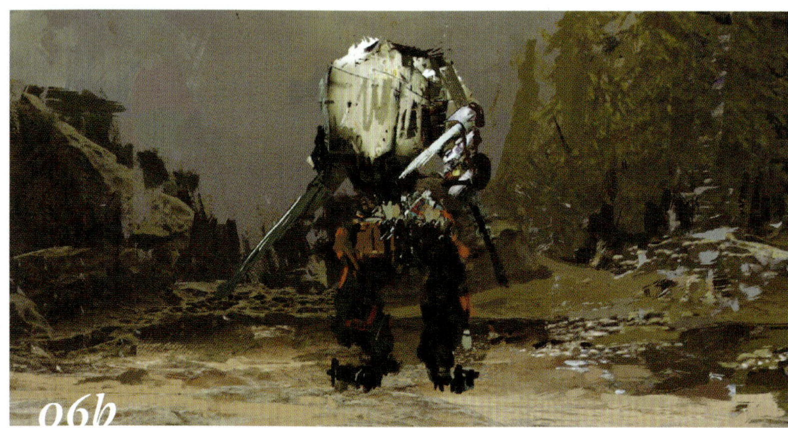

▲ Your design may change from the original silhouette

06: Clipping masks and details

Find some reference images or textures to add details to the mech; I use images of old car engines (**image 06a**). Make a clipping mask of the silhouette using each texture – vary the blend modes and Transparency to add variation. When I create something technological I always use this method because it reduces the overall working time and assists with the design and structure (**image 06b**). Erase any details which are unnecessary or don't match your design. The basic work pattern for this stage is a combination of

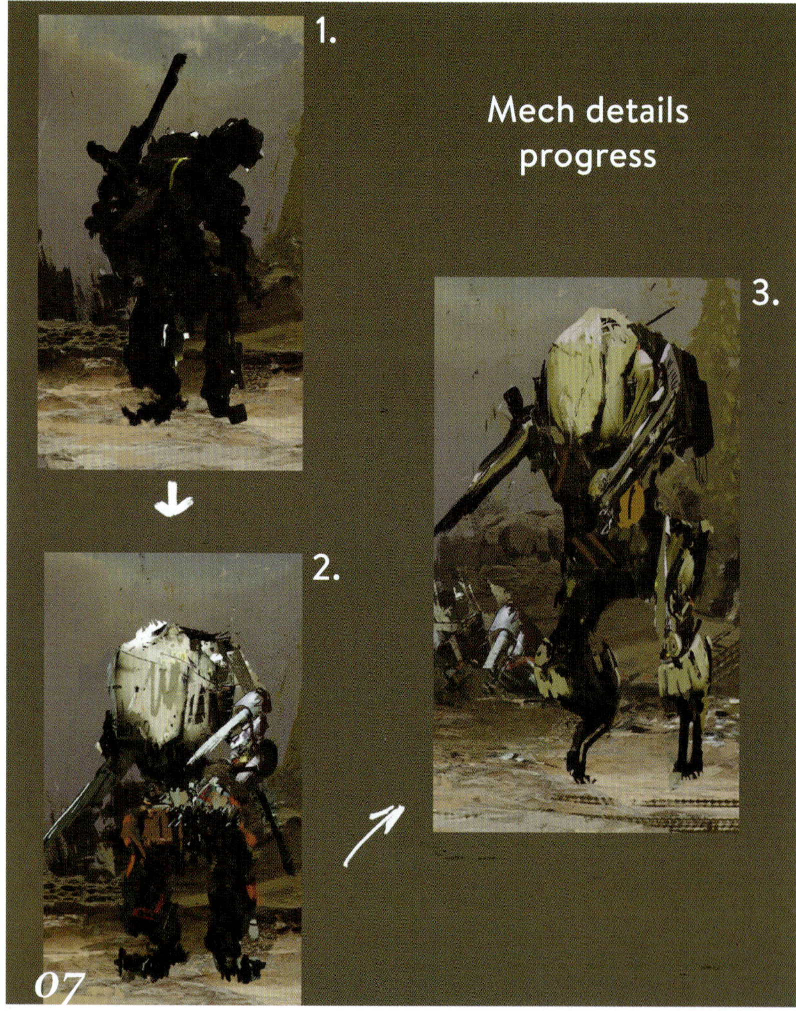

▲ The progression of the mech

brush, texture, erase, brush – it is a perfect method for objects such as vehicles or transportation. Don't forget to adjust the texture using the various settings (Levels, Color Balance, and Match Color).

07: Mech details progress

Take a moment to look at how your mech is progressing and whether you need to make any changes. I want to make my mech a bit taller; also his feet need adjusting so that they sink into the sand rather than sit on top. This will add a sense of weight, making him appear more believable. You can play around with Levels and Curves to make your mech fit more harmoniously with the environment.

08: Characters and additional details

With the mech finished you can begin setting the stage and adding extra details. Use a dry mixer brush to create fine details such as rocks, stones, and fragments. Add some small parts of the textures to add detail and depth to the whole scene (**image 08a**). Apply them in the Darken blend mode and adjust the levels to suit.

This is the time to add some characters to the image. They serve a couple of functions, firstly as part of the narrative and secondly to give a sense of scale (**image 08b**). Paint simple silhouettes for the characters with a few highlights.

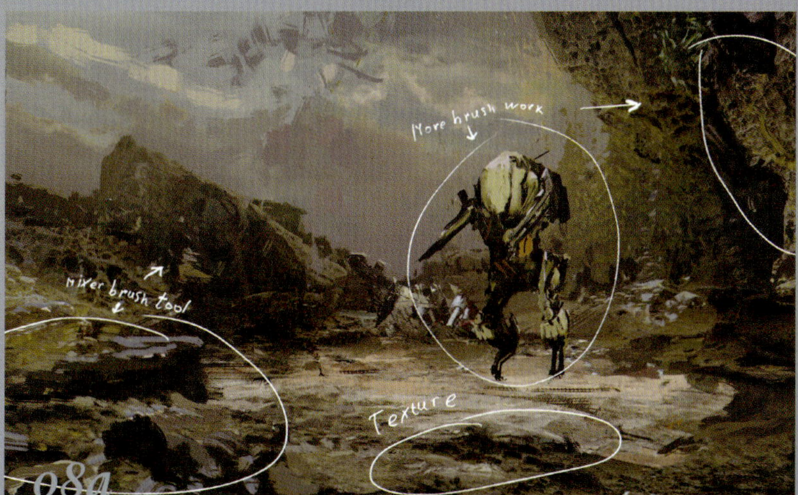

▲ Adding more texture and brush work gives the scene more depth

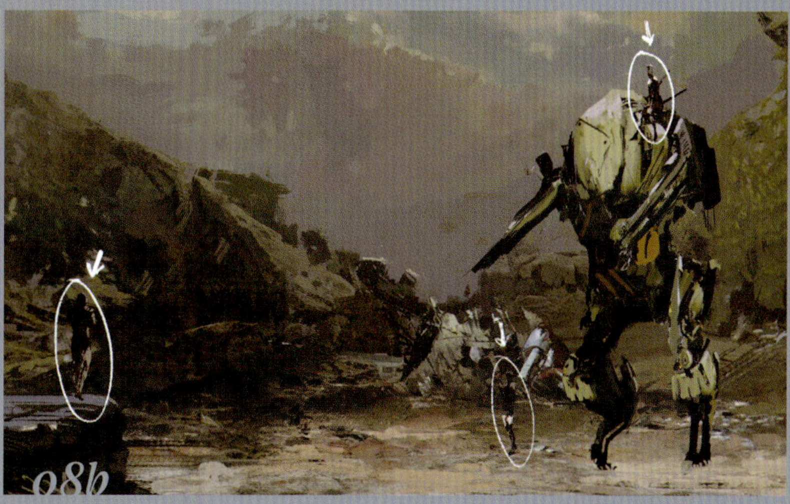

▲ Characters give a sense of epic scale

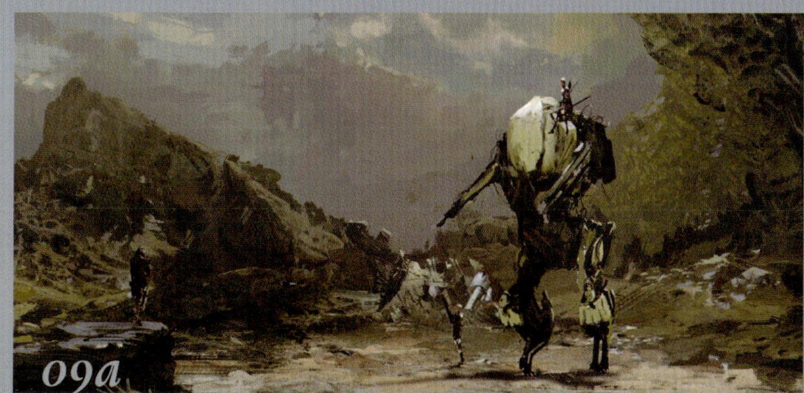

▲ Shadows can make or break a painting

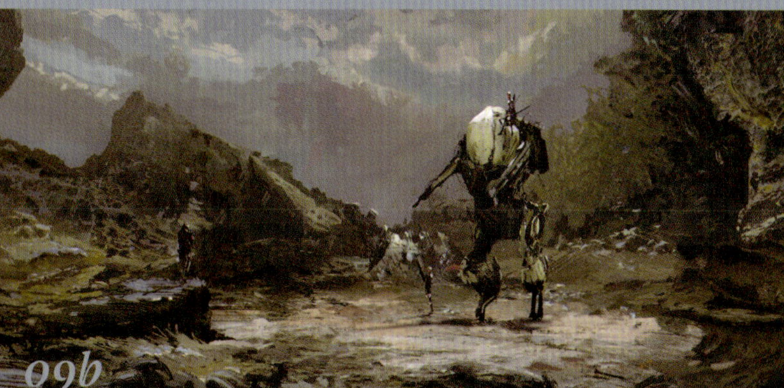

▲ Use Burn and Color Dodge to add depth

It is amazing how these tiny details add depth to a scene. The story has changed from the original: now the mech is broken and a piece of its mechanism is lying forgotten on the ground.

09: Lighting

The work is almost done. The last few things to do are to adjust the lighting, gamma, and contrast. Since the light comes down from above, you need to create shadows under the robot and characters (**image 09a**). For the shadows use the default Soft brush and apply Gaussian Blur. After manipulating the shadows add some more small details in areas of rock and sky. Use the Burn tool to darken the foreground and use Color Dodge for the background – again this is for perspective and depth (**image 09b**).

10: Final touches

In this last phase you only really need to make some adjustments and edits to the settings (Levels > Color Balance). Try making the overall tone a bit warmer and add more light to the ground using Color Dodge. As a final touch, apply some noise (2.5%). This adds a stylized look to the work and gets rid of the areas of extra contrast.

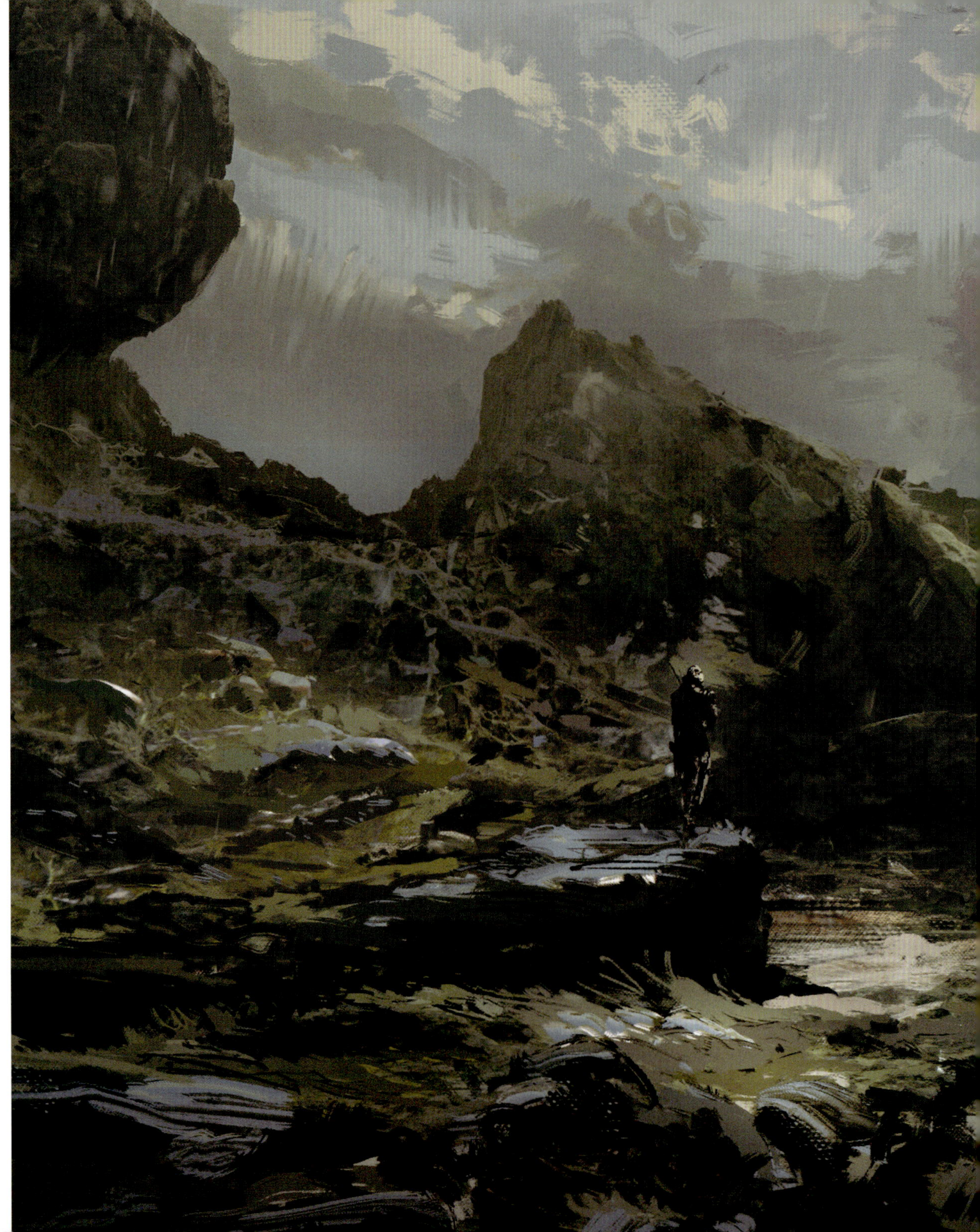

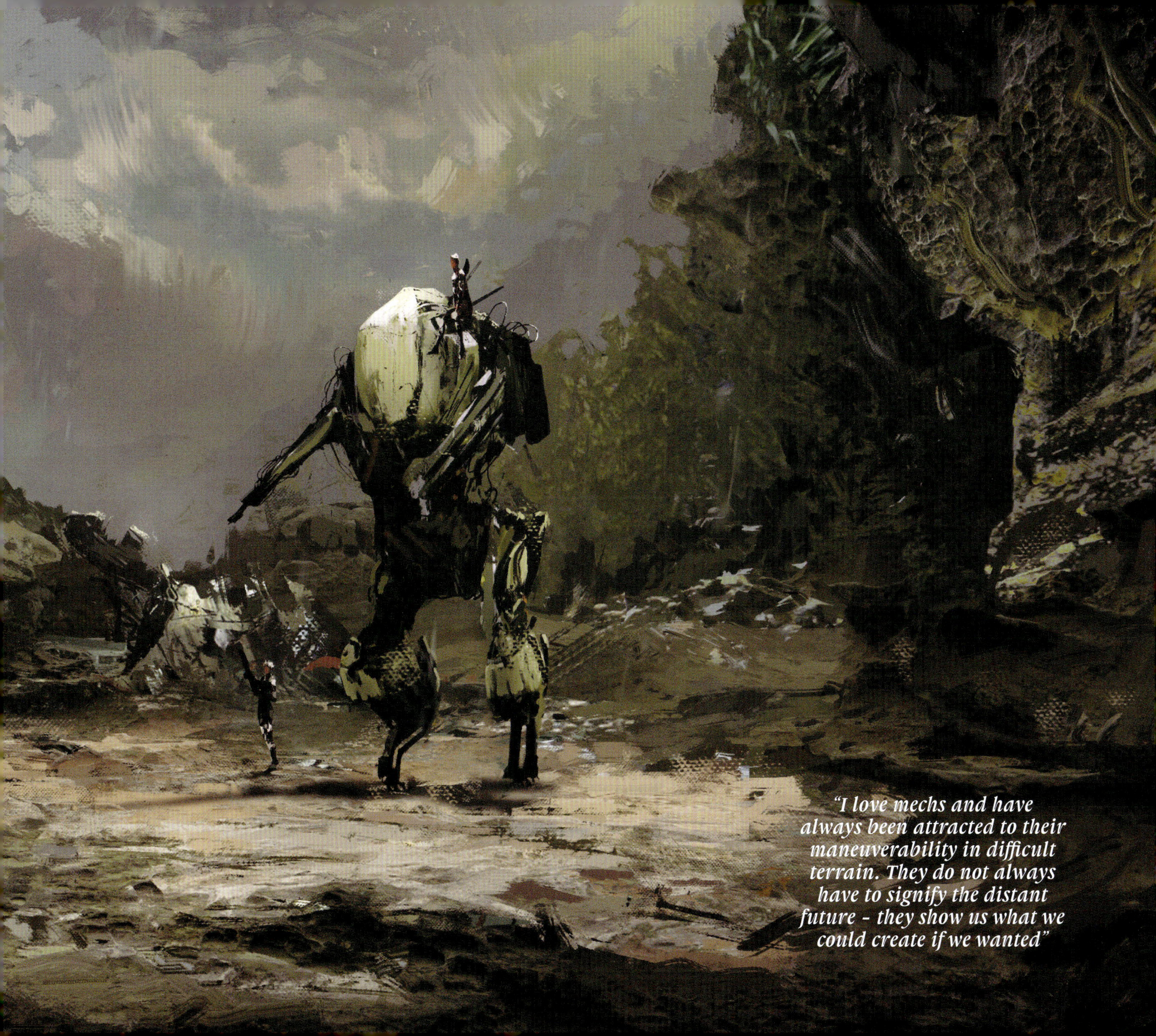

"I love mechs and have always been attracted to their maneuverability in difficult terrain. They do not always have to signify the distant future – they show us what we could create if we wanted"

REAL WORLD: SEASCAPE

by Katy Grierson

Speed paintings can have a particular aesthetic about them, often relying on the use of photos to produce a finished image in a short space of time. While this is incredibly useful in some industries and for just getting an idea down, reliance on photos can be an issue and, for certain projects that require a more painterly aesthetic, can even be a hindrance. It is always a good idea to practice merely painting without photos to cover any problem areas. In the following tutorial minimal photo use is the goal while still coming out with a pleasing speed painting.

01: Thumbnails and starting your piece

It is always a good idea to work out ideas by beginning with a few thumbnails (see **a–c** in **image 01a**). To help focus on the shapes, color palette, and atmosphere of your work keep in mind your theme – in this case a seascape. As well as working out composition, thumbnails allow ideas to flow better and can be used to warm up before moving on to the main painting.

With your thumbnails done you can pick the one which speaks to you the most. I choose the one shown in **image 01b** to be the base thumbnail because the cliffs framing the image have the most interest and potential. Resize the image to about 6000 × 2400 pixels at 300 dpi; this should be an ample size, especially if you decide to take the painting to a finished illustration. I think that if your machine can handle it, you should always try to work big as it is much easier to shrink an image than to make it bigger!

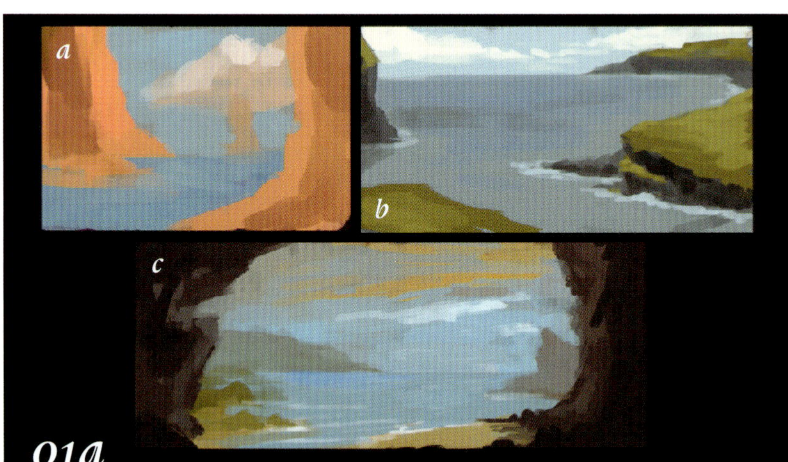

▲ Quick thumbnails to iron out composition and get ideas down can be very helpful

02: Add the photos

To introduce more color you can use reference photos which can be found with a quick online search or by taking your own. If you look at **image 02, a** and **b** are two photos I have taken on a smartphone. These will be mostly painted over so the resolution isn't important. If the intention is to leave the photos intact then the source material would need to be of a high resolution.

Paste the reference photos in a separate layer on top of your base image. You may need to edit the images to fit

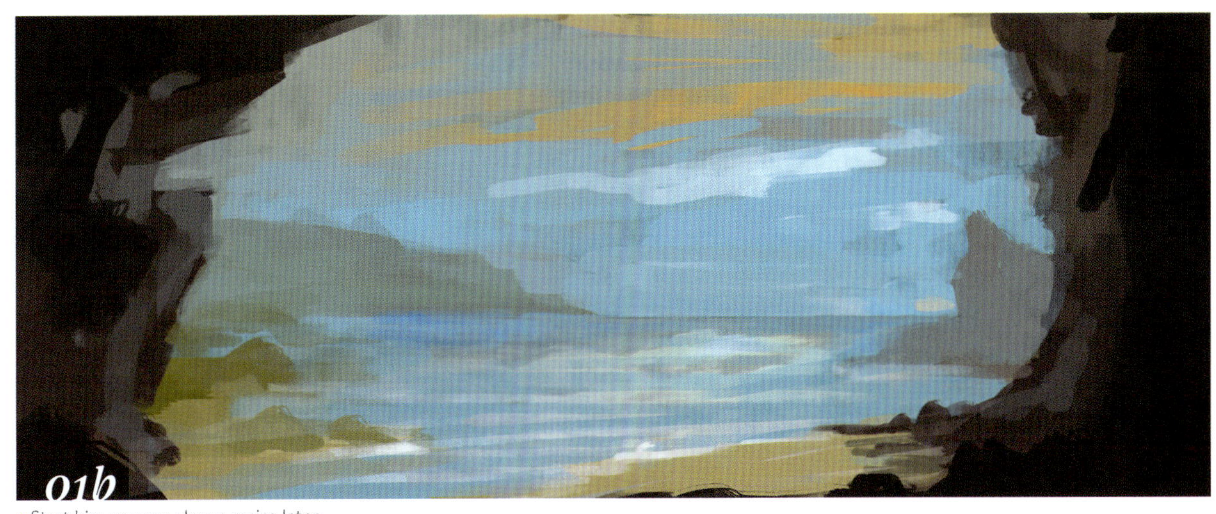

▲ Start big; you can always resize later

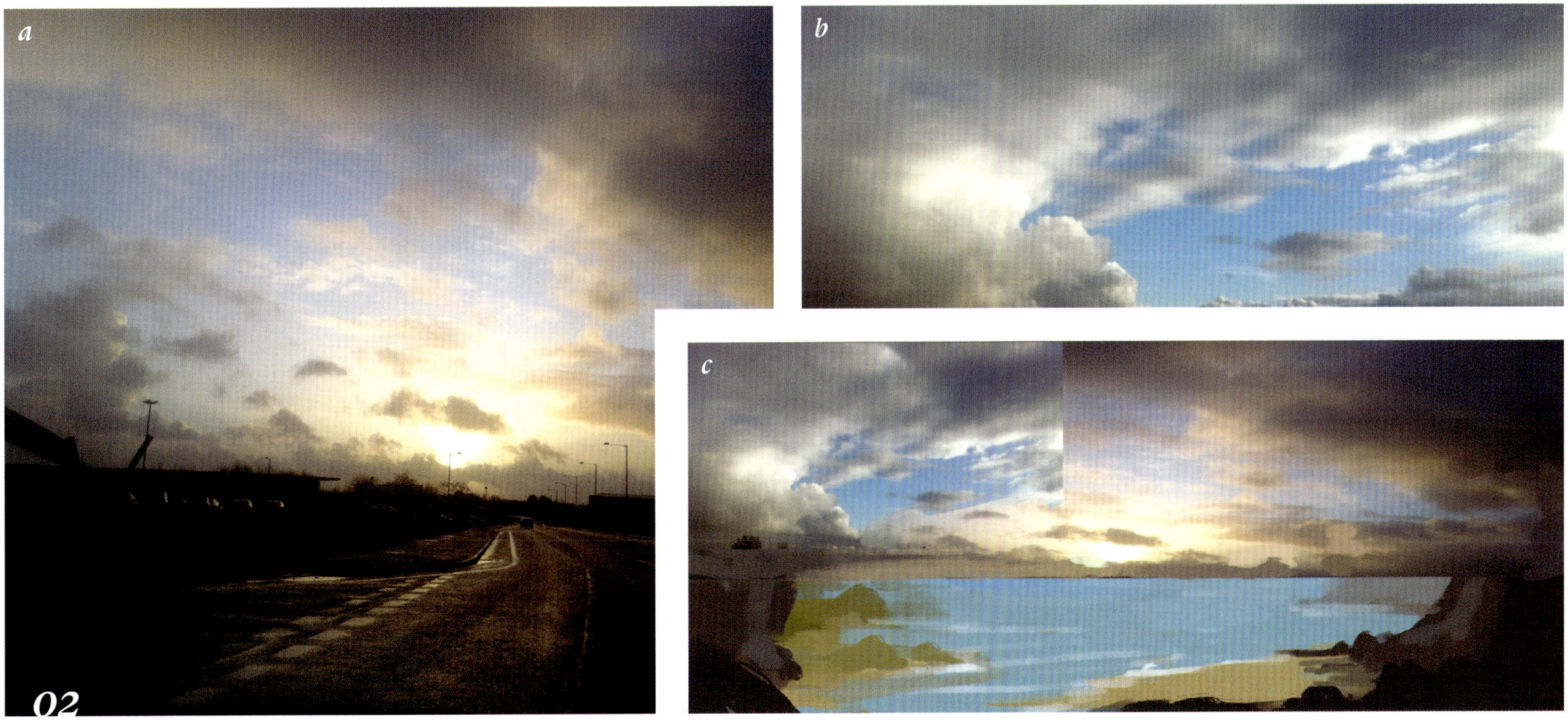

a

b

c

02

▲ Make sure you pick the correct source material for your intentions

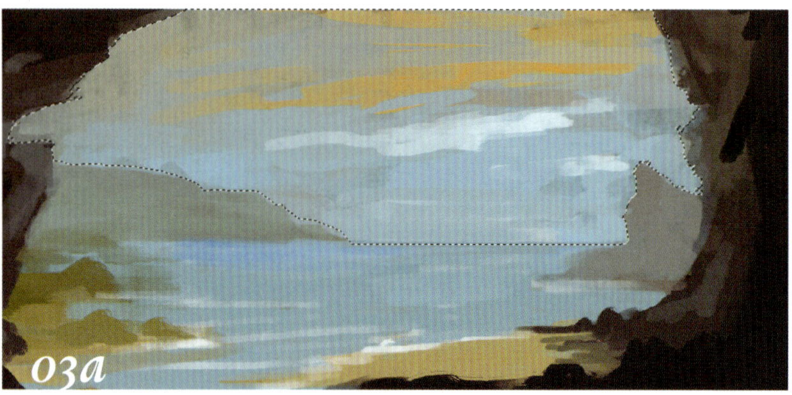

▲ Use the digital masking tools to edit the photo layers

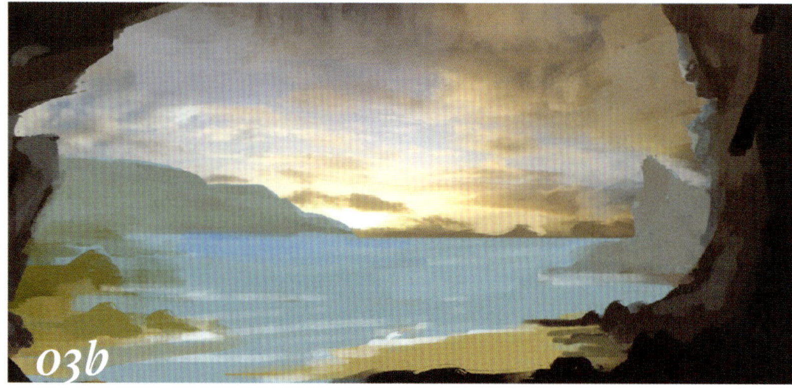

▲ The image once the photos have been added in

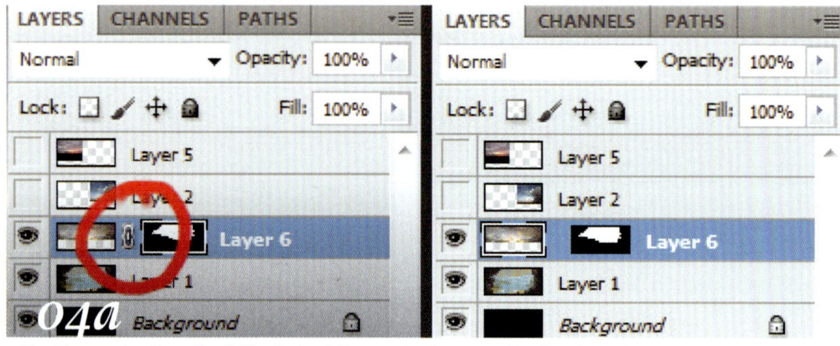

▲ Masking tools allow flexibility in deciding on the best use for the photo layer

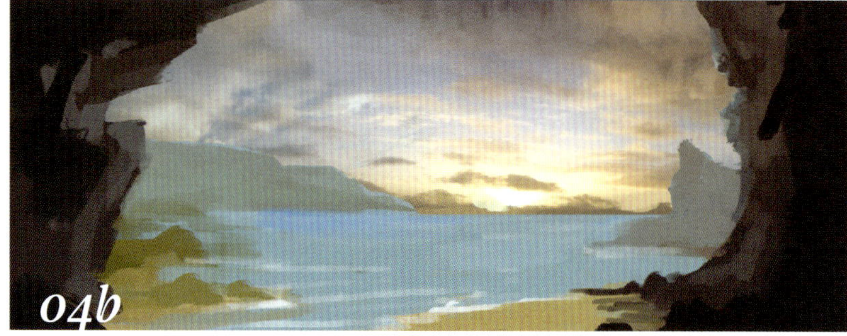

▲ The image once the photo has been moved

your idea. I stretch the sunset photo and partially paint over it to edit out the street lights and other erroneous material (see **c** in **image 02**).

03: Fit the photos in

After erasing some of the smaller cloud image so that it fits in, turn off the photo layers and go back to the thumbnail image. Select the sky area that will be replaced with the photo using the Magic Wand or Selection tool. This does not have to be too neat at this stage as it will be painted over later. Once this selection is made, create a layer mask. This will mask out anything not in the selection.

04: Use layer masks

Layer masks are incredibly useful as they enable quick editing of layers without destroying what is in the layer itself. Both mask and layer can be edited independently by simply clicking on either one in the Layers panel. In this instance however we need to move the photo but not the mask to make full use of that sunset. Click the link between the photo and mask in the Layers panel (**image 04a**). This unlinks them and allows us to move the photo slightly to the right. If we had simply deleted what was not in the selection before, this would not have been possible (**image 04b**).

05: Integrate the photo

Duplicate the photo layer, complete with mask. No longer needing the mask it is simply a case of dragging the mask itself to the trash bin on the Layers panel. This will bring a pop-up that asks if you want to keep and apply the mask or delete it. In this case we can delete it as it is no longer needed for this layer. Applying the mask will remove the editing capabilities that the mask allows and simply delete the non-visible aspects. Mirror the photo layer, turn down the opacity, and place over the water and erase as needed.

06: Back to painting

Once the photo is in place we can begin painting. Start a new layer and, using a large textured brush, start re-adding elements to the piece. Color picking from the photo can help a great deal as it begins to tie the photo and painting

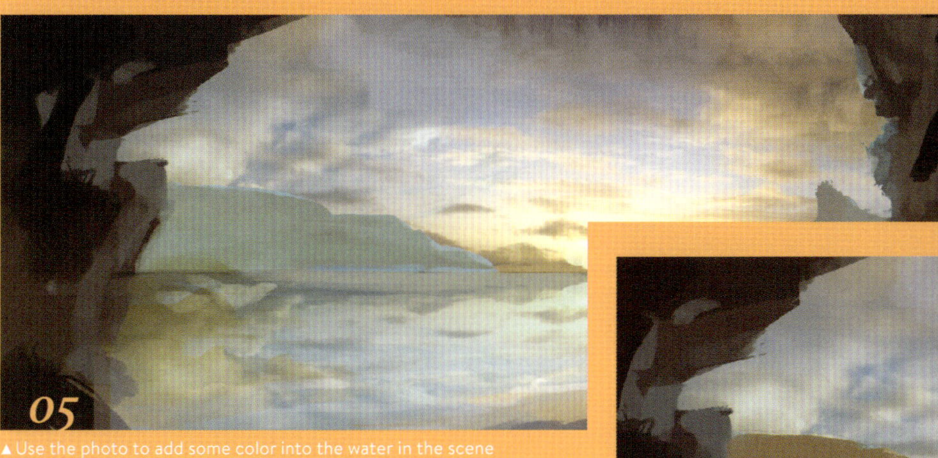
▲Use the photo to add some color into the water in the scene

▲Color pick from the photo to tie the image together

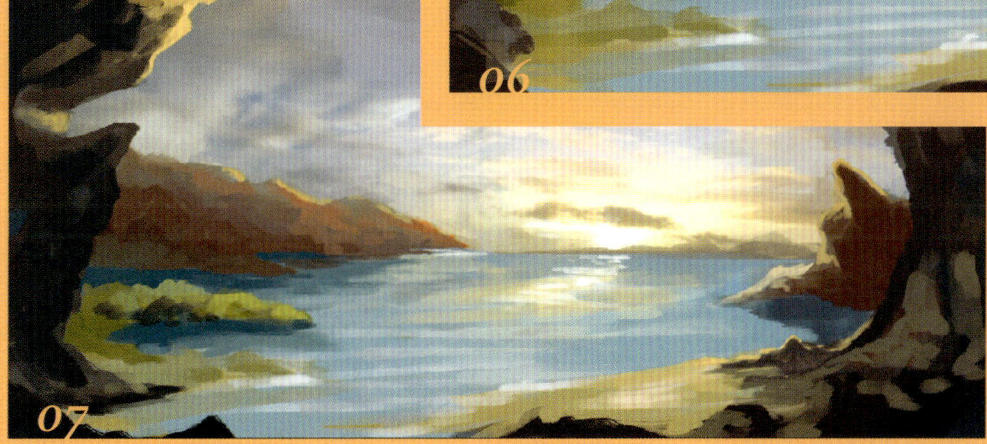
▲Keep in mind that aspects like atmospheric perspective add more realism to your images

together. Keep in mind where the light will be coming from based on the photo that is being used. This will greatly influence the colors of your scene based on the time of day and the local color and texture of the surfaces.

07: Paint atmospheric perspective

This scene deals with a large distance going into the canvas. One of the easiest ways to add depth is to remember that for things further away there is more atmosphere between us and the object. This means that it will almost always need to be desaturated, slightly blue, and have less detail compared to the foreground. Keep this in mind when choosing color and tone in the scene.

08: Add some lighting

The lighting in your scene can easily add interest to your piece; it would be easy in this instance to simply make the foreground rocks dark and in shadow. By adding the highlights at the top of the

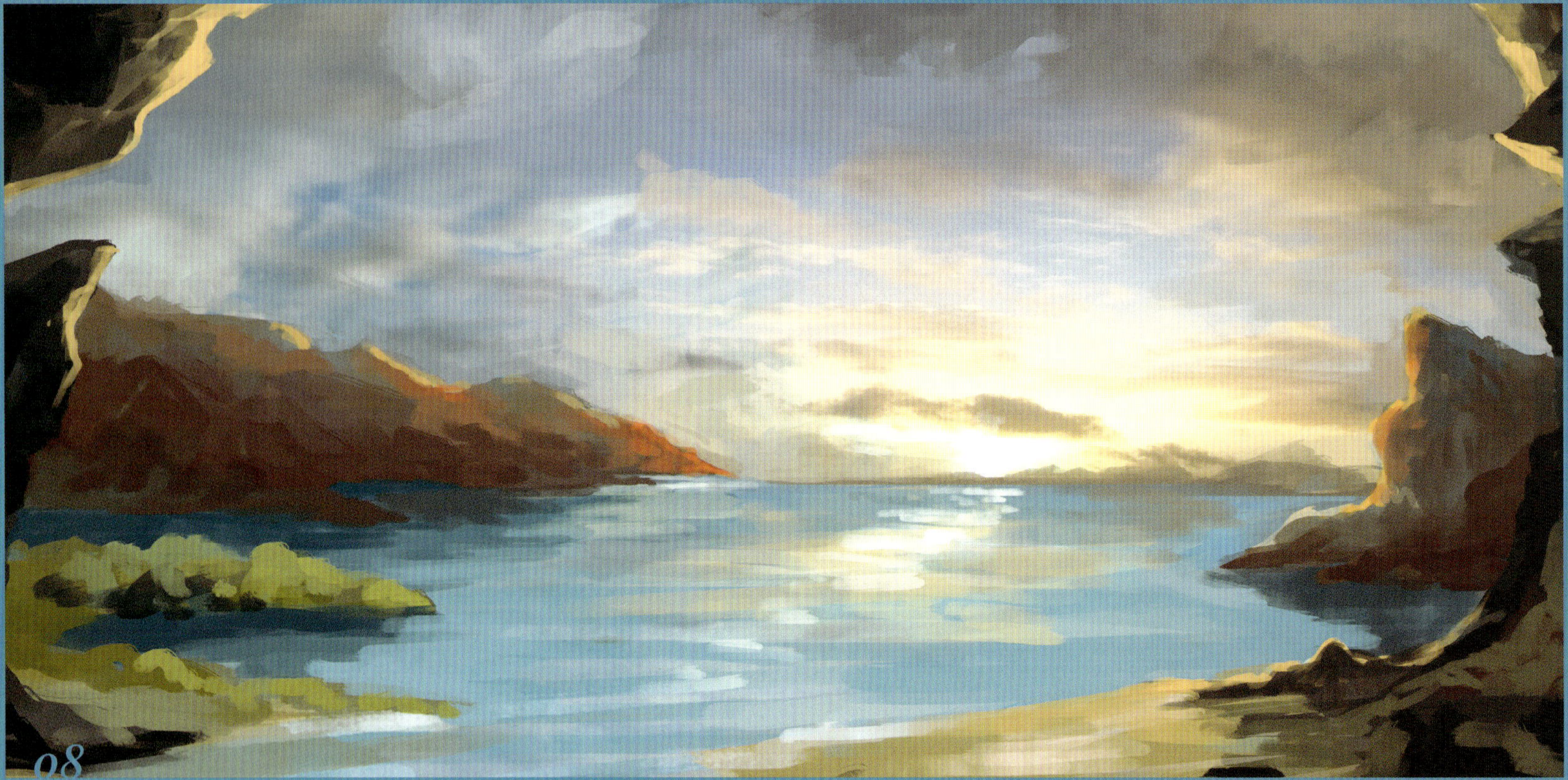

▲ Use lighting to your advantage to create interest and drama

cliffs in the foreground, however, we stop the eye disregarding the rocky frame completely. Now is a good time to add some shadow as well. Steer clear of using blacks and grays as they wash out the image. Darkening and *adding* saturation, especially in cooler colors, can really add depth without losing detail.

09: Even out the color

Once the main color and lighting scheme has been decided there will undoubtedly still be some areas that are looking drab and lackluster. Making use of color layers provides a quick and simple solution. Here a Soft Light layer is used to just tint the color (**image 09a**); it is akin to a wash color on an oil painting. A large soft airbrush often works best for

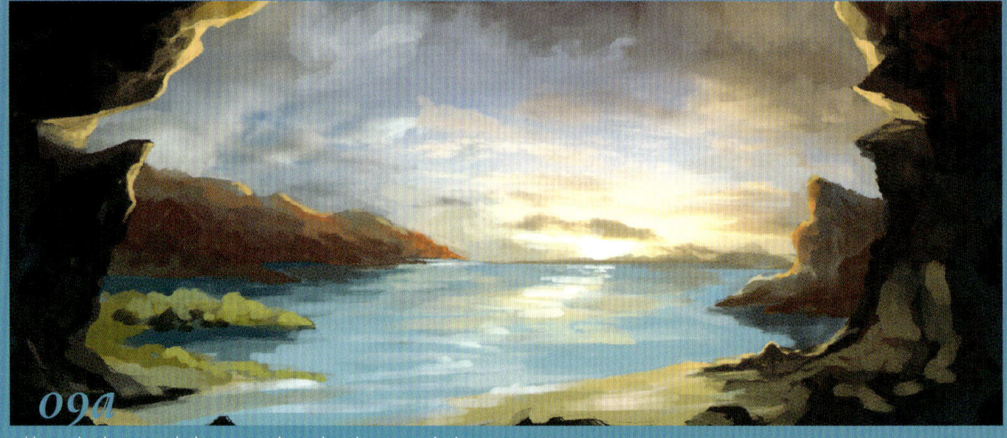

▲ Use color layers to balance out the colors in your painting

this as hard edges can leave artifacts that look distracting when the layers are flattened later (**image 09b**).

10: Detail the image

Once the colors have been adjusted, we can begin adding more detail. Switching to a harder brush at this juncture will provide some harder edges and therefore much more detail and contrast, especially in the foreground on the rocks and cave entrance.

Adding contrasting but subtle greens also creates interest in the rocks. Using a hard brush prevents over-rendering which can eat up time during speed painting. A single brushstroke denoting color and tone is much faster than fussy repeated strokes with a lighter, softer brush.

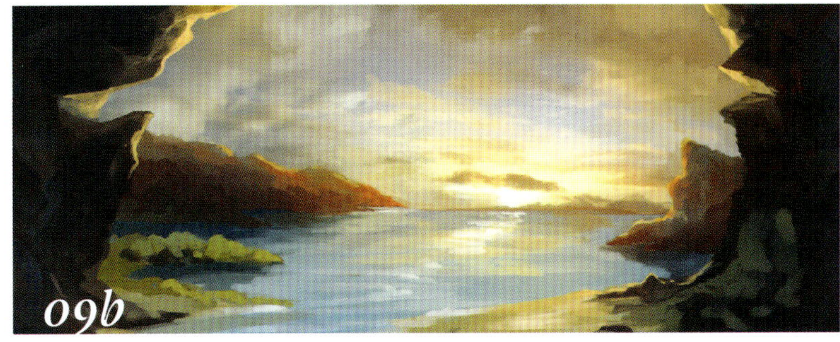

▲ Use a large airbrush to even out the colors in your image

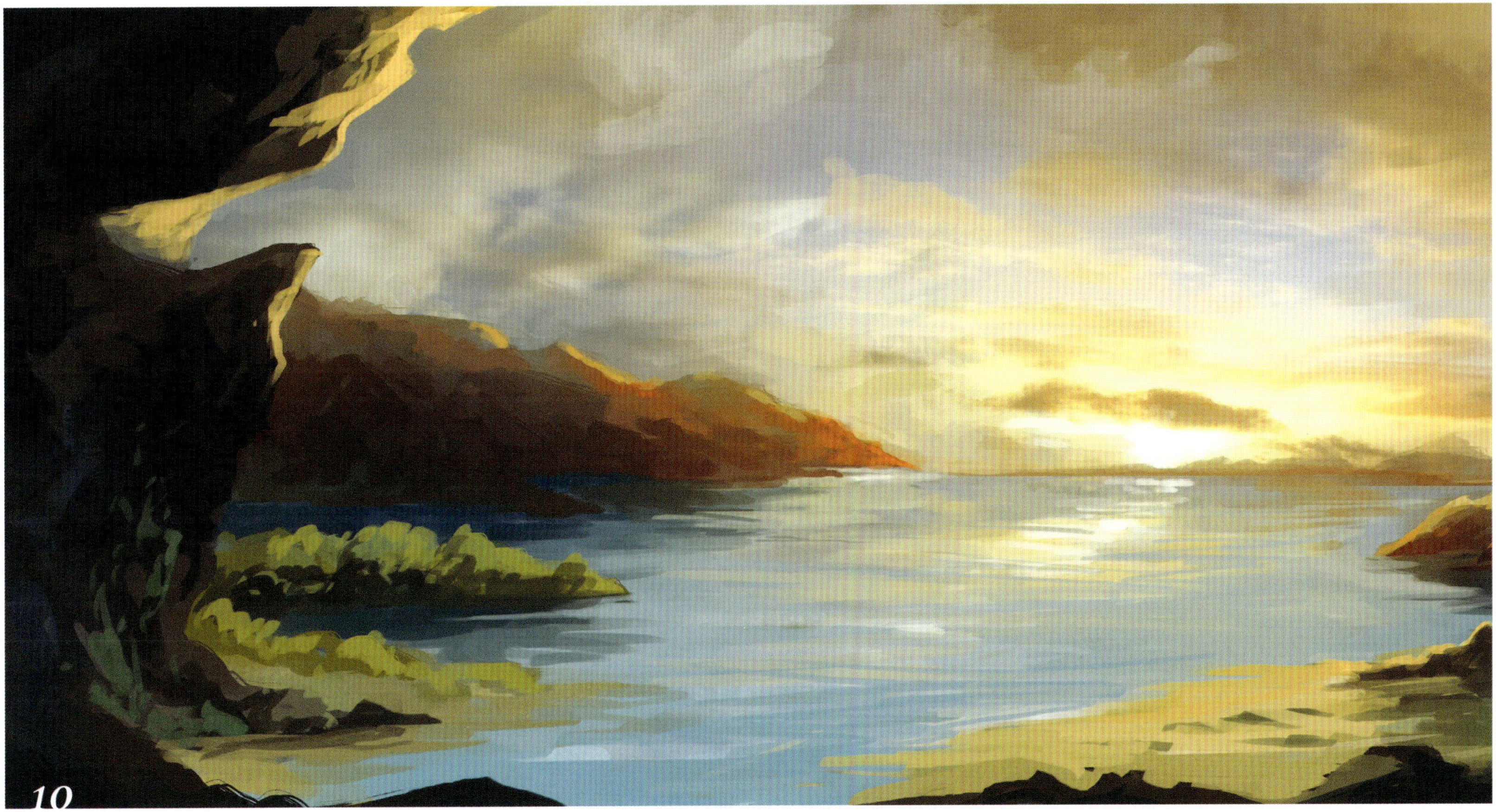

▲ Learn to use single brushstrokes rather than repeated ones to denote color and tone

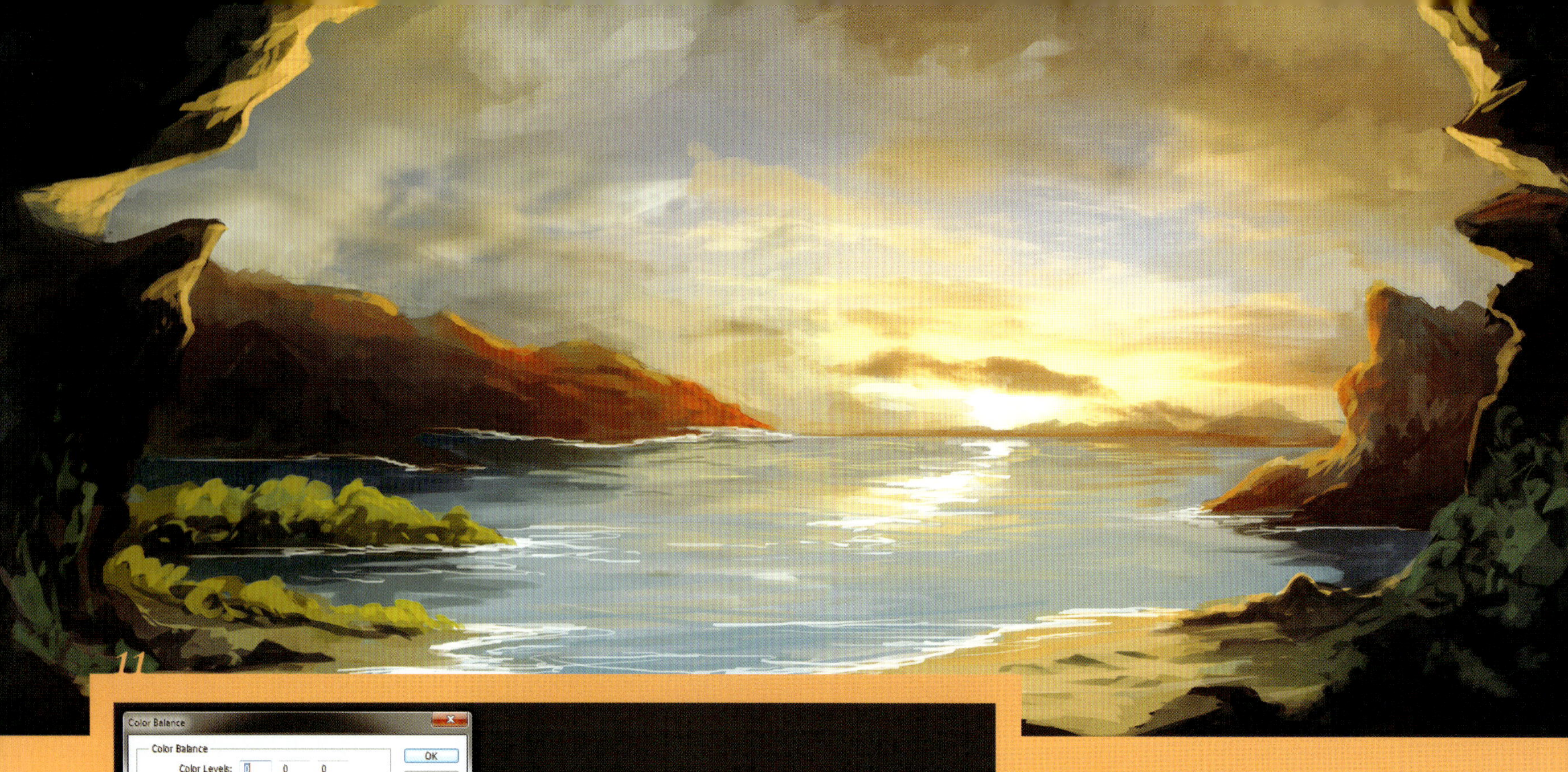

11: Create the water

Water can be tricky to paint quickly; doing studies of different water conditions can be highly useful as well as informative as there are so many variables to consider – lighting, water type, environmental factors like wind or gravity, local color of the water, and how clear it is to name but a few. In this instance the water is a calm but moving coastal body of water so simply adding white edges to the blue of the water instantly gives the impression of waves lapping gently up the shore.

12: Check it is working

Flipping the image horizontally is one of the quickest ways to see if the composition is working; doing this at all stages can really help show any issues. At this point it is also a good juncture to use the software's tools to once again tweak the overall mood of the image. I use Color Balance which is available in Photoshop through Image > Adjustments > Color Balance

12a

▲Use the editing tools to make the most of the image

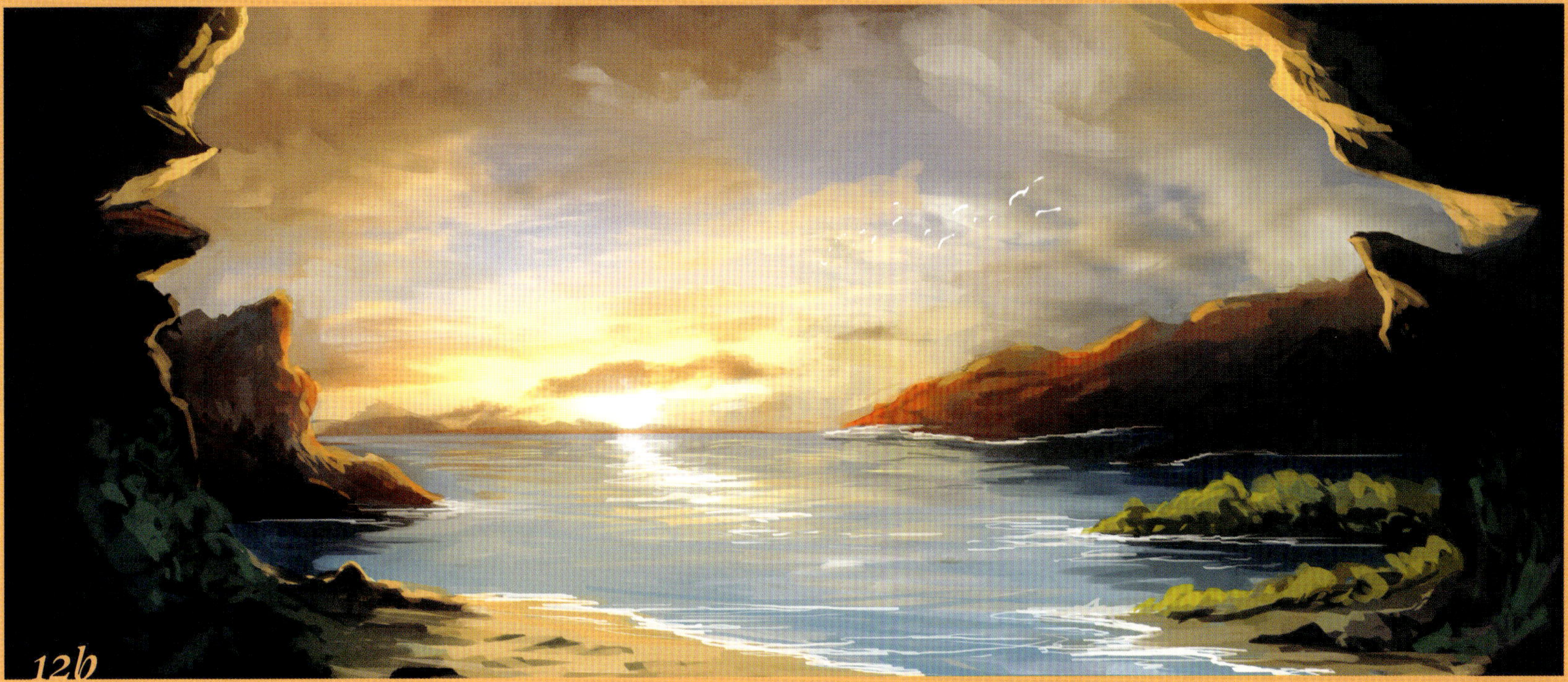

▲ Use color to make the most of the sunset

(**image 12a**). Here the blues and pinky oranges are pronounced to really make the most of that sunset sky (**image 12b**).

13: Finishing touches

The speed painting is mostly complete now and time is running short for the two-hour goal. There could easily be several more hours spent on rendering the rocks in the foreground but at this stage it is about priorities. Therefore I decide to spend more time on the water as it is a seascape. Adding little wave splashes with a splatter-type brush and more highlights on the water itself really adds a sense of that moving, ever-changing water. A little more detail and color variation on the foliage also just adds that little something extra.

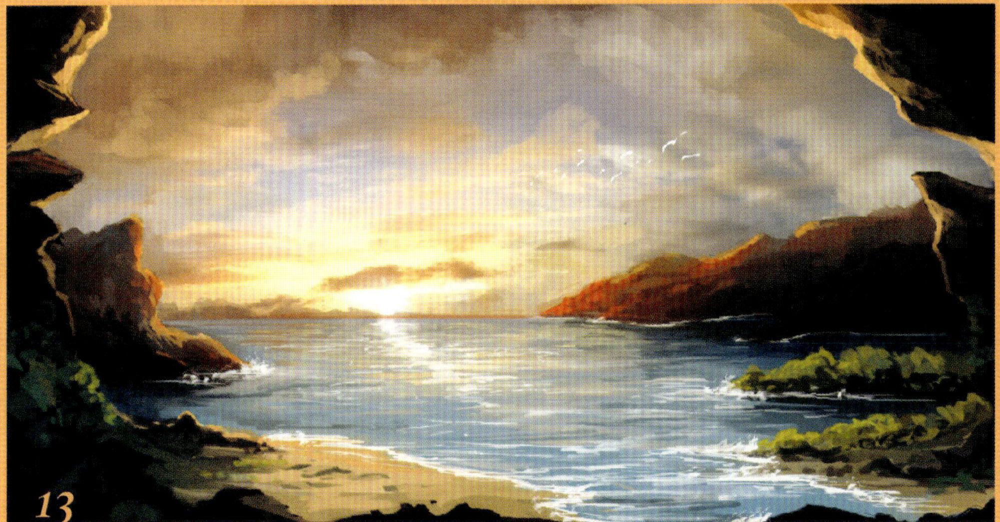

▲ Choose what is important in your image to add some final finishing touches

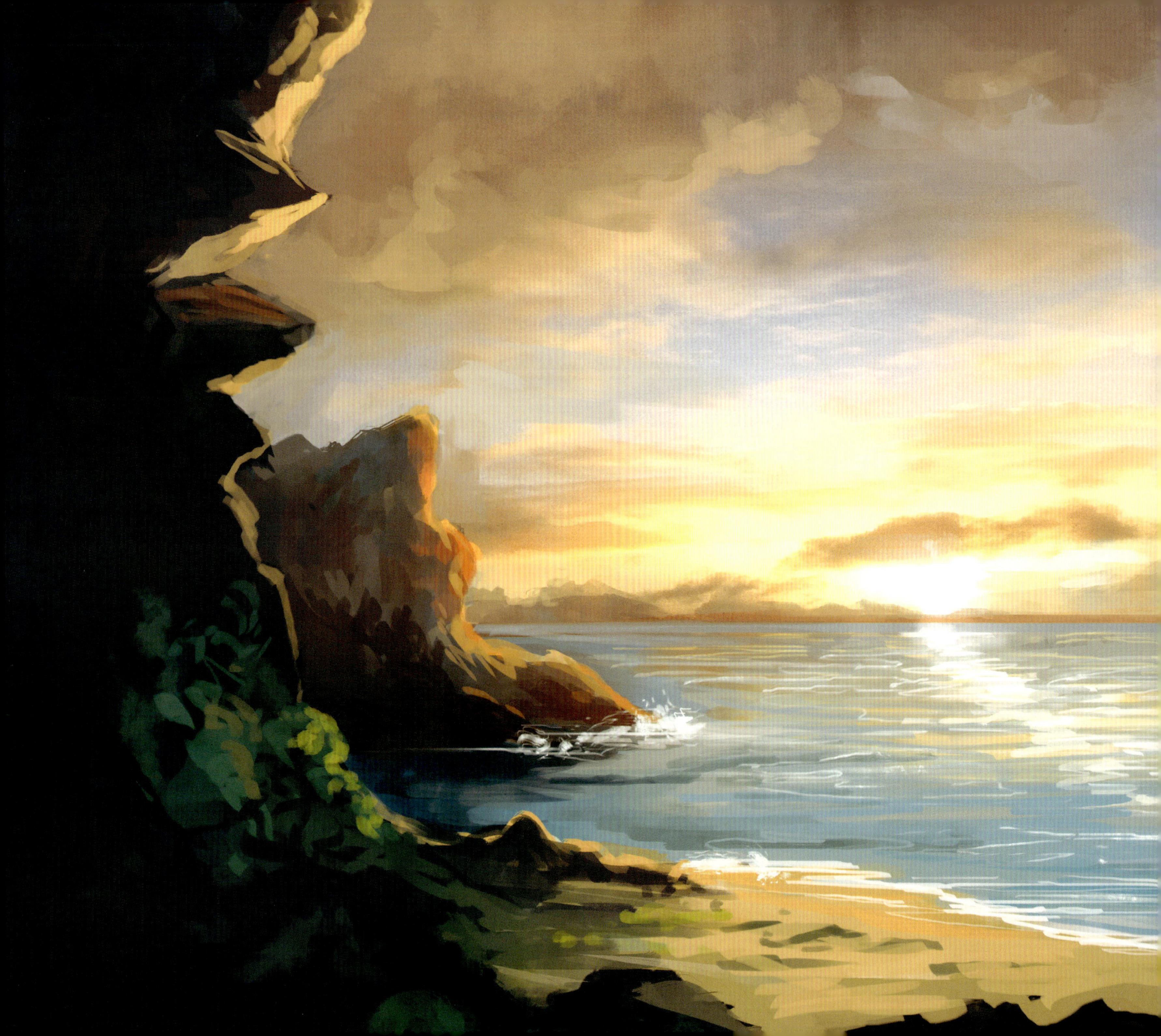

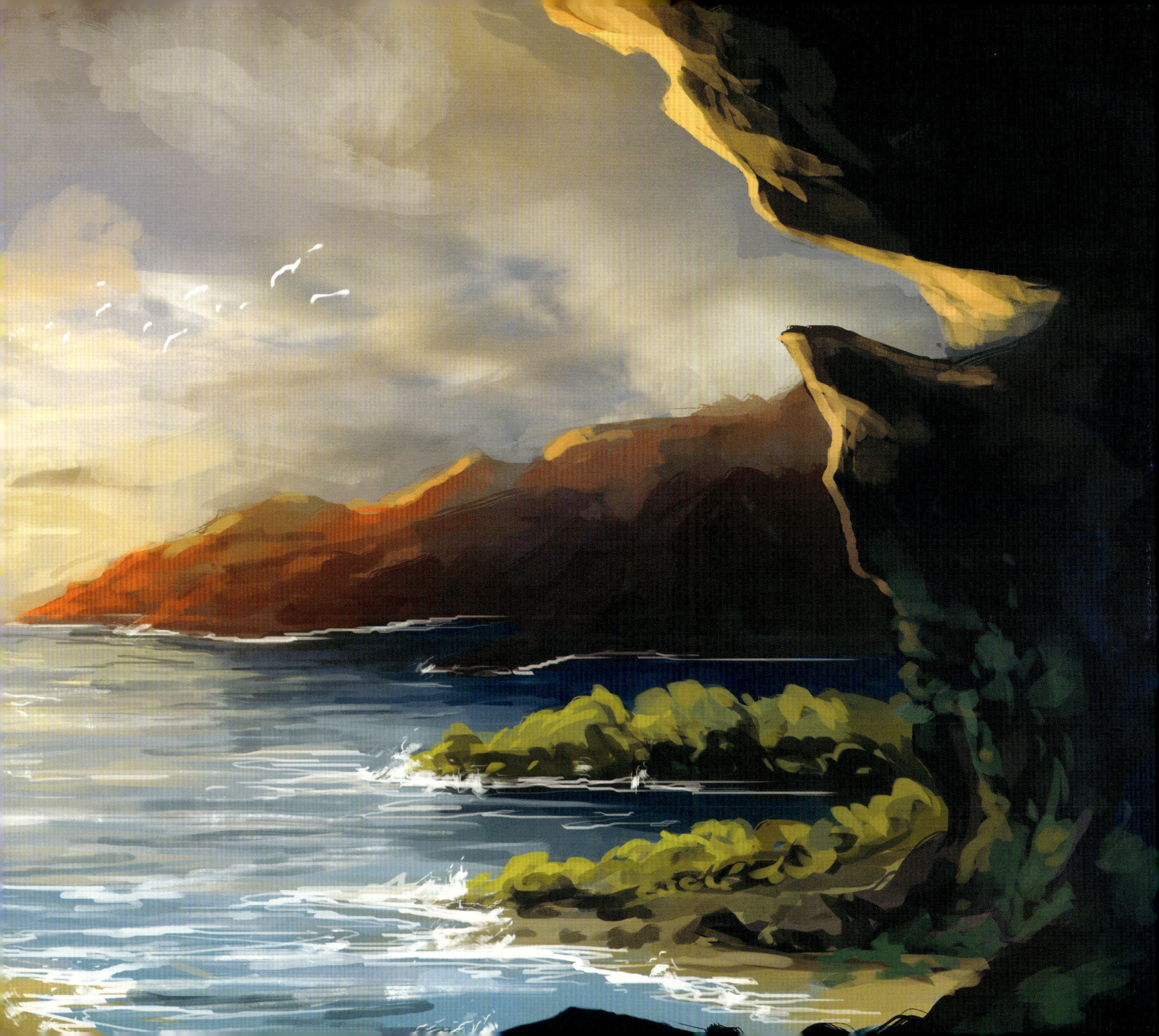

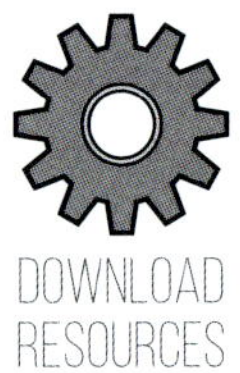

FANTASY: NIGHT STORM
by Stephanie Cost

Every artist has a rich and unique history of experience that contributes to their work. My particular history involves dark country skies, crisp air, catching fireflies, adventure stories, and chalk pastels. I prefer vastness, sweeping gestures, and color. When I sit down to make a piece like this one, I may not know anything more than that, but it's enough to give the next idea a personal twist. Landscape art is about forcing the viewer into a single moment, for example imagine turning a corner or cresting a hill, and seeing the world turn and being illuminated by a new light. For this tutorial I will be going back and forth between Photoshop and Corel Painter, just as I go back and forth between sharp and loose rendering.

01: Ideas and thumbnails

For this piece we are going to create a simple composition. It will have a ship, clouds, and be set at night. To get your ideas going try making a list of descriptive words and juxtapositions such as: still/churning; big/small; the calm before the storm; and ominous.

With words to hand make a few loose line thumbnails to capture a sense of motion. I like to do several two-value ones and isolate the ones that appeal to me the most – in this case I like the simple graphic compositions best. When you are ready, commit to just one thumbnail.

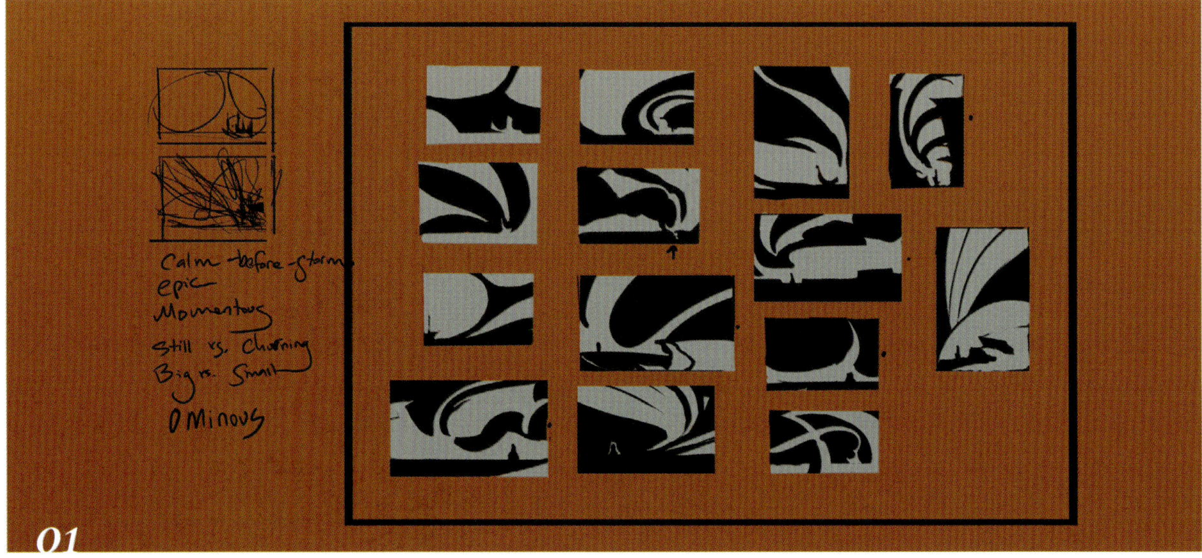

▲ I like to use colored backdrops when doing this initial stage as I think it gives pieces a "feel" before they begin

02: Rough brush build-up

When you have settled on a composition, enlarge it, make a new Photoshop layer, and paint over the top of the thumbnail. Use the Magic Wand tool to keep the main elements of the thumbnail. Don't worry, you will get to be messy soon! Use custom brushes with rough edges that trail off nicely and utilize high-contrast, gritty textures; any type of brush will work for this stage as long as it is big. You need to make big, bold shapes and strokes.

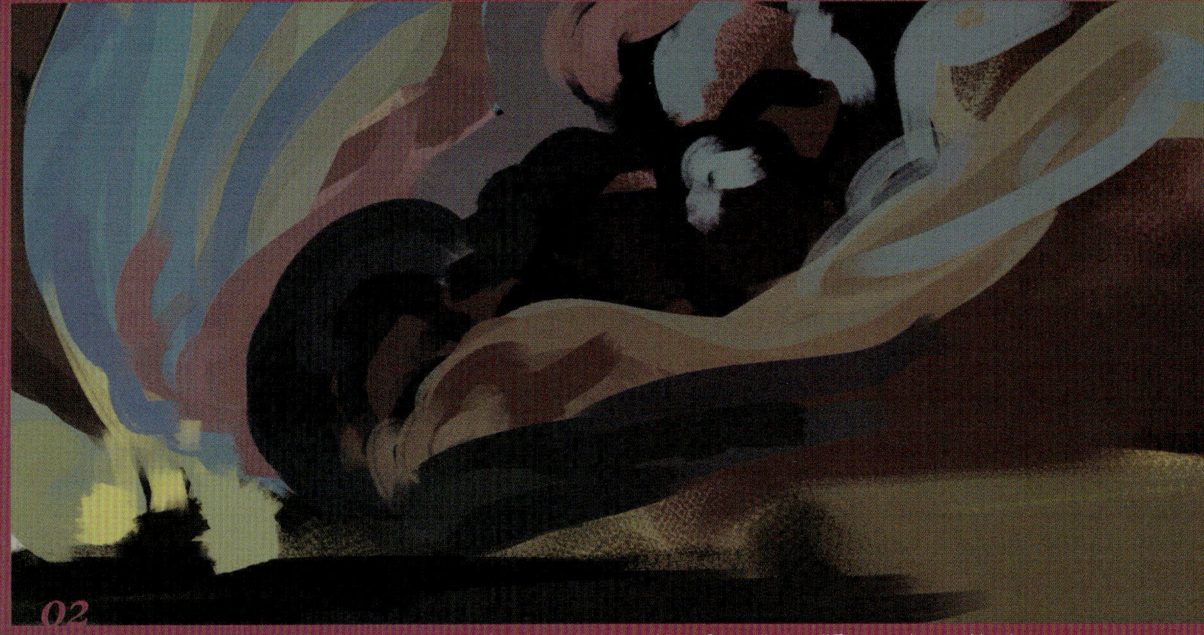

▲ Don't worry too much about keeping the composition perfect – experiment and have fun exploring different color combinations

03: Added complexity

To add complexity to your painting you should make full use of textures and custom brushes – there are hundreds of free ones on the internet. Find yourself a nice variety such as a rounded lizard-skin-esque one, a smooth chalk-like one, or maybe a chunky, rough gravel brush. They are great for breaking up the internal shapes of your composition. You can try using a soft flat brush with Hue Jitter on each stroke; this is good for harder edges and unexpected colors.

To explore different approaches to making shapes you can try the Acrylic and Sponge tools in Painter, or the Mixer brush in Photoshop. Although this is an abstract piece at the moment, it is still a good time to study reference images as you start to break up the big shapes (**image 03a**).

I prefer to color blend in Corel Painter (**image 03b**) because the tapering effects on the brushes are good for blending color naturally and finding new, rich hues. I find

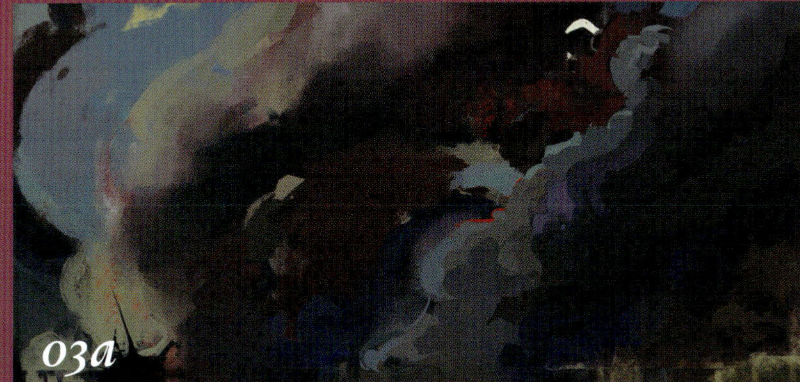

▲ Exploration is good for weeding out bad compositions

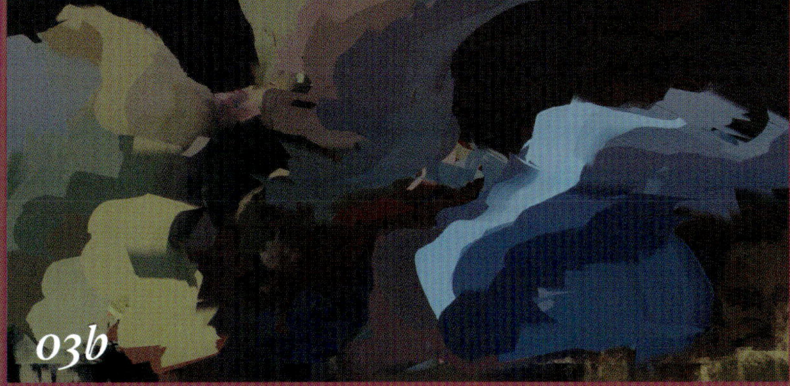

▲ The Painter brushes blend colors naturally

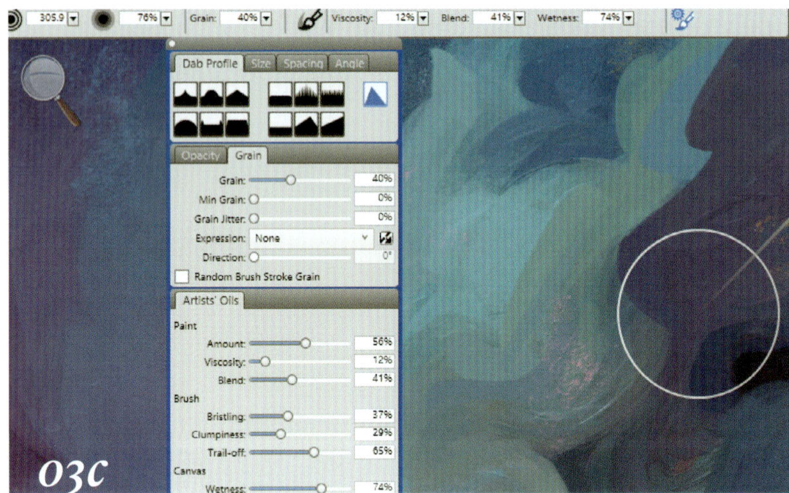

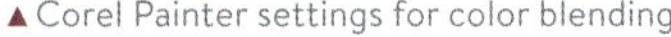

▲ Corel Painter settings for color blending

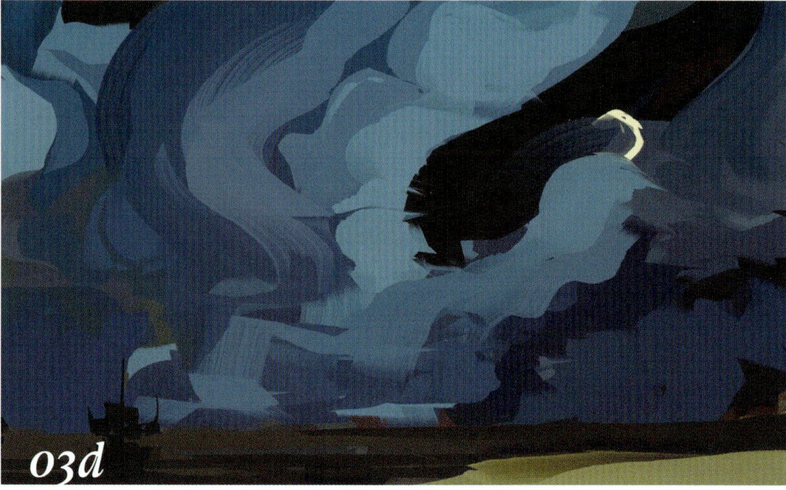

▲ Now I have a color palette I can refocus the composition

that the Clumpy Thin Flat Acrylic brush set to a large size with varying levels of viscosity and blend percentage is a really great brush for blending colors (**image 03c**).

The previous steps may be hidden beneath the top layer but they are still there and you can go back to them to find elements that you want in your composition. Now is a good time to narrow down your color palette (**image 03d**).

04: Focus the composition

With your exploration of composition and color palette done, hopefully you will now have an idea of the mood and movement of your work. If it is how you want it to be you can bring back some of the hues from other steps. To do this stretch the Acrylic tool's viscosity setting; this will achieve slick, natural color shifts.

Try to work on one layer by consolidating the layers. Use Copy, Undo, and Paste so that you can still access old material but have a solid layer of colors to work on. This helps with the way Painter samples color and "pushes" pixels around, and it's also a commitment to be bold in the process.

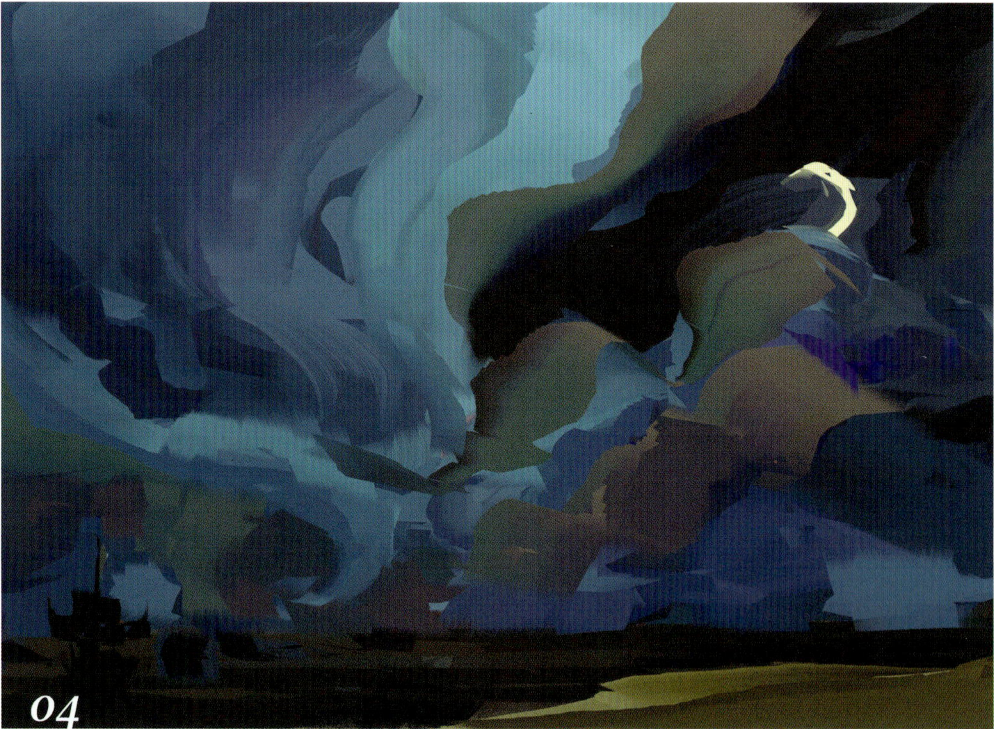

▲ I love playing with neutralized oranges; I like the way they interact and vibrate with every color

"I also use big round brushes with softer contrast for a rolling, organic succession of forms"

05: Chalk brushes and the palette knife

I always use a high contrast of texture within my imitation-chalk brushes. I use concrete and metal as textures a lot and sometimes keep the size (which affects how often it "repeats") low for hits of light and detail. I also use big round brushes with softer contrast for a rolling, organic succession of forms that plays off the more gritty chalk brushes.

Again I start with a fun exploration of saturated colors and move to forms that are more neutral, tight, and dynamic (**image 05a**). I continue to study references at this stage to get ideas for variety and believability within clouds.

Using Painter for molding forms is useful and the Pointed Palette Knife Jitter tool is excellent for digging into the piece and bringing energy to certain areas that you want the viewer's eye to linger on and explore.

It's important to remain visceral with your work and remember the emotion and thoughts behind your initial inspiration. I find it useful to search for a sense of movement and energy in the forms and a high level of drama. Although a risky stage, it can be rewarding to experiment with the strengths of Photoshop and Painter side by side (**image 05b**).

Pro tip: Values

Periodically check the grayscale version of your piece to evaluate how the composition is looking and also look at the RGB channels individually; these can inspire interesting value compositions to work toward. Preserving your first tiny thumbnail in the corner of your file is also useful to refer back to. Although the composition can change during the course of the work, the emotional impact survives in the final version.

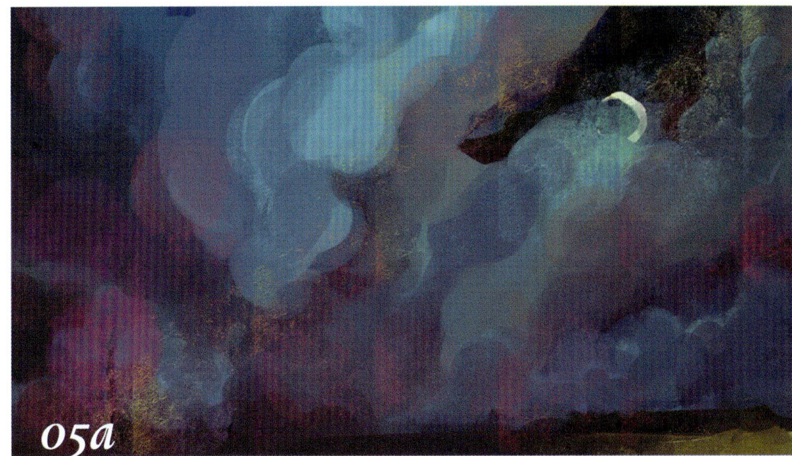

▲ I want a clear read of movement and direction. I want my forms to be varied but not distracting

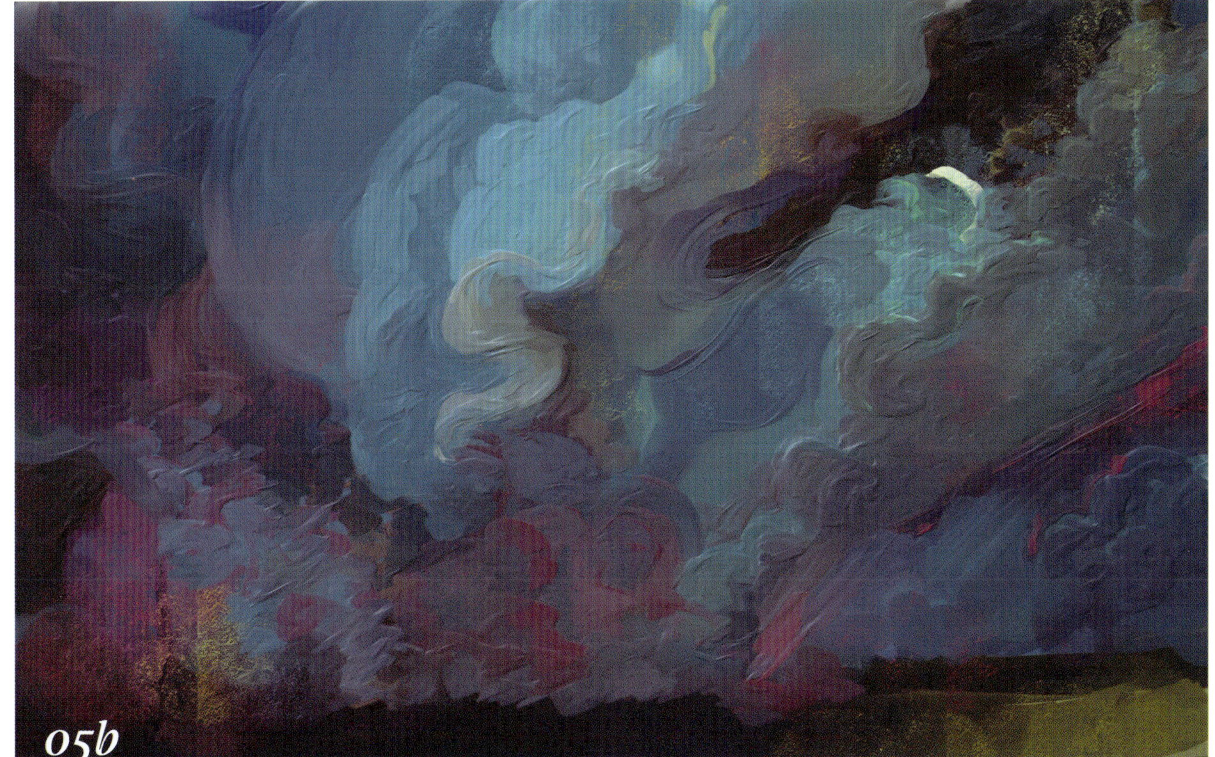

▲ Try to avoid obscuring the forms and blotting out textures

06: Bring back broad strokes

In many ways this is the most challenging stage for me because it is delicate and if overdone will ruin the balance of energy and unity that I'm working toward. Go back to Photoshop and with the lizard-skin and Chalk brushes soften some of the edges, tone down the distracting areas, and return to larger brushstrokes to counter the uniformity of the Palette Knife strokes.

Slow down for this step but be careful not to over-soften the image to the point of flatness.

07: Linear gradients and Painter

Linear gradients are brilliant for achieving greater depth in your painting. Simply fill a new layer with an indigo gradient coming in from the top (110% scale, 26% Fill, and Overlay blend mode), and make another

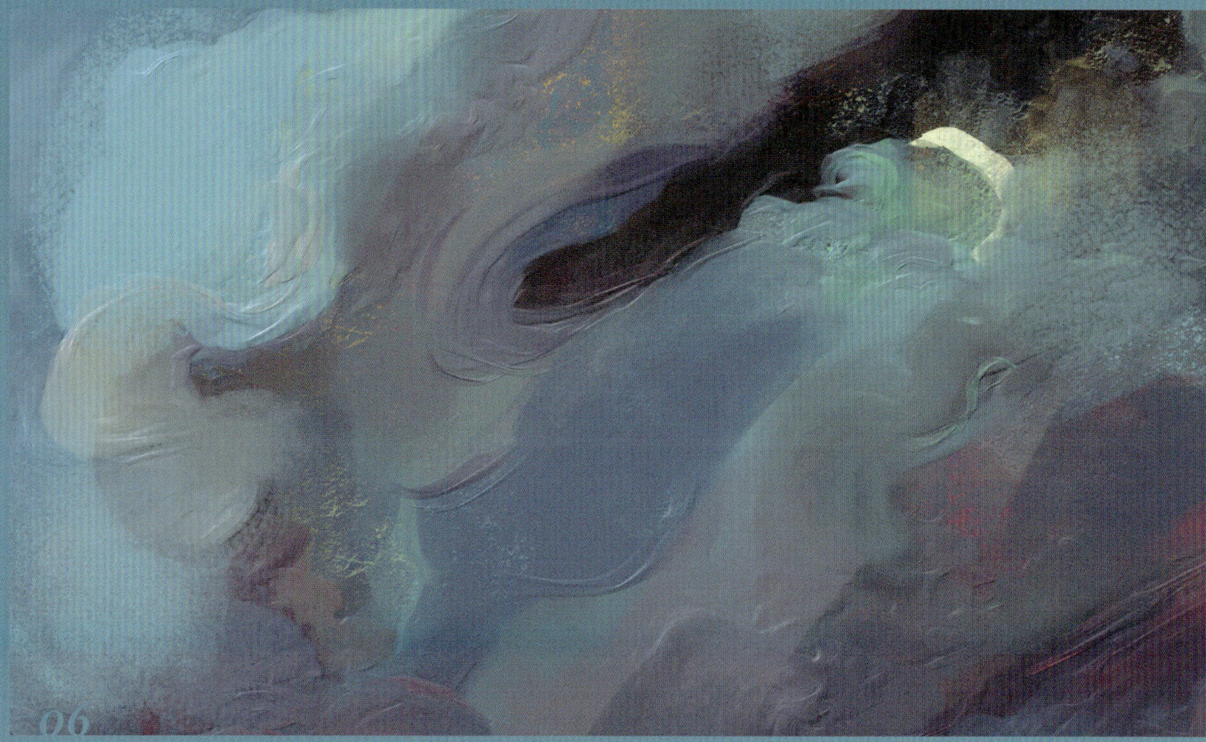

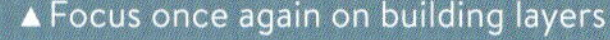
▲ Focus once again on building layers

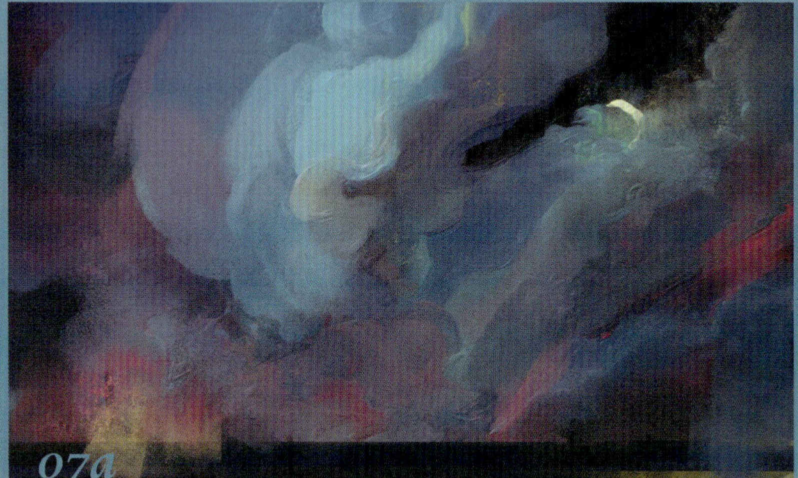

▲ Use gradients to add subtle depth without messing with the strokes

▲ Clarify the delineation between light and dark forms

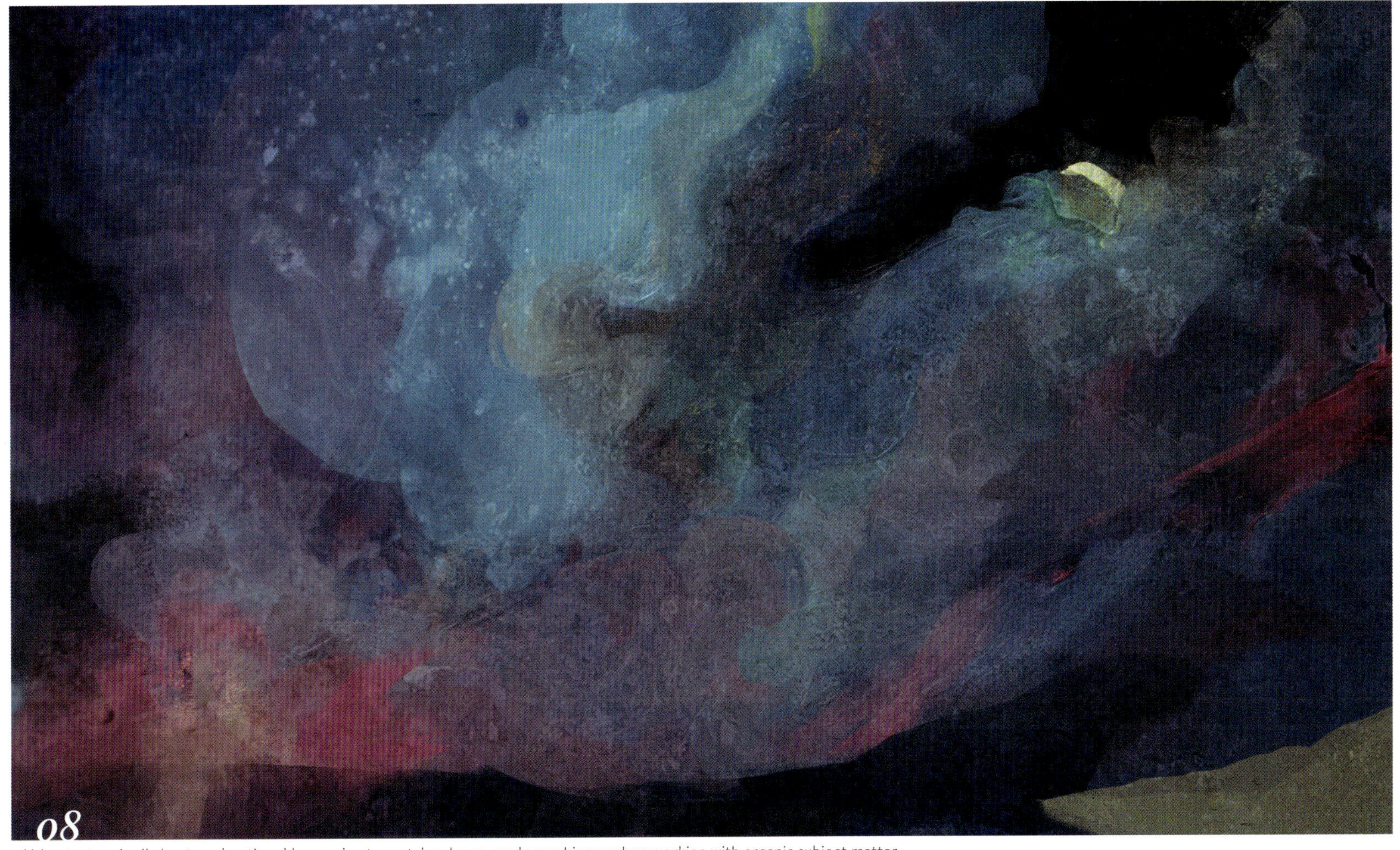

▲ Using texture is all about exploration. I love going to metal and man-made machinery when working with organic subject matter

gradient coming in from the bottom in a rich gold color (130% scale, 60% Fill, and Color Dodge blend mode). To keep the image from flattening put layer masks on both gradients. Then paint in with a black chalky brush to remove pigment from the areas you want to preserve (**image 07a**). Back to Painter and the Clumpy Thin Flat Acrylic tool – set with 24% Grain, 27% Viscosity, 31% Blend, and 64% Wetness. Paint into areas that are disjointed or rough. It's important to consolidate all layers for this and duplicate the new background layer to preserve it because this effect works best on a layer with all pixels present (**image 07b**).

08: Textures

I almost always expand textures past the bounds of the canvas because I appreciate the unifying effect that they have on the entire piece, regardless of what is later masked off. In this step I use two textures: the first one is a rusty bluish metal texture with an interesting yellow bit that I rotate around until it coincides with my moon, set to Overlay and 24% Fill; the second texture is an abstract, blurred image that has a diagonal that I lined up with my lower clouds' bottom line, set to Linear Light and 8% Fill. Combined, these balance grit against slickness.

Pro tip: Recycling material

Abandoned stages of the working file, as well as old unused sketches and studies, are perfect for adding inspiration and visual interest to a struggling composition. I experiment with size, rotation, filter effects, and saturation levels of my in-progress images to inspire entirely different pieces.

09: Hard lines and hue shift

After masking away most of the textures, go back to brush work. This step is for defining billowing forms and, in a larger size, calming down large shapes that serve as rest points for the eye.

One of my favorite brushes in Photoshop is created with an irregular shape at 19% Spacing, no texture, and just 3% Brightness, Saturation, and Hue Jitter under Color Dynamics. Previously, I've used many broad sponge-like atmospheric brushes, but my "key shift" brush is smaller and pressure-controlled with a nice forked tail to the stroke that still allows blending.

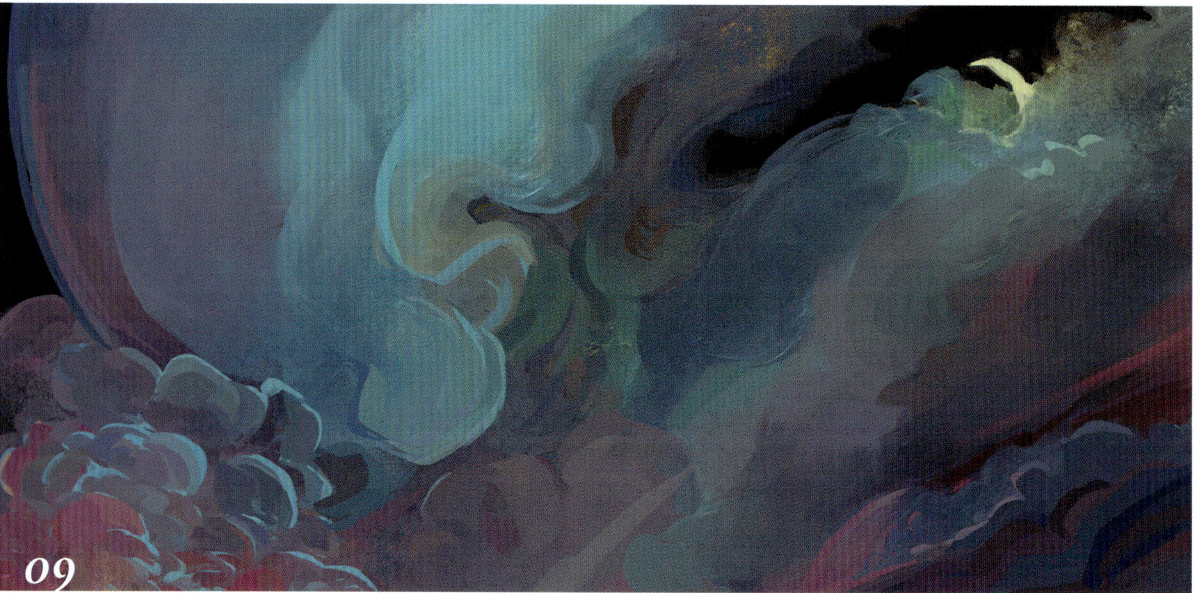

▲ Experimenting with Color Dynamics on any Photoshop brush is useful; happy accidents occur in colors as well as marks

10: Crisp versus flowing

At this stage you need to be aware of how every mark affects the whole composition. Use an Acrylic brush with very low viscosity and high wetness to make strokes that act like ink or smoke; use it to unify neighboring areas and bring fluidity to the bottom of the canvas. You don't want the viewer to be distracted unnecessarily so use a texture brush to add flecks along the

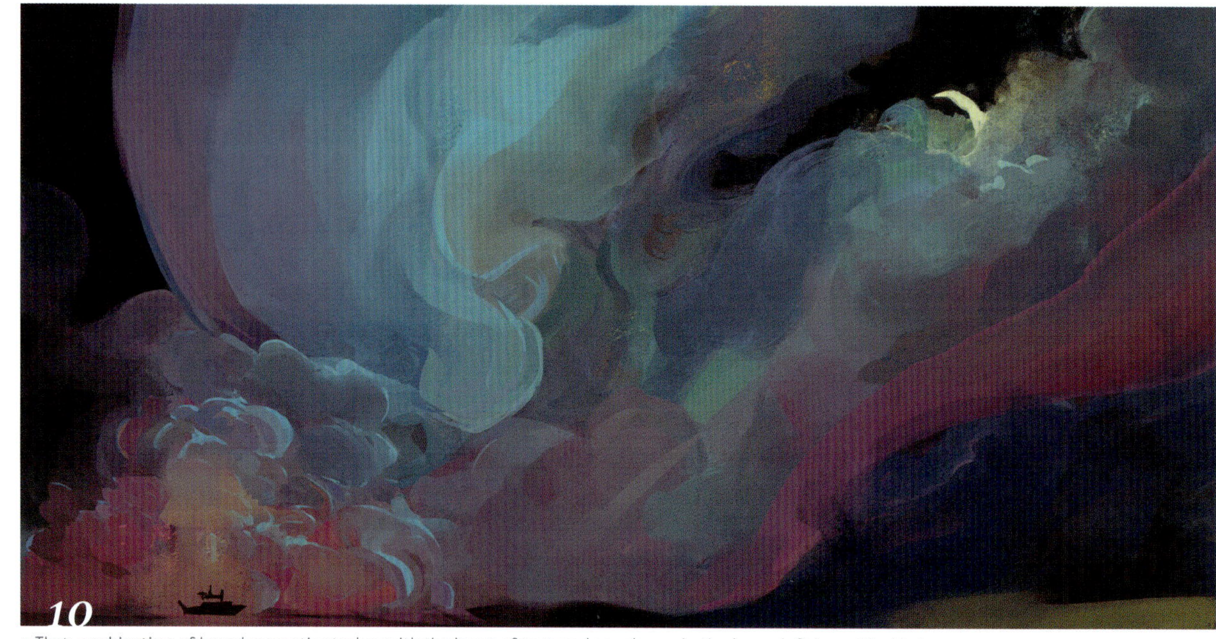

▲ That combination of broad romantic strokes with the burst of textured roughness in the lower left is my ideal balance

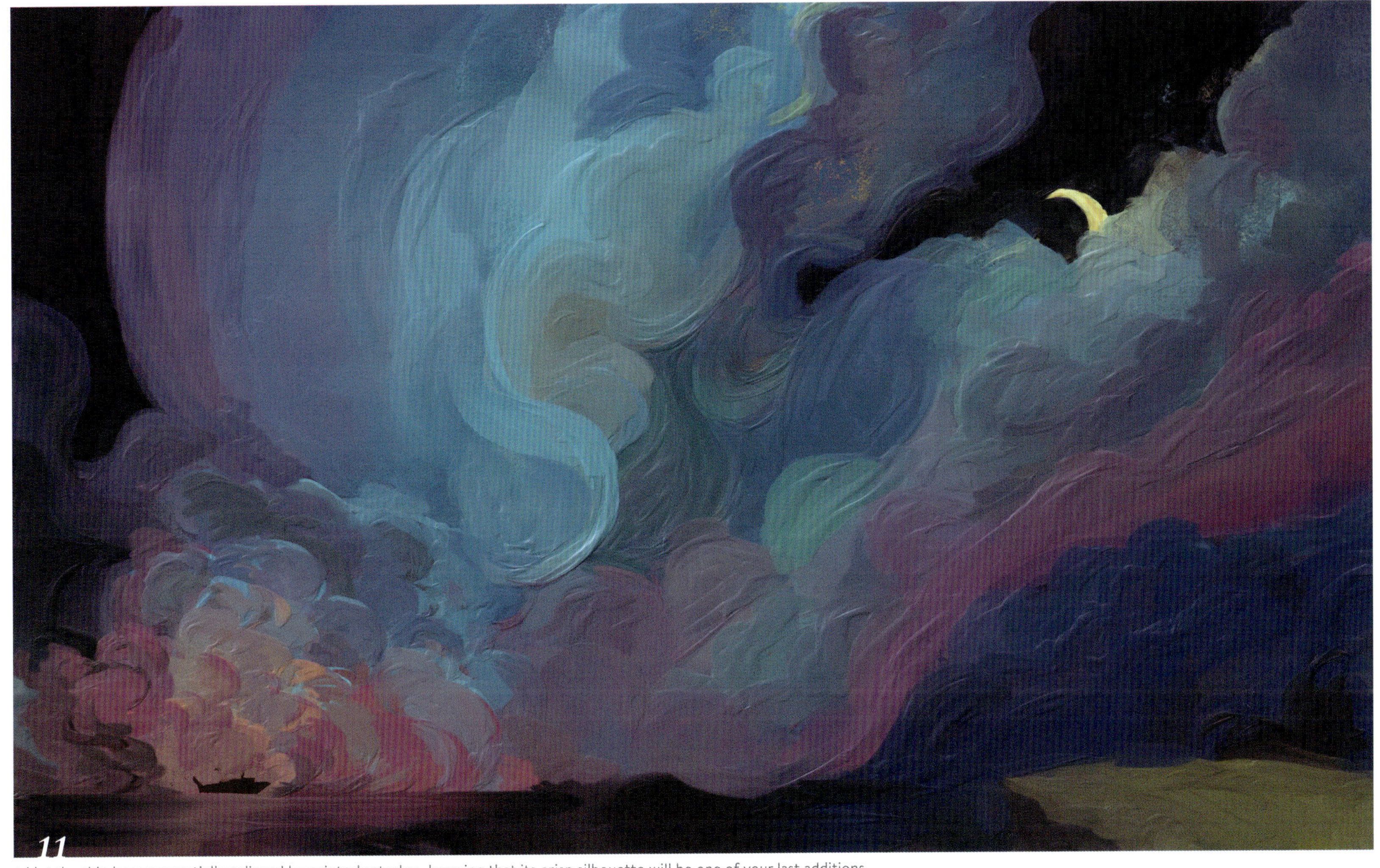

▲ I let the ship become partially eclipsed by painterly strokes, knowing that its crisp silhouette will be one of your last additions

line of interest (from the two points of focus). Add a silhouette of a little ship to tie the composition together.

11: Vibrancy

When you are happy with the overall composition you can then turn your focus to working on the mood and subtlety of the painting.

I find that an excellent tool to use at the end of a piece is Vibrance (which you can find in Layer > New Adjustment Layer in Photoshop). It really adds richness to your colors and atmosphere. An alternative method you can try is to incorporate another texture with very low opacity and set to Overlay; however, I want to add details by hand later in the process so I am going to ramp Vibrance up to +36 in this case.

"When you are happy with the overall composition you can then turn your focus to working on the mood and subtlety of the painting"

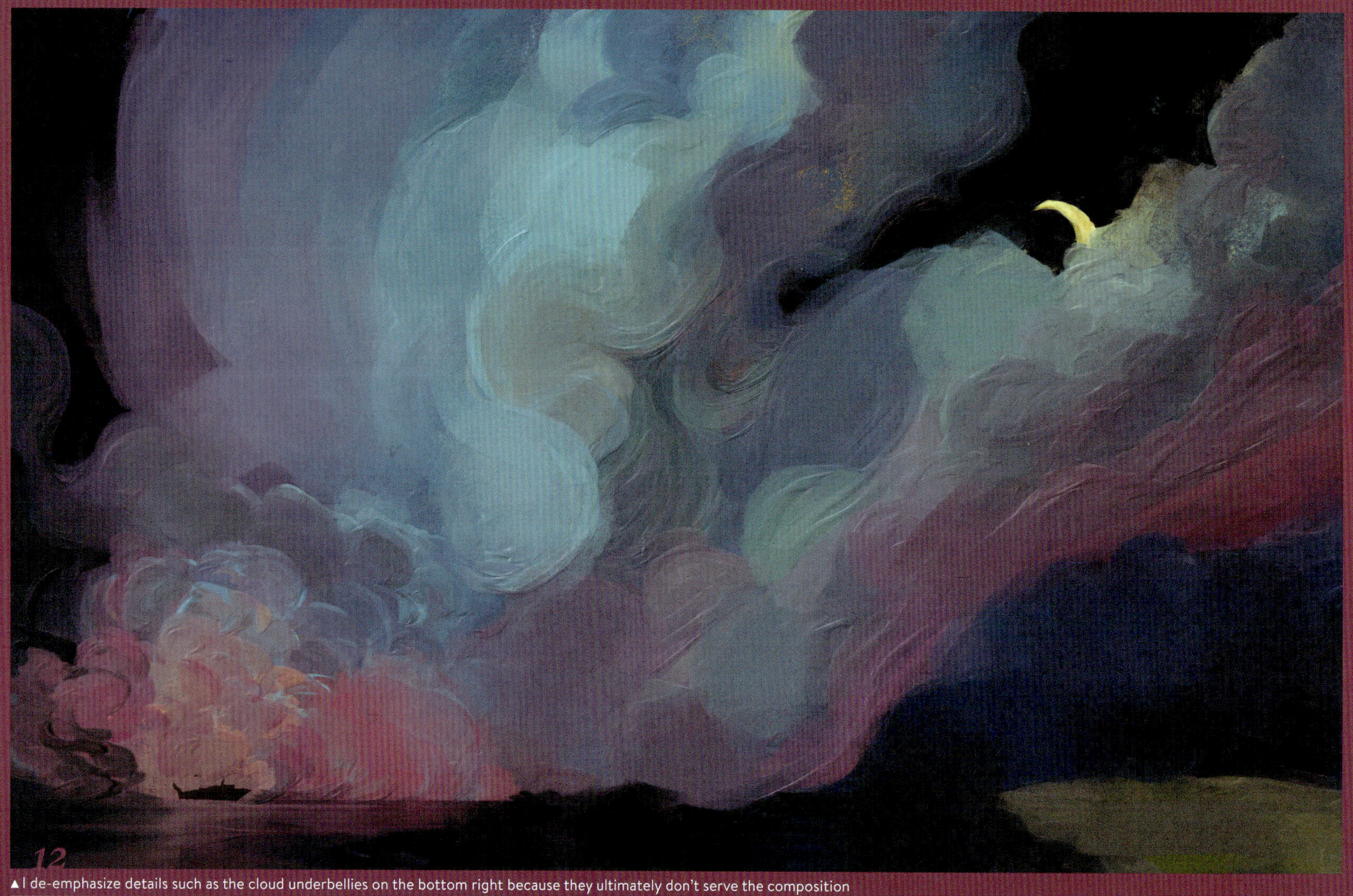

▲I de-emphasize details such as the cloud underbellies on the bottom right because they ultimately don't serve the composition

12: The Palette Knife returns

Head back into Painter to do one final pass with the Palette Knife Jitter tool. When we used the Palette Knife in step 05 we were going for energy and explosive movement; now the movements should be slower and more carefully measured in order to make the jagged edges of the strokes less distracting while you clean up the negative spaces and use the Color Picker to create subtle transitions in the billowing shapes.

13: Rhythm and shape variety

Now use the Magic Wand tool to select the newly cleaned-up negative spaces and transfer that selected area to the bottom layer (the preserved consolidation from a few steps ago that remained untouched). Simply copy and paste to create a ghost image with a low Fill percentage. On top of this bring in an imitation chalk or pastel brush to smooth over some of the rougher brushstrokes, as well as repeat shapes and break up others. This calms

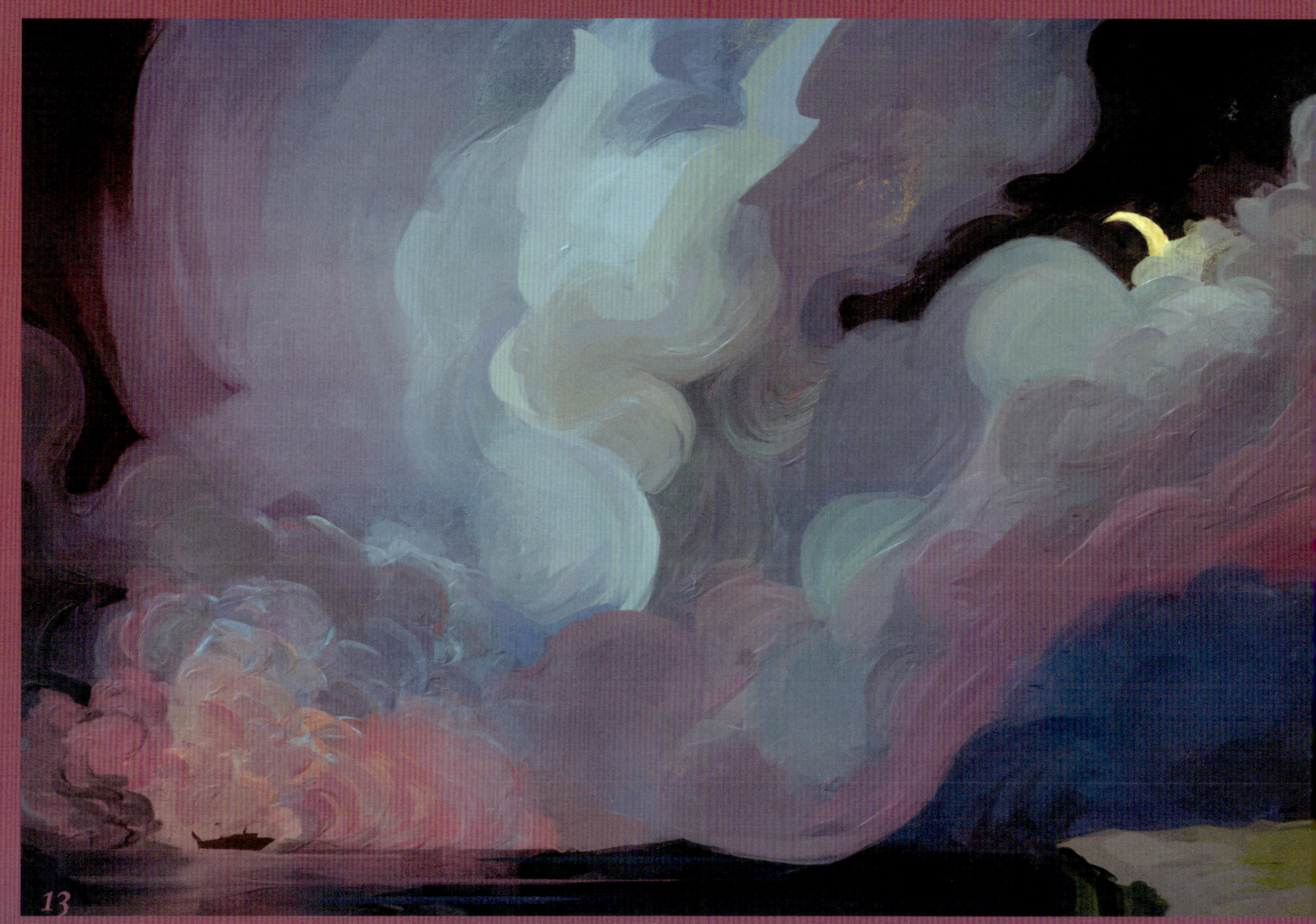

13

▲The lower purple shape is deceptively simple looking. I'll revise brushstrokes repeatedly until I hit the perfect simple curve

down "resting point" areas and brings a rhythm to chosen, repeating shapes.

If your shapes are a little too uniform at this stage you can always go back in with the "key shift" brush (step 09) to add in abstracted strokes that are more linear and serve as visual arrows.

You can also carve back into the negative space around the moon and maybe introduce some size difference between the cloud shapes. You might want to darken the bottom of the image and make it a horizontal plane, which will act as a counterbalance to the vertical and diagonal clouds.

14: Tweaks and final touches

Finally it's time to address the ship. Draw a very simple silhouette over the broken base from before. Set it to 59% Fill to de-emphasize this area of focus and make the ship recede into the billows behind it. If your image still looks a little too slick then you can add another layer of brightly colored chalk marks and mask it away to leave just a hint of texture. I now have a hard decision to make: do I keep the landmass in the lower-right corner or do away with it? I think I'll get rid of it to free the space as an area of stillness.

There are a few final touches we can make to really bring the composition to life. Add +30 Vibrance and use Painter's Bulge tool under the FX brush menu to warp the shape of the moon into a sharper, more elegant silhouette.

Also use the Acrylic tool to add another fluid rim of light to the little billowing forms on the bottom left, and add a little punch to the secondary focal point by using a subtle Airbrush set to Hard Light and 36% Fill.

Lastly add a subtle indigo Glow (another FX in Painter) to tie it all together and really exaggerate the mysterious atmosphere.

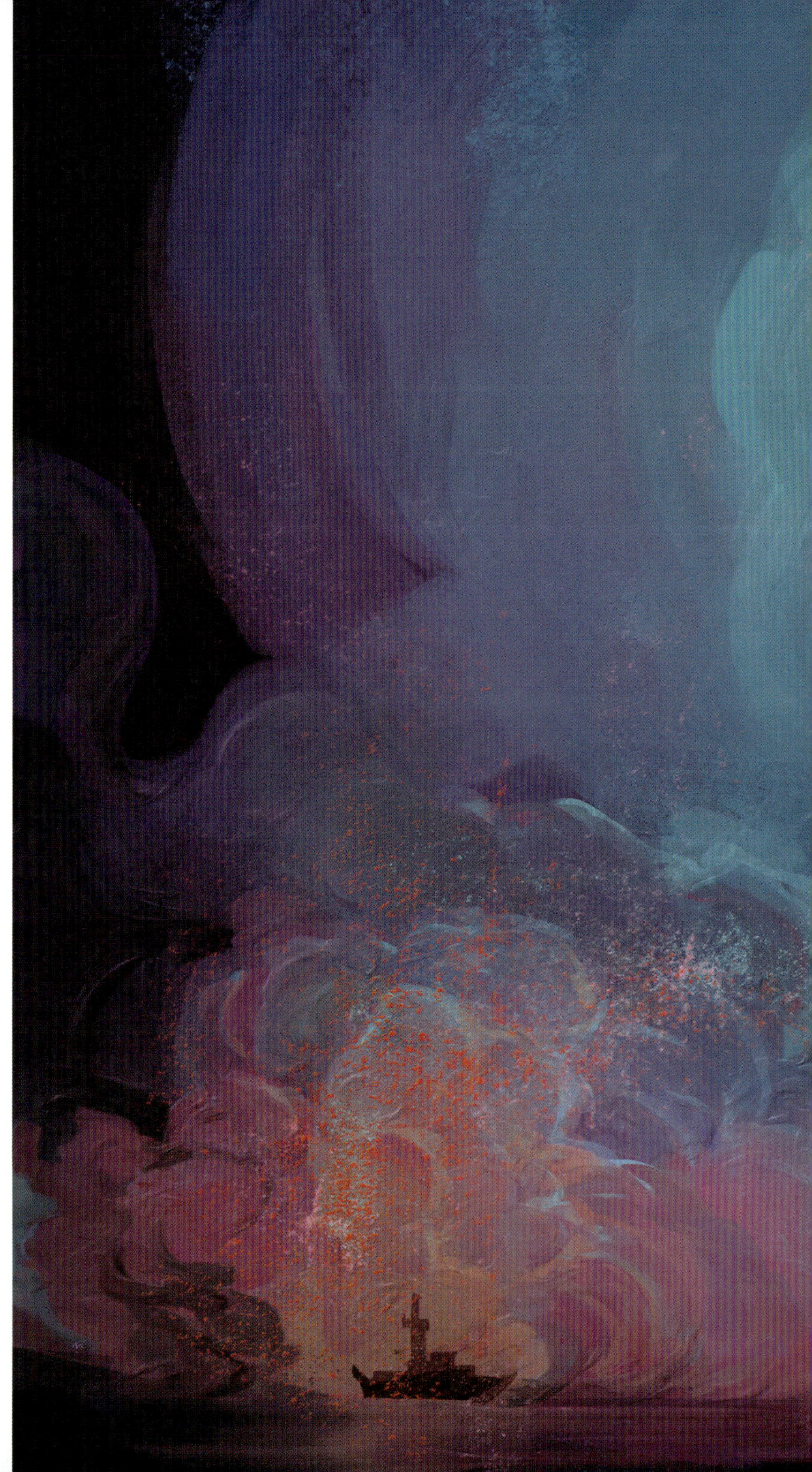

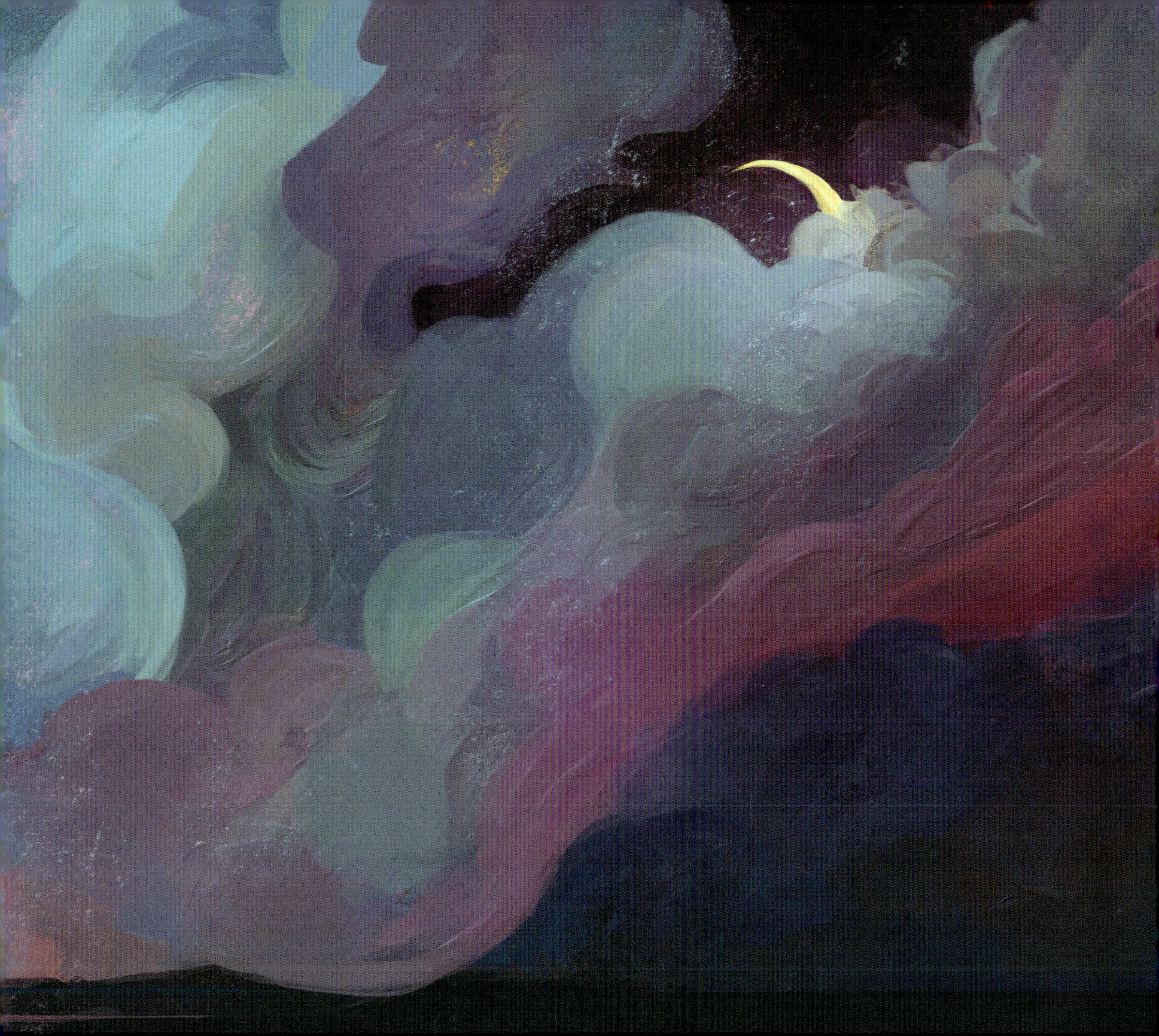

FANTASY: THE DOME

by Ioan Dumitrescu

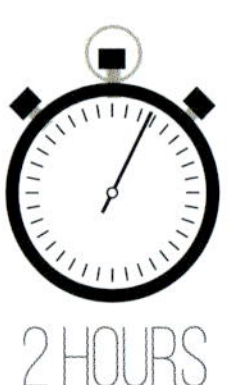

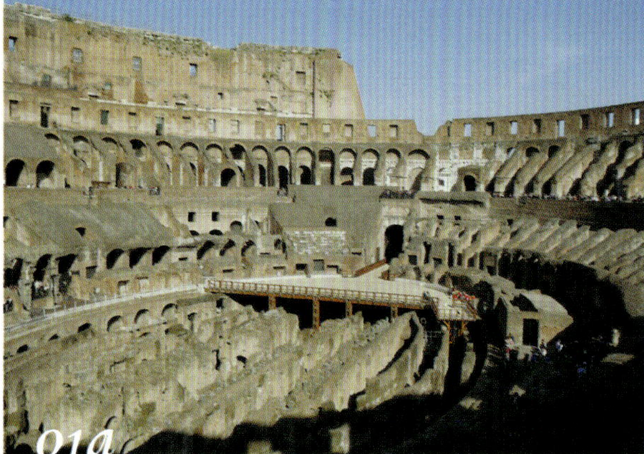

▲Find source references that fit with your intended theme

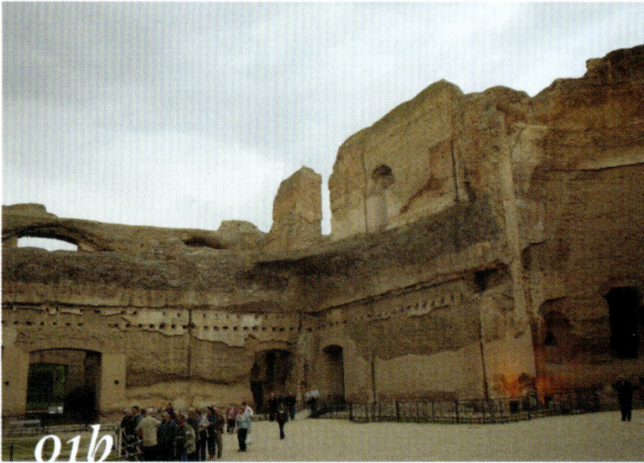

▲References will help you select the color and lighting

I usually start speed-painting exercises with a couple of ideas already in mind, and for this piece I have gone with ancient times, fallen civilizations, and how I can show a central meeting ground left to become dust after the civilization has gone!

I start this speed painting with the antiquity of enormous amphitheaters, spas, and historic public buildings where people gathered around to watch epic spectacles and cheer their favorite gladiators. Speed paints are a great way to train your eye in composition, light, and color. Following a time frame, in this case of only two hours, makes you think about what is important, conscious of your decisions, and consider what you can do in order to finish on time.

01: Source references

This speed painting is based on the ancient world and you will therefore need to gather references to help with recreating the architecture and constructions of a fallen civilization. I use my own photos taken on a trip to Rome as references (**images 01a–1c**).

Spend some time looking at how the huge structures were built without the benefits of modern building methods. Although they have deteriorated over time, many of the

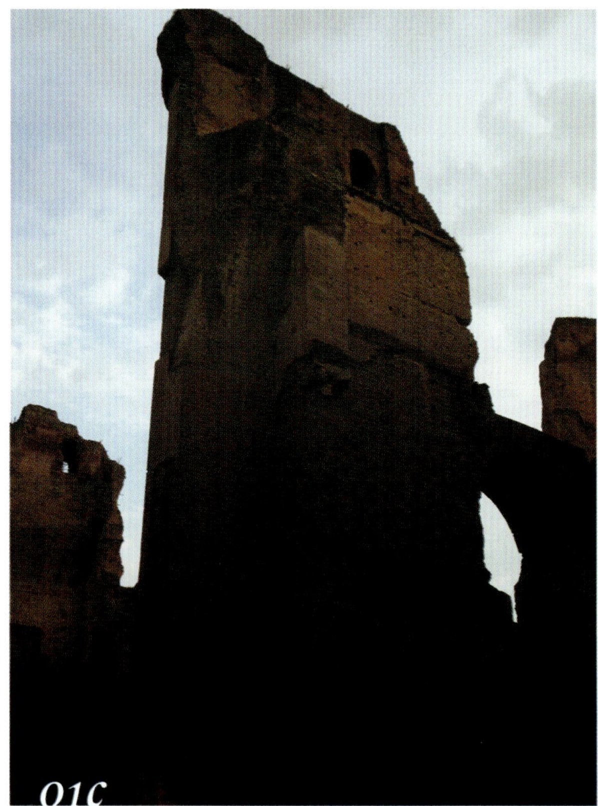

▲They can also provide some interesting shapes for your scene

structures are still standing. Scale is a very important factor in this painting and so things will need to be simplified because time is of the essence.

02: Create basic color

Using the references you can put down some big shapes for the color sketch. I go for one of those late spring afternoons with beautiful cyan skies and when the sunlight is very crisp and clean. I want to create a coliseum-esque structure with a huge dome that has crumbled away in places, as well as some ruins in which some people might still dwell.

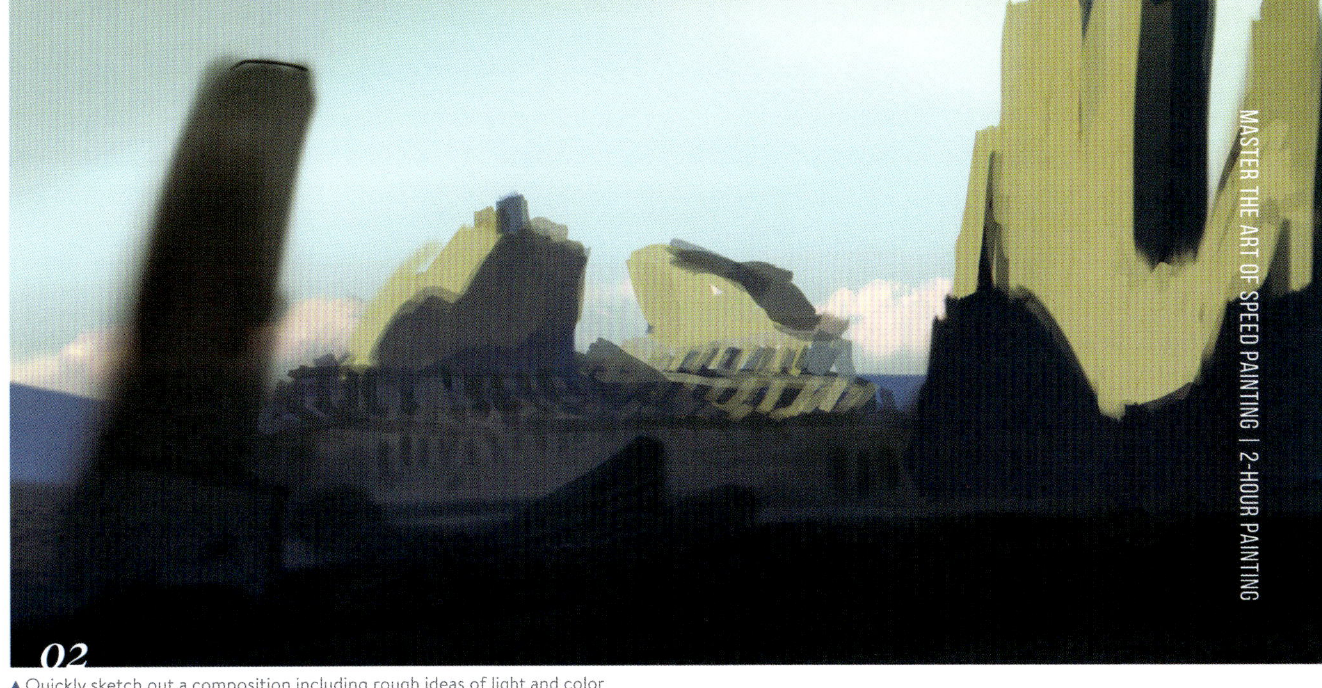

▲ Quickly sketch out a composition including rough ideas of light and color

Put in a basic ground texture and adjust the values and color to imply a shadowed land – you can add a few large ruins towards the foreground. Make sure the light hits the big dome in the background. The colors give the whole scene a desert-like feel. You can also add some long-abandoned and ruined boats in the foreground. They could act as a reminder of a time when this place might have had a lush landscape filled with rivers and oceans, and small docks lining the banks of the long-gone waterways. Maybe along the arena there was a huge market place!

03: Add some references

You can make use of the references you collected by dragging them in and adjusting the colors until they fit the scene. Try to let the base color bleed through the blues and yellows; this will help you to achieve a more realistic look in the end.

Now you can start to define the composition and spatial layout of the scene and objects. I don't think my first sketch is epic enough so I scale things up to take over the canvas and overwhelm the viewer. Try to find cool shapes for the ruins and create their shadows because the play between light and dark is very important for the whole composition. If you want to go for a painterly but real look, you will need to cover up most of the references – but don't let the references dictate what the image will be.

Use the time constraint to your advantage and try to create mystery, to actually let the viewer fill in the details

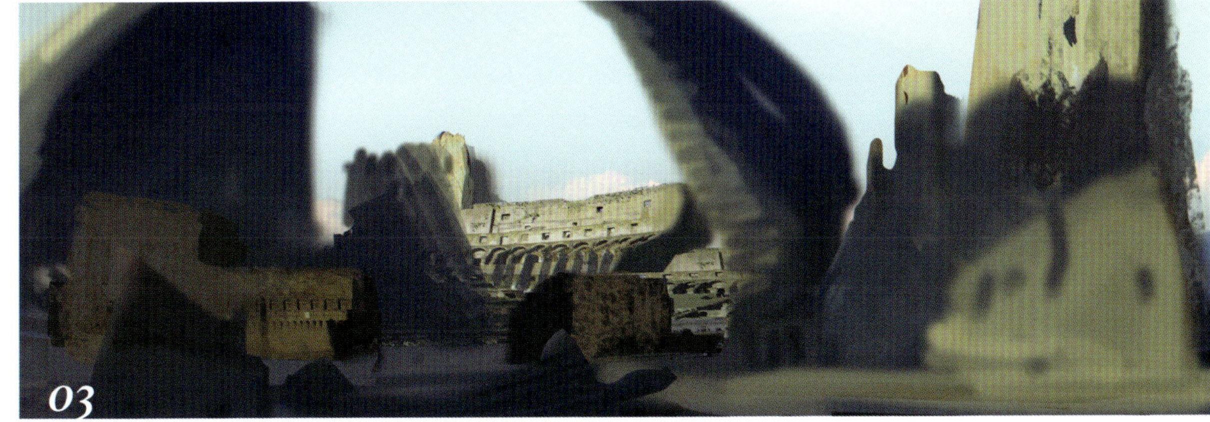

▲ Adding references to your sketch is a quick way to build up the image

and information. The ruins become screens, showing only snapshots of what is behind them – a glimpse of what the world was and how beautiful it must have been. I certainly look for evocative images in my work, images that speak out to the viewer and play on their emotions.

04: Add interest

At this stage of a painting I flip the image horizontally and vertically; I don't hold on to anything in it because otherwise things can become too forced; I want the image to flow naturally.

So, the scene is starting to build up and you can add more textures and play with the colors. Maybe add in a bit more of the red brick with dark saturated blues and columns and arches on top of the coliseum – hinting at multiple levels and what could lie beyond it. I decide to break up the mass on the right-middle ground, so the eye is encouraged to slow down towards the edge of the frame, rest, and then go back following the shadow and light play.

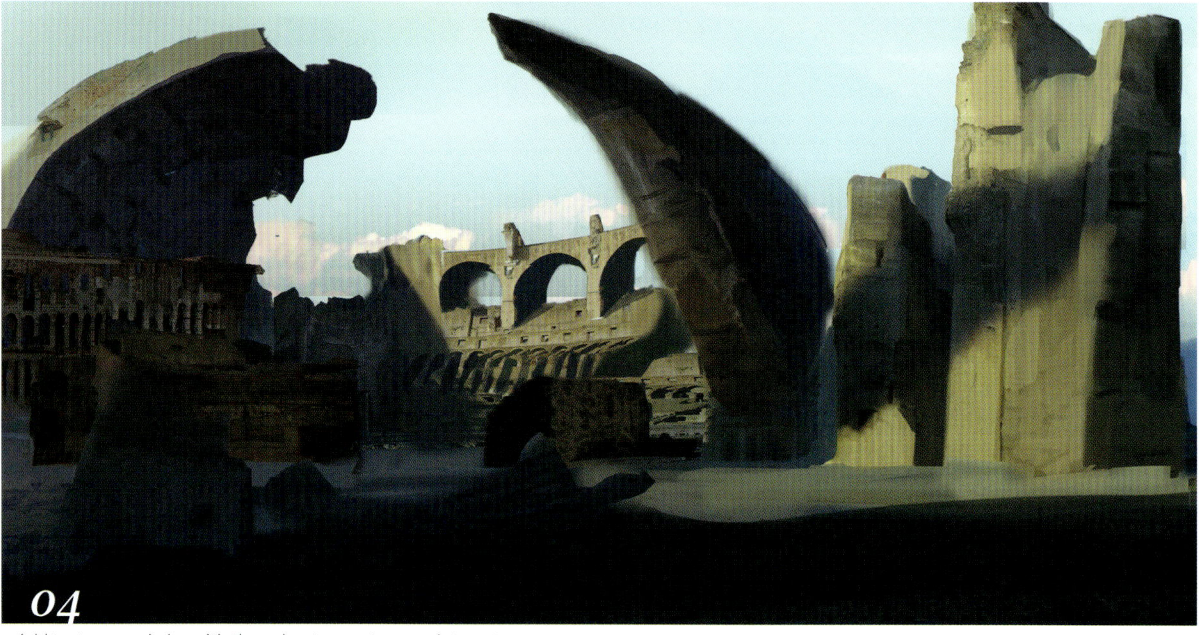

▲ Add textures and play with the colors to create more interest

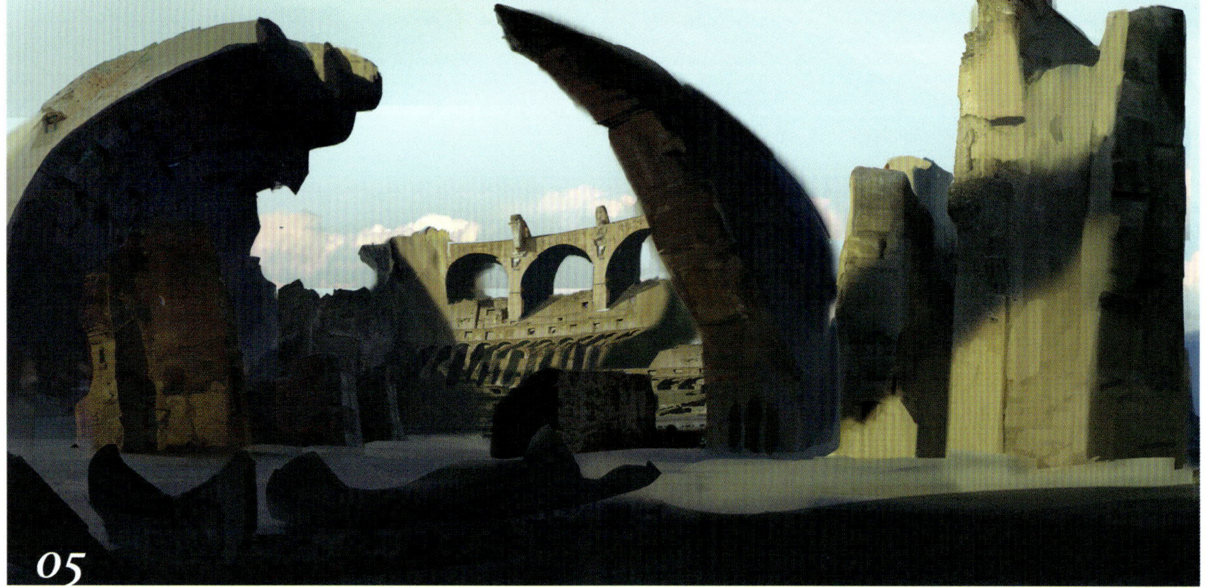

▲ Add depth to the ruins and check the scale of the image

05: Refine structural shapes

You need to be careful that some of the buildings don't ruin the scale; I feel that the group of buildings on the left is blocking the background view and is too flat for my liking – they may have worked to show a circle perimeter but that isn't what I am going for. I therefore decide to cut through it and place three pillar-like structures that might have supported the building before the dome crashed.

In **image 05** you can see that there are a lot of warm browns to reflect the desert setting and also to show off the ambience from a streak of light on the ground, leading to the structures on the right of the middle ground.

06: Seek structural realism

The sharp break in the ruin of the dome is defying gravity and scale a bit so it needs to be changed to be something more massive and solid. That way it will have real weight and reflect the extreme forces that this building had to support in the past (**image 06a**). Collapsing domes are very common throughout history as domes are an incredibly difficult architectural feature to master. They only reached their full potential in buildings such as the Pantheon and Saint Peter's Basilica.

Add masts to the ships to further block the edge of the frame and, with the help of the broken dome, draw the focus on what matters in the image. You can see in **image 06b** how the composition leads the viewer's eye around the image.

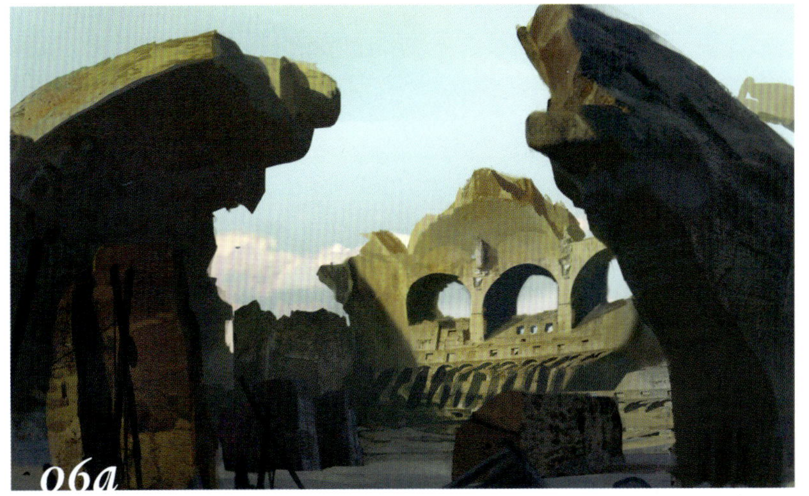

▲ Build up the broken dome so that it looks like a structure that might have physically existed

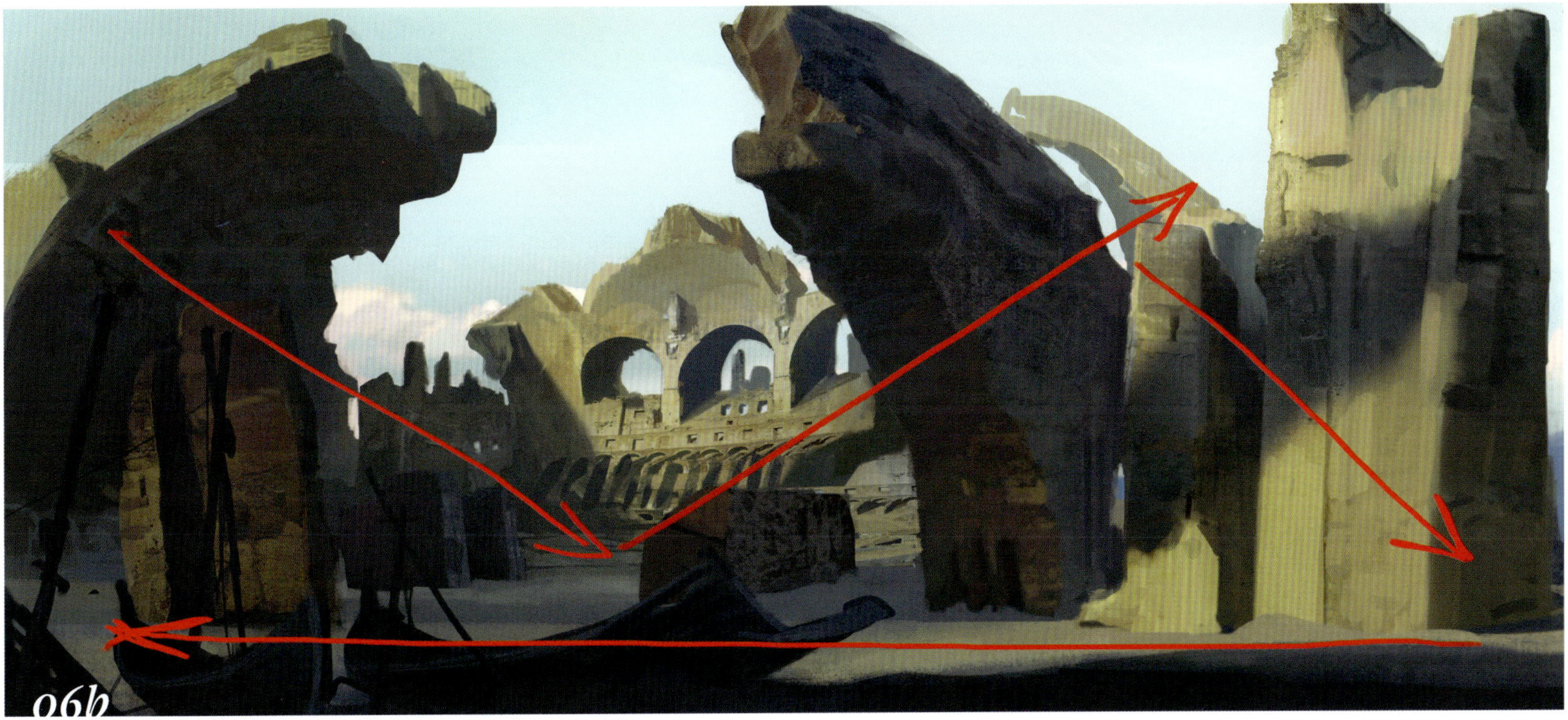

06b

▲ The red lines show how the viewer's eye will travel around the image

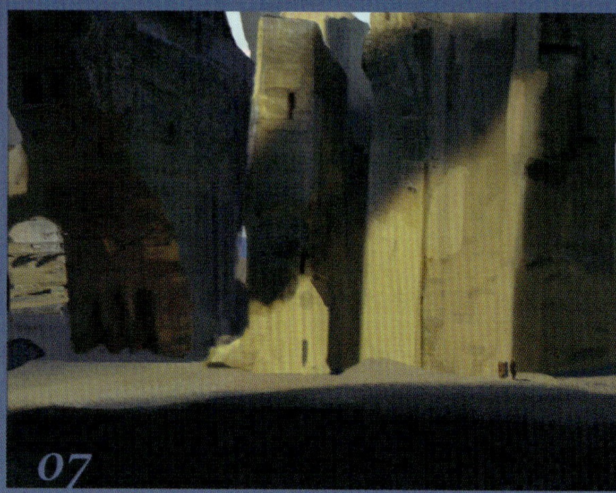

▲ Adding two tiny people near the lower right side of the image provides a sense of scale

07: Add people for scale

Now it's time to add some tiny humans to the image at the bottom edge of the middle-ground structure. Adding a few characters will really show off the epic scale of the surroundings. I group my characters together having a discussion, completely oblivious to their surroundings as if they are nothing special to them – it is a sad fact that humans often have a tendency to not appreciate the great things that are around them.

Continue to add further details along the dome structure and bring certain parts that are of interest in to focus; those that aren't can recede into the shadows.

08: Finishing touches

This is when you can add a few final touches to spice the image up. The lit portion of the middle-ground structure is a bit too similar to the background. To add more of an atmosphere to the piece you could make the light a bit more filtered and use darker red tones. You can do this on the ground as well – this could be from all the red bricks basically turning to dust over the eons.

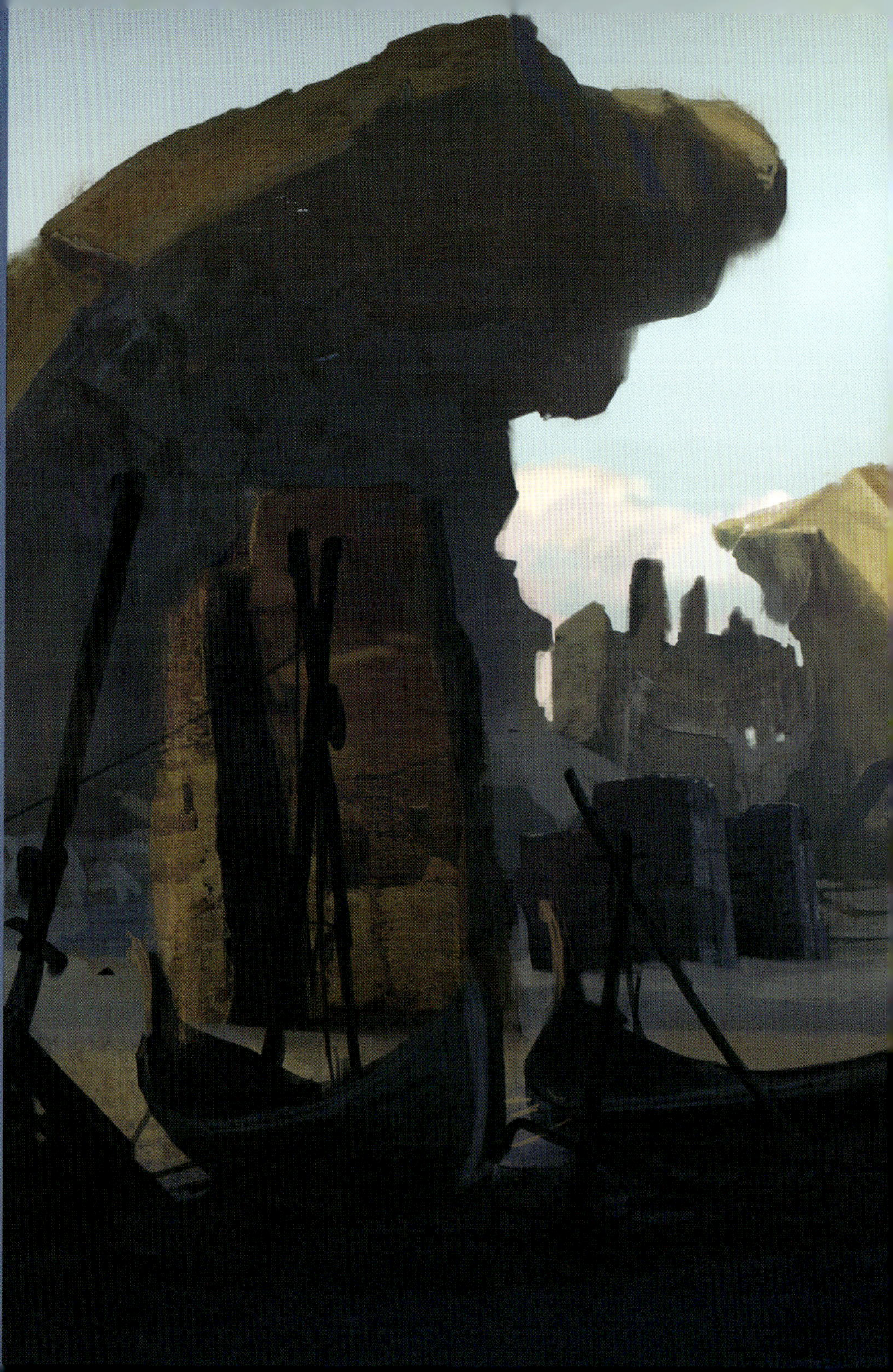

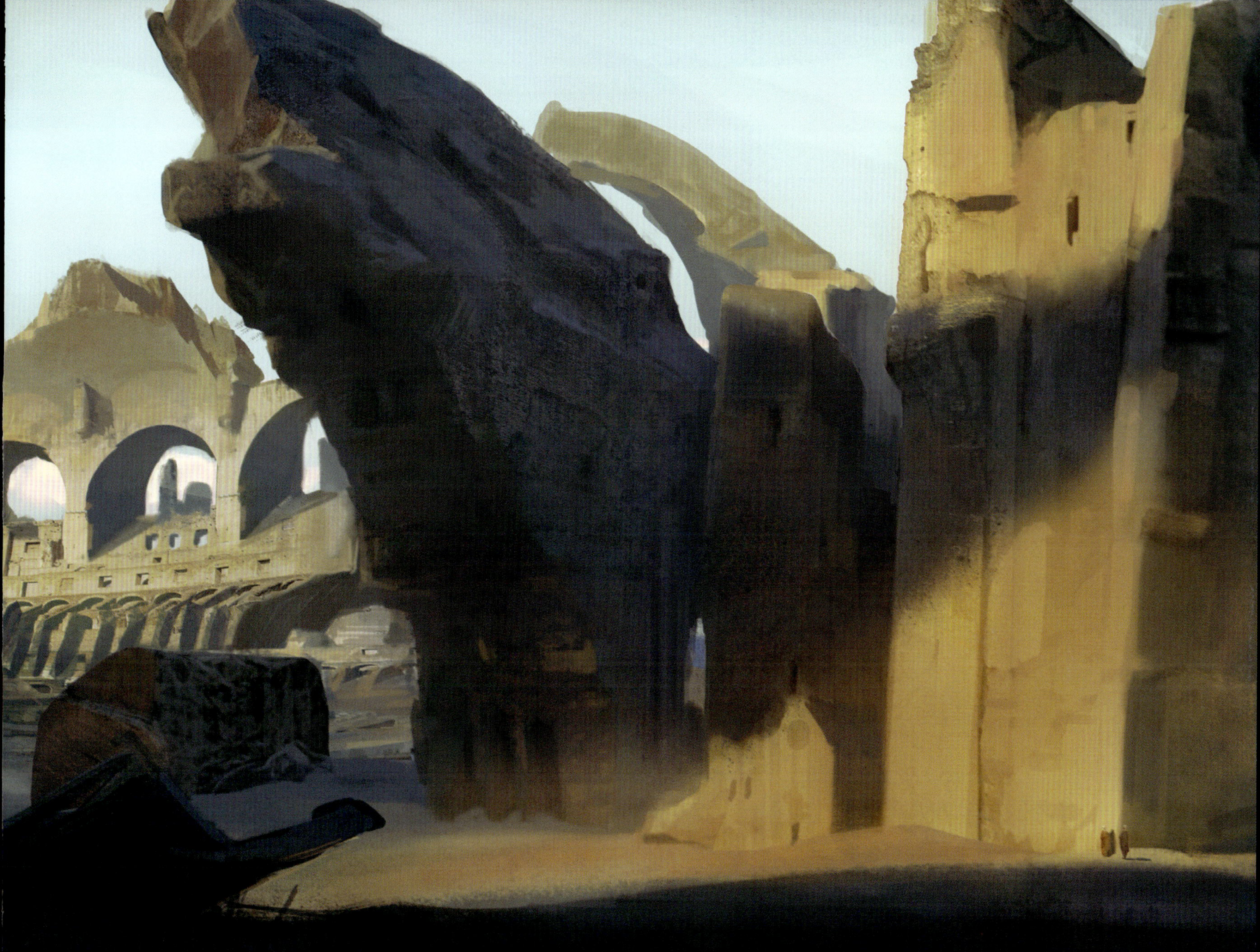

FANTASY: SERENITY
by Ioan Dumitrescu

In this tutorial we will paint another historical fantasy landscape, but this time the painting will be set in a universe with little correlation to human history. I create for myself a tale of magical lands, with materials bent to the will of man in ways that are only imaginable.

Here I want to show that you don't need to use subject-related photo references for your ideas. What you need is to just let yourself see things; allow your imagination to dictate the terms and follow your instincts and you will come up with ideas that you did not think of at first.

For all of this, patience is essential. Do not be overwhelmed by a blank canvas or a lack of ideas. Instead try to see them as an advantage, or as an opportunity for the unexpected! Taking chances and accepting failure is the only way to learn. Spending two hours to try to

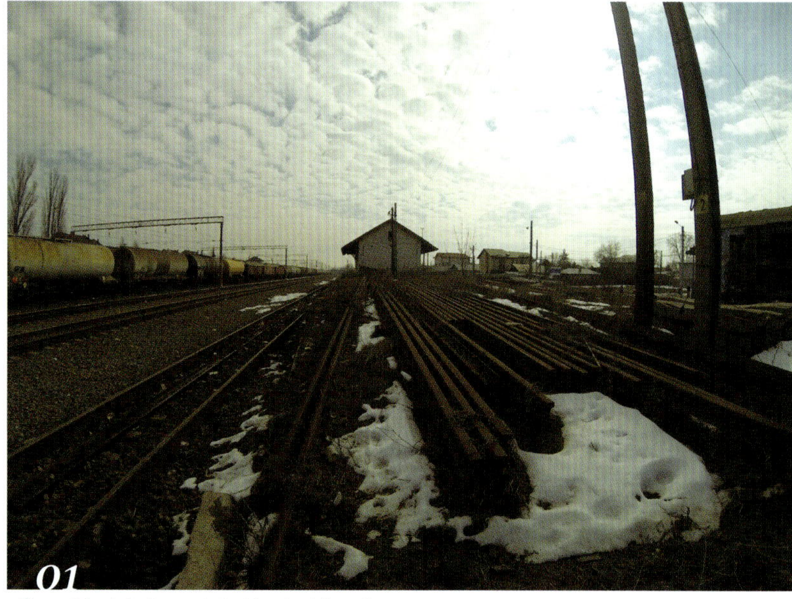

▲ The original photograph that inspired *Serenity*

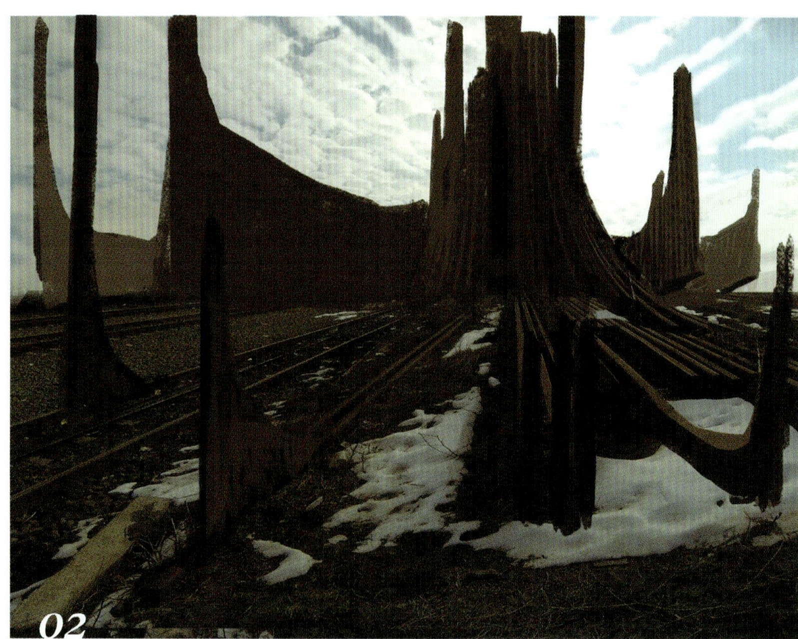

▲ Once an idea has been settled on and a reference has been chosen, start painting!

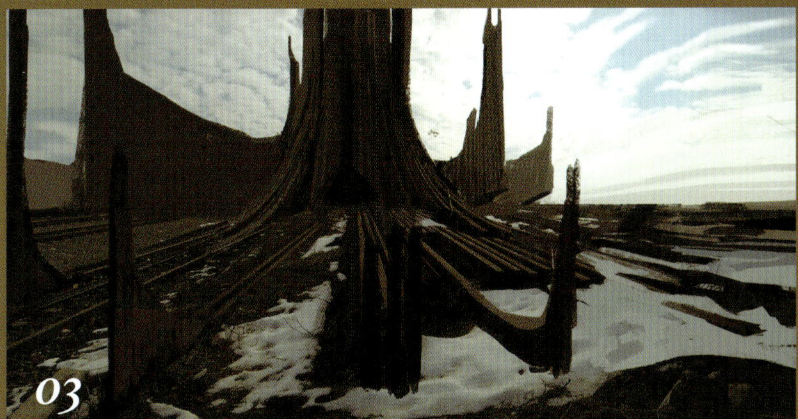

▲ Enlarge the canvas to the right to stop the scene becoming overcrowded

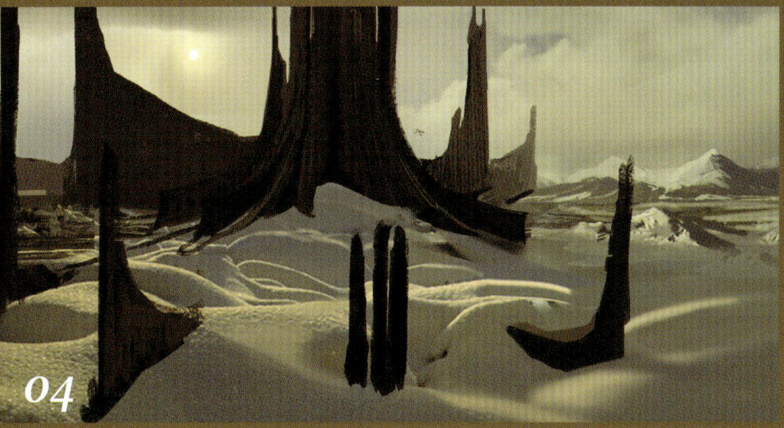

▲ To give a sense of serenity the sky is changed and snow is added to the ground

explore the many potential ways to express a mood or a feeling through your image is definitely worth it!

01: Find a reference

For this tutorial I don't start with looking at a specific reference, I just scroll through my own images to see if I can find anything to inspire myself. I quickly see a cool photo of a railway, and the tracks laid aside after being changed.

What I like is the feeling it gives me, a scarce serene environment, and the rusted tracks make up a cool pattern. The picture was taken with a tiny GoPro camera, ideal for keeping in your pocket for the time when something comes up in your daily walks.

02: Start painting!

You can start painting immediately, sampling in the colors and keeping to the image's current perspective for now. I start imagining a huge citadel of steel. I interpret the lines towards the camera and on the sides as the structural foundation for the citadel, "feeding" off the ground and into the skies. To add to this deserted land you could also make it menacing and abandoned, while still conveying a past shadow of its former self.

03: Enlarge the canvas

I notice that I have crowded a few too many elements into the scene so I enlarge the canvas to the right to make way for further development. Nothing can restrict me here. You could consider the sketch done at this stage as far as the idea goes. But we have two hours to make it more interesting, so we shall see what can be found.

04: Alter the atmosphere

I feel that the image at this point is a bit too muddy for my intent. In the end I want an epic yet peaceful look. To do this you can keep the structure as the main element of contrast and work around it. The scale has to be huge, but we will sort this at the end. Change the sky to more of a sunset look, full of clouds and mist.

Looking back at the original photo, I realize snow would make a great choice to fill the field with. I choose an old mobile shot of some snow in the winter for this. I bring it across and cover the structure and the fields. What I like about the photo are the shapes of the piled snow, so I change the tones and colors to fit the environment. Think of an environment that sort of meshes with the sky, unifying the serenity of it all.

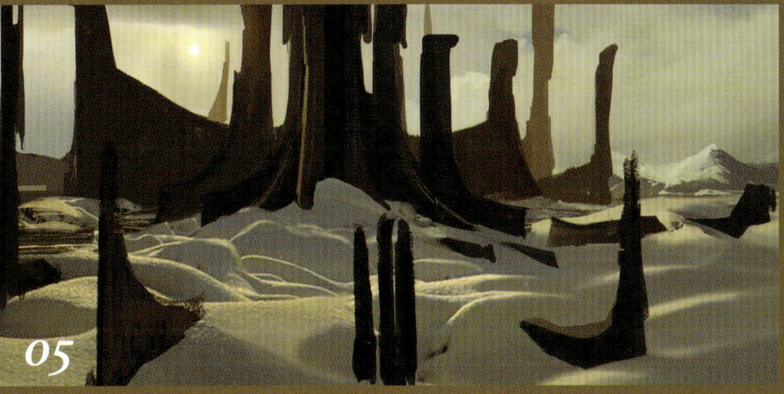

▲ Refine the shapes to improve the connection between the structures and the ground

05: Refine the shapes

Now it's time to refine the shapes. The scene needs to represent something a bit

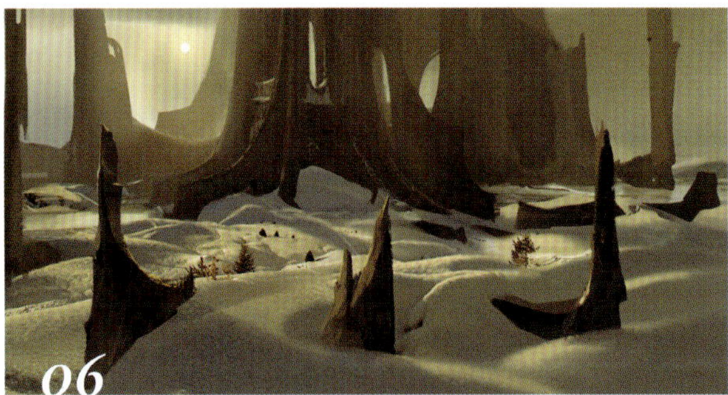

▲Add to the atmosphere by playing with the sunlight and mist

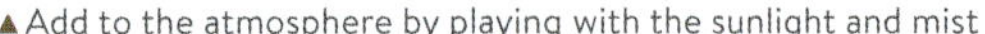

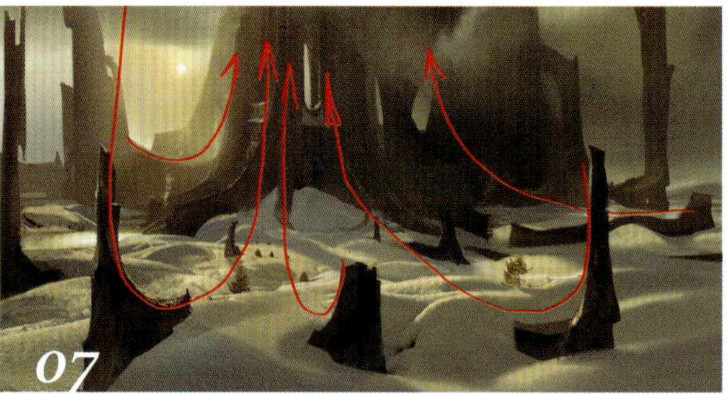

▲The shapes in the foreground help to direct the viewer's eye

less abstract, which will be a challenge. Don't pressure yourself too much. What I manage to solve is enough. If you hit a creative wall, move on to something else and see if you can solve something there instead. When you feel more confident go back to the first problem you had.

For now these pillar-like structures around a central core do not do it for me. Maybe in another situation it would have worked. Try to connect the structures better to the ground and snow, further refining shapes here and there.

06: Adjust the structure and add to the atmosphere

I begin arranging the main structure, suggesting an immense citadel of metal. Once you get a good silhouette going, puncture it to give it more depth and scale. Go ahead and put in atmosphere to further separate the structures from one another.

Things definitely need a bit more atmosphere so try playing with the sun and the mist to give a richer feeling to the piece. Adding small highlights, ridges, and pieces of metal that catch the light will give more volume. Laying snow on top of the extrusions helps with perspective and further polishes the volume.

07: Direct the viewer's eye

Further polishing of the snow on the ground and the protruding metal pillars helps the eye to home in on the main central structure of the scene. Now the composition is in place and we've marked the main lines, the viewer's eye will follow the curves around the image. They block the borders and focus on the center of the image. The fragments coming out of the snow recede into the distance and help suggest the huge scale of things. The atmosphere helps with this as well, so I add in clouds of mist towards the top to engulf the citadel.

08: Imply scale and finish!

Now it is time for the final details. The best way to show the relative scale of things is to place a human being. I place several wandering warriors, heading towards the citadel. They help to tell a story and engage the audience into believing what's happening. They are also something the viewer can associate themselves with.

Another thing I watch for at this stage is the hard edges and soft edges of things. The flow of composition is helped by the variation of these, letting the eye rest and move along. You'll notice this clearly on the left side of the citadel, around the sharp sun, around the soft forms of the clouds, and around the main structure. Below the citadel there are sharp edges. Soft marks in the snow also indicate wind gusts taking snow with them.

The symmetry of the foreground pillars is bothering me, so I enlarge the right one. Balance doesn't always need to come from equality and symmetry. It's all about balancing the big with the small, left and right, across all of the image. You should always try to keep a good rhythm and flow to everything, to allow the viewer's eye to smoothly move around the image to get the best view.

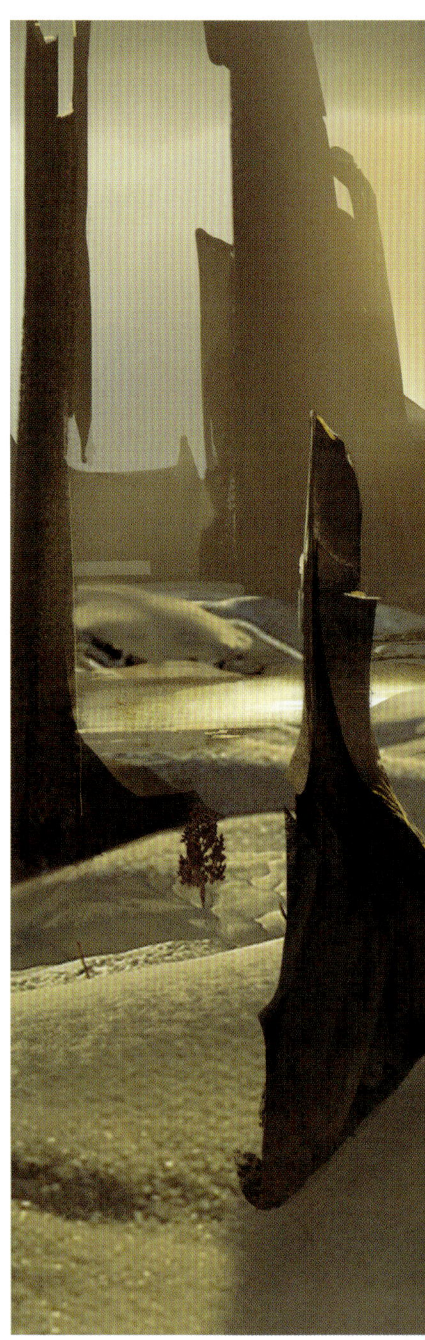

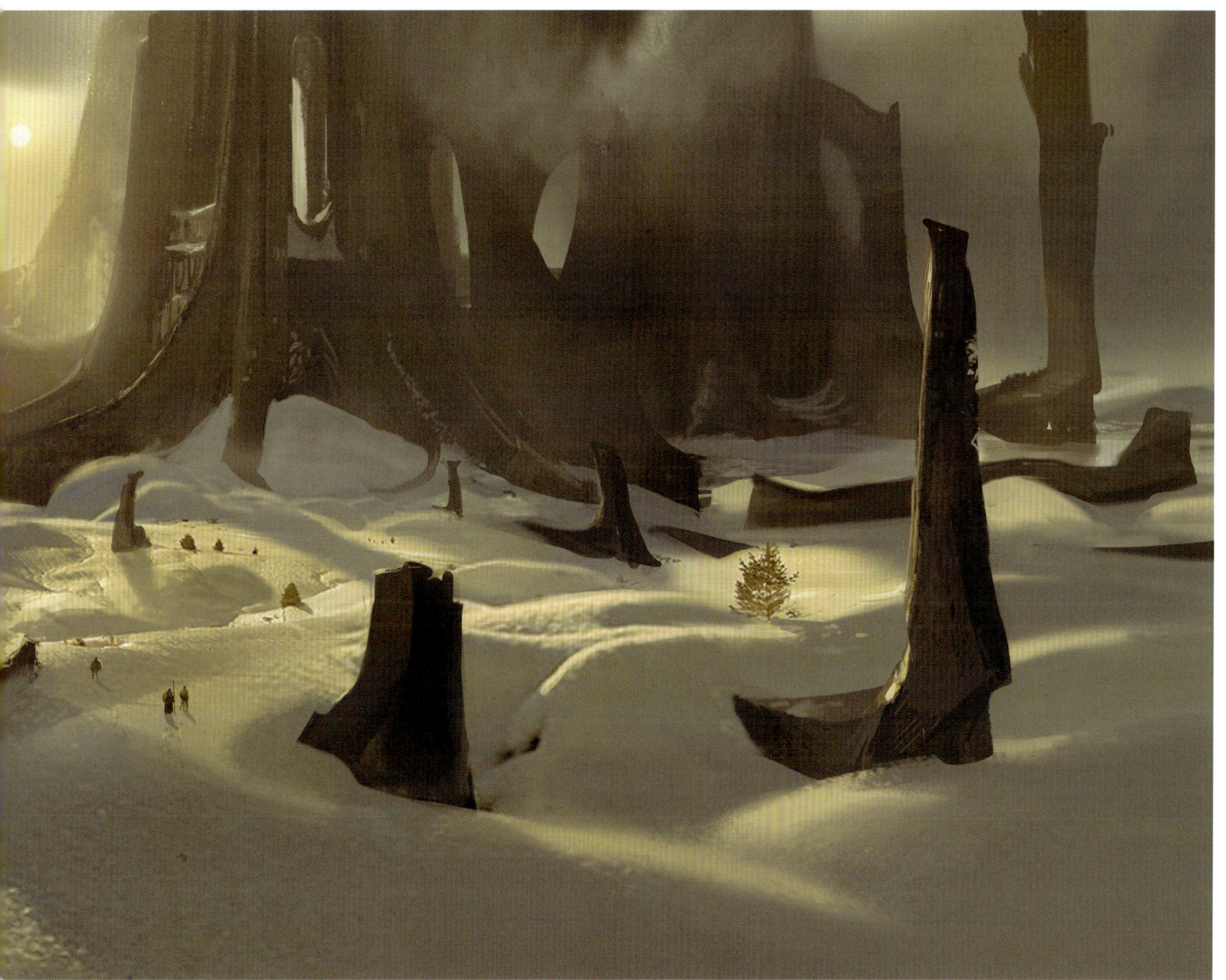

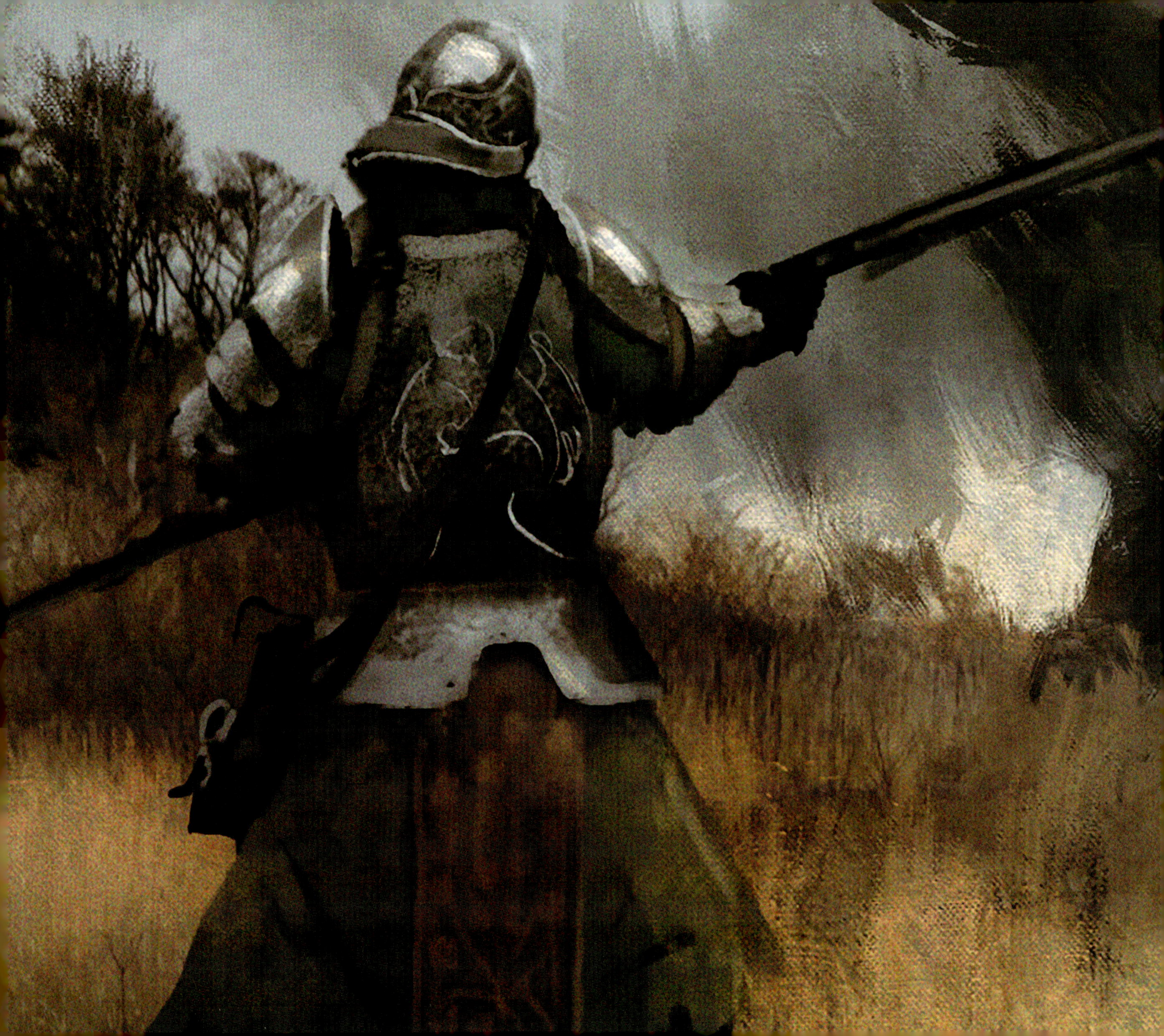

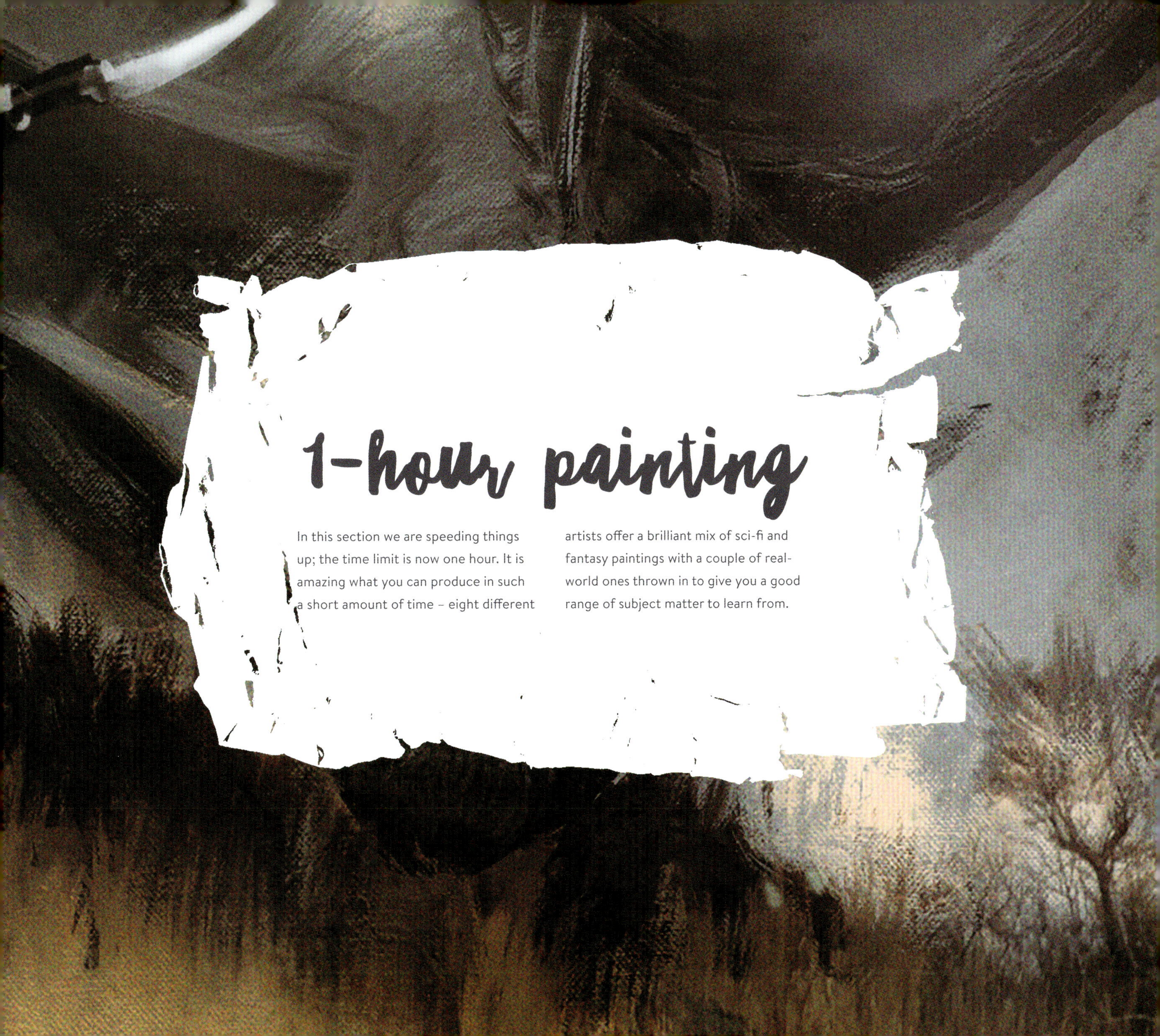

1-hour painting

In this section we are speeding things up; the time limit is now one hour. It is amazing what you can produce in such a short amount of time – eight different artists offer a brilliant mix of sci-fi and fantasy paintings with a couple of real-world ones thrown in to give you a good range of subject matter to learn from.

1 HOUR

SCI-FI: FORGOTTEN EXPLORERS

by Florian Aupetit

Speed painting is a useful tool for finding a mood for an illustration and to speed up your productivity. But it is mainly a kind of sketch or study for a future and better painting. This tutorial will guide you through the speed-painting process. I will share my personal three-step workflow which will hopefully give you another way of working. The time limit for this painting is one hour and the genre is sci-fi. It will not be a heavily technical tutorial as some of the emphasis will be on the pre-production and thought processes behind the painting. I will also share a few tips during the speed-painting process.

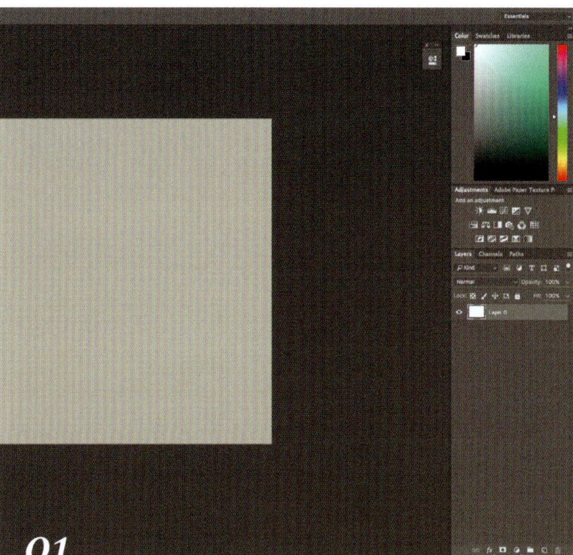

▲ Build a clean interface with only the tools you need, especially if you work on a small screen

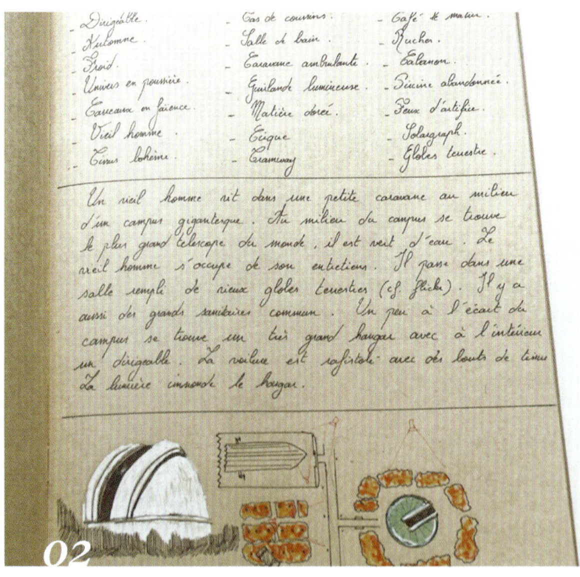

▲ Here is my three-step workflow. I really try to work hard on narration and develop all the background stories

Science fiction
Greenish blue
Scale
Hidden world
~~Deep space~~
Cold
~~Aseptic~~
Discovery
~~Alien~~
Explorers
Shuttle
~~Black hole~~

03

▲ This first step aims to collect your objectives in just a few words, so it helps us to avoid becoming lost in too many ideas

04/26/2410.

Back on Earth and after months of hard work a team of scientists and explorers have finally found our ancestors.

28.626572 -80.620543

04

▲ Pitch your painting; try to describe it in a couple of sentences. Create a little universe for your character(s) or environment

"Having a solid workflow is essential to increase your productivity. I've developed my own three-step workflow by learning from my mistakes. It helps to add a narrative to your work"

01: Set up the interface

Setting up your interface is a crucial part of any speed painting because having easy and fast access to what you need saves time. Knowing as many shortcuts as possible (especially for the primary tools) is also important; that's why the first thing I do is hide the Tool panel in Photoshop.

Only keep what you really need. I have the Color Picker in the top right and below it the Adjustments toolbar, and finally below that the Layers palette. This may not be the ideal interface but it's the most effective for me; your interface has to reflect your workflow.

02: Three-step workflow

Having a solid workflow is essential to increase your productivity. I've developed my own three-step workflow by learning from my mistakes. It helps to add a narrative to your work. I usually use it for illustrations or concept art but you can apply it to speed painting or any type of picture you have to produce (however here some of the process will be mental; if you have any spare time try putting your ideas on paper and write down details for each of the steps).

03: 1 - Keywords

The first step is "Keywords." Start by thinking of words that relate to your topic or theme. The easiest way to find your story is to write a couple of random words related to the theme. For now, try not to visualize the image but think of what you would like to create in the next hour. This could be a color, feeling, place, or object.

You will hopefully now have an idea of what it is that you want to paint. You can delete any words that are useless or irrelevant.

04: 2 - Story

For me the most important part of any picture (no matter what the technique or medium used) is the narrative it shows the viewer. A good question to ask yourself is "why?" Why this picture? Why did I choose this story instead of another one?

The choices I made in the previous step show that my story is about spaceships, a cold environment, and a discovery. Generally I like to write a short story of what the painting will show; if I had more time now I would write several versions to find the right one. For this painting we have a team of explorers who have traveled far to find their ancestors.

05: 3 - Location

Now it's time to decide on a location in which to set your story. My story is set on Earth, which is completely covered in snow and ice (perhaps during a bitter ice age). The main focus is a rocket buried deep in a huge cave made of greenish ice. To help you figure out your camera angle you should take the time to make a couple of quick sketches showing the scene from a few different angles.

06: Environmental references

One of my favorite parts of the process is finding reference images. As the story is set in a cold and icy environment you'll need to look for references of ice and ice-caves such as ones in Iceland and pictures of flipped icebergs. Try to find some references that show how the sunlight reacts with the walls of ice.

07: Find the rocket

I am a huge fan of space exploration so I know what kind of rocket I want to

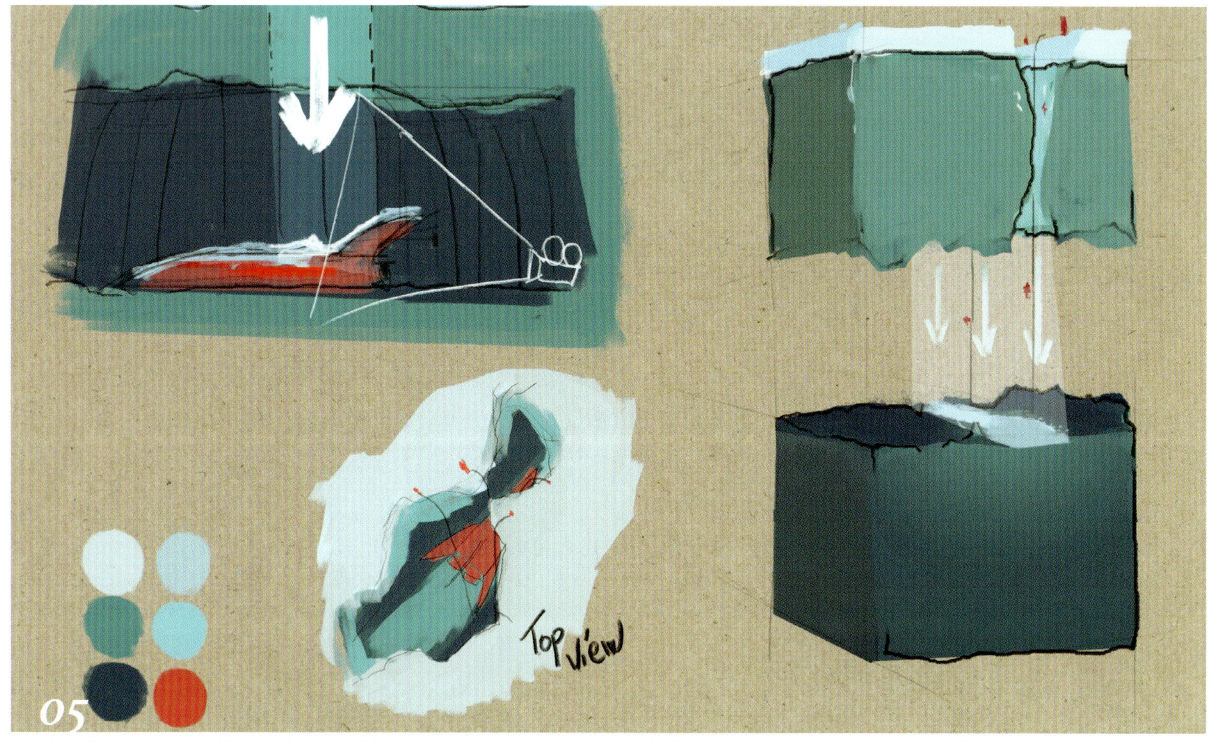

▲ Sketch different views of the environment (side view, top view, and so on) to get a better idea where you can put your "cameras"

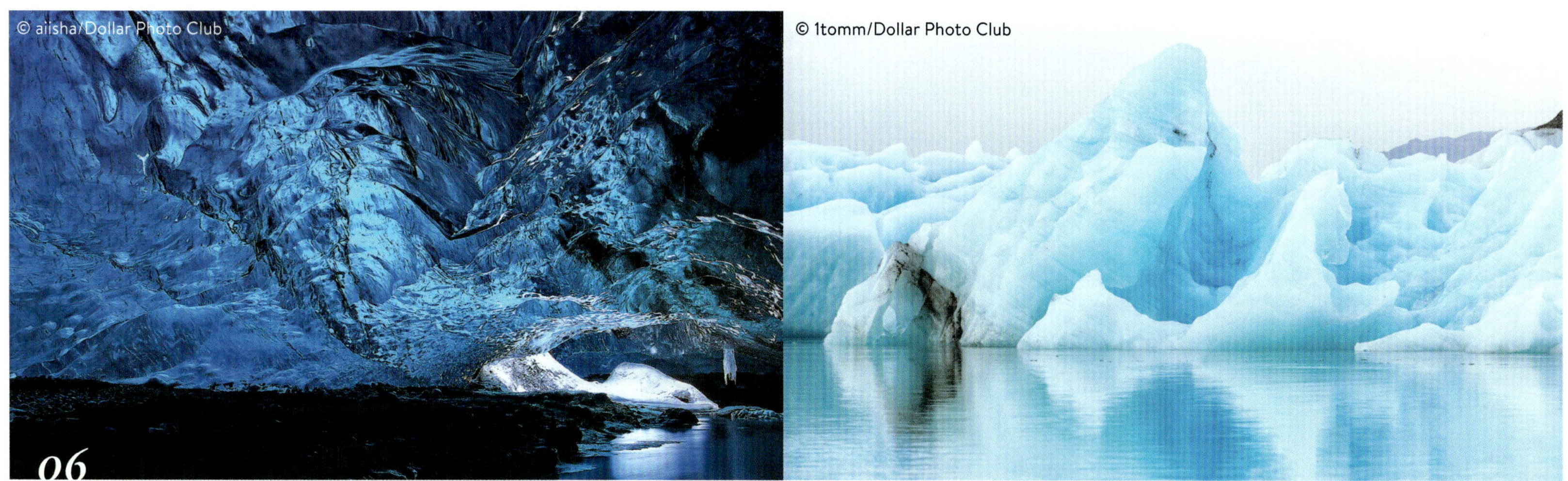

▲ Take your time to collect a lot of different references – these will be really helpful during the next steps

paint – it is obviously the Saturn V, the tallest and most powerful rocket we have ever built. Luckily, there is a full-scale version (restored) of the Saturn V rocket at Florida's Kennedy Space Center so you shouldn't have any problems finding fantastic reference pictures. You want to get as many as you can and taken from lots of different angles.

If you know which position your rocket will be lying in you can concentrate on that angle. My rocket will be lying on its side with bits broken off and scattered around; fortunately you can find plenty of images of the component parts of the rocket too, which makes life so much easier!

"I have a very particular process I like to use to find the mood or atmosphere of a painting – I use a series of thumbnails to find the best mood"

08: Create effective mood

Lighting is a powerful tool for storytelling. You can learn a lot about a situation by observing the light in the scene. How the "good" or "bad" characters are lit or the color of the light can reflect the mind of a character or a place.

I have a very particular process I like to use to find the mood or atmosphere of a painting – I use a series of thumbnails to find the best mood. It is quite simple; start in black and white with a big smooth brush and paint different kinds of lighting in a row of thumbnails, but keep the shapes very simple, almost as if you're squinting your eyes. Then do a second line of thumbnails, this time with colors, using the same process but with even more blur.

Finally duplicate the two lines of thumbnails; put the black-and-white thumbnails on top with a Color Dodge layer. You can see some of the ones I came up with in **image 08**.

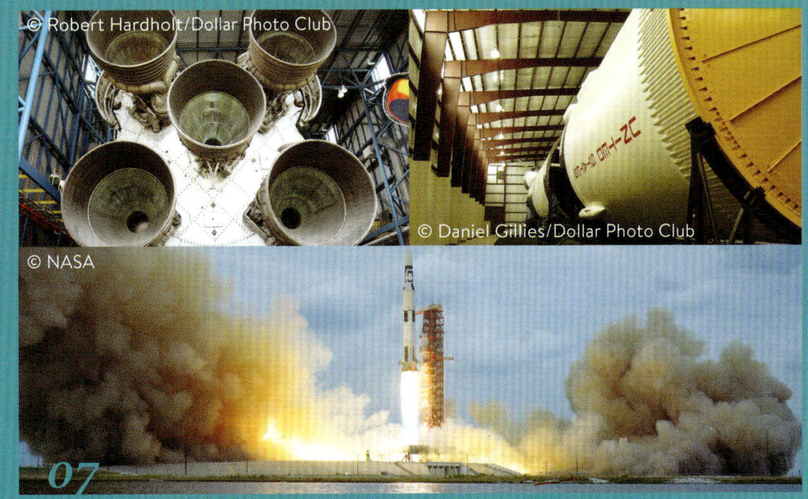

▲ I am a big fan of space exploration so I knew I needed to include the Saturn V rocket

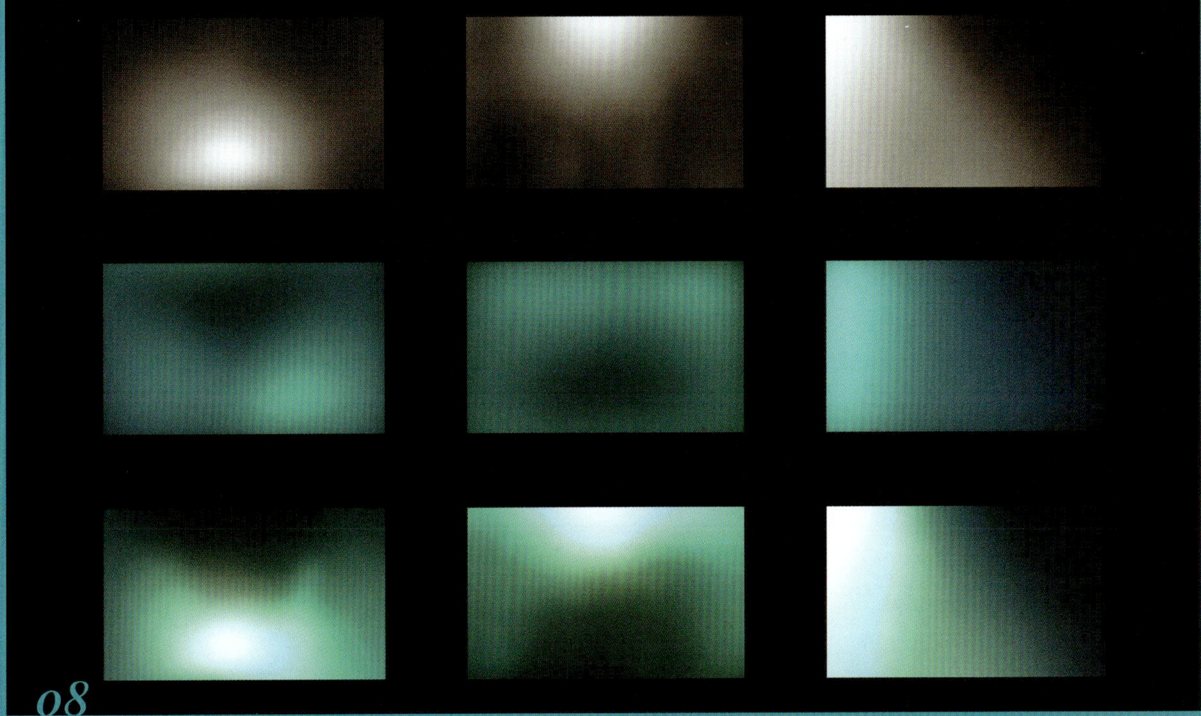

▲ Imagine your lighting as if you are squinting your eyes. Use a big smooth brush to roughly paint the mood you want

09: The famous composition thumbnails

It's time to work on the composition of the painting. This is a necessary step toward achieving a solid picture (you can do it without thumbnails but you will lose time and/or quality). You have to use all the previous steps and simplify them in a little sketch, so think of the story, lighting, environment, characters, and feelings that you want to deliver to the viewer. Quickly paint six thumbnails. You can do this in black and white or use a bit of color, there are no rules. I choose C in **image 09** because of the use of the space.

10: Block the shapes

When you have validated your thumbnail you have to block in the big shapes of your painting. Work on your values and on the mass of the shapes. Find a good balance between your dark and light values. For me, the light values will be in the background (the main source of light comes from the top left) and the foreground will be darker than the rest. Correct the perspective if you need to – the rocket might need a bit of work. Also add some depth with another source of light far in the background.

11: Time to use colors

So far you have worked in black and white but you may want to quickly see it with the mood from step 08. Use the Gradient Map adjustment and the Camera Raw filter to tweak the contrast

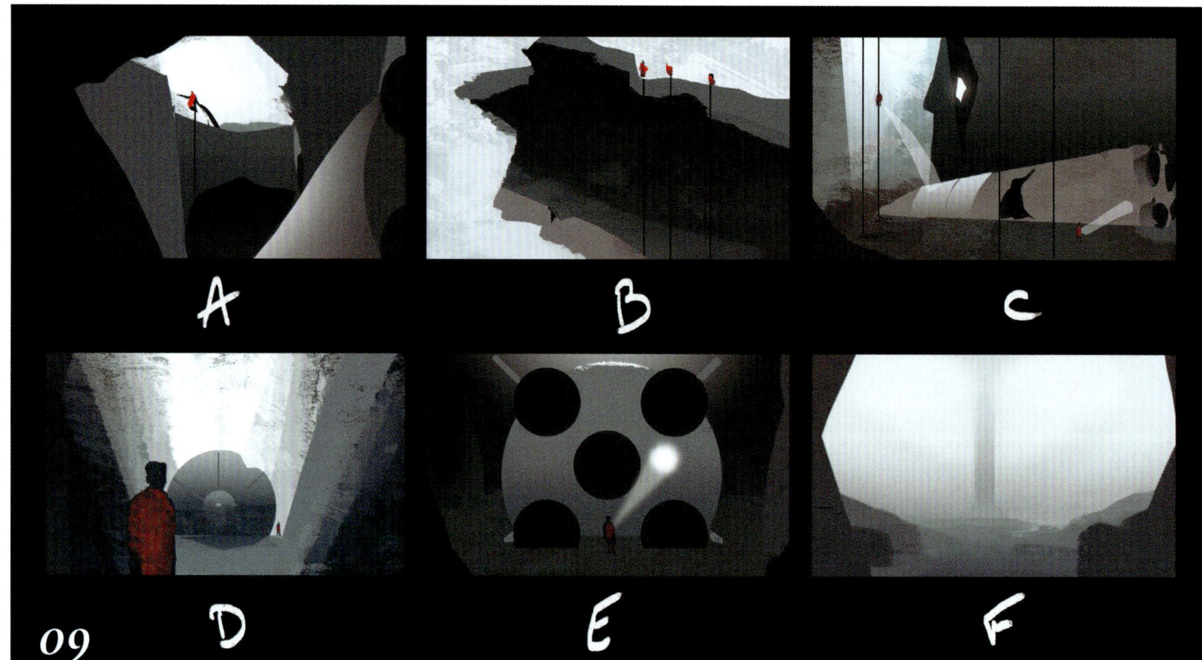

▲Composition is crucial for having a readable picture. During this step try to play with perspective to get very different compositions

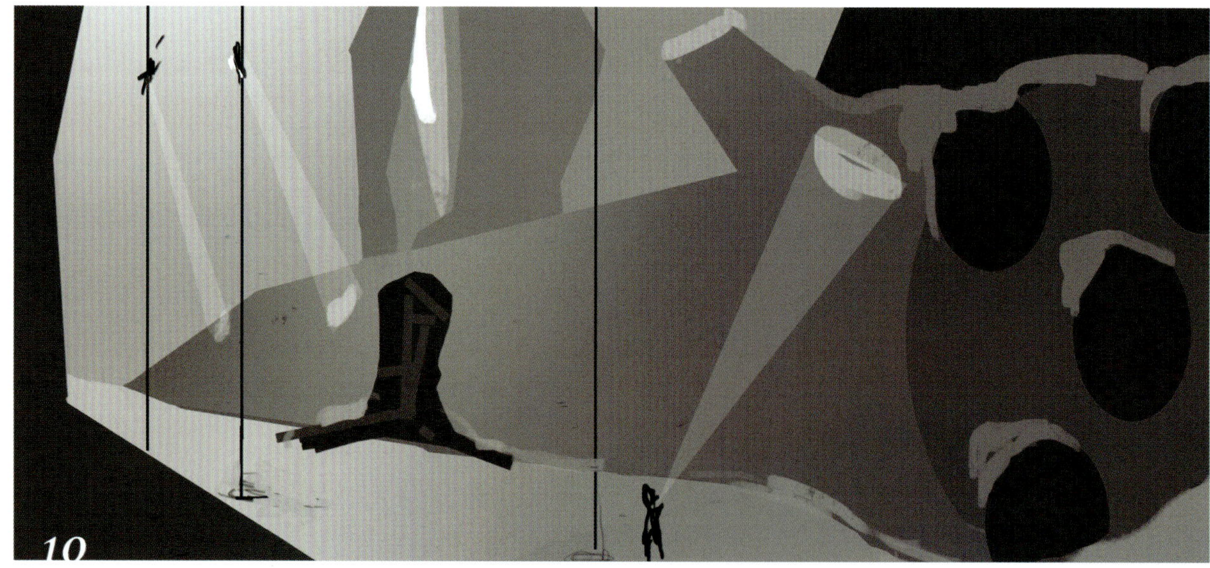

▲Use the Lasso tool to block your shapes. Squint your eyes again to get a global view of your painting

and the colors. First add a Gradient Map adjustment layer and click on the gradient to add the light and dark values. Then merge all the layers, create one on the top (Ctrl+Alt+Shift+E), and apply the Camera Raw filter (Ctrl+Shift+A) to adjust the contrast (note that this filter has only been available since the CC version of Photoshop).

You also have the potential to create new settings with a gradient as a mask so that it only changes the temperature in a particular area of your painting.

12: Give me some ice

Put your references on another screen (if you have one) to be able to go back and look at them. The main source of light is on the top-left of the painting so the colors will be lighter and vibrant (because ice scatters a large amount of light) compared to the wall in the dark part of the cave, which is almost opaque. The main tools you need to quickly blend the colors are the Lasso, Gradient, and Mixer Brush.

Pay attention to your edges; you have to play with hard and soft edges which is why I use the Lasso (for the hard edges) and the Mixer brush (for the soft ones).

"I prefer to work with a small canvas (maybe at 50% zoom). This gives me a global point of view of my painting"

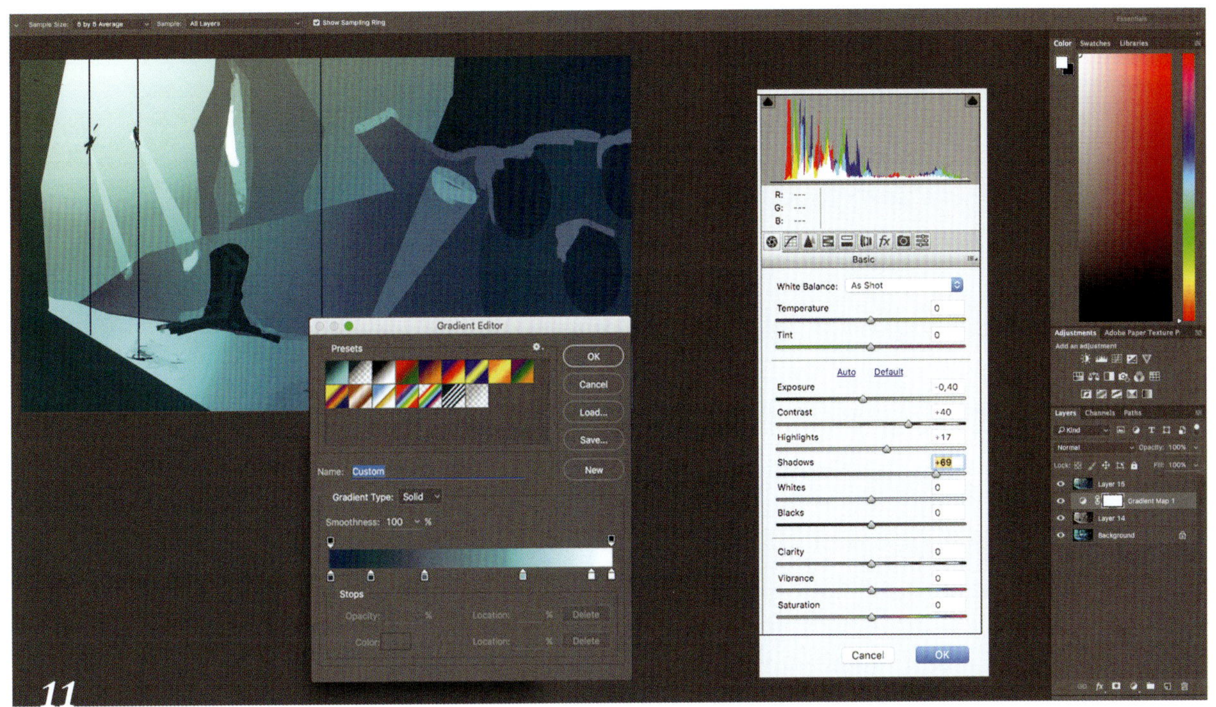

▲ The Gradient Map adjustment layer is good for applying tints

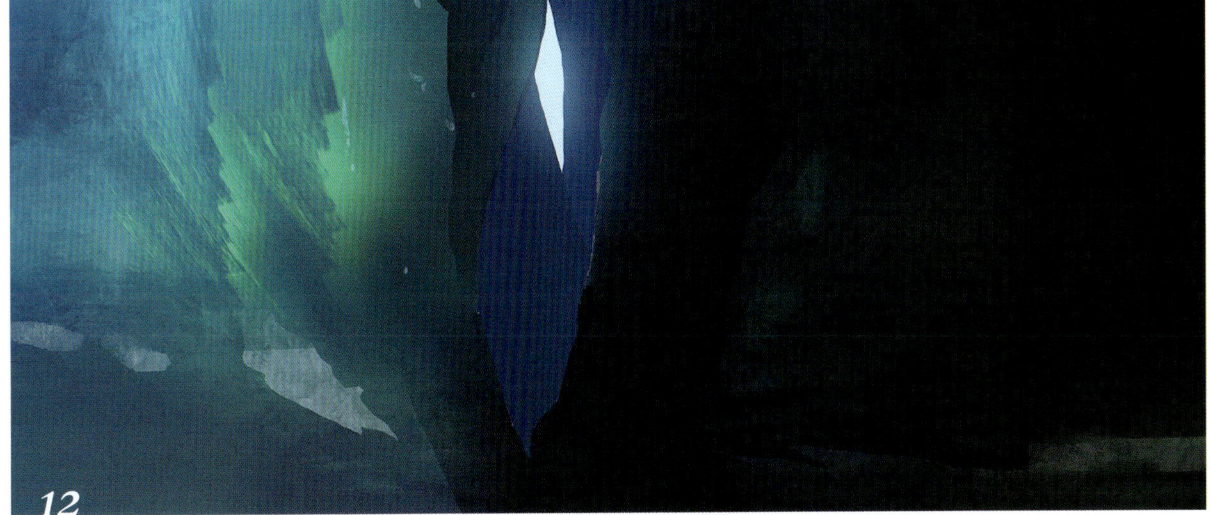

▲ Use your references to roughly paint the wall. Look at how the light reacts on the surface and how it changes the colors

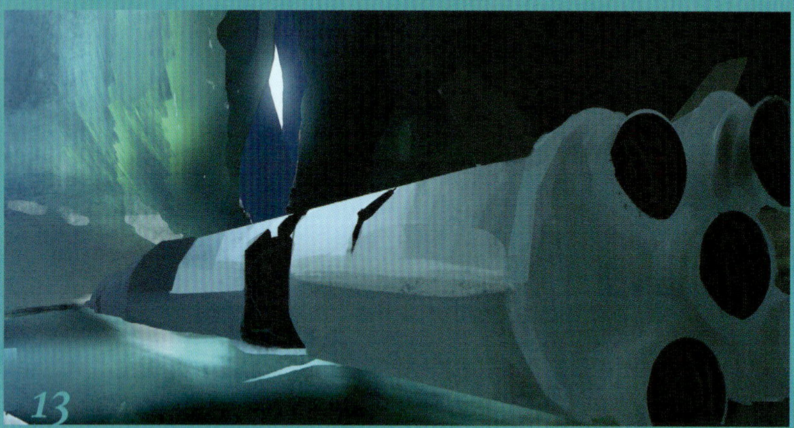

▲ Not the most difficult step of this painting – the engines are basically cylinders so find your vanishing point and follow your guidelines

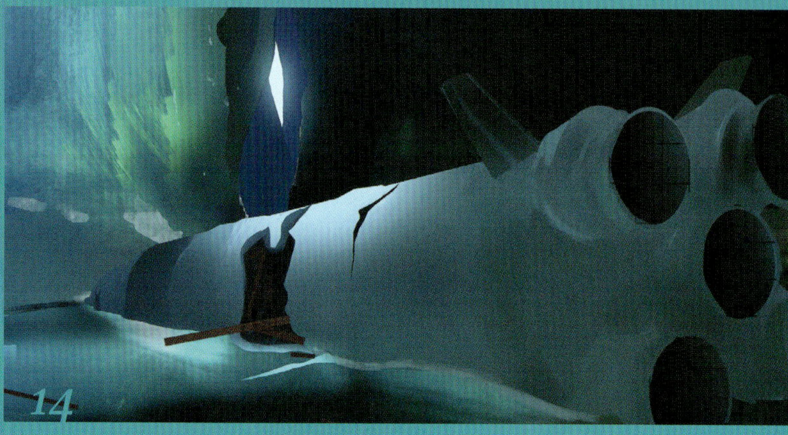

▲ This is when you can spend a little time refining the rocket. Add some details such as girders or beams using custom shapes

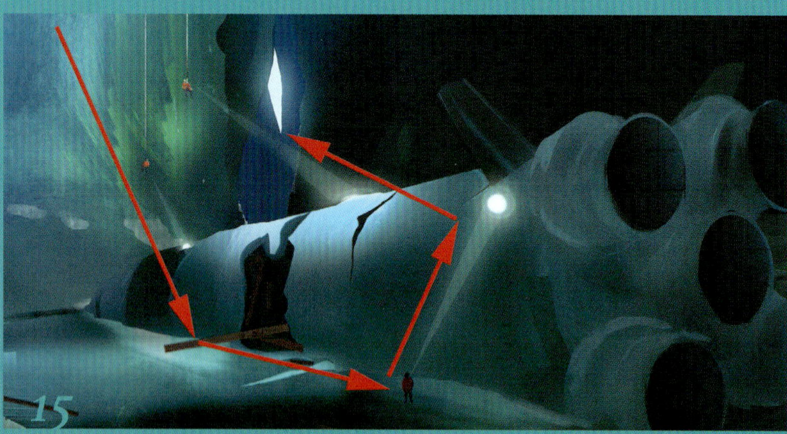

▲ Find a purpose for your characters to build a better composition. I will use the light of their torch to lead the eye of the viewer

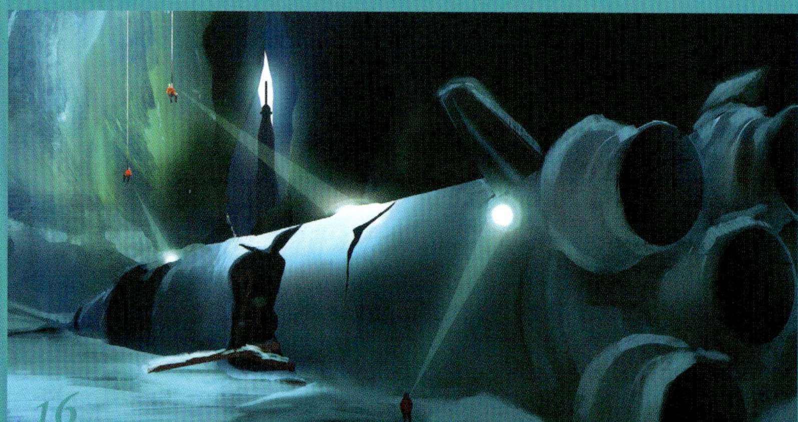

▲ Snow is rarely pure white; it always takes the color of its environment (usually the sky), in this case the ice cave

13: Add the rocket

The rocket is basically a cylinder so this isn't really the challenging part. Put the vanishing point on the left and add some guidelines with the Line tool. The Saturn V rocket is almost completely painted light gray so inside the ice cave it will appear a bit bluish/greenish because the ice scatters the light before it hits the rocket surface.

Draw some dark ellipses for the engines and add some different cracks in the body to show its age. For now, don't think about the second light bounce; focus only on the main shape of the rocket.

14: Refine the rocket

I prefer to work with a small canvas (maybe at 50% zoom). This gives me a global point of view of my painting. However for this step I will break this rule!

Start to smooth the body of the rocket using the Mixer brush and also add the rebounded light at the bottom of the body. Then refine the rocket engines and finally add some details such as the shell of the metal case near the holes and some red metal pieces (which are the remainder of the launch pad). You could also put some hard edges on the fin. Your references will again be useful here.

15: Abseil down the cliff

When adding characters to your composition, don't just add them as a simple silhouette on top of your painting; use them to tell your story. In my case I think it might be useful to use the light beams from their torches to lead the viewer's eye around the composition. The ropes will be the first guide, then the intersection of the rocket and the ground to the character far on the right. Finally the fin and the light ray of the middle character will lead to the rocket in the background.

16: Let it snow!

As you probably know snow is almost never pure white. It takes on the color of the environment so here it will be a light cool gray because of all the ice around the rocket. Now the quick sketches of the location you made in step 05 will help you to find where you need to add more snow. There is a big hole in the cave (where the characters come in from above) so the area just below this hole will have a cover of snow. Add some frost on the ground. Also add some small heaps at the top of the engine and inside the bottom exhaust ports.

17: Add atmospheric effects

Atmospheric effects are really important for setting up the mood. For example fog helps you to add a bit of mystery into the narrative of your painting. Use a big Smooth brush with low opacity and pick a light color (the color of the snow for example) to add some fog in the background, in front of the vertical rocket, and also near the light source in top-left of the frame.

18: Detail the ice

Use your reference pictures (on another screen) to work on the reflections on the ice in more depth. Pick a light blue color (never use a pure white or pure black in your painting) and add some specular points on the parts facing the different light sources. Use the Lasso tool to make selections and add

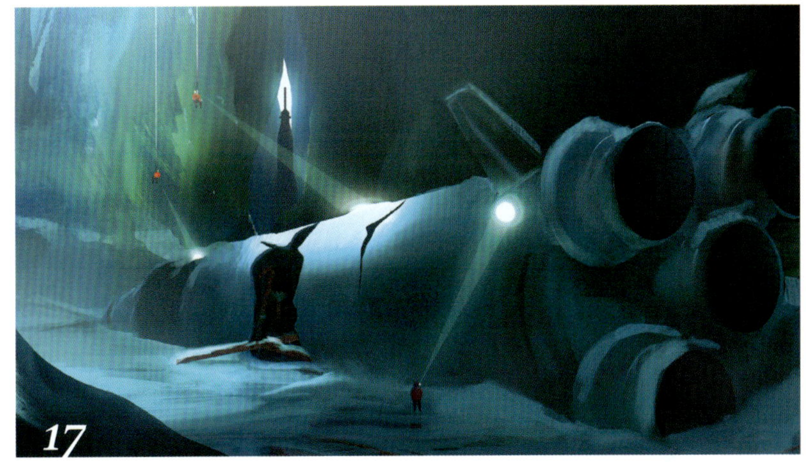

▲ Add some atmospheric effects like fog to give a cold feeling and a bit of mystery

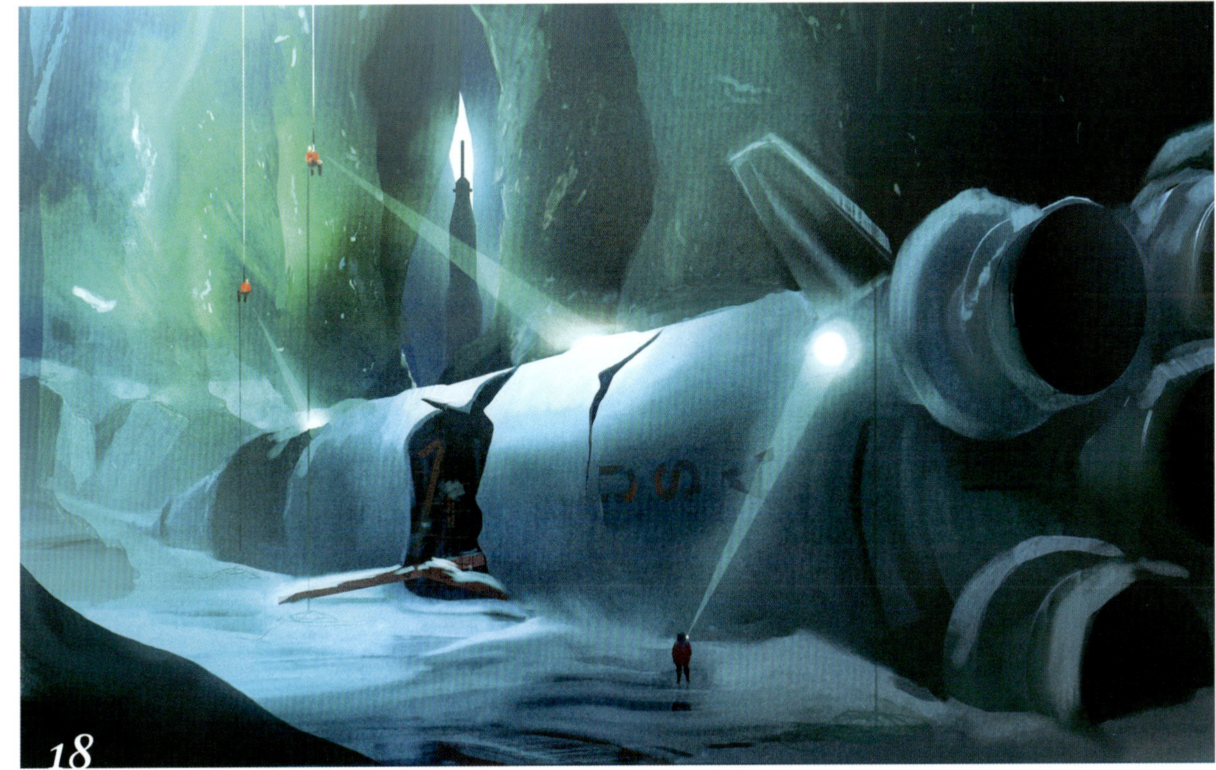

▲ Use the references you found earlier to help you detail the ice

Pro tip: Flip your painting

Everyone has a stronger eye (around two-thirds of people are right-eye dominant and the other third are left-eye dominant). That means you can unconsciously accentuate your perspective in one side of your painting. To avoid this just create a shortcut to flip your canvas horizontally.

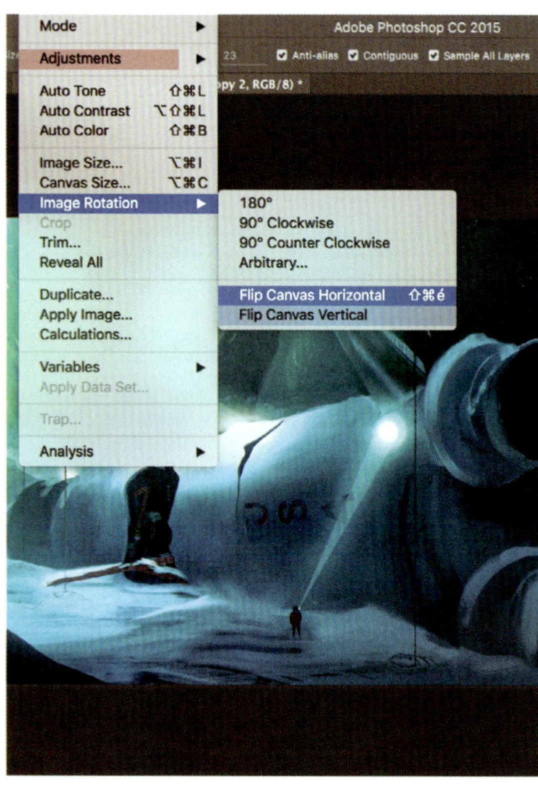

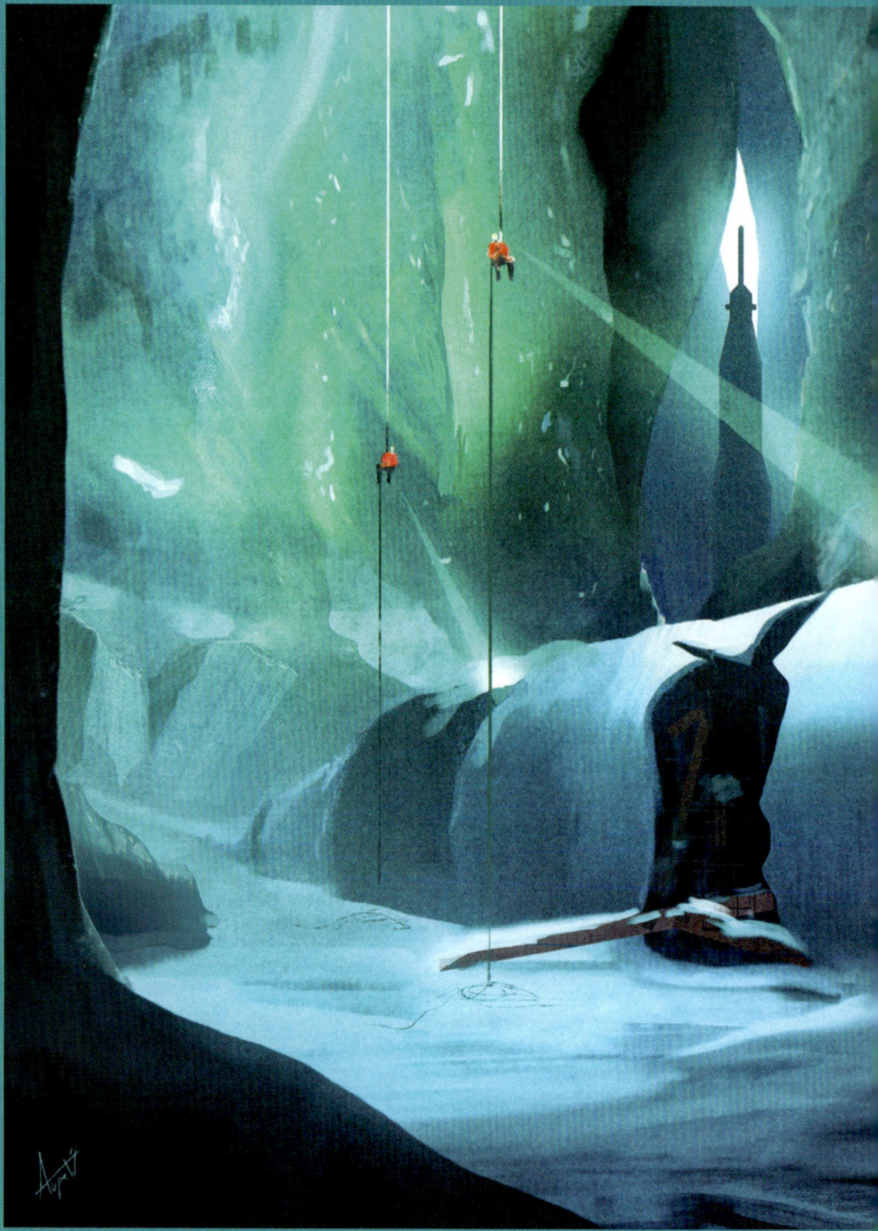

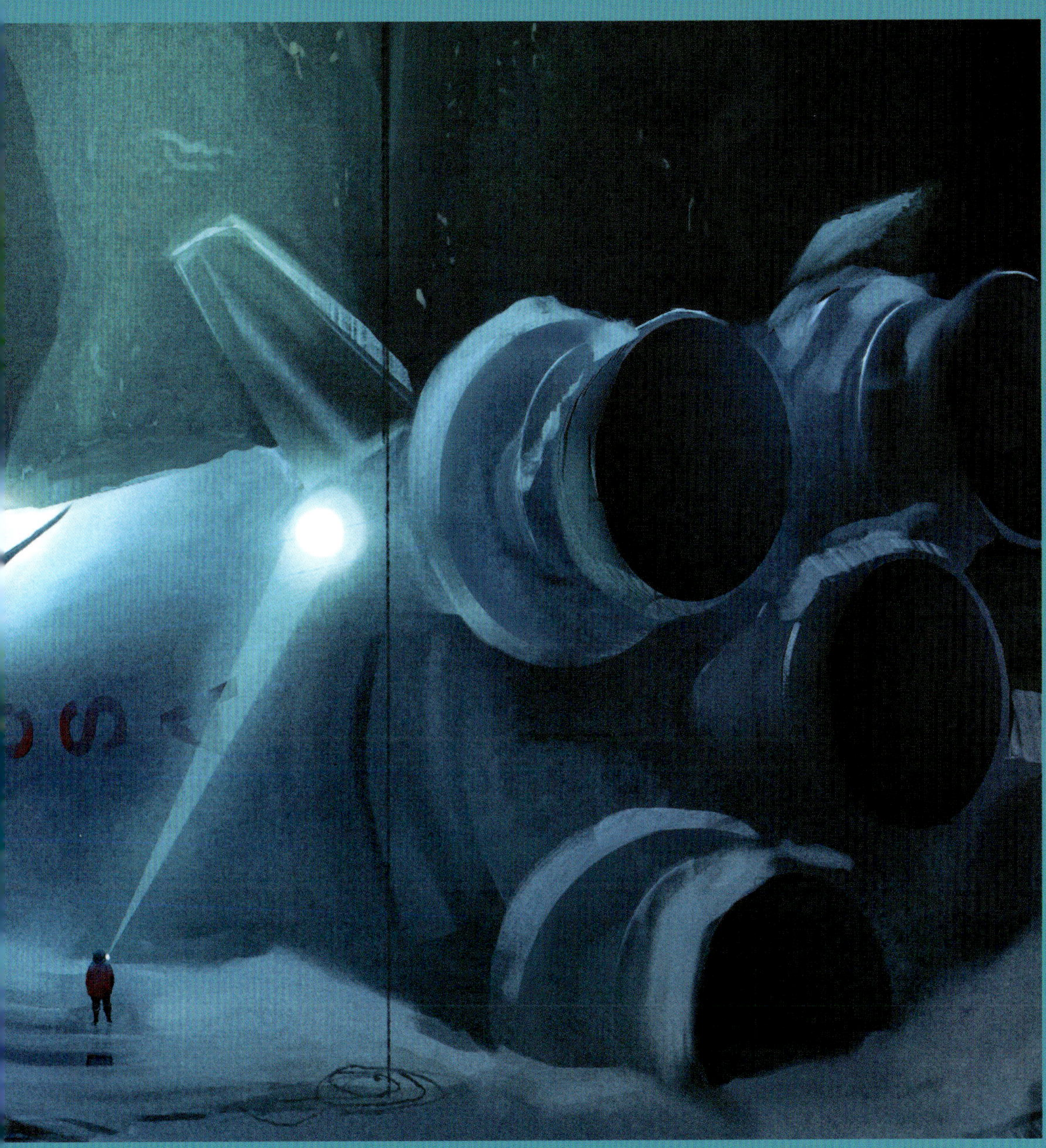

a bit of depth to the crevices in the wall; use the Gradient tool in Multiply mode to fill parts of the selections.

The time should be around fifty-five or fifty-eight minutes so your painting is almost done, it just needs a bit of color correction.

19: Final adjustments and conclusion

With a couple of minutes left, use the Camera Raw filter to lower the exposure, adding contrast and increasing the high values. Change the white balance to give your picture a cooler feel. The Grain filter is also useful for unifying your painting so create a new layer set to Overlay and fill it with a 50% gray. It should be invisible at the moment but will show up when you apply a Noise filter and decrease the opacity.

Now try a little trick to add more grain in the dark values: duplicate your painting (Ctrl+J), desaturate (Ctrl+Shift+U), invert (Ctrl+I), and use this picture as a layer mask for the second grain layer.

I hope this tutorial will be helpful not only for the technical aspects of speed painting but also for all the process before you start the first brushstrokes. Telling a story is crucial for us – a picture with a story will be always better than a painting without.

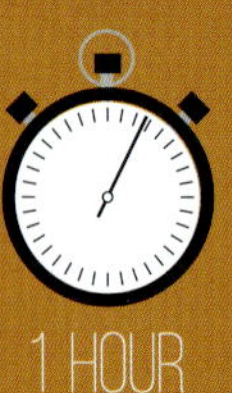

1 HOUR

SCI-FI: MARS FACTORY
by Massimo Porcella

▲Build up your composition using tonal values

In this tutorial we will quickly create a one-hour sci-fi speed painting using textures, color, and structural shapes.

01: Idea and sketch

Having an initial idea is one of the most important parts of any painting; from here you can build on it to work towards a final image. As we are going to create a sci-fi themed painting we need to start with the initial shapes and composition. This not only builds on the concept but also lays the foundations for the actual scene.

Using a simple soft round brush, roughly sketch in your composition. Change over to a flat brush to build up volume on the architectural structures. You should see your composition coming together. On separate layers you can bring in some tonal values to define the planes and atmospheric perspective to give the piece a sense of depth. The values should be lightest at the back and darkest at the front.

02: Shape

This is my favorite part of the process – I love it and for me it is definitely the most creative. You need to create structural shapes that will act as the skeleton or backbone of the sketch. Think about what it is you want to show; I go for gigantic structures that dominate the environment like some sort of factory on Mars (**image 02a**).

Simply make a new layer and create an interesting and futuristic shape using the Polygonal Lasso and Brush tools.

▲I love creating interesting structural shapes

When you are happy, duplicate it and use the Transform tool to stretch it into a new and interesting shape; repeat this process a few times and use these building blocks to develop your concept. Place the shapes on each of the plane layers and pick up the corresponding tonal values from step 01 (**image 02b**).

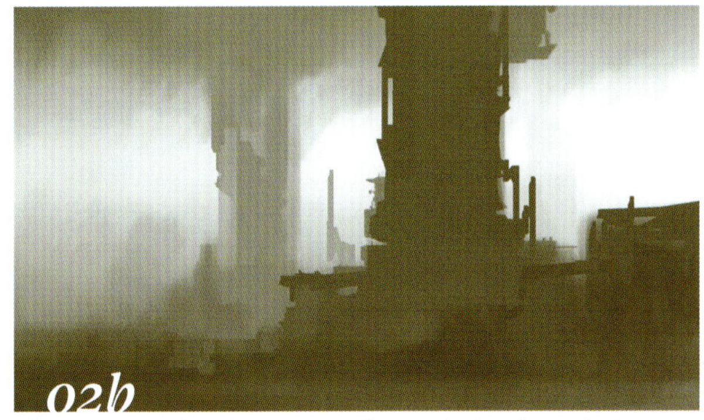

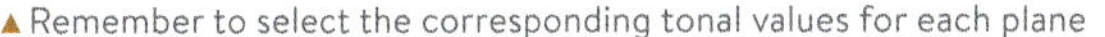
▲ Remember to select the corresponding tonal values for each plane

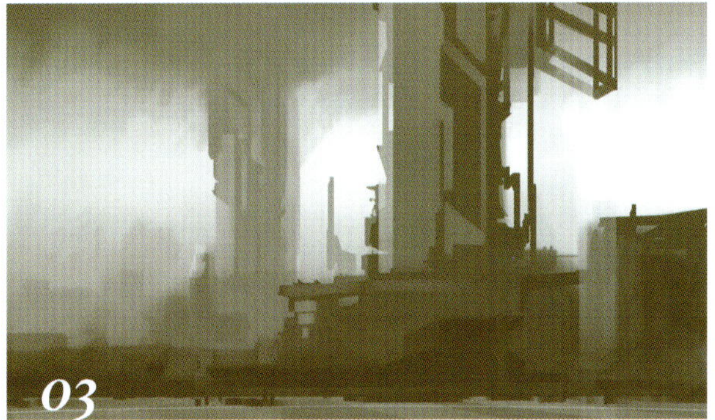

▲ Build up the volume of the buildings to bring depth to your image

"To keep the sci-fi feel you will need to design the structures with straight architectural lines"

03: Painting and volume

This is where you need to paint some volume and dimensionality onto your structures to give them a feeling of depth and bring realism to the whole sketch.

Go back to the tonal values to define not only the depth of the environment, but also the color palette of the whole painting. Use the Eyedropper tool to select the volume colors.

To keep the sci-fi feel you will need to design the structures with straight architectural lines; do this by holding down the Shift key when using a flat-tipped, hard-edged brush.

04: Contrast and definition

Time to add some contrast to the scene using Curves (Layer > New Adjustment Layer > Curves...). The idea is to add definition and to up the heavy martian atmosphere by color picking and painting layer after layer. By pulling out the darks and lights and building on the small and big volumes, you can further contrast the image and create a greater sense of depth to describe the background, middle ground, and foreground.

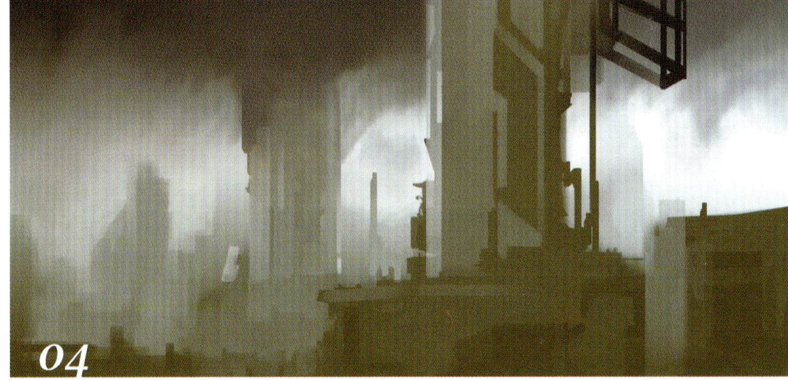

▲ Build up the heavy martian atmosphere

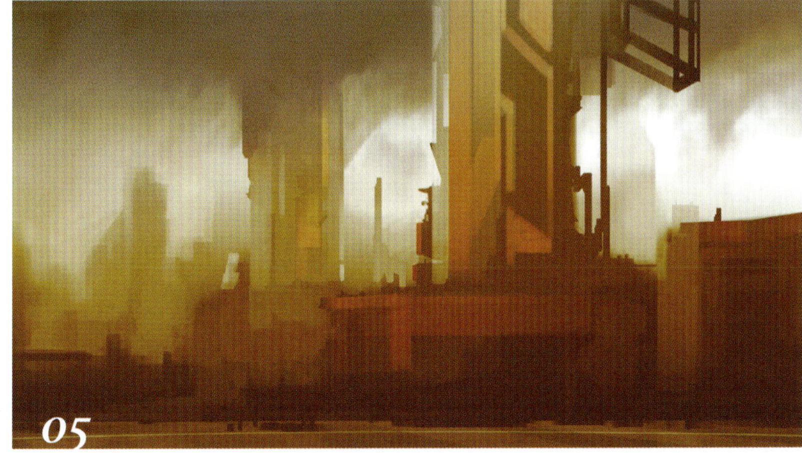

▲ Use the Gradient tool to add a base color

05: Base color

You've got the tonal values of your image now so you need to add a base color. As this illustration is set on Mars, a warm orange is a great choice. Use the Gradient tool and different blend modes such as Color, Soft Light, or Overlay – pick whichever you prefer or whichever goes with the tonal values.

The Gradient tool is perfect here because you can choose the color for every part of the sketch, starting from the ground, at the base of the buildings, moving to the skyline shade, and finally picking up a color to define the shade between land and sky. For an even color palette, use the Eraser tool to blend all the colors together.

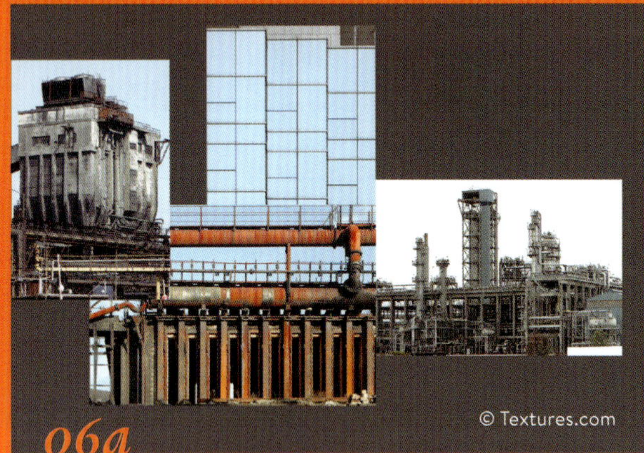

06a

▲A small sample of the textures I use

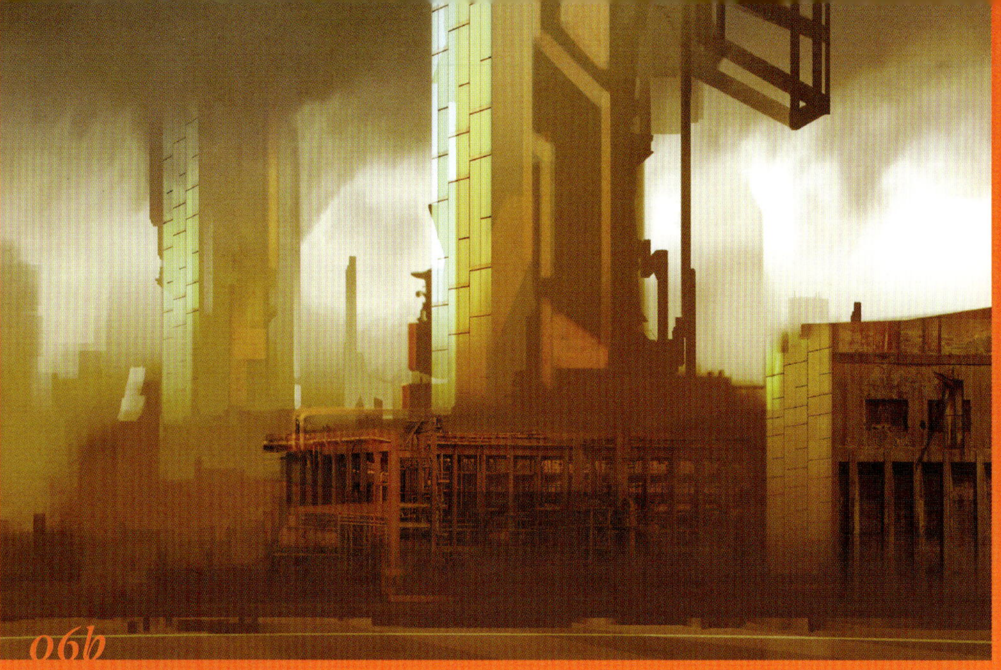

06b

▲The textures really bring the painting to life

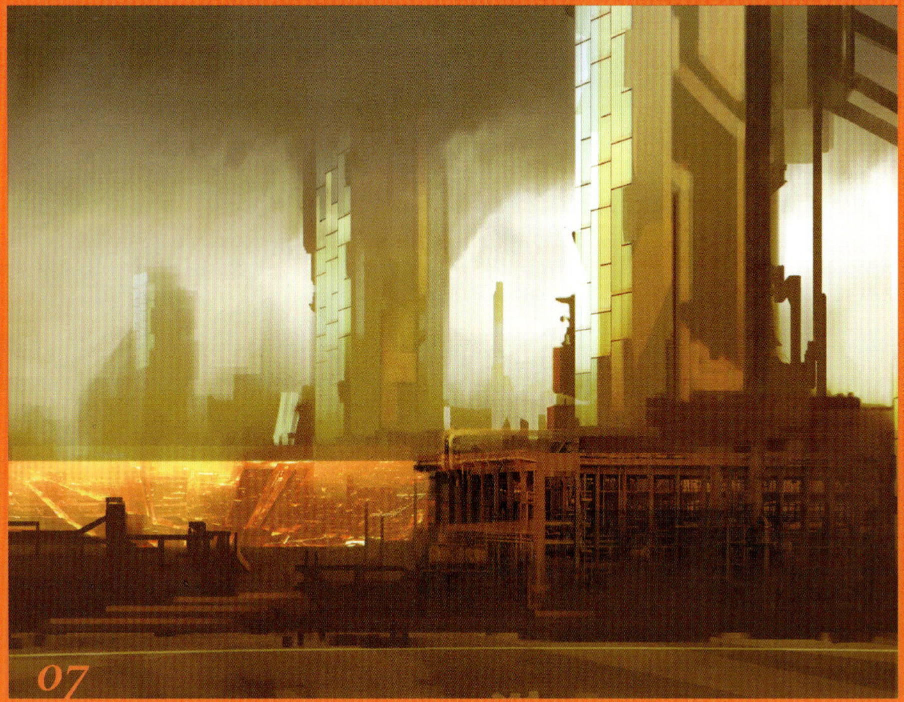

07

▲Keep applying textures and painting over them

06: Texturing

We have arrived at another one of my favorite parts of the working process – texturing; it is also one of the quickest. As with nearly all art projects you will need to spend a little time gathering reference pictures and textures based on the look you are going for (**image 06a**). With references in hand use interesting parts of them, with a variety of blend modes, to add texture to the different planes – mostly the middle and foregrounds. Use the Polygonal Lasso tool to select the parts of the painting you are interested in and apply a texture using a Soft Light blend mode; this will keep the color palette but mix them with the texture tones. Again, the Eraser tool can help you to clean up the bits you don't need (**image 06b**).

07: Add more textures and brushstrokes

Keep going with the texturing process and also on a new layer add some brushstrokes. This process is very important because it allows us to blend the texturing and painting together in order to define the basic anatomy of the image. Add texture to the areas where you want to have realistic detail and, in a new layer, paint in more of the image, remembering to base the color on the texture's tonal values to give the appearance of the continuation of the texture. This method is great for getting alternate versions of the same texture to add both continuity and variation to the image.

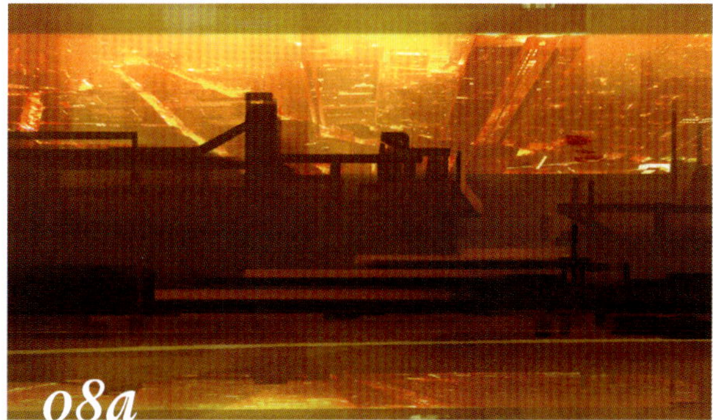

▲ A shiny and reflective floor adds more depth to your scene

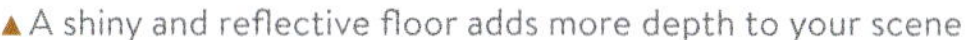

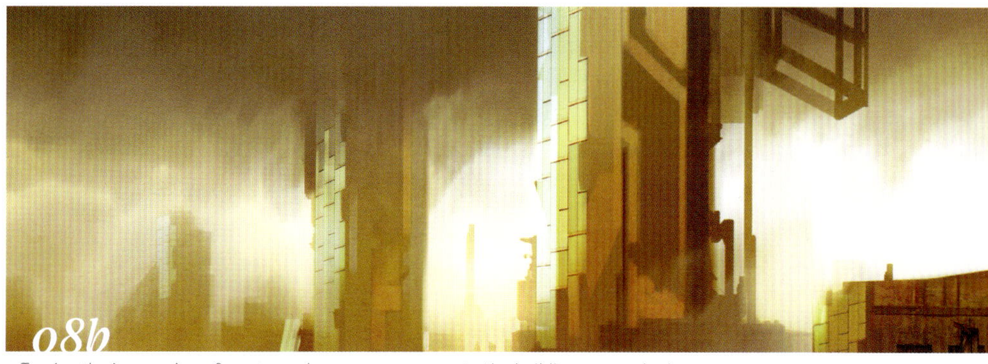

▲ To give the impression of an atmosphere you can separate the buildings on each plane

08: Mood and light

At this stage you might want to spend time building up the mood and atmosphere of the painting, which will have a positive effect on the depth of field.

Use a particle effect brush in between the two buildings to give an impression of smoke or fog. Create a shiny and reflective floor by mirroring and flipping the scene above it (**image 08a**). To separate the foreground from the middle ground, and increase the depth, draw a quick solid structure just above the reflection.

Moving onto the top half, use the Lasso tool to select the upper building, and with a soft brush add a little light. Use an Overlay layer to separate the structures on the different planes to create a sense of atmosphere (**image 08b**). The look you are going for is like that of a busy city at dusk when there is a lot of pollution in the air – you can almost touch it. The light is very soft and diffuse.

09: Contrast and midtones

Let's now play with the contrast again to bring the darks slightly lower. This is a really useful trick for giving the sense of a thicker atmosphere. Open up the Curves tool on the adjustment layer panel and add three points for the dark, mid-, and light tones (**image 09a**). I bring down the midtones to mix and integrate the planes together and to blend the texturing and painting, bringing them closer in style to create some interesting effects.

Keep the light tones low at this point, as you will work on them in the next step. This method is not only quick and allows you to play with the contrast, it also helps to create an even mood, making the whole environment feel "alive" and realistic (**image 09b**).

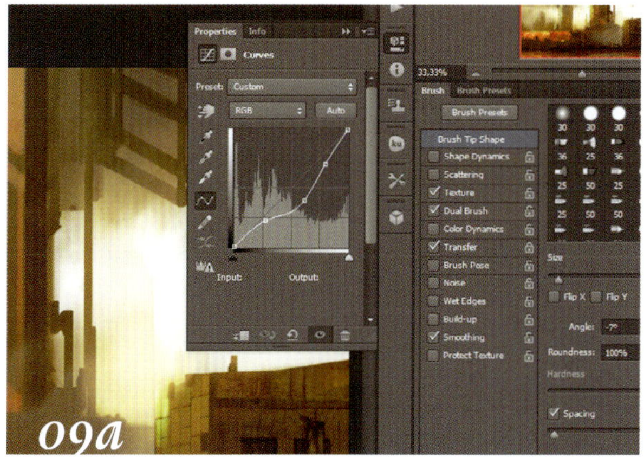

▲ Use Curves to play with the contrast

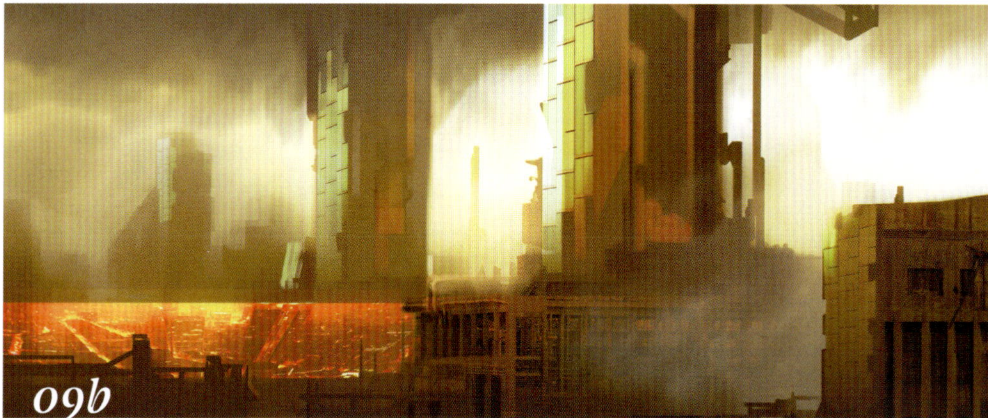

▲ This is a great way to give your work a more realistic feel

"Use a soft brush to carefully blend the light edges, not only the ray of light but also where the light is reflected onto the surface of the structures"

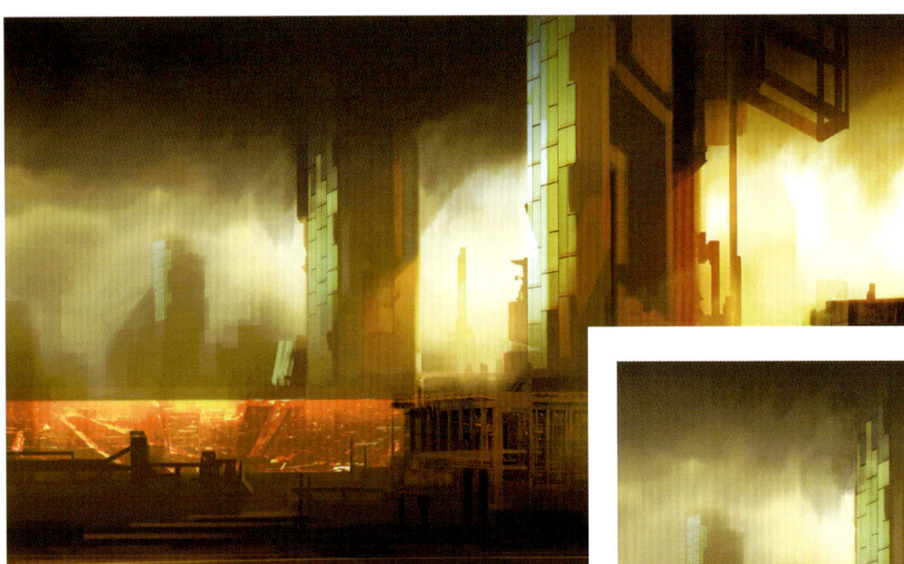

▲ Color Dodge is a great tool for adding light to a painting

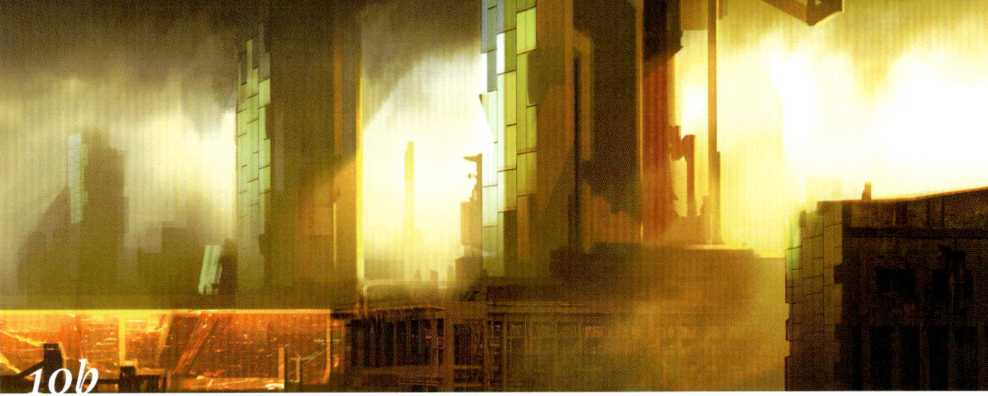

▲ Use rim lighting to add even more realism

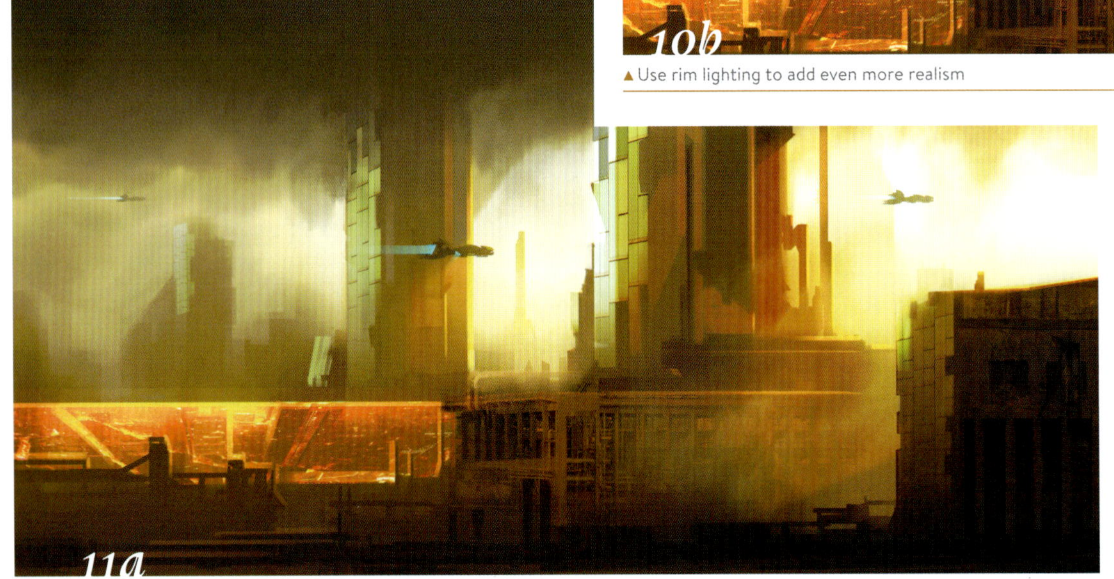

▲ Add little ships to show scale and bring the composition to life

10: Light

Time for some color dodging! Use the Eyedropper tool to pick the orange color of the image and create the light in between the buildings and structures (**image 10a**). Draw perspective lines that fall on them with the Polygonal Lasso tool.

In a new layer set to Color Dodge, paint the rim light to really make the building's silhouettes stand out from the surrounding areas. After doing this use a soft brush to carefully blend the light edges, not only the ray of light but also where the light is reflected onto the surface of the structures. This will add even more realism and visual effects (**image 10b**).

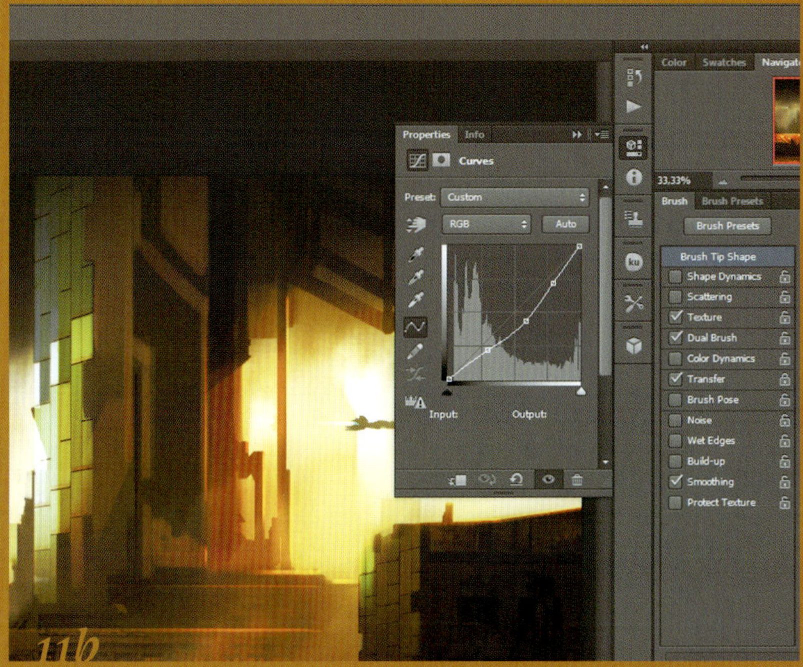

▲ Once again play around with the contrast

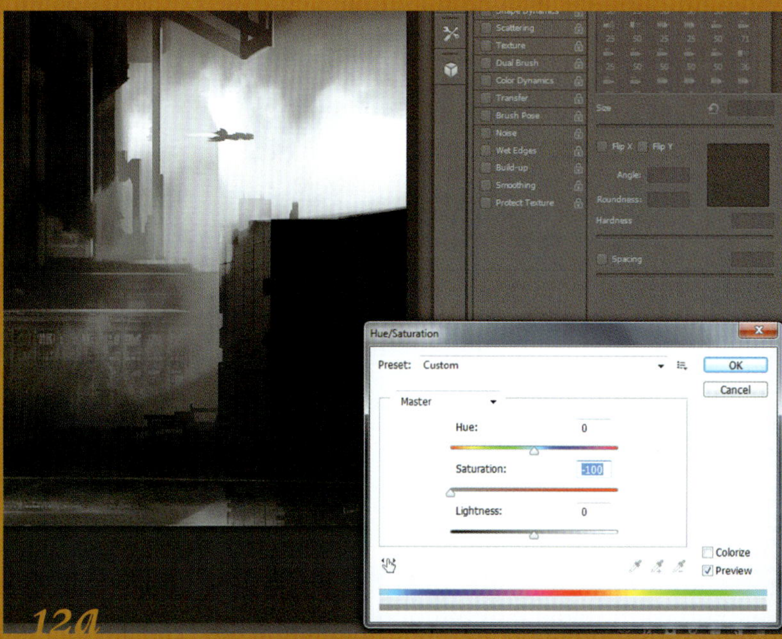

▲ Use the Hue/Saturation tool to desaturate the painting

11: Ship

With the main parts of the painting done you can move on to adding extra detail to make the scene more dynamic and alive, and also to give it a sense of scale. Draw simple silhouettes on a separate layer to give the impression of spaceships flying around. With the silhouettes of the base of the ships done, block the layer and pick up colors from the main body of the painting to add color and details to the ships. This helps them to fit into the scene much more realistically (**image 11a**).

Now repeat what you did with Curves in step 09 to add contrast and blend in the midtones once again (**image 11b**). This will help to re-integrate the light, mixing it with the atmospheric mood and incorporating the ships even further into the composition. Finish this stage by pushing the lights up a little to make the sky brighter.

12: Shadow and blur

This will be the last phase of the process. Merge all the layers into one layer (Ctrl+Alt+Shift+E). Completely desaturate it using Hue/Saturation (**image 12a**) and Curves and Levels in the adjustment layer panel; you want to capture the brightest white and darkest black – basically contrasting the image as much as possible (**images 12b** and **12c**).

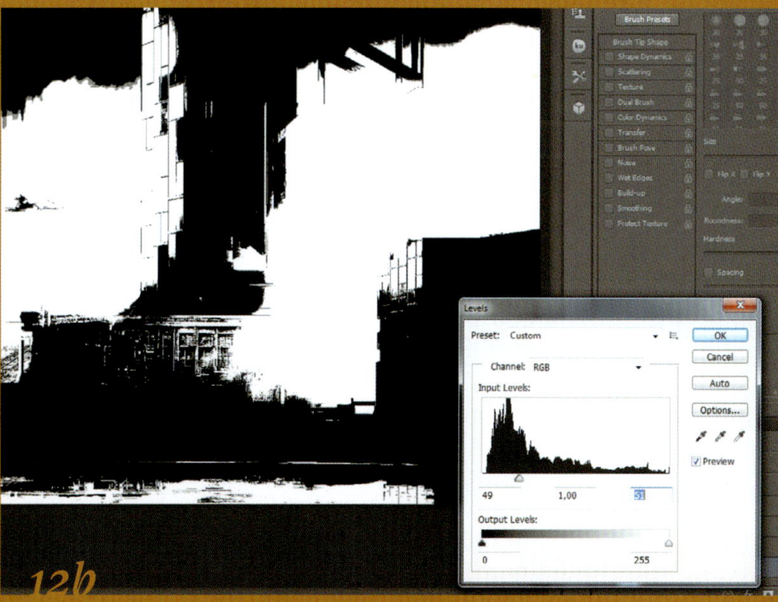

▲ Use Curves and Levels to bring out the darkest blacks

▲ The darkest blacks and brightest whites

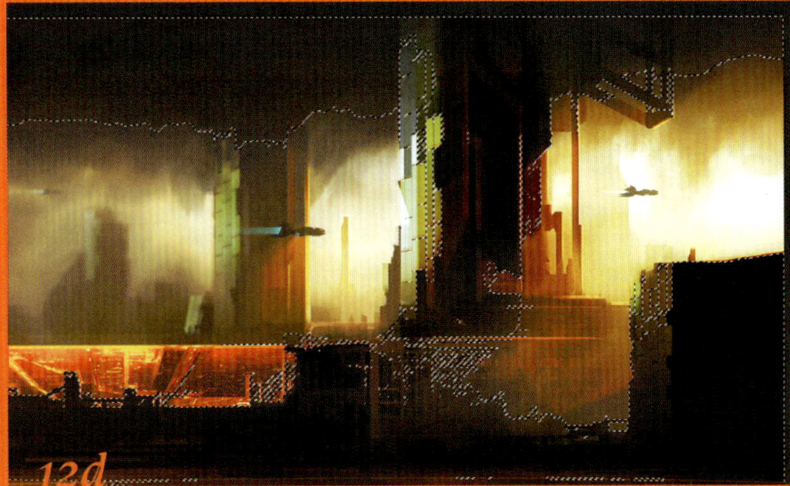

▲ The mask selection over the colored image

Use the Magic Wand tool to select just the blacks and create a mask selection of them (**image 12d**). Then on a new layer paint with the Gradient tool and the mask. Do this to get more control of the parts you want to darken, which will add contrast and a depth of field to the composition. The very final thing is to add a little blur to the furthest part of the image to add an even greater sense of depth and to enhance the mood. And that's it, you are done!

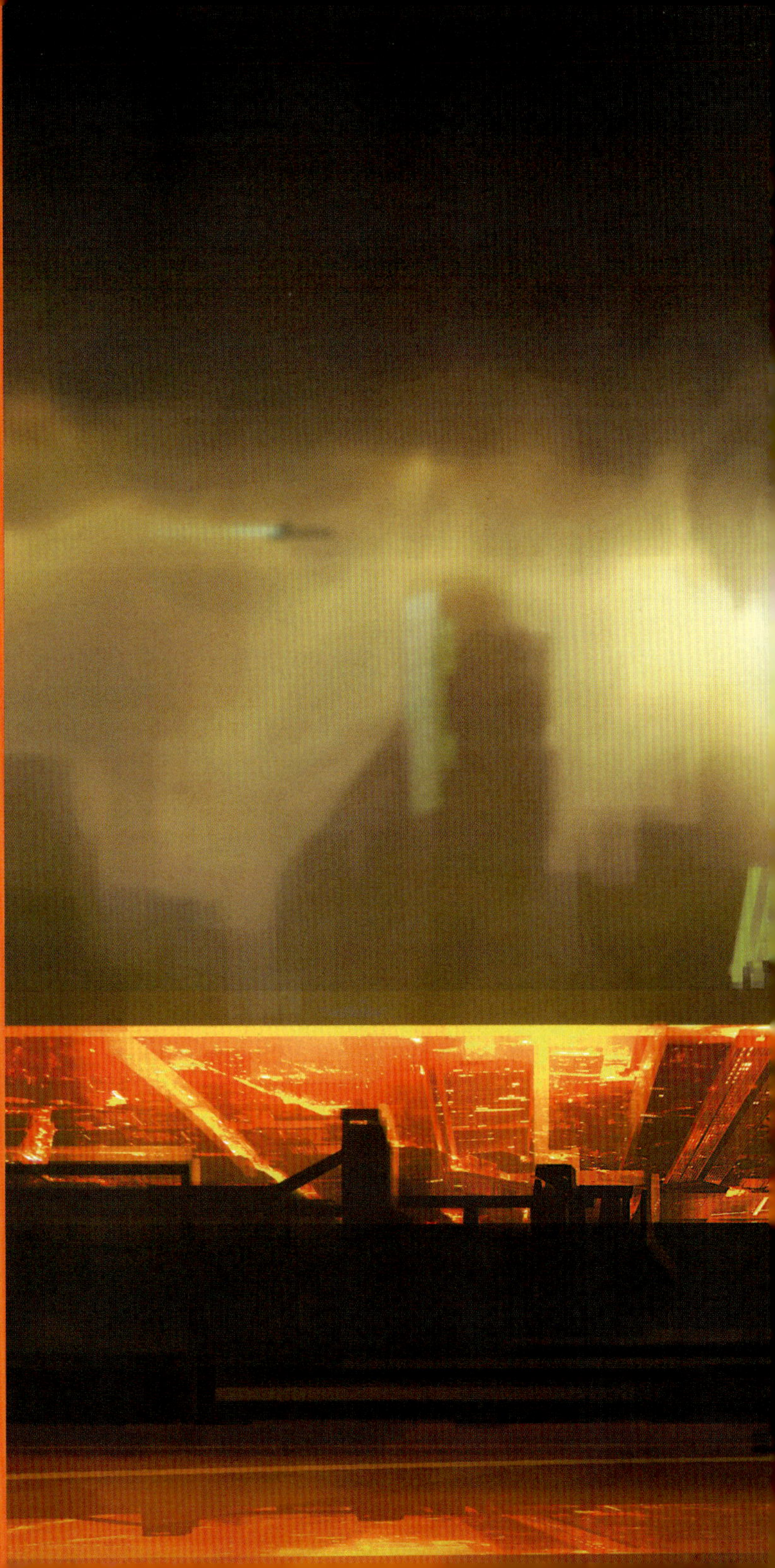

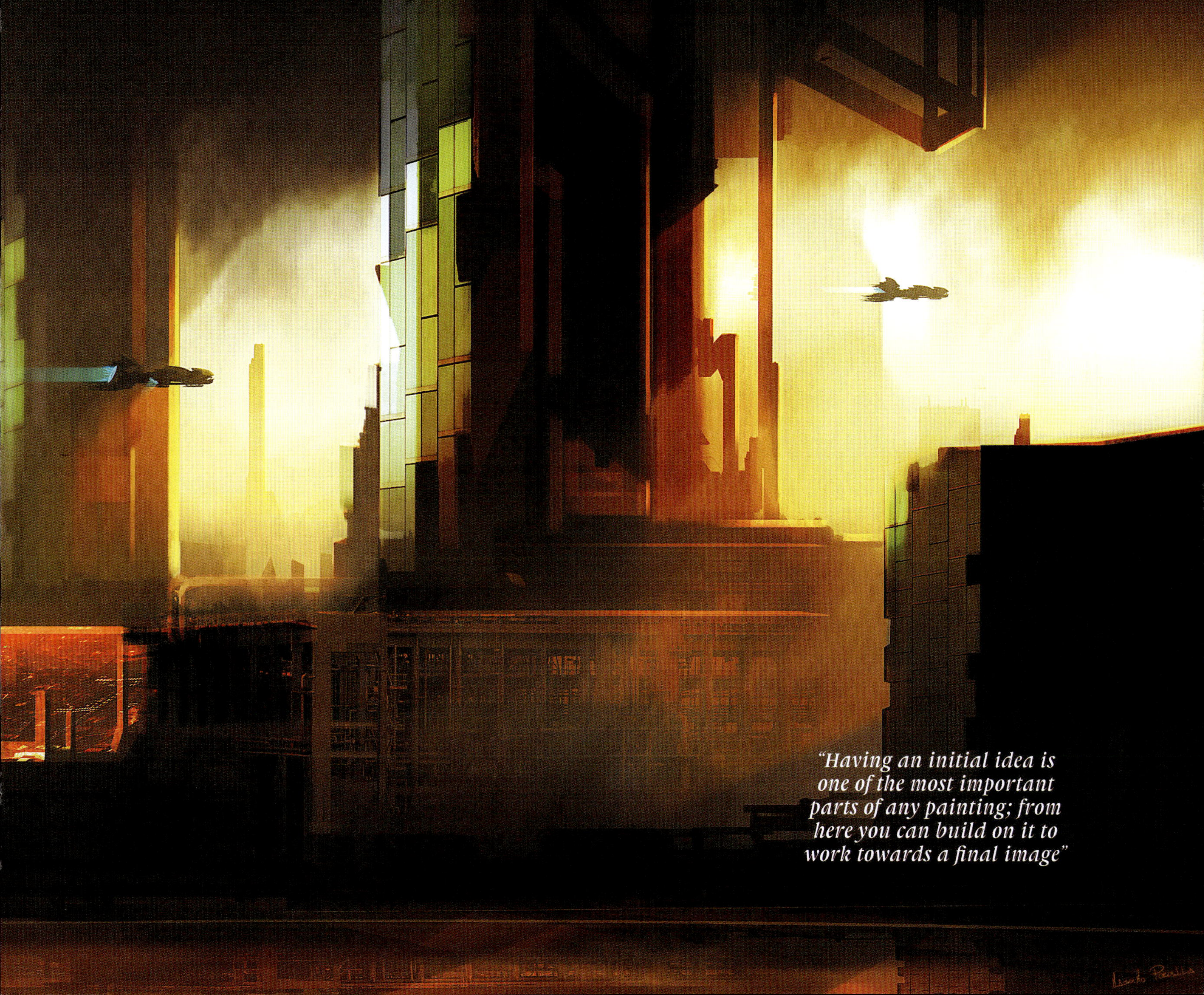

"Having an initial idea is one of the most important parts of any painting; from here you can build on it to work towards a final image"

1 HOUR

FANTASY: FACE YOUR FEARS

by Alex Olmedo

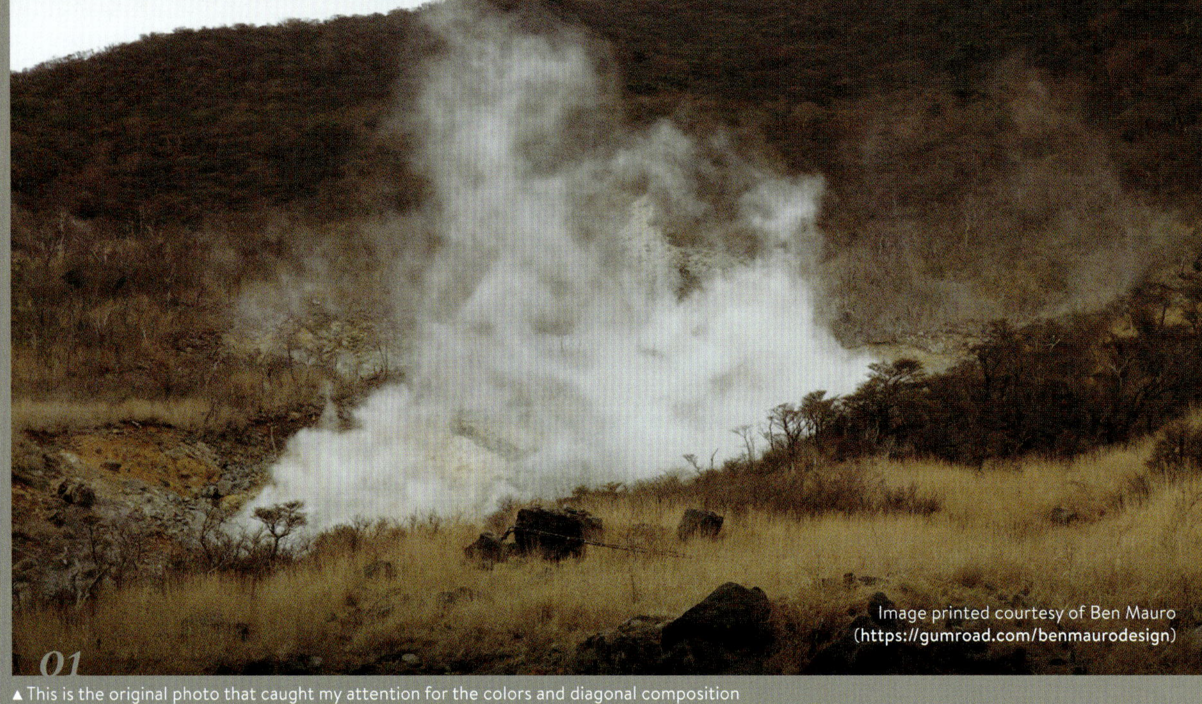

Image printed courtesy of Ben Mauro (https://gumroad.com/benmaurodesign)

▲ This is the original photo that caught my attention for the colors and diagonal composition

This tutorial will show you how to create a speed painting with a painterly traditional feel. Speed paintings are a great way to help improve your skill level because they force your imagination and also show you which techniques are best to use to realize your ideas quickly.

The techniques you will use will help you take any photograph and turn it into a fantasy painting. This will be done by utilizing the colors and textures from the reference photo. You will start off loose, gently and slowly bringing the forms to life in order to give your painting the atmosphere and narrative you want.

01: Reference images

It is so easy to find references. You can take your own or you can do a quick online search or use image collection sites such as Tumblr and Pinterest to build up a reference library. You can also buy (quite cheaply) big packs of reference images on websites such as **www.photobash.org**.

I look through my collection of images and choose the one shown in **image 01** for its interesting colors and atmosphere – it is taken from Ben Mauro's Matte Painting reference pack, available from his Gumroad page.

"A really great way of finding new shapes is through 'happy accidents'"

02: Transform the photo

The first thing to do is resize and move the reference image on the canvas using the Transform tool (Ctrl+T) to find a good composition. Try not to distort it too much as you don't want it to become blurry or unfocused.

Following the basic rules of atmospheric perspective, you want the background to be brightest, the middle ground to be warm, and the foreground to be dark.

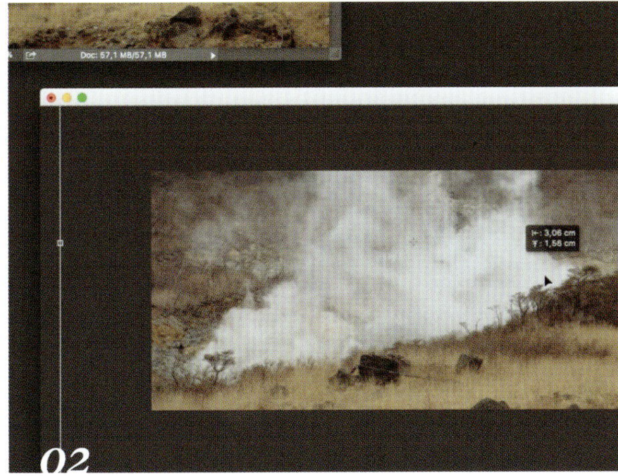
▲ Transform the image paying attention to the composition and the quality of the textures that you will probably use later

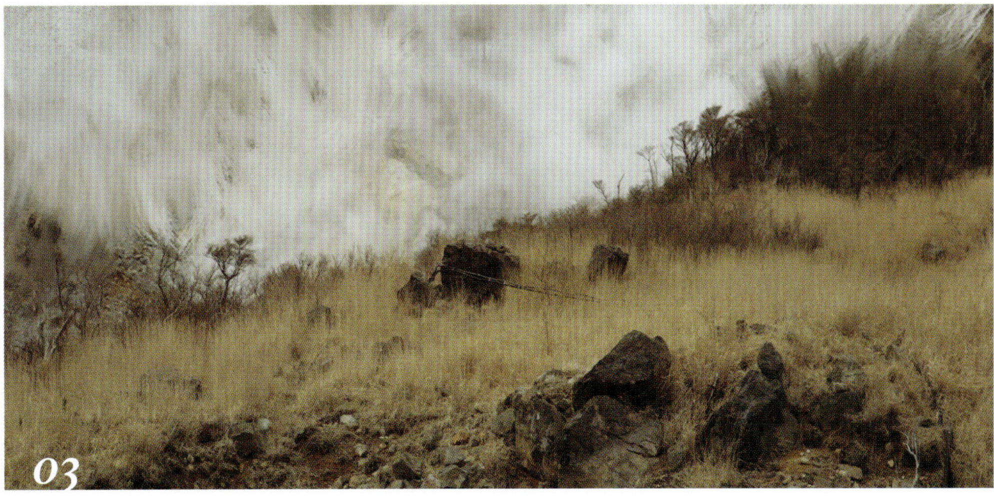
▲ Use the Mixer brush impulsively and with energy to create realistic brushstrokes imitating traditional media

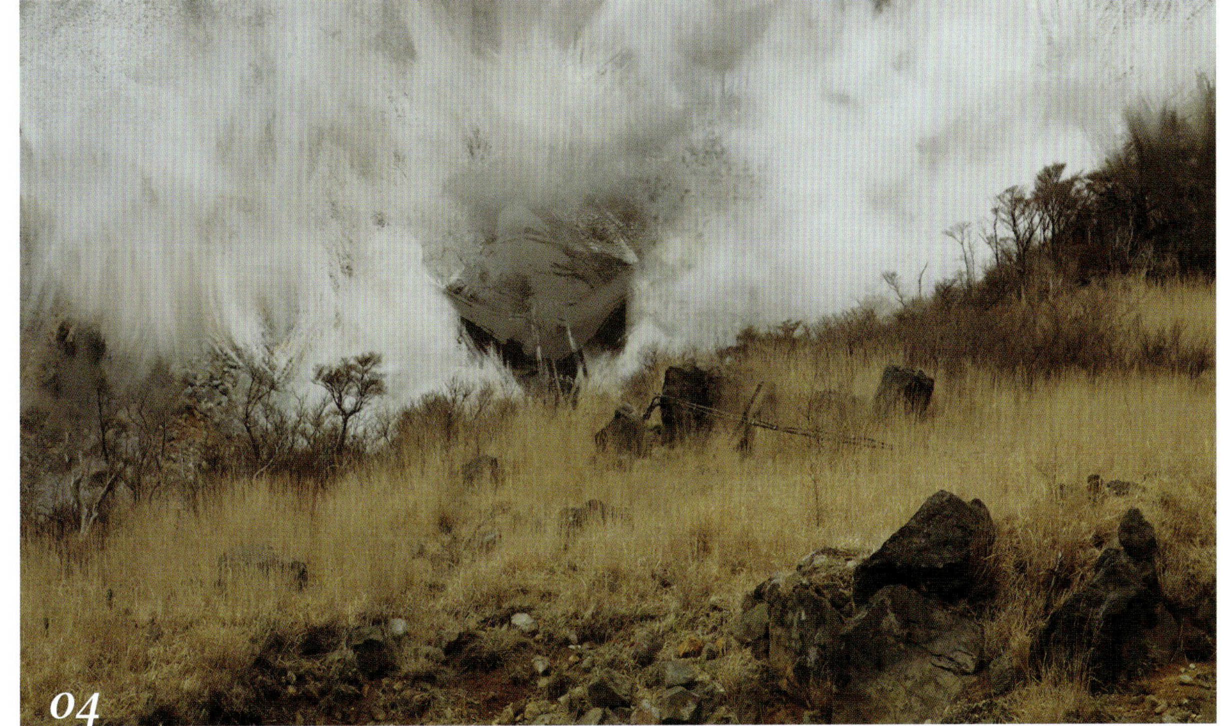
▲ Sometimes the shapes just appear as you are painting

03: Add the first strokes

Use the Color Picker to select the color of the smoke and on a new layer put down some big brushstrokes with your favorite brush. You don't need to be too concerned with defining a particular shape, just be impulsive and painterly. You can play with the same brush in Mixer Brush mode to soften the edges and add more color mixing – this mode is great for a more traditional look for your work.

04: Happy accidents

A really great way of finding new shapes is through "happy accidents"; this can happen when you are playing around with the brushstrokes (or adding photo textures) and you see something interesting, such as a person or a creature. The first of the darker smokey strokes revealed a creature's head, so I continue to work on it until a dragon shape appears.

05: The pose of the dragon

So you have your dragon head and the rest of the body is starting to appear, what next? You should think about what the dragon is doing, is he walking or attacking? I go for attacking! Paint the wings spread out in a menacing pose – they will lose their definition in the background. Work with the Brush and Smudge tools to give a mysterious atmospheric feeling.

06: Emphasize the mood

The mood of the painting is given through the colors, lighting, and shapes. As this photo is overcast we have more room to play with the variables. Losing the shape of the dragon with the background makes it appear darker and more mystical, leaving it up to the viewer's imagination to complete the story behind the image. This means we can draw the viewer further into the image and increase their interest.

You can always try flipping the image as an option if the composition doesn't feel right; it is amazing what a difference this can make.

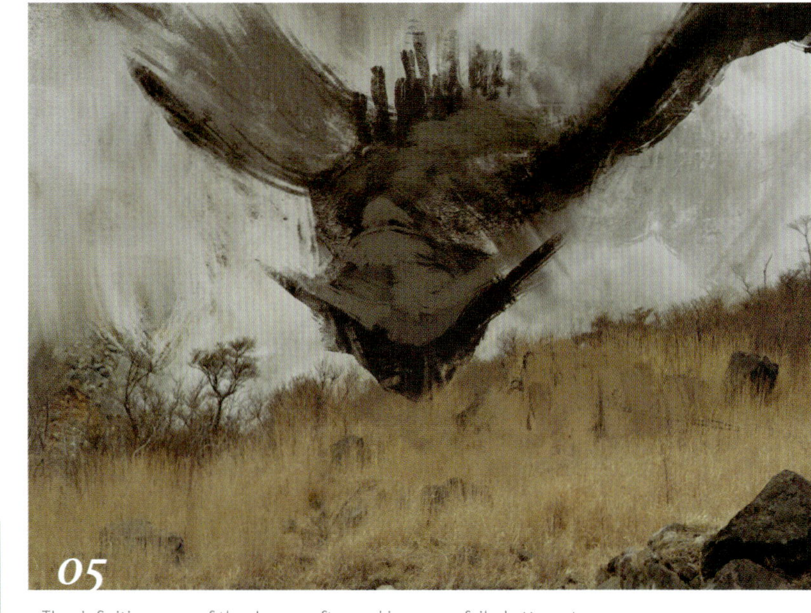

▲ The definitive pose of the dragon after making some failed attempts. This one leaves more room for the imagination

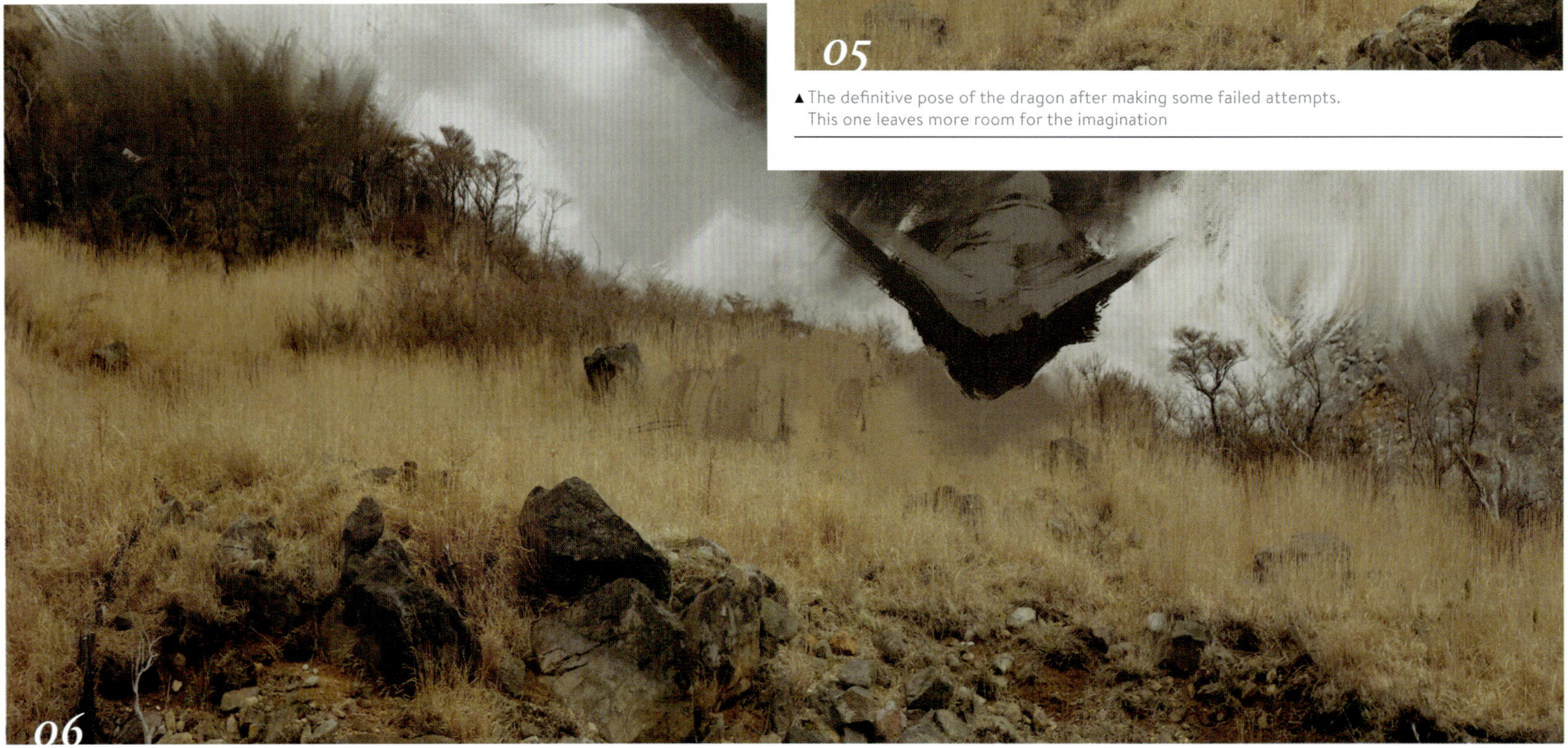

▲ Using the Smudge tool you can soften edges to integrate them into the background, giving a greater sense of atmosphere

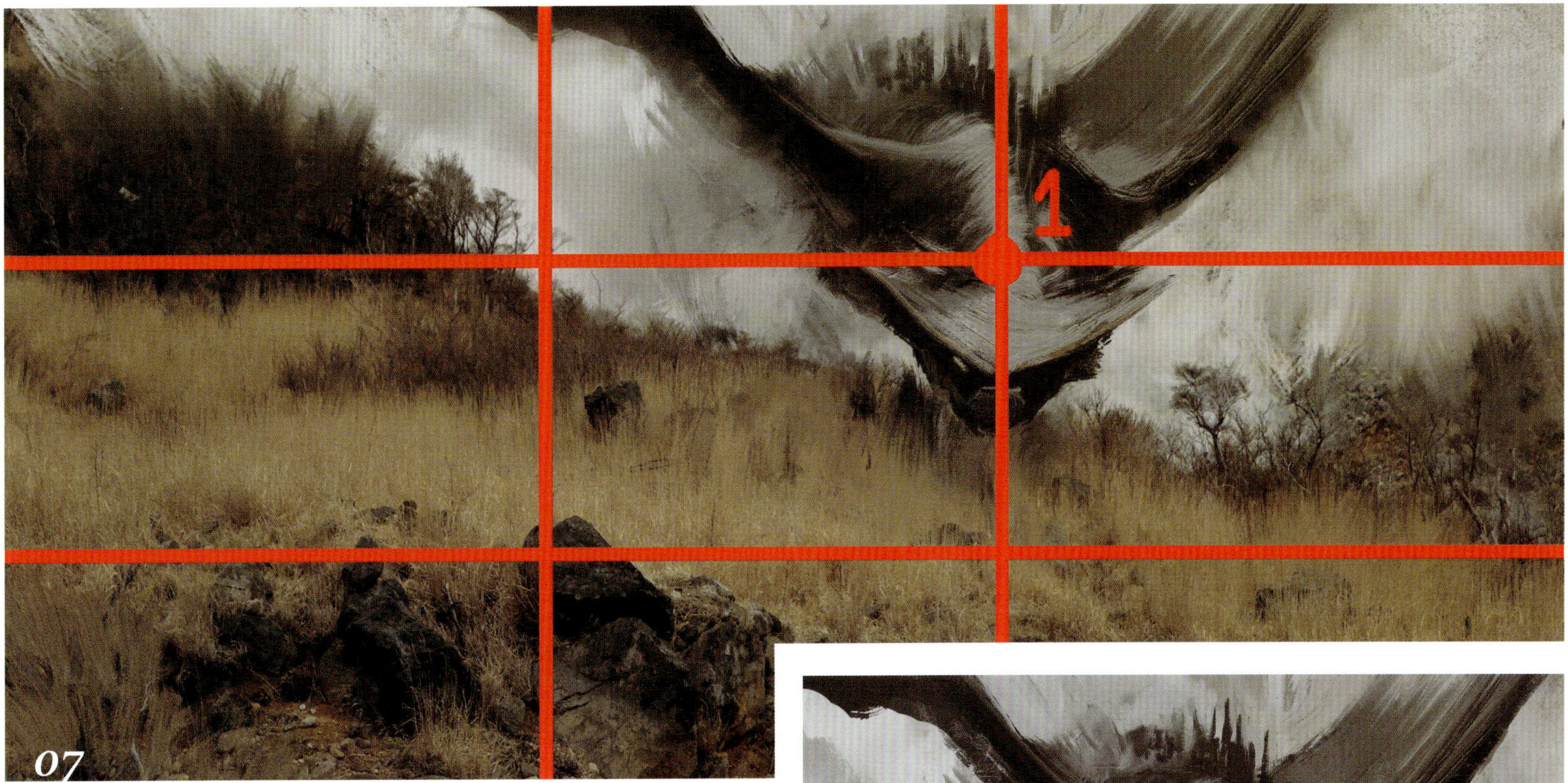

▲ Placing the main subject close to one of the four focal points helps the viewer to quickly look at it

07: Focal point

Using the most basic tenets of composition, the rule of thirds, paint the dragon head on one of the focal points; you need to add more detail to areas where you want the viewer's eye to rest.

Using both the Standard and Mixer brushes, add details to the dragon head, such as scales, horns, and the suggestion of eyes and a mouth. Even though this is a focal point you don't want it to be too defined to maintain the painterly look.

08: Define the body

Now that we are sure about the position and the intention of the dragon, it is time to place him in the environment. It is not always good to constantly look at references, but instead be more spontaneous and original. I decide to go with the classic "ready to attack" pose of felines which is something most people can easily recognize. I also keep working on the rest of the body, redefining some forms and paying close attention to the strokes to achieve more bulky forms.

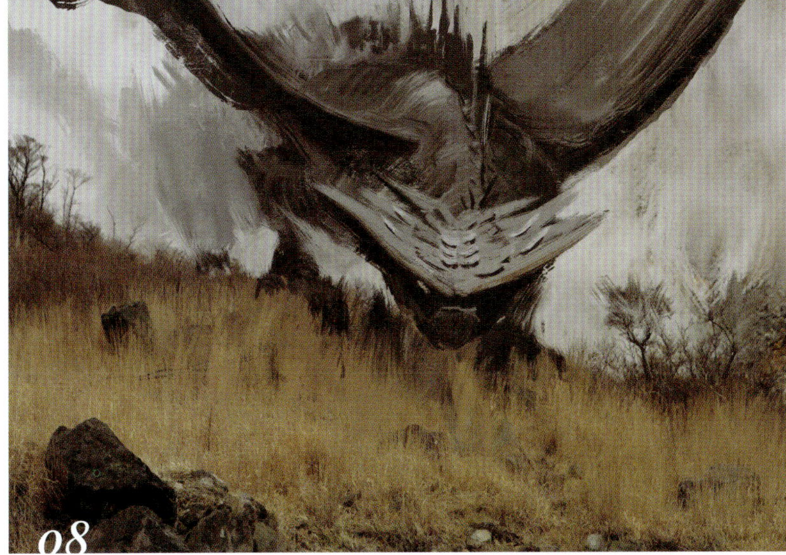

▲ The dragon is almost done

09: Flip the canvas

Flipping the canvas is one of the best techniques for avoiding mistakes in the composition and balance of your paintings. When you are looking at the same picture for long periods of time your brain starts to get used to it and it will fail to see any errors in the composition or proportions. I highly recommend you set up a shortcut for rotating your image; it will save time and also improve the results of your work.

10: Color palette

Use a neutral and desaturated color palette; you can get the dragon's colors from the environment and with slight changes to the values and hues make a harmonious painting. It is also important to consider the reflective light – adding some oranges and browns to the bottom of the body and the brighter grays of the sky to the highlights will give your main subject the color vibrancy necessary to make it more interesting to the viewer.

11: Secondary main subject

If you are happy with the background, you can now focus on a secondary subject. As there is an hour time limit you will need to simplify your options. You could go with a dragon hunter – maybe riding a horse or standing in the field, getting ready to attack the big dragon. When adding a character try starting with the basic shape of the silhouette, using a hard brush. This will make it easier to see the proportions and pose.

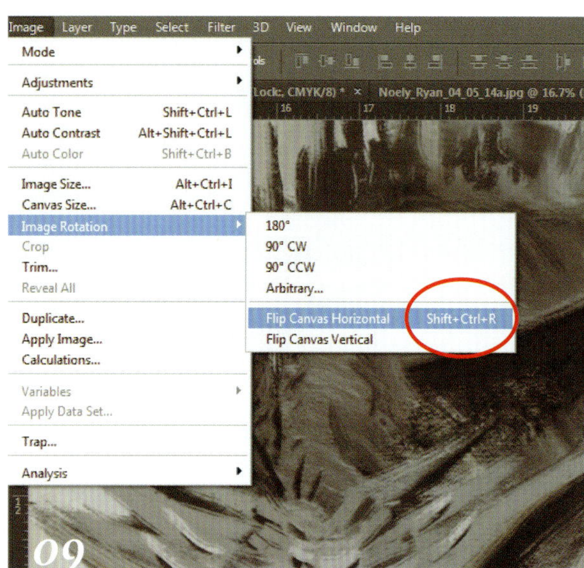

▲ Choose an easy shortcut to remember so you can quickly refresh your perspective of the painting

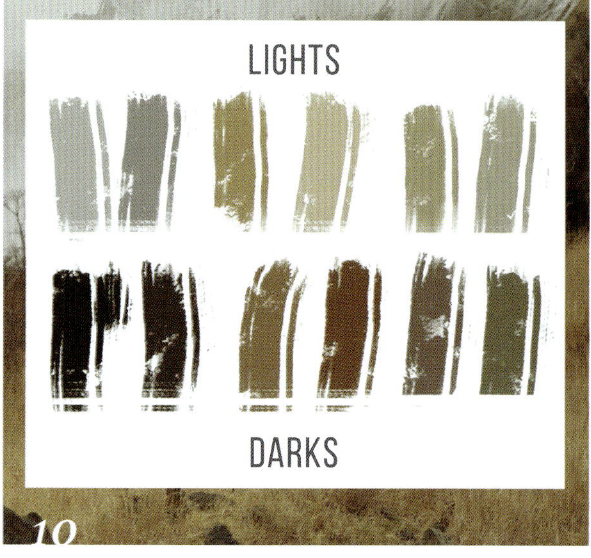

▲ Neutral and desaturated colors give the painting more serenity and harmony

12: Describe the secondary subject

When you are happy with the silhouette you can play around with the Free Transform tool to distort and stretch the figure to fit into the scene. To add more detail lock the transparent pixels and start adding some colors, again using the colors from the surrounding area. Suggest some of the forms with only light and shadow. To make the shape crisper use a hard eraser to give a nice clean edge.

13: Costume design

Taking advantage of the colors added in the previous step, start playing with more hues and values, adding more volume and details. As a dragon

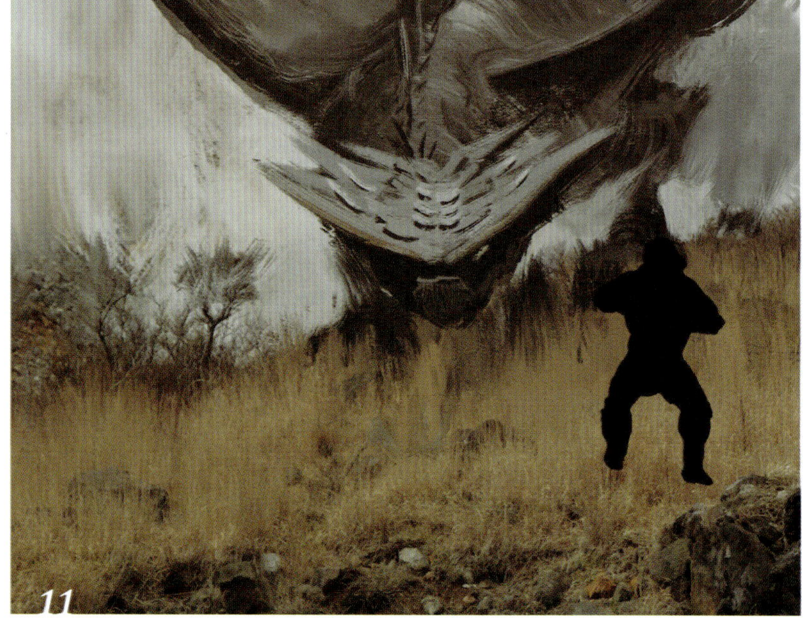

▲ A silhouette helps you to get the right post for your character

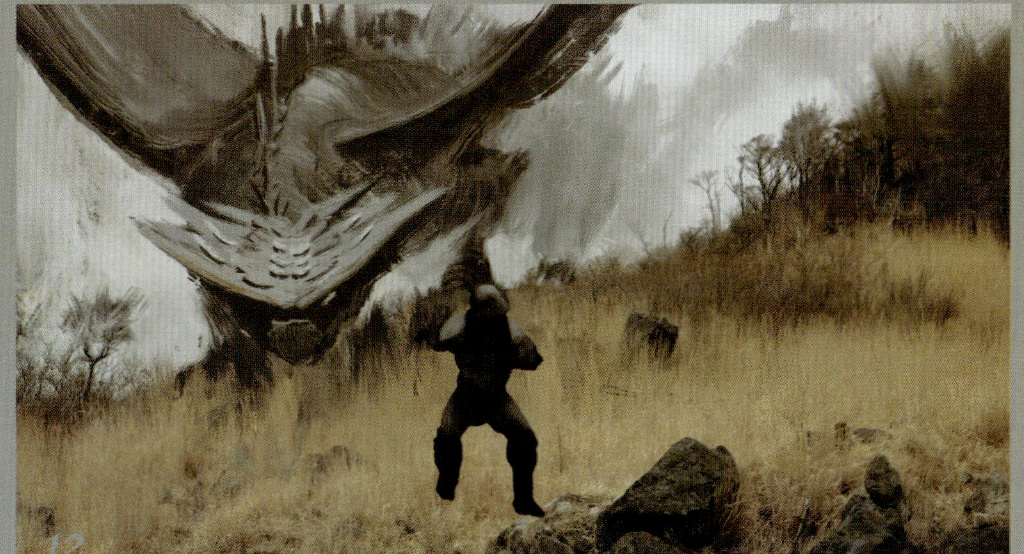

▲ Using a clipping mask or locking the pixels of your layer is a good way to start adding colors to it

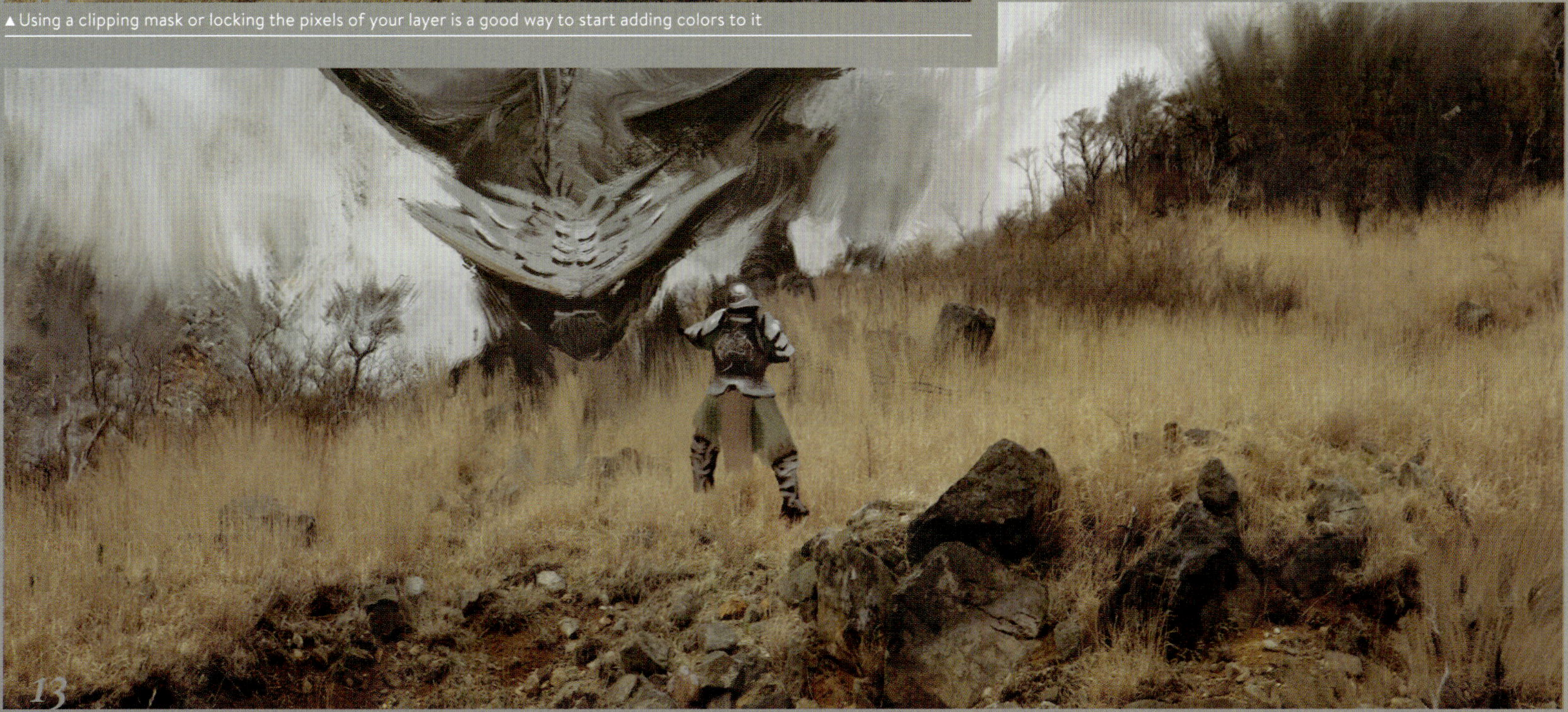

▲ Try to break the silhouette by adding things that seem to hang and lean on the body, making it more believable

hunter, he needs to have some kind of armor and a helmet. Using the same brush as the rest of the painting along with some scattered texture brushes, you can start defining the different parts of the armor and clothes. This is a good opportunity to introduce a new hue – the green tones of the dress coat make for an eye-catching outfit for the hunter.

14: Correct the composition

If you are not happy with the placement of your character you can easily correct the composition by stretching and moving him until he is in a better place. In a new position in **image 14**, he is bigger and closer to the viewer. He is in the opposite focal point to the main subject, the dragon, giving the painting a better balance and flow, following the diagonal composition I liked in the original photo.

15: Refining phase

Now that the painting is almost complete you can start adding the last little details. Zoom in closer, although not too much, to the parts that you think need more detail. You don't want to waste time messing with non-vital elements and unnecessary details. Keep up with the spontaneous style from the beginning right through to the end, but still think carefully about when and where you are going to put the brushstrokes.

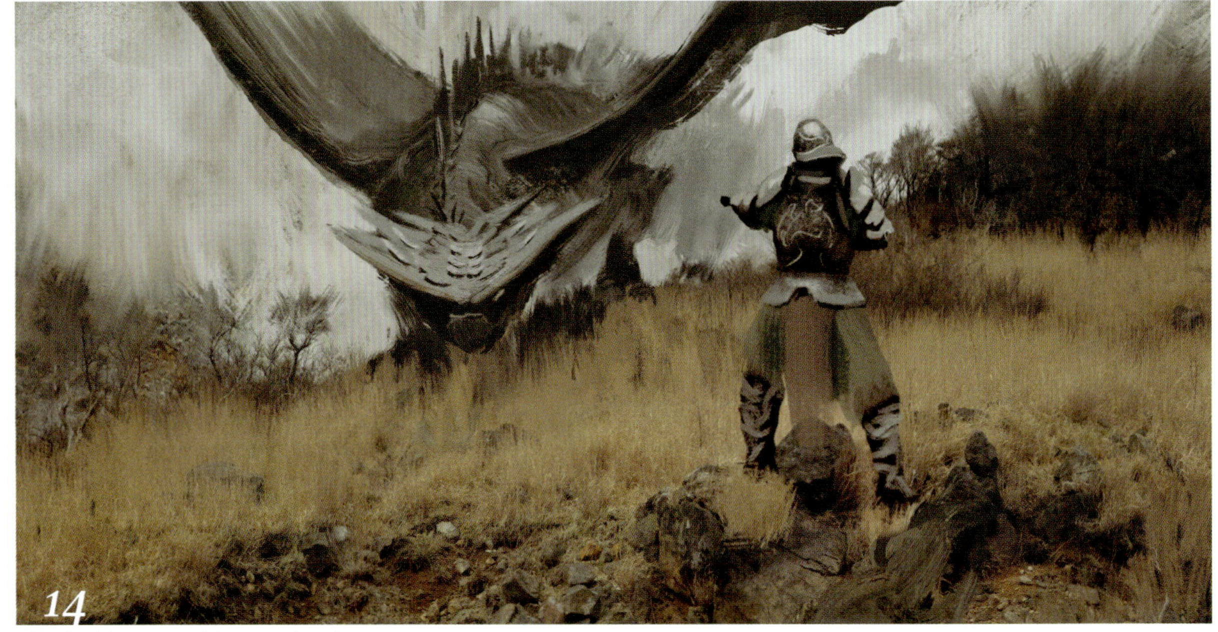

▲ The final placement of the secondary character

16: Separate the main subjects

Near to the end of the process is the time to add some final touches balancing the whole image. Duplicate the dragon hunter layer and go to Image > Adjustments > Brightness/Contrast..., and play with the sliders to get the values you want. This will give the appearance that the two focal points are farther apart – atmospheric perspective at play again.

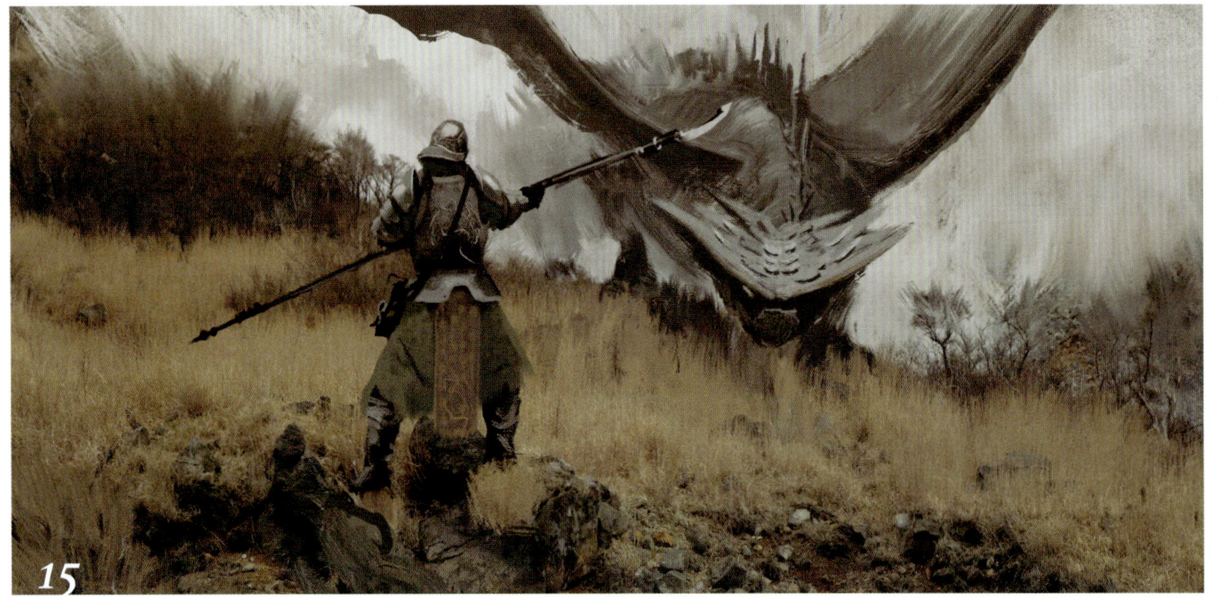

▲ Using textured brushes I suggest more details on the character, through the patterns on the coat for example

17: Add more drama

You need to add balance to the image after darkening the dragon hunter to add more drama. One of the easiest ways is to duplicate the whole image (Ctrl+Alt+Shift+E), adjust the Curves (Ctrl+M or Image > Adjustments > Curves...), and make it much darker. Then create a layer mask painted black where you want the image to be brighter. This way you can better control the light without painting over everything again. I decide to add light to the dragon's

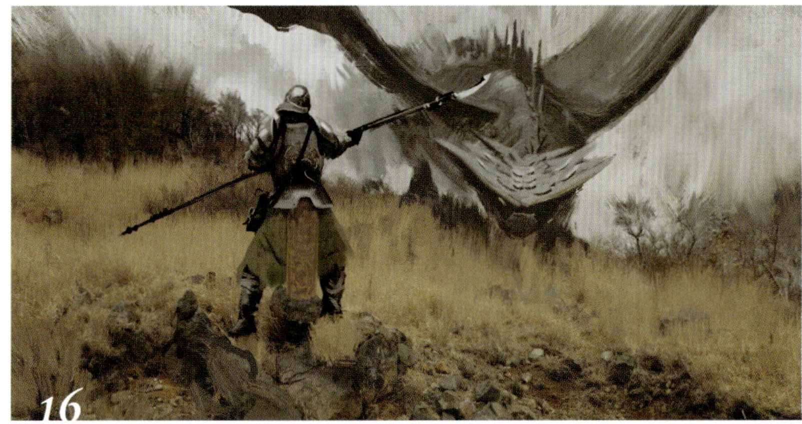

▲ With more contrast the foreground elements look closer to the camera/viewer

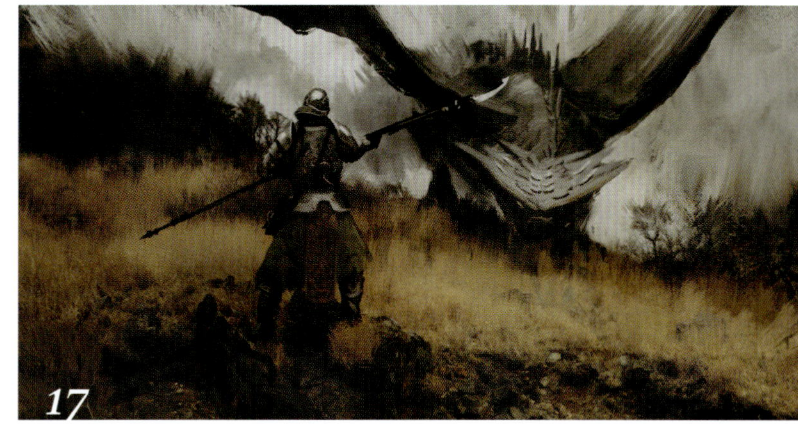

▲ With the intention of making the dragon more sinister and striking, I darken the image

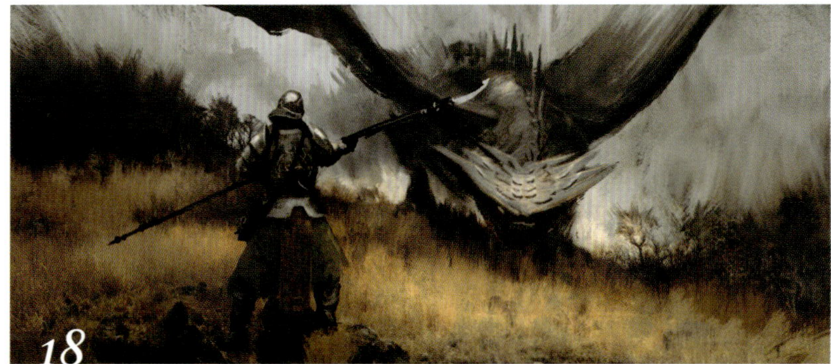

▲ I add warms colors in the lights to make a richer and more colorful image that previously was a bit monochromatic

head and between the two subjects, adding a darker frame to the picture.

18: Warm light

Adding warm colors to the lighter areas of an image can emphasize the lighting to contrast with the cool shadows – a Color Dodge layer is perfect for this. Fill it with black, choose the light color you want, and paint slowly and carefully in the places where you want the contrast to pop. Again, add the most contrast near the dragon head. In fact the warm light behind his arms makes me think of a background on fire or something more sinister, helping with the storytelling.

19: Unify the scene

The last step I usually do with some of my paintings is to add an Overlay layer with a lot of noise on top of everything. Create a new layer filled with gray set to 50%

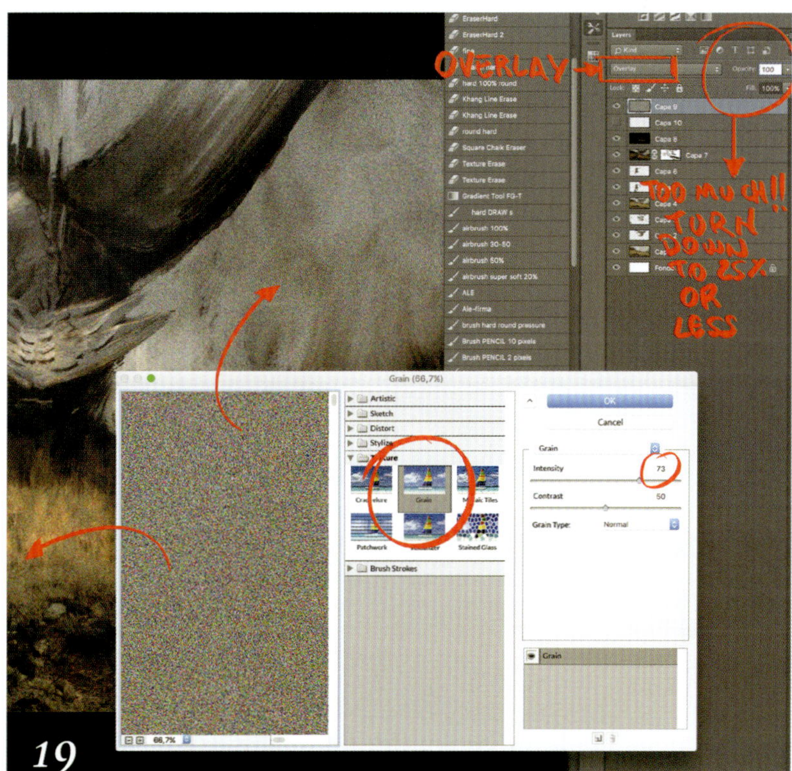

▲ Add noisy or textured Overlay layers on top your image to unify and add depth to your paintings

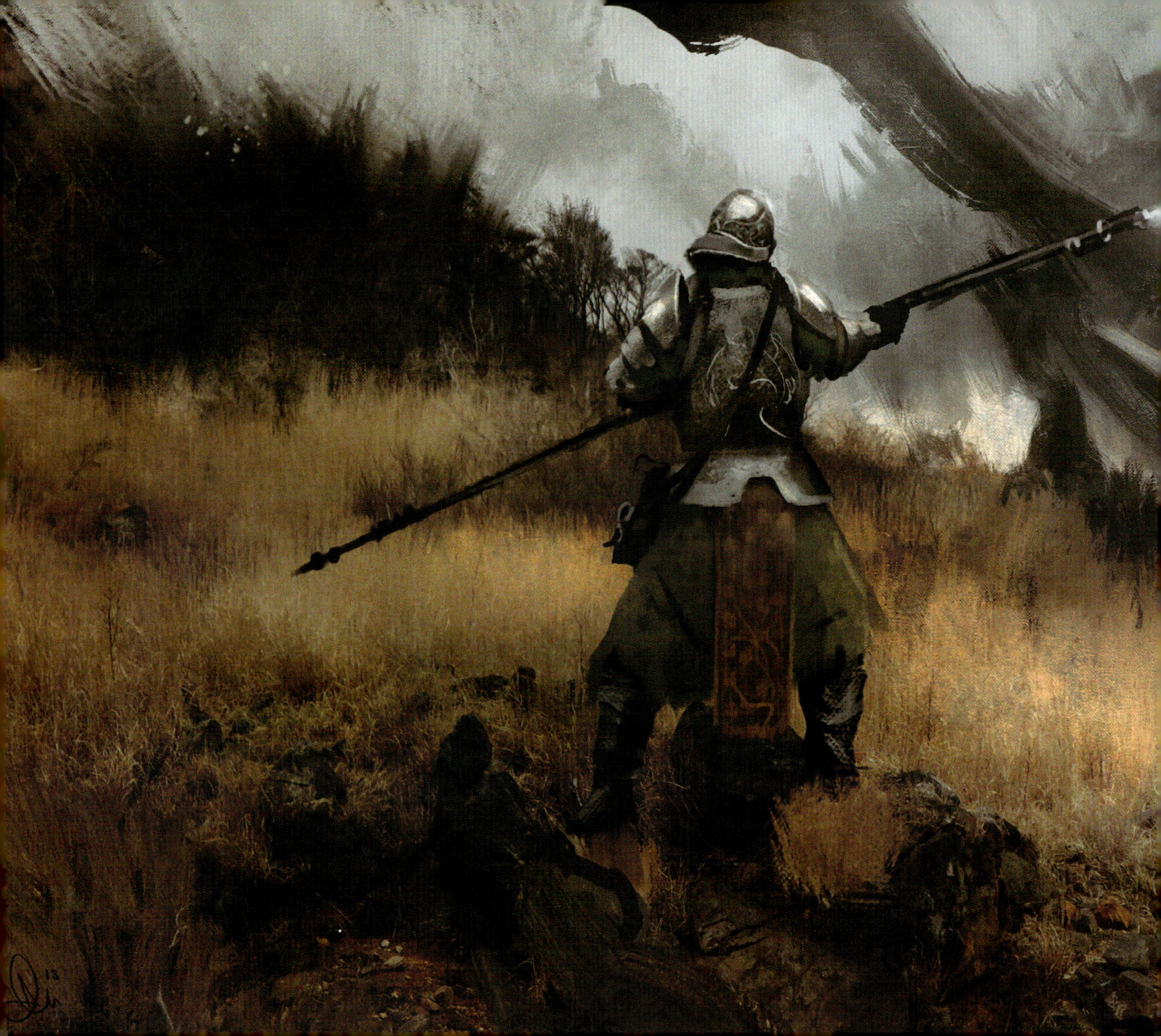

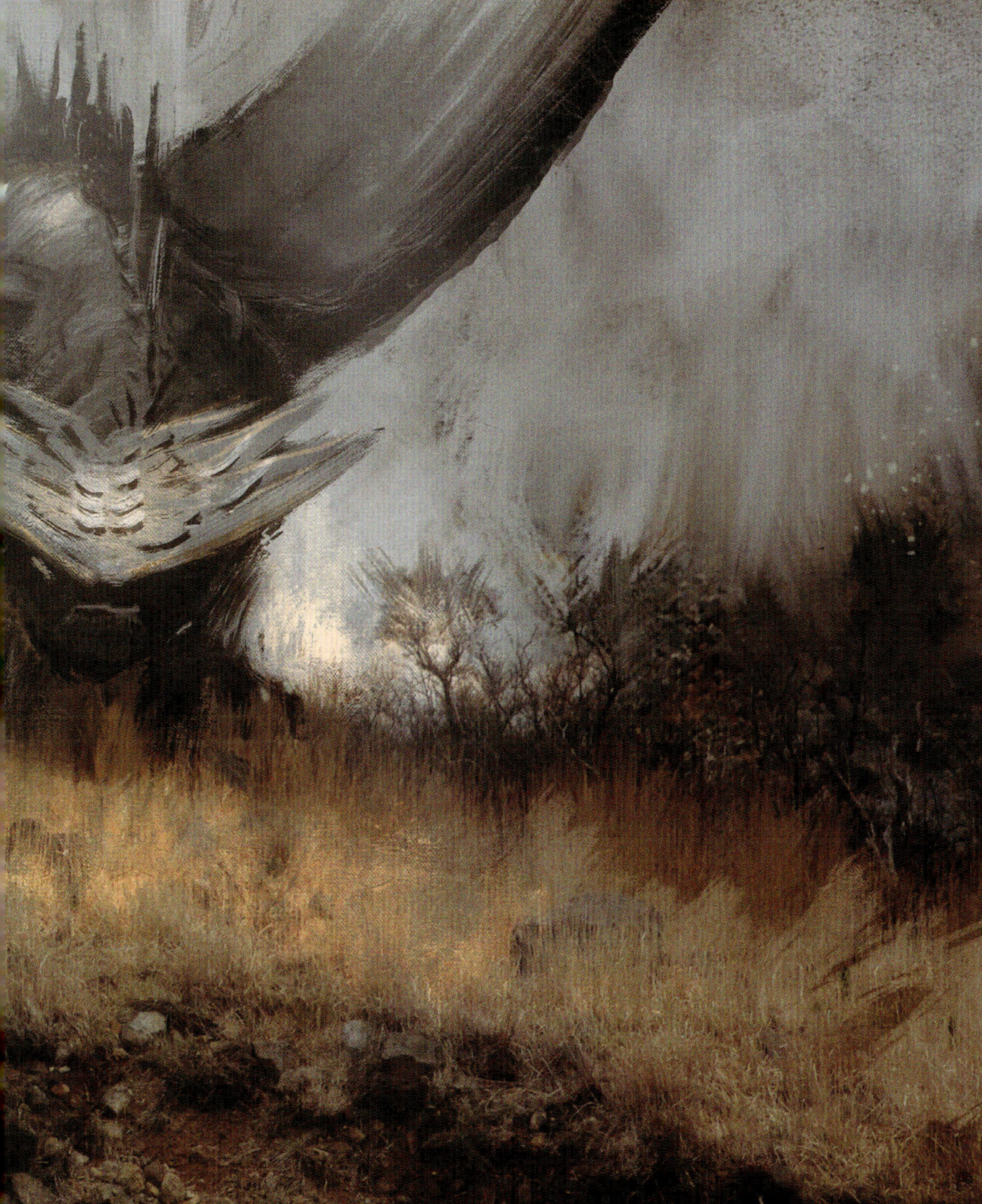

and turn it into an Overlay layer, then go to Filter > Filter Gallery... > Grain and add lots of Grain. Finally, change the opacity of the layer to 20–25%. Doing this will unify the colors and edges of the painting, making it more attractive to the viewer.

20: Final touches

In the last two steps I change the values of some parts of the body of the dragon. I try to tone it down with some atmosphere, adding some light rays coming from the top of the image.

I also use some of my custom brushes to add more detail to the atmosphere as dots and particles. This makes the painting more dynamic and realistic. Just add a little highlight on the armor and finish.

Pro tip: Be spontaneous

When talking about sketches, concepts, and speed paintings it is really important to let your hand paint alone. Sometimes you fail and sometimes you succeed. The first ideas are usually the best! When going into detail it is easy to forget the basic idea of the painting.

SCI-FI: A MODERN INTERIOR

by Ian Jun Wei Chiew

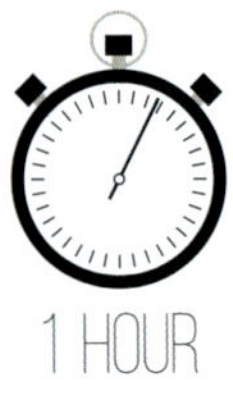

1 HOUR

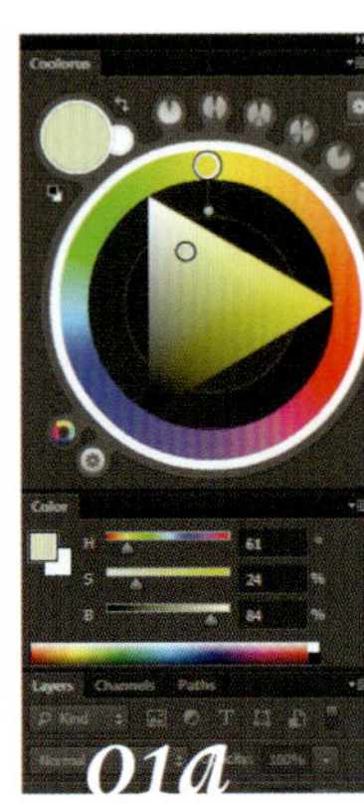

01a

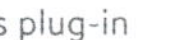

▲ Coolorus plug-in

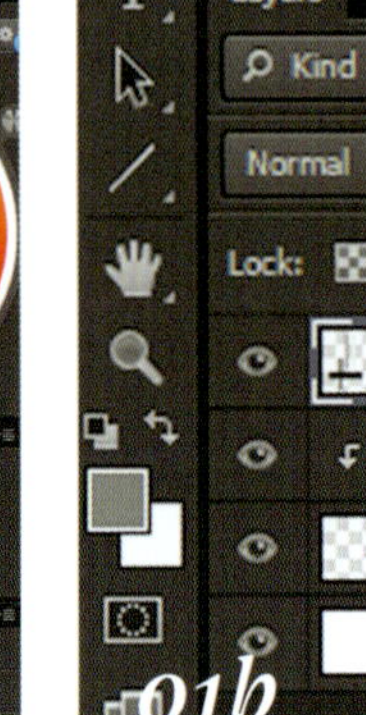

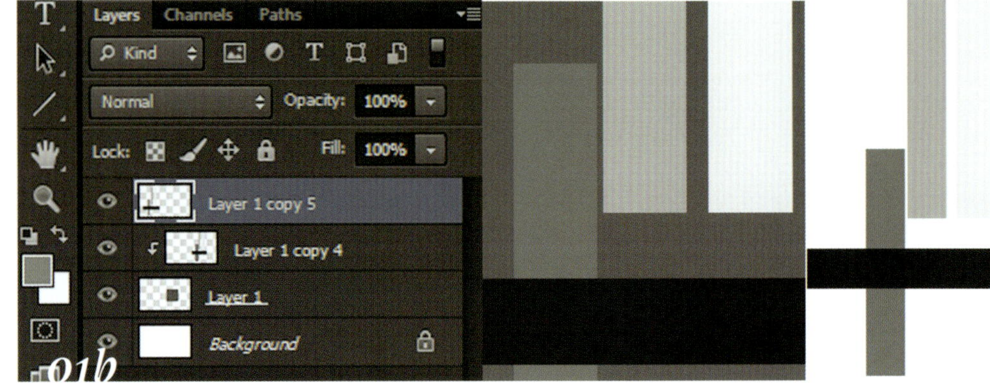

▲ The Navigator and Layers palette help you to keep an eye on the image progression

The theme for this piece is a modern sci-fi interior of a lounge or lobby – partly because I'm inspired by contemporary and modern architecture. I have chosen to go with a warm color palette. Once I've got an idea in my head, I start hunting for reference images; in this case most are modern hotel lobbies and sushi bars. The reason for the sushi bars is because they usually have wooden counters and tables, which have a nice warm color palette.

I make a big composition image that consists of all the reference images in a collage. I always do this so that I can have all the images open in a single JPEG file that fills up my second monitor, instead of having to either individually open each image or open them all with many windows. I also do some value and color adjustments on all the images so that they feel more unified and because I will be going for the warmer palette. I also do some color tweaks to give me a better representation of what I want the final result to look like.

> *"I enjoy creating abstract shapes and use them as assets for the painting"*

01: Set up the interface

I have my tool bars moved from left to right just so that I can access them within the same vicinity as my layers. I use a plug-in called Coolorus which gives me a nice color wheel on the top right (**image 01a**). The Navigator is a great window to have in your interface because you always want to check and see if your image reads well in a thumbnail size, so I occasionally take a glance at it instead of zooming in and out all the time.

I keep my Layers palette at the bottom as I use it very often and prefer to have the adjustment itself on its own layer instead of having it directly applied on the layer that I'm working on (**image 01b**). This is so that I can have more control with the opacity and masks of that adjustment layer.

I also have my F1 hot-keyed to flip the canvas horizontally. I use this often to give me a fresh eye whenever I get too deep into my image. Finally, I have Actions at the bottom. Actions help speed my process up a lot as they basically record a set of actions/menu items that I can just map to a single button.

02: Create initial shape assets

I enjoy creating abstract shapes and use them as assets for the painting. Do this by first blocking out a silhouette with the Lasso and Marquee tools, making a new layer, and then clipping it to the silhouette layer. Keep making lots of abstract, geometric shapes; they should stay within the silhouette.

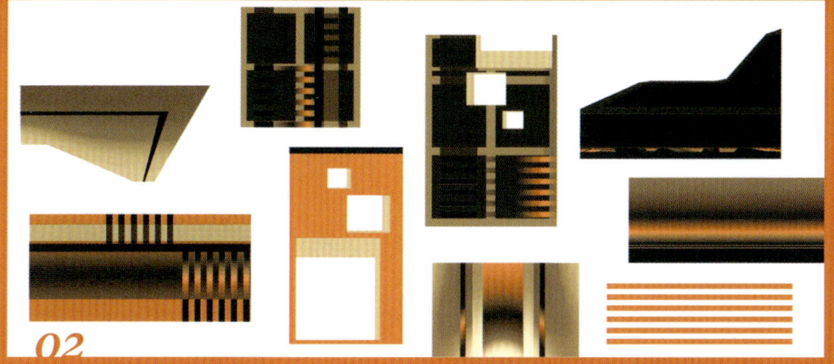

▲Create a number of abstract shapes to become assets for the painting

Pro tip: Experiment

I change up my process every so often depending on the subject matter, but the tools I use are pretty much the same. The Transform, Clipping, and Smudge tools are essential to my workflow as I prefer to create a collage and find shapes, rather than painting right from the get go. I find this method to be more fun and experimental, which can lead to ideas and compositions you would never think of developing. There are endless possibilities with Photoshop; you can find a new use for any existing tool. At the end of the day, what makes a good image is your own personal knowledge of the foundations such as composition, values, color, and lighting.

To clip a layer to another one below, hold Alt and hover your cursor in between the two layers, then left-click. You can also transform a single abstract shape and clip it into the same silhouette to create countless shapes and variety. Then add a basic color scheme to them. As we move forward you will see how the Transform, Lasso, and clipping layers tools are essential to this workflow.

03: Compose the image with assets

I set up my document with the canvas at the bottom and have the asset sheet on the top keeping each individual asset on its own layer. This is so that I can easily look and pick which assets to use to start composing my image.

First add a gradient to the background and then copy an asset to the bottom and transform it into a shape. In this case, I take one and transform it to look like a one-point perspective ground plane.

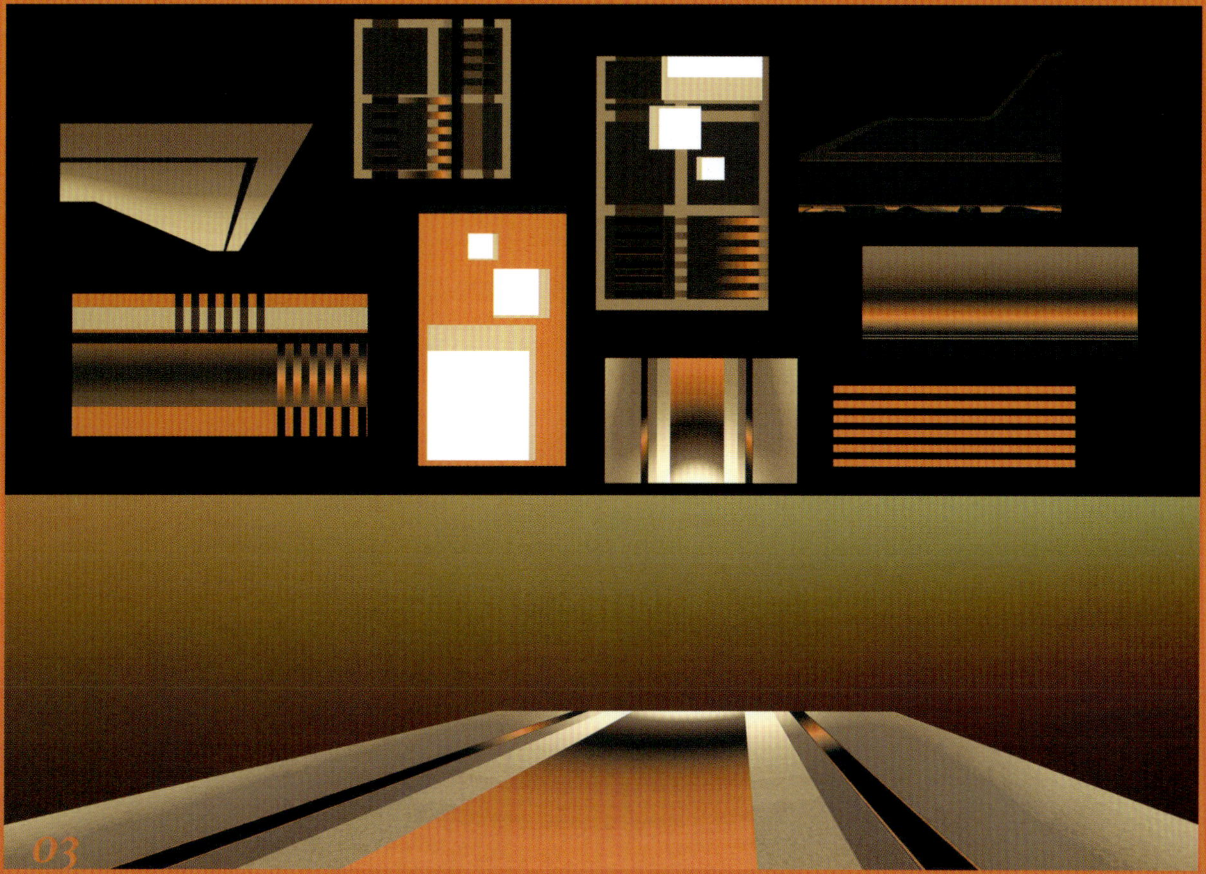

▲Compose your image by adding a background gradient, duplicating and transforming your shape assets

▲Play with the composition to find a focal point in the foreground and middle ground

04: Composition focal point

I try to incorporate all my assets and transform them in place to get a basic composition down. Having those assets already made speeds things up a lot, which at the end gives me more time to explore different shapes and compositions.

In this case I keep the image in a simple one-point perspective as we look down a lobby towards the focal point in the center. I also make a new silhouette and clip multiple assets in for quick detail and interest.

I make the center focus consist of more vertical and horizontal lines, which contrasts well with all the angled shapes in the foreground and middle ground.

05: Clean up perspective issues

I generally prefer to add my perspective guidelines a little further into the painting process rather than from the start. This is because if I have guidelines at the very beginning, I tend to be very restricted in what I put down on the canvas and have to follow every detail of the guidelines. Therefore they slow down the entire process as well as restrict the development of compositional ideas. Once I have a sketch down and ready to move forward, I add the guidelines then and clean up all the perspective errors, even changing the angle of view slightly.

06: Apply color adjustments

I've got my basic color palette down from the colors already on the individual assets

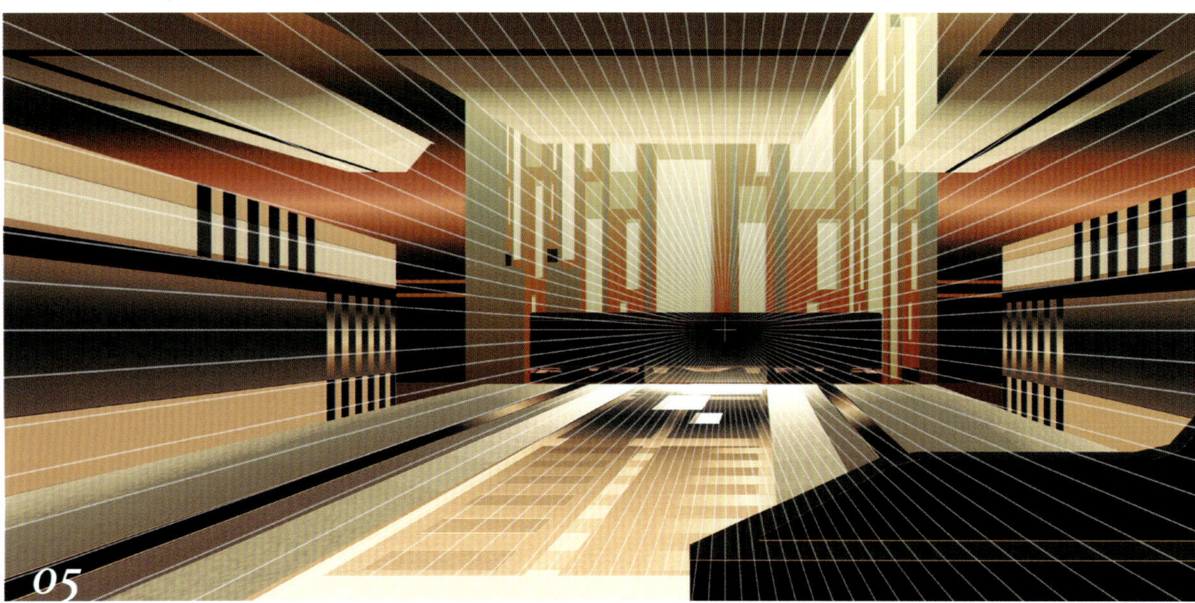

▲After the basic composition, perspective lines can clean up any perspective issues

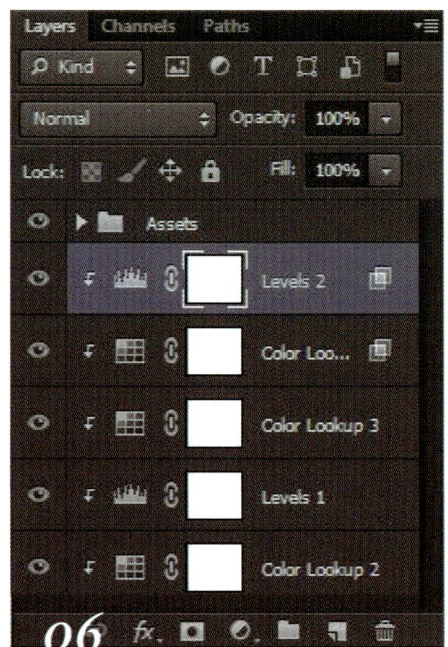

▲Set layers in a group and clip new adjustments to the group

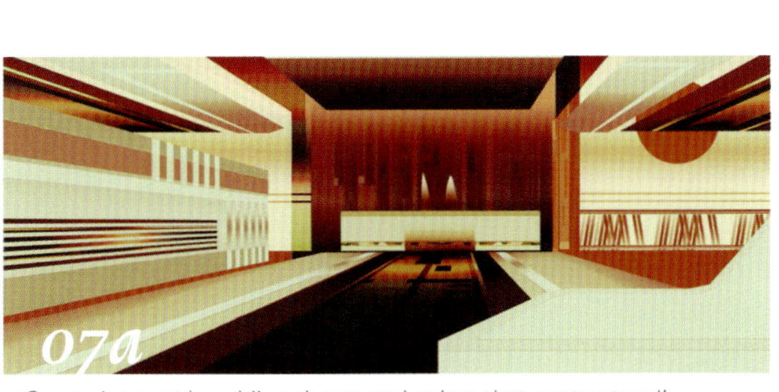

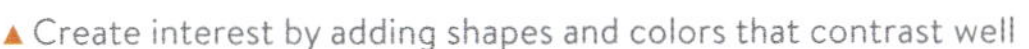

▲ Create interest by adding shapes and colors that contrast well

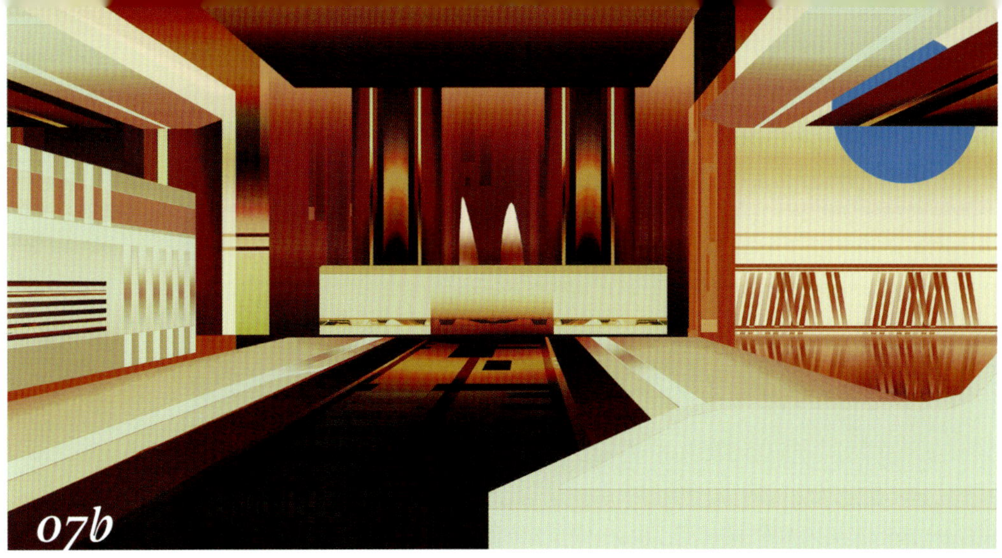

▲ You can also vary the amount of detail in different areas to create contrast

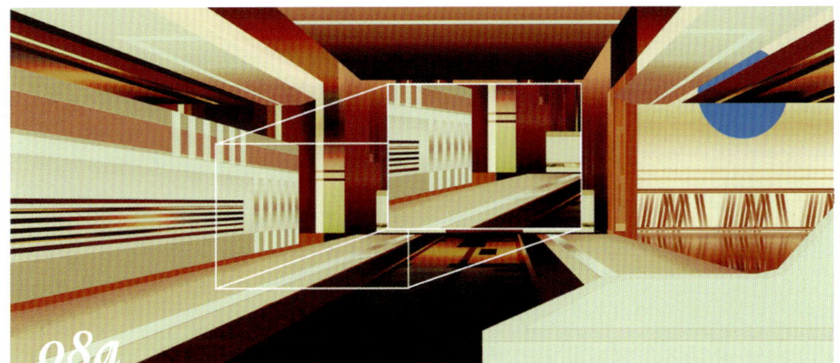

▲ Copy a section of the image and transform it to find interesting details

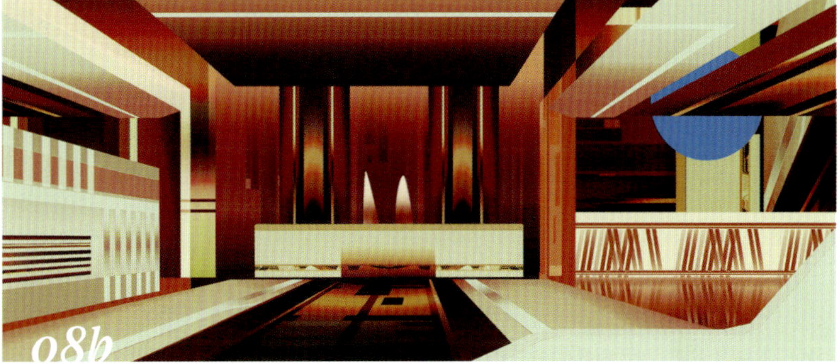

▲ I paste a section on the right-hand side of the image

but I feel the scheme needs a kick. Play around with adjustments such as Hue/Saturation, Levels, and Color Lookup to get something brighter, adding more saturated warmth to the overall tone. I have all my layers set into a group and clip the adjustment layers to that group.

07: Detail passes

Now it's time to add some more visual interest around the image. I start by just thinking about what shapes and colors would contrast well with the current state of the image. In this case, I add a circle shape to contrast with all the angular ones (**image 07a**).

I also remove the wall on the right as I think it feels too busy. This creates a nice break for the eye to rest on. I select the same asset for the ground plane and use it as a framing element for the figure at the counter. This helps focus the image to the center as well as provide more interesting shapes. I also add some kind of railing towards the right to get some small concentration of detail which contrasts well with the open space (**image 07b**). I think that blue contrasts well with the reds and oranges, so I add this to the scheme as well.

08: Ctrl+Shift+C

During the early sketch stage, I often experiment with Ctrl+Shift+C, which copies everything in a selection regardless of what layer I am in. This is a quick way to copy a certain part of an image and keep all layers intact. You can then move the selection around the image and transform with layer adjustments to get an abstract look which can help you find "happy accidents" in terms of its position (**image 08a**). I copy a section of my painting and move it to the right as well as rotating it 90 degrees counter-clockwise (**image 08b**). I also add some value adjustments and some quick details in the background.

09: The Smudge tool

The Smudge tool is great for filling up blank areas and for creating complex shapes. Set the Smudge tool to 100% Opacity and move sections around. A hard brush is best for this. I tend to use a square brush as it gives straight and clean edges.

Add a blue circle at the center (the center needs a strong focus point and to provide interesting contrasts). The bottom-right corner looks odd because the thickness of that patterned line is the same width as most of the lines throughout the painting. By smudging parts of that line downwards, not only do you fill up that area, it also looks a lot more unified with the pattern.

10: Reflections

To make reflections, simply copy whatever you want to reflect (Ctrl+Shift+C), flip it upside down, move it into the reflection area, and apply a vertical Motion Blur to it. You can then erase or mask out certain parts of the ground that are not reflective. Fortunately, you can control where you want the reflections. In the Layer Style menu you can control the transparency of lights and darks of your current layer (**image 10a**). You can also control the dark or light values of the underlying layer to show through. This is great for masking out reflections that are not supposed to show on a dark (or light) surface instead of having to manually lasso and mask out areas, as the material shape could be very complex (**image 10b**).

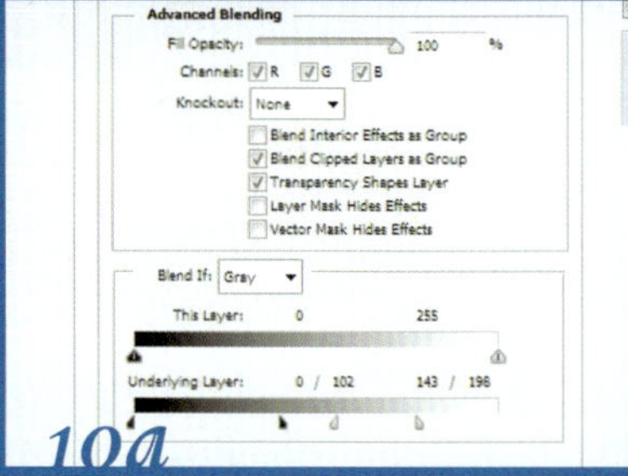

▲ Sliders in the Layer Style tool allow you to control the light and dark values of a layer

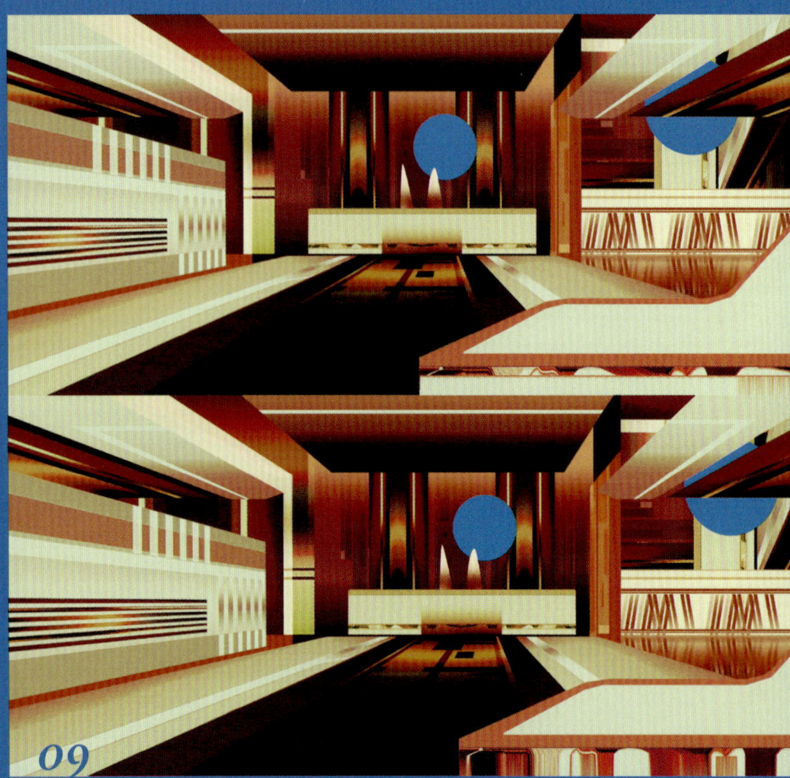

▲ Details such as another blue circle are added and the pattern in the bottom-right corner is smudged

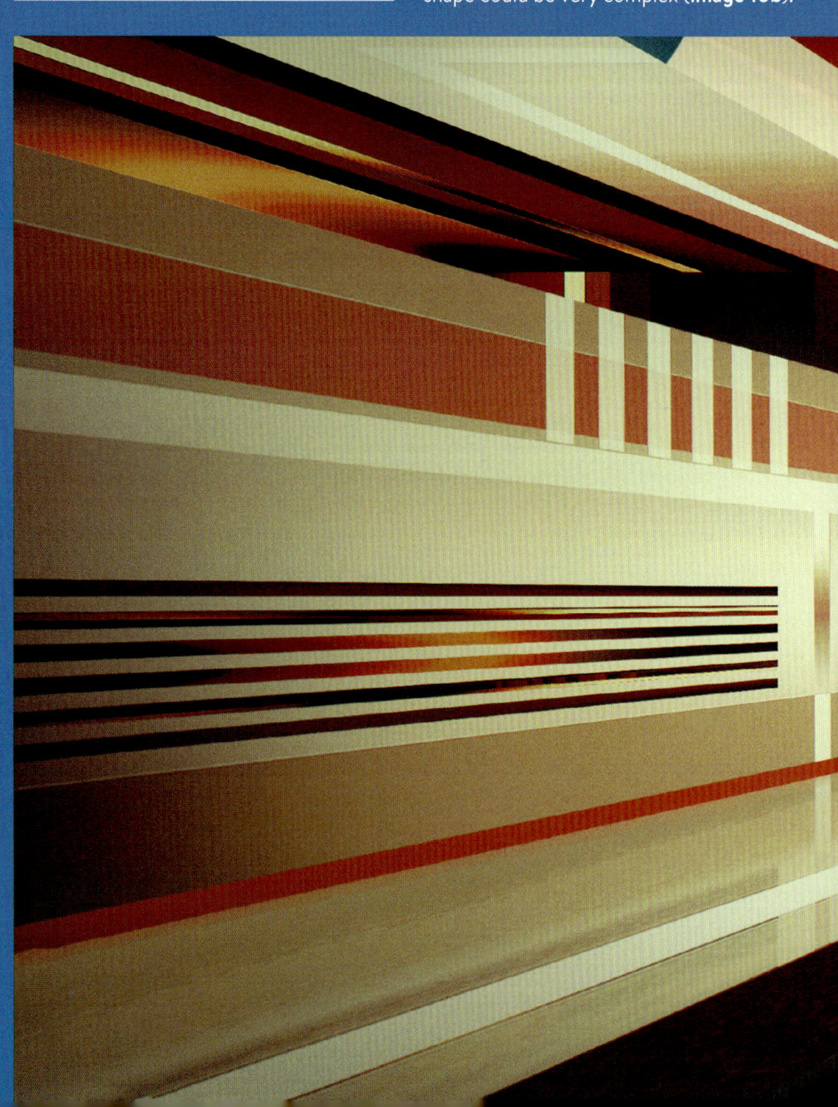

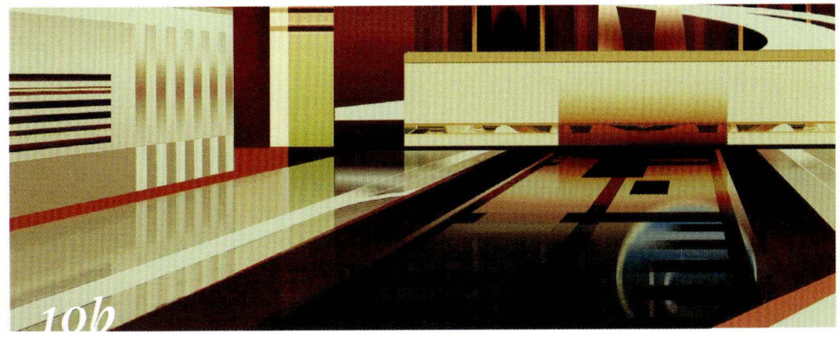

▲ Adding reflections can make or break an image

11: Final touches and details

Add in some more blue circles in order to add more contrast and interest. Also add an arc shape right behind the counter as the overall flow of the image is too stale. This will lead the eye to the figures and logo that I have created.

Darken the edges of the image so that the contrast is higher towards the center, which makes a better focal point. To add even further to the contrasts, add a slight warm Color Dodge to the center, which effectively brightens up and saturates that area, adding to the overall atmosphere of the room.

I tend to add a noise layer right at the end just so that it unifies the entire image slightly. I sign it off, and I'm done!

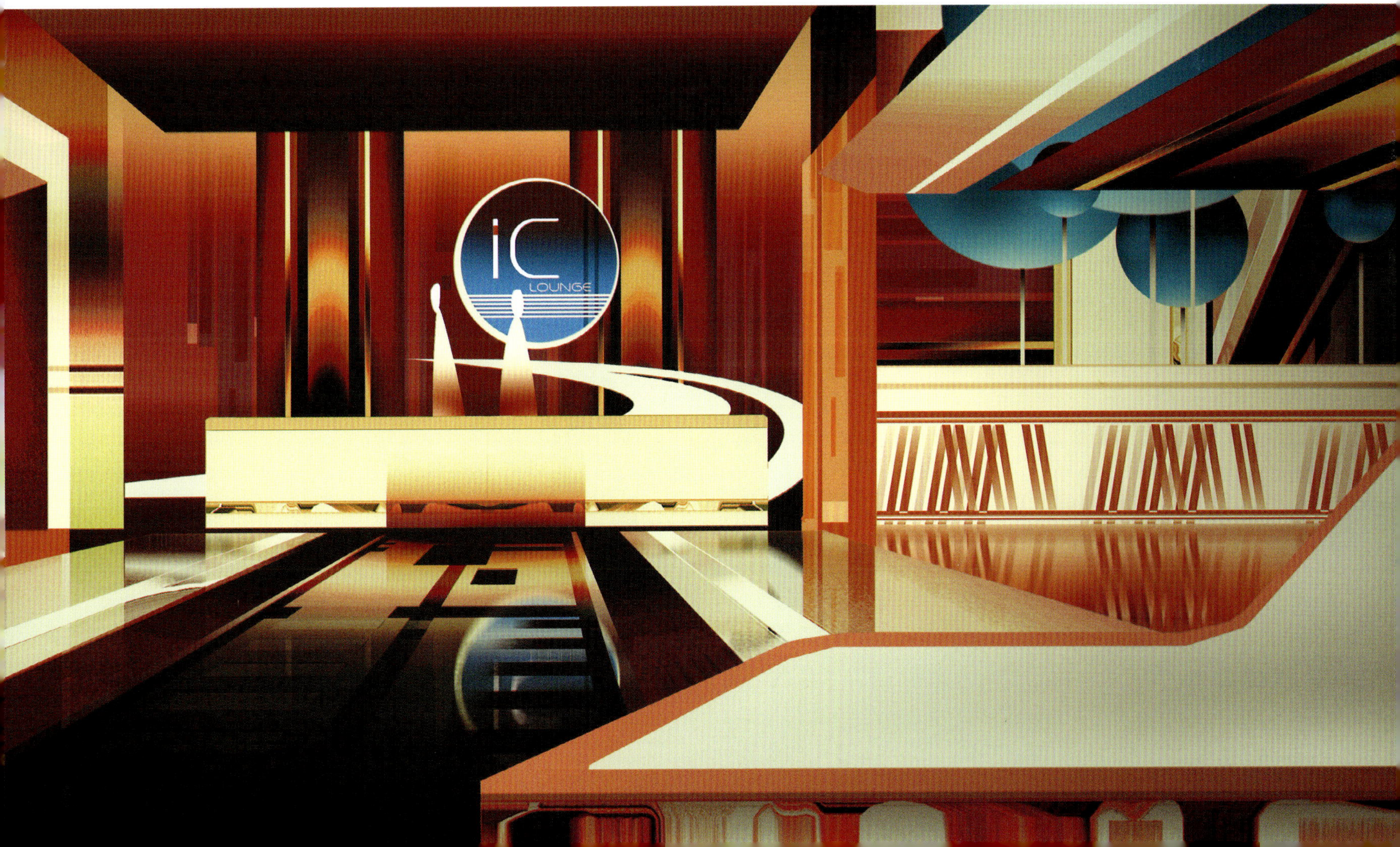

1 HOUR

SCI-FI: THE FUTURE

by Ioan Dumitrescu

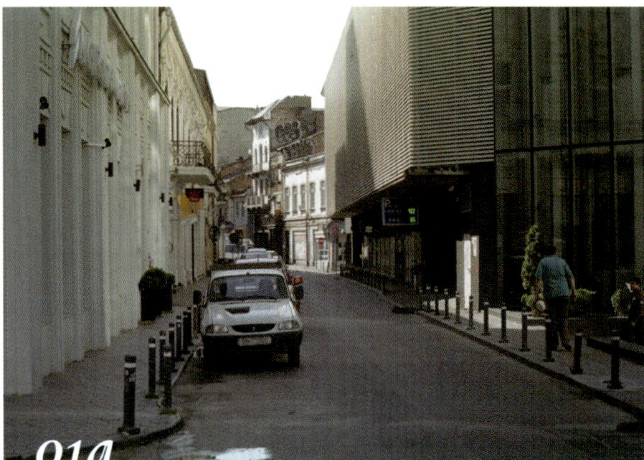

▲ A dull city street ready for digital transformation

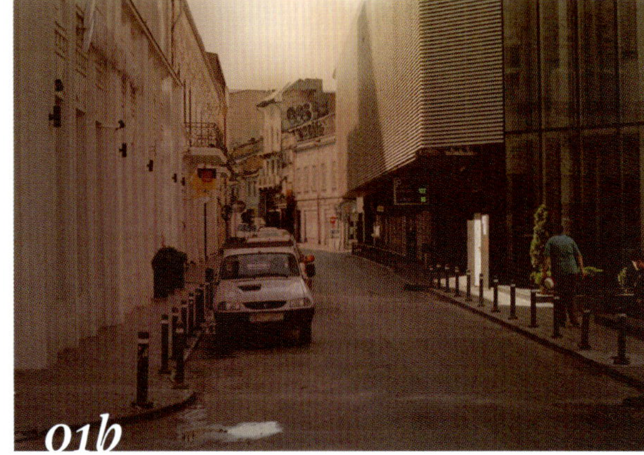

▲ Adding color effects can change the mood of a photo

In this tutorial we are going to do a paintover of a photograph. This is a good technique to use if you are given a photo of a film set or location and you have to make it look cool; you may not have the whole day to work on it as the production designer might only give you a couple of hours.

01: Get started

I don't want to make the task easy, so I have chosen a rather dull city street – nothing special here, right (**image 01a**)? But as a concept designer you are asked to make something out of it, to build on top of it.

Normally you will be working for a client, who will give you the theme, but for this tutorial I have selected the theme and degree of freedom for changing the piece. In today's digital world anything can be changed to suit the vision of the property, be that for games or films.

Inspiration can be found anywhere, including books. I've been reading *The Martian* by Andy Weir so let's bring some Mars tones into the piece. In my mind I know I want to add some sort of tram and a lot of people to create a scene similar to the pictures you see of Asia, with people in all directions and lots of traffic.

> *"As we are going for a futuristic scene you should find images of buildings with Brutalist architecture that will work with the desired atmosphere"*

Start by adding some color effects. Use the Round brush to lay some colors down. As we are going for a dry, desert, Mars-inspired color scheme, warm colors such as oranges and soft magentas are perfect (**image 01b**). I extend the canvas as I feel the scene needs to be longer.

02: Change the mood

Photobashing saves a lot of time, but it can also use up a lot of time when integration is involved; here we are going for something in the middle. As we are going for a futuristic scene you should find images of buildings with Brutalist architecture that will work with the desired atmosphere (see the right-hand side of **image 02**).

You can make adjustments to the tones in the left-middle ground and center background. The tones should be more uniform and have areas that pop. Take advantage of the original photographs to help you decide on the lighting.

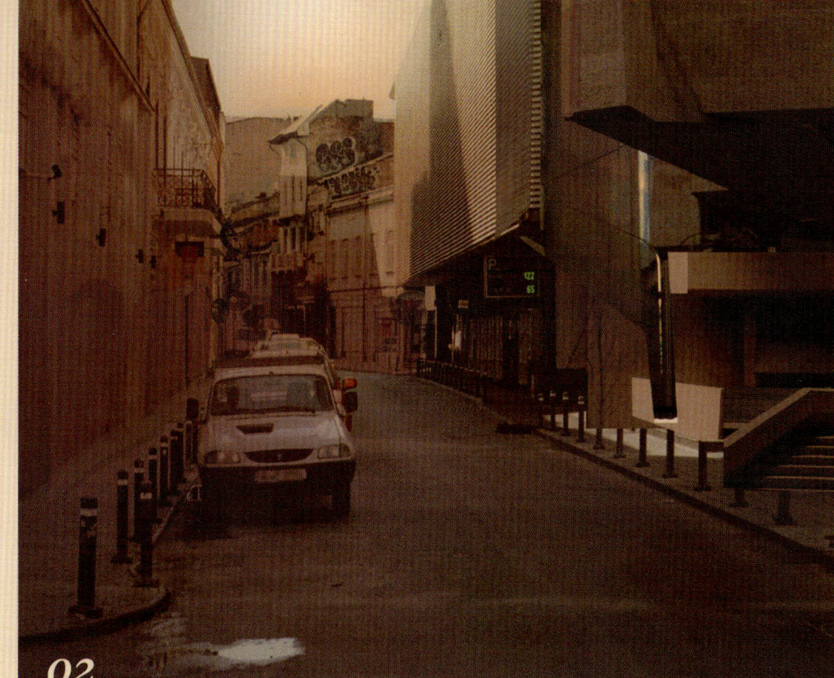
02

▲ Photobashing can completely change the look and mood of a scene

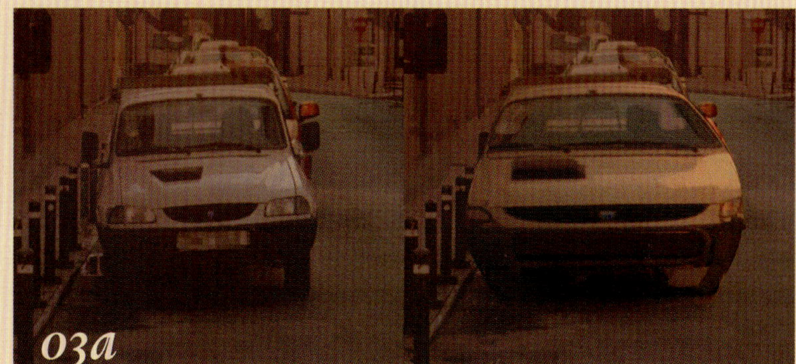
03a

▲ Transform existing parts to fit the theme

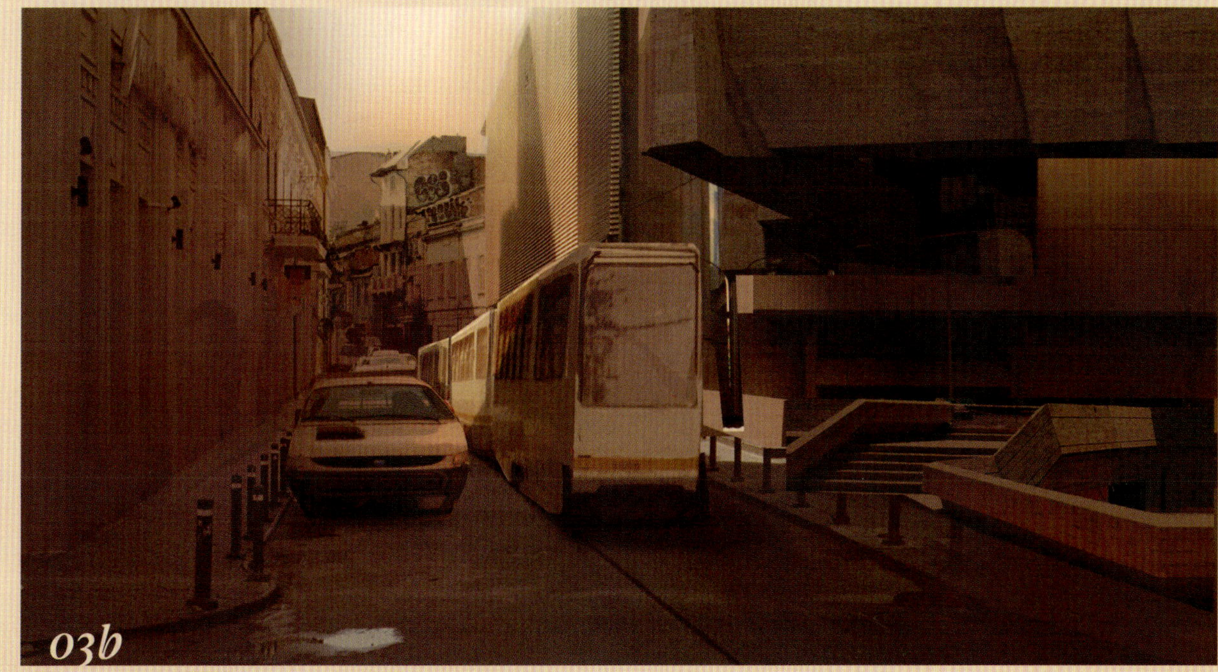
03b

▲ Adding highlights to parts of your image creates contrast and interest

03: Traffic

It's time to bring some life into the scene by adding in some traffic elements. The parked car at the front of the picture is quite ugly and doesn't have a futuristic feel about it. Select the car as a separate layer, then warp and transform it into shape to give it the appropriate look (**image 03a**).

Adding more traffic elements busies up the scene, so in this case I add a tram. You can use the same process to alter the proportions of the tram as you used for the car; select different parts and use the Transform tool to warp its features. You can add contrast and interest to your image by bringing parts of the tram out of the shadows and adding some highlights (**image 03b**).

04: Detail the background

The environment now needs to suit the near-future look, so adjust the left side with an aluminum finish and add the silhouettes of skyscrapers against the harsh sun in the background. The smog and dust in the atmosphere create this beautiful atmosphere, which is rich with colors. I bring in pools of light to the stairs on the right. This will help the viewer's eye to jump around the image and still find it appealing. Colors can be tricky to choose, so make a new layer and start trying colors out whenever you aren't sure. You can always change it by adjusting the Levels and Hue/Saturation, for example.

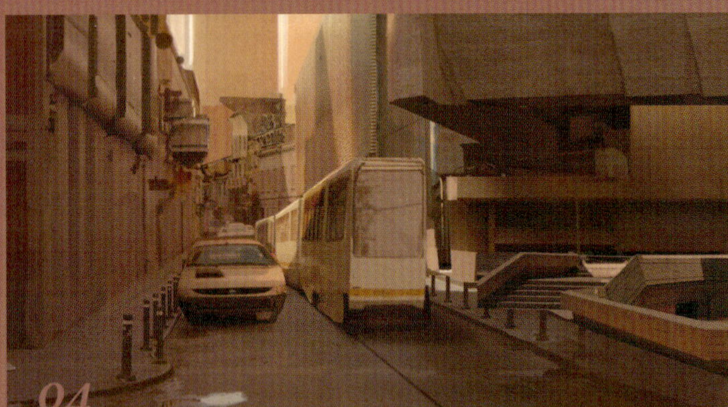

▲ Extra details in the background bring added depth

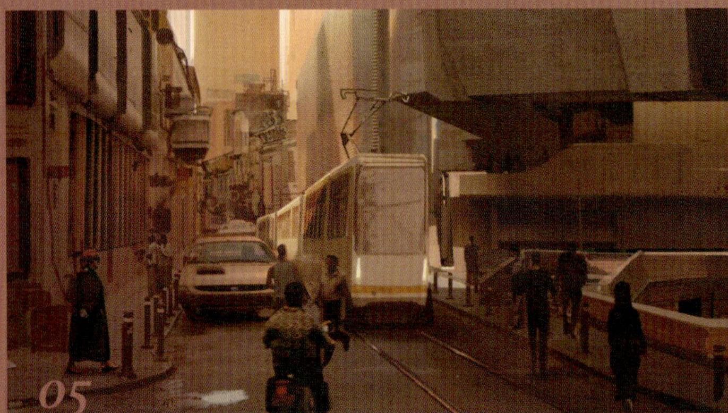

▲ Populating your scene with people really brings it to life

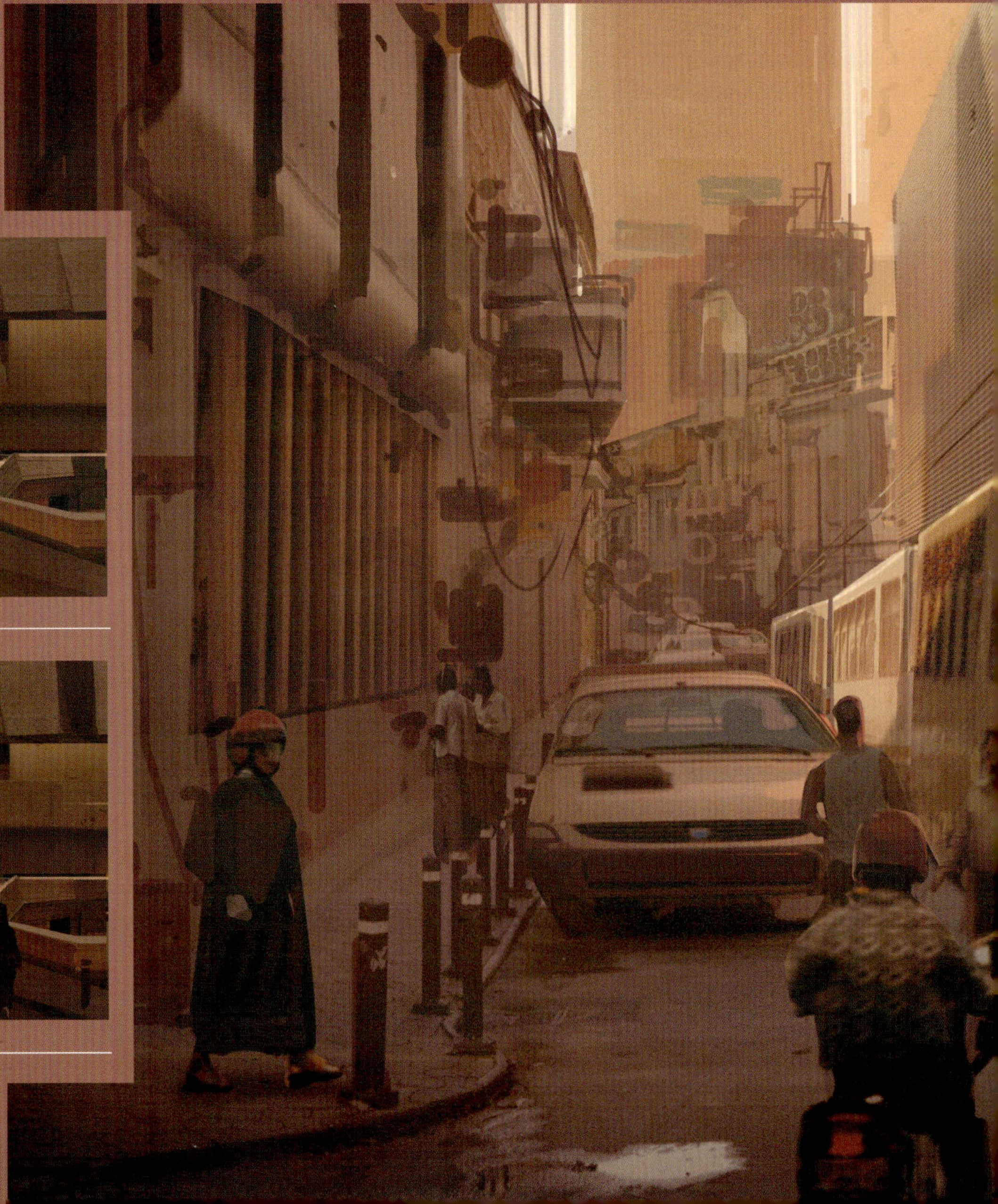

05: Bring the scene to life

Now it is time to really bring this piece to life. Start adding people from a reference. I use my reference from a trip to Thailand. I decide that the scene around the tram will be my main focus so I place the people to encircle it in a way. Keep a space in front of it to allow the eye to pause and rest. Note how the guy on the scooter coming from the foreground connects and draws the viewer in.

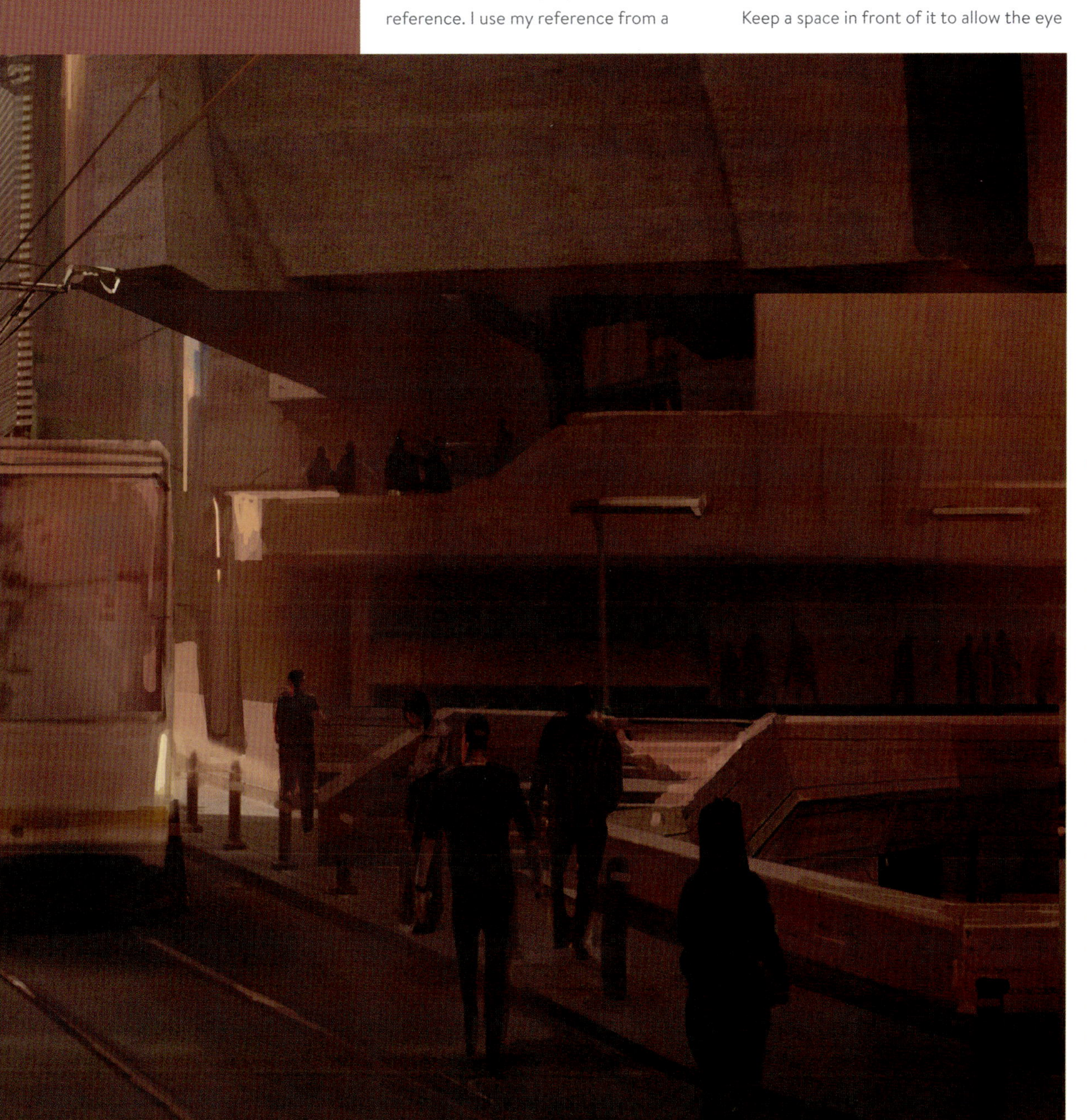

We've kept enough areas clean so we can start creating noise in the background. Add signage and pipes, all indicated with the normal round brush. There's no need to bring in photos for these. The brain will fill in the gaps if you feed it enough, or in this case just play around enough with darker saturated magentas and burgundy; it's such a nice color scheme.

For functionality, the tram needs the connecting pole between the power line and itself, so we can add this in.

06: Final touches

The background is quite chaotic so add some noise to the middle ground to balance it out. The right side, which is calm, brings a nice resting point for the eye. Darken the tram's front window as its reflection needs to be darker to fit the environment. Also bring the digital display from the original photo to give the tram an identification number. It's good to add little details that actually have a function.

Note that the people's heads aren't on the same horizontal plane. I wanted to suggest a slight tilt in the road with the tram basically going up towards us, which is why it's a more angular perspective. This adds an interesting dimension to the piece. To finish, I add in a bit of noise filter, and decrease its opacity.

1 HOUR

FANTASY: MONUMENTAL RUIN

by James Paick

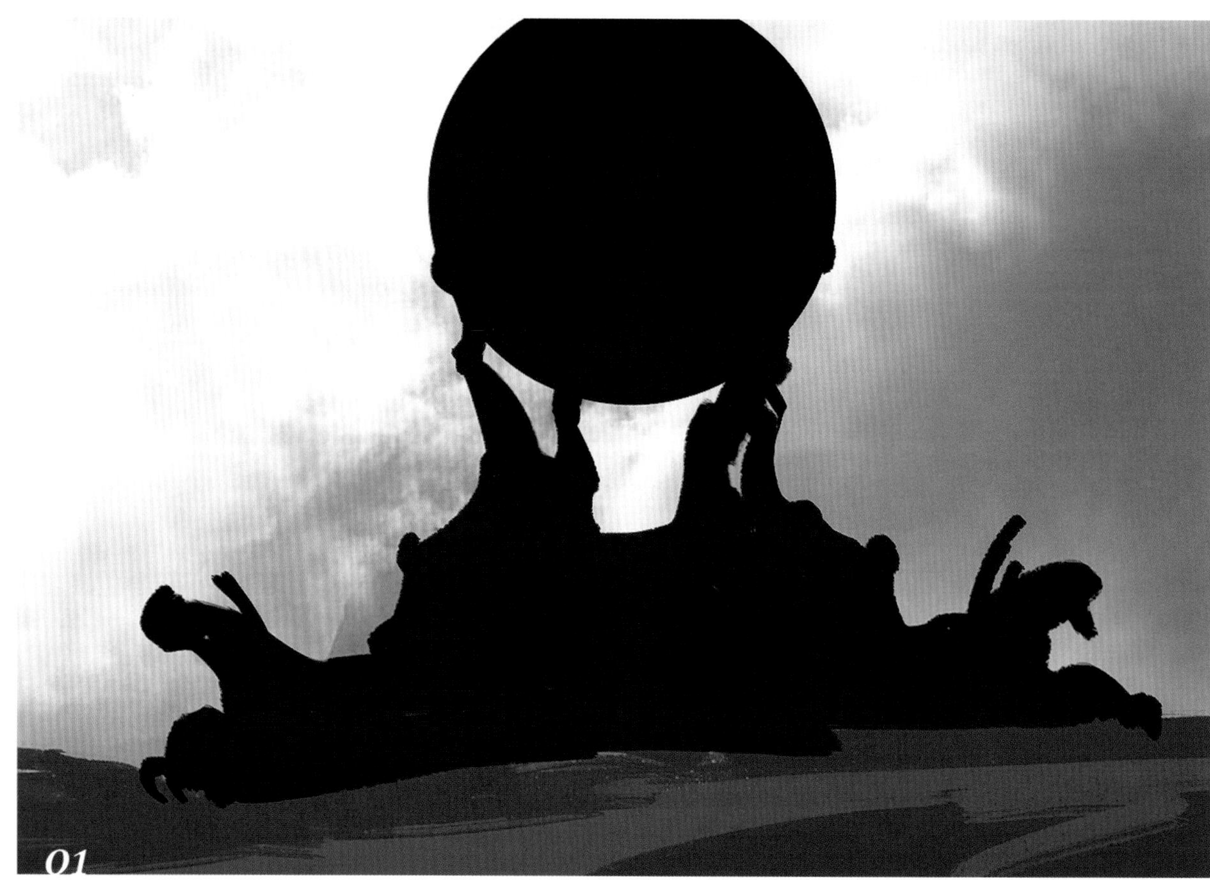

▲ Start with a compelling shape backlit on a moody sky

In this tutorial I will show you how I create monumental fantasy ruins using photo textures I found in my personal photo library. I can't stress enough the importance of having a good photo reference library. You can find plenty on the internet but nothing beats going out there and taking your own. You can get the right exposure, scenery, and contrast to work with your current piece, or just interesting landmarks or cloud formations which might spark a new idea and build the imagination. Don't limit yourself to the natural world; there are so many fascinating and elaborate architectural elements on buildings and other human-made things.

01: Begin with a silhouette

For this initial phase, think about what concept you are going for; I'm going with a concept of a ruin in a natural landscape with moody lighting. Find a suitable reference to use for your backdrop – as I said in the introduction there are lots of options you can choose from. I have a photo from a photo shoot I recently went on with my friend and it is perfect for the backdrop sky.

Make a silhouette of your ruin. You can compose it from any architectural textures that pique your interest. I

"It is important to adjust values and Hue/Saturation when doing this. You do not want your texturing to be the wrong hue and temperature compared to the environment"

am using different round and arching shapes for a feel of something human-made yet organic at the same time.

02: Fill in the silhouette

While on the same reference photo gathering trip, I took a photo of a building facade which is perfect for filling in the silhouette. First start by filling in the main sphere with a repeating texture; then copy the sphere and shrink it using the Transform Tool. Place this smaller shape on the corners of your ruin. Find an interesting section of a texture to use on the base then copy and mirror it to create an interesting design. It is

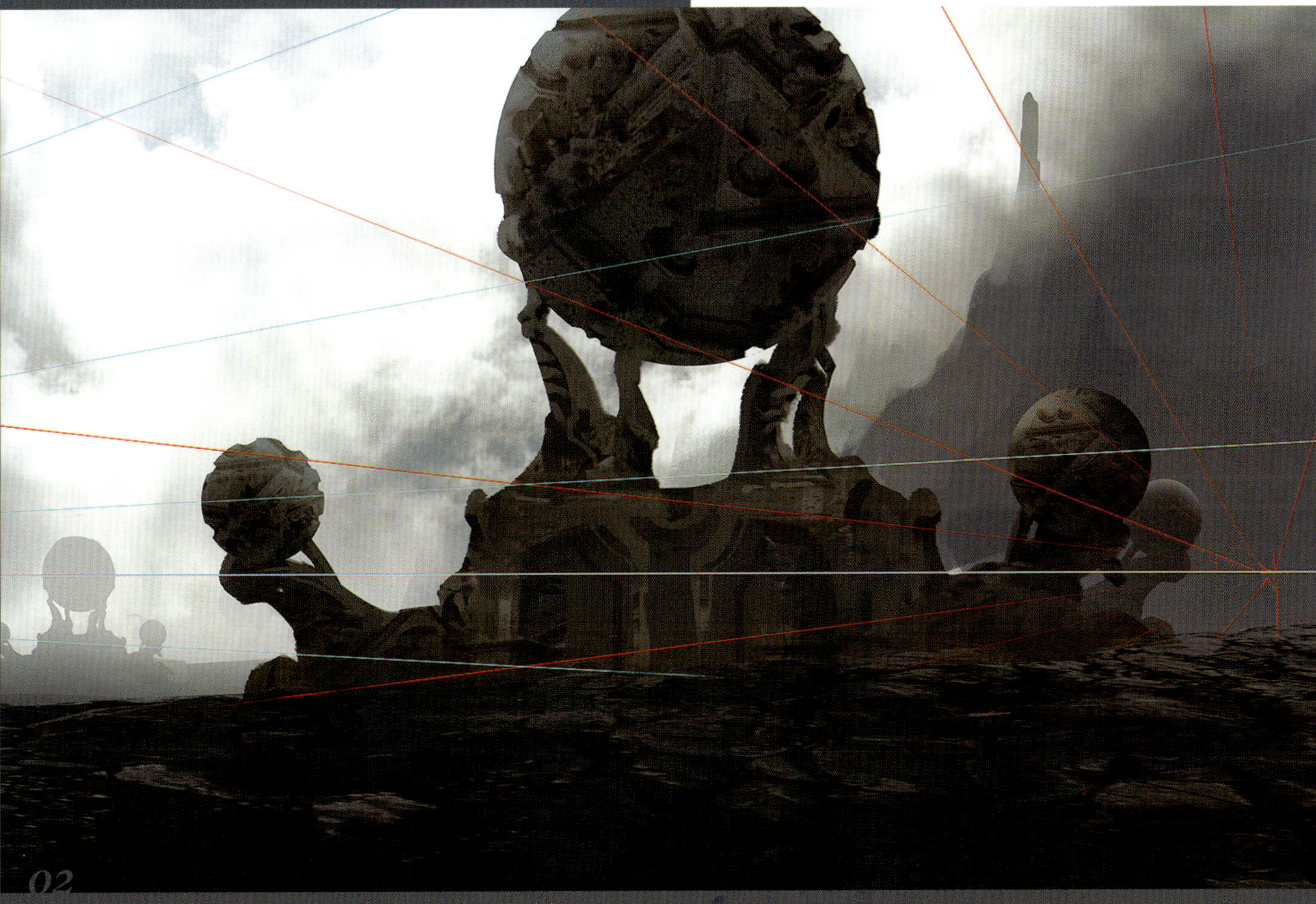

▲ Design the interior shapes in the silhouette with texture and repeated shapes

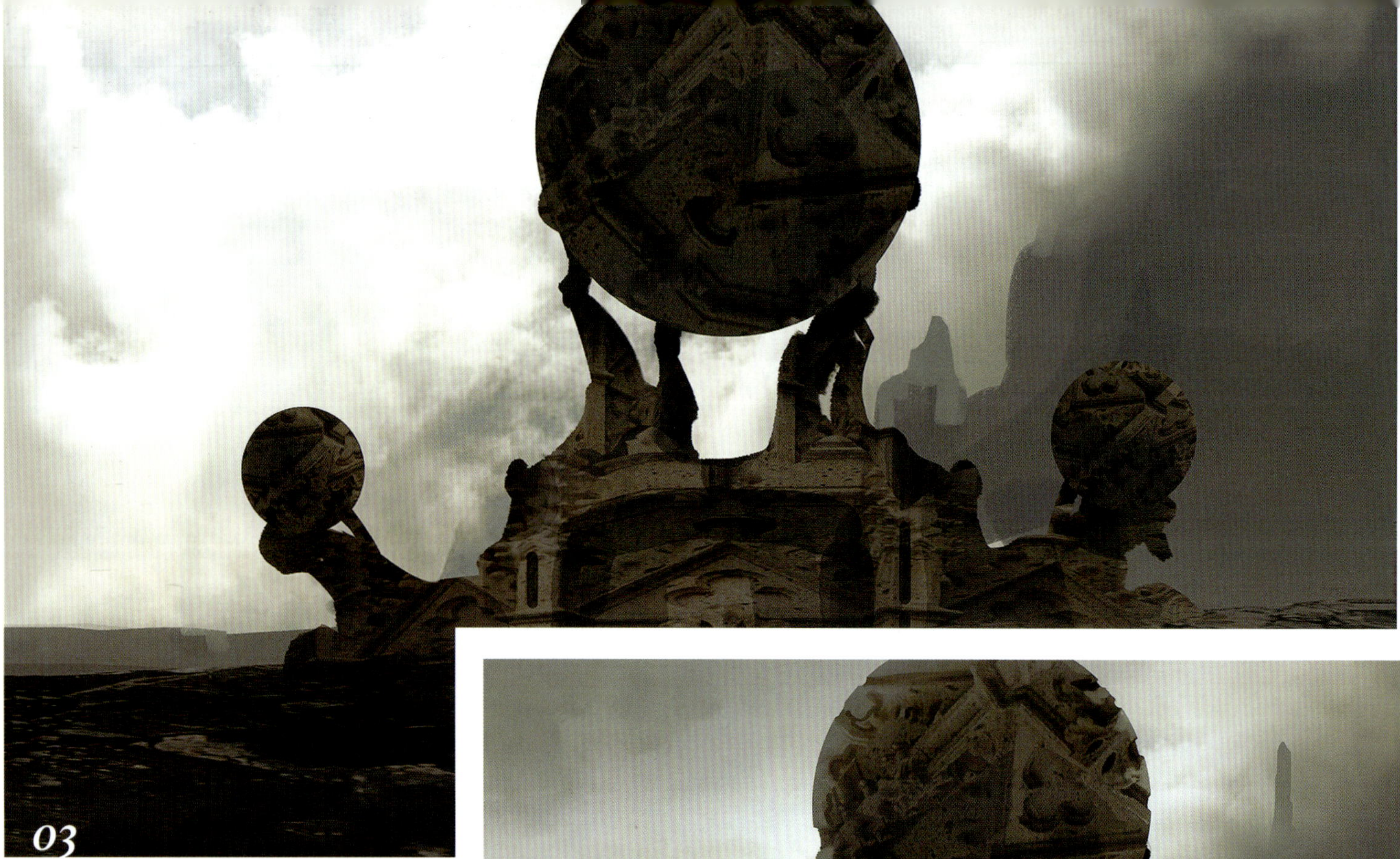

▲ Use repeated shapes and motifs to enhance the ruin feel

important to adjust values and Hue/Saturation when doing this. You do not want your texturing to be the wrong hue and temperature compared to the environment. I recommend that you use perspective lines to ensure your textures are lying on the correct surface plane.

03: Analyze, adjust, and fix

Take a few minutes to step back and look at your overall design; see if there are any ways you could adjust, enhance, and push the design to the next level. Sometimes it's good to take a moment to look at a source of inspiration

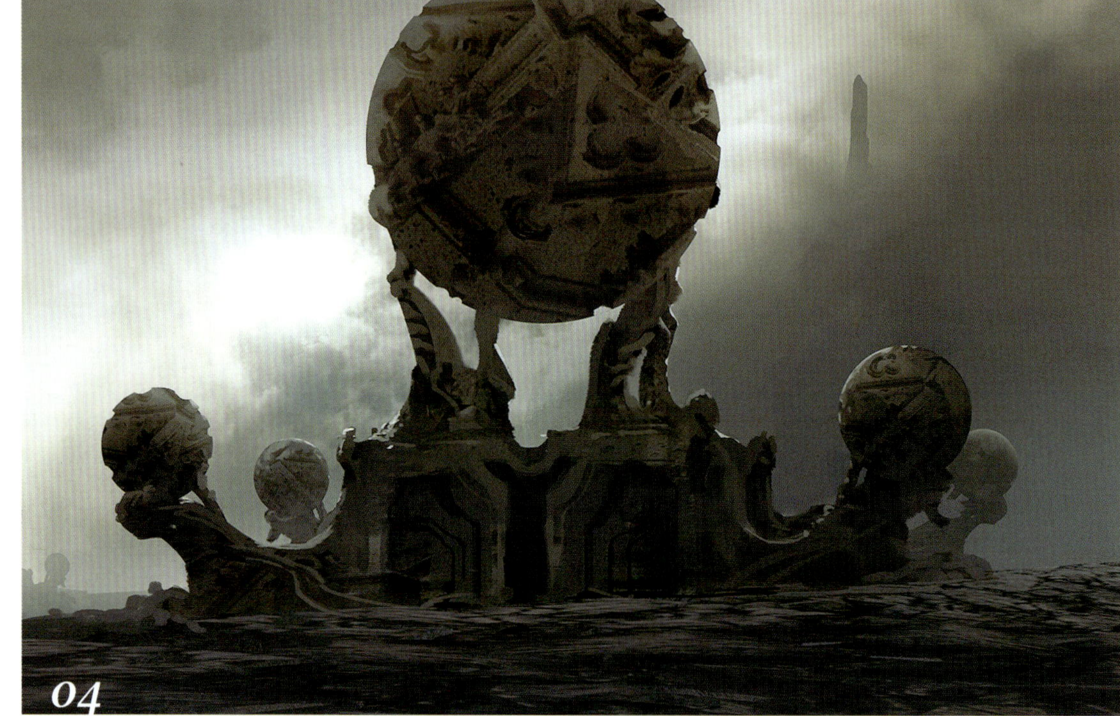

▲ Explore more shapes and rhythms to create design aesthetics for a fantasy feel

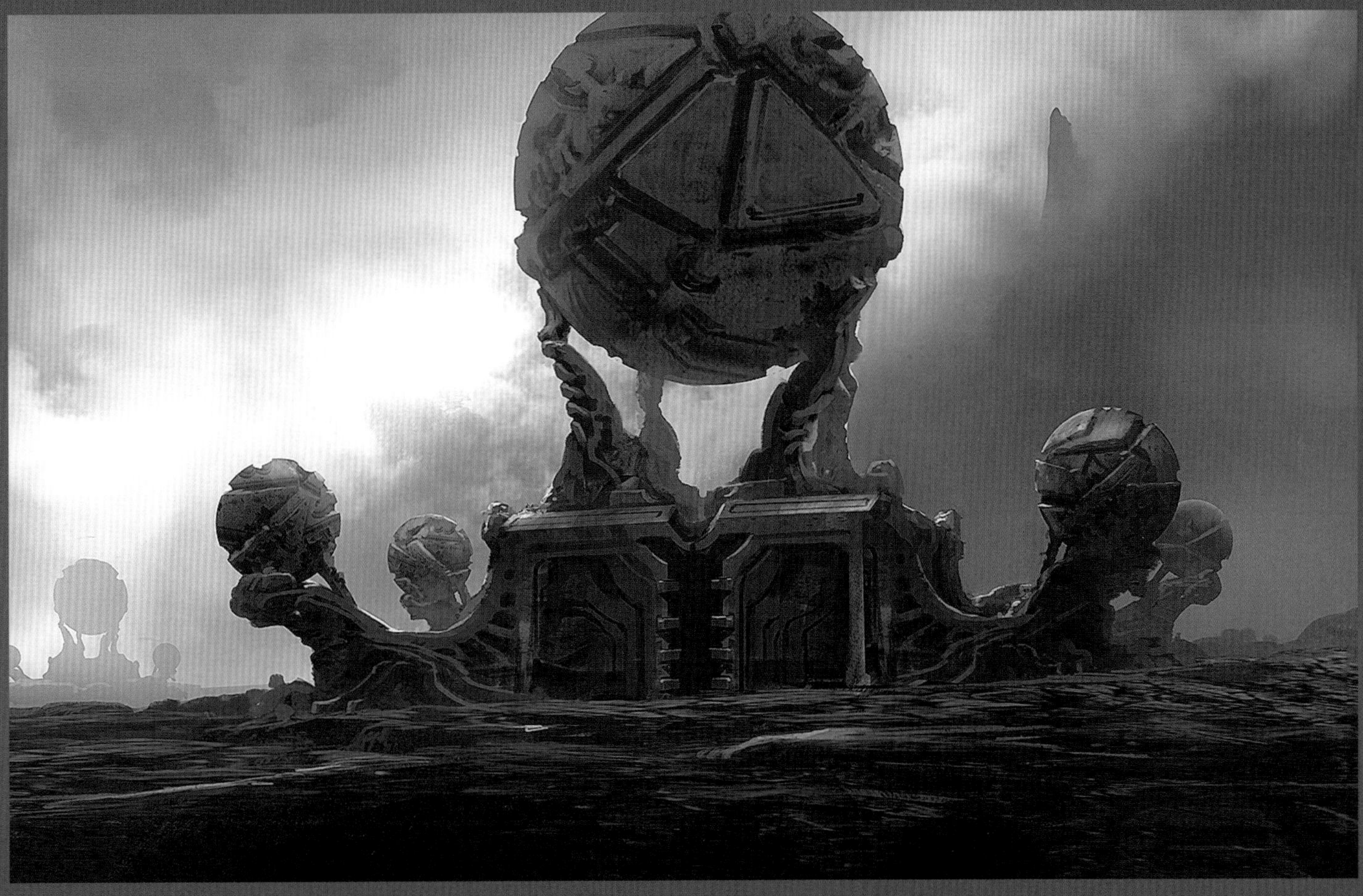

or just think about what you've got in your head. I can see that I need to push the shadow accents and some of the repeated shapes to make the design fit more closely with the concept in my mind. Keep pushing and fixing until you are content with your design.

04: Refine the design

Take a brush and refine the design while illustrating the painting with further detail. This stage is what I like to call the "stitch" because you "stitch" the photo texture and design together with paint. Add details in concentrated areas, as well as having areas where the viewer's eye can rest with simple shapes. You are trying to refine the design to have an organic yet human-made feel with repeated shapes and design elements.

> ***"When speed painting, try to keep the canvas small to reduce the temptation to over render"***

05: Lighting and touch ups

After the design is established, concentrate on enhancing the lighting, atmosphere, and those last few touch ups. Here I mainly focus on surface material and surface details. This stage is the last phase of the overall painting but can often take the longest to accomplish. When speed painting, try to keep the canvas small to reduce the temptation to over render. Try to focus on the overall concept and not the illustration.

FANTASY: ICE WORLD
by James Paick

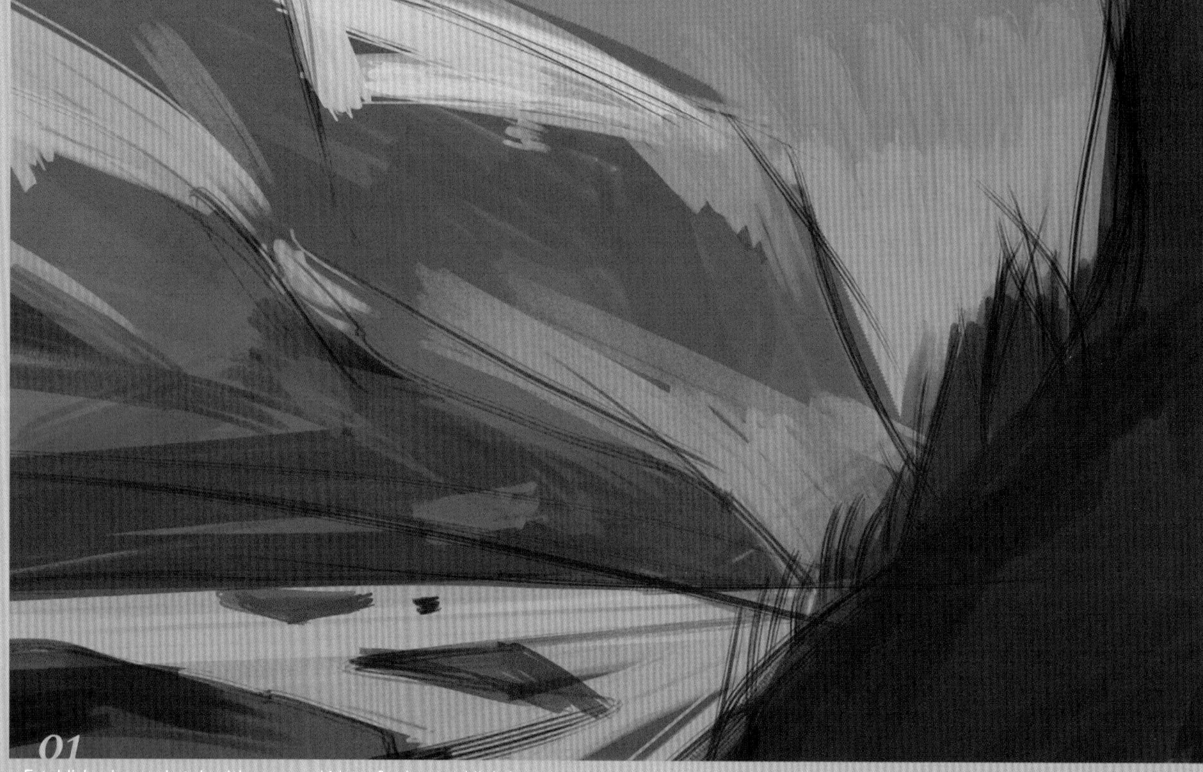

▲Establish a loose sketch with a general idea of values and lighting

In this tutorial we'll explore the process of creating a fantasy ice world using a mix of photo textures and painting techniques. Composition is a very important part of any artwork, and even more so for speed painting, in order to get the overall impression and desired impact in a short amount of time.

At first, try to work just the simple idea in a rough form. I use this method with personal as well as client work. While exploring the process, allow yourself to try new things and experiment so as to not become too rigid with a singular idea. Allow "happy accidents" to happen and enjoy the ride! Details are the last finishing touches and will add your personal flair and style to the piece.

01: Lay it in - establish your environment

At this beginning stage, it is ideal to have a general direction for the concept illustration in mind. Being loose and general is important as it will give you room to play and explore so you can make those happy little accidents and exciting discoveries. I like to establish the composition with a rough sketch and lay in the general value structure and lighting. You also need to keep in mind the overall concept of showcasing a fantasy structure. Choose the ideal composition that best shows off your concept.

02: Pull the trigger - start building the world

Establishing the tones and colors is a very important phase of the painting; it is where decision making comes into play. Once the "lay-in" (step 01) is established, you can begin to "pull the trigger" and focus on the lighting and atmosphere. With a combination of photo texture and painting techniques you can massage and build the image into an appealing world. Look at the graphic design of small shapes contrasted with large simple shapes. Keep a photo reference of the ideal image that you are aiming towards to one side.

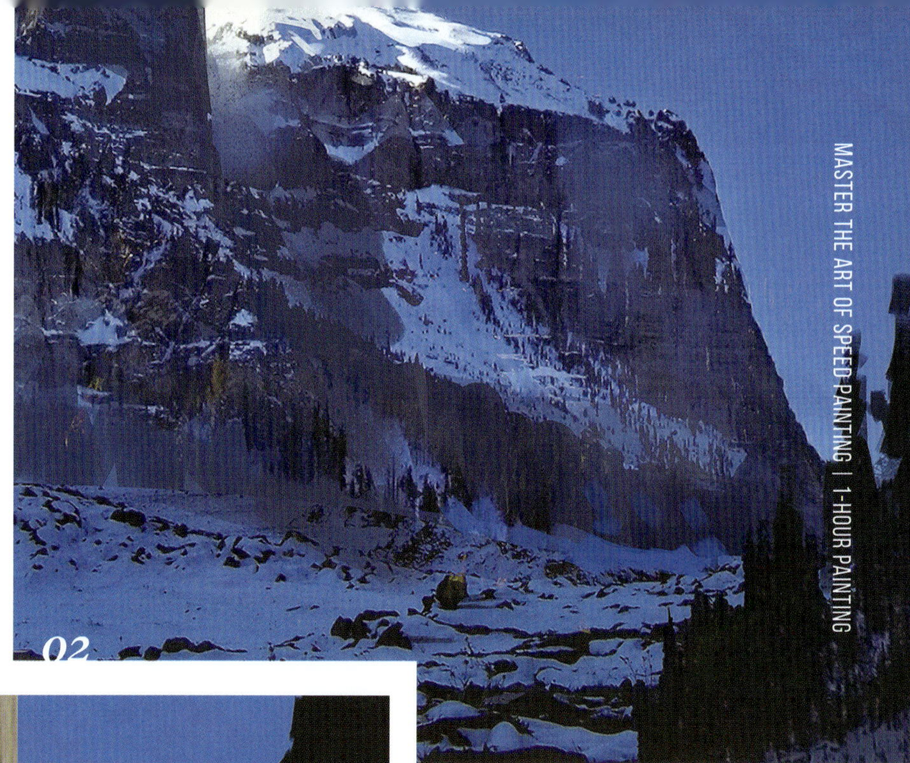

▲ Build the world by establishing the color palette and graphic design

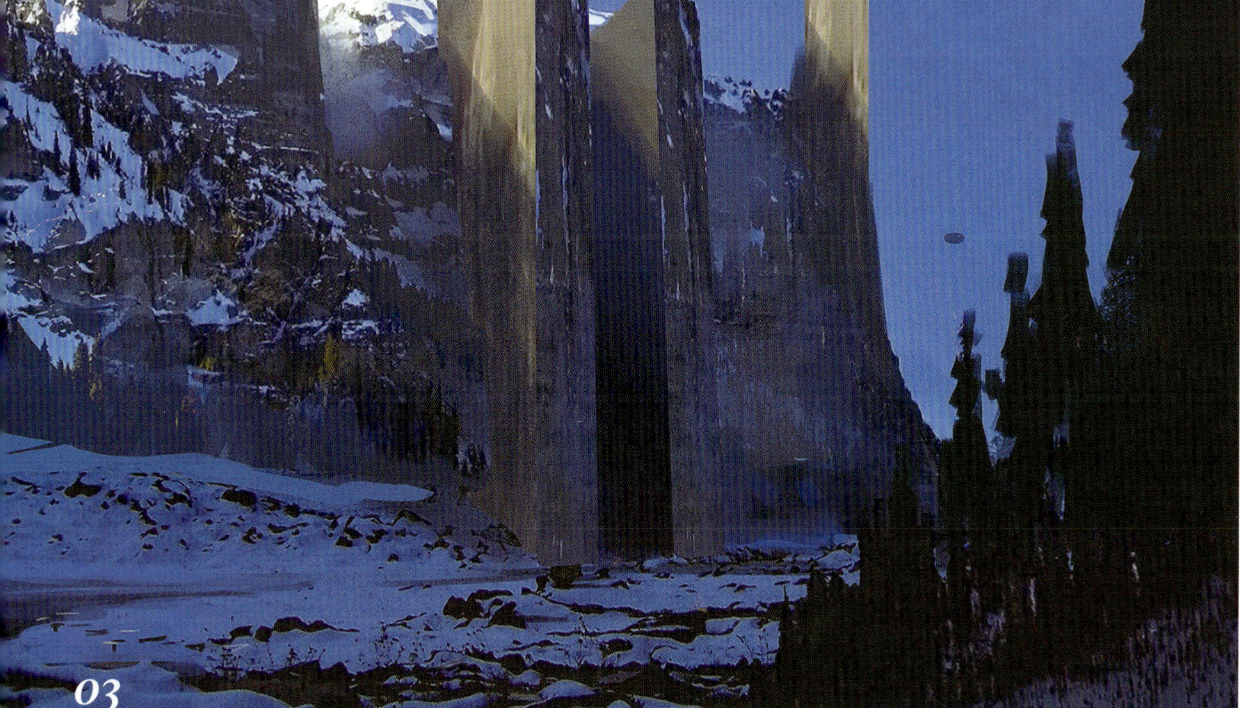

▲ Establish your design by making a bold focal point

03: What are we looking at? Establish a design

As the overall painting begins to come together, set aside the "illustration" phase and start to push the conceptual aspect of the painting.

I add in two huge pillars that are carved into and from the mountain. It is important to showcase the epic scale of the pillars with the use of tightly concentrated shapes placed directly next to the large, simple shape of the pillars. Make a bold statement with your design and focal point – in this case the pillars – as that is the whole point of the image!

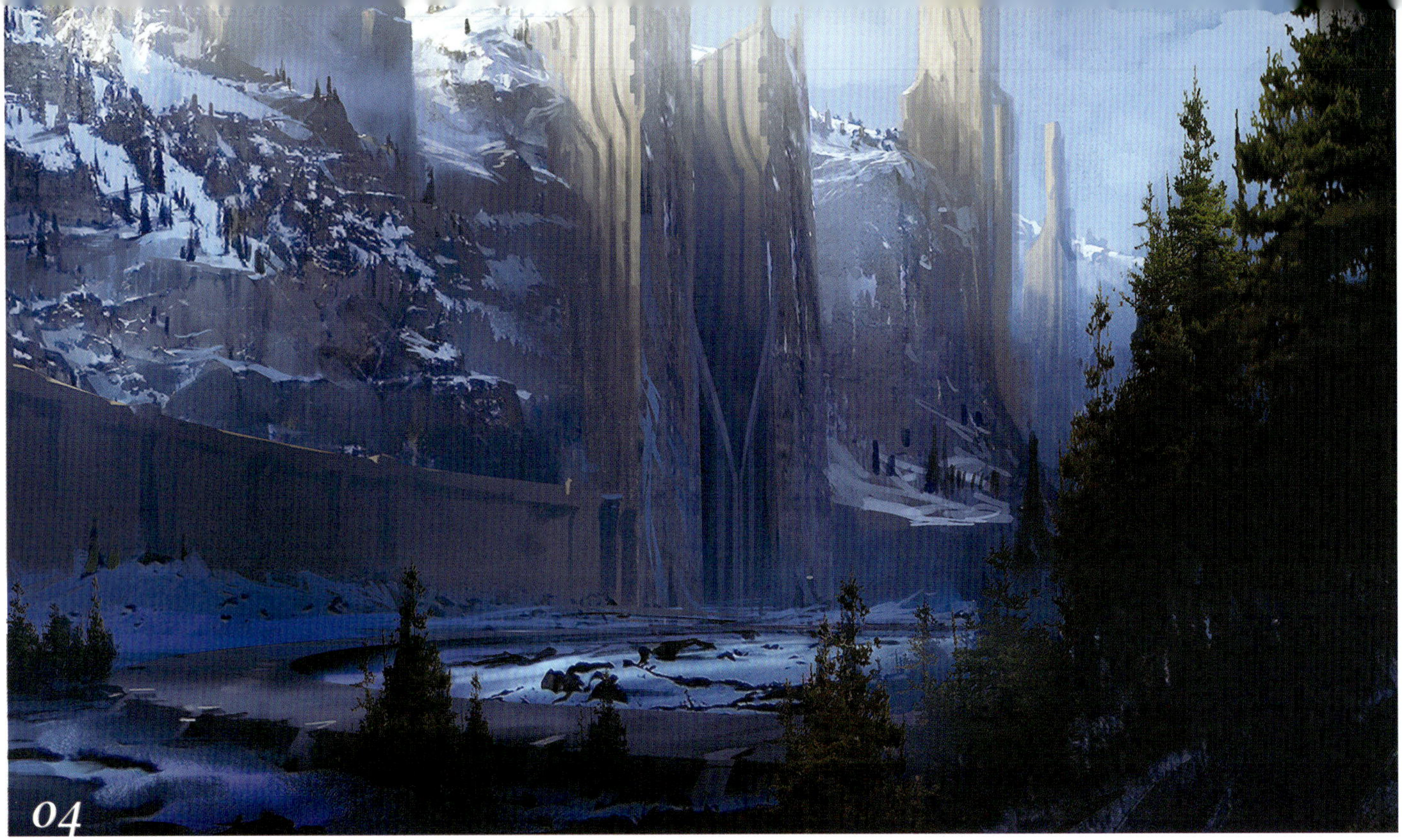

▲Push the design to help explain the concept

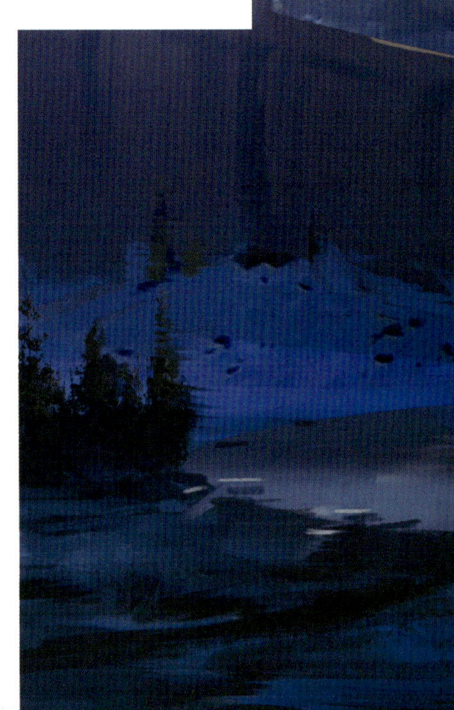

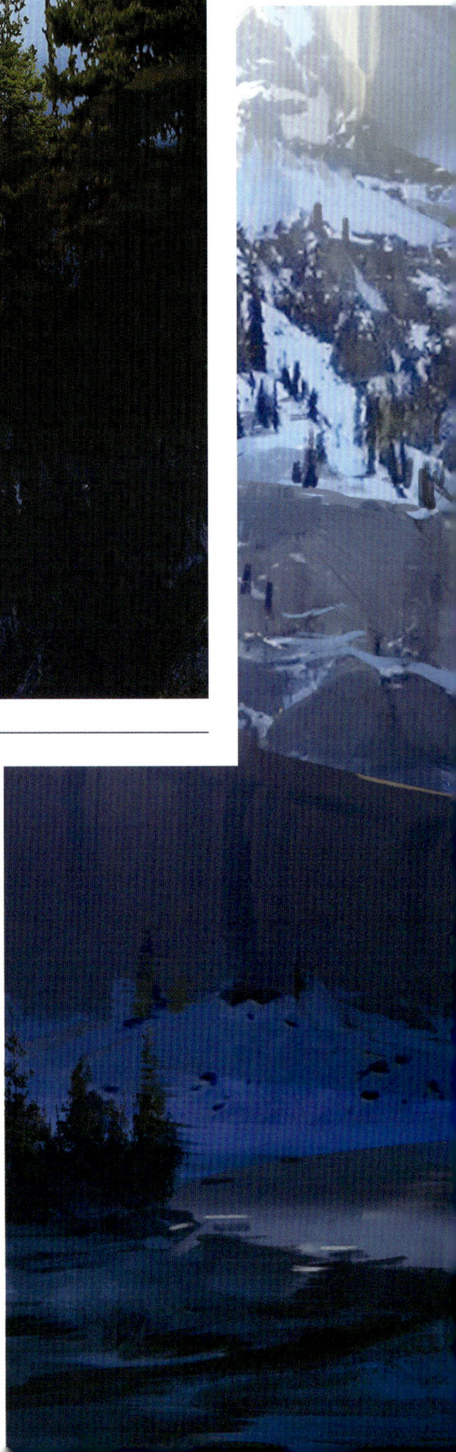

04: Push the design further

Now that you have something on the canvas, you can think about turning it into an appealing and convincing concept. Push the design further by adding elements of interest, such as repeated design elements on the surface of the pillars. Also establish details along the focal point, for example add in fortified walls and a pathway. This will help to create rhythms that lead the eye around the page.

This is also a good time to think about what additional elements you could use that would help to explain the setting, design, and concept; atmosphere and foliage are good choices for this.

05: The icing on the cake

Composition, colors, lighting, the concept, and the cool factors – check! Now you can add the icing on the cake. For some final touches, add in the indication of a group of torches and people; use these along with some separation in the foreground trees to enhance the depth. For a speed painting, keeping the details loose and suggestive will allow the imagination of the viewer to fill in the gaps. As the image progresses, keep the idea simple and remember not to overdo it!

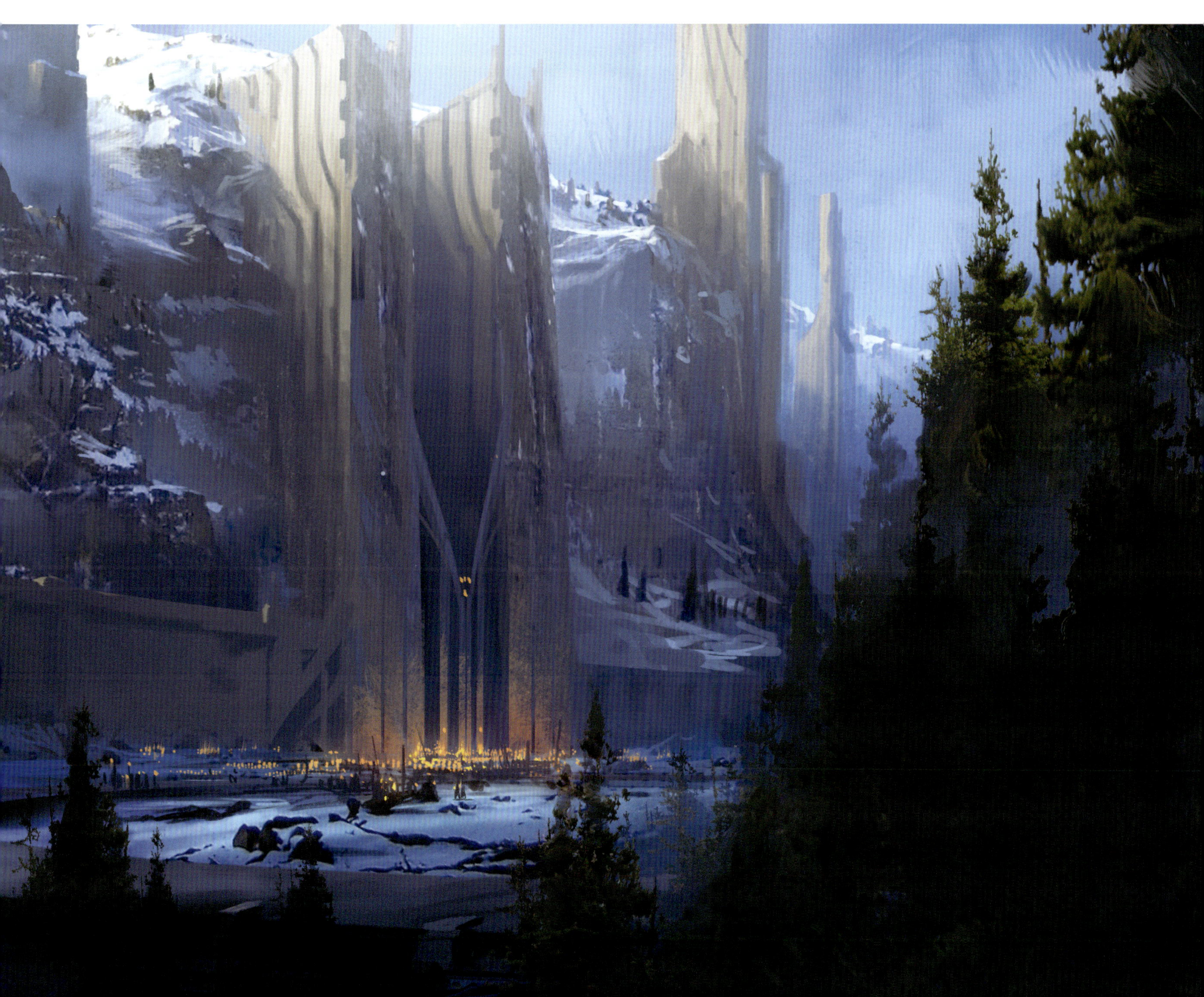

1 HOUR

REAL WORLD: URBAN SKETCHING

Danilo Lombardo

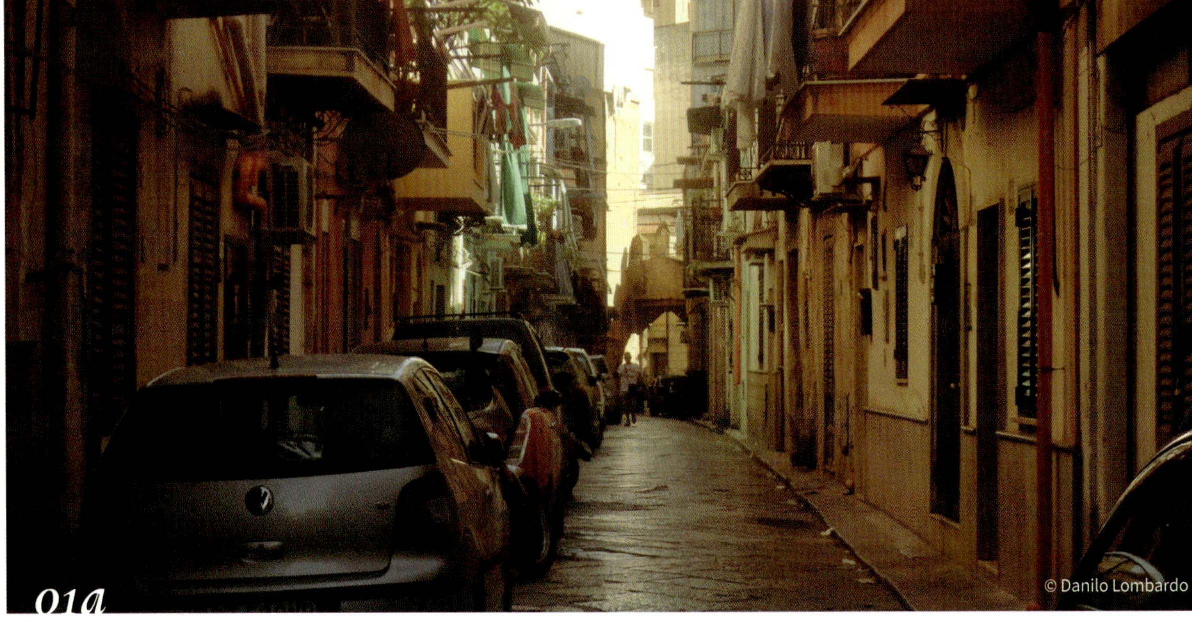

▲ Reference photo

In this tutorial I will show you my method for capturing fast environment sketches using ArtRage. Lighting is important for my 3D art, where I usually work on environments and sets; I find quick color sketches a vital step when lighting a 3D shot, which is a time-consuming but necessary task. Looking at how light behaves in real life and how it affects color is important because it adds depth and believability, as well as creating the desired mood or suggestion of emotion needed for good storytelling.

To realize a descriptive but quick sketch we will use a synthesis technique where details will only be suggested to the observer, using fast strokes and the right tone combinations. This was the technique used by Macchiaioli painters, whose paintings attempted to capture natural light, shade, and color. They were the Italian counterpart of the Impressionists and "macchia" in Italian means "stain" or "spot." This exercise is good for studying how light behaves in real life as well as how it can affect colors. The synthesis process will force us to focus only on primary shapes and elements and will improve our perceptive capability.

01: Set up the document

I have chosen one of my photos of my home town Palermo, Italy, to use as a reference image (**image 01a**).

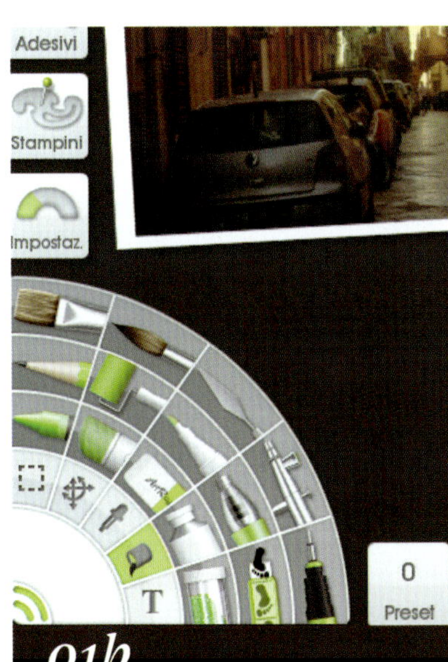

▲ ArtRage has a nice, clean user interface. Right-click anywhere on the screen to hide it

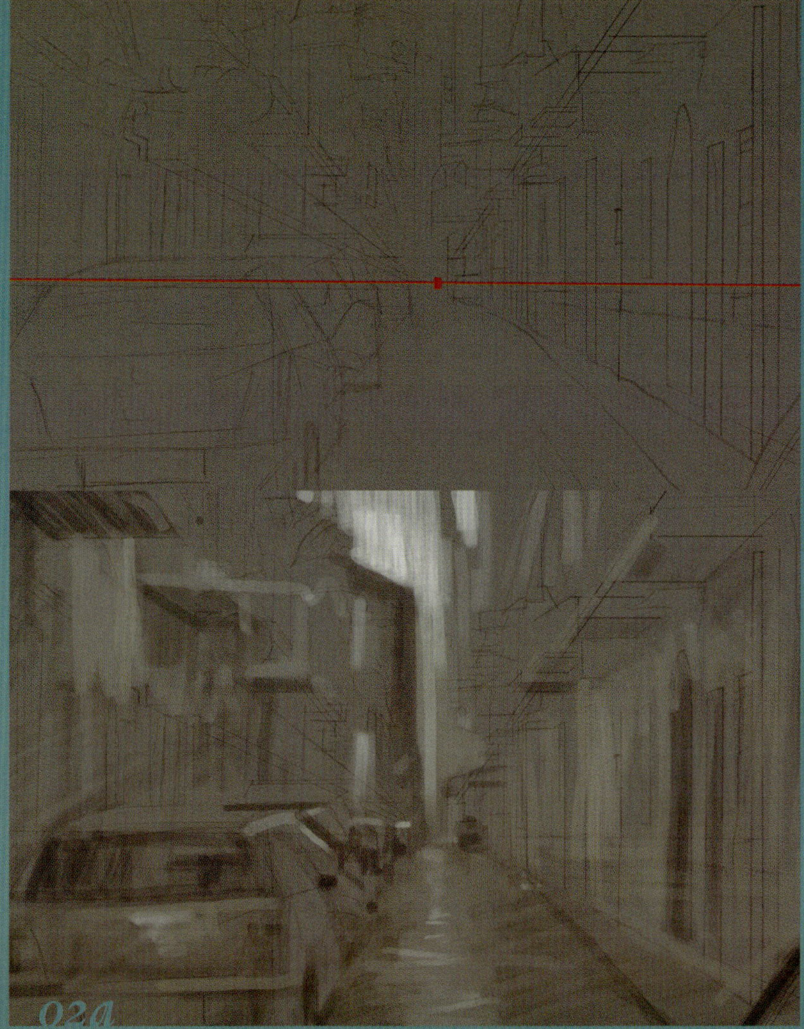

▲ Draw a quick pencil sketch

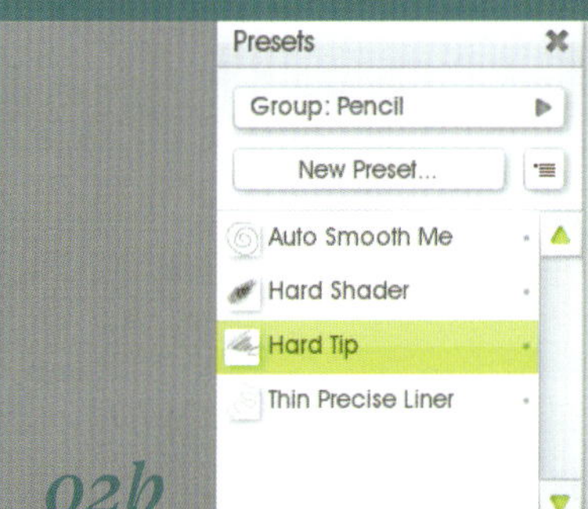

▲ Pencil presets

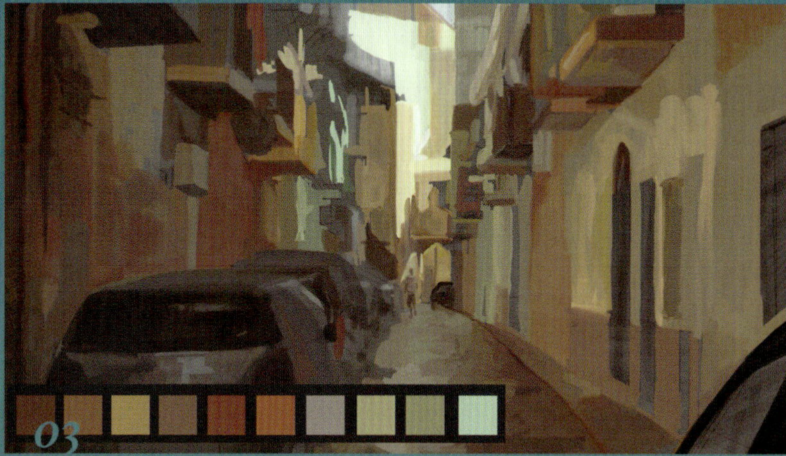

▲ Fast, broad strokes achieve this first impression of colors

ArtRage has some very nice and easy-to-use tools which suit my mixed technique (**image 01b**). To start, set up an ArtRage document at 7000 × 3900 pixels, or multiples of the reference photo size you are using. Having a large document allows you to work at a good resolution and gain an extra bit of definition when resizing the image. Using the reference panel, import the reference photo into the software, then start by filling a layer with a flat gray – this will allow for a better contrast between the canvas and the colors.

02: Initial sketch

You might find it useful to start with a preliminary sketch to act as a guide for placing all the elements in the space. Draw a line to act as the horizon and mark the focal point, which is slightly off center (see the red line in **image 02a**). Using one-point perspective, draw the principle lines with the Pencil tool (Presets > Pencil > Hard Tip; **image 02b**). It's important to vary the line weight to give a sense of depth, so the foreground should have a thicker line than the background. The huge amount of detail can be represented by abstracting the shapes with simple lines and marks.

On a second layer add some quick shading just to gain information about major shadows, midtones, and highlights using the Hard Shader.

03: Color blocking

At this stage focus on light, contrast, and values. Don't work at full size at this point; just have an overview of the canvas. On a separate layer set to 70% Opacity, use the Oil brush to add color in quick, broad strokes. Instead of doing a perfect representation of light we will use a scale (see the color chart in **image 03**) to represent a "feeling" of lighting.

The reference photo will decide the initial color palette; you can use it to directly extract the important colors using the Color Sampler. Try to keep your palette limited to help with precision. When you have decided on your palette you can paint a simplified version of the scene which should be made of light and shadows.

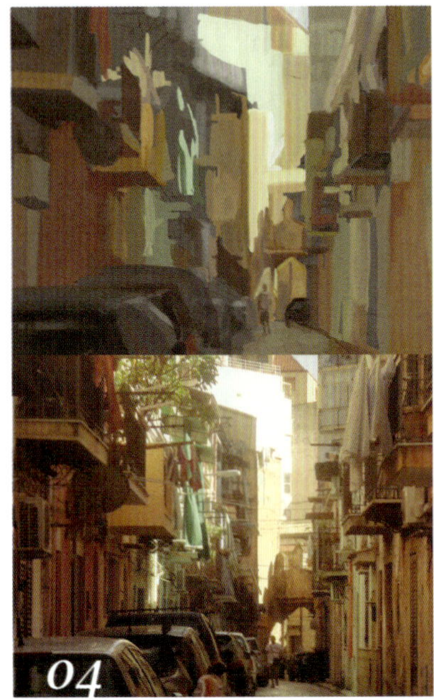

▲ Comparing the canvas and reference shows the major color spots are in the correct place

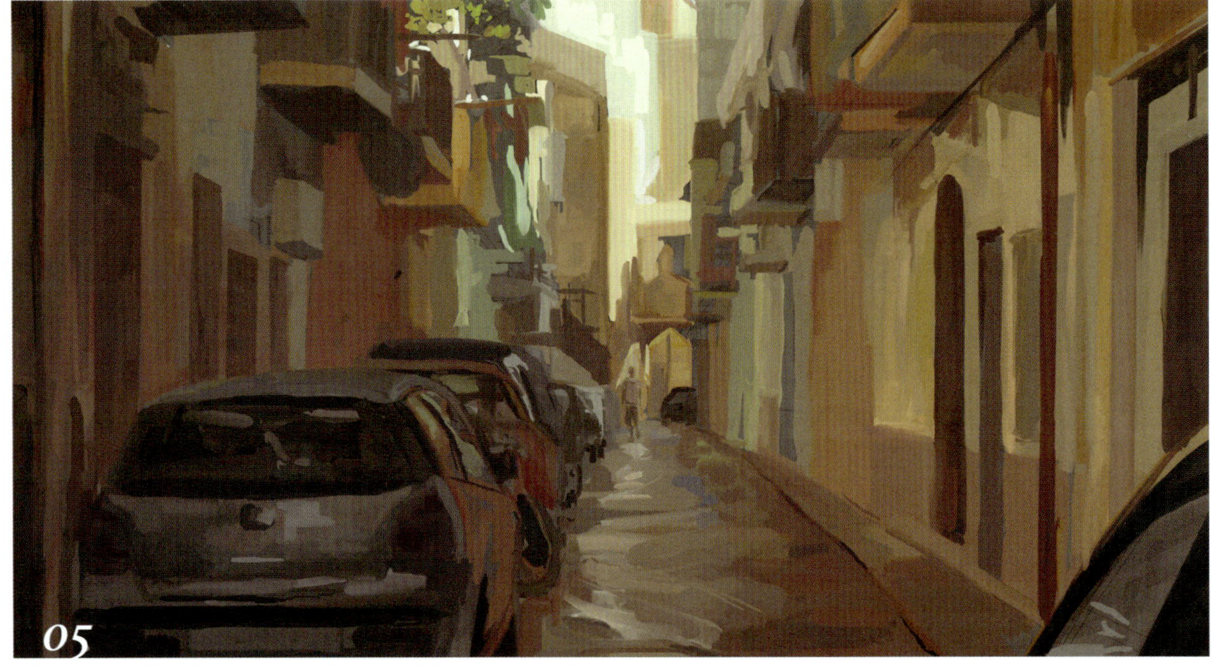

▲ Start to use bold strokes to separate elements and demonstrate depth

04: Lighting and values

It is crucial to observe and understand the right value relationship between colors. When a ray of light hits a surface it bounces all over until it stops, so in terms of color everything is influenced by this light bouncing, even the stronger shadows.

In this process it is important not to over saturate the tones on strong highlights and shadows, because this can distract our eyes and make us have less control. Everything needs to transmit a sense of blending as it is light that dominates color, so we can't always represent blue using blue or red using red under different lighting conditions. We have to understand and study where the light is coming from, and how and why it is reflecting in a certain way on a certain surface, to be able to simplify it.

This image is made primarily of warm tones, but we can introduce cold tones like greens and blues to create vibrant and playful lighting. Instead of using white for pure light I use a very light green.

05: Depth and contrast

To test the rough blocking you have at this point, start to cut some elements from the background. On another layer paint only some major lines and colors with the intention of adding depth and contrast to the painting. Focus on some secondary elements like doors and plants; start refining the cars and some buildings and introduce stronger shadows.

Also use a few dark, hard lines to suggest the shape of objects and to increase the depth of your image. Using a diversification of intensity in the lines, we

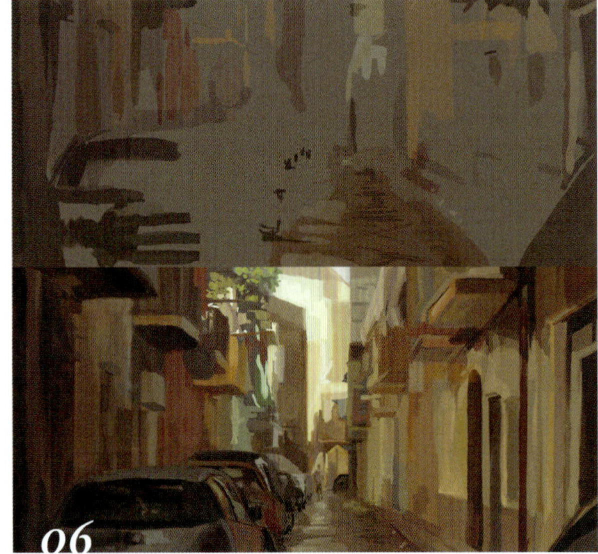

▲ The glazing layer and the result of it

can suggest the motion of the shapes we are drawing. Try to use only those strong predominant lines that will help you create the illusion of depth.

06: Glaze with layers and opacity

We can make our painting uniform by applying some glazing to blend all the tones together. To do this create a new layer on top of your stack with Opacity set to something like 40%. You will need this to paint those elements that you want to be on top of the first blocking and to level all your tones.

Introduce a stronger contrast between the foreground and the background using shadows and paint more graduations of color in the midtone range. On another layer (at 20% Opacity) you can finish this kind of polishing by adding warmer tones.

"The goal here is to refine the 'first impression' of the painting and make it look uniform"

07: Refine the color blocking

At this point I have used only the Oil brush, because I personally like its behavior in this kind of sketch, however ArtRage offers a wide range of tools and you should not feel limited from exploring more.

In my opinion the Pencil tool works perfectly along with oils for this method. Create another layer and this time, using the Hard Shader pencil preset, paint some corrections on top of your work.

Looking at the reference and working with a zoomed-out canvas, you can gain that first impact and correct those things that keep breaking the uniformity of your painting. Introduce some shadows and lights to enhance depth and paint some more values, trying to improve the ground and the reflection effect on it. The goal here is to refine the "first impression" of the painting and make it look uniform.

08: Tertiary shapes

The color sketch at this point is very dirty, and it represents only the major forms (primary and secondary shapes like walls, doors, windows, and ground); it's missing all the details on the windows, doors, and cables.

We need to stay rough, and not fuss over the individual details. Having all the primary shapes sketched out will make it very easy to add many details after (tertiary shapes). I accentuate some strong points like the lines of the car silhouettes, or on the sidewalk, to make some elements, and the space itself, more readable.

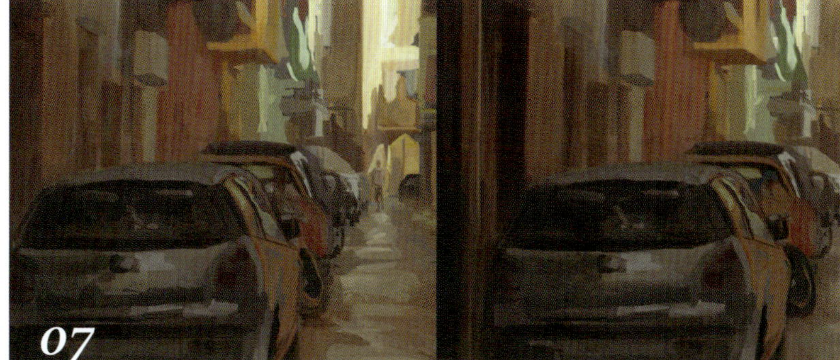

▲ The Pencil tool does a great job of making the colors uniform and adding more precision

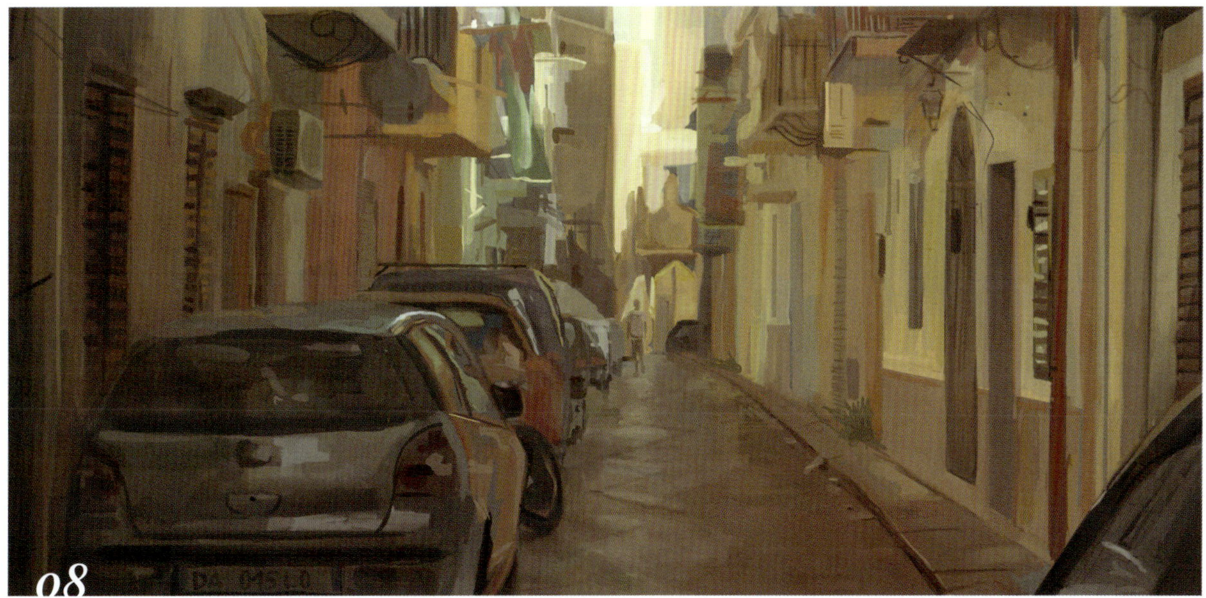

▲ Once you have the bases, this is where the image details can finally come out

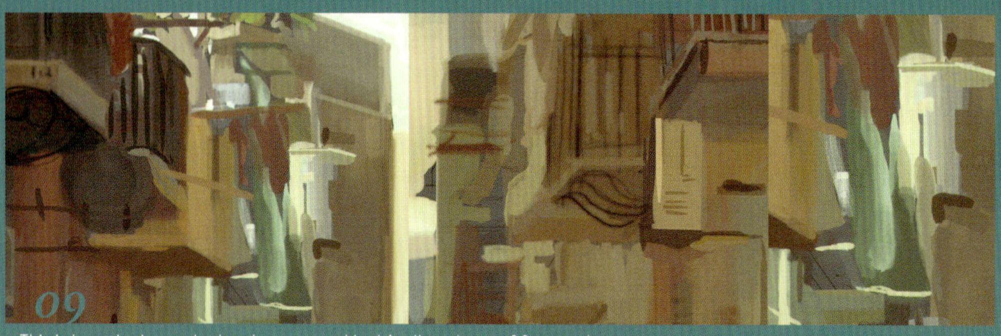

▲ This is how the image looks when zoomed in. It's all made up of fast marks

09: Signature and style

Even if we are just copying from a photo – I personally look at this as an exercise to develop skills, understand light, and be able to draw more personal concepts – we can introduce our "signature" or "style" embedded in the visual language of the image. All the lines, dots, and strokes are pieces of the grammar of the painting.

Style is an important aspect to take into consideration when we are dealing with a speedy work such as this, and we can use our stylistic choices to be even more fast and dirty, while at the same time maintaining a good aesthetic and keeping the image interesting.

10: Photoshop and final conclusions

In ArtRage I export my image in PNG format and then import it into Photoshop. On a layer set to Multiply with 57% Opacity, I import a "grunge texture" from **www.textures.com**. I use it to add a universal shadowing on the foreground, so I delete the upper part of the texture with the eraser.

I use the same process to add a general light, a sort of glow on the upper part of the image, but this time my merging mode is set to Screen. On a separate layer I paint a quick "fog" to separate the buildings in the distance and I refine the ground reflection. My image is a little bit too red so I add a Color Correction layer to adjust the tones and saturation and make it more yellowish. You can see the final image on the right here.

In my opinion the goal of practicing speed painting is not to be a faster painter. Concept art is not about perfect paintings, it is more about design, about building a visual language to communicate a story. To do research on shapes, colors, patterns, character design, and lighting, it's important to be able to explore as many variants as possible, so speed is a tool you can use to communicate an idea quickly to yourself or your team.

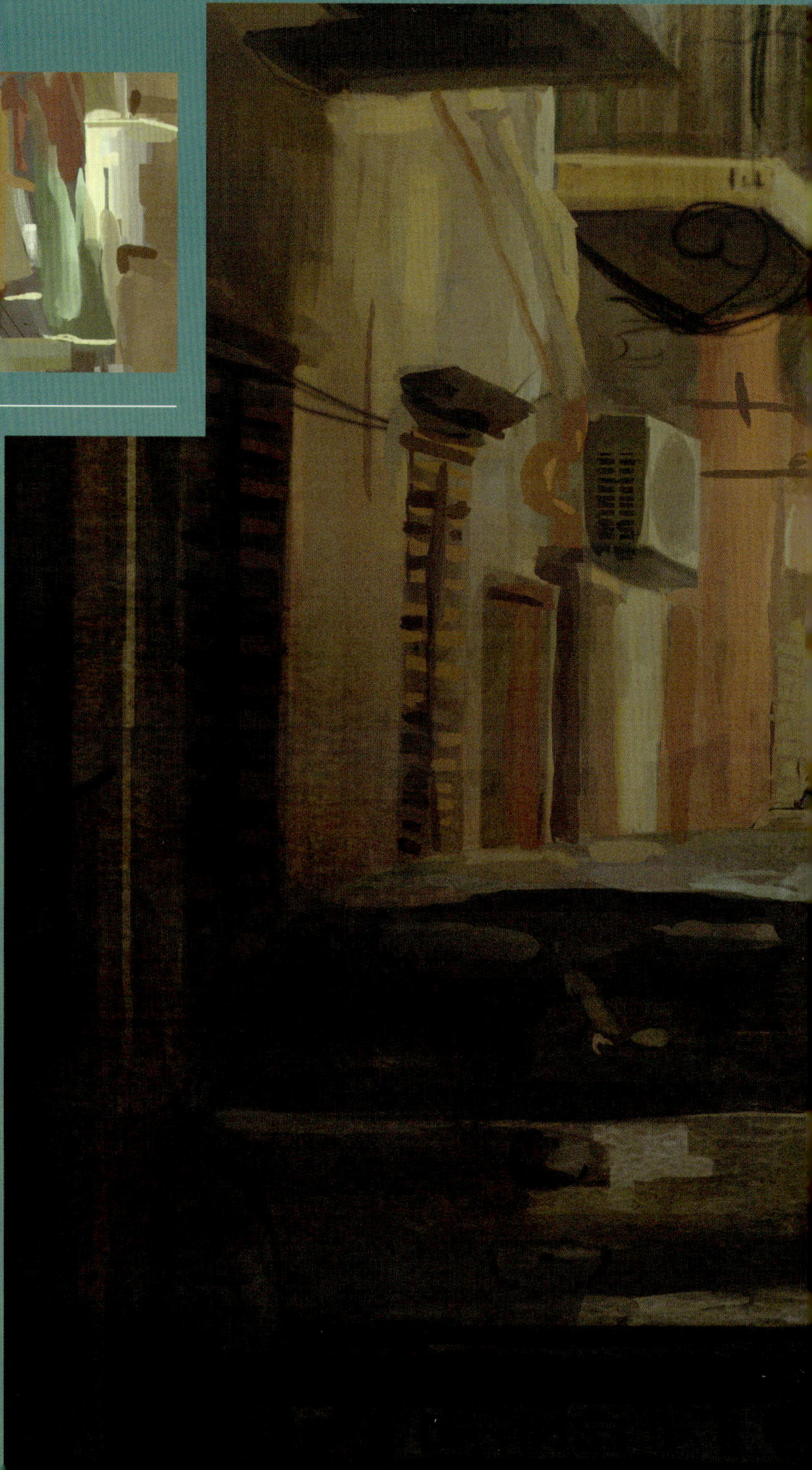

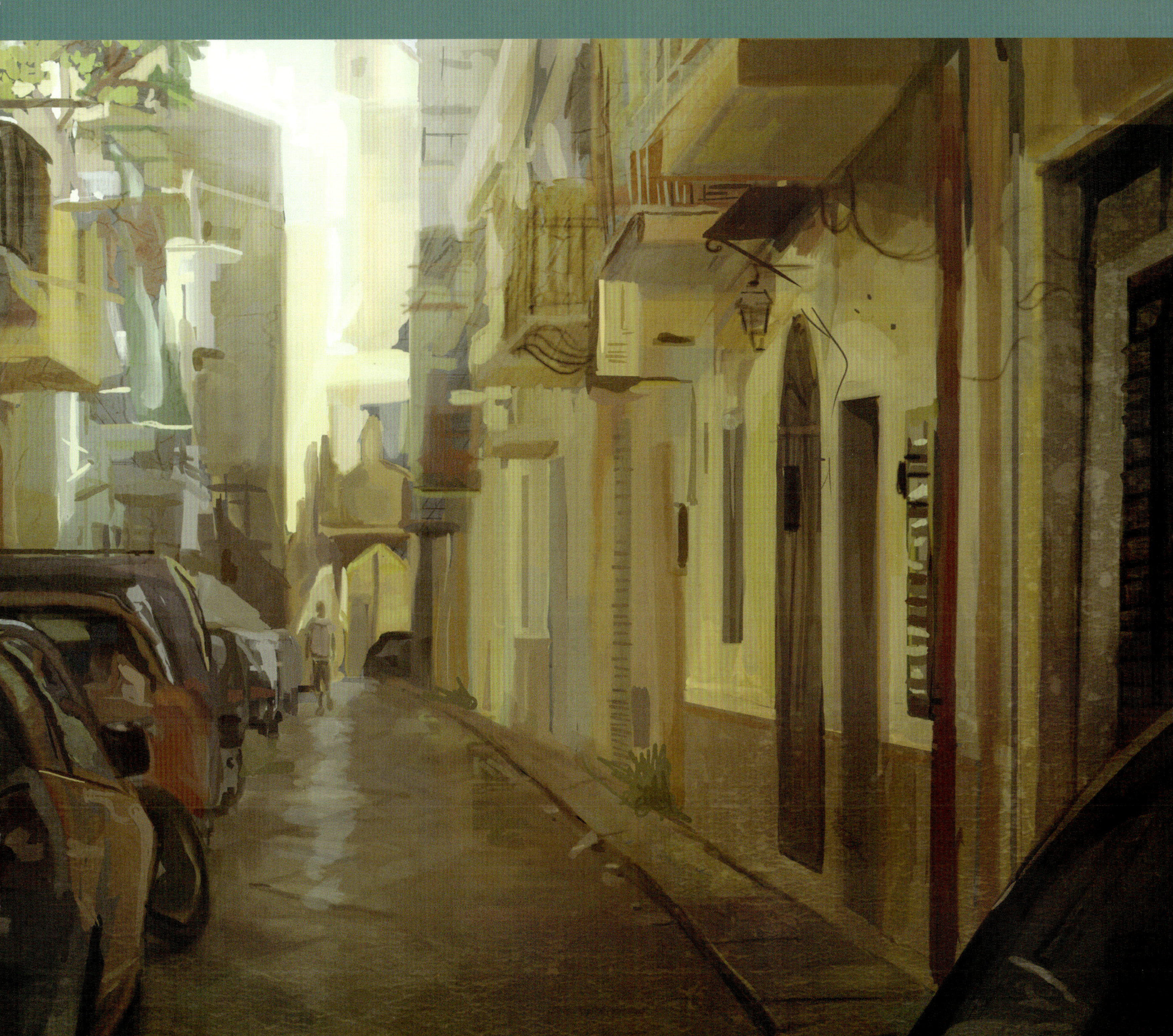

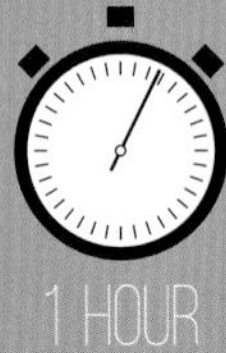

REAL WORLD: NIGHT SCENE

by Danilo Lombardo

This tutorial will look at composition and low light illumination using painting techniques and photobashing. When working as a concept artist you need to be fast and have a workflow that allows you to do different versions of the same scene relatively quickly. For this tutorial I want to make a classic foggy night scene, set in a secret factory in a huge industrial zone. I imagine having to make a painting to show the mood and composition for a movie scene.

01: Tools

When working on this type of art I like to use as few tools as possible. For example I use a rectangular brush (**a** in **image 01**) with a hard and soft side, which allows it to be used almost like a marker pen – and obviously it is good for rectangular strokes!

To get a painterly effect you can simply mix and vary the strokes by using the Smudge tool (**b**). Set the hardness to 35–40%. You can use the Brush panel (F5) to make changes to the parameters to suit your needs, such as changing the angle of the strokes (**c–e**). The Lasso tool is very handy when you want to make selections on the fly to create interesting shapes (**f**). The Levels tool (Ctrl+L) is great for modulating the tones of certain areas of interest. Finally, the Eraser tool can be used to cut some parts or modulate the opacity of certain areas.

02: Composition, lines, and rhythm

Composition is important to a successful image; you need to create a visual harmony that will be enjoyable for the viewer. Good balance is the way in which elements are put together. Space is also very important when thinking about composition – how to use it effectively and not be limited by the physicality of the canvas.

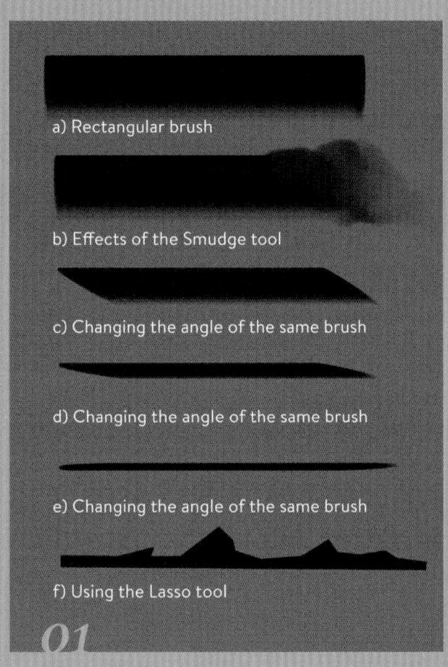

▲ A selection of the different brushstrokes I use for this image

When visualizing the scene, we have to make use of invisible lines that lead the viewer towards certain areas. In my painting the composition is very horizontal, so most of the invisible lines

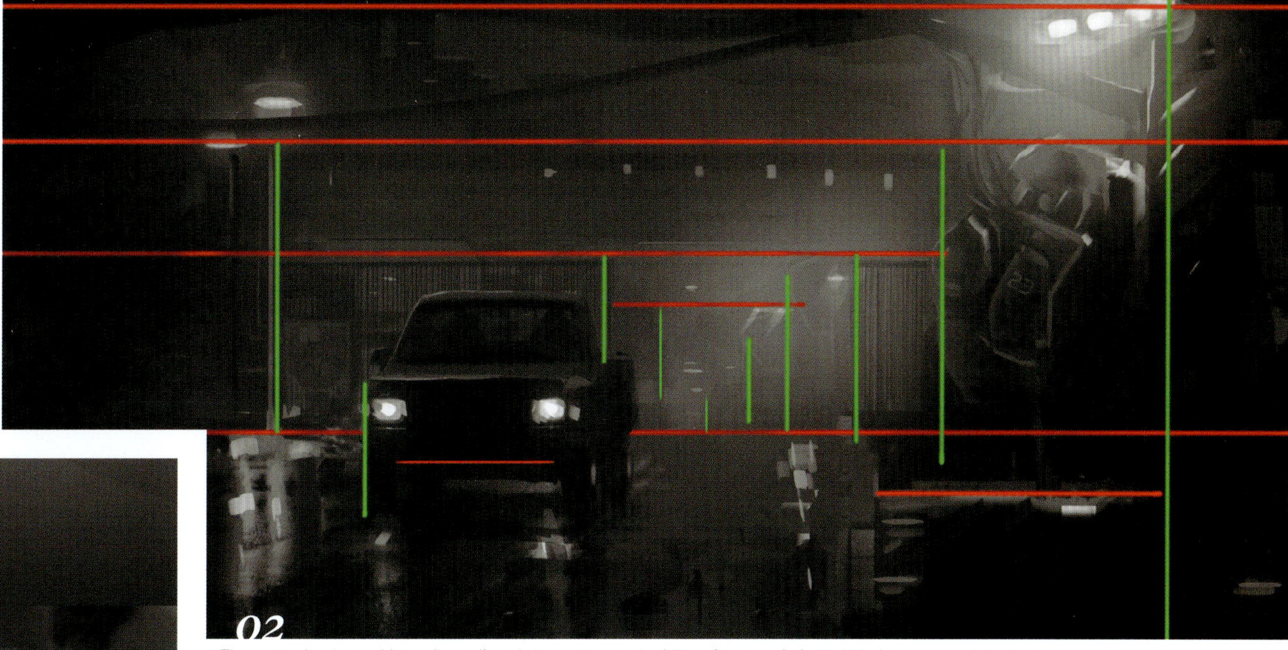

▲ The major horizontal lines (in red) and the major vertical lines (in green) that will help us to read the image

are horizontal as well. This is because the image's purpose is to transmit a sense of quiet in a shady situation, and also a sensation of secrecy. This is one of the most common compositions – the camera is very static, but we can add compositional interest creating a rhythm in the interaction of lights and shadows as well as using various levels of depth.

03: Thumbnails

Thumbnails are a great start to any piece of art (**image 03a**), but sometimes you just know what you want to make and a quick preliminary sketch is all you need. Concept art is more about design than painting skills. I paint very fast pieces with the canvas zoomed to 25%, which gives me a great overview of the whole piece.

"Develop a good atmosphere using only shape and light"

To start fill your Photoshop canvas with gray and use the Lasso tool to create a road with a gradient on top. Quickly block in a car shape with fast strokes to give the general shape of the car. At this point your main focus should be on the framing and composition of the piece, with the car as the focal point (**image 03b**).

Let the shapes form the image. Try to make this process as organic as possible; you should be able to develop a good atmosphere using only shape and light. What do the shapes suggest to you? In mine I could see a bridge or tunnel. Build up your thumbnails until you are happy with the composition, but remember you can change your mind at any point!

03a

▲ A breakdown of my thumbnail sketch – framing is in red and focal point in yellow

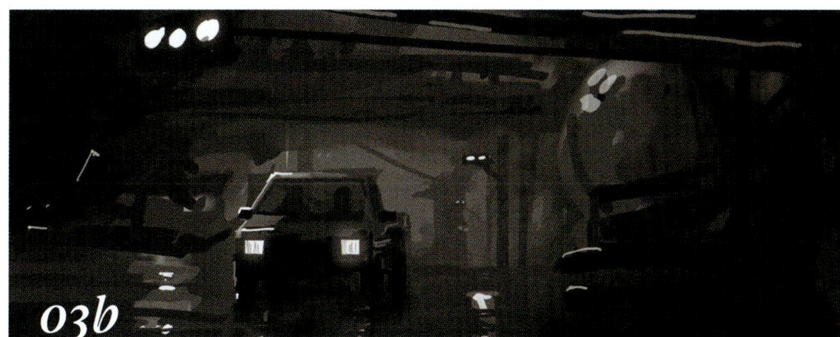

▲ The car is the focal point of the image, so make sure you frame it properly

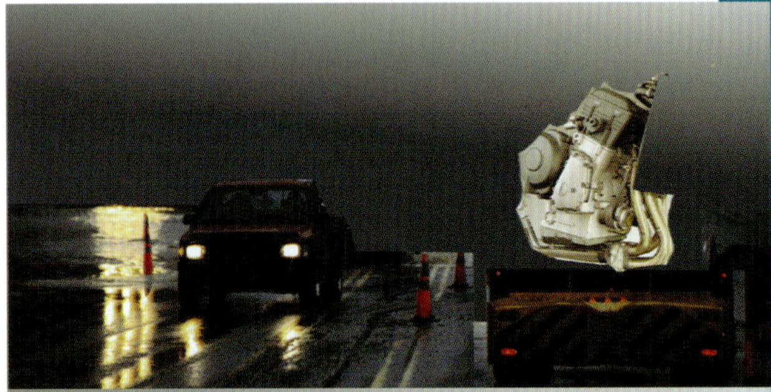

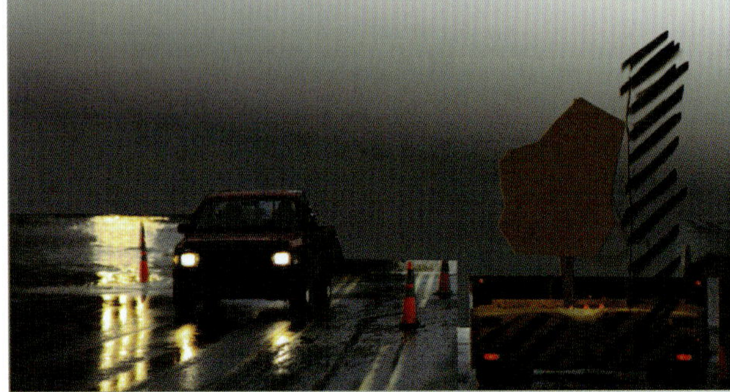

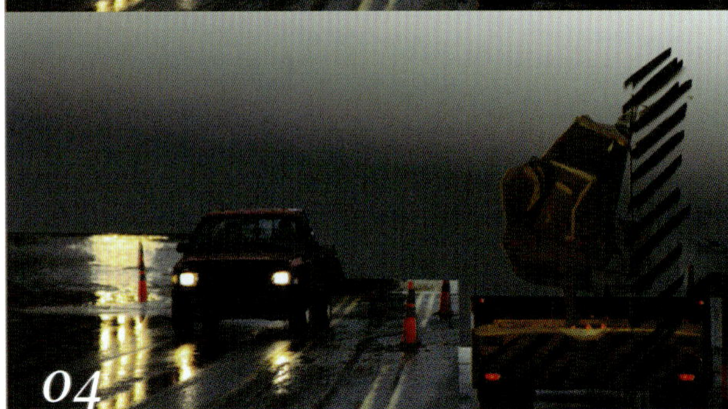

▲ The three-step process for photobashing

04: Photobashing

Photobashing is a great way to speed up the process, using a selection of reference images to make the scene.

As a base, start by adding a gradient and importing your chosen photos. They can be modified to fit as needed using the Transform tools.

I use the following three steps to add an extra element into the image.

1. Import and position the photo.

2. Use the Polygonal Lasso tool to make a selection of the shape and fill with the main color you want.

3. Finally, in a Multiply layer, put the photo on top of the color blocking, making adjustments as needed.

05: Lighting

Surfaces stop light in three different ways:

- **absorption** – all the light is absorbed by the surface (see **a** in **image 05**);
- **reflection** – light bounces off the surface (**b**; the angle of reflection depends on the material's properties);
- **refraction** – lights travel inside the surface (for example with glasses) (**c**).

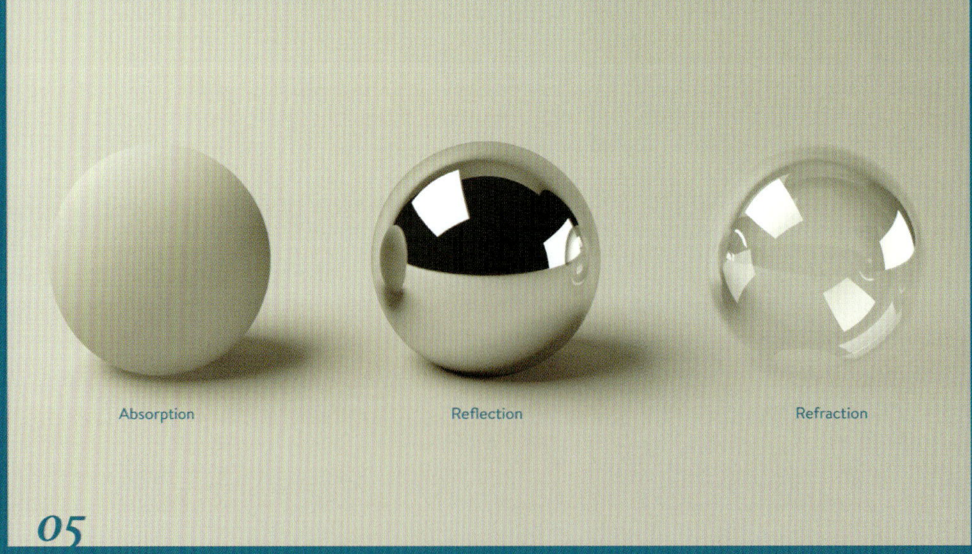

▲ I made this quick 3D render to show the different ways light can interact with a surface

Everything is lit by a certain amount of direct and indirect (bounced) light. On an overcast day, we do not see distinct rays of light, but light bouncing around, filtered by clouds, giving a uniform and soft light with diffuse shadows. A bright sunny day will produce hard shadows, and you will be able to see the direct light coming from the sun. We need to think about these properties in our image.

06: Low light situation

A low light situation does not mean a total absence of light. In our scene we can still see in these conditions because of the large amount of scattered light bounced from the moon, although the light has lost much of its intensity and has become diffuse.

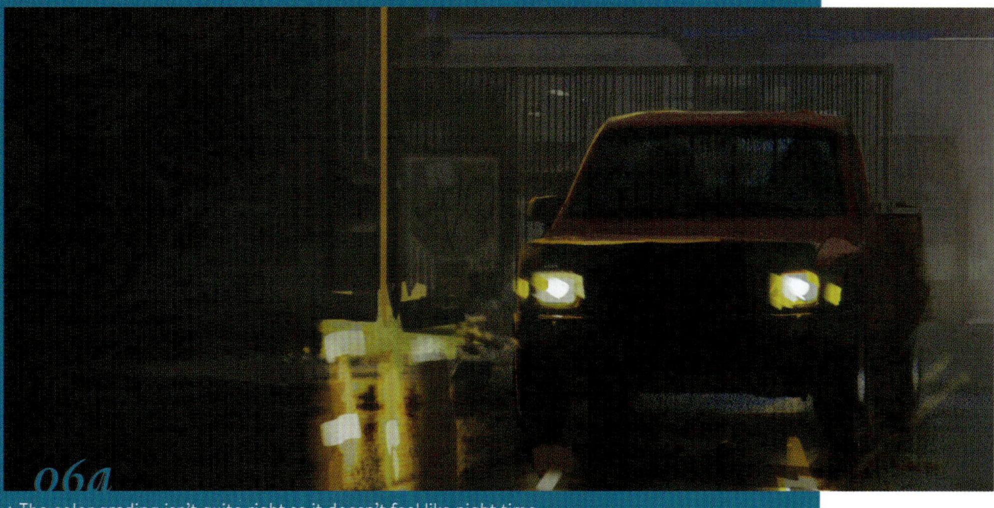

▲ The color grading isn't quite right so it doesn't feel like night time

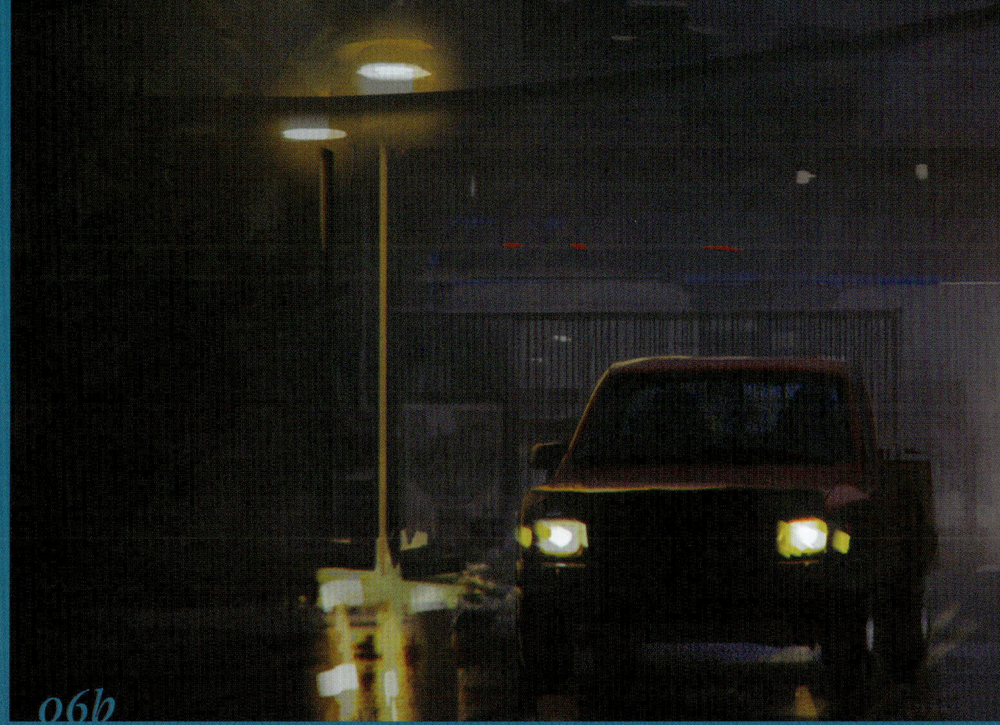

▲ The diffuse base light contrasts nicely with the strong orange artificial lights

In cinematography and television, color grading the night is often codified as blue or green. You can use this system to give your art the expected color representation. Paint the diffused scene using blues and add warm orange tones for the artificial light sources such as headlamps (**images 06a** and **06b**). Orange and blue are complementary colors and very pleasing to the human eye, while the contrast between the two colors adds a touch of realism to the image.

07: Values and color temperature

At this stage it is good to use very desaturated colors to allow you to

"There can be different color temperatures within the same object, for example in fire, where the colors usually go from white to yellow to orange to red"

work on the values rather than the hues. Limit your palette to build the scene in an organic way; add the layers of elements while trying to stick to the main dominant color.

For each different light try to use a different color temperature, for example the difference between bright midday sun and a candle flame. There can be different color temperatures within the same object, for example in fire, where the colors usually go from white to yellow to orange to red. Once you know where the lights are going to go you can use very fast strokes to paint the effect that the light has on the scene. Keep it simple and rough; your goal should be to block everything out and give depth to the scene.

08: Atmospheric effects

Adding a glow around the lights will give the image extra depth, as does atmospheric perspective. This is where colors are less saturated and contrasted the further away an object is, for instance if you look at

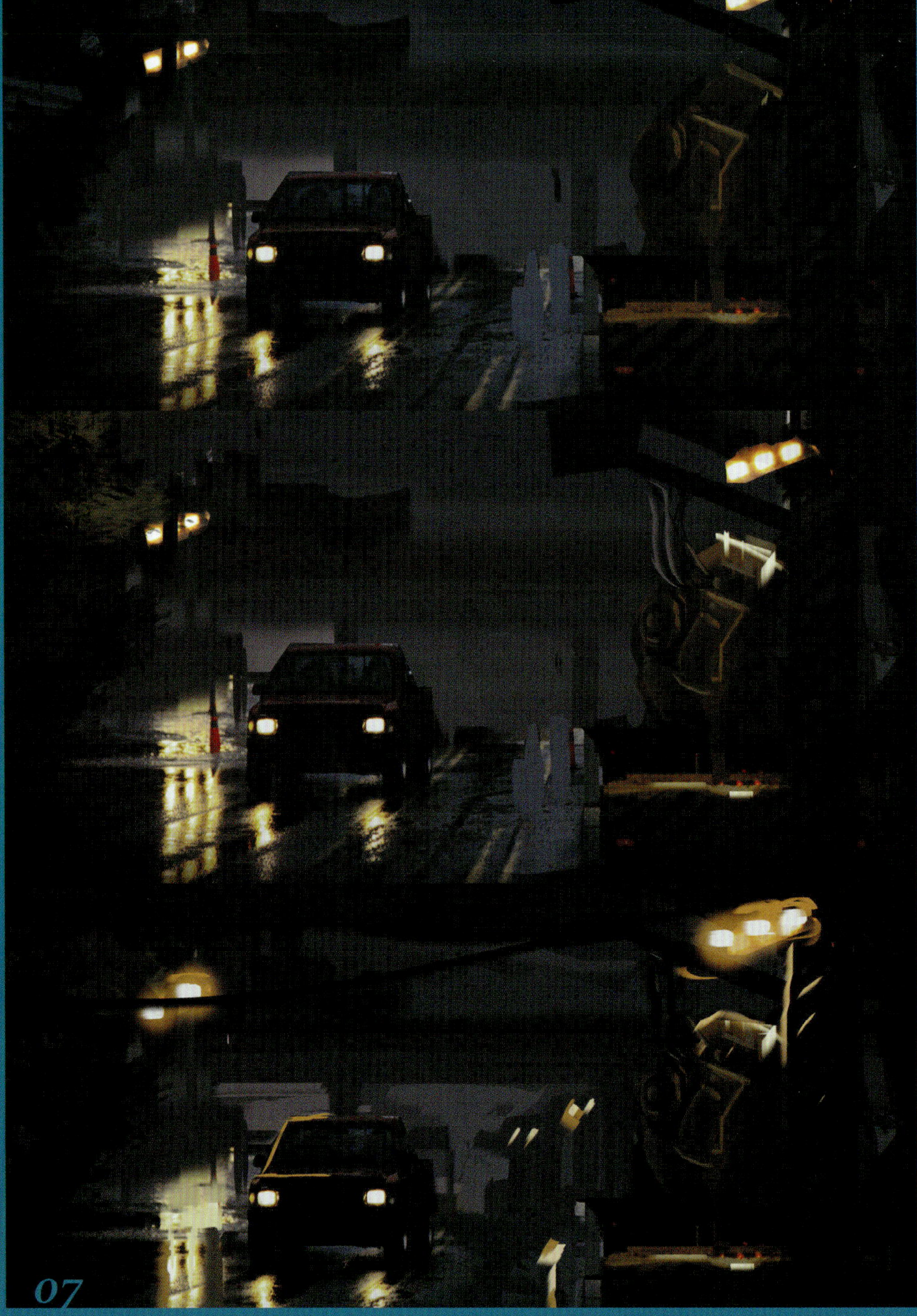

▲ Try using different color temperatures for each light source

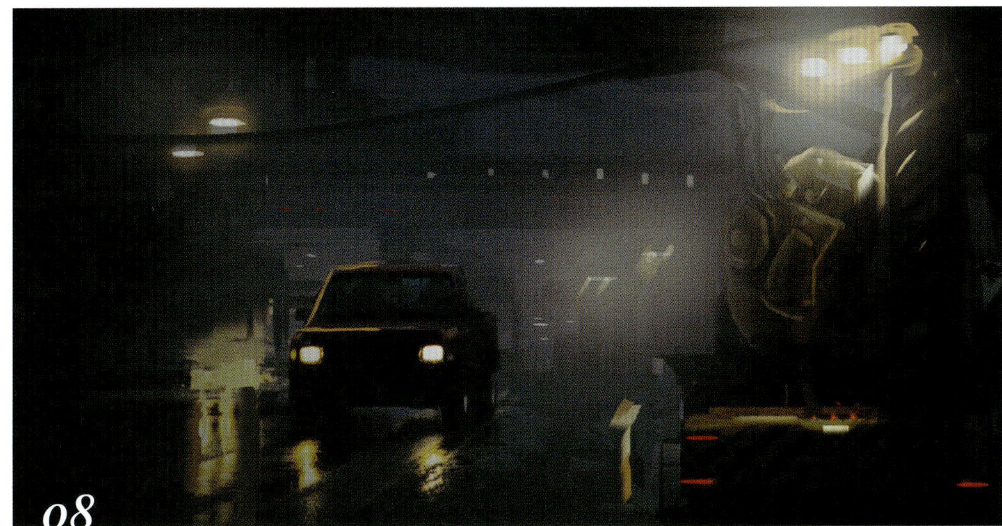

▲ Adding atmospheric perspective enhances the sense of depth

a distant mountain range the colors almost blend with the background.

You can see the interaction between particles in the air and the lights, especially on foggy nights. To achieve this illuminated fog effect, open a new layer and paint the soft glow using a soft round brush with low opacity. The image will be more distinct in the foreground, which will make the space look much deeper, as well as having the effect of unifying the lighting.

09: Texture and detail

As the image colors are quite dark and desaturated you can incrementally increase the saturation by using a Color Correction layer. I prefer this method instead of doing color corrections in the image panel, as it is non-destructive and you can always go back.

"A rim light is a good way to highlight a subject, making it pop out against the background"

To add textures and details you can simply import a texture from your collection and transform it to fit the painted elements. This is a very quick way to add interest and detail to an image. It is easy enough to break any false perfection by erasing bits of the texture and changing the opacity.

Continue to add different textures and details, gradually refining every aspect, such as adding highlights to make it "pop" from the scene, for example on the rim light on the car. A rim light is a good way to highlight a subject, making it pop out against the background. I also paint a gate, using just straight lines.

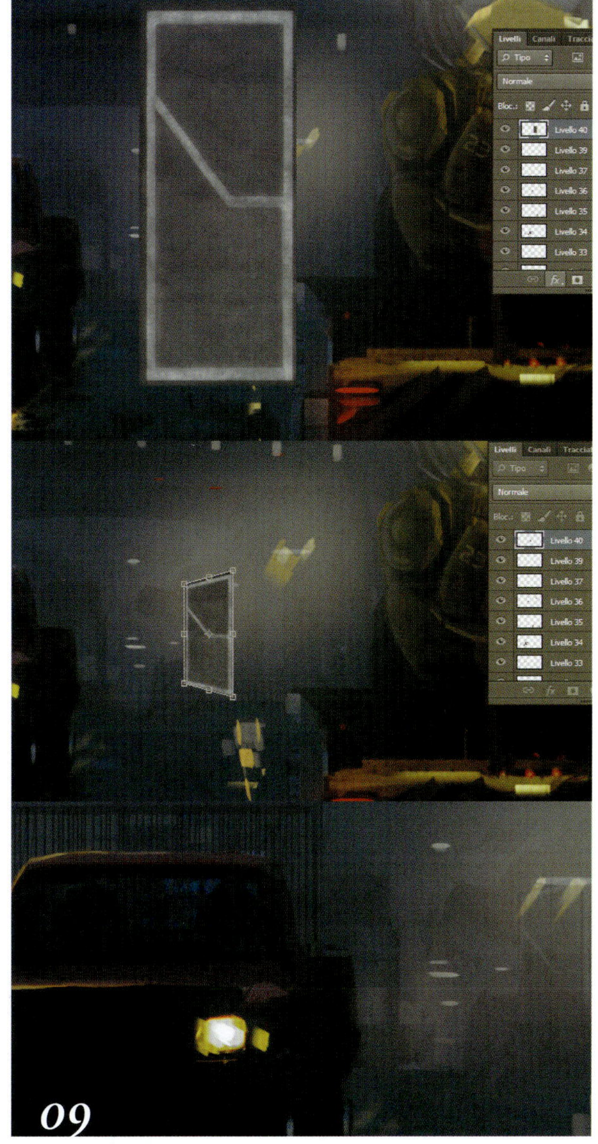

▲ Change the overall coloration and saturation using a Color Correction layer

10: Color correction

In digital art, we are not limited by the possibilities of colors, pigments, and tools, we are painting on screens using just light. Though the fundamentals are the same, digital painting uses light (in the form of pixels) instead of pigments, so anything we don't like about an image can easily be changed. As a final touch carry out a color correction to eliminate the strong blue in the scene; do this by adding a Color Balance layer and decreasing the blue contribution by 20%, which will increase the yellow. Now the image has a more a greenish tint. Carry out this operation on the midtone level so that the highlights and shadows remain the same. Exaggerating the color corrections can easily lead to undesirable results, such as very dark shadows or overexposed lights. Experimentation is the key; keep going until you find what you like.

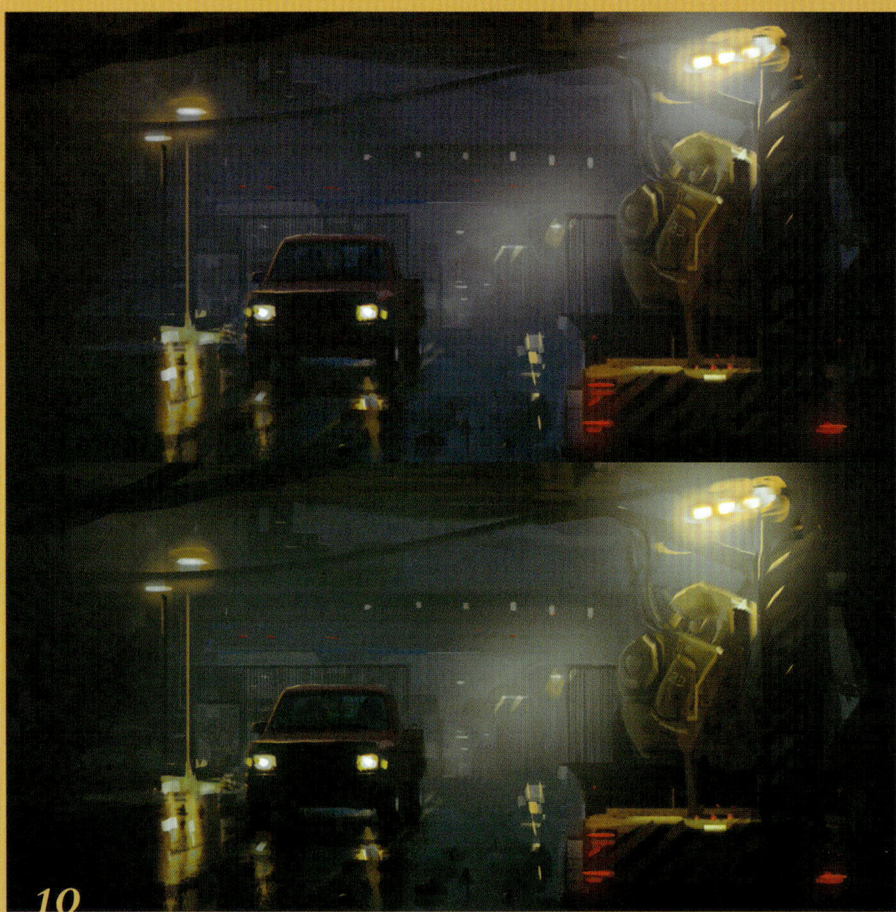

▲ Before and after color correction

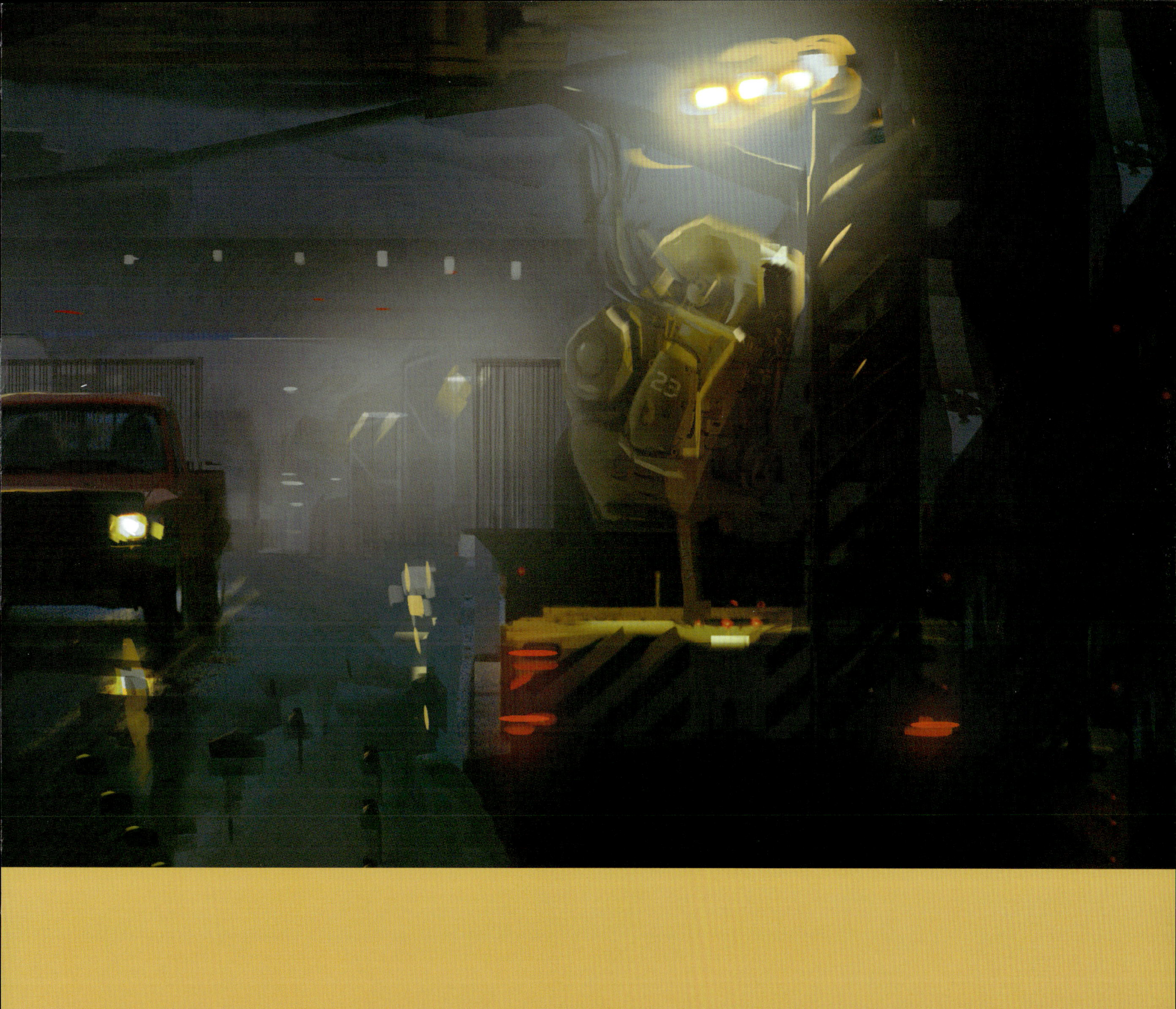

FANTASY: THE WATERWAY

by Sung Choi

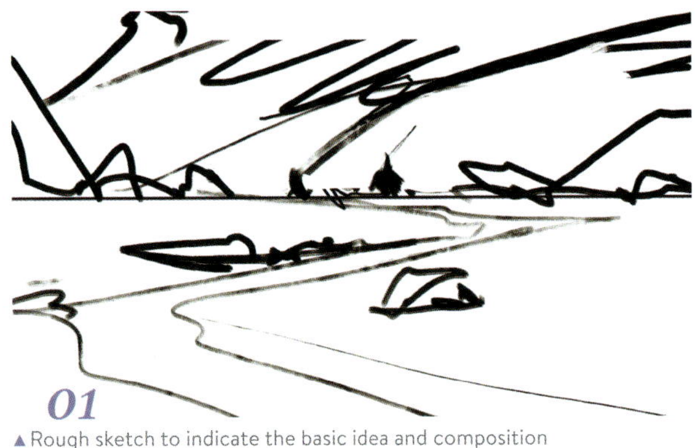

▲ Rough sketch to indicate the basic idea and composition

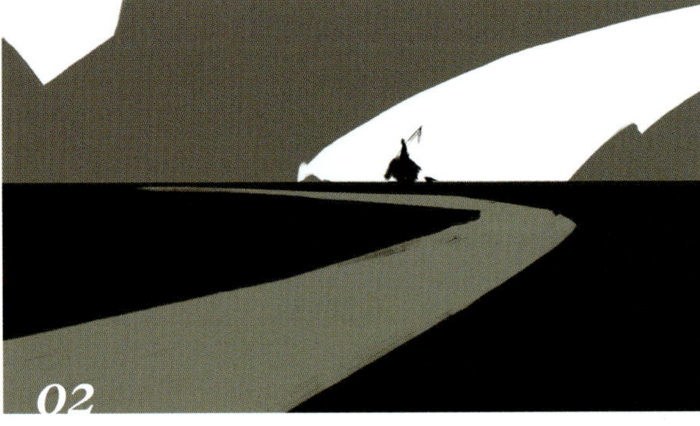

▲ Block out the major shapes

This tutorial is an introduction to my speed-painting process. Speed painting is the perfect tool for those times when you have an exciting idea or visual in your head and need to capture it and get it down quickly. This can happen when you've randomly seen something that sends inspiration hurtling around your brain.

With an idea in hand, I like to start my paintings with a simple black-and-white sketch because I find that using these two values enables you to capture both an appealing composition and the lighting at the same time. For me, this part of the process is the most important and I like to spend a lot of time on it so that I can clearly visualize the final outcome.

01: Initial rough sketch

The very first thing to do before anything else is to make a really rough line drawing. It doesn't need to be detailed because at this stage you only need to give a general idea of the narrative and composition.

My initial concept is for a vast waterway network in an alien environment with a character and mountable creature in the distance.

02: Block out the shapes

Using your rough sketch as a guide you can start to block out some of the major shapes; each shape should be a different opaque value and on a separate layer. I find it easier to have the shapes with 100% transparency so that there isn't any overlap between them when I paint on top.

This is also a good opportunity to work out the lighting, and focus more on the composition of the whole scene, with the use of minimal values. Sometimes I can devote more than an hour to finding just the right sketch.

For creating shapes, use a very simple 100% Opacity brush. You can use the Round brush, which is one of the default brushes in Photoshop.

03: Color experimentation

After blocking out the shapes, begin with some color experimentation and work on a scheme. As we will have earthy

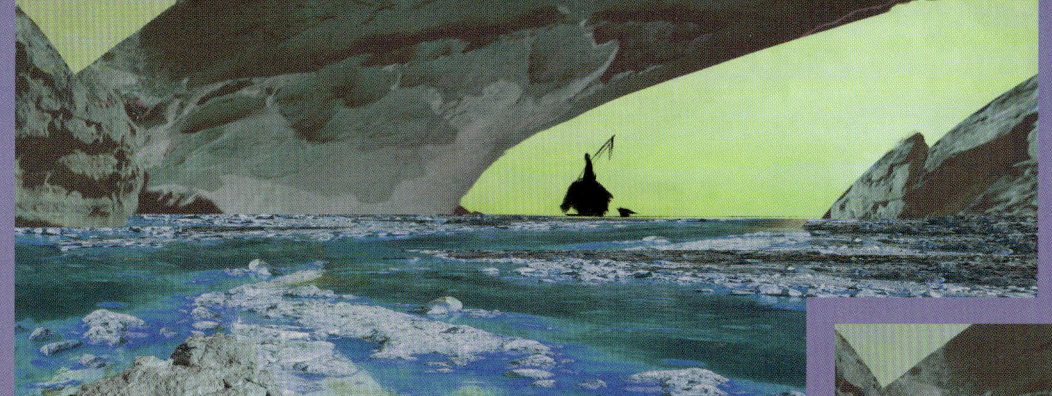

▲ Experiment with color and texture

colors elsewhere in the image, I try a completely different color palette. At the same time experiment with different textures from reference photos.

04: Add reflections

I add reflection by making a layer, applying the entire image, flipping it vertically, clipping it to the water shape layer, then moving it to fit on the horizon line.

Though you are trying out different color schemes you need to make sure that it still makes sense and goes with the narrative. Colors are always relative in an environment so the color on the sky and the ground is very important. Don't go too crazy – keep it harmonious so the sky reflections on the water don't look out of place.

05: Variations

After some slight variation in the sky color, I decide to have a purplish color as an ambient sky. This helps prevent the painting from being too monochromatic. Touch up some of the rock shapes based on the texture you have. You can also add some little red leaves on the ground to create color variation.

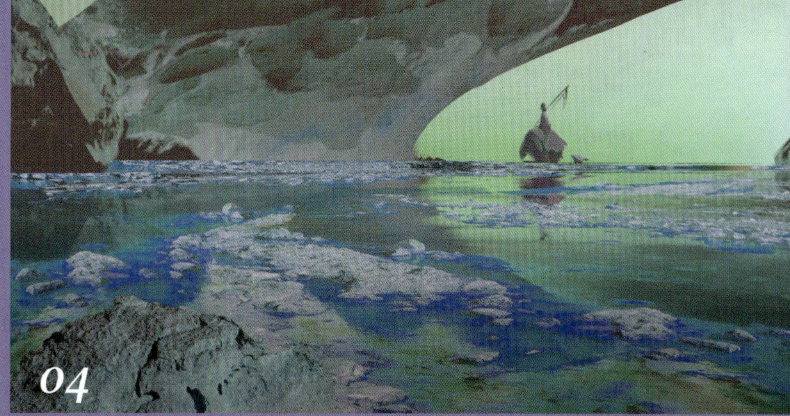

▲ Reflections are a great way to add depth and realism to a painting

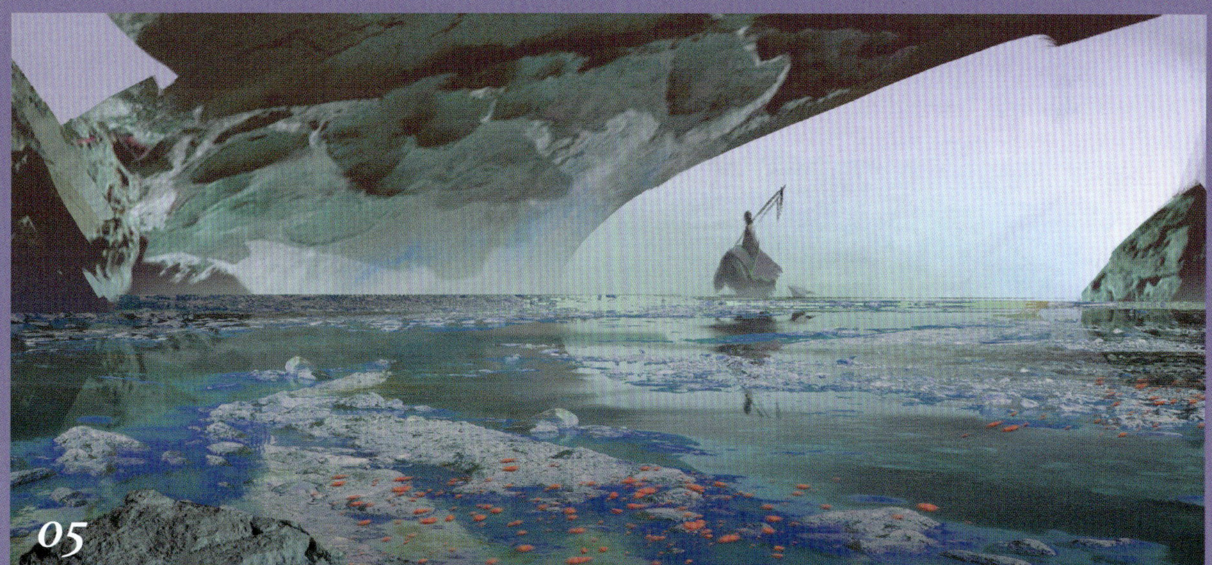

▲ Variation is a key element in any image as you don't want the viewer to be bored

06: Rocks and vegetation

Time to add some extra details such as a rock in front of the large canopy. Be careful with values here. I find the values from step 05 to be too high compared to the original ones, so spend a few minutes adjusting them if needed.

Add background elements such as vegetation to create more areas of interest; try to keep them light because you don't want them to mess up the composition. For vegetation use a custom brush to paint in bunches of tall grass in different green values (use Color Dynamics in the Brush menu).

07: Finishing touches

After you have collated all the elements that need to be in the painting you can spend a little bit of time cleaning up some of the rough edges and shapes. This stage comes at the very end and is all about cleaning up the painting and keeping all the elements consistent.

After this, you can add some contrast by playing around with Levels and Color Balance, although not too much. Make one final new layer and clean those edges one last time with the Mixer brush. The speed painting is now complete.

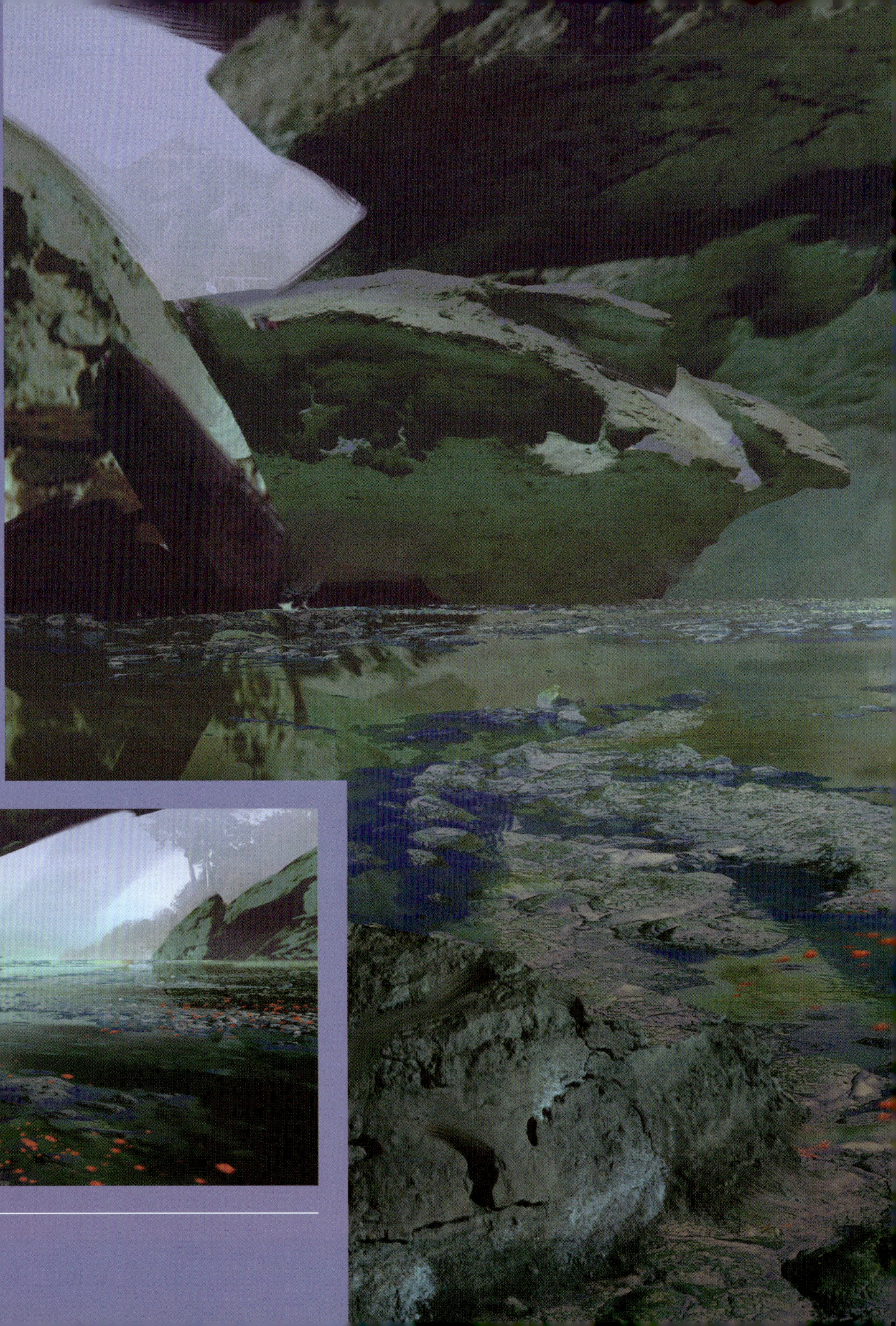

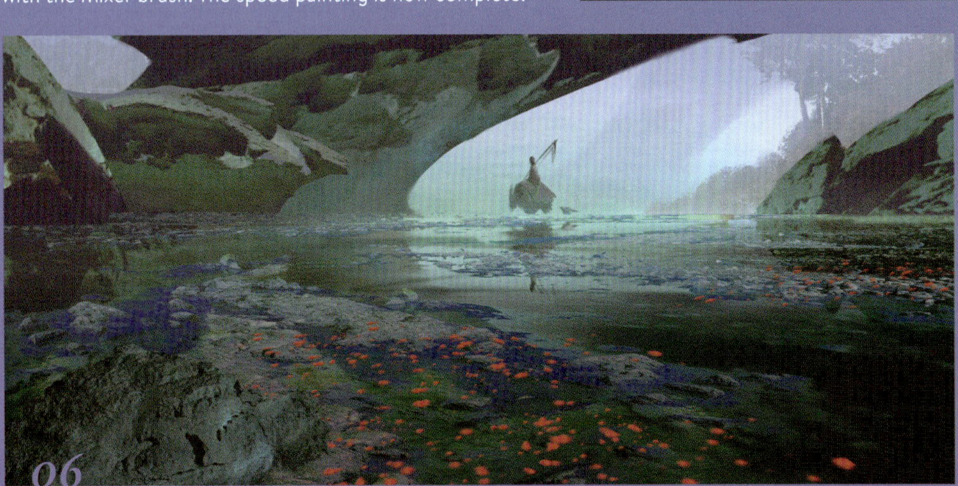

▲ Adding vegetation and rocks brings the image together

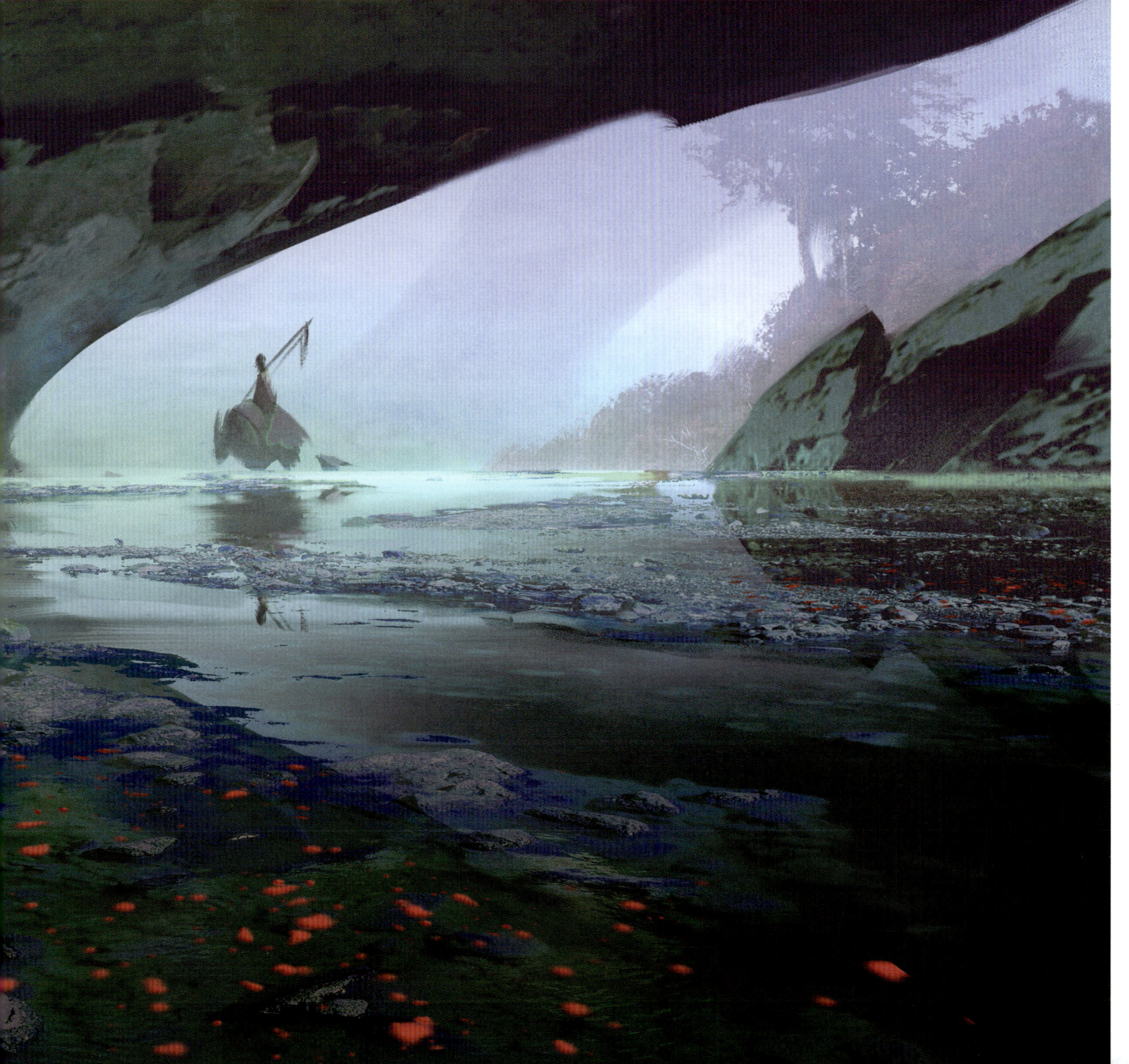

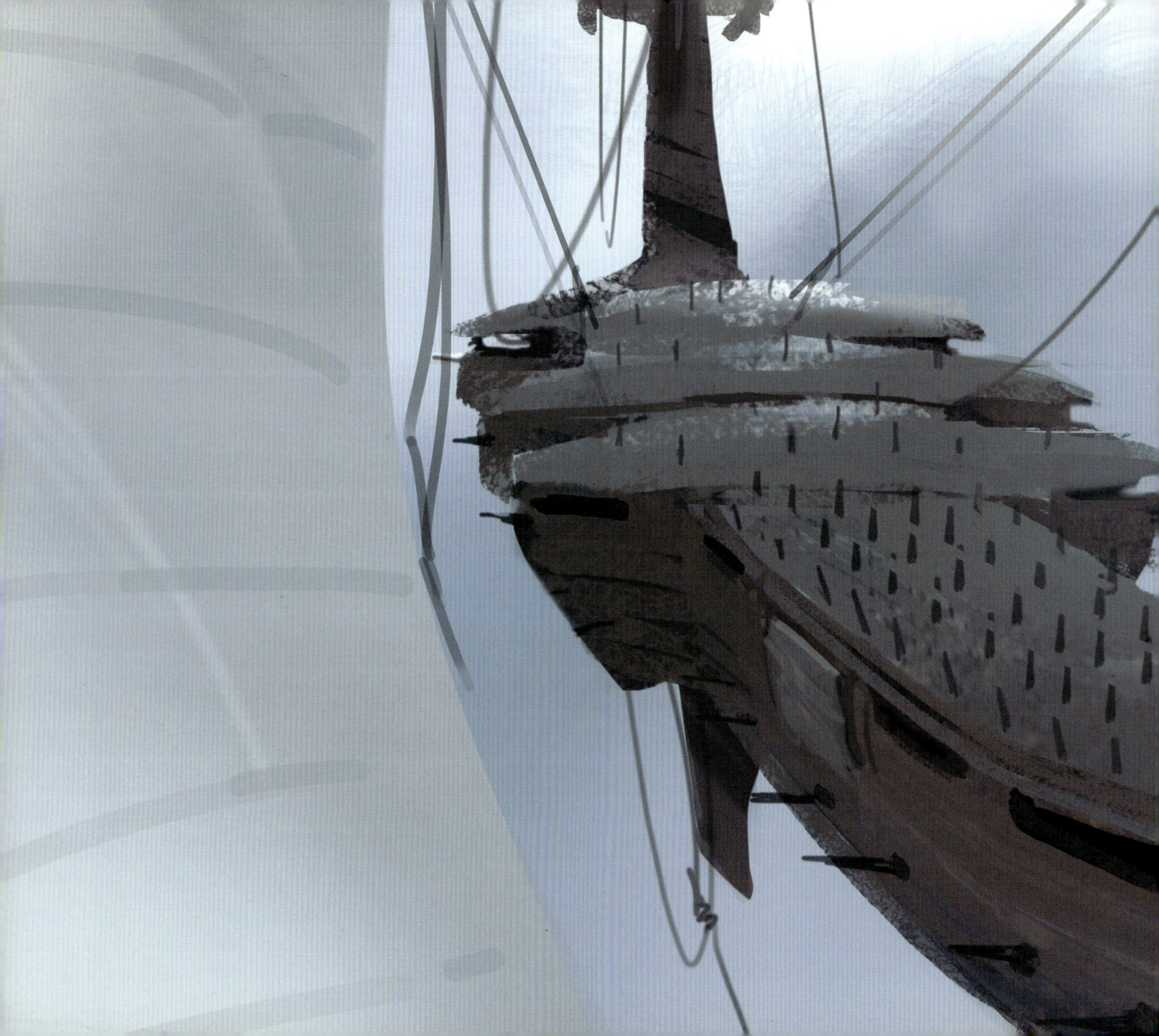

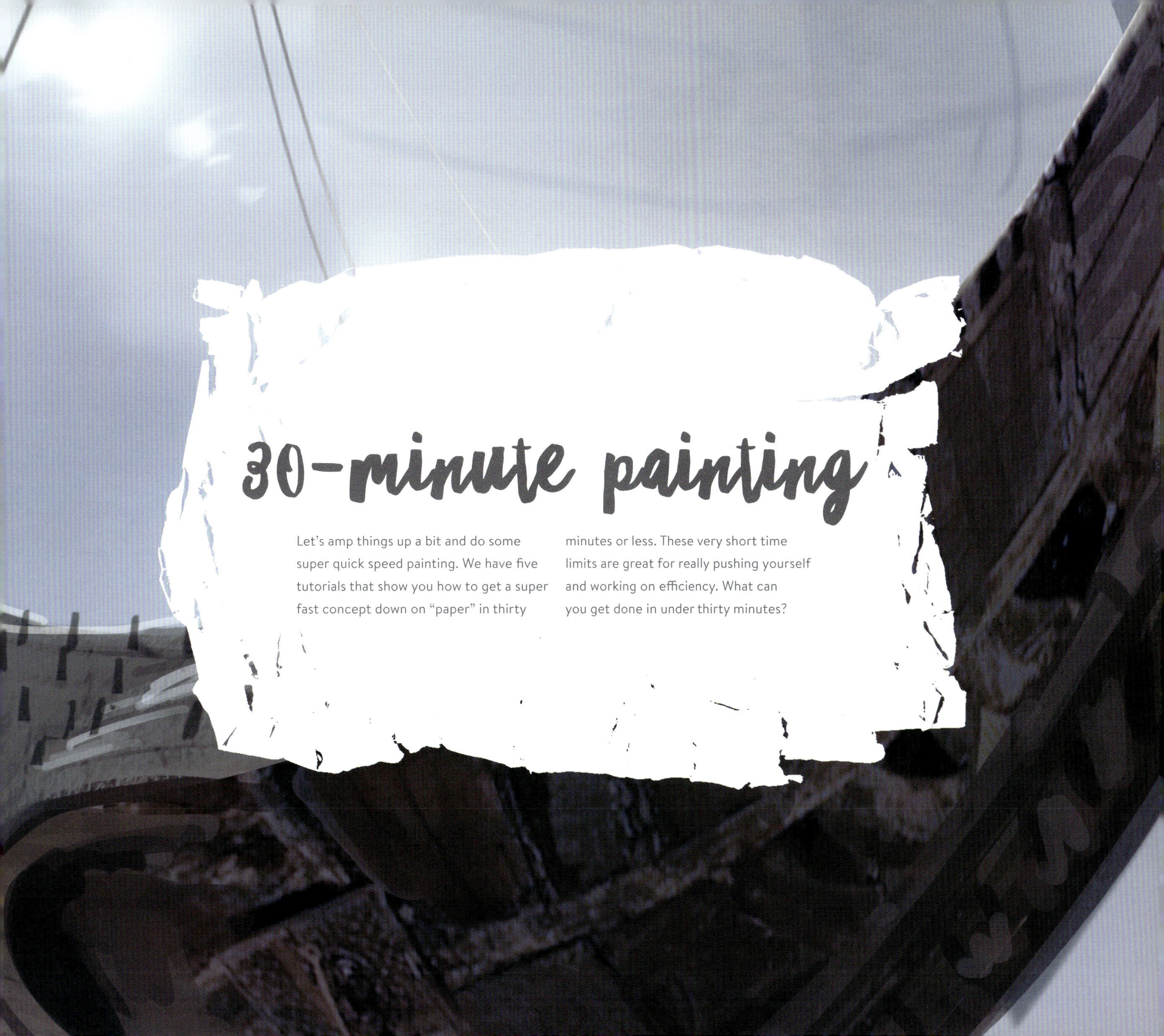

30-minute painting

Let's amp things up a bit and do some super quick speed painting. We have five tutorials that show you how to get a super fast concept down on "paper" in thirty minutes or less. These very short time limits are great for really pushing yourself and working on efficiency. What can you get done in under thirty minutes?

SCI-FI: MOBILE LAB
by Sung Choi

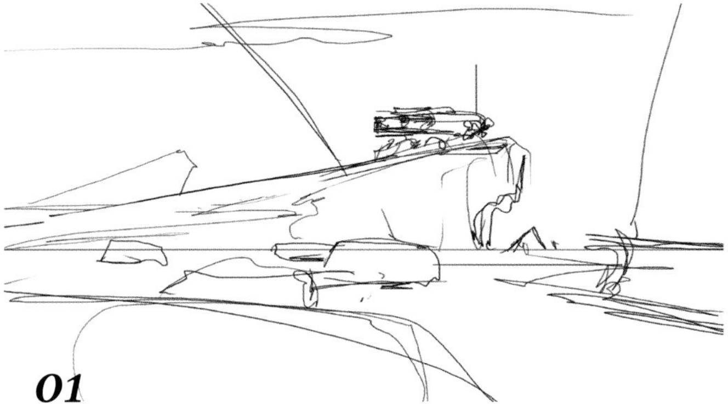

01
▲A quick sketch can lead to all sorts of possibilities

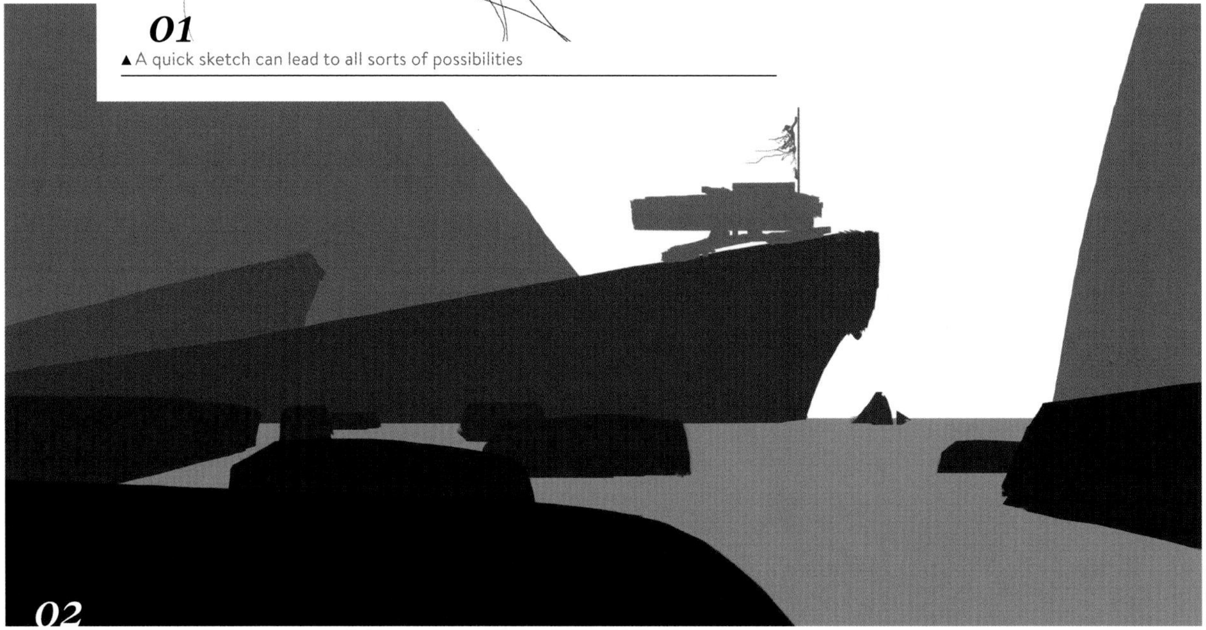

02
▲Blocking the shapes in separate layers helps to organize the composition

For this thirty-minute tutorial we will look at my process for making a super speedy sci-fi landscape which could potentially be used as a basis for a future painting. It is a simpler workflow than my previous one (page 202) as the time is so limited.

As always we will start with a simple two-tone sketch to capture a good composition and the lighting.

To make the most of the thirty minutes we will stick to black and white and minimal texturing so we don't waste time worrying about different colors and textures. Instead the main focus will be on making full use of gradients and contrast to build up the mood and atmosphere of the painting.

01: Idea sketching

Roughly lay down what's in your head. This simple line drawing should take a few minutes and will help you to see what's going on in the shot by placing the key features. I am going for an environment where acid eats away at the terrain and where there is some sort of mobile laboratory perched on top of a rock.

02: Shape blocking

After establishing a sketch, you can start blocking out the shapes in separate layers. This helps to organize and keep the layers in order, and also to see the image as simplified value groups. As you can see **image 02**, the overall composition is simple with one interesting shape which is the lab. I intentionally make the silhouettes of the mountains have a clean directional line that is pointing down to the lab.

03: Values

You can make this painting even simpler by darkening the values. Add some light shapes on top of the base layer to show that there is a slice of light coming through from the sky. To add a spooky element to the image, make it overcast with other areas that are very dark.

Paint all the light shapes on new layers, on top of their base layers, then use a clipping mask, which will allow you to paint without going out of the silhouette's lines.

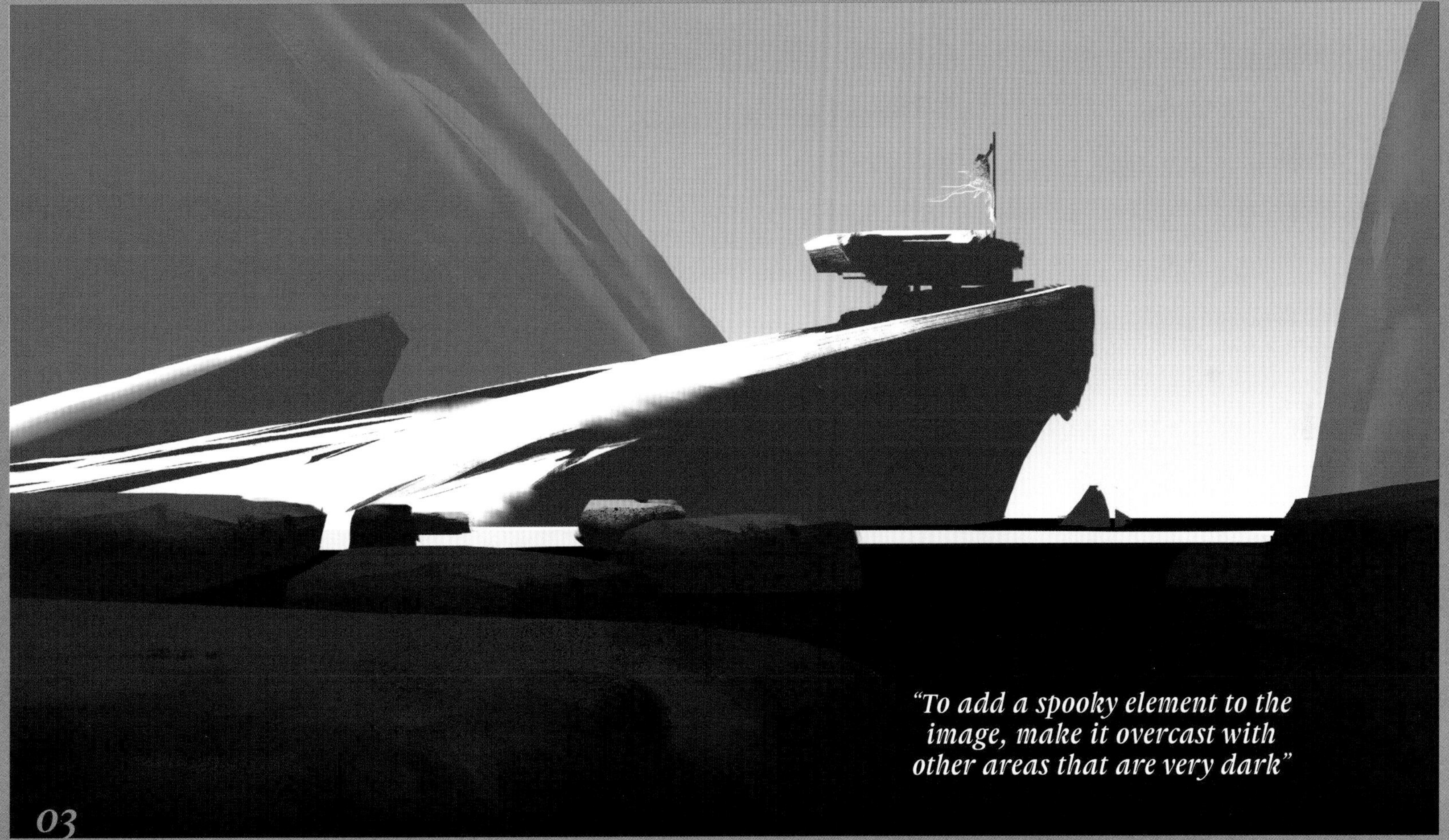

"To add a spooky element to the image, make it overcast with other areas that are very dark"

03

▲Darkening the values can make the scene appear shadowy and eerie

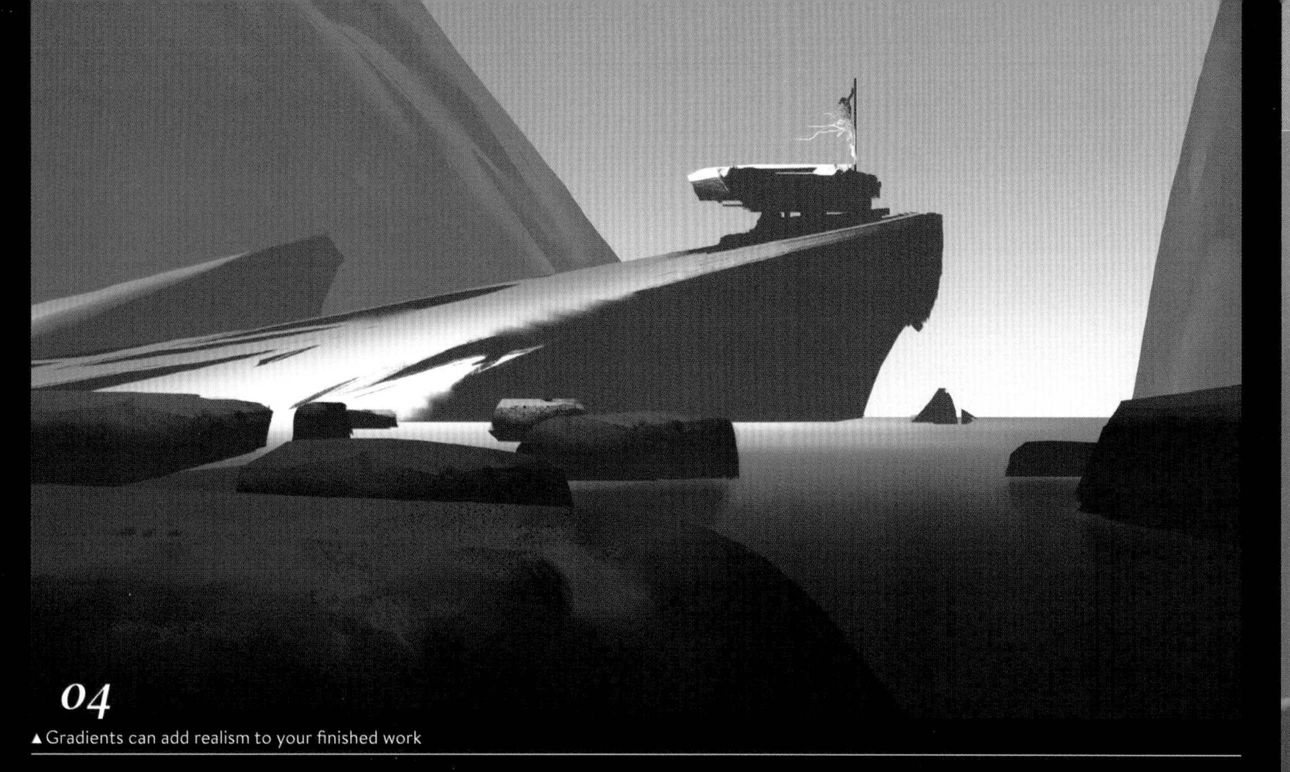

04

▲ Gradients can add realism to your finished work

04: Gradients

After painting light shapes you can add some gradients to give them a more realistic look. This will give you an idea of what the final image will look like and whether you need to add to the overall mood of the piece or not. I don't use gradients unless I feel strongly that the shapes and compositions I have are working well. Practicing the sketch without using gradients and gray values helps a ton.

05: Finishing touches

I add some misty clouds on top of the frame and the reflection on the acid water. Then I add some smoke coming out of the surface of the water to hint that this water is not good for drinking. I also clean up some edges that are too sharp when they are not the focus of the image. Now this can be a sketch (or a map) for a more finalized painting.

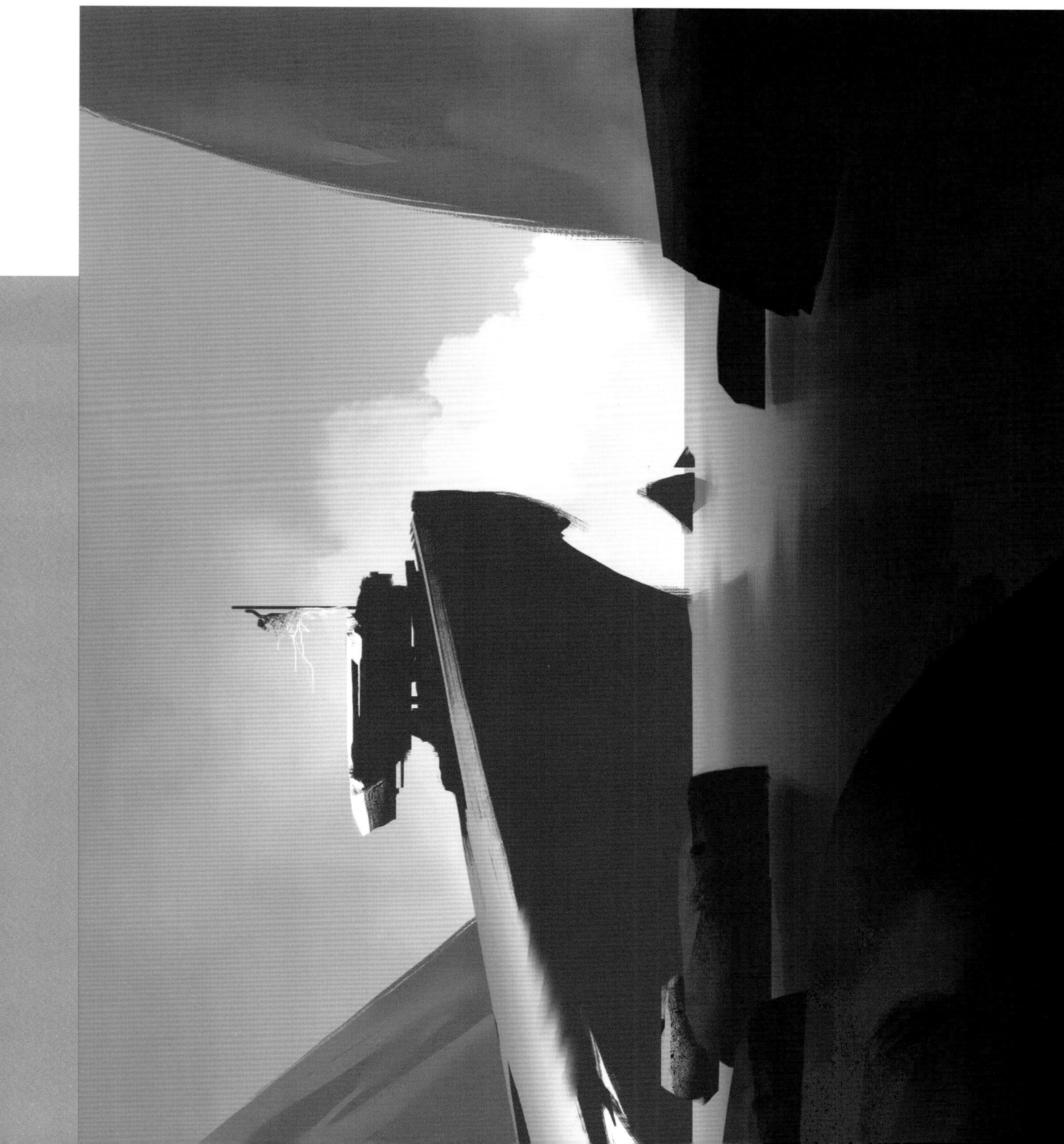

SCI-FI: CHECKPOINT ON MARS

by Massimo Porcella

In this tutorial you will learn how to quickly create a 30-minute sci-fi speed painting using structural shapes, texturing, and color.

01: Idea

First use the Gradient tool to add a shade to the canvas, then use a hard brush and actively transfer paint to the ground. Dark grays are a good choice because they help to give a sense of volume and depth.

Use a custom cloud brush to make a sky. It doesn't need to be detailed or fancy; simple cloud shapes will be fine.

Make a huge structure which dominates the background of the page but is not the main focal point of the piece. The Polygonal Lasso tool is good for making geometric structures.

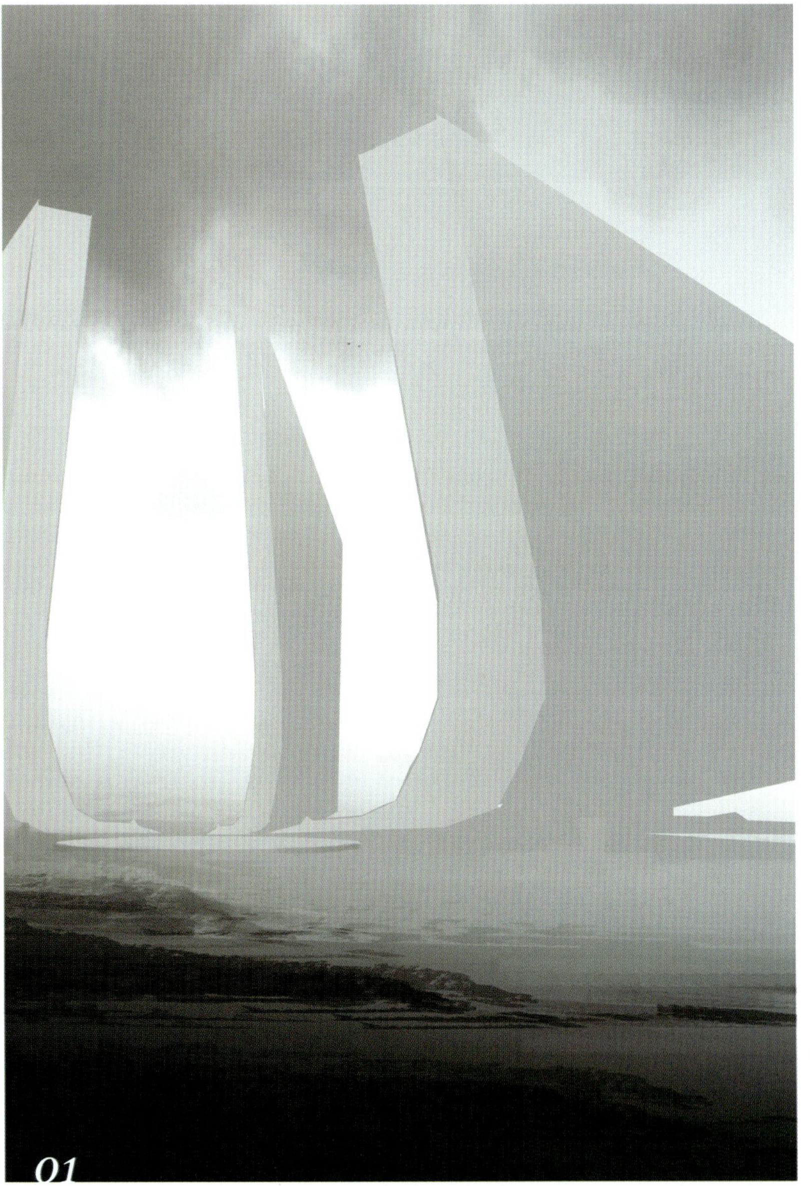

▲ Build up the layers of the background

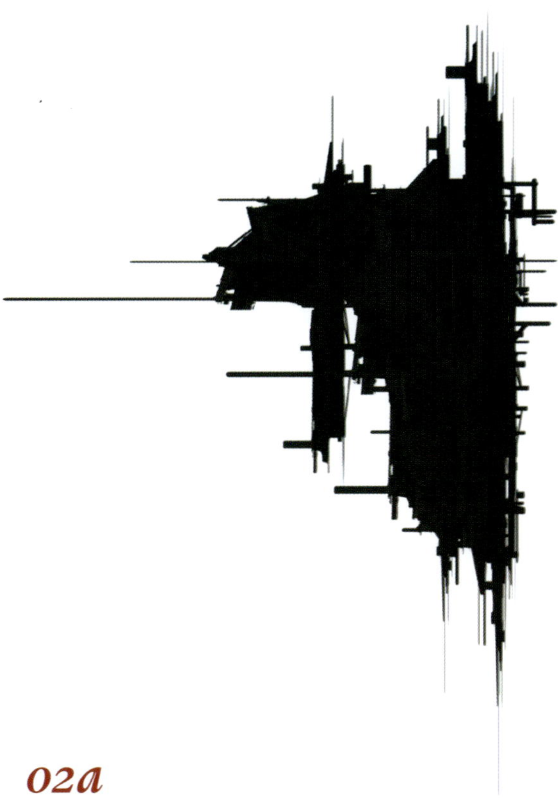

02a

▲A structural shape that will add interest

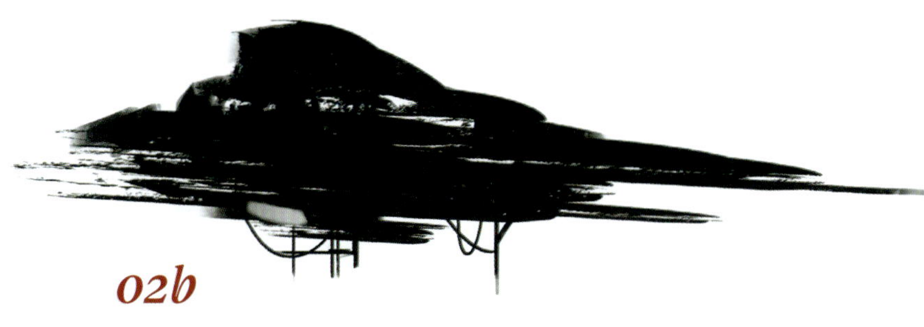

02b

▲The ship shape

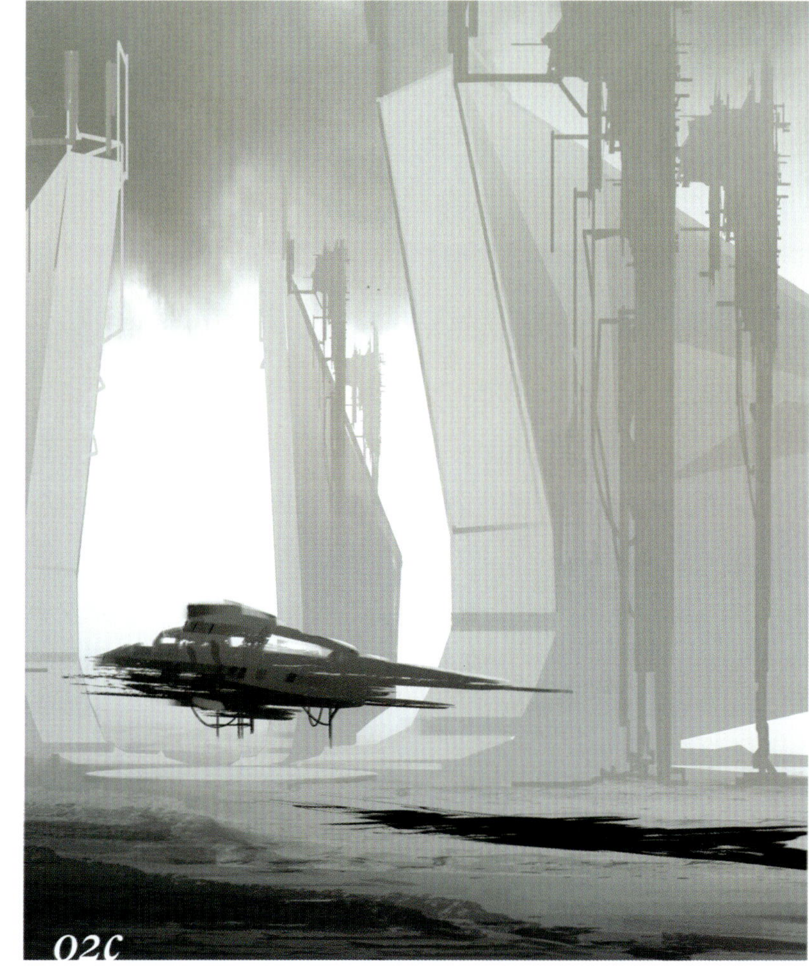

02c

▲Bring the structural elements together in the image

"You can create new and different shapes from these bases simply by playing with the Free Transform tool"

02: Shapes

Now you need to make two more structural shapes: one will add interest to the huge background structures (**image 02a**) and the other will be a spaceship to balance out the composition (**image 02b**).

On separate layers use the Polygonal Lasso tool to create random geometric shapes, then copy and paste to duplicate them. You can create new and different shapes from these bases simply by playing with the Free Transform tool – stretch and adjust them as needed.

With your shapes made, place several copies of the structural shape to act as struts for the huge background structure, adjusting the size and tone of each one according to atmospheric perspective. Place the ship shape on one of the rule-of-thirds intersection points to act as the main focus of the painting; I put mine in the lower-left corner (**image 02c**).

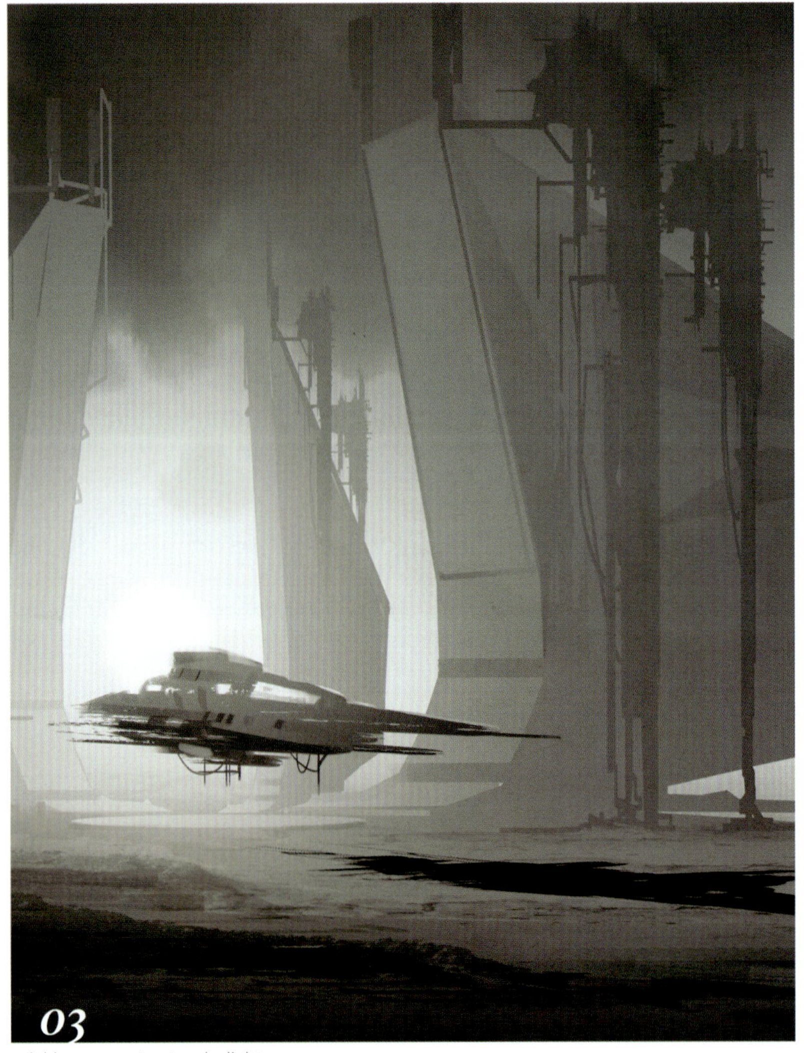

▲ Add some contrast and a light source

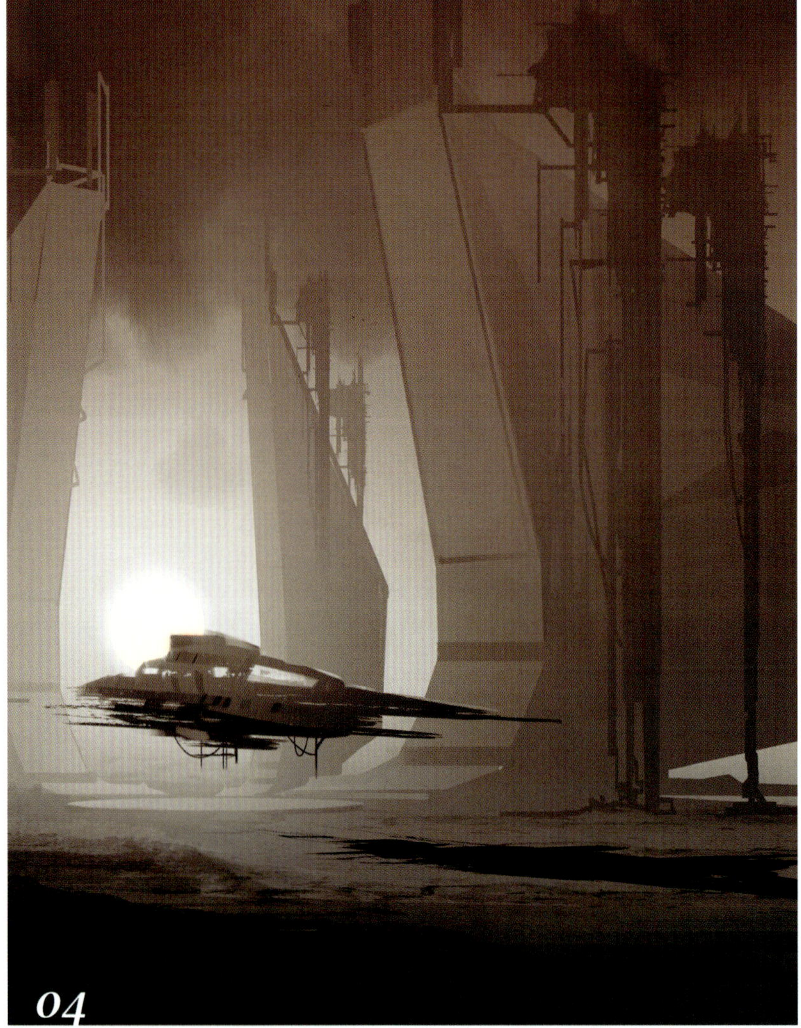

▲ A well-chosen base color will set the scene

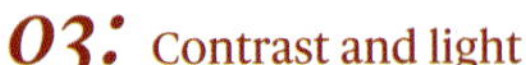

03: Contrast and light

Add contrast to create a depth of field and a sense of volume using the Curves tool to pull out the lights and darks. Add a light source just behind the ship – in this case it is the Sun. By putting the light low on the horizon you are adding more drama and increasing the atmosphere. Remember that the low angle of the light will elongate and distort the shadows. To paint the sun use a hard brush for the middle of the sun and on a separate layer, using a soft brush, create a hazy halo effect.

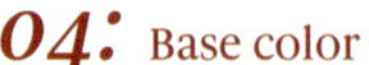

04: Base color

As with step 01, use the Gradient tool to add a base color. Go for a muddy red in order to bring to mind a martian sunset. Use different blend modes to find the effect you like best. Make sure you choose your base color well because it will set the scene and tone for the whole painting.

05: Ground

Merge the layers into one (Ctrl+Alt+Shift+E), desaturate it by turning it black and white (**image 05a**), and use Levels adjustments to capture the brightest whites and darkest blacks – basically contrasting the image as much as possible.

Use the Magic Wand tool to create a mask selection of the darkest black areas (**image 05b**) and on a new layer with the mask you've just created, paint a gradient using the base color as a guide. This will give you control of the parts you are going to paint on, contrasting even more and adding depth to the planes by enhancing the atmospheric perspective (**image 05c**).

Now you should have a much better reading of the scene because the light source and focal points are emphasized (**image 05d**). Add some blur to the furthest parts of the image to increase the depth of field. Your painting should now have a very atmospheric and dramatic feel.

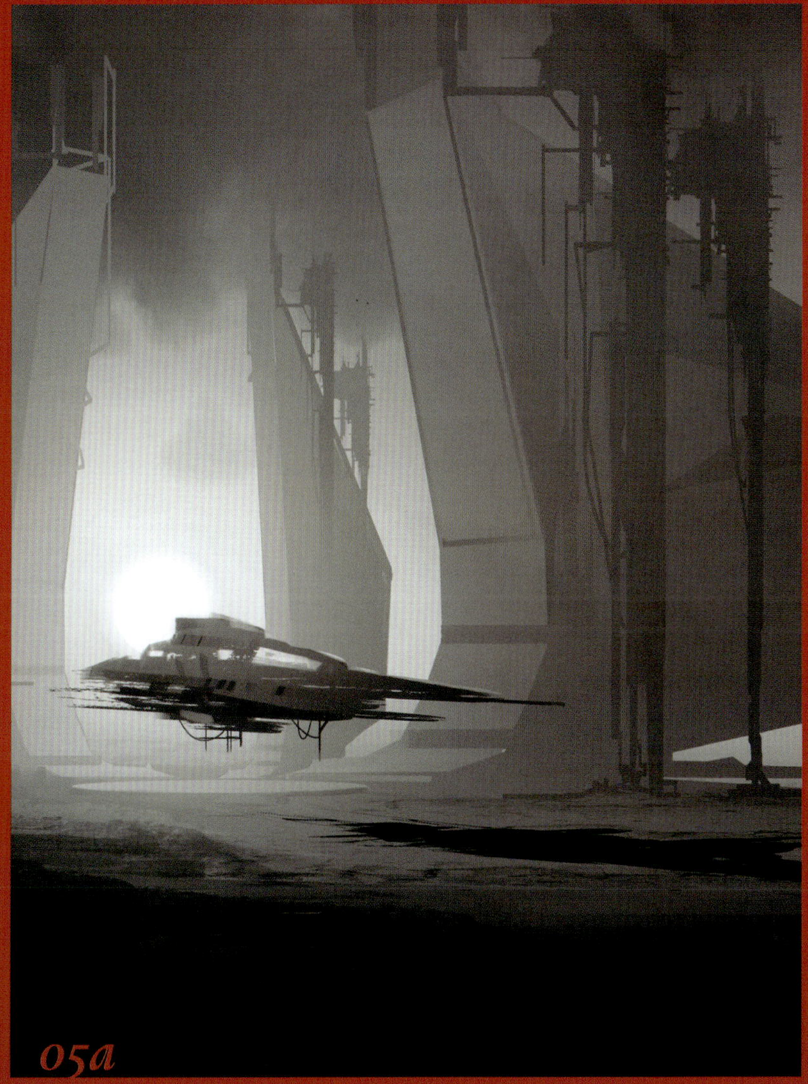

▲ Use an adjustment layer to desaturate the image

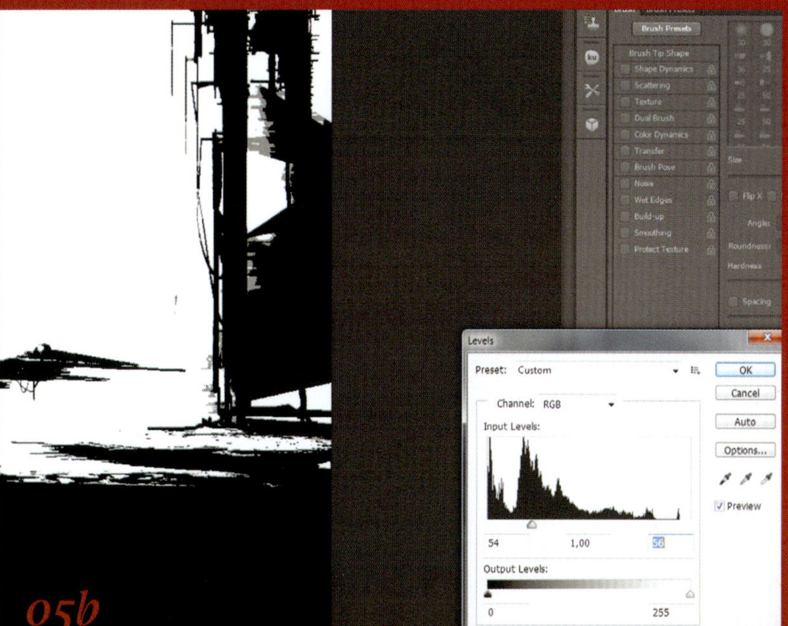

▲ Create a mask selection of the blacks

▲ Painting with a gradient will increase the sense of atmospheric perspective

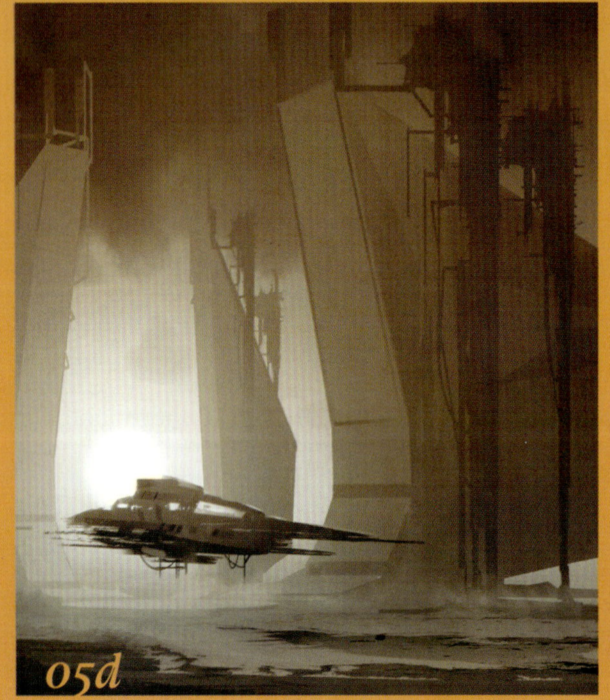

▲Use lighting to direct the viewer's eyes

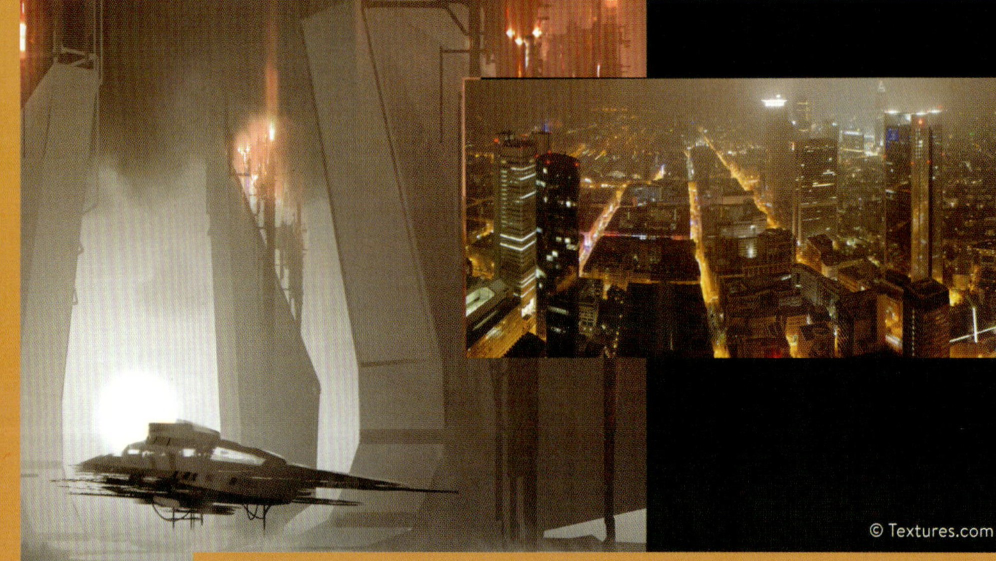

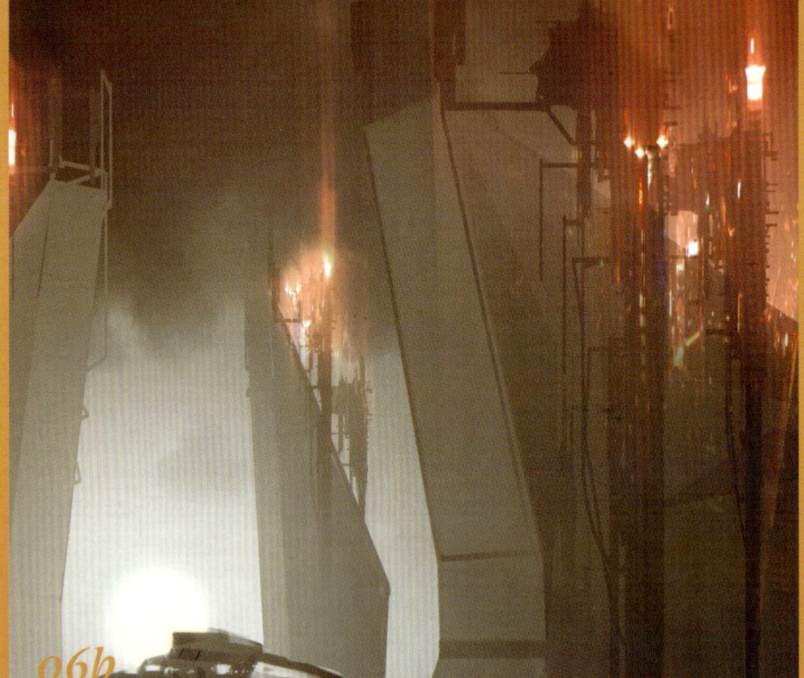

▲Using photos of city lights is a quick way to add interest to any painting

06: Texturing for artificial light

Find a reference photo of a city at night; this will create the artificial lights. You will have to stretch and squash it to match up with the background structure and the struts on the side. Apply it in Color Dodge blend mode to get rid of the black, only keeping the lights. Use a slightly blurred brush to create streams of light going upwards (**images 06a** and **06b**). This method of adding lights is also useful when designing concepts of cities, or to add interesting lights to sci-fi interiors.

"Weathering the structures and adding dirt to the walls will help them fit in with the overall mood"

07: Age with a textured brush

With the main elements of the composition in place you can start to add some definition. Try adding some aging details (using a textured brush) that reinforce the initial concept. In this case the painting is set on the surface of an alien desert planet. Weathering the structures and adding dirt to the walls will help them fit in with the overall mood.

Similarly, use a rust pattern on the ship in order to give it a dirty and

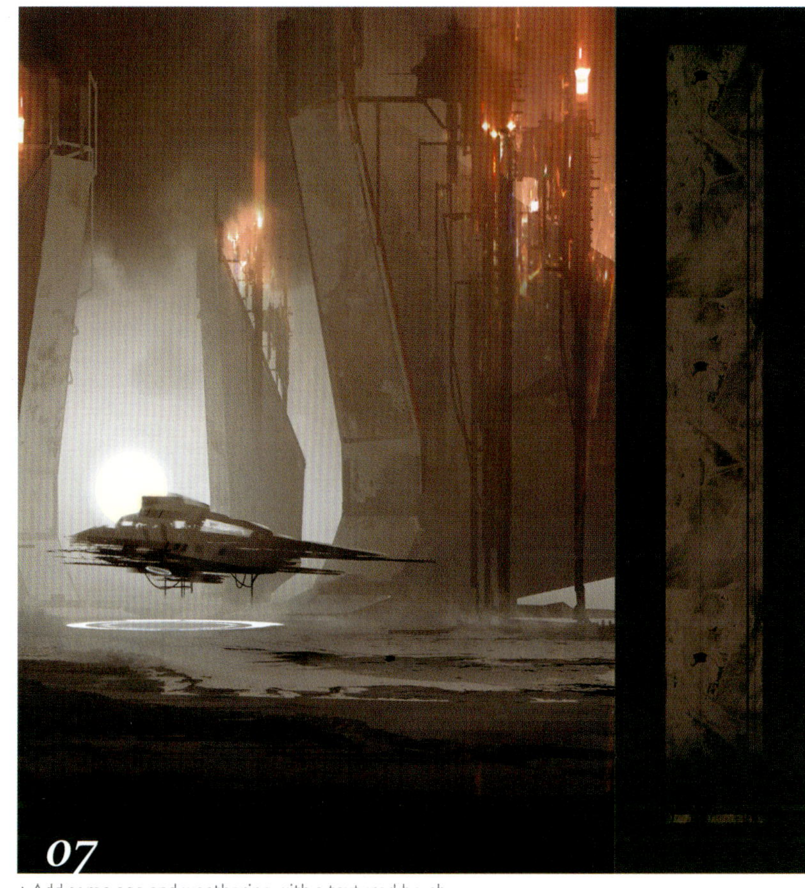

▲ Add some age and weathering with a textured brush

decaying feel. This will make the ship more interesting by quickly adding a random rusty pattern. Apply the rust directly with a square brush.

08: Contrast, refining, and Color Dodge

Back to contrasting to darken the whole painting; use Curves to lower the blacks and strengthen the whites (only slightly!). Pulling out the lights and darks not only adds contrast but also adds more volume and depth to each of the planes. This will help to focus the viewer on the brightest point – the ship.

To brighten the main focal point and make it stand out you need to build up the lighting details: open a new layer set to Color Dodge and use a hard-edged brush (lower the hardness slightly). Finish it off by adding some particle effects.

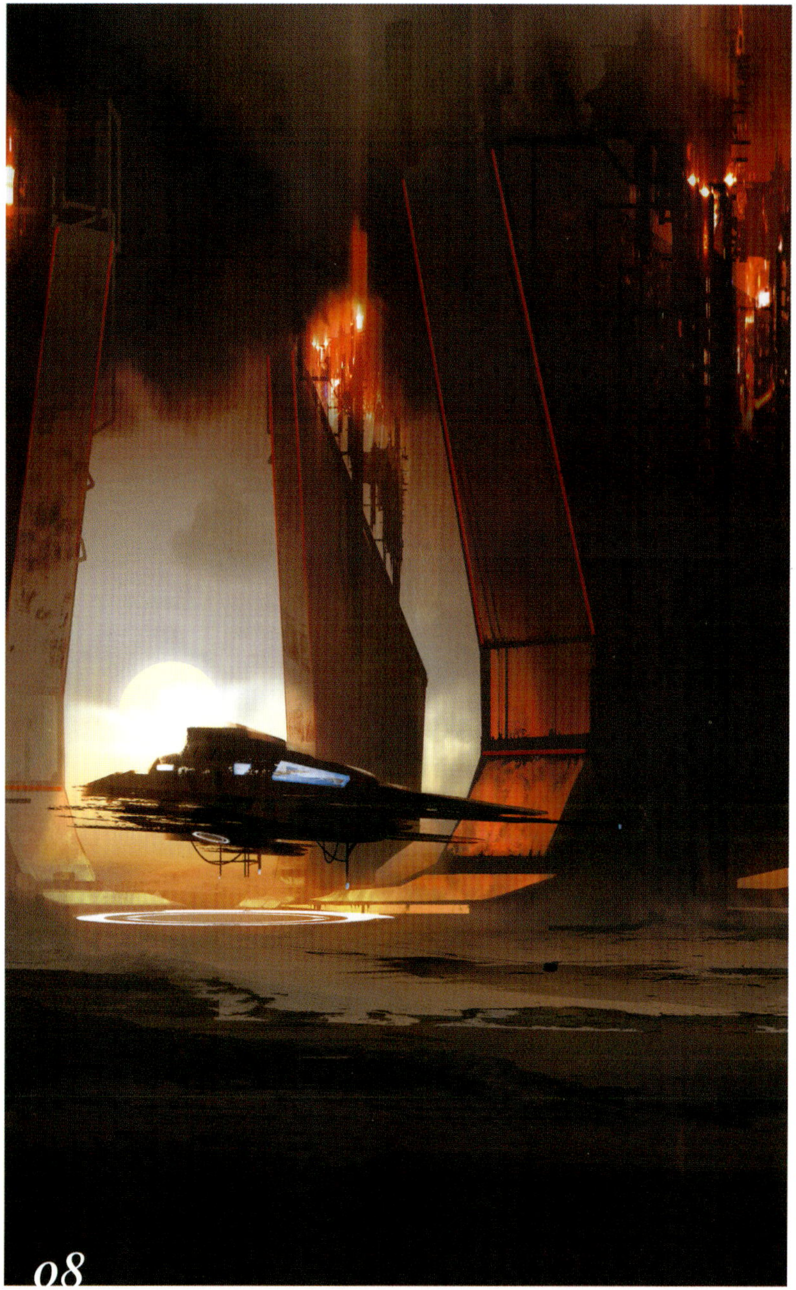

▲ Increase the attention on the focal point of the image

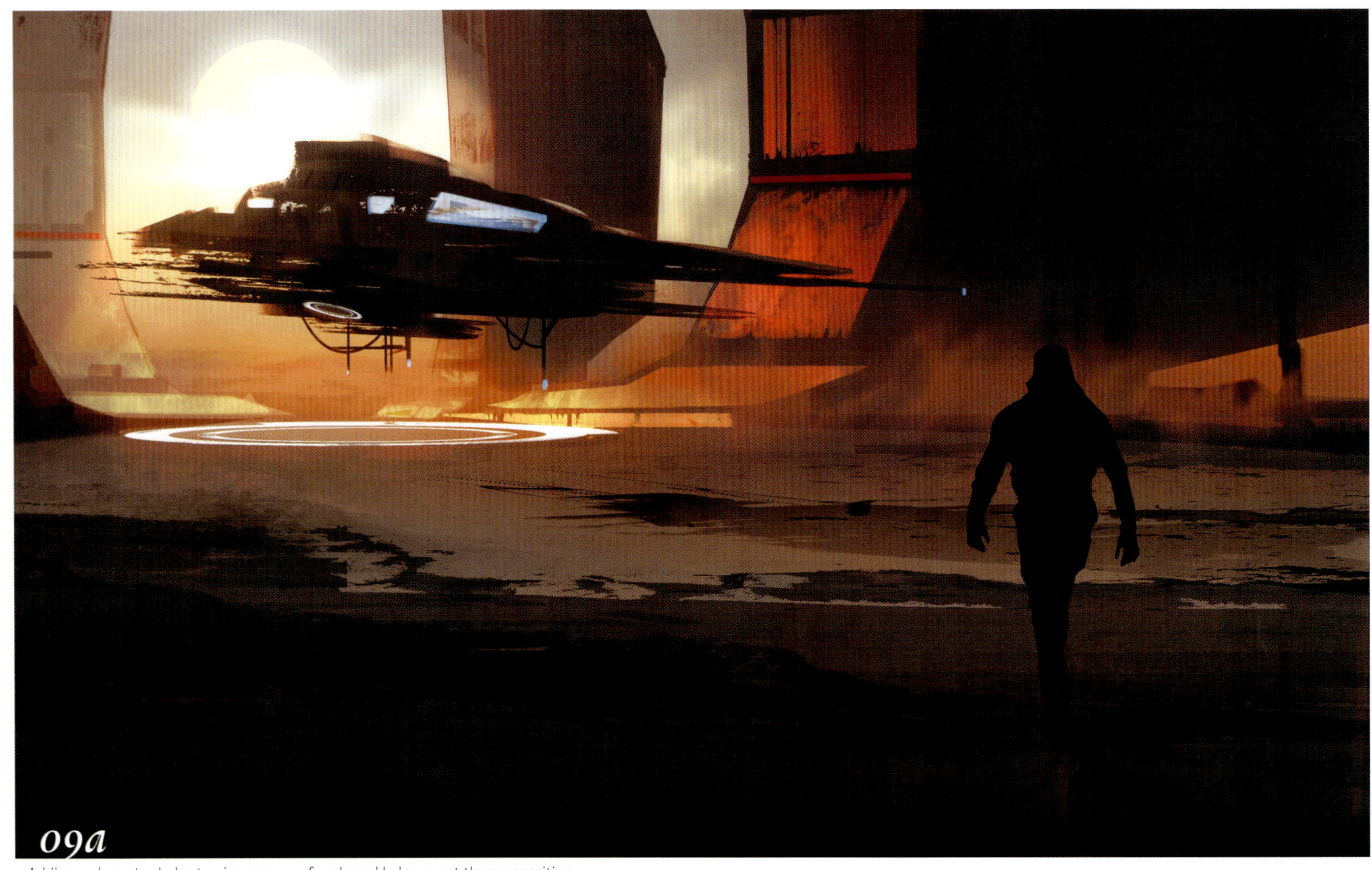

▲Adding a character helps to give a sense of scale and balance out the composition

"My advice is to draw the character on a separate layer and adjust the size and position later; doing it this way will give you a global view of the character in relation to the environment and also allow you to move him about with ease"

09: Character and finalizing process

We need to add something to balance out the composition and add a sense of scale – what is better than a character? He will also bring some life to the barren scene. Use a hard-edged brush with no Transfer to draw a silhouette of the character. My advice is to draw it on a separate layer and adjust the size and position later; doing it this way will give you a global view of the character in relation to the environment and also allow you to move him about with ease (**image 09a**).

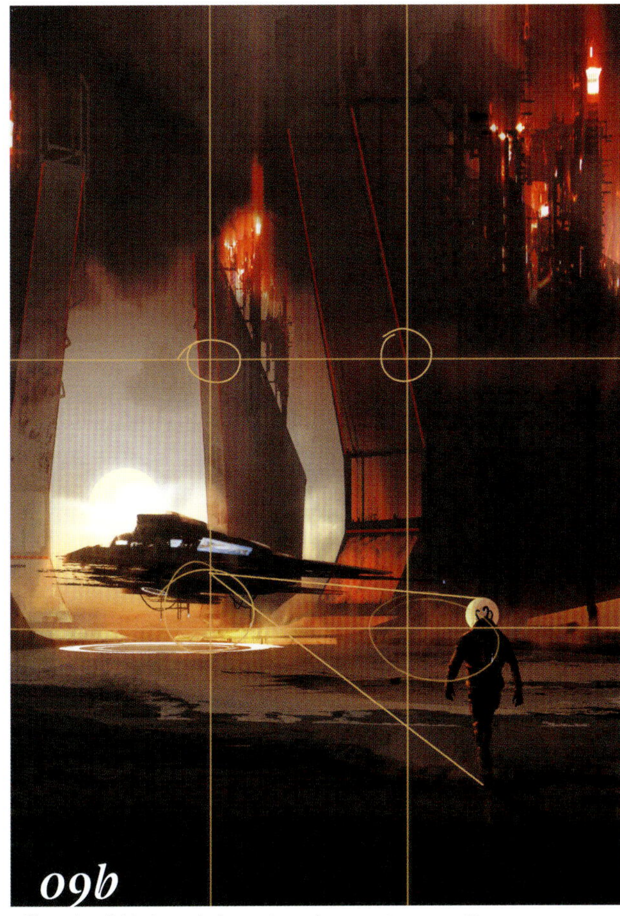

▲ The rule of thirds can help you to make a great composition

To make the character part of the environment block out the silhouette and quickly paint. Use the Eyedropper tool to select colors from the painting and add some lines to suggest his three-dimensionality. Use the rule of thirds to get a balanced composition when placing the character in the environment. Roughly sketch in a three-by-three grid if you want to check the character's placement (**image 09b**). To integrate him properly with the ground blend the area between the legs and ground with a volumetric particle effect. With that you are finished!

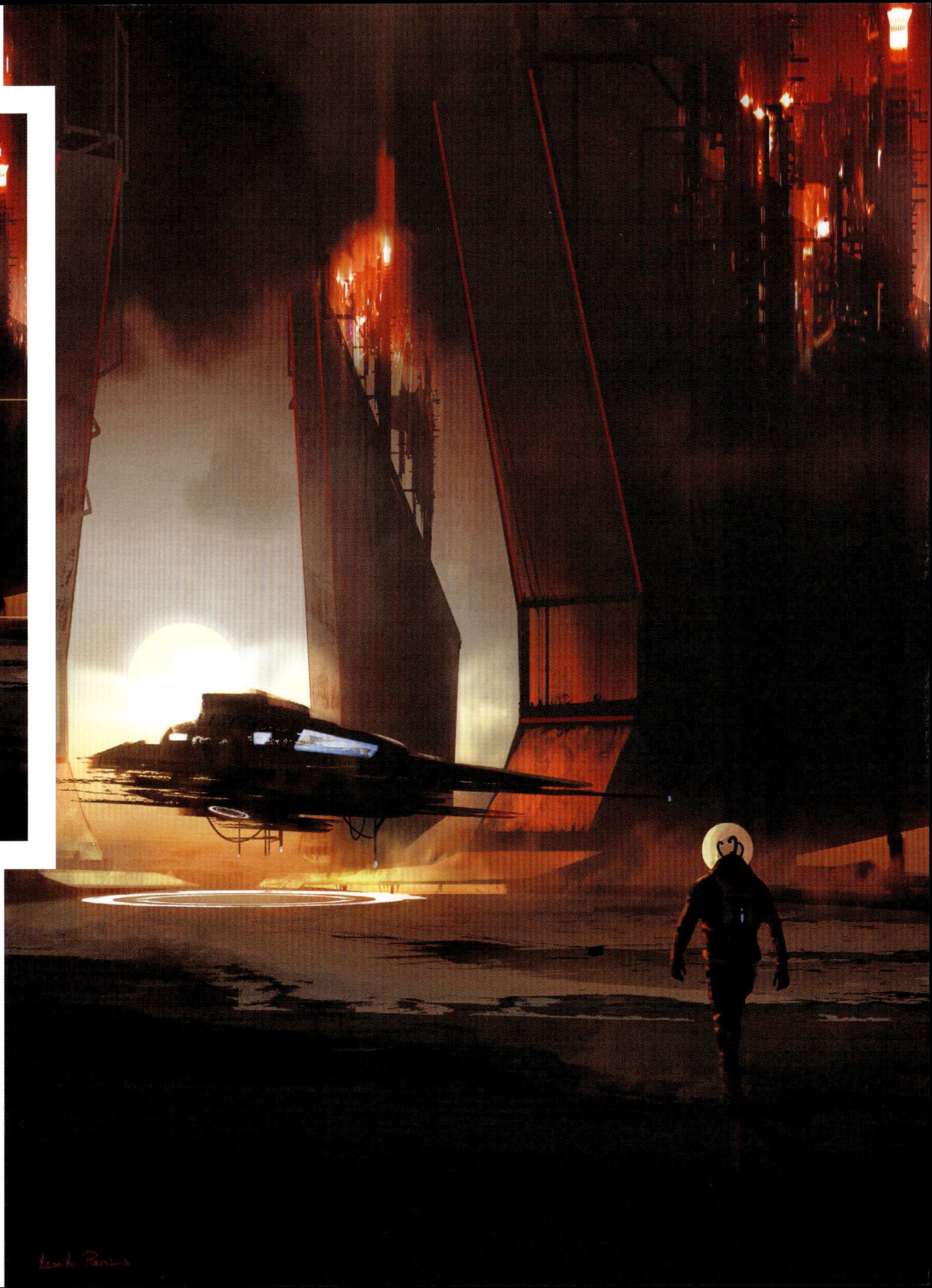

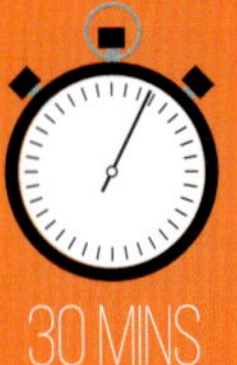

FANTASY: LETTING IT FLOW

Katy Grierson

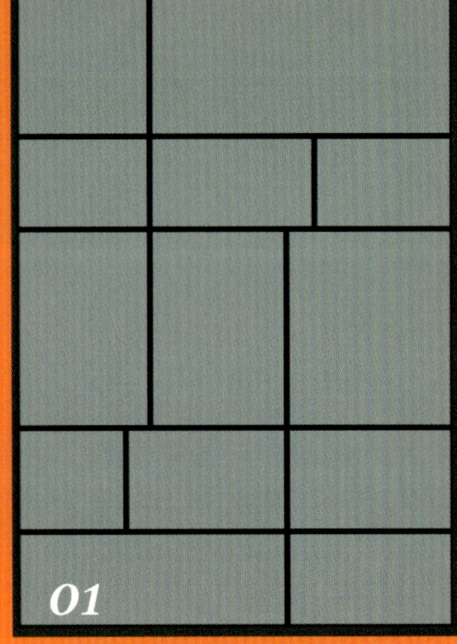

▲ Set up your canvas with a series of boxes on a new locked layer

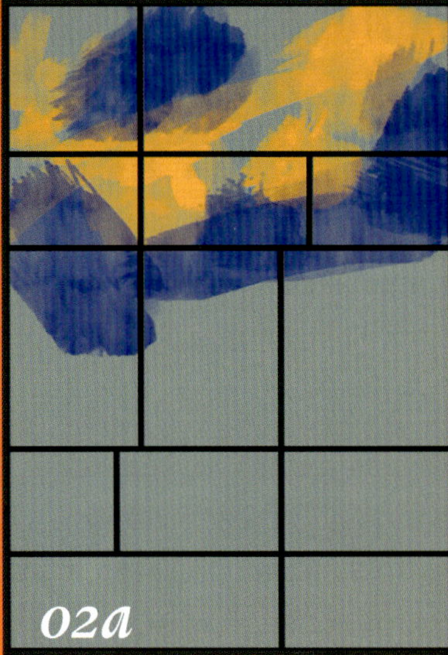

▲ Don't think; just get some brushstrokes down!

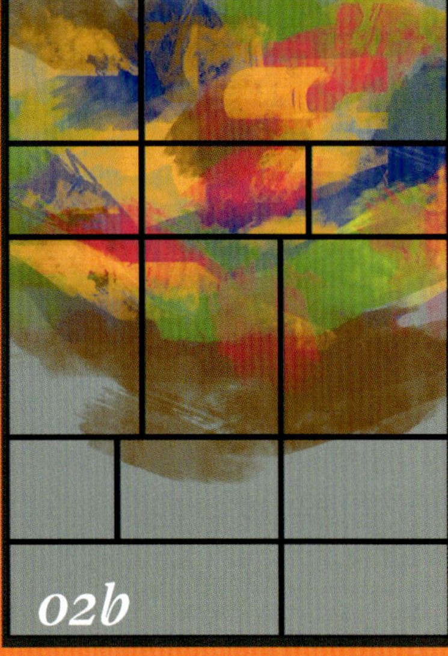

▲ Lay those colors down to get a variety in texture and tone

Sometimes when you sit down to draw or paint something you lack inspiration, or experience the opposite – too much inspiration. It can be difficult to let go of the idea that you have to draw something, anything; but it can also be incredibly useful and rewarding. Once you get into the right mindset speed painting, concepting, and thumbnailing become a much more open-ended process, allowing you to explore ideas that are at first "happy accidents" but lead to very strong images as you take the picture further.

01: Set up

I like to set up my canvas to A4 print size (2480 × 3508 pixels) because it allows me to place a reassuring restriction on endless possibilities and ideas. You might find it easier on the eye to change the background color from a stark white to a softer color, such as mid-gray. On a new layer create a series of box borders with transparent insides – they can be any size or ratio but try to keep them varied. Lock this layer so you don't accidentally paint on it.

02: Start painting

On a layer underneath the boxes, use a big Brush tool to lay down some strokes of varying color, tone, texture, and opacity. Try not to paint anything specific, just fill the canvas with color and texture. You can switch brushes but try to keep the size quite large – this is good for speed and preventing the urge to paint something specific. This initial letting go can be the hardest thing to master but the effects are worth it in the end **(image 02a)**.

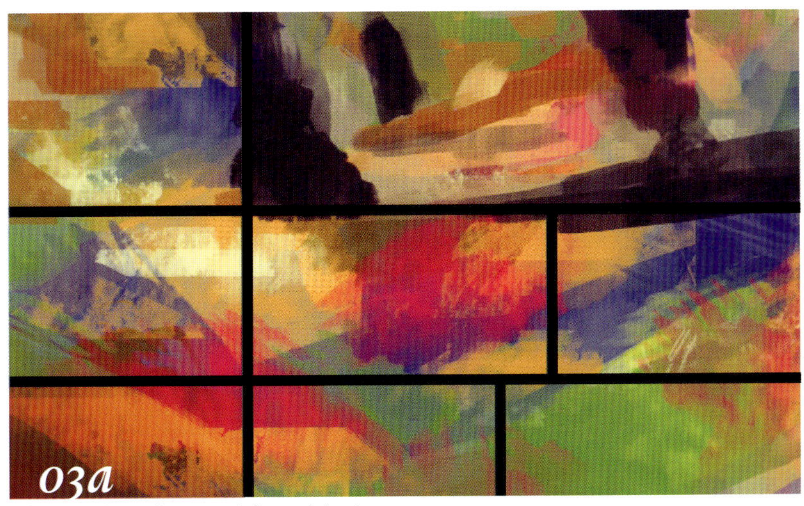

▲ Slowly pick out shapes to define and develop

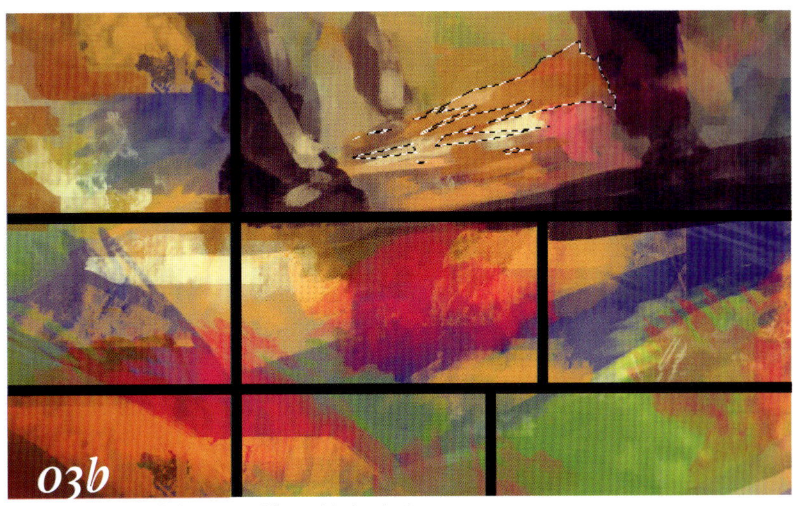

▲ Use the Lasso or Selection tool for quick, hard edges

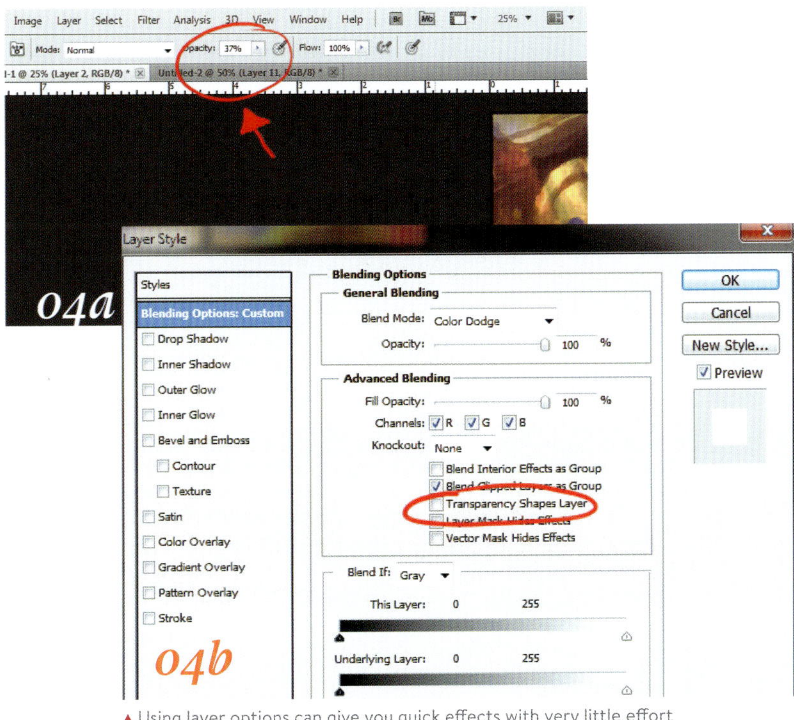

▲ Using layer options can give you quick effects with very little effort

Keep going until you have filled your boxes (you don't have to fill them all). It should still look quite abstract – the colors might clash horribly. This will be the base for your thumbnails. By starting this way there is less pressure to fill a blank white canvas, which can be a hindrance to creativity (**image 02b**).

03: Seeing shapes

Pick a box and focus on it, excluding all the others. Continue to add more shapes and colors within its confines with a big brush. Keep going until something pops out at you – this is similar to seeing objects in cloud formations – the color and shapes become a tree or a rock, a creature or a person. Once you see something you like you can start defining and developing it. There is no right or wrong way to do this (**image 03a**).

Spend a few minutes repeating this for each of the boxes. Don't get bogged down in the details by zooming in to define the shapes. I like to use the Lasso or Selection tools to get harder edges; they are both great tools for making hard edges when speed painting (**image 03b**).

04: Move on

I am going to work on the top-left thumbnail. I really like the tree-like structures; they seem to form a tunnel through the center.

Make a new layer set to Color Dodge (**image 04a**). If you are in Photoshop make sure you turn off the Transparency Shapes Layer box (**image 04b**) as well as turning down the opacity on your brush. This prevents it from misbehaving and taking over.

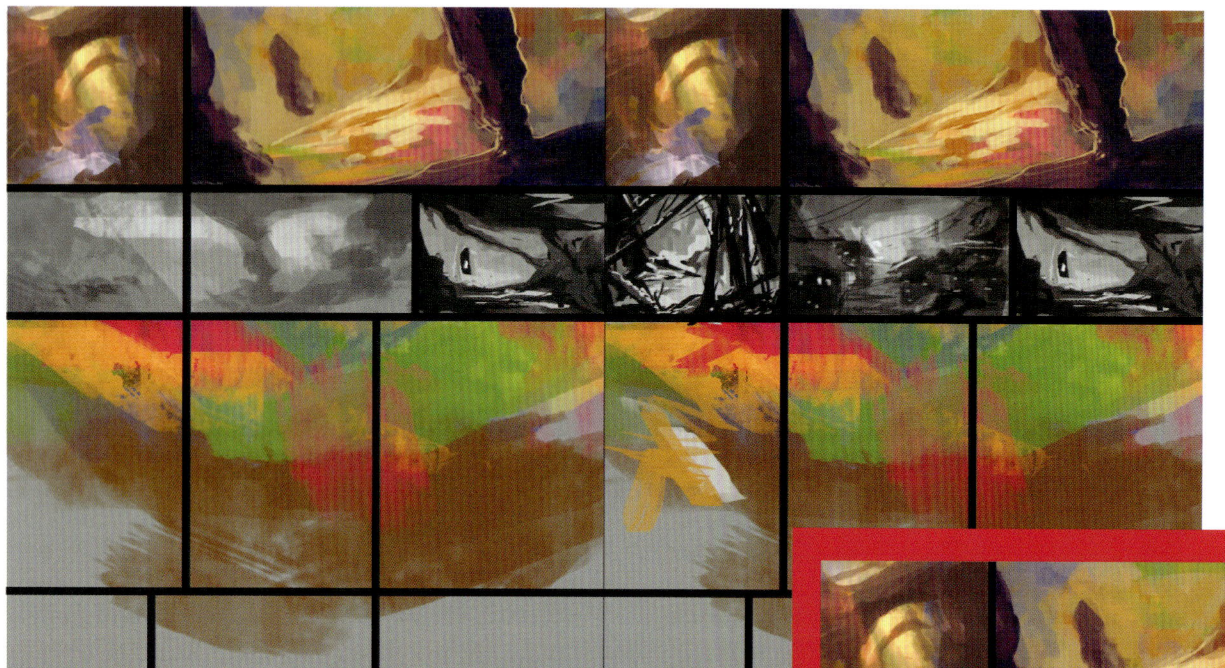

▲This technique can also be used to create grayscale paintings

"Changing your tools like this can prevent you from getting into too much of a comfort zone"

05: Painting in grayscale

Painting in grayscale is a great method for creating thumbnails. You simply need to desaturate a box or boxes and follow the same process you have been using so far but without color. However, I recommend you use a color as a base then desaturate, this way you will get a richer variety of gray tones (**image 05**).

I change brushes here, picking a flatter textured brush to create the village and a harder brush with no opacity for the forest. Changing your tools like this can prevent you from getting into too much of a comfort zone.

06: It doesn't work every time

Not every box will yield a workable result – sometimes the colors just aren't working or the composition fails to inspire. When this happens you can just give up on the box altogether – as the time invested so far is only a matter of minutes it is easier to let go and move on than spend another half an hour and still have an image that isn't working. The more you

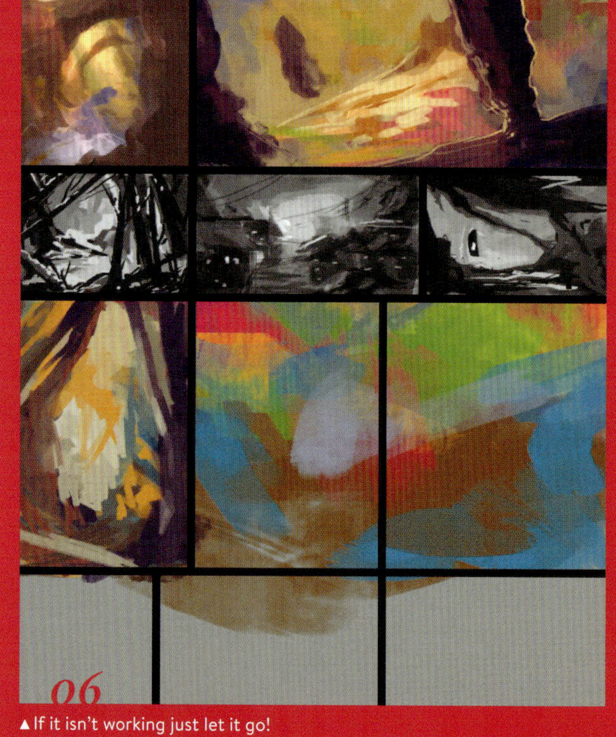

▲If it isn't working just let it go!

"I find that these methods can sometimes bring a box back from the brink with minimal fuss and expended time"

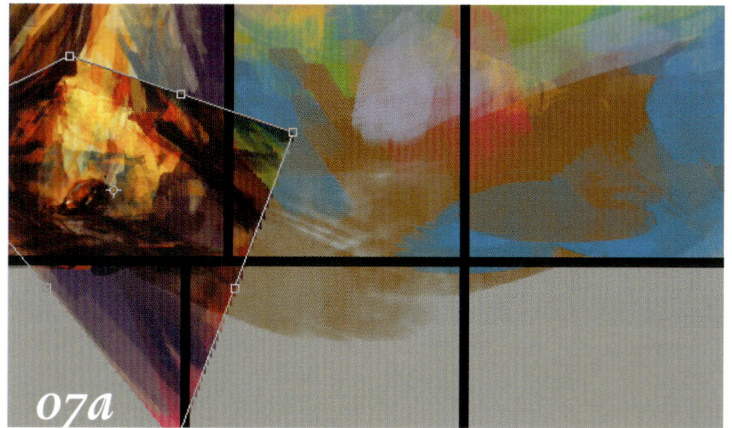

▲ Use editing tools to quickly and easily make something out of failing boxes

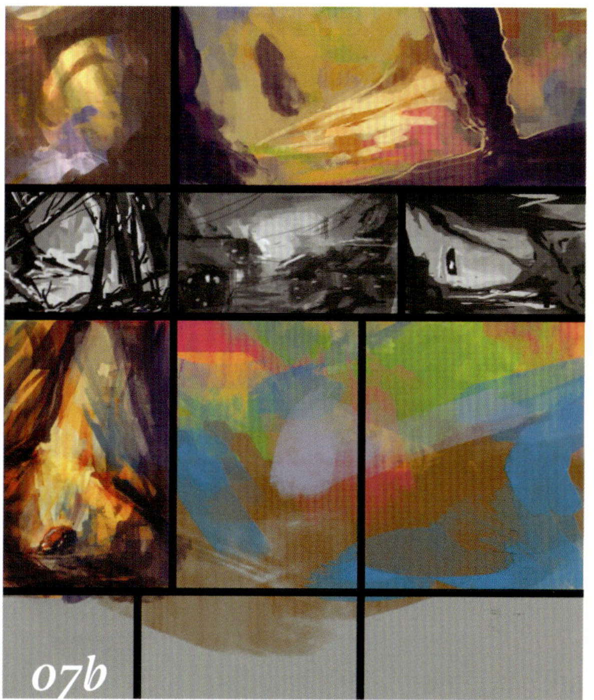

▲ Bringing a box back from the brink is sometimes worth the effort

practice with this method the fewer boxes you will have that "don't work."

07: Rescuing a box

There are, however, a couple of things you can try if you're unsure about a box. You can try copying a box onto a new layer with the Blend mode set to Overlay and warp the shapes using the Free Transform tool.

You can also erase some of the hard edges or use the Soft Light layer option to rescue a box. I find that these methods can sometimes bring a box back from the brink with minimal fuss and expended time (**images 07a** and **07b**).

08: Play around

Having no goal in mind for the painting experimentation means that the thumbnails happen much more freely and naturally, but not all of them will be a success and have potential. As you can see in **image 08**, I give up on the lower-middle image before it is even vaguely recognizable and moved on – it just wasn't working. However, in less than fifteen minutes I have eight thumbnails and perhaps three or four which I can take further.

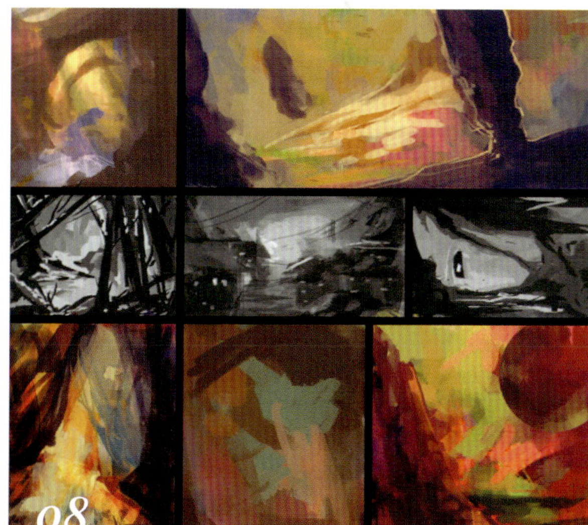

▲ Experimenting allows you to explore ideas more quickly

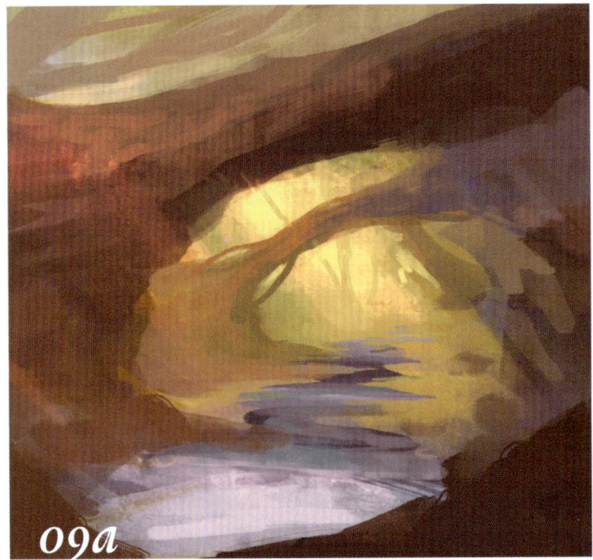

▲ By zooming out you can get an idea of what the finished piece will look like

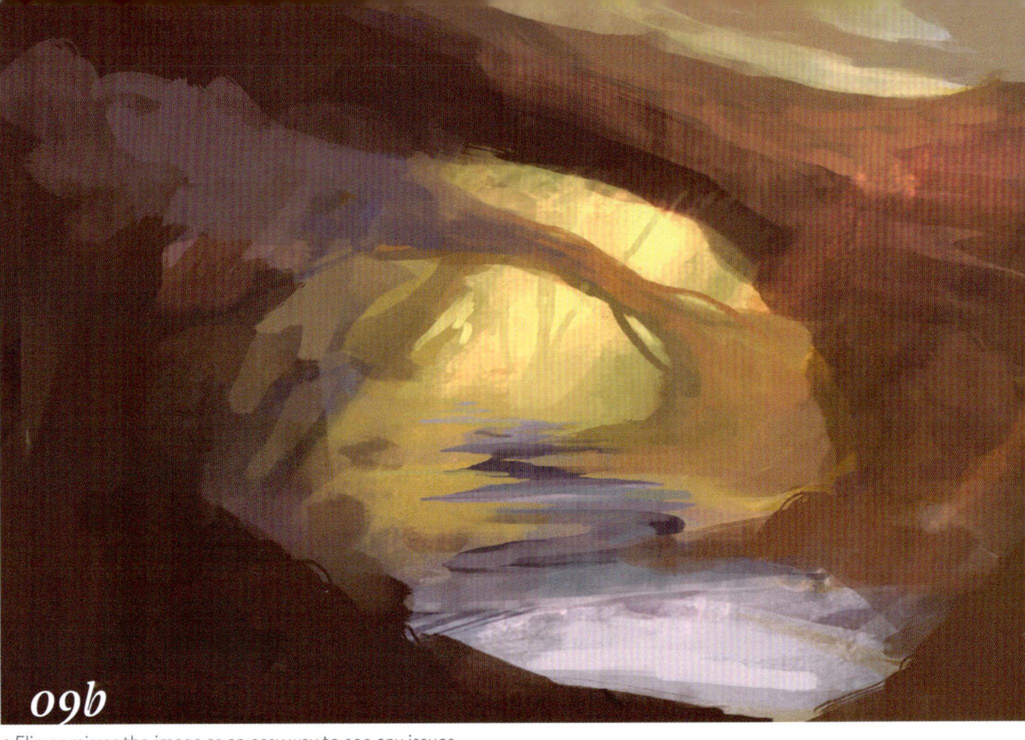

▲ Flip or mirror the image as an easy way to see any issues

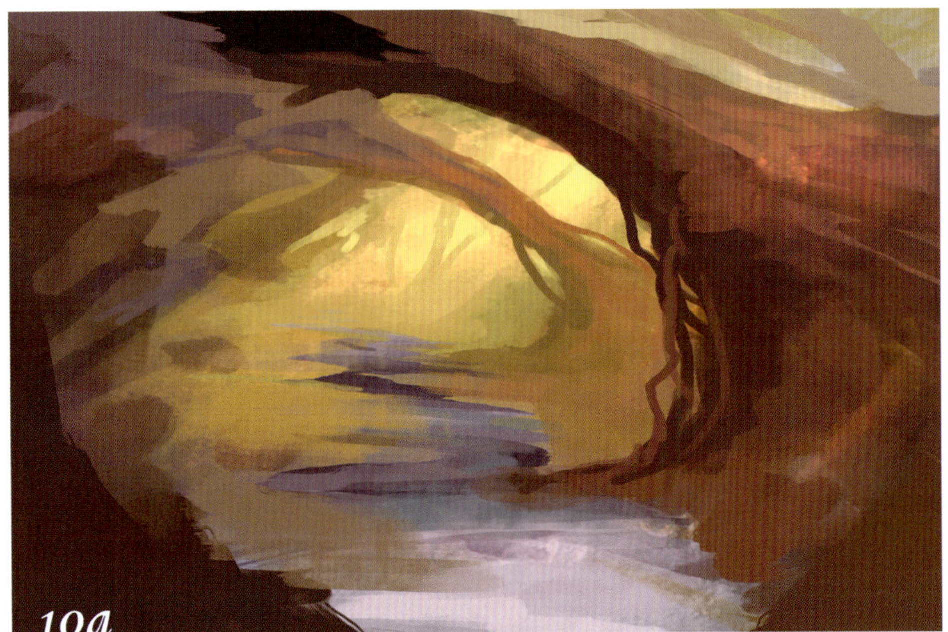

▲ Experiment using the software's distortion tools to get the best out of your speed painting

09: Take it further and improve

Pick one of your thumbnails to take further (I choose the top-left thumbnail) and transfer it to a new file. I set my canvas to 6000 × 4000 pixels and change the orientation to landscape. So, less than half way through your thirty-minute painting you have what could easily be mistaken for a finished painting (**image 09a**).

A great trick to check your composition and to spot any potential issues is to flip your image (**image 09b**). If this was a longer speed painting I would add some photo textures to add more detail to the image.

10: Keep experimenting

Be careful not to simply settle for what is in front of you if flipping it produces something nice (**image 10a**). There are a number of other things you can try, such as using distortion tools like Free Transform (Ctrl+Alt) to go beyond simple scaling. Don't be afraid to duplicate, rotate, or add perspective to see what happens (**image 10b**).

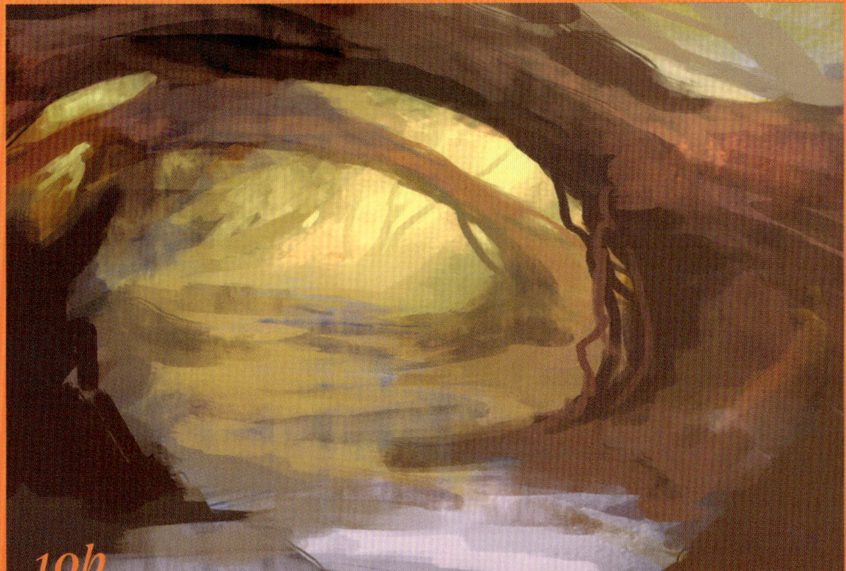

▲You may find a better composition when experimenting

11: Almost there!

We have almost reached the time limit for this speed painting but there is still time to do some last-minute fleshing out. Here you could flip the image back to its original orientation and add some darker trees to the foreground and lighter ones to the background to give the image depth, as well as add some extra foliage and bark detail in the middle ground. Using a textured brush here is a great help because it adds detail with very little effort.

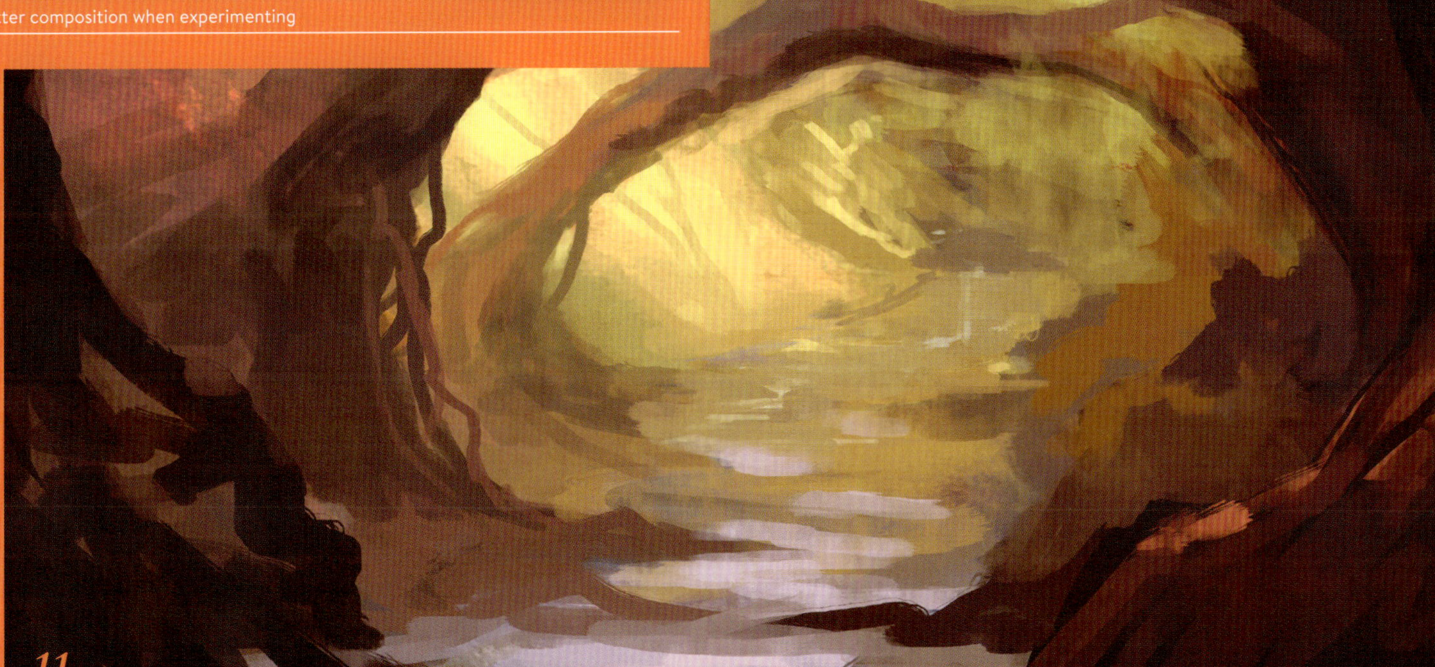

▲Finally getting to the details

12: Color depth

Using layer effects to your advantage creates interest and really makes the image "pop." Try using Soft Light and Overlay, along with a textured airbrush on low opacity to drop some more subtle color into the image; specifically blues and purples in the shadows, and oranges and pinks in the lighter areas. This is a quick way to make your image pop and make a great base for painting on should the speed painting be taken into a more finished image. At this point it is also a good stage to use tools like Color Balance and Levels, and tweak the Hue/Saturation levels to even out the image.

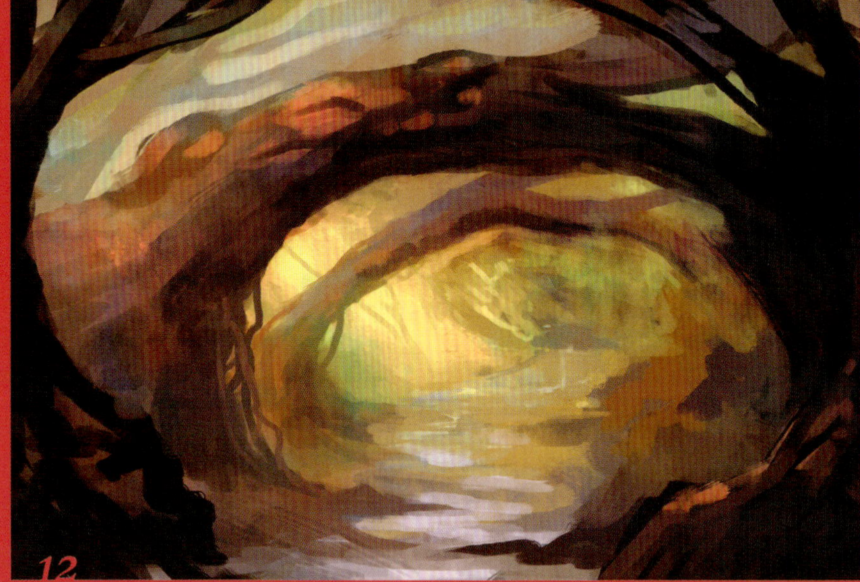

▲ Use layers to add subtle tones and colors

13: Finalize

Using the same technique as we did in the thumbnail stage using the Color Dodge layer (step 04), add light shafts and pick out a few of sunlight spots to keep the eye moving. Add foliage with a leaf brush and some quick vines to add detail. Finally add some birds to really draw the viewer into the image. As a speed painting this could be considered finished, though there is a lot of room to spend a great deal more time on it.

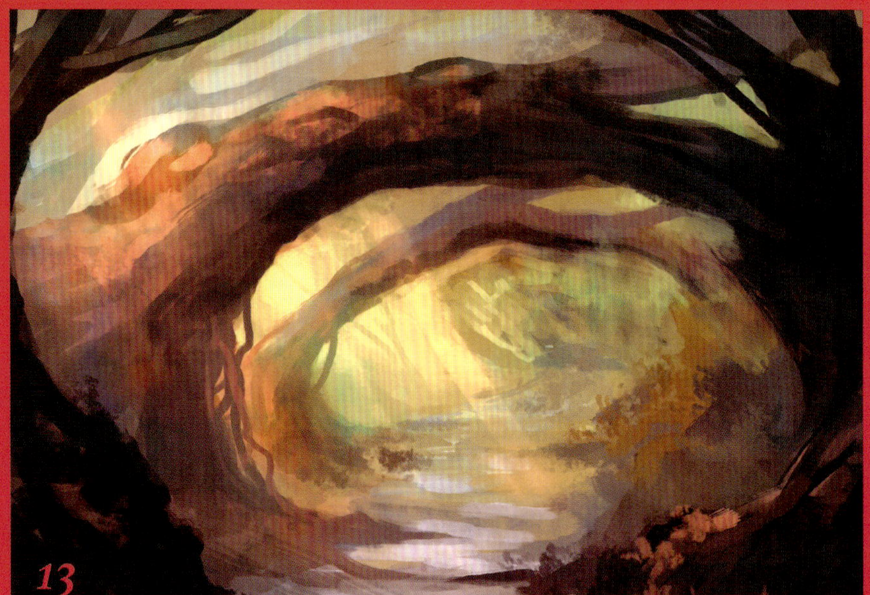

▲ Small but quick details really finish off the image

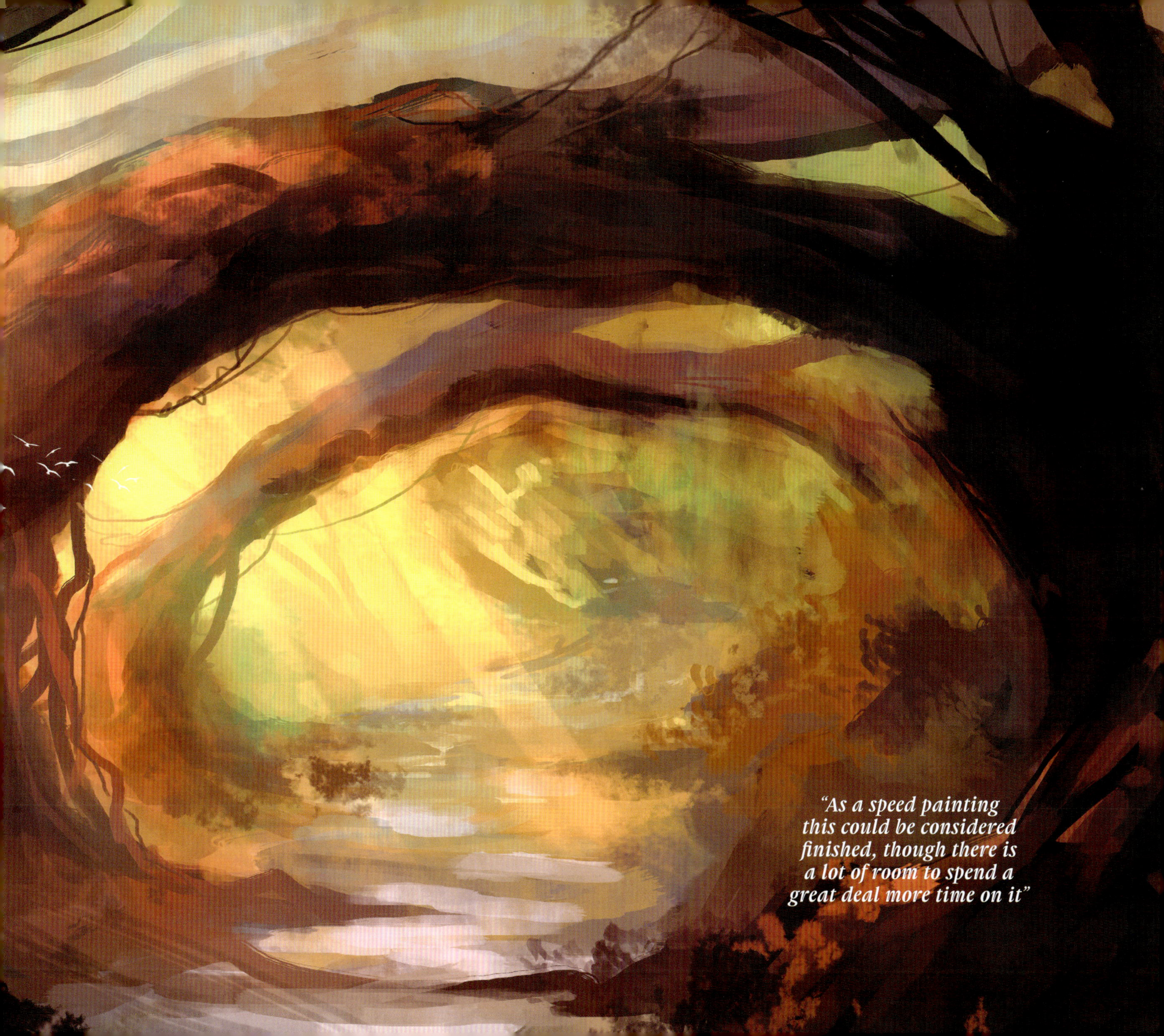

"As a speed painting this could be considered finished, though there is a lot of room to spend a great deal more time on it"

FANTASY: FLYOVER
by Ioan Dumitrescu

▲ Start by painting an epic dynamic sky

In this tutorial we will do a thirty-minute speed painting of a fantasy vehicle. It's not something you should be intimidated by. What I do (unless I already have a good idea in mind) is start scribbling with the Round brush, leaving things blurred so I can extract ideas from them.

It's important to think of something that you can actually describe in this time. There is no point saying "I'll paint an epic space battle with a hundred ships and five fighting characters in the foreground." It's not that it definitely can't be done but you'll be left high and dry after the pressure you've put on yourself and will find that it will be a bit of a mess and need another hour to actually make it clear to someone that isn't in the art field or just yourself.

01: The sky

As the title suggests we are going to create an airship, so the most obvious thing to start painting is the sky. The perspective needs to be very dynamic to make an interesting image. Use the clouds to help you portray a three-point perspective.

You can use a Color Dodge layer at the end to make pockets of bright light pop out, as if the sun is peeping through breaks in the clouds.

02: The ship

I decide that the view of the ship should be head on, breaking through the clouds like the old sail ships used to break the waves. This will give the image a much more dynamic look.

Start off by painting in the basic shapes – an elongated hull and two billowing sails. This is a good opportunity to have some of the sunlight catch on the surface of the ship and disperse.

There will most probably be moisture up there settling on all the surfaces so everything will have a touch of reflection and highlights from the water droplets.

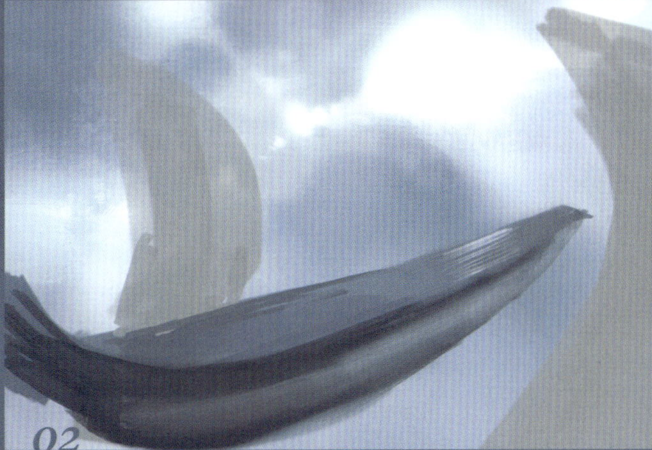

▲ Paint a simple silhouette of the ship and add some sails

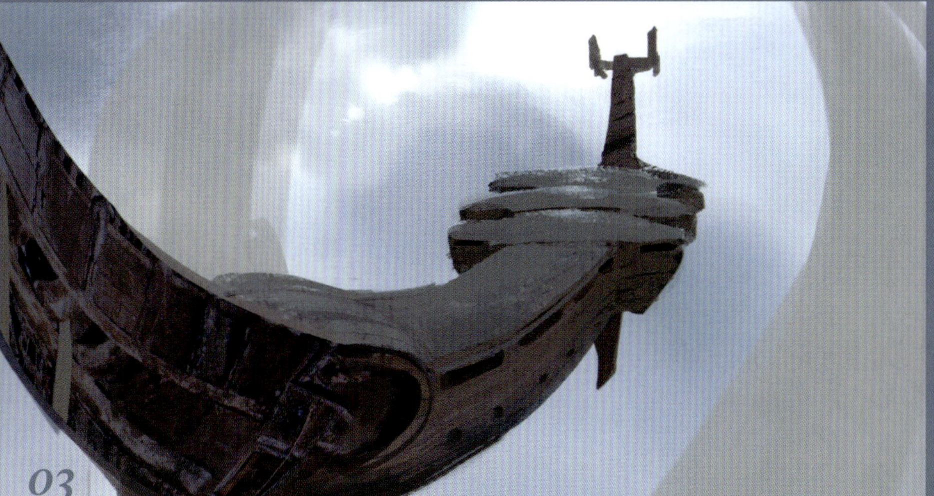

▲ Make your ship big and imposing, think of the heavily armored Korean turtle ships

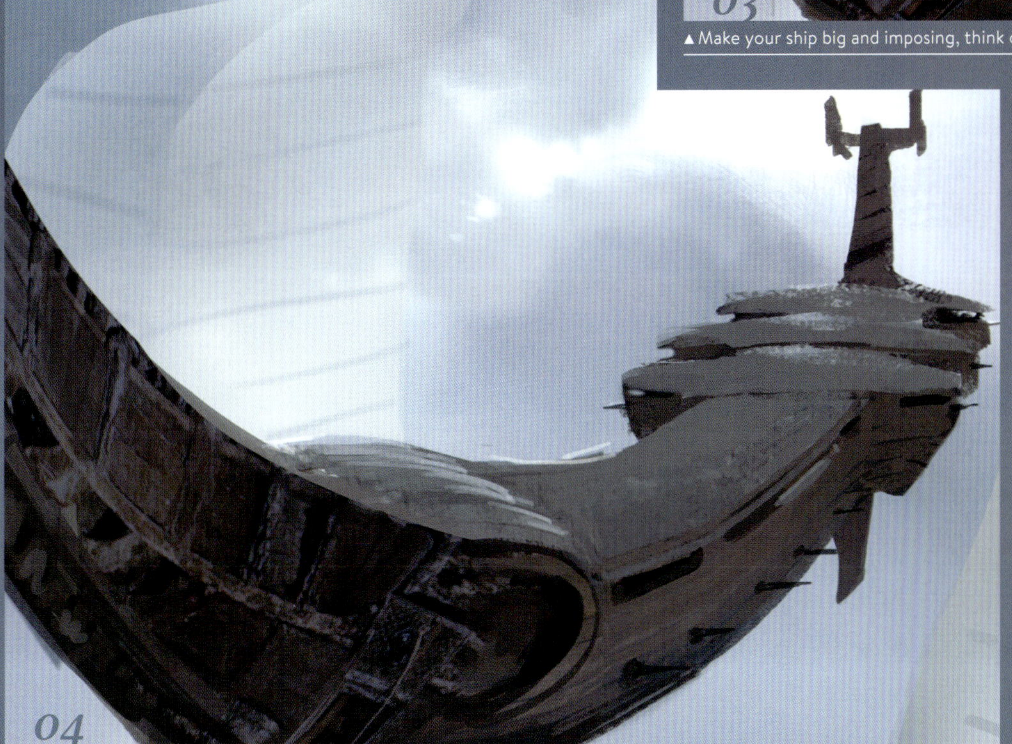

▲ Adding lots of defences reinforces the narrative of this being a warship

03: A bigger ship

You might want to switch the camera angle so that it is much wider; this will give a bigger, more imposing front. Making use of the curvature of the original composition will help you shape the curve of the hull.

04: Add details and sails

Now you can start adding some details to the ship. As this is an airship you want to go for something battle worthy.

As mentioned in the caption of **image 03**, think of Korean turtle ships, named for their protective shell-like armor. Look for good references so you can accurately describe the shapes and overall look of the nature of your design.

The sails are a good place to look at next. You need to make sure the light comes through the canvas. Also adding seams will add to the appearance of volume and texture. Add spikes to the sides of the ship – you can add them to the top of the ship as well; again, remember to look at your reference images.

05: Flip your canvas and final touches

Flipping your canvas gives you a whole new perspective on your work; in this case it makes the image more powerful so I decide to leave it like that. Now you are almost done – all that is left to do is to add all those little extras.

The sails need an indication of their functionality; how do the sails pull? They need masts and rigging (**image 05a**). Add a central mast and some sort of contraption held by ropes for the side sails. This is where I add in the rooftop spikes (**image 05b**) and a bit of cloud mist at the front. The speed painting is complete.

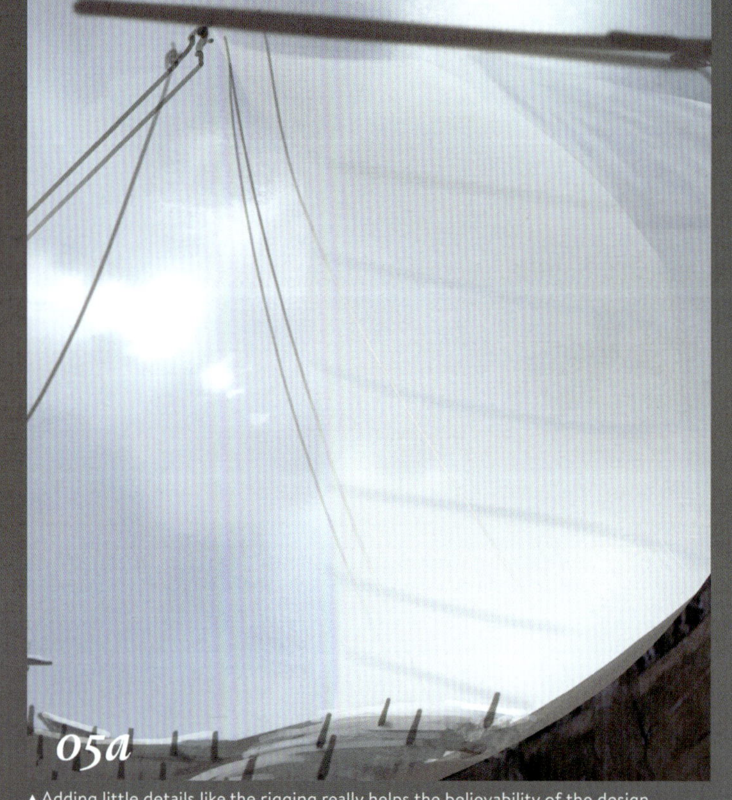

▲Adding little details like the rigging really helps the believability of the design

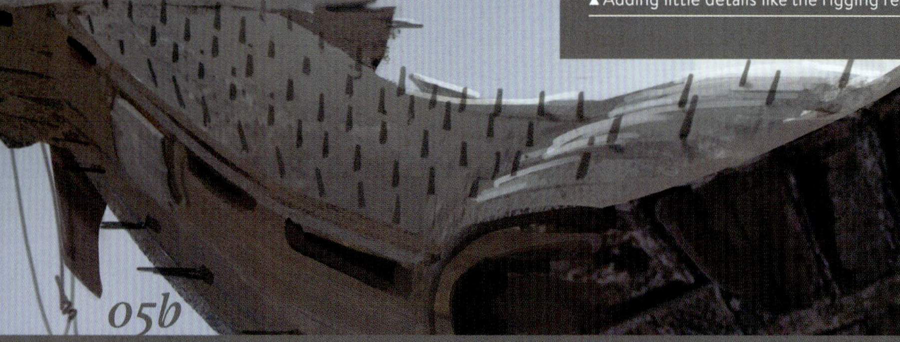

▲The roofing spikes give the airship a more menacing appearance

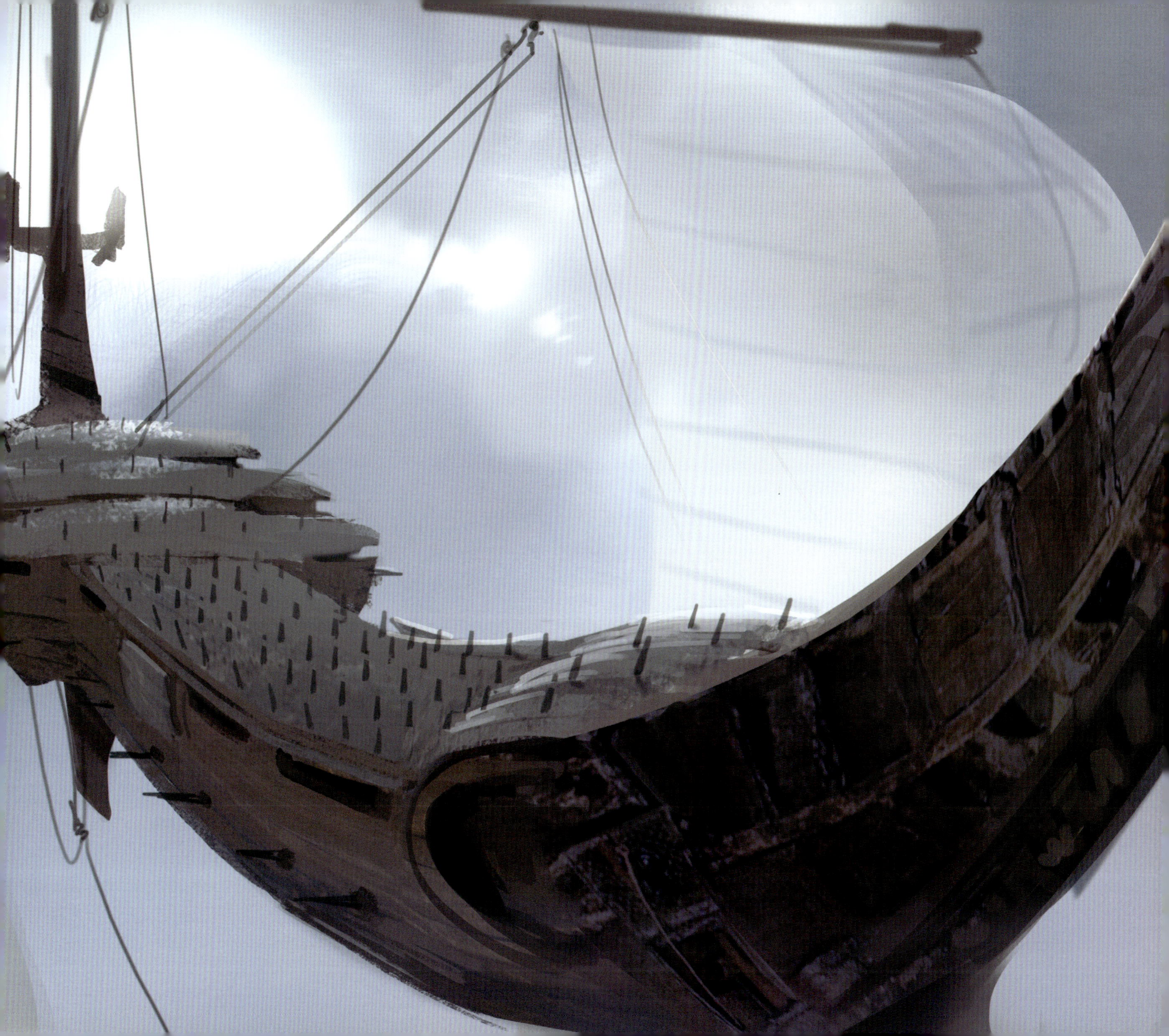

FILM NOIR: BANG
by Ioan Dumitrescu

In this tutorial we will be doing a super quick speed painting. It is really more of a short sketch, especially as every second counts. Film noir is one of my preferred genres because of its striking roughness, gritty lighting, and dramatic angles. It is the source of inspiration for an endless list of games, movies, and anything visual.

01: Contrast

We have a ten-minute time limit, so let's begin as we have nothing to lose! As well as having roughness and dynamism in your speed painting, why not add contrast to that list and draw a splash of light on a black background?

02: Atmosphere

You have started with contrast; now let's add some atmosphere to the image. What I envisage here could have come straight out of an old gangster movie. A classic vehicle pulling up in the pouring rain and the main character pointing a gun at somebody just out of frame.

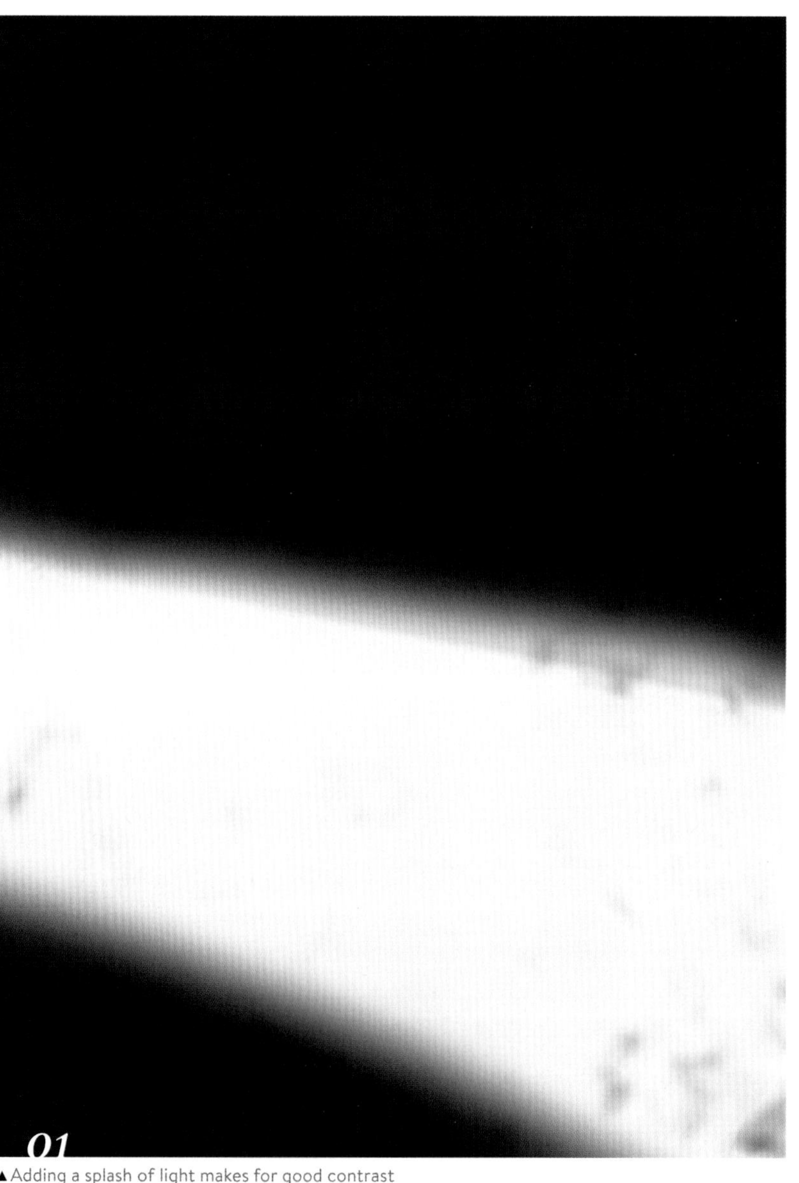

▲ Adding a splash of light makes for good contrast

▲ Adding a vehicle and headlights adds to the atmosphere

Sketch in a simple vehicle shape and add headlights; refine them to get a good basis for the atmosphere to bounce off. It is important to give the main character plenty of opportunity to look dramatic.

03: Add the main character

We have contrast and atmosphere so next we need a main character. For me the old "private dick" story of being in the wrong place at the wrong time will never grow old! To flesh him out start with a simple black silhouette and add details to bring him to life. He is lit from above and the side is bright with the intense headlights from the vehicle.

When you are happy with your character you can add some noise (Filter > Noise). Desaturate the noise to black and white and apply Motion Blur to suggest falling rain.

To give movement and even more life to the rain, paint on top of everything with some brushes. I do everything on a single layer, which should usually be avoided, but I can cut out elements if required.

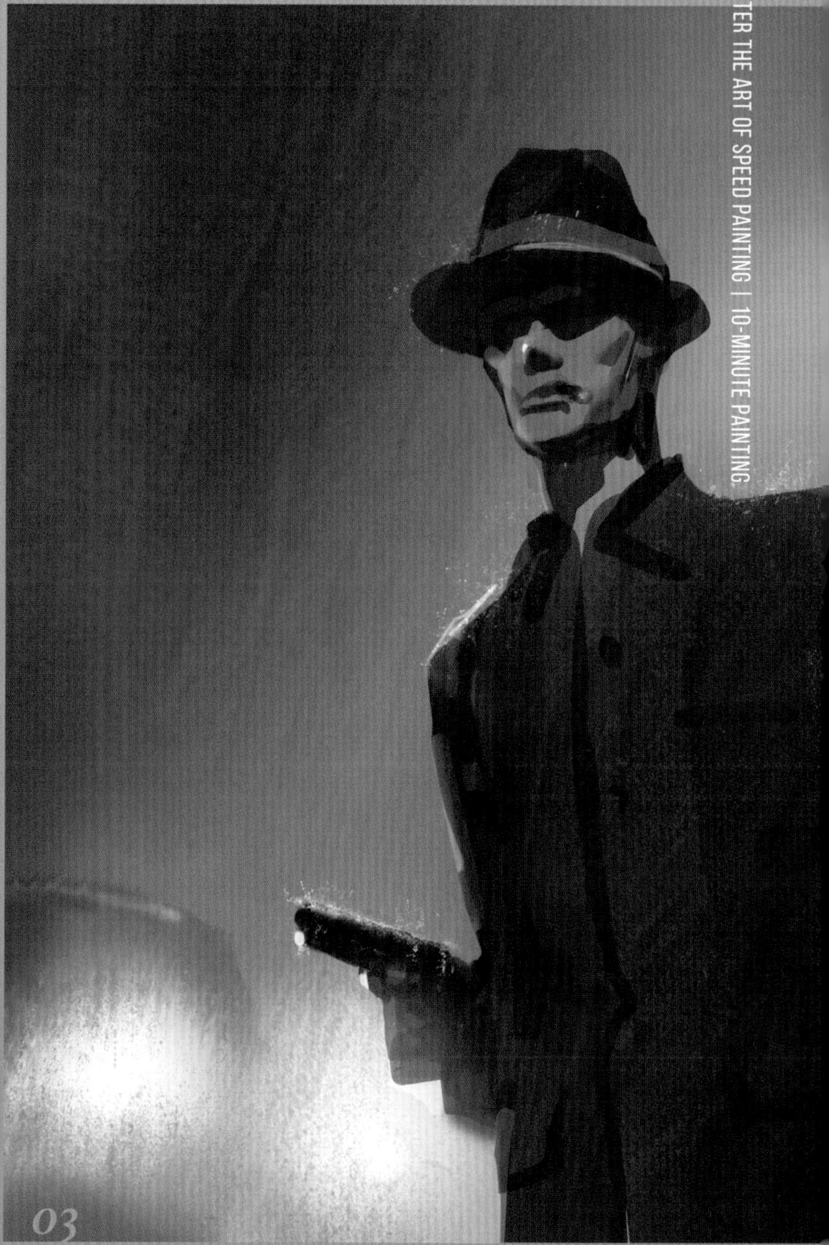

▲ Give the scene life by adding the character and some rain

"Remember that this is a quick ten-minute painting so you shouldn't worry about every tiny little detail; try to be loose and enjoy yourself"

04: The little details

This is where you can add those little details which can make or break a painting. Definition can often be lost when adding noise, so this is the perfect time to add some back in.

As our guy is in a heavy downpour, I pop his collar as if the wind had just blown in, although he is still focused on his target. The drips of rain from his shoulders and gun catch the headlights, as does the rim of his fedora.

05: A touch of sepia

Remember that this is a quick ten-minute painting so you shouldn't worry about every tiny little detail; try to be loose and enjoy yourself. As a final touch you can modify the color to give it a slight sepia tone, as if it is a still from an old movie.

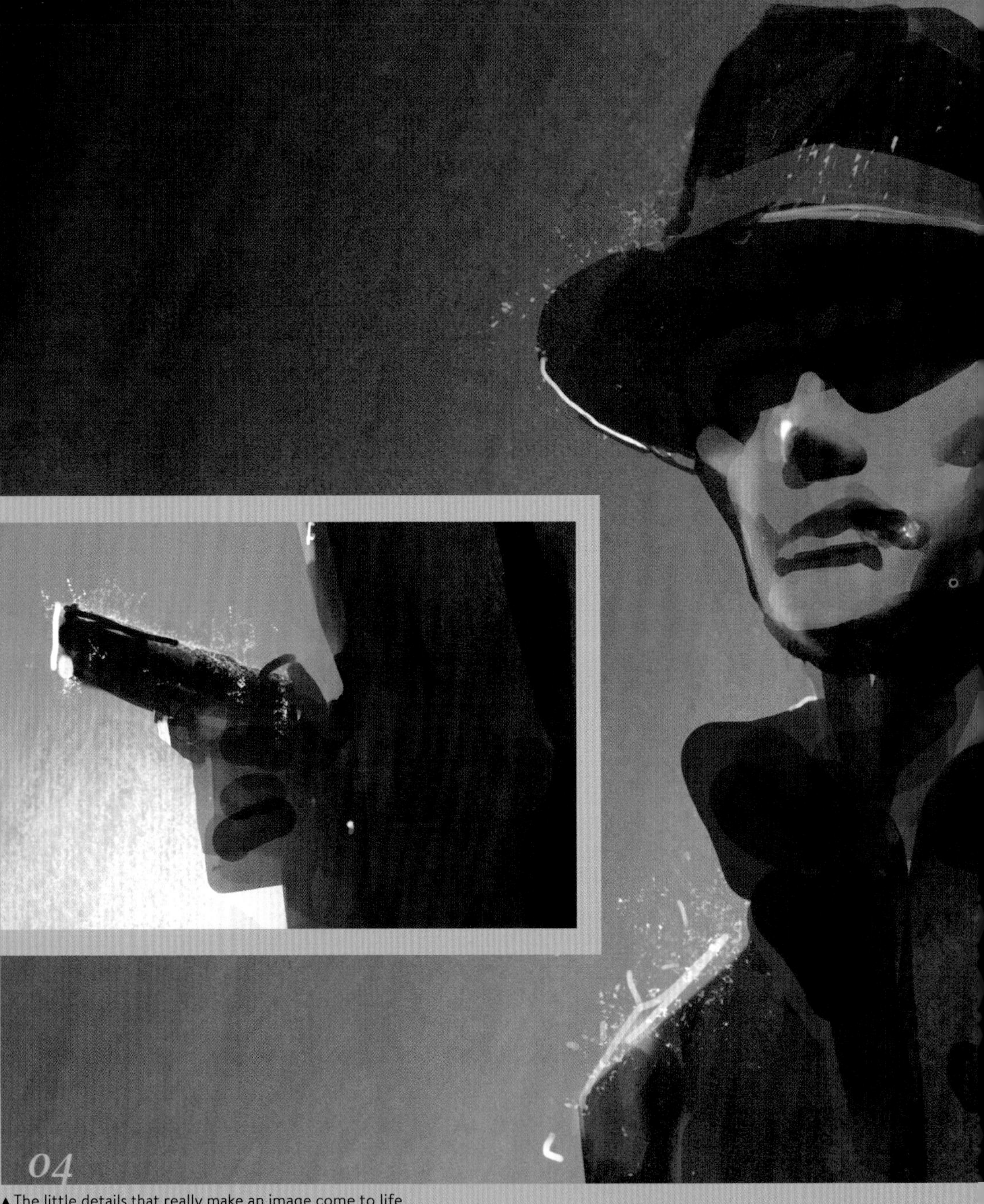

▲ The little details that really make an image come to life

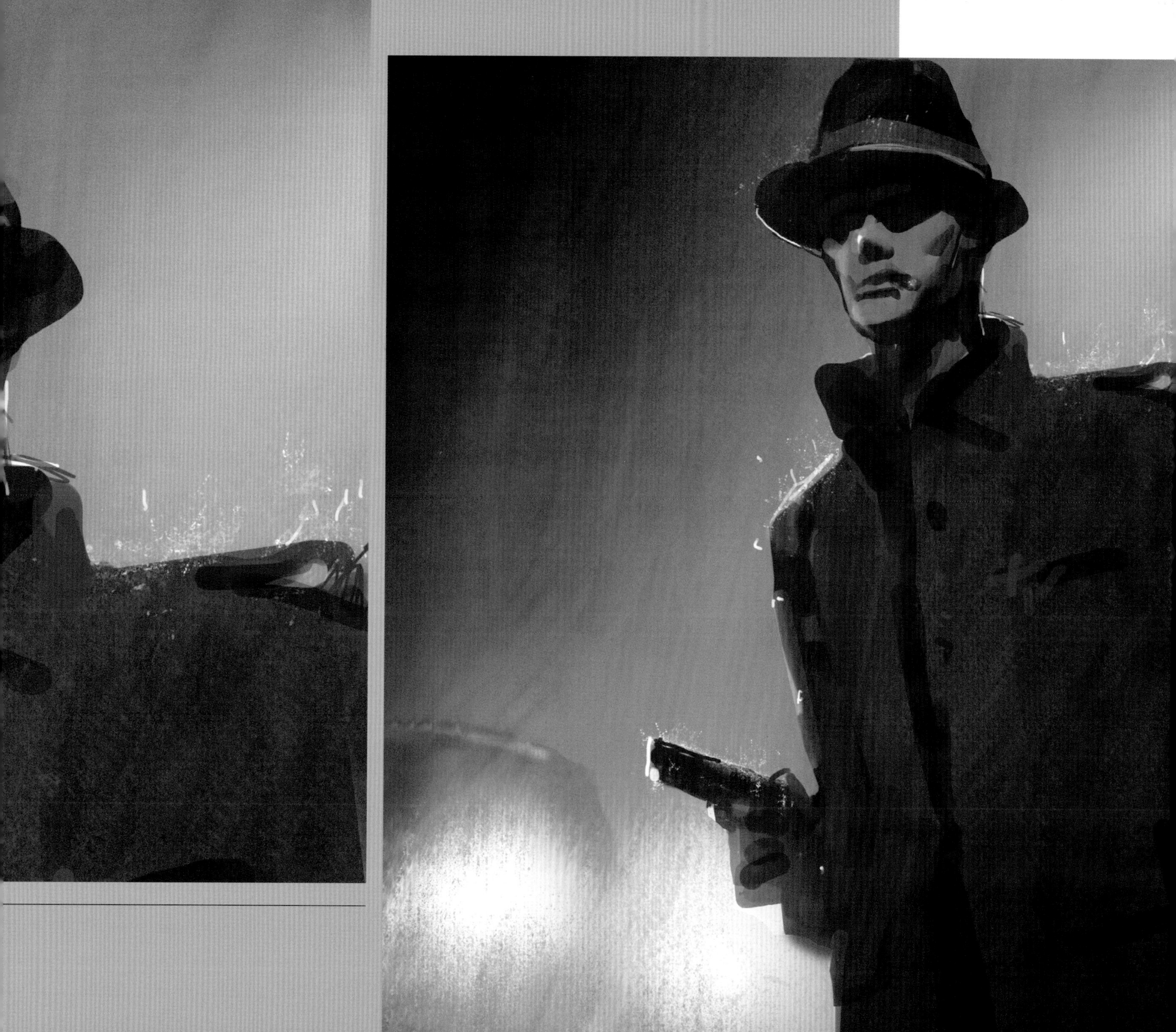

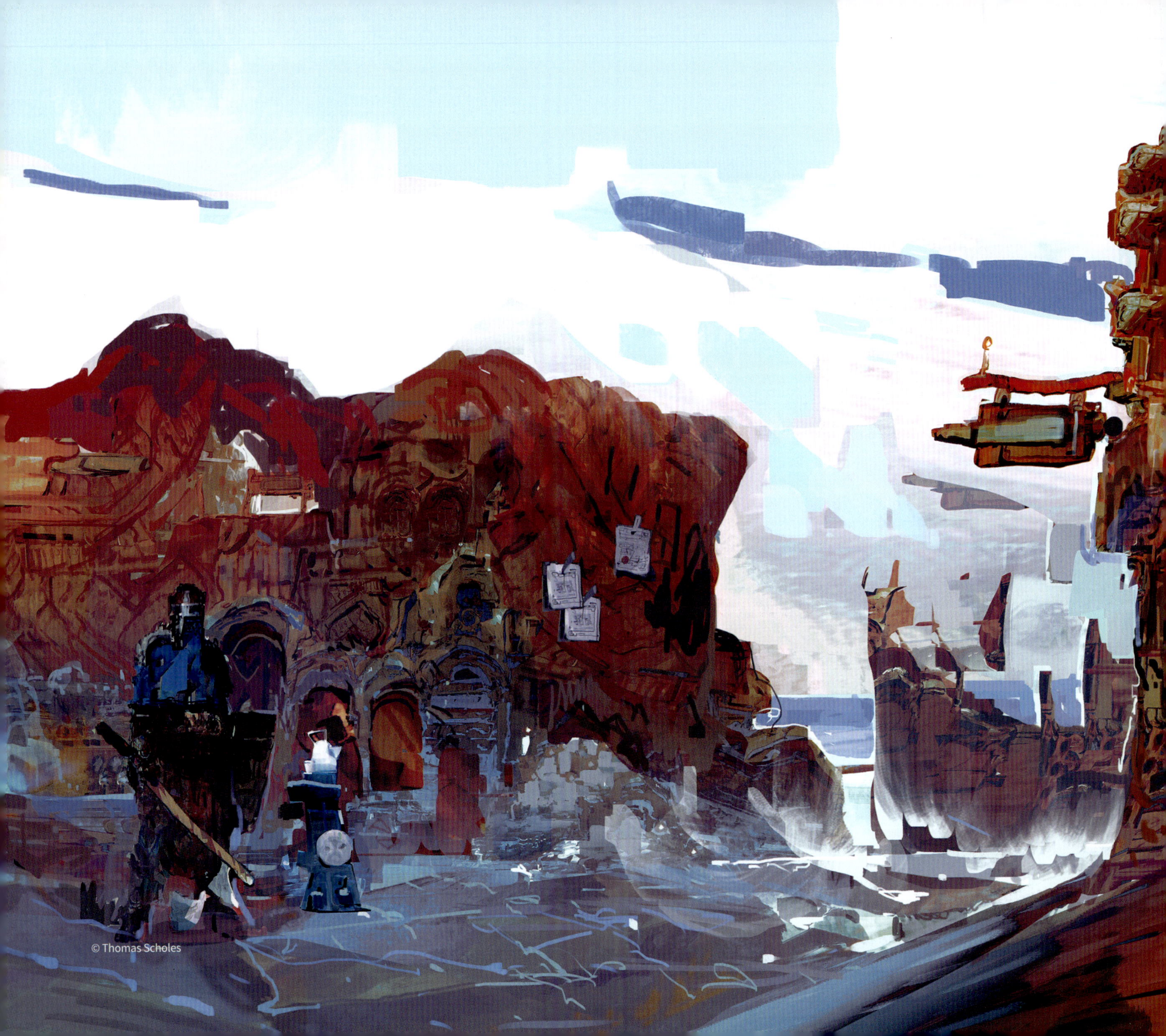

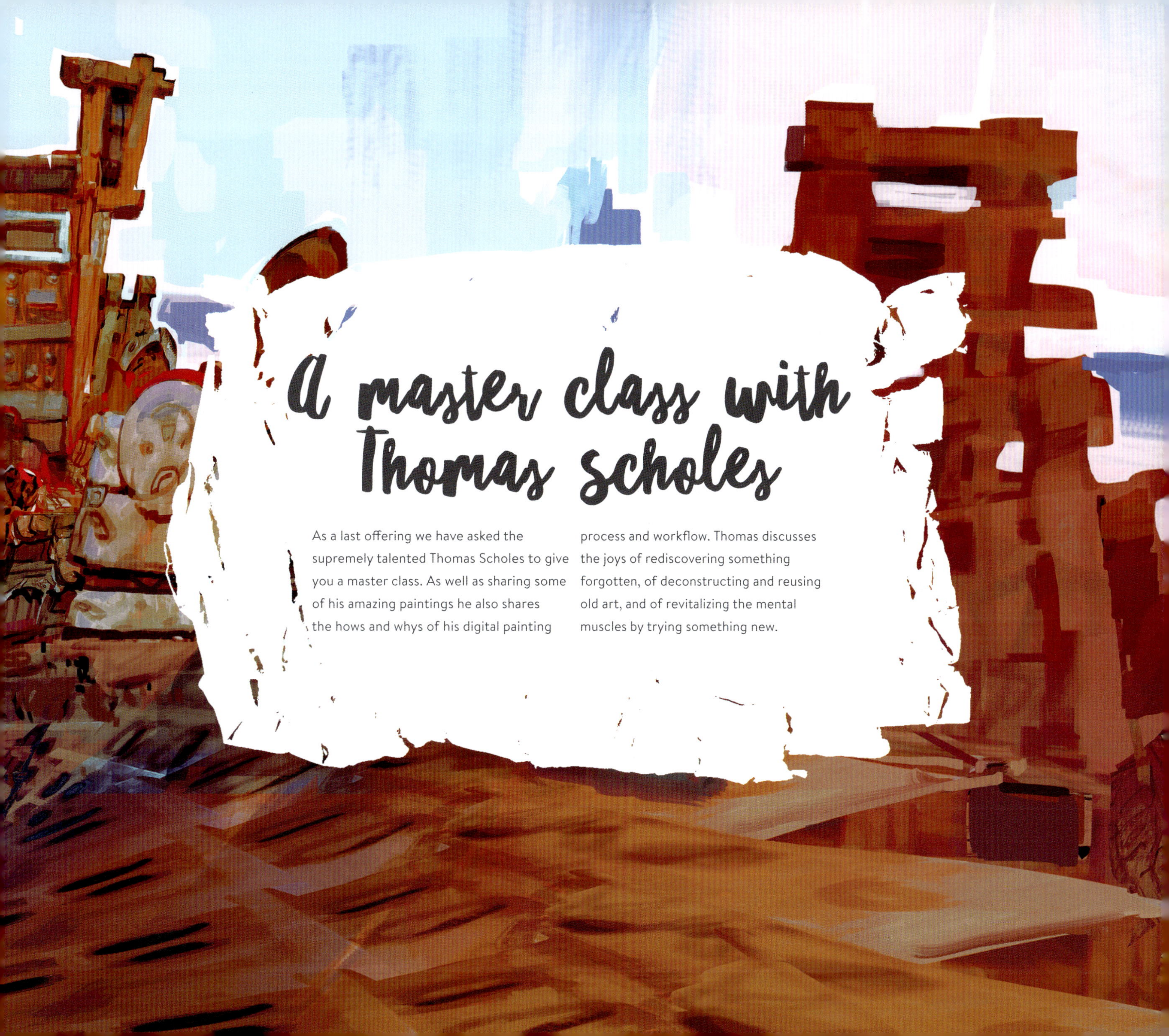

A master class with Thomas Scholes

As a last offering we have asked the supremely talented Thomas Scholes to give you a master class. As well as sharing some of his amazing paintings he also shares the hows and whys of his digital painting process and workflow. Thomas discusses the joys of rediscovering something forgotten, of deconstructing and reusing old art, and of revitalizing the mental muscles by trying something new.

A MASTER CLASS WITH THOMAS SCHOLES

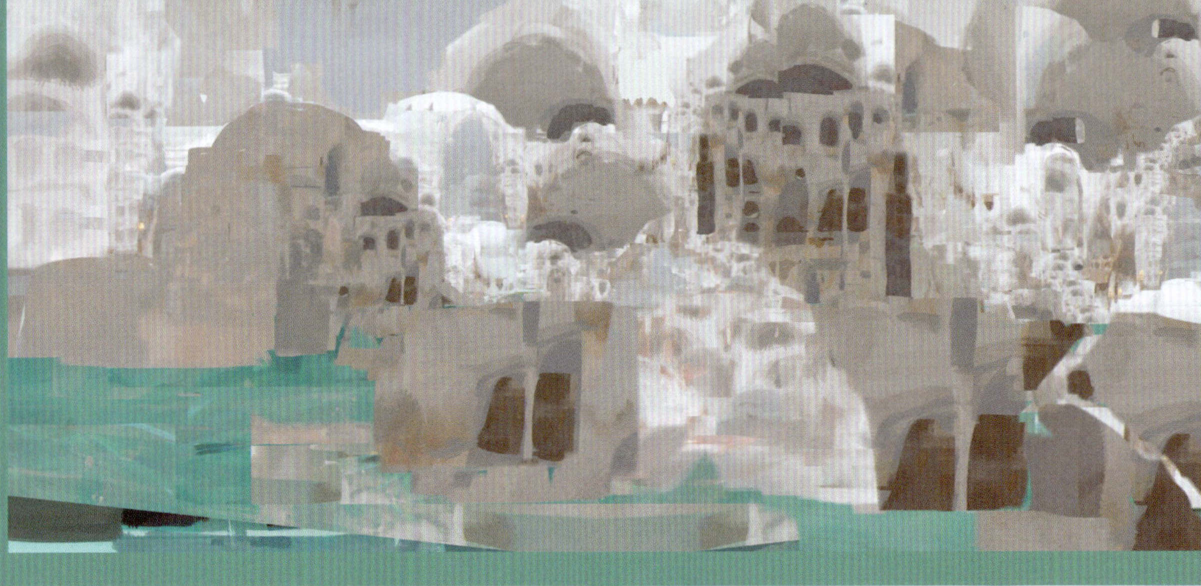

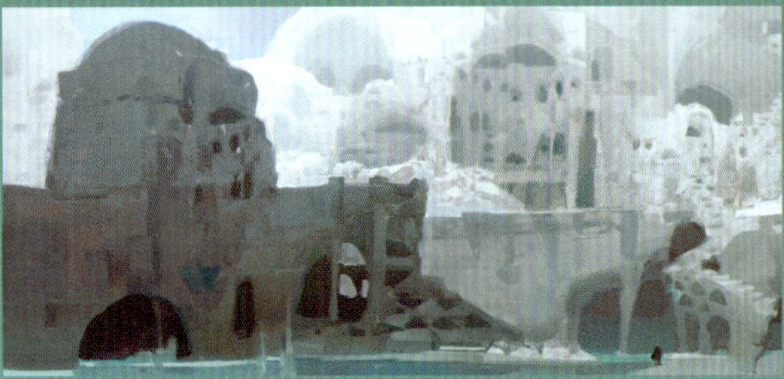

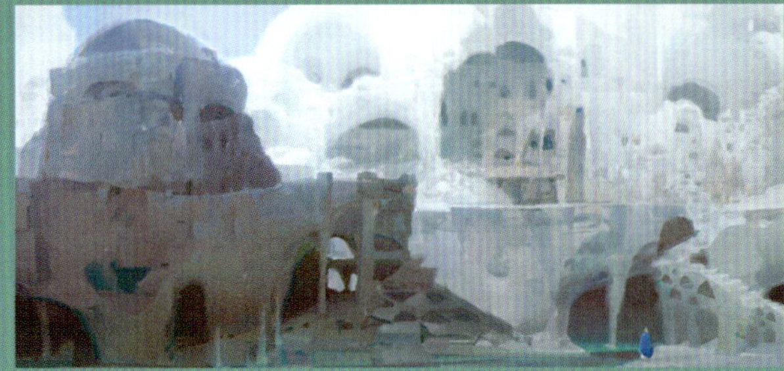

Even after a hard day's mental labor I often find myself thirsting for further creative satisfaction, with so little time left to invest and often just before a necessary and healthy night's rest.

What is one to do with these few spare moments? What can an artist do in an hour or two? Or, more importantly: what can an artist do within this time that creates value? I should hope that, whatever your personal variant of this question or its answer, you spend your artistic free time wisely.

That we spend this time we have away from our work with either purpose of experimentation and self-expression, or as exercise towards progressing our knowledge and broadening our experience. Outside our studies I believe we receive the added bonus that most clients will immediately appreciate and benefit from the agility of an artist who is able to adapt and change a scene, or design, dynamically to better suit the client's vision, the ever-evolving requirements of the brief or script, as well as the needs of the audience.

Rather than run ourselves ragged with an additive and linear process, let's work exponentially, iteratively, and even recursively. Why consider any work final when there is still much to learn from existing structure and value? Why must everything, including our procedures as artists, be so linear, so permanent? Time need not be an element that we introduce to the realm of digital painting. The medium will never dry, nor will it always remain pliable. Mistakes can be rewound; but redone if we don't learn from our histories.

Caveat

To be clear, I do not often find that I am able to complete a work of much satisfaction in less than several hours. I do, however, think two hours is more than enough time to accomplish some progress on existing works or worlds, and plenty of time for experimental and artistic exercises. It is important to recognize this as an investment, and consequently it is of vital importance that any sketch or experiment of value be saved, and that this value either be refined or extracted. I hope that you agree with me that waste is a waste; so what would be wasted should, instead, be converted or repurposed to create new opportunities and potential. Even a humble few blades of well-rendered grass can provide countless further explorations, reinvestments, or timesavings.

Evolution

In this spirit I have, within my own personal archives, hundreds of paintings from the last several years that continue to live on as I often return to breathe new life into them or their descendants. This practice could, at a sideways glance, appear to be at odds with a more standard practice of speed painting – that the work should be completed (start to finish) within the time allowed – but all of my sessions start with the simple and honest intent to emphasize one or two key ideas or elements that have caught my interest in the time allowed. I should hope it is alright with you, the reader, if I were to expand the definition of speed painting to include this, if for no other reason than you may find it useful to your own process and motivation. Even if you never directly employ these methods in your workflow I think you may benefit from it as exercise to strengthen your relationship with your own intuition.

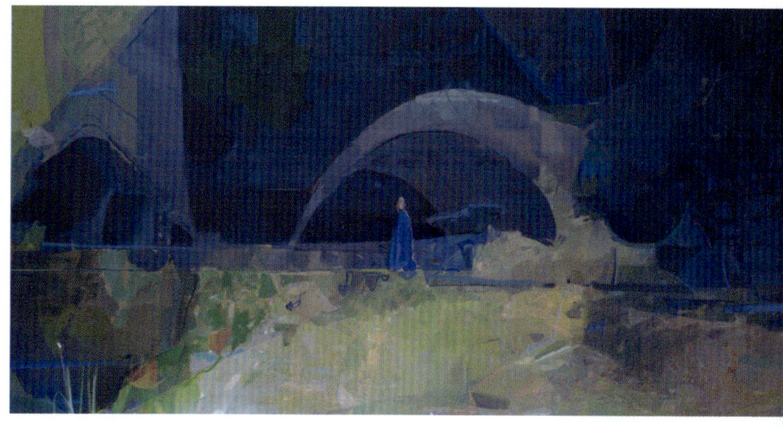

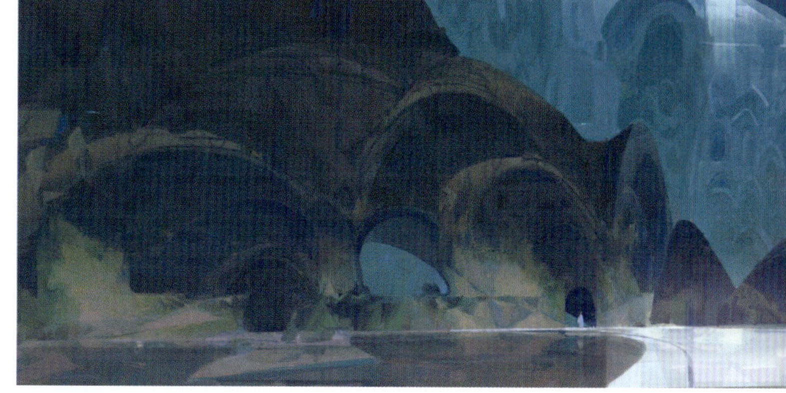

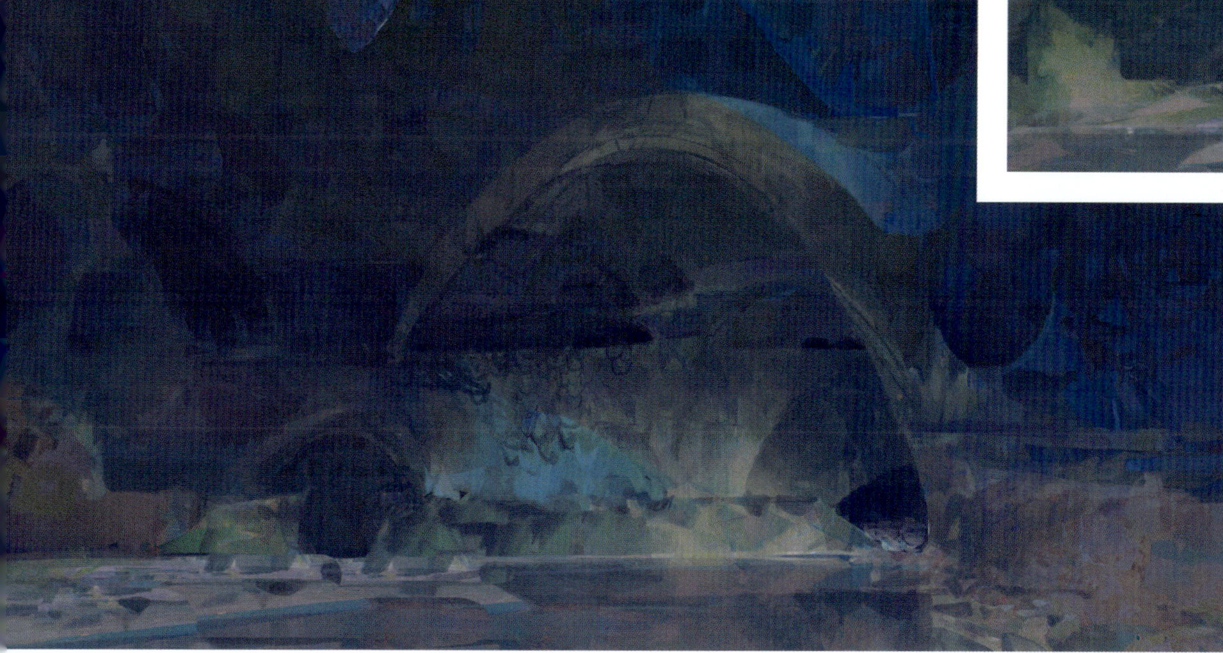

Generation

At times these sessions may incorporate assets compiled over multiple years of previous work in the form of a collage, in others it is one or many paintings overlaying another. Others still may be the iterative mutation of a favored selection from a stalled painting, which itself may even return life to the original work or instead go on to create new and divergent work.

These methods may be less than linear, and at times at odds with a more traditional or orthodox process but this does not mean it is not beneficial (commercial or otherwise) to earnestly follow the flow of our interests, the honest potentials of the image, what we want for the work and what little control we may have achieved of the overall craft.

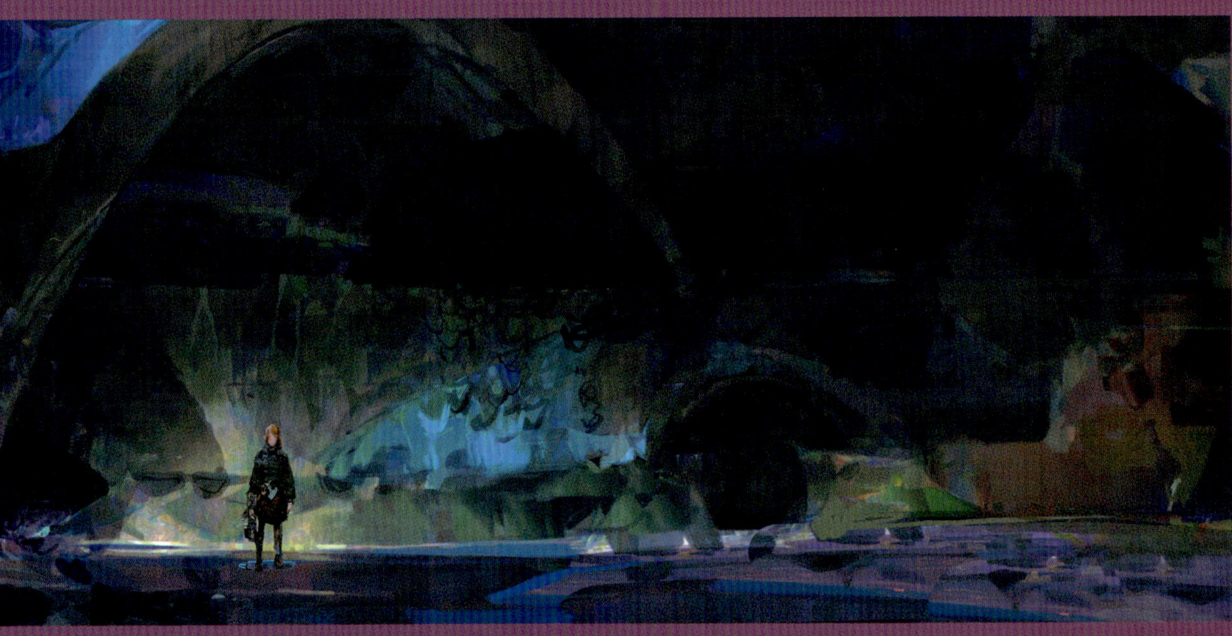

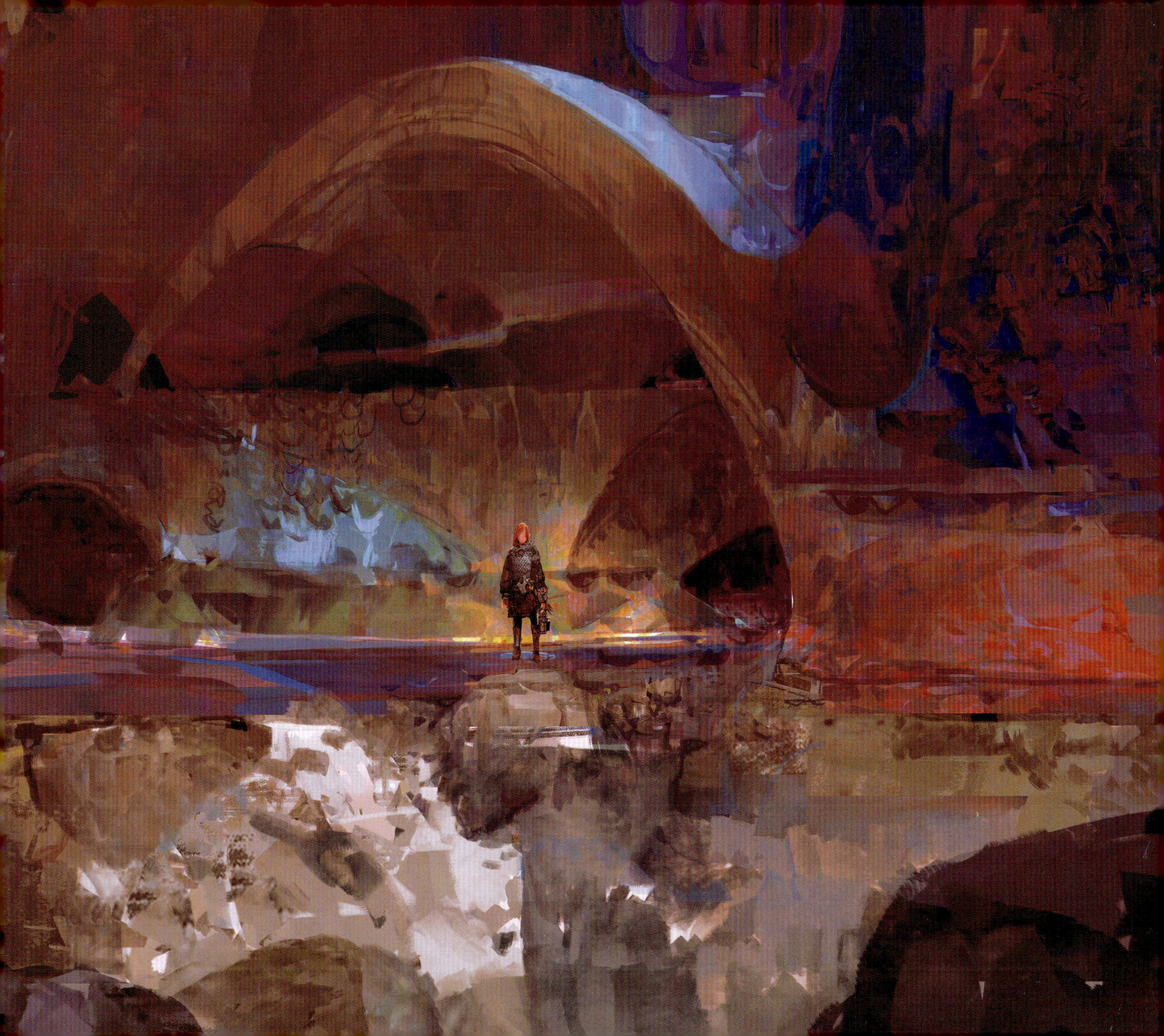

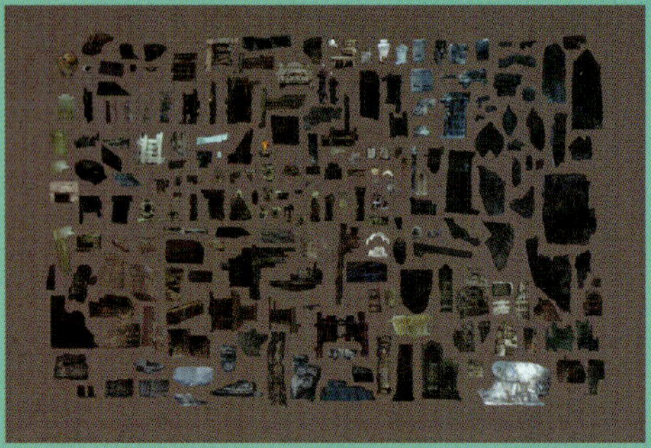

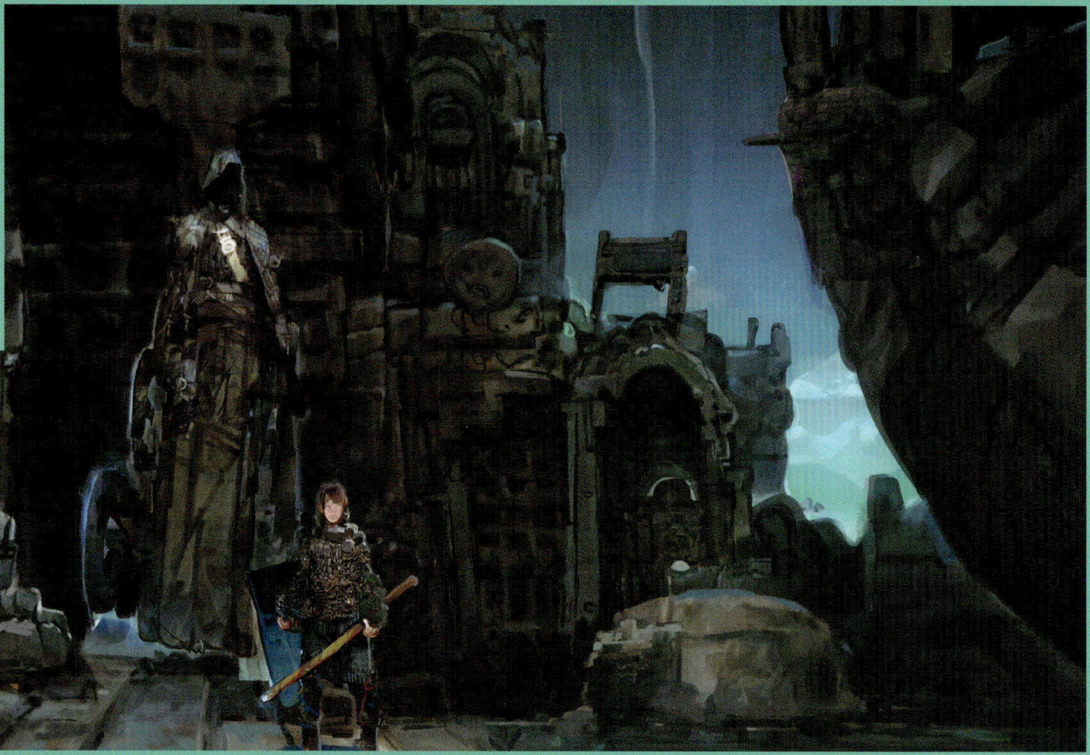

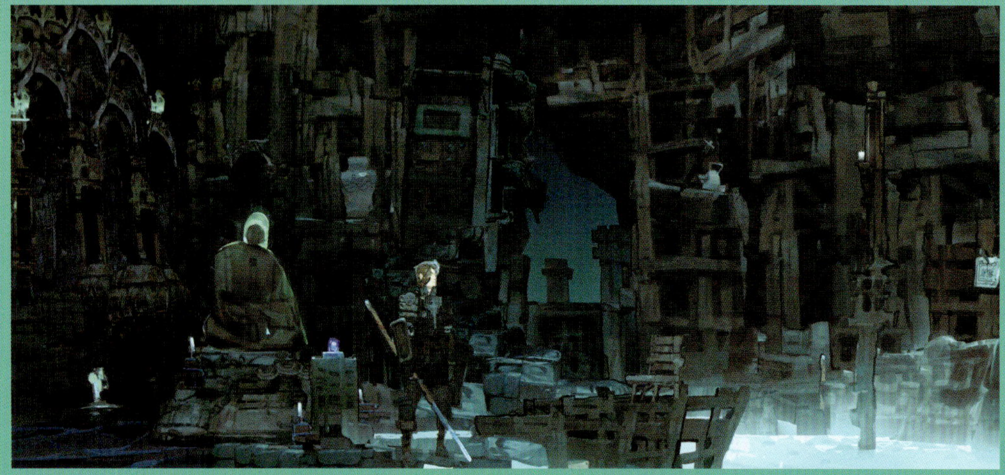

Variety and growth

If you want different results, you must work differently. An artist must be creative with their tools, subjects, and their mindsets to remain truly creative. However, without some standardization of process this is of course far too chaotic to give relatable and pragmatic results. Diversity and mutation are essential to evolution and interest but so too are structure and stability to growth and communications.

I often find that it is these restraints and parameters, as well as many others, that may impede rampant creativity but also provide the framework upon which the truly interesting and innovative can be built. Such parameters can, outside of work, come in the form of time constraints, but can also manifest as limits on subject matter, brushes, color palette or any other method, medium or technique.

Repetition one

Repetition of existing elements does, of course, present an obvious issue; although, if desired this can be readily converted into rhythm visually and within a series of paintings can become thematic variations or iterative in nature and appropriate for rapid prototyping towards visual and conceptual subjects. To anyone who grew up playing computer games, these techniques should feel familiar as the reuse and camouflage of familiar assets is quite similar to the techniques born out of the extremely low memory capacity of early gaming hardware and is still a limitation and challenge even today.

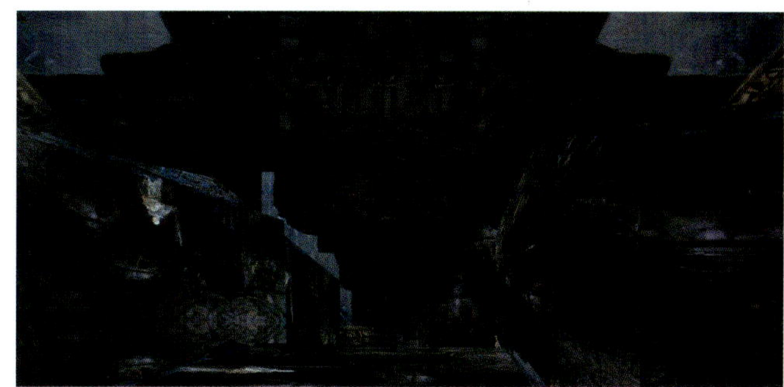

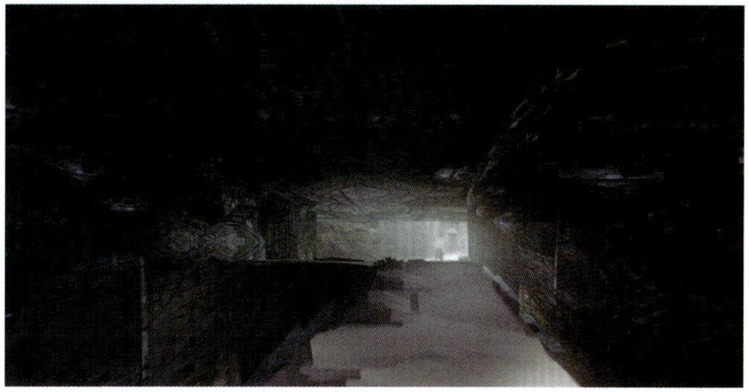

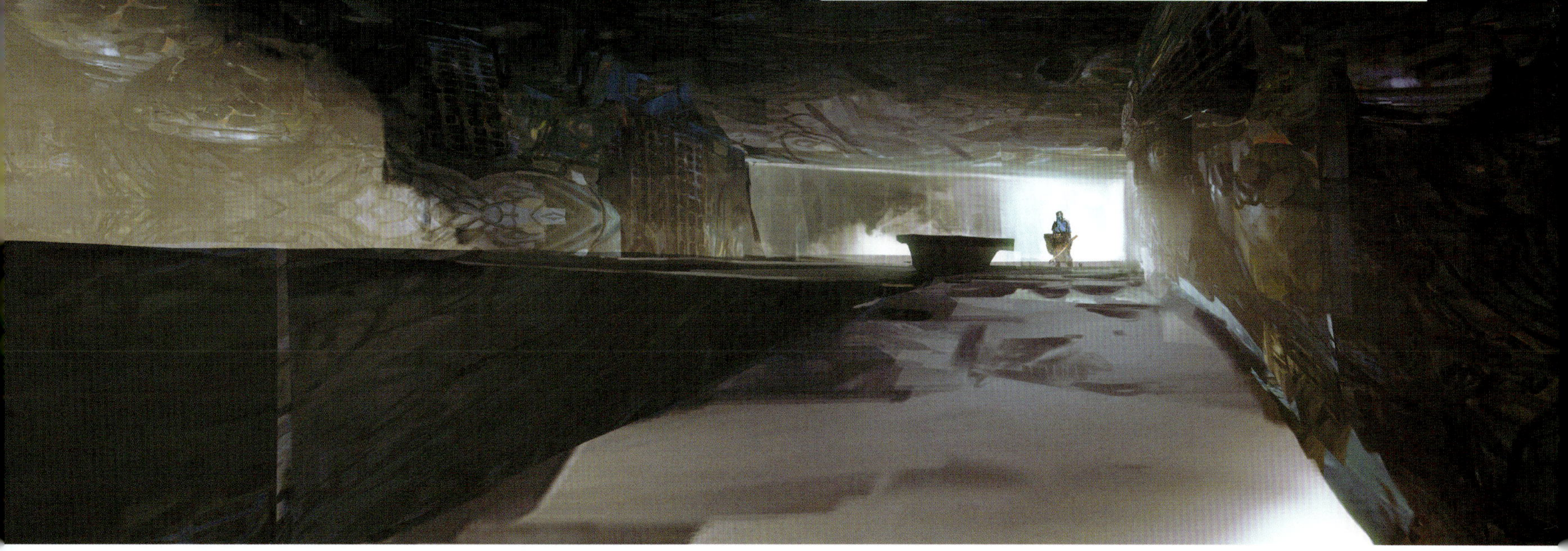

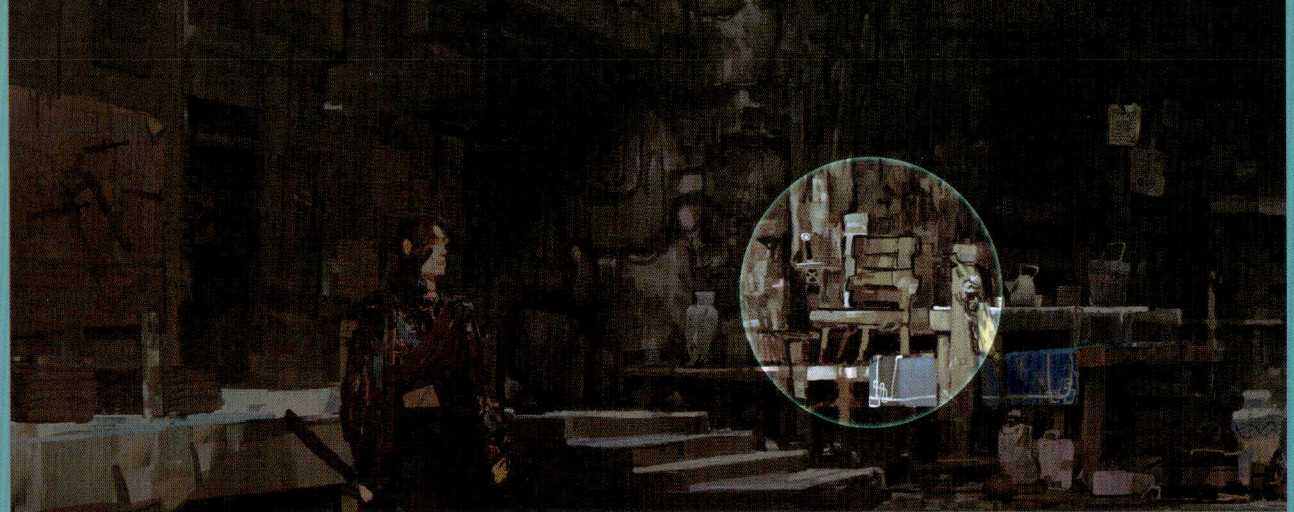

Repetition 1

I would argue the repetition of objects and props over time is impromptu sequential art and has within it the catalysts for narrative. Indeed there are a few props within my painted asset library that, when I find a new home for them, is like visiting an old friend as I get to re-experience all the places and scenes in which that prop has visited over the years. Think of the furniture in your own home and the stories of past apartments or houses that they carry with them.

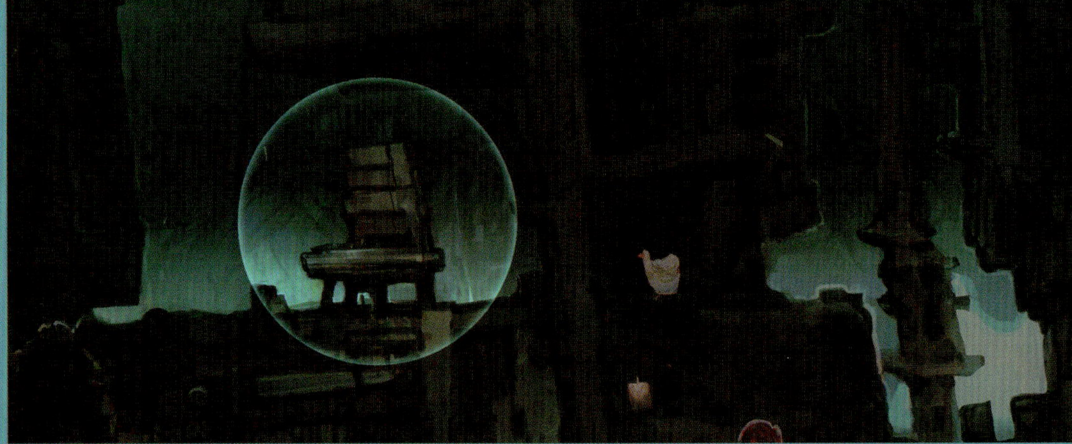

Returning to digital painting, I have this one wooden chair that has been with me and my work for a few years now – it is practically the main character of its own traveling narrative and needs only a motive to make it official. Another example are simple bulbs of garlic that have had so many incarnations, or perhaps it's just one string of bulbs passed along from location to location, hung up here and there, perhaps with the aid of the aforementioned traveling chair.

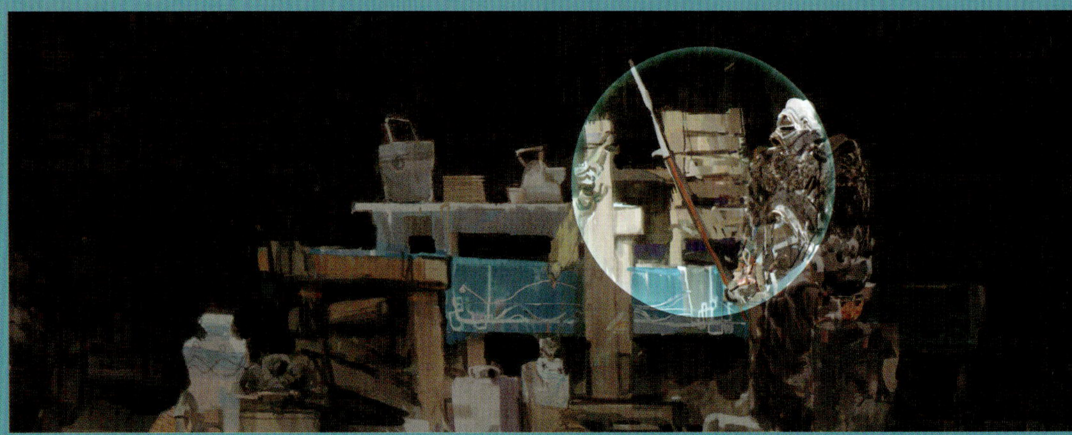

I also enjoy the deconstruction and reuse of lumber from a previously rendered table; often I imagine the inhabitants of my created worlds would also salvage things when times are dire and materials scarce. In this way the process matches the product, naturally and definitively; and I also believe it matches an efficient production.

Life is short

For many of these pieces it wouldn't be much more work to paint them again from scratch but as time is of the essence – not just for a two-hour time frame but life in general – my goal is not only to learn to paint, but to design and compose a scene, environment, or world with enough rapidity and grace to (hopefully one day) create work with inherent emotion and gesture of vitality so that the audience may not only process the work but feel it within their own selves.

In this way, I imagine, exercise in the visual arts is quite like training muscle memory: we must practice and improve until our reaction becomes instinctual, perhaps subconscious, and therefore born out of our very being. Those preferential towards a rationalist mindset may disagree, but I would ask them to deny that there is within themselves and their work a voice or imprint of theirs alone no matter how soft the whisper or loud the arena.

In resting the paintbrush and instead utilizing collage, we are able to flex an alternative mental muscle group and let the usual ones rest and heal. I find benefit not only in this exercise of another method, but also in the recovery of enthusiasm for old tools. This may be a case of "absence makes the heart grow fonder," basic retreat and regroup, or of the branch feeding the trunk; I'll leave the metaphor up to the reader presently involved.

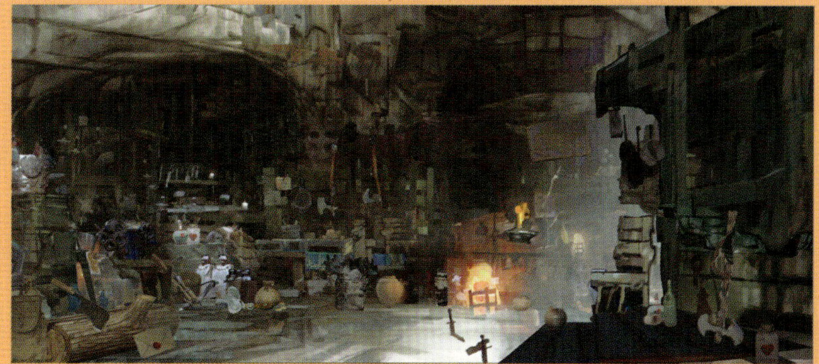

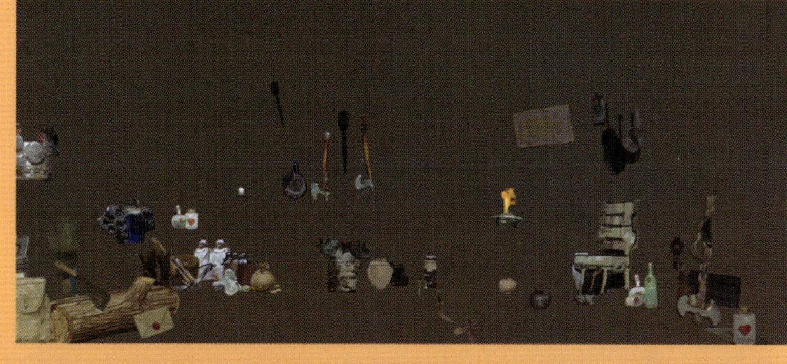

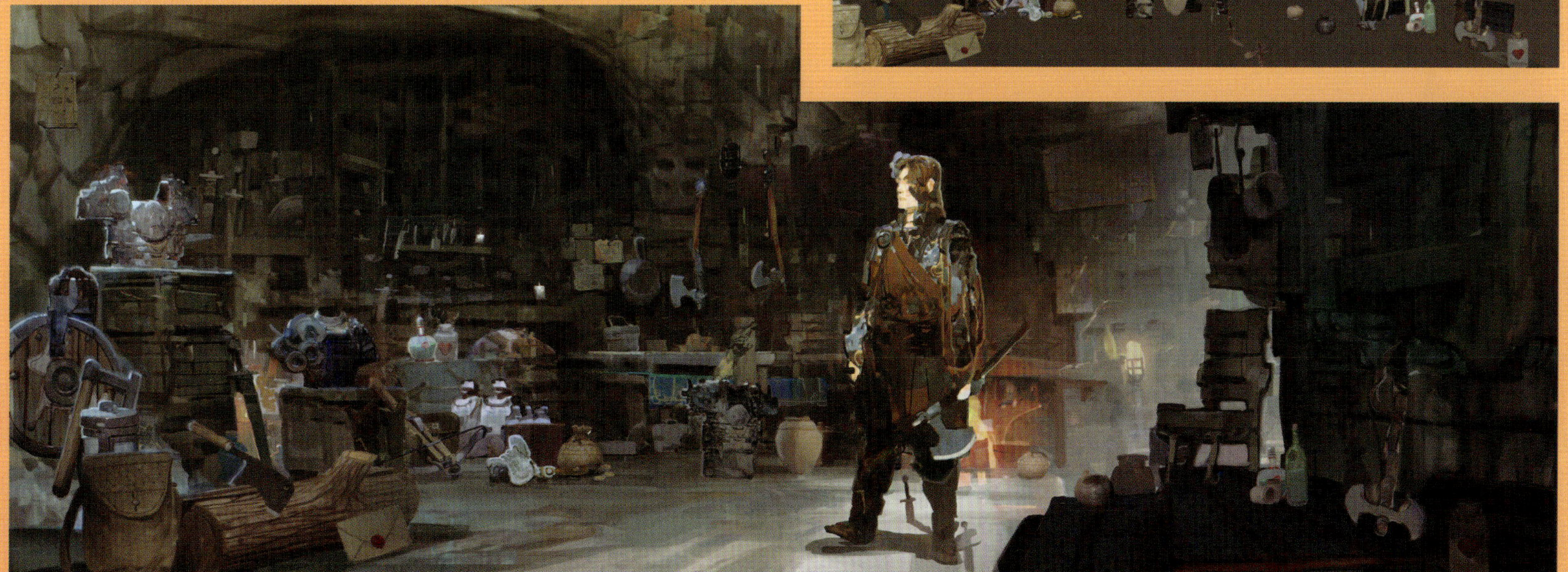

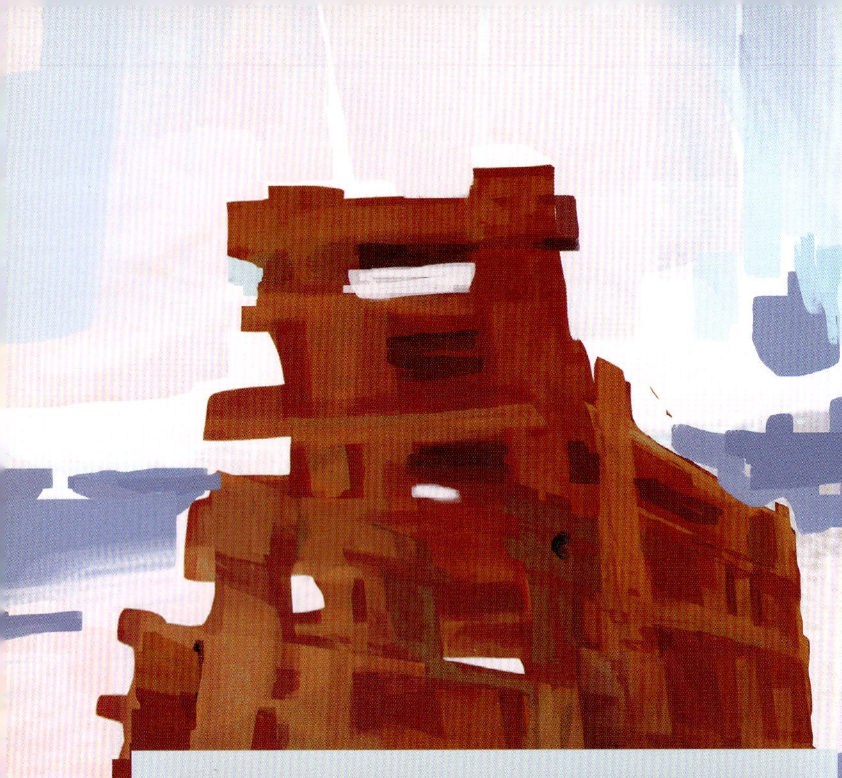

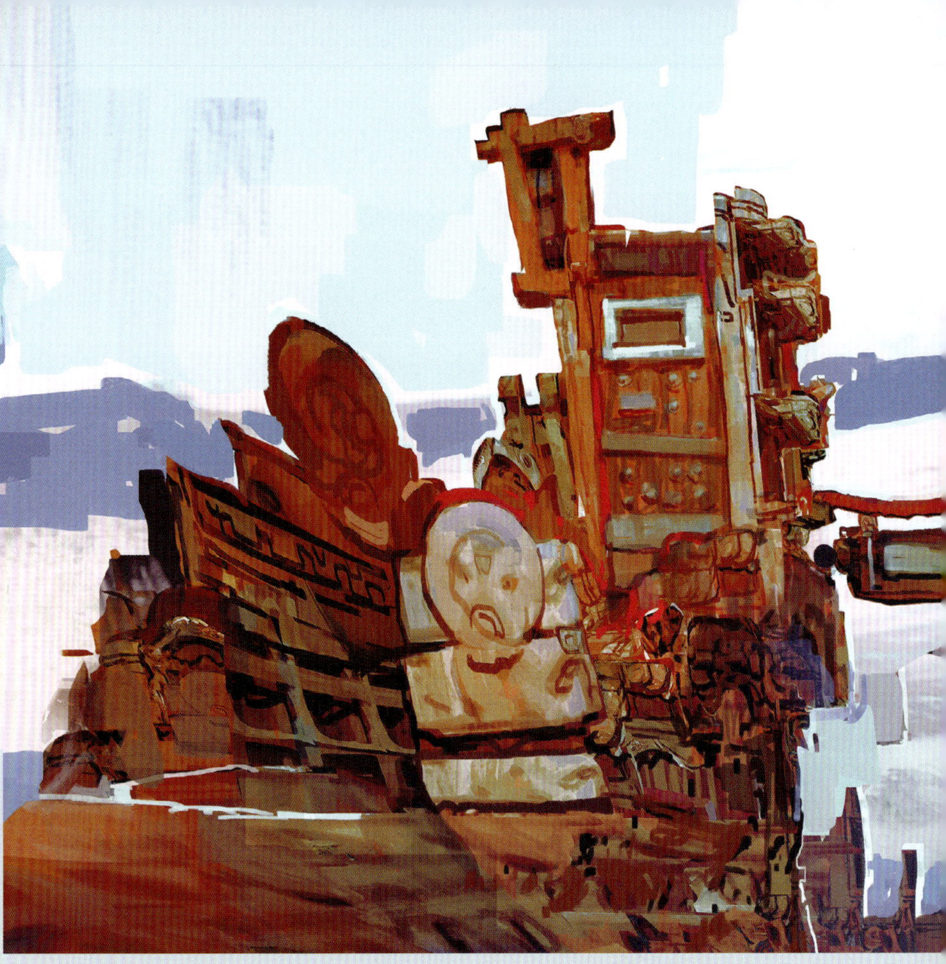

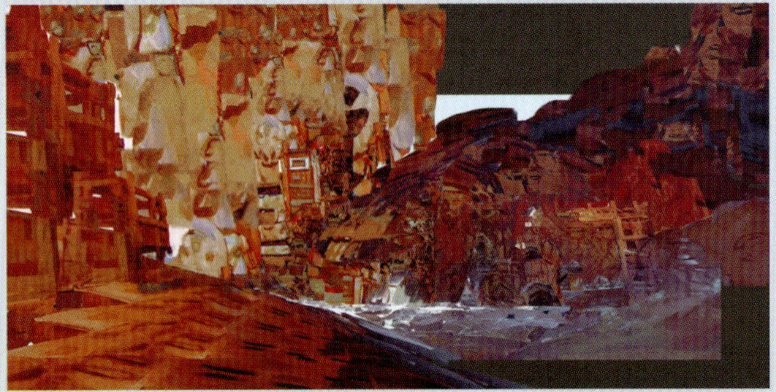

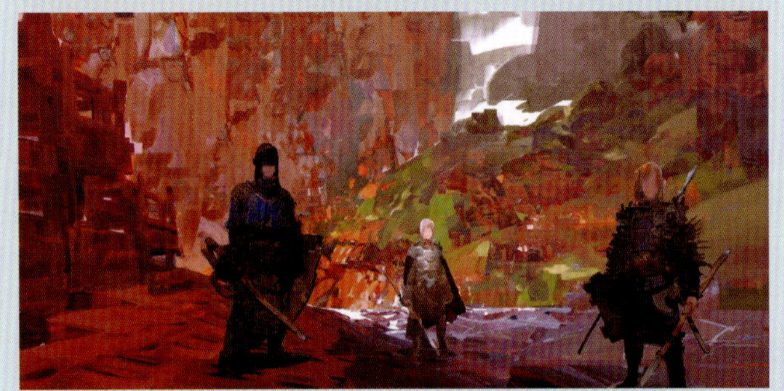

Matter and mixed metaphor

A digital painting can still dry out motivationally, just as any idea can become tired I find that as a painting forms, its essential material becomes less fluid and eventually slows near to a solid as my ability to improve it, my interest in it, and my daily energy diminish.

Sometimes a short break allows it to thaw. Other times when I return it has become rock solid. Rather than force it, I say let it rest until you, your skills, and motivation are ready again.

I think it's very important to have a healthy relationship with your work. Treat it as an individual. Be respectful to what it "wants" or has the potential to do. Other times you'll be better off if you let the work ferment; sometimes it needs to rest, as do your perceptions and expectations of it. I'm sure this particular paragraph reads as especially silly to some, but this sort of creative wrapper, frame, or metaphor has always been useful to me and my understanding of the world.

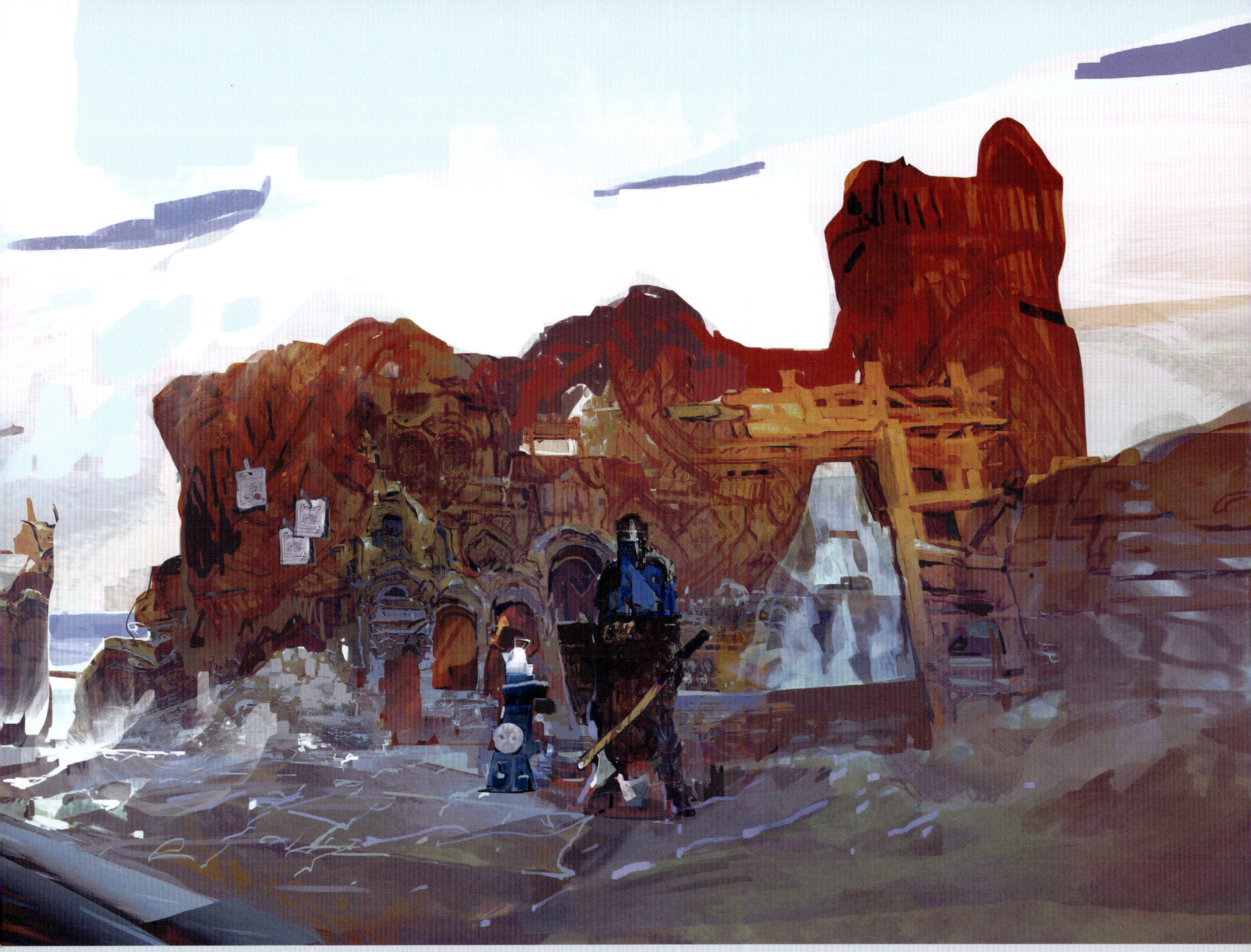

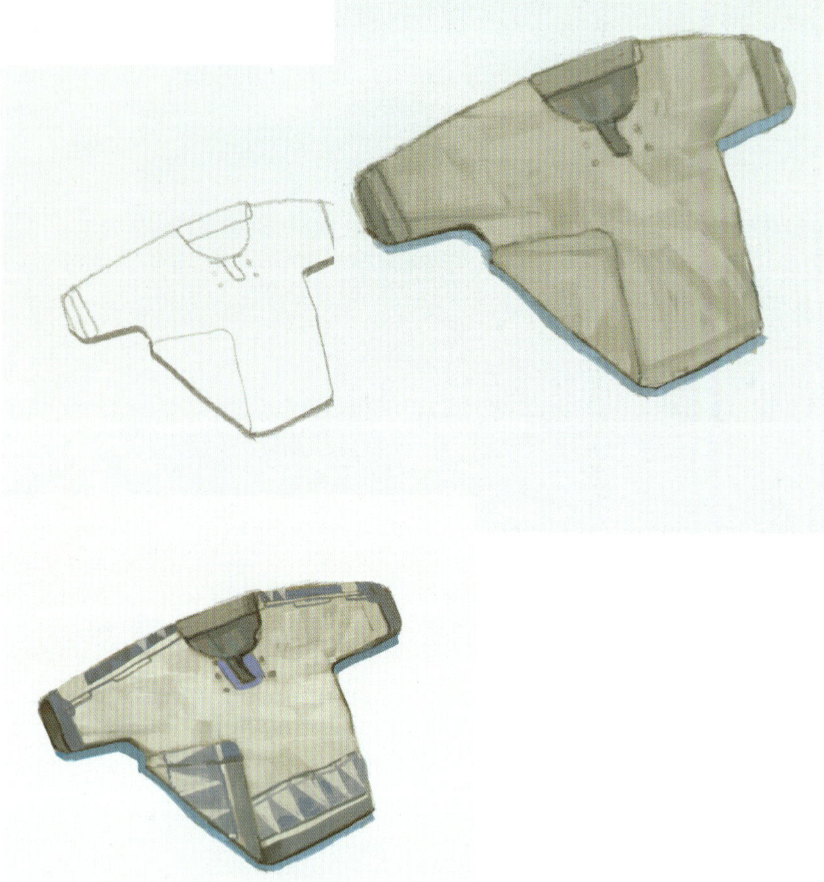

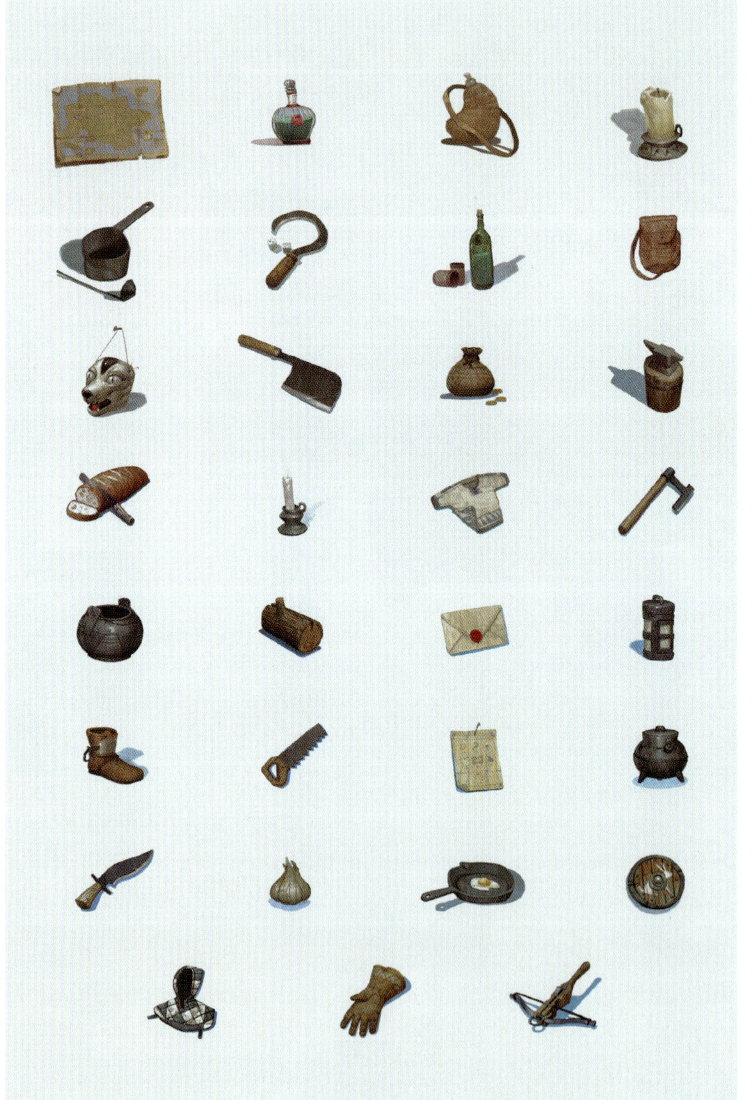

Retrograde

Truly, there's no reason even an artist using more traditional mediums and methods couldn't translate much of this workflow into physical reality. However, it may be generally more productive for one to use these digital tools as preparatory aides; or to more readily reintroduce one's intuition past a stalled or stale original at the easel; or perhaps to experiment and collect data for solutions to other traditional problems you can't traditionally Ctrl+Z Undo. This is not an occasion for any artist to rush, nor is it a case to not treat each mark with intent and respect but it is a case for the benefits of moderation and variety. Practice makes perfect and there are methods of practice unique to digital painting as, of course, with any and all mediums.

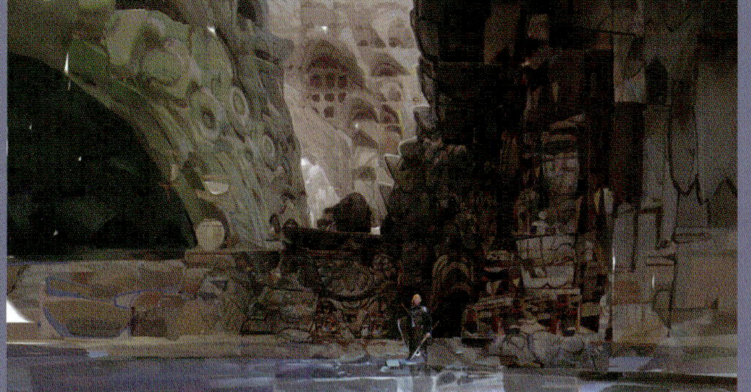

Efficiency and salvage

Don't Delete, instead use Cut and Paste. Much of what you might remove from a painting can be salvaged and used somewhere that either aids the concept, subject, or aesthetic complexity, harmony or composition. Remember that waste is generally a sign of inefficiency, ignorance, or mismanagement.

Spend time getting organized and automated. One of the latest digital adjustments I've made is to program one key to hide/unhide my Perspective Grids. One of the latest physical adjustments I've made is to take notes. Go make some of your own and send me an email with your best and we'll chat and trade some more tips. Whatever doesn't get passed along is lost. We ourselves are responsible for the state and health of our community and as such I believe we must all be good neighbors, allies, and economists.

Some unsolicited advice

Some techniques are designed to help others communicate their ideas, and some are more helpful in finding what you yourself would like to express or discover. Whether visual author or visual translator, an artist must be fluent in the language in order to communicate. I would encourage you to experiment with everything of interest; as you will often find the answers you seek in the most unlikely of places. Therefore, I believe we must always be very careful of the terminology we place upon ourselves and our work; others and theirs. These stereotypes and judgments are, at times, useful for efficient or heuristic mental processing in simplified or directed systems, but are mere tokens of our complex realities and needs.

In closing, compare yourself not to others but to yourself of yesterday, last week, or month; have you made enough healthy progress? If not, get back to work. If so, go play – it will help you work even harder tomorrow.

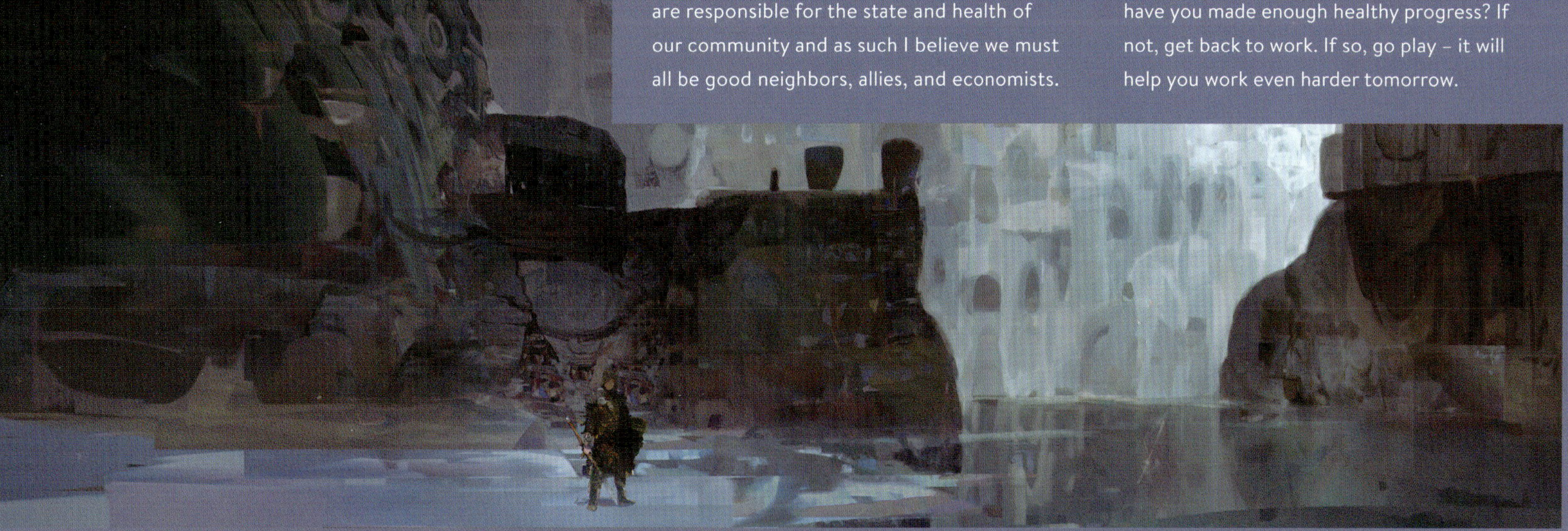

Meet the artists

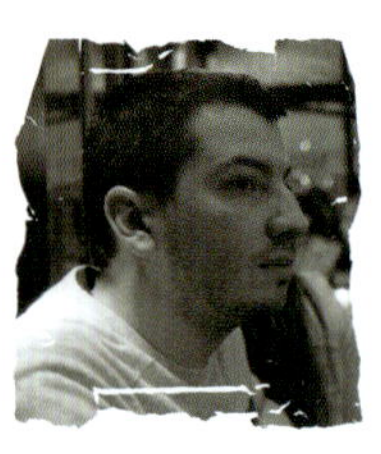

Florian Aupetit
www.florianaupetit.com

Florian Aupetit is a 3D generalist based in Paris, France. He also works as a freelance illustrator and concept artist. He is interested in everything, especially old master paintings and photographs.

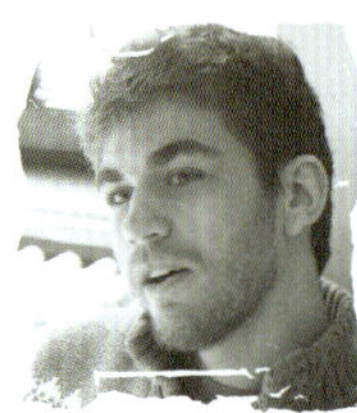

Ioan Dumitrescu
www.ioandumitrescu.com

Ioan Dumitrescu is a finishing architect working in the movie and games industry. He mainly works on creating new worlds and telling stories through his art.

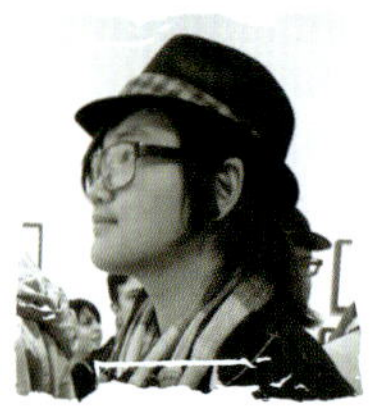

Ian Jun Wei Chiew
www.ianchiew.com

Malaysian national Ian Jun Wei Chiew is a concept artist working in the film and gaming industry. He is currently working at Sony's Sucker Punch Productions in Seattle, USA, and freelances on various projects.

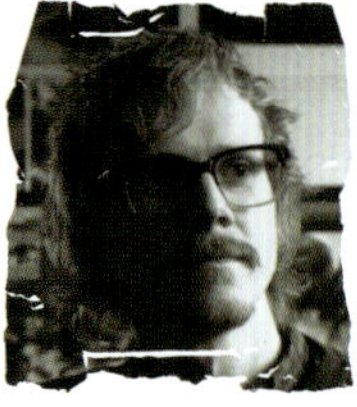

Jesper Friis
www.artstation.com/artist/maaskeikke

Jesper Friis is a Danish artist who primarily focuses on fantasy environments, but likes to experiment with all forms of visual art and design. He likes the idea of being lost and not knowing where he is!

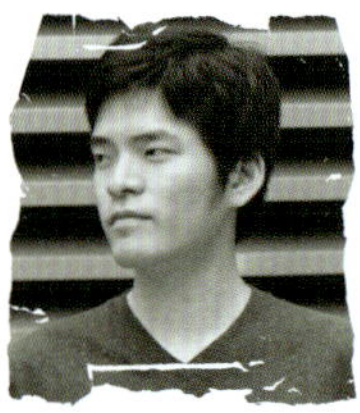

Sung Choi
www.sung-choi.com

Sung Choi (Sunghun Choi) is an award-winning concept artist from South Korea currently working at Bungie in Washington. He specializes in world design and illustration for the entertainment industry.

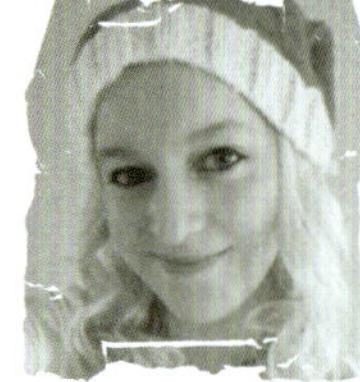

Katy Grierson
www.kovah.co.uk

Katy has been drawing and painting for as long as she can remember and feels especially privileged that it is her job. She has always had an active imagination and take greats pleasure in building worlds and sharing her creations.

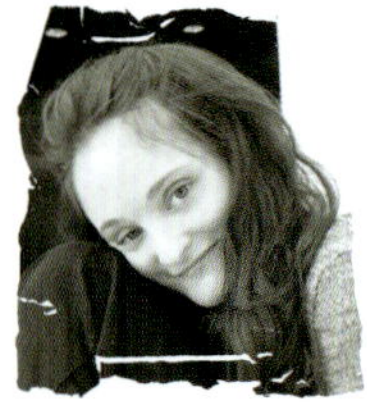

Stephanie Cost
www.stephaniedraws.com

Stephanie Cost currently freelances as an illustrator and loves landscape painting. She is influenced by both mythology and pop culture and her art is often a reflection of her wanderlust and love of exploration.

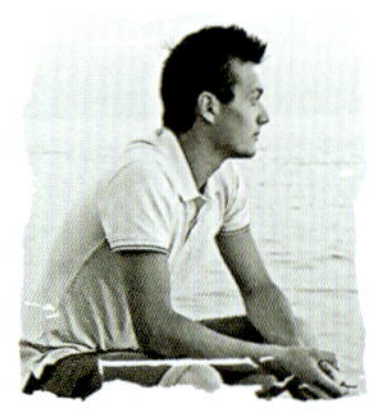

Wadim Kashin
www.artstation.com/artist/septicwd

Wadim Kashin hails from Moscow, Russia. He is mostly self-taught and is the only artist in his family. He started out using traditional media such as pencils and paint, but has moved on to digital.

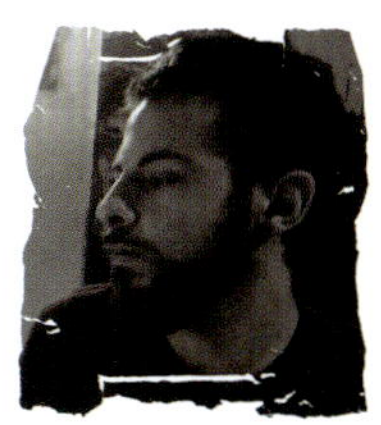

Danilo Lombardo
https://danilolombardo.allyou.net/2209622

Danilo Lombardo is an Italian self-taught digital artist. He is currently working as a lighting technical director and CG generalist for films, commercials, and game cinematics.

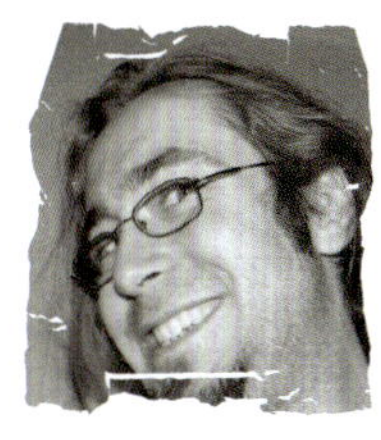

Marcin Rubinkowski
www.artstation.com/artist/marcinrubinkowski

Originally from Poland, Marcin Rubinkowski is a freelance senior concept artist and illustrator, most active in the movie and games industry. He specializes in environment design and is dedicated to the principle of passion!

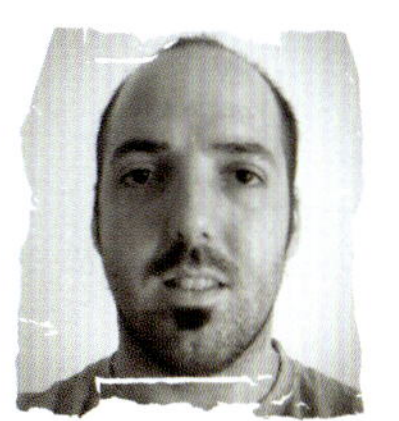

Alex Olmedo
www.artstation.com/artist/alex_olmedo

Alex Olmedo is a Spanish concept designer and illustrator who is very passionate about natural landscapes. He first discovered digital painting three years ago and hasn't looked back since.

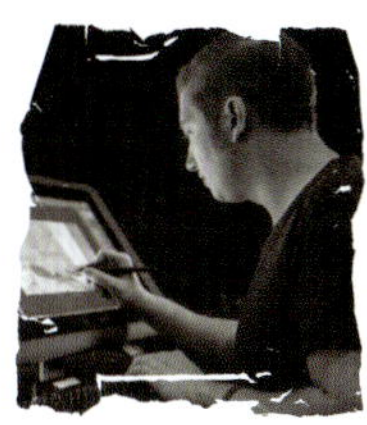

Thomas Scholes
www.artofscholes.com

Thomas currently works as a freelance artist in concept art/visual development, specializing in environments and pre-production. He is most interested in natural environments, architecture, cultures, moods, and style.

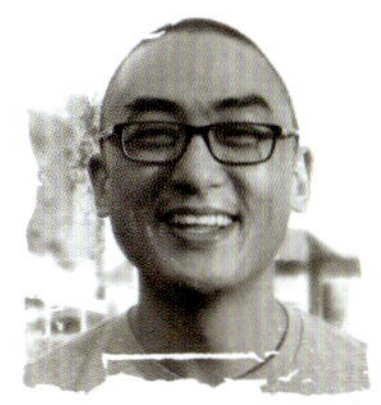

James Paick
www.jamespaickart.com

James is the Founder and Creative Director at Scribble Pad Studios and Co-Founder of Brainstorm School in Burbank, CA, along with John J. Park, focusing on concept art education for people looking to design for games and film.

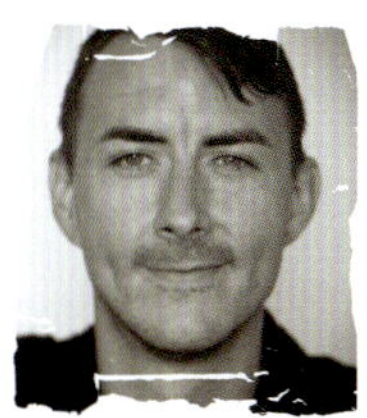

Noely Ryan
www.artstation.com/artist/enor

Noely works in the film and TV industry at Egg Post Production, where he works on large products for some awesome clients. He thinks it's great to be able to do what you love for a living and works hard to be able to continue to do so.

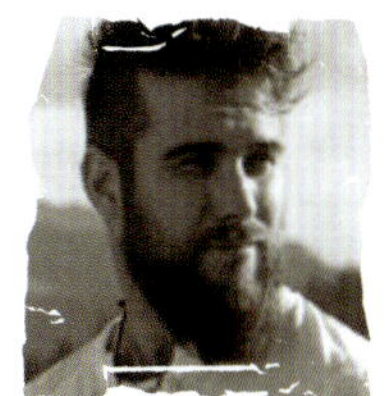

Massimo Porcella
www.artstation.com/artist/max

Born and raised in the Italian town of Genoa, Massimo started exploring digital and concept art from an early age. He is largely self-taught, although has attended several advanced master classes and workshops.

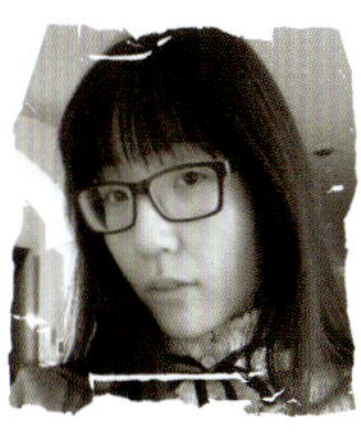

Donglu Yu
www.artofdonglu.wix.com/home

Donglu currently works at WB Games Montréal as Lead Concept Artist. She has worked on many great titles, including *Deus Ex: Human Revolution*, several *Assassin's Creed* games, and *Far Cry 4*.

Index

N

R

S

T

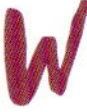

Z

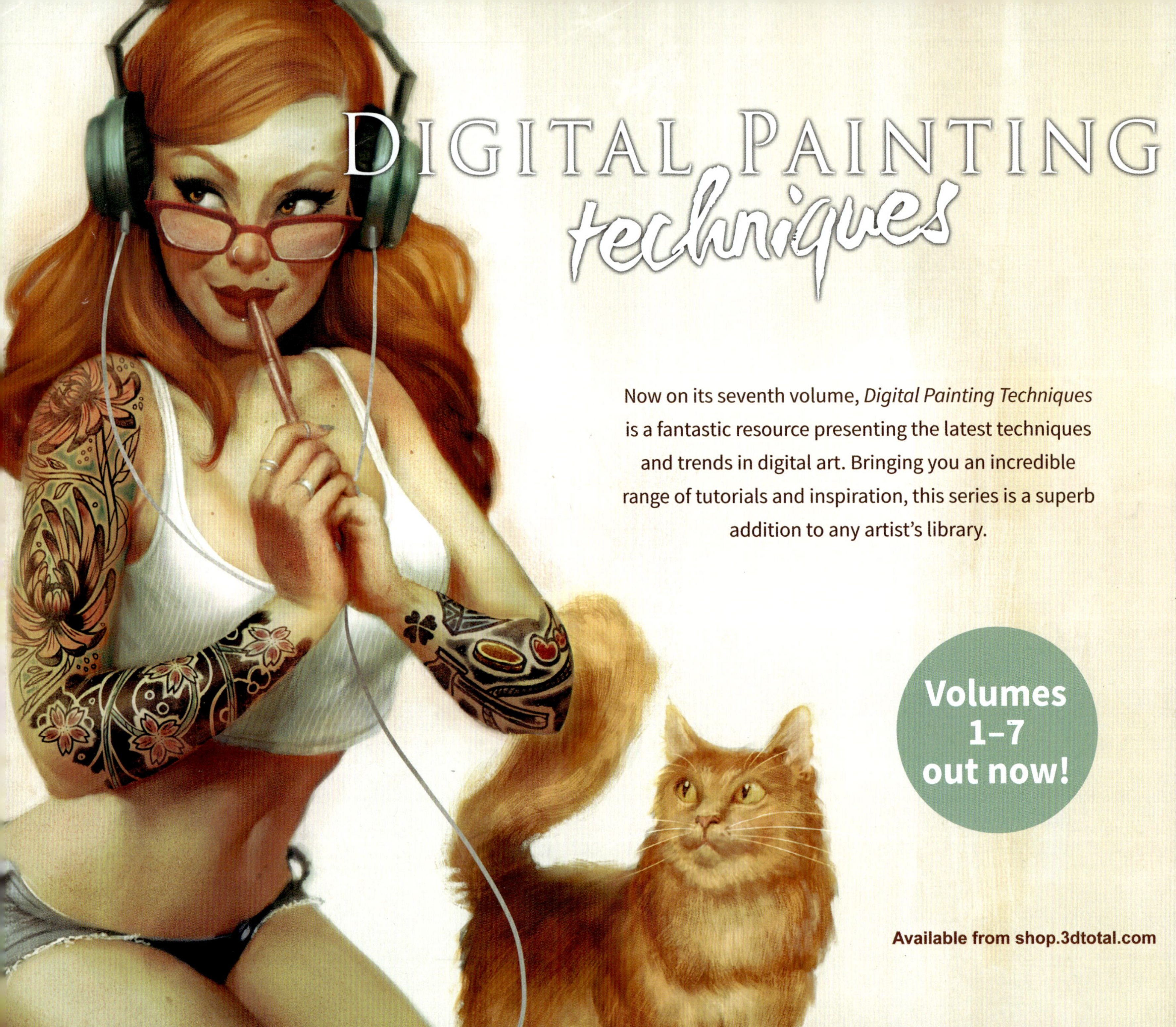

Digital Painting
techniques
Now on its seventh volume, *Digital Painting Techniques* is a fantastic resource presenting the latest techniques and trends in digital art. Bringing you an incredible range of tutorials and inspiration, this series is a superb addition to any artist's library.
Volumes 1–7 out now!
Available from shop.3dtotal.com